رياض الصالحين

RIYADH-US-SALEHEEN

ARABIC-ENGLISH

Vol. II

Compiled By

IMAM ABU ZAKARIYA YAHYA BIN SHARAF AN-NAWAWI

Translated By

S. M. MADNI ABBASI

KITAB BHAVAN
New Delhi-110002

KITAB BHAVAN
Publishers, Distributors, Exporters & Importers
1784, Kalan Mahal, Darya Ganj,
New Delhi - 1100 02 (India)

Phones : (91-11) 23277392/93, 23274686, 32906494
Fax : (91-11) 23263383

Website : www.kitabbavan.net
: www.kitabbavan.com

Email : nasri@vsnl.com
: nusrat@bol.net.in

1st Published in India : 1984
11th Edition : 2014

ISBN : 81-7151-242-9 (Set)
ISBN : 81-7151-244-5 (Vol. II)

Book Code No. : (set) 0003

Printed & Published in India by :
Nusrat Ali Nasri for KITAB BHAVAN
1784, Kalan Mahal, Darya Ganj,
New Delhi - 1100 02 [India]

CONTENTS

VOLUME II

BOOK OF MERITS AND EXCELLENCES OF HOLY QURAN 510

* * * * * * *

PREFACE

This is the second and last volume of the English translation of Riadh-us-Saleheen of Imam Abu Zakaria Yahya bin Sharaf An-Nawawi. The first volume was published in February 1983 and has been well received.

Reviewing the first volume in the Muslim World Book Review, Leicester (U.K.) in its issue No. 1 of 1983, Mr. Ahmed von Denffer, a German Muslim and a scholar of repute, has observed that :

> "Many young Muslims in the West and many Westerners 'on the path' towards Islam will be extremely grateful to both the translator as well as the publisher for having brought out this first part (of two parts) of Riyadh-us-Saleheen in English, together with its Arabic text. ... ...
>
> The list of contents for Part I is very detailed and helpful, because it is subdivided into 'books' and 'chapters'. ... ...
>
> Abbasi's translation has a more detailed introduction (Preface) and includes a useful short biographical account of Imam Nawawi. On the whole it appears that Abbasi has attempted to remain much closer to the Arabic text, both with regard to the chapter headings and to the ahadith themselves. This is of advantage to the student of hadith, who has only little or no knowledge of Arabic, since he will not miss many details. ... ...
>
> There is no doubt that Abbasi's translation of the Riyadh-us-Saleheen will soon be one of the most widely used translations of any collection of ahadith among English-speaking Muslim."

The translator has taken care to be faithful to the original Arabic text and closer to the meaning and underlying idea of the original. Nothing has been omitted from the original, nor meaning and central idea of any hadith altered, twisted or changed in any way. With this end in view, the original Arabic version has also been given along with the translation, to enable the reader to refer to the original if necessary.

Moreover, since millions of Muslims read these traditions with keenness and devotion, the translator and the publisher of this book have taken special care to present the same with its original charm and spirit without any alteration or interpolation. There is a growing desire among the Western people these days to know and understand Islam, and it is hoped this book will help them to appreciate Islam and its virtues, and come nearer to it.

English translation of the Quranic verses cited in this book (both the volumes) are those of the Holy Quran translated by Mr. Mohammad Marmaduke Pickthall.

Improvements suggested in the review on volume I, have been carried out. It is therefore hoped that this attempt of ours will be appreciated by the distinguished readers.

As usual, Mr. Akhlaq Husain, Managing Director, International Islamic Publishers Ltd., Karachi, was of great help to me in the compilation of this book. He found time to examine the manuscript and corrected and revised the same wherever necessary. I am greatly indebted to him for this help.

Karachi.
23rd September, 1984.

S.M. MADNI ABBASI

INTRODUCTION BY THE COMPILER OF RIADH--US--SALEHEEN

In the name of Allah, the Beneficent, the Merciful.

All praise is due to Allah, the One, All-Powerful, *Dominant* Most Forgiving and Sparing, Who brings night after day, so that it may serve as a mild reproof and caution to those persons who are endowed with a (clean) heart and nice perception and as a reminder and an advice and a beacon signal to those who are prudent and foreseeing. Allah is One Who picked up persons from amongst His servants and awakened them from the deep slumber, and gifted them with the blessing of piety and made them capable of deep thinking and discerning, meditation and observation with the eyes of heart; and He made them capable to repent on wrongs done by them and to accept (sound) advice and to retract, and He made this practice as an essential part of their life. He gifted these chosen persons with the capacity to worship Him and make preparations for the Hereafter, and then enabled them to be regular and steadfast in this discipline. I eulogise this Being (Allah) in most elocutionary terms and pure words which cover all the good qualities and virtues. I affirm that there is no god but Allah, Who is Virtuous, Noble, Kind and Merciful and Worthy of worship. I affirm that our master and leader (Holy Prophet Muhammad S.A.W.) is His bondsman and Messenger, His friend and beloved; he guides us on the right path and calls towards the true religion. May Allah have mercy on him and all the prophets and virtuous persons and their children.

Object of the creation of the mankind and the correct method of achieving that object.

After glorifying Allah and invoking His blessings (upon His Messenger S.A.W.), it is stated that Allah has said that :

> "I created the jinn and humankind only that they might worship Me. I seek no livelihood from them, nor do I ask that they should feed Me." (51:56-57).

This holy verse unequivocally proves that the object of the creation of jinn and mankind, is only the worship of Allah. As such, it is incumbent upon them to keep the purpose of their creation (always) in view; they should not get attracted towards the charms and decorations of the world; because this abode has no permanence nor it is fit for permanent living. This world is transient, and a conveyance to transport (us) to another place. It is not a place where one should feel happy and pleased. The thoroughfare of our life will forsake us at a turning point; it is not a path to remain with us permanently. Hence, those people are attentive who are passing their time (life) in worshipping and obeying (Allah); and those people are sagacious and knowledgable, who have made forbearance and virtue as the mode of their life.

The Holy Quran portrays the pricture of the impermanence of the world thus :—

> "The similitude of the life of the world is only as water which We send down from the sky, the earth's growth of that which men and cattle eat mingleth with it till, when the earth hath taken on her ornaments and is embellished, and her people deem that they are masters of her, Our commandment cometh by night or by day and We make it as reaped corn as if it had not flourished yesterday. Thus do We expound the revelations for people who reflect."
> (10:25)

There are a number of Quranic verses on this topic. How apt is a poet in this connection :—

> "There are a number of prudent servants of Allah, who have retired from the world, and are afraid of the mischiefs (of the world). They have scanned the world very thoroughly, and they were convinced that it was not the real home of the man. They considered it (the world) as a fathomless sea, and disanchored ships equipped with virtuous deeds in this sea."

Therefore when the impermanence of the world is like this, and the object of our creation is that which I have just stated, then it becomes incumbent upon every mature and prudent Muslim that he should follow the foot-steps of those persons who are (virtuous and) liked by others, and follow the same creed which is followed by the wise and prudent men; and should make preparations for the object towards which I have drawn (your) attention. The most suitable and feasible method to achieve this object, is the following and obedience of the Holy Prophet (S.A.W.)

Allah the Almighty has called upon us "Help ye one another unto righteousness and pious duty." (5:2) And an authentic tradition of the Holy Prophet (S.A.W.) reported by Imams Muslim, Nisai and Tirmizi, says that: "So long as a Muslim remains busy helping his Muslim brother, Allah the Most High, continues to help him (the former)." The Holy Prophet (S.A.W.) has further said: "A person who invited anybody to do a good thing, will get recompense equivalent to the person who does so." (Muslim and Abu Daud) And said: "Anybody who invited (somebody) towards good, will get merit equal to his follower, and there will be no mitigation of merit of either." (Muslim and Abu Daud)

The Holy Prophet (S.A.W.) is reported to have said to Hazrat Ali (R.A.A.) :" O Ali ! If Allah enables (even) one man to get guidance (towards the right path) through thee, then the same will be better for you more than many red camels." (Red camels in Arabia were considered to be very precious) *(Bukhari and Muslim)*

In view of these Quranic verses and the traditions of the Holy Prophet (S.A.W.) I felt inclined to collect and summarise such authentic traditions of the Holy Prophet (S.A.W.) which may help a reader to make his passage to the Hereafter easy and enable him to achieve a system or method of life, both internal and external, comprising of *ambitions* temptations and warnings and all the discipline of the life of the pious persons, like piety, penance, improvement of morals, correction of deeds and purity of hearts.

I have ensured that only authentic and clear traditions drawn from reputed and distinguished sources, will find place in this book. Each chapter will begin with appropriate verses from the Holy Quran. To elucidate a point, the reader has been guided towards the hidden meaning of some items. The phrase "agreed" at the end of a tradition means a reference to "Bukhari and Muslim"

With the grace of Allah, I am sanguine that if this book is completed, then it will help its reader to reach towards goodness and virtue, and will save him from evil and ruination. I request my brother who derives some benefit from this book, his indulgence to remember me, my father, my teachers, friends and all the Muslims in prayers. I rely entirely on Allah the Most Kind, I believe in Him and I entrust myself to Him. To me my Allah is sufficient, and He is the best Maker of my affairs. Nobody has power to save us from evil and to lead us towards virtue except Allah the Most High and Supreme.

This introduction was intended to be included in the First Volume of this book, but it was omitted inadvertently.

ABBREVIATIONS USED

1. S.A.W. *Sal-lal-laho 'Alaihi wa Sal-lam* (Peace be upon him)

2. R.A.A. *Radi Allaho 'Anhu — or 'An'huma — or 'An'hum.* (Allah was pleased with both of then — or with them).

3. R.A. *Rahmat-Allah-e-'Alaih* (Allah's mercy be upon him).

بسم الله الرحمن الرحيم

CHAPTER 144

VISITING A SICK PERSON, ACCOMPANYING A FUNERAL PROCESSION, OFFERING PRAYERS FOR THE DECEASED, PRESENCE ON THE OCCASION OF BURIAL, AND TO STAY NEAR THE GRAVE AFTER BURIAL

٨٩٤ – عن البَرَاءِ بن عازِبٍ رضي الله عنهما قال : أَمَرَنَا رسولُ اللهِ صلى اللهُ عليهِ وسلم بعِيَادَةِ المَرِيضِ ، وَاتِّبَاعِ الجَنَازَةِ ، وَتَشْمِيتِ العَاطِسِ ، وَإِبْرَارِ المُقْسِمِ ، وَنَصْرِ المَظْلُومِ ، وَإِجَابَةِ الدَّاعِي ، وَإِفْشَاءِ السَّلام. متفقٌ عليه .

894. This Hadis has already been covered in S.No. 239 of Chapter 27.

٨٩٥ – وعن أبي هريرة رضي الله عنه أن رسول الله ، صلّى اللهُ عليهِ وسلّم ، قال : « حَقُّ المُسْلِمِ عَلى المُسْلِمِ خَمْسٌ : رَدُّ السَّلام ، وَعِيَادَةُ المَرِيضِ ، وَاتِّبَاعُ الجَنَائز ، وإجَابَةُ الدَّعْوَة ، وَتَشْمِيتُ العَاطِس » متفقٌ عليه .

895. This Hadis is the same as mentioned in S. No. 238 of Chapter 27.

٨٩٦ – وعنه قال : قالَ رسولُ الله ، صلى اللهُ عليهِ وسلّم : « إنَّ اللهَ عَزَّ وَجَلَّ يَقُولُ يَوْمَ القِيَامَةِ « يَاابْنَ آدَمَ مَرِضْتُ فَلَمْ تَعُدْنِي ! قال : يَارَبِّ كَيْفَ أَعُودُكَ وَأَنْتَ رَبُّ العَالمِين ؟! قال : أَمَا عَلِمْتَ أَنَّ عَبْدِي فُلاناً مَرِضَ فَلَمْ تَعُدْهُ ؟ أَمَا عَلِمْتَ أَنَّكَ لَوْ عُدْتَهُ لَوَجَدْتَنِي عِنْدَهُ ؟ يَاابْنَ آدَمَ اسْتَطْعَمْتُكَ فَلَمْ تُطْعِمْنِي ! قال : يَارَبِّ كَيْفَ أُطْعِمُكَ وَأَنْتَ رَبُّ العَالمِينَ ؟! قال : أَمَا عَلِمْتَ أَنَّهُ اسْتَطْعَمَكَ عَبْدِي فُلانٌ فَلَمْ

تُطْعِمْهُ ، أَمَا عَلِمْتَ أَنَّكَ لَوْ أَطْعَمْتَهُ لَوَجَدْتَ ذلكَ عِنْدي ؟ يَاابْنَ آدَمَ اسْتَسْقَيْتُكَ فَلَمْ تَسْقِنِي ! قال : يَارَبِّ كَيْفَ أَسْقِيكَ وَأَنْتَ رَبُّ الْعَالَمِينَ ؟! قال : اسْتَسْقَاكَ عَبْدِي فُلانٌ فَلَمْ تَسْقِهِ ! أَمَا عَلِمْتَ أَنَّكَ لَوْ سَقَيْتَهُ لَوَجَدْتَ ذلكَ عِنْدِي ؟ » رواه مسلم .

896. Hazrat Abu Hurairah (R.A.A.) relates that the Holy Prophet (S.A.W.) said: Allah, the Lord of honour and glory, will say on the Day of Judgement: 'O Son of Adam! I was sick and you did not visit me! The man will submit. My Lord! How could I have visited Thee when Thou art Sustainer of the world ? Allah will say: 'Did you know that My servant so and so was sick and you did not visit him? Did you not realise that if you had visited him you would have found me with him? O Son of Adam! I asked you for food but you did not give me food The Man will submit: 'O My Sustainer! How could I have fed Thee when Thou art the Sustainer of the World ?Allah will say: Did you not know that My servant so and so asked you for food but you did not feed him? Did you not realize that if you had fed him you would have found your reward with me?' 'O Son of Adam! I asked you for water but you did not give Me water. The man will submit, "My Sustainer! How could I have given Thee to drink when Thou art the Sustainer of the Worlds?' Allah will say: 'My servant so and so asked you for a drink but you did not give him water. Did you not realize that if you had given him to drink you would have found its reward with Me? *(Muslim)*

٨٩٧ — وعن أبي موسى رضي الله عنه قال : قالَ رسولُ اللهِ ، صلى اللهُ عليه وسلم : « عُودُوا المَرِيضَ ، وَأَطْعِمُوا الجَائِعَ ، وَفُكُّوا العَانِي » رواه البخاري .

897. Hazrat Abu Musa Ash'ari (R.A.A.) relates that the Holy Prophet (S.A.W.) asked us to visit the sick, feed the hungry, and procure the freedom of the captives. *(Bukhari).*

٨٩٨ — وعن ثَوْبَانَ ، رضي اللهُ عنه ، عن النبيِّ ، صلّى اللهُ عليهِ وسلم ، قال : « إنَّ المُسْلِمَ إذا عادَ أخاهُ المُسْلِمَ لَمْ يَزَلْ في خُرْفَةِ الجَنَّةِ حتّى يَرْجِعَ » قِيلَ : يا رسولَ اللهِ وَمَا خُرْفَةُ الجَنَّةِ ؟ قال : « جَنَاهَا » رواه مسلم

898. Hazrat Sauban (R.A.A.) relates that the Holy Prophet (S.A.W.) said: 'When a Muslim visits a brother Muslim who is ailing, he remains among the Khurfah of Paradise till he returns from his visit. The Holy Prophet (S.A.W.) was asked: 'O' Messenger of Allah! What is the *Khurfah* of Paradise? He answered: 'Its fruits.' *(Muslim)*

٨٩٩ ـ وعن عَليّ ، رضي الله عنه . قال : سَمِعْتُ رسولَ الله ، صلى اللهُ عليه وسلم ، يقولُ : « مَامِنْ مُسْلِمٍ يَعُودُ مُسْلِماً غُدْوَةً إلاّ صَلّى عَلَيْهِ سَبْعُونَ أَلْفَ مَلَكٍ حَتّى يُمْسِي ، وَإِنْ عَادَهُ عَشِيَّةً إلاّ صَلّى عَلَيْهِ سَبْعُونَ أَلْفَ مَلَكٍ حَتّى يُصْبِحَ ، وَكَانَ لَهُ خَرِيفٌ في الجَنَّةِ » رواه التّرمذي وقال : حديث حسن .

899. Hazrat Ali (R.A.A.) relates that he heard the Holy Prophet (S.A.W.) say. When a Muslim visits an ailing Muslim in the morning, seventy thousand angels keep invoking blessings for him till the evening. and if he visits him in the evening seventy thousand angels keep on invoking blessings for him till the morning, and he is allotted an orchard of fruit trees in Paradise. *(Tirmizi)*

٩٠٠ ـ وعن أنسٍ ، رضي اللهُ عنه ، قال : كَانَ غُلامٌ يَهُودِيٌّ يَخْدُمُ النَّبيَّ ، صلّى اللهُ عليهِ وسلم ، فَمَرِضَ ، فَأَتَاهُ النَّبيُّ صلى الله عليهِ وسلم يَعُودُهُ ، فَقَعَدَ عِنْدَ رَأْسِهِ فقالَ لَهُ : « أَسْلِمْ » فَنَظَرَ إلى أَبِيهِ وَهُوَ عِنْدَهُ ؟ فقال : أَطِعْ أَبَا القَاسِمِ ، فَأَسْلَمَ ، فَخَرَجَ النَّبيُّ ، صلّى الله عليه وسلم ، وَهُوَ يقولُ : « الحَمْدُ لله الّذي أَنْقَذَهُ مِنَ النّارِ » رواه البخاري .

900. Hazrat Anas (R.A.A.) relates that a Jewish boy who used to serve the Holy Prophet (S.A.W.) fell ill, and the Holy Prophet (S.A.W.) visited him and sat down near his head and said to him. 'Accept Islam.' 'Accept Islam.' The boy looked towards his father who was close to him and answered: 'Obey, Abul Qasim,' whereupon the boy declared his acceptance of Islam. When the Holy Prophet (S.A.W.) left him, he affirmed: All praise is due to Allah Who has delivered him from the Fire. *(Bukhari)*

* * * * * * *

CHAPTER 145

HOW TO PRAY FOR THE SICK

٩٠١ — عن عائشة ، رضي الله عنها ، أنّ النبيّ ، صلّى الله عليه وسلم ، كانَ إذا اشتكى الإنسانُ الشّيءَ منه ، أو كانت به قَرْحَةٌ أو جُرْحٌ ، قال النّبيُّ ، صلّى الله عليه وسلم ، بأُصْبُعِهِ هكذا ، ووَضَعَ سُفْيانُ بنُ عُيَيْنَةَ الرّاوي سبّابتَهُ بالأرْضِ ثُمّ رفعَها وقال : « بسْمِ الله ، تُرْبَةُ أرْضِنا ، بِرِيقَةِ بَعْضِنا ، يُشْفَى به سَقيمُنا ، بإذْنِ رَبّنا » متفقٌ عليه .

901. Hazrat Ayesha (R.A.A.) relates that when any one complained to the Holy Prophet (S.A.W.) of pain or suffered from a boil or an injury on his person, he (S.A.W.) would touch the earth with his forefinger, and then raise it and say: 'In the name of Allah, I seek blessing from the dust of our earth which contains the saliva of some of us whereby our sick are healed by the command of Allah.'

(Bukhari and Muslim)

٩٠٢ — وعنها أن النبيّ ، صلى اللهُ عليهِ وسلّم ، كانَ يَعُودُ بَعْضَ أهْلِهِ يَمْسَحُ بِيَدِهِ اليُمْنَى ويقولُ : « اللّهُمّ رَبَّ النّاسِ ، أذْهِبِ البَأْسَ ، واشْفِ ، أنْتَ الشّافي لا شِفاءَ إلاّ شِفاؤُكَ ، شِفاءً لا يُغادِرُ سَقَماً » متفقٌ عليه .

902 . Hazrat Ayesha (R.A.A.) relates that when the Holy Prophet (S.A.W.) visited any member of his family who was sick, he would touch the patient with his right hand and would supplicate: 'O' Allah, Lord of mankind, remove the affliction and bestow healing. Thou art the Healer, there is no healer save Thee, a healing that leaves no ill behind.'

(Bukhari and Muslim)

٩٠٣ — وعن أنسٍ ، رضي الله عنه ، أنه قال لِثابِتٍ رحمه الله : ألا أرْقيكَ برُقْيَةِ رسولِ الله ، صلى الله عليه وسلم ؟ قال : بَلى ، قال : اللّهُمّ رَبَّ النّاسِ ، مُذْهِبَ البَأْسِ ، اشْفِ أنتَ الشّافي ، لاشافيَ إلاّ أنْتَ ، شِفاءً لا يُغادِرُ سَقَماً . رواه البخاري .

903. Hazrat Anas (R.A.A.) relates that he said to Hazrat Sabit (R.A.A.): "Shall I not repeat spells over thy ailment as the Holy Prophet (S.A.W.) used to do. He said: 'Certainly do so', whereupon Hazrat Anas (R.A.A.) supplicated. 'O' Allah, Lord of mankind, Remover of affliction, bestow healing for Thou art the Healer, there is no healer save Thee, a healing that leaves no sickness behind.' *(Bukhari)*

٩٠٤ — وعن سعدِ بن أبي وقّاصٍ ، رضي الله عنه ، قال : عادَني رسولُ اللهِ ، صلّى اللهُ عليهِ وسلّم ، فقال : « اللّهمَّ اشْفِ سَعْداً ، اللّهمَّ اشْفِ سَعْداً ، اللّهمَّ اشْفِ سَعْداً » رواه مسلم .

904. Hazrat Sa'd ibn Abi Waqqas (R.A.A.) relates that the Holy Prophet (S.A.W.) visited him during his illness and supplicated: 'O Allah, bestow cure on Sa'ad. He repeated it thrice. *(Muslim)*

٩٠٥ — وعن أبي عبد اللهِ عثمانَ بنِ أبي العاصِ ، رضي الله عنه ، أنهُ شكا إلى رسول الله ، صلّى اللهُ عليهِ وسلّم ، وَجَعاً يَجِدُهُ في جَسَدِهِ ، فقال له رسول الله ، صلّى اللهُ عليهِ وسلّم : « ضَعْ يَدَكَ عَلى الذي يَأْلم مِن جَسَدِكَ وَقلْ : بِسمِ اللهِ — ثَلاثاً — وَقُلْ سَبْعَ مَرَّاتٍ : أَعُوذُ بِعِزَّةِ اللهِ وَقُدْرَتِهِ مِنْ شَرِّ مَا أَجِدُ وَأُحَاذِرُ » رواه مسلم

905. Hazrat Abu Abdullah Usman bin Abul 'Aas (R.A.A.) relates that he complained to the Holy Prophet (S.A.W.) of a pain that afflicted his body. He (S.A.W.) told him: 'Place thy hand on the part of thy body that aches and say, *Bismillah* three times, and then repeat seven times: *A'oozo Be'izzatillahe Wa Qudrat'-e-hi Min Sharr-e-Ma Ajido Wa Uhaziro'* (I seek the protection of the Honour and Might of Allah from the evil that afflicts me and that I apprehend.) *(Muslim)*

٩٠٦ — وعن ابن عباسٍ ، رضي الله عنهما ، عن النبيِّ ، صلّى اللهُ عليهِ وسلّم ، قال : « مَنْ عَادَ مَرِيضاً لَمْ يَحْضُرْهُ أَجَلُهُ ، فقالَ عِنْدَهُ سَبْعَ مَرَّاتٍ : أَسْأَلُ اللهَ العَظِيمَ رَبَّ العَرْشِ العَظِيمِ أَنْ يَشْفِيكَ : إلاَّ عَافَاهُ اللهُ مِنْ ذلكَ المَرَضِ » رواه أبو داود والترمذي وقال : حديث حسن ، وقال الحاكِم : حديث صحيح على شرطِ البخاري .

906. Hazrat Ibn Abbas (R.A.A.) relates that the Holy Prophet (S.A.W.) said: 'If a person visits a patient who is not on the verge of death, and supplicates seven times: *as alulla-hal 'Azeema rabbal arshil azeem ain-yash fika* (I beseech Allah the Glorious, Lord of the Glorious Throne, to bestow cure on thee). Allah will cure him of his sickness.

(Abu Daud and Tirmizi)

٩٠٧ ــ وعنه أنَّ النبيَّ ، صلَّى اللهُ عليهِ وسلَّم ، دَخَلَ عَلى أعْرابيٍ يَعُودُهُ ، وَكانَ إذا دَخَلَ عَلى مَنْ يَعُودُهُ قال : « لابَأسَ ، طَهُورٌ إنْ شاءَ اللهُ » رواه البخاري .

907. Hazrat Ibn Abbas (R.A.A.) relates that the Holy Prophet (S.A.W.) visited an Arab from the rural area who was ailing. Whenever he visited a sick person he used to say: *La Basa tahurun Insha Allah.* (Have no fear. The ailment will prove purifying if Allah wills so.)

(Bukhari)

٩٠٨ ــ وعن أبي سعيد الخُدْرِيِّ رضي الله عنه أن جبْريلَ أَتَى النَّبيَّ ، صلَّى اللهُ عليهِ وسلَّم ، فقال : يَا مُحَمَّدُ اشْتَكَيْتَ ؟ قال : « نَعَمْ » قال : بِسْمِ اللهِ أَرْقيكَ ، مِنْ كُلِّ شَيْءٍ يُؤْذِيكَ ، مِنْ شَرِّ كُلِّ نَفْسٍ أَوْ عَيْنِ حَاسِدٍ ، اللهُ يَشْفِيكَ ، بِسْمِ اللهِ أَرْقيكَ » رواه مسلم .

908. Hazrat Abu Saeed Khudri (R.A.A.) relates that Gabriel once came to the Holy Prophet (S.A.W.) and inquired: 'Muhammad (S.A.W.), do you feel anything to complain? He (S.A.W.) answered: 'Yes'. Gabriel said:

'In the name of Allah, I wipe thee of all that troubles thee, from the mischief of every person and every envious eye. May Allah cure thee. In the name of Allah, I wipe thee. *(Muslim)*

٩٠٩ ــ وعن أبي سعيد الخُدْرِيِّ وأبي هريرة ، رضيَ اللهُ عنهما ، أنَّهُمَا شَهِدَا عَلى رسولِ الله ، صلَّى اللهُ عليهِ وسلَّم ، أنه قال : « مَنْ قال : لاإلهَ إلّا اللهُ وَاللهُ أَكْبَرُ ، صَدَّقَهُ رَبُّهُ ، فقال : لا إلهَ إلّا أَنَا وَأَنَا أَكْبَرُ . وإذا قال : لا إلهَ إلّا اللهُ وَحْدَهُ لاشَريكَ لَهُ ، قال : يقول : لا إلهَ إلّا أنا وَحْدي لاشَريكَ لي . وإذا قال : لاإلهَ إلّا اللهُ لَهُ المُلْكُ وَلَهُ الحَمْدُ ، قال : لاإلهَ إلّا أَنَا لِي المُلْكُ وَلِيَ الحَمْدُ . وإذا قال : لاإلهَ إلّا اللهُ وَلا حَوْلَ وَلا قوَّةَ إلّا

بِاللهِ ، قال : لا إلهَ إِلّا أنَا وَلاحَوْلَ وَلا قُوَّةَ إِلّا بي » وَكانَ يقولُ : « مَنْ قالَها في مَرَضِهِ ثُمَّ مَاتَ لَمْ تَطْعَمْهُ النَّارُ » رواه الترمذي وقال : حديث حسن .

909. Hazrat Abu Sa'eed Khudri (R.A.A.) and **Hazrat Abu Hurairah** (R.A.A.) both bear witness that the Holy Prophet (S.A.W.) said: If a person says: *La Ilaha Illal-laho WAllaho Akbar.* (there is no god save Allah ,Allah is the Greatest), His Sustainer responds to him and affirms— there is no god except Me and I am the greatest;

and when he says: *La Ilaha Illal-laho Wahdahu La Sharika Lahu.* (there is no god save Allah,the One, He has no associate), Allah the Exalted affirms this and says: there is no god save Me Who is Alone and has no associate.

When he says: *La ilaha Illal-laho Lahul Mulko Wa Lahul Hamd* (There is no god save Allah. His is the sovereignty and His is the praise) Then Allah affirms this and says: there is no god save Me, Mine is the praise and Mine is the sovereignty.

When he says: *La Ilaha Illal-laho Wa La Haula Wa La Quwwata Illa Billah* (there is no god save Allah, and there is no strength nor power except that with Allah), He affirms this also and says: there is no god save Me, and there is no strength nor power except that with Me.

The Holy Prophet (S.A.W.) used to say. One who says this in his illness and dies thereafter, will not be consumed by the fire of the Hell. *(Tirmizi)*

* * * * * * *

CHAPTER 146

ENQUIRIES ABOUT THE SICK FROM HIS FAMILY MEMBERS

٩١٠ – عن ابن عباسٍ ، رضيَ اللهُ عنهما ، أنَّ عليَّ بن أبي طالب ، رضيَ اللهُ عنهُ خرجَ مِنْ عِنْدِ رسولِ اللهِ ، صلَّى اللهُ عليهِ وسلَّم ، في وَجَعِهِ الَّذي تُوُفِّيَ فيهِ ، فقالَ النَّاسُ : يَا أبَا الحَسَنِ ، كَيفَ أصْبَحَ رسولُ اللهِ صلَّى اللهُ عليهِ وسلَّم ؟ قال : أصْبَحَ بِحَمْدِ اللهِ بَارِئاً . رواه البخاري

910. Hazrat Ibn Abbas (R.A.A.) says that Hazrat Ali ibn Abu Talib (R.A.A.) came out of the chamber of the Holy Prophet (S.A.W.) during the illness of the latter which proved fatal, and the people asked him: 'O' Abul Hasan! How the Holy Prophet (S.A.W.) passed the night?' He answered: 'Praise be to Allah — he passed the night well.' *(Bukhari)*

* * * * * * *

CHAPTER 147

WHAT ONE SHOULD SAY WHEN DESPAIRED OF HIS LIFE

٩١١ – عن عائشة رضيَ اللهُ عنها قالت : سَمِعْتُ النبيَّ صلّى اللهُ عليهِ وسلّم وَهُوَ مُسْتَنِدٌ إليّ يَقُولُ : « اللّهُمّ اغفِرْ لي وارْحمني ، وأَلحِقني بالرَّفِيقِ الأعْلى » متفق عليه .

911. Hazrat Ayesha (R.A.A.) relates that she heard the Holy Prophet (S.A.W.) say, when he was resting against her in his last illness: *Alla-hum-magh-firli War ham-ni, Wa al-hiq-ni Bir-Rrafiqil A'la* (O' Allah: forgive me and have mercy on me and join me with the Exalted companion.) *(Bukhari and Muslim)*

٩١٢ – وعنها قالت : رَأَيْتُ رسولَ الله صلى الله عليهِ وسلّم وَهُوَ بالموْتِ ، عِندَهُ قَدَحٌ فيهِ ماءٌ ، وَهُوَ يدخِلُ يَدَهُ في القَدَحِ ، ثم يَمسَحُ وَجْهَهُ بالماء ، ثم يقول : « اللّهُمّ أَعِنّي عَلى غَمَرَاتِ المَوْتِ وَسَكَرَاتِ المَوْتِ » . رواه الترمذي .

912. Hazrat Ayesha (R.A.A.) relates that she observed the Holy Prophet (S.A.W.) when he was in the throes of death, put his hand in a large cup of water which was close to him and wipe his face with it, saying: *Alla-humma A'Inni 'ala ghama-ratil maute wa Sakara'til maut.* ('Allah, help me over the hardship and agony of death.) *(Tirmizi)*

* * * * * * *

CHAPTER 148

TO ADVISE THE MEMBERS OF THE FAMILY OF THE SICK AND HIS ATTENDANTS TO TREAT THE PATIENT KINDLY, AND ALSO TO TREAT WITH KINDNESS ONE WHOSE DEATH IS IMMINENT OR HAS BEEN SENTENCED TO DEATH

٩١٣ – عن عِمرانَ بن الحُصَيْنِ رضي الله عنهما أن امْرَأَةً مِنْ جُهَيْنَةَ أَتَتِ النّبيَّ صلّى اللهُ عليهِ وسلّم وَهِيَ حُبْلى مِنَ الزِّنَا ، فقالت : يا رسولَ الله ، أَصَبتُ حَدّاً فأَقِمهُ عَلَيَّ ، فَدَعَا رسولُ اللهِ صلّى اللهُ عليهِ وسلّم وليَّهَا ، فقال : « أَحْسِنْ إِليْهَا ، فإذا وضَعَتْ فَأْتِني بِهَا » فَفَعَلَ ، فَأَمَرَ بِهَا النبيُّ

صلّى اللهُ عليهِ وسلّم . فشُدّتْ عليها ثيابُها . ثُمّ أمرَ بها فرُجمتْ ، ثُمّ صلّى عليها . رواه مسلم .

913. This Hadis has been covered in the first part of S. No. 22 of Chapter 2.

* * * * * * *

CHAPTER 149

PERMISSION TO THE PATIENT TO GIVE VENT TO FEELINGS OF AGONY, PROVIDED THE SAME IS NOT THE RESULT OF DESPAIR AND DANGER.

٩١٤ ــ عن ابنِ مسعودٍ رضيَ اللهُ عنه قال : دخلتُ على النّبيّ صلّى اللهُ عليه وسلم وهوَ يُوعَكُ . فمسستُهُ . فقلتُ : إنّكَ لتُوعَكُ وعكاً شديداً . فقال : « أجلْ إنّي أوعَكُ كما يُوعَكُ رجلانِ منكُمْ » متفق عليه

914. This Hadis has already been covered in S. No. 39 of Chapter 3.

٩١٥ ــ وعن سعدِ بن أبي وقّاصٍ رضيَ اللهُ عنه قال : جاءَني رسولُ اللهِ صلّى اللهُ عليهِ وسلّم يعودُني منْ وجعٍ اشتدّ بي . فقلتُ : بلَغَ بي ماترى . وأنا ذُو مالٍ . ولا يرثُني إلاّ ابنتي . وذكر الحديث . متفقٌ عليه .

915. This Hadis has already been covered in the first part of S. No. 6 of Chapter 1.

٩١٦ ــ وعن القاسمِ بن محمدٍ قال : قالتْ عائشةُ رضيَ اللهُ عنها : وارأساهُ فقال النّبيُّ صلّى اللهُ عليهِ وسلّم : « بلْ أنا وارأساهُ » وذكر الحديث . رواه البخاري .

916. Hazrat Qasim Ibn Muhammad (R.A.A.) relates that Hazrat Ayesha (R.A.A.) said: 'Oh, my headache,' whereupon the Holy Prophet (S.A.W.) said: 'Rather I would say: Oh, my headache.' *(Bukhari)*

* * * * * * *

CHAPTER 150

URGING A DYING PERSON TO AFFIRM THE KALIMA.

٩١٧ – عن معاذ رضي الله عنه قال: قال رسول الله صلى الله عليه وسلم «من كان آخر كلامه لا إله إلا الله دخل الجنة»

رواه أبو داود والحاكم وقال: صحيح الاسناد.

917. Hazrat Mu'az (R.A.A.) relates that the Holy Prophet (S.A.W.) said. 'A person whose last words are the affirmation of Kalima *la-ilaha il lal-lah* (there is no god save Allah) shall enter Paradise.

(*Abu Daud* and *Hakim* have reported this tradition and its chain of transmission).

٩١٨ – وعن أبي سعيد الخدري رضي الله عنه قال: قال رسول الله صلى الله عليه وسلم: «لقنوا موتاكم لا إله إلا الله» رواه مسلم.

918. Hazrat Abu Sa'id Khudri (R.A.A.) relates that the Holy Prophet (S.A.W.) said: 'Exhort your dying ones to affirm *La ilaha-Illallah* (There is no god save Allah). *(Muslim)*

* * * * * * *

CHAPTER 151

WHAT TO SUPPLICATE AFTER CLOSING THE EYES OF A PERSON WHO HAS DIED.

٩١٩ – عن أم سلمة رضي الله عنها قالت: دخل رسول الله صلى الله عليه وسلم على أبي سلمة وقد شق بصره، فأغمضه، ثم قال: «إن الروح إذا قبض، تبعه البصر» فضج ناس من أهله، فقال: «لا تدعوا على أنفسكم إلا بخير، فإن الملائكة يؤمنون على ما تقولون» ثم قال: «اللهم اغفر لأبي سلمة، وارفع درجته في المهديين، واخلفه في عقبه في الغابرين، واغفر لنا وله يا رب العالمين، وافسح له في قبره، ونور له فيه» رواه مسلم.

919. Hazrat Umm Salamah (R.A.A.) relates. 'The Holy Prophet (S.A.W.) visited Abu Salamah (Her husband) when his eyes had become hard (due to death). He (S.A.W.) closed them and said' 'When the soul of a person is taken away, the vision of the eye also goes away'. Thereupon the members of Abu Salamah's family started lamenting for him. The Holy Prophet (S.A.W.) asked them: 'Pray for only that thing which may be good for yourselves, for the angels on your supplications say 'Amen'. Then he prayed: 'O Allah! Forgive Abu Salamah and enhance his position among those who are properly guided and make some of his successors to succeed him. 'O' Lord of the Worlds forgive him and all of us, and make his grave spacious enough for him and illumine it for him.' *(Muslim)*

* * * * * * *

CHAPTER 152

WHAT SHOULD BE SAID NEAR A PERSON ON DEATH BED AND WHAT TO SAY TO THE BEREAVED FAMILY

٩٢٠ ـ عن أمِّ سَلَمَةَ رضيَ اللهُ عنها قالت: قالَ رَسُولُ اللهِ صلّى اللهُ عليهِ وسلم: « إذا حَضَرْتُمُ المَرِيضَ، أوِ المَيِّتَ، فَقُولُوا خَيْراً؛ فَإنَّ المَلائِكَةَ يُؤَمِّنُونَ عَلى مَا تَقُولُونَ » قالَتْ: فَلَمَّا مَاتَ أبُو سَلَمَةَ، أتَيْتُ النَّبيَّ صلّى اللهُ عليهِ وسلَّم فَقُلْتُ: يارسُولَ اللهِ، إنَّ أبَا سَلَمَةَ قَدْ مَاتَ، قالَ: « قُولي: اللّهُمَّ اغْفِرْ لي وَلَهُ، وَأعْقِبْني مِنْهُ عُقْبَى حَسَنَةً » فقلتُ: فَأعْقَبَني اللهُ مَنْ هُوَ خَيْرٌ لي مِنْهُ: مُحَمَّداً صلى اللهُ عليهِ وسلَّم. رواه مسلم هكذا: « إذا حَضَرْتُمُ المَرِيضَ » أوِ « المَيِّتَ » عَلى الشَّكِّ، ورواه أبو داود وغيره: « المَيِّتَ » بلا شَكٍّ.

920. Hazrat Umm Salamah (R.A.A.) relates that the Holy Prophet (S.A.W.) said: 'When you visit a sick person or one who has died, say only that which is beneficial, for the angels say 'Amen' on your utterances.' She adds: 'When Abu Salamah (her husband) died I went to the Holy Prophet (S.A.W.) and said: 'O' Messenger of Allah, Abu Salamah has died.' He asked me to pray, 'O' Allah, forgive me (Umm Salamah) and him, and bestow upon me a better return. I supplicated as he had directed, and Allah bestowed upon me one better than Abu Salamah i.e. the Holy Prophet Muhammad (S.A.W.)' *(Muslim)*

٩٢١ — وعنها قالت : سمعتُ رسولَ اللهِ صلّى اللهُ عليهِ وسلّم يقول : « مَامِن عبدٍ تُصيبهُ مُصيبةٌ ، فيقولُ : إنّا للهِ وإنّا إليه راجِعُون : اللّهمّ آؤجُرْنِي فِي مُصيبتي . وأخْلُف لي خيراً منها . إلا أجرهُ اللهُ تعالى في مُصيبتِه وأخلفَ له خيراً مِنها . قالت : فلمّا تُوفّي أبُو سلَمَة ، قلتُ كما أمرَني رسولُ اللهِ صلّى اللهُ عليهِ وسلّم . فأخلَفَ اللهُ لي خيراً منهُ رسولَ اللهِ صلّى اللهُ عليه وسلّم . رواه مسلم

921. Hazrat Umm Salamah (R.A.A.) relates. 'I heard the Holy Prophet (S.A.W.) say: 'When a person suffers from some misfortune and supplicates thus: *'Inna Lillahe Wa Inna Ilaihe Raje-'oon,'* To Allah we belong and to Him shall we return: 'O Allah! make good the loss in my misfortune (grant me recompense) and grant me something better than that which I have lost: 'Allah then compensates him for his loss in his misfortune and gives him a better substitute than the one he has lost. Hazrat Umm Salamah (R.A.A.) adds: When Abu Salamah died, I supplicated as the Holy Prophet (S.A.W.) had directed me, and after him Allah bestowed upon me a better person than the one whom I had lost, that is, to say, the Holy Prophet (S.A.W.). *(Muslim)*

٩٢٢ — وعن أبي موسى رضي الله عنه أنّ رسولَ اللهِ صلّى اللهُ عليهِ وسلّم قال : « إذا مَاتَ وَلدُ العَبدِ ، قال اللهُ تعالى لمَلائِكتِهِ : قَبَضْتم ولدَ عَبْدِي؟ فيقولُونَ : نَعَم ، فيقولُ : قَبَضتُم ثَمرَةَ فُؤادِهِ ؟ فيقولونَ : نَعَم . فيَقُولُ : فَمَاذا قال عَبْدِي؟ فيقولُونَ : حَمِدَكَ واسْتَرْجعَ ، فيَقُولُ اللهُ تعالى : ابنُوا لِعَبْدِي بَيتاً في الجنّة ، وَسَمّوهُ بيتَ الحَمدِ » رواه الترمذي (٥) وقال : حديث حسن .

922. Hazrat Abu Musa (R.A.A.) relates that the Holy Prophet (S.A.W.) said: When a servant of Allah loses his child, Allah asks His angels: Have you snatched away the child of my servant (i.e. taken possession of his soul)? They reply, Yes Sir. Then Allah further asks: 'Have you taken possession of the flower of his heart? They answer: Yes Sir. Then He inquires: 'Then what was the reaction of my servant? The angels say: He praised Thee and affirmed: *Inna lillahe wa inna ilaihe raje'oon.* (To Allah we all belong and to Him we shall return). On this Allah calls upon the angels: 'Build for My servant a mansion in Paradise and call it: Bait-al Hamd: i.e. the House of Praise." *(Tirmizi)*

٩٢٣ — وعن أبي هُريرةَ رضي اللهُ عنه أنَّ رسولَ اللهِ صلَّى اللهُ عليهِ وسلَّم قال : يقولُ اللهُ تعالى : ما لِعَبْدِي المُؤْمِنِ عِنْدِي جزَاءٌ إذا قبَضْتُ صَفيَّهُ مِنْ أهْلِ الدُّنْيَا ، ثُمَّ احْتَسَبَهُ إلاَّ الجَنَّةَ » رواه البخاري .

923. Covered in S. No. 32 of Chapter 3.

٩٢٤ — وعن أُسامة بن زيدٍ رضي الله عنهما قال : أَرْسَلَتْ إحْدى بَناتِ النبيِّ صلَّى اللهُ عليه وسلَّم إليْهِ تَدْعُوهُ وتُخْبِرُهُ أنَّ صَبيّاً لها — أوْ ابناً — في المَوْتِ فقال للرَّسول : « ارْجِعْ إليْها، فأَخْبِرْها أنَّ للهِ تعَالى مَا أخَذَ ولَهُ ما أعْطَى ، وكُلُّ شَيْءٍ عِنْدَهُ بأجَلٍ مُسَمّىً ، فَمُرْهَا، فلْتَصْبِرْ ولْتَحْتَسِبْ » وذكر تمام الحديث . متفقٌ عليه .

924. Covered in S. No. 29 of Chapter 3.

* * * * * * *

CHAPTER 153

SHEDDING OF TEARS ON DEATH WITHOUT CRYING AND BEATING

٩٢٥ — عن ابنِ عُمرَ رضي الله عنهما أنَّ رسُولَ اللهِ صلَّى اللهُ عليهِ وسلَّم عاد سَعْدَ بنَ عُبادَةَ ، ومَعَهُ عَبْدُ الرَّحمنِ بنُ عَوْفٍ ، وسَعْدُ بنُ أبي وقَّاصٍ ، وعَبْدُ اللهِ بنُ مَسْعُودٍ رضي الله عنهم ، فبَكى رسولُ اللهِ صلَّى اللهُ عليهِ وسلَّم ، فلمَّا رأى القَوْمُ بُكاءَ رسولِ اللهِ صلَّى اللهُ عليهِ وسلَّم ، بكَوْا ، فقال : « ألا تَسْمَعُونَ ؟ إنَّ اللهَ لا يُعَذِّبُ بِدمعِ العَيْنِ ، ولا بِحُزْنِ القَلْبِ ، ولكِنْ يُعَذِّبُ بِهذا أوْ يَرْحَمُ » وأشَارَ إلى لِسَانِهِ . متفقٌ عليه .

925. Hazrat Ibn Umar (R.A.A.) relates that the Holy Prophet (S.A.W.) visited Hazrat Sa'd ibn Ubadah (R.A.A.) during his illness. He was accompanied by Hazrat Abdul Rahman ibn Auf, Hazrat Saad ibn Abi Waqqas and Hazrat Abdullah ibn Mas'ud (R.A.A.). The Holy Prophet (S.A.W.) on seeing the critical condition of Hazrat Sa'd (R.A.A.) began to weep, and his companions also started weeping. He (S.A.W.)

told them: Listen! Allah does not punish for shedding tears of the grief of the heart, but punishes or forgives the utterances of this; and he pointed to his tongue. *(Bukhari and Muslim)*

٩٢٦ — وعن أُسامَةَ بنِ زَيْدٍ رضي الله عنهما أنّ رسول اللهِ صلّى اللهُ عليهِ وسلّم رُفِعَ إليهِ ابْنُ ابنتِهِ وهُوَ في الموْتِ . فَفاضَتْ عَيْنا رسولِ اللهِ صلّى اللهُ عليهِ وسلّم . فقال له سعدٌ : ماهذا يارسولَ الله ؟! قال : « هذهِ رحمةٌ جعلها اللهُ تعالى في قلوبِ عبادِهِ ، وإنّما يرْحمُ اللهُ مِنْ عبادِهِ الرُّحماءَ » متفقٌ عليه .

926. This Hadis has been covered partly in No. 29 of Chapter 3.

٩٢٧ — وعن أنسٍ رضيَ اللهُ عنه أنّ رسُولَ اللهِ صلّى اللهُ عليهِ وسلم دَخلَ عَلى ابْنِهِ إبْراهِيمَ رضي الله عنه وَهُوَ يَجُودُ بنَفْسِهِ فَجَعَلَتْ عَيْنا رسولِ اللهِ صلّى اللهُ عليهِ وسلّم تَذْرِفانِ . فقال له عبدُ الرّحمن بنُ عوْفٍ : وأنت يارسولَ الله ؟! فقال : « يَا ابْنَ عَوْفٍ إنّها رَحْمَةٌ » ثُمّ أتْبَعَها بأخْرَى ، فقال : « إنّ العَيْنَ تَدْمَعُ والقَلْبَ يَحْزَنُ ، ولا نَقولُ إلا مايرْضِي رَبَّنا . وإنّا بفِراقِكَ يَا إبْراهيمُ لمَحْزُونُونَ » .

رواه البخاري ، وروى مسلم بعضه .

927. **Hazrat Anas** (R.A.A.) relates that the Holy Prophet visited his son, Hazrat Ibrahim (R.A.A.) when he was dying; seeing this, his eyes began to flow; on this Hazrat Abdur Rehman ibn Auf (R.A.A.) remarked: 'O Messenger of Allah! even you (are weeping). The Holy Prophet (S.A.W.) said: 'Ibn Auf, this is simply mercy, the softness of the heart, so saying he started weeping again, and said: The tears trickle from the eyes, and the heart is full of sorrow, but we say only that which may please our Lord. We are indeed grieved, O Ibrahim, by thy passing away ' *(Bukhari, Muslim* reported some portions)

* * * * * * *

CHAPTER 154

KEEPING SECRET KNOWLEDGE OF THE CONDITION OF A DEAD BODY.

٩٢٨ ــ عن أبي رافع أسلمَ مولى رسول الله صلّى اللهُ عليه وسلّم أنّ رسول الله صلى اللهُ عليه وسلّم قال : « مَنْ غَسَّلَ مَيِّتاً فكَتَمَ عَلَيْه، غَفَرَ اللهُ له أرْبعينَ مَرَّةً » رواه الحاكم وقال : صحيح على شرط مسلم .

928. Hazrat Abu Rafi' Aslam (R.A.A.) a freed slave of the Holy Prophet (S.A.W.) relates that the Holy Prophet (S.A.W.) said: 'He who washes a dead body and keeps secret (his knowledge of its condition) is forgiven by Allah forty times.' *(Hakim)*

* * * * * * *

CHAPTER 155

JOINING FUNERAL PRAYERS AND PROCESSIONS AND PRESENCE ON BURIAL, DISAPPROVAL OF WOMEN ACCOMPANYING FUNERAL PROCESSIONS.

٩٢٩ ــ عن أبي هُرَيْرةَ رَضِيَ اللهُ عنه قال : قالَ رسولُ اللهِ صلّى اللهُ عليه وسلّم : « مَنْ شَهِدَ الجنَازَةَ حتّى يُصَلّى عَلَيها ، فلَهُ قيرَاطٌ ، ومَنْ شَهِدَهَا حتّى تُدْفَنَ ، فلَهُ قيرَاطَانِ » قيلَ : ومَا القيراطَانِ؟ قال : «مِثْلُ الجَبَلَيْنِ العَظِيمَيْنِ » . متفقٌ عليه .

929. This Hadis has already been mentioned in No. 36 of Chapter 3.

٩٣٠ ــ وعنه أنّ رسولَ اللهِ صلّى اللهُ عليهِ وسلّم قال : «مَنِ اتَّبَعَ جَنَازَةَ مُسْلمٍ إيمَاناً وَاحتِساباً ، وكَانَ معَهُ حتّى يُصَلّى عَلَيها ويَفرُغَ مِنْ دَفنِها ، فإنّهُ يَرْجِعُ مِنَ الأجْرِ بِقيرَاطَيْنِ كُلُّ قيرَاطٍ مِثلُ أُحُدٍ ، ومَنْ صَلّى عَلَيهَا ، ثم رَجَعَ قَبْلَ أن تُدْفَنَ ، فإنّهُ يَرجِعُ بِقيرَاطٍ » رواه البخاري

930. This Hadis is the same as No. 37.

٩٣١ – وعن أمِّ عَطِيَّةَ رضيَ الله عنها قَالَتْ : نُهينا عَنِ اتِّبَاعِ الجَنَائِزِ ، ولَم يُعزَمْ عَلَيْنَا » متفقٌ عليه

931. **Hazrat Umm Atiyah** (R.A.A.) says: 'We were not allowed to accompany funeral processions, but this prohibition was not strictly enforced. *(Bukhari and Muslim)*

* * * * * * *

CHAPTER 156

DESIRABILITY OF LARGE CONGREGATION IN FUNERAL PRAYERS AND FORMATION OF THREE OR MORE LINES OF THOSE WHO PRAY.

٩٣٢ – عَنْ عائشةَ رَضِيَ اللهُ عنها قَالَتْ : قالَ رسولُ اللهِ صلَّى اللهُ عليه وسلَّم : مَامِنْ مَيِّتٍ يُصَلِّي عَليهِ أُمَّةٌ مِنَ المُسْلِمِينَ يَبلُغُونَ مائَةً كُلُّهُم يَشْفَعُونَ له إلا شُفِّعُوا فيهِ » رواه مسلم .

932. **Hazrat Ayesha** (R.A.A.) relates that the Holy Prophet (S.A.W.) said: If as many as a hundred Muslims join in funeral prayer for a person, and all of them pray to Allah for his salvation, their recommendation would be granted. *(Muslim)*

٩٣٣ – وعنِ ابنِ عباسٍ رضيَ الله عنهما قال: سَمِعْتُ رَسُولَ اللهِ صلَّى اللهُ عليهِ وسلَّمَ يَقُولُ : «مَا مِنْ رَجُلٍ مُسْلِمٍ يَمُوتُ، فيَقومُ عَلى جَنَازتِهِ أَرْبَعُونَ رَجُلاً لايُشرِكُونَ بِاللهِ شَيْئاً إلاَّ شَفَّعَهُمُ اللهُ فيهِ » رواه مسلم

933. This Hadis is the same as No. 430 of Chapter 51

٩٣٤ – وعن مَرْثَدِ بن عبدِ اللهِ اليَزَنِيِّ قال : كانَ مَالِكُ بنُ هُبَيْرَةَ رضي الله عنه إذا صَلَّى عَلى الجَنَازَةِ ، فتَقَالَّ النَّاسَ عَلَيها ، جَزَّأَهُمْ عَلَيها ثَلاثَةَ أَجزَاءٍ ، ثم قال : قالَ رَسُولُ الله صلَّى اللهُ عليهِ وسلم : « مَنْ صَلَّى عَلَيهِ ثَلاثَةُ صُفُوفٍ ، فَقَدْ أَوْجَبَ » [١٨٨]

رواه أبو داود ، والترمذي وقال : حديث حسن .

934. Hazrat Marsad bin Abdullah Al-Yazani (R.A.A.) relates that when Hazrat Malik bin Hubairah (R.A.A.) while leading a funeral prayer noticed that the number of participants was less, he divided them into three rows, explaining that the Holy Prophet (S.A.W.) had said: 'If three rows of supplicants pray for the deliverance of a deceased person, he would be admitted to Paradise.'

(*Abu Daud* and *Tirmizi* said it is of good chain,)

* * * * * * *

CHAPTER 157

WHAT SHOULD BE RECITED IN FUNERAL PRAYERS.

يُكَبِّرُ أَرْبَعَ تَكبيرَاتٍ : يَتَعَوَّذُ بَعْدَ الأُولى ، ثُمَّ يَقرأُ فَاتِحَةَ الكِتَابِ ، ثُمَّ يُكَبِّرُ الثَّانِيَةَ ، ثُمَّ يُصَلِّي عَلَى النبيِّ صلَّى اللهُ عليهِ وسلَّم ، فيقول : اللَّهُمَّ صَلِّ عَلَى مُحَمَّدٍ ، وَعَلَى آلِ مُحَمَّدٍ . وَالأَفضَلُ أن يُتِمَّهُ بقوله : كَمَا صَلَّيْتَ عَلَى إبراهِيمَ . . إلى قولِهِ : إنَّكَ حَمِيدٌ مَجِيدٌ .

ولايفعَلُ ما يفعلُهُ كثيرٌ مِنَ العوَامِّ مِنْ قِرَاءَتِهِم (إنَّ اللهَ وَمَلائِكَتَهُ يُصَلُّونَ عَلَى النَّبيِّ) الآية[الأحزاب: ٥٦]فَإنَّهُ لاتَصِحُّ صَلاتُهُ إذا اقتَصَرَ عليهِ .
ثم يُكَبِّرُ الثَّالِثَةَ،ويَدعُو للمَيِّتِ وللمُسْلِمينَ بِمَا سَنَذكُرُهُ من الأحاديثِ إن شَاءَ اللهُ تعالى ، ثم يُكَبِّرُ الرَّابعةَ ويَدعُو ، ومِنْ أحْسَنِهِ : اللَّهُمَّ لاَ تَحْرِمْنَا أَجْرَهُ ، ولا تَفتِنَّا بَعدَهُ ، واغْفِرْ لَنَا ولَهُ .

والمُختَارُ أنه يُطَوِّلُ الدُّعاءَ في الرَّابعةِ خِلافَ مايَعتَادُهُ أكثَرُ النَّاسِ ؛ لحديث ابن أبي أَوفى الذي سنَذكُرُهُ إن شاءَ اللهُ تعالى .

فَأمَّا الأَدْعِيَةُ المَأثُورَةُ بَعْدَ التَّكْبِيرَةِ الثالثة ، فمنها :

Note:- Imam Nawawi says that in a funeral prayer (service) four Takbirs should be recited. After the first Takbir "*Ta'awwuz*" (i.e. *A'aoozo-billahe* is to be read followed by Surah *Fateha*; and then the second *Takbir* is to be recited followed by *Salat* on Holy Prophet (S.A.W.) It is better to recite the Salat (Benediction upon the Holy Prophet (S.A.W.) in full i.e.

"Allahumma salle 'ala Muhammadim-wa 'ala aale Muhammad-in kama sallaita 'ala Ibraheema wa 'ala aale Ibraheema wa barik 'ala saiyaidina Muhammadim wa 'ala aale Muhammad-in kama barakta 'ala Ibraheema wa 'ala aale Ibraheema innaka Hameedum Majeed."

"O' Allah! Bless Muhammad and the people of Muhammad, as Thou didst bless Abraham and the people of Abraham. And bless Muhammad and the people of Muhammad, as Thou dids't bless Abraham and the people of Abraham, verily Thou art Praiseworthy, and Glorious."

Recitation of *Salat* is necessary, otherwise the prayer will be defective.

After this the third *Takbir* is recited, and prayer for the salvation of the deceased and the entire Muslim community, and then the fourth *Takbir* should be recited and the supplication. Of all the prayers the best prayer is:-

"Allahumma la tahrim-na ajrahoo wa la taftinna ba' adahoo waghfir lana wa lahoo."

"O Allah! Do not deprive us from its reward and do not involve us in some trouble hereafter and grant us and to the deceased salvation."

It would be still better to prolong the supplication in the **Takbir** According to Hanafi and Maliki schools the recitation of Surah *Fateha* in funeral prayers is not warranted by the tradition of Holy Prophet (S.A.W.). According to them rather the supplication should be read after the first ***Takbir***.

٩٣٥ – عن أبي عبدِ الرحمنِ عوفِ بن مالكٍ رضي الله عنه قال : صلّى رسولُ اللهِ صلّى اللهُ عليهِ وسلّم على جِنازةٍ ، فحفِظتُ مِنْ دُعائِه وهُوَ يقُولُ : « اللّهُمَّ اغفِرْ لهُ ، وارحمْهُ ، وعافِهِ واعفُ عنْهُ ، وأكرِمْ نُزُلَهُ ، ووسِّعْ مُدخَلَهُ ، واغسِلْهُ بالماءِ والثّلجِ والبَرَدِ ، ونقِّهِ منَ الخطايا ، كما نقّيْتَ الثّوبَ الأبيضَ منَ الدّنَسِ ، وأبدِلْهُ داراً خيراً مِنْ دارِه ، وأهلاً خيراً من أهلِهِ ، وزوجاً خيراً مِنْ زوجِهِ ، وأدخِلْهُ الجنّةَ ، وأعِذْهُ من عذابِ القبرِ ، ومِنْ عذابِ النّارِ » حتّى تمنّيْتُ أنْ أكونَ أنا ذلكَ الميّتَ . رواه مسلم .

935. Hazrat Abu Abdur Rehman Auf ibn Malik (R.A.A.) say: The Holy Prophet (S.A.W.) once led the funeral prayer of a deceased person and I committed this prayer in my memory. The Holy Prophet (S.A.W.) supplicated thus :-

> *"Alla-hum-maghfir lahu war ham-hu wa 'afehi wa'fi 'anhu wa akrim nuzu-lahu wa wasse' mud-khalah-hu, wagh-silhu-bil ma'e was-selji wal barade wa naq-qiho minal khataya kama naq-qatas-saubal abyaza minad-danase, wa abdil-hu daaran khairam-min daarihi wa-ah-lan khairam-min ahle-hi wa zau-jan khair-ram min zau-jihi wa ad-khil-hul jan-nata wa a'iz-hu min'azabil qabre wa min'azabin-nar.*

'O' Allah, do forgive him and show mercy to him and keep him safe and sound and excuse him for his faults, and grant him respectable place in the heaven, and make his grave spacious, and wash him with water, snow and ice and purify him of all his sins as a piece of white cloth is cleared of dirt, and grant him a new house better than his (old) house and a family and a wife better than his wife, and allow him to enter the Paradise, and protect him from the torture of the grave and the Hell.

Hearing this supplication, I wished I had been that dead person. *(Muslim)*

٩٣٦ – وعن أبي هُريرة وأبي قَتَادَةَ ، وأبي إبْرَاهِيمَ الأَشْهَلِيِّ عَنْ أبيه – وأبُوه صَحَابِيٌّ – رضي الله عنهم ، عَنِ النبيِّ صلّى الله عليه وسلّم أنّه صَلّى عَلى جِنَازَةٍ فقال : « اللَّهُمَّ اغفِرْ لِحَيِّنَا وَمَيِّتِنَا ، وَصَغيرِنَا وكَبيرِنَا ، وَذَكَرِنَا وَأُنْثَانَا ، وَشَاهِدِنا وَغَائِبِنَا . اللَّهُمَّ مَنْ أَحْيَيْتَه مِنَّا ، فَأَحْيِهِ عَلَى الإسْلامِ ، وَمَنْ تَوَفَّيْتَه مِنَّا ، فَتَوَفَّهُ عَلَى الإيمانِ ؛ اللَّهُمَّ لا تَحْرِمْنا أَجْرَهُ ، وَلا تَفْتِنَّا بَعْدَهُ » رواه الترمذي من رواية أبي هُرَيْرَةَ وَالأَشْهَلِيِّ ، رواه أبو داود من رواية أبي هريرة وأبي قَتَادَةَ . قال الحاكم : حديث أبي هريرة صَحيحٌ على شَرْطِ البُخاريِّ ومُسْلِمٍ ، قال التِّرمِذيُّ : قال البخاريُّ : أصحُّ رواياتِ هذا الحديث روايةُ الأَشْهَلِيِّ . قال البخاري : وَأَصَحُّ شيءٍ في الباب حديث عَوْفِ بن مالكٍ .

936. Hazrat Abu Hurairah (R.A.A.) **Hazrat Abu Qatadah** (R.A.A.) and **Hazrat Abu Ibrahim Ashali** (R.A.A.) on the authority of his father (who was also a companion of the Holy Prophet S.A.W.) relate that the Holy Prophet (S.A.W.) supplicated in a funeral as follows:-

'O' Allah, forgive our living and our dead, our young and old, our men and women and those of us who are alive and those of us who are dead. 'O Allah, one whom Thou dost grant life from among us, let him live in accordance with Islam and one whom Thou dost cause to die from among us, let him die on faith (Iman). Allah do not deprive us of his reward and do not put us on trial after him.'

(Abu Daud and Tirmizi)

٩٣٧ – وعن أبي هُرَيْرَةَ رَضِيَ اللهُ عَنْهُ قَالَ : سَمِعْتُ رَسُولَ اللهِ صلّى اللهُ عليهِ وسلَّم يقول : « إذا صَلَّيْتُمْ عَلى المَيِّتِ ، فَأَخْلِصُوا له الدُّعاءَ » رواه أبو داود

937. Hazrat Abu Hurairah (R.A.A.) relates that he heard the Holy Prophet (S.A.W.) say: 'When you pray for a dead person, do so sincerely!

(Abu Daud)

٩٣٨ – وعَنْهُ عَنِ النَّبِيِّ صلّى اللهُ عَلَيْهِ وسلَّم في الصَّلاةِ عَلى الجَنازَةِ : « اللّهُمَّ أَنْتَ رَبُّهَا ، وَأَنْتَ خَلَقْتَها ، وَأَنْتَ هَدَيْتَها لِلإسْلامِ ، وَأَنْتَ قَبَضْتَ رُوحَهَا ، وَأَنْتَ أَعْلَمُ بِسِرِّهَا وَعَلانِيَتِها ، جِئْنَاكَ شُفَعَاءَ لَهُ ، فاغفِرْ لهُ » رواه أبو داود

938. Hazrat Abu Hurairah (R.A.A.) reports the following supplication from the Holy Prophet (S.A.W.) in a funeral prayer:

'O Allah! Thou art his Lord and Thou hads't createdhim andguided him to accept Islam, and Thou hast taken possession of his soul, and Thou knowest well his hidden and open acts. However, we have come before Thee as his intercessor, so forgive him. *(Abu Daud)*

٩٣٩ – وعن وَاثِلَةَ بنِ الأَسْقَعِ رضيَ اللهُ عنه قال : صَلَّى بِنَا رسولُ اللهِ صلّى اللهُ عليهِ وسلَّم عَلى رَجُلٍ مِنَ المُسْلمينَ ، فَسَمِعْتُهُ يقولُ : « اللّهُمَّ إنَّ فُلانَ ابْنَ فُلانٍ في ذِمَّتِكَ وَحَبْلِ جِوَارِكَ ، فَقِهِ فِتْنَةَ القَبْرِ ، وَعَذَابَ النَّارِ ، وَأَنْتَ أَهْلُ الوَفَاءِ والحَمْدِ ؛ اللّهُمَّ فاغفِرْ لهُ وَارْحَمْهُ ، إنكَ أَنْتَ الغَفُورُ الرَّحيمُ » رواه أبو داود

939. Hazrat Wasillah ibn Al-Asqa'a (R.A.A.) say: The Holy Prophet (S.A.W.) led the funeral prayer of a Muslim when we were also among the congregation. I heard the Holy Prophet (S.A.W.) supplicating:

'O Allah, son of so and so is under Thy protection and in the neighbourhood of Thy (mercy), save him from the torture of the grave and the punishment of the Hell. Thou art the Master of faith and worthy of all praise. 'O Allah! do forgive him and have mercy on him. Undoubtedly Thou art the Most Forgiving and Most Merciful.

(Abu Daud)

٩٤٠ – وعن عبد الله بن أبي أوفى رضي الله عنهما أنَّهُ كبَّرَ على جنازةِ ابنةٍ لهُ أربعَ تكبيراتٍ، فقامَ بعدَ الرَّابعةِ كقدرِ ما بينَ التكبيرتينِ يستغفرُ لها ويدعو، ثُمَّ قال: كانَ رسولُ اللهِ صلَّى اللهُ عليهِ وسلَّمَ يصنعُ هكذا.

وفي رواية: «كبَّرَ أربعاً، فمكثَ ساعةً حتَّى ظننتُ أنَّهُ سيكبِّرُ خمساً، ثُمَّ سلَّمَ عن يمينهِ وعن شمالهِ. فلمَّا انصرفَ قلنا لهُ: ما هذا؟ فقال: إنِّي لا أزيدكُم على ما رأيتُ رسولَ اللهِ صلَّى اللهُ عليهِ وسلَّمَ يصنعُ، أو: هكذا صنعَ رسولُ اللهِ صلَّى اللهُ عليهِ وسلَّمَ»

رواه الحاكم [1] وقال: حديث صحيح

940. About Hazrat Abdullah ibn Abu Aufa (R.A.A.), it is reported that while leading the funeral prayer of his daughter, he pronounced four takbirs, *and* at the end of fourth takbir, he remained standing for as long as the time spent between two takbirs, seeking Allah's forgiveness for her and praying for her. When he finished he said: 'The Holy Prophet (S.A.W.) also used to do like this.'

According to another version: He said four takbirs and then paused in prayer for a while till I thought, he would call the takbir for the fifth time but thereafter he saluted to his right and left. When he turned after completing the prayers, "What is this?" we asked him. He said 'I would not add anything to that which I saw the Holy Prophet (S.A.W.) performed like this. (***Hakim*** has reported this and said this is correct.)

Note. Most of the scholars are unanimous that there are only four takbirs in a funeral prayer. The traditions which attribute more than four takbirs to the Holy Prophet (S.A.W.) relate to the early period. Subsequent traditions mention only four takbirs, which prove that calling of more than four takbirs has been revoked.

* * * * * * *

CHAPTER 158

SPEEDY BURIAL OF THE DEAD

٩٤١ – وعن أبي هُرَيْرَةَ رَضِيَ اللهُ عَنْهُ عَنِ النَّبيِّ صلّى الله عليه وسلَّم قال : « أَسْرِعُوا بِالجَنَازَةِ ، فَإِنْ تَكُ صَالِحَةً ، فَخَيْرٌ تُقَدِّمُونَهَا إِلَيْهِ ، وَإِنْ تَكُ سِوَى ذلِكَ ، فَشَرٌّ تَضَعُونَهُ عَنْ رِقَابِكُمْ » متفقٌ عليه

وفي روايةٍ لِمُسْلِمٍ : « فَخَيْرٌ تُقَدِّمُونَهَا عَلَيْهِ » .

941. Hazrat Abu Hurairah (R.A.A.) relates that the Holy Prophet (S.A.W.) said: Be quick in taking a coffin (to the graveyard), because if the coffin is that of a virtuous and good person, you would hurry him towards good, and should he be otherwise, you should lay down evil from your necks. *(Bukhari and Muslim)*

According to a version of *Imam Muslim* it is benevolence towards which you are taking him.

٩٤٢ – وعن أبي سعيدٍ الخُدْرِيِّ رضي اللهُ عنه قَالَ : كَانَ النَّبيُّ صلّى اللهُ عليهِ وسلَّمَ يَقُولُ : « إذا وُضِعَتِ الجَنَازَةُ ، فَاحْتَمَلَهَا الرِّجَالُ عَلى أَعْنَاقِهِمْ ، فَإِنْ كَانَتْ صَالِحَةً . قالَتْ : قَدِّمُونِي ، وَإِنْ كَانَتْ غَيْرَ صَالِحَةٍ ،قَالَتْ لِأَهْلِهَا : يَاوَيْلَهَا أَيْنَ تَذْهَبُونَ بِهَا ؟ يَسْمَعُ صَوْتَهَا كُلُّ شَيْءٍ إلاَّ الإنْسَانَ ، وَلَوْ سَمِعَ الإنْسَانُ لَصَعِقَ » رواه البخاري

942 This Hadis is the same as No. 444 of Chapter 53.

* * * * * * *

CHAPTER 159

QUICK PAYMENT OF THE DEBTS OF A DECEASED AND SPEEDY BURIAL OF THE DEAD BODY BUT IN CASE OF SUDDEN DEATH TO DELAY TO ASCERTAIN THE FACT OF DEATH

٩٤٣ – عن أبي هريرة رضي الله عنه ، عن النبيِّ صلّى اللهُ عليهِ وسلَّم قال : « نَفْسُ المُؤْمِنِ مُعَلَّقَةٌ بِدَيْنِهِ حَتَّى يُقْضَى عَنْهُ »

رواه الترمذي وقال : حديث حسنٌ .

943. Hazrat Abu Hurairah (R.A.A.) relates that the Holy Prophet (S.A.W.) said: The soul of a deceased believer remains suspended (from his entry into heaven) till the payment of his debt. *(Tirmizi)*

٩٤٤ — وعن حُصَيْنِ بن وَحْوَحٍ رضيَ اللهُ عَنْهُ أنَّ طَلْحَةَ بنَ البَرَاءِ رَضِيَ اللهُ عَنْهُ مَرِضَ، فَأَتَاهُ النَّبيُّ صَلَّى اللهُ عليهِ وسلَّمَ يَعُودُهُ فقَالَ: إنِّي لا أرَى طَلْحَةَ إلاَّ قَدْ حَدَثَ فيهِ المَوْتُ فَآذِنُونِي بِهِ وَعَجِّلُوا بِهِ، فَإِنَّهُ لايَنْبَغِي لِجِيفَةِ مُسْلِمٍ أنْ تُحْبَسَ بَيْنَ ظَهْرَانَيْ أهْلِهِ » .

رواه أبو داود

944. Hazrat Husain ibn Wahwah (R.A.A.) relates that Hazrat Talha bin Bra'a bin 'Aazib (R.A.A.) fell (seriously) ill and as such the Holy Prophet (S.A.W.) visited him to inquire about his health. After he had seen him he said: 'I think that Talha's death is imminent. Therefore let me know when he dies and make haste with his funeral, for it is not proper that the dead body of a Muslim should remain (unnecessarily) with his family.' *(Abu Daud)*

* * * * * * *

CHAPTER 160

EXHORTATION NEAR A GRAVE

٩٤٥ — عن عليٍّ رَضِيَ اللهُ عنه قال: كُنَّا في جَنَازَةٍ في بَقِيعِ الغَرْقَدِ فَأَتَانَا رَسُولُ اللهِ صلَّى اللهُ عَلَيْهِ وسلَّم فقَعَدَ، وَقَعَدْنَا حَوْلَهُ وَمَعَهُ مِخْصَرَةٌ فنَكَسَ وَجَعَلَ يَنْكُتُ بِمِخْصَرَتِهِ، ثم قال: مَا مِنْكُمْ مِنْ أحَدٍ إلّا وَقَدْ كُتِبَ مَقْعَدُهُ مِنَ النَّارِ ومَقْعَدُهُ مِنَ الجَنَّةِ، فقالوا: يا رَسُولَ اللهِ أفَلا نَتَّكِلُ عَلَى كِتَابِنَا؟ فقال: « اعْمَلُوا، فَكُلٌّ مُيَسَّرٌ لِمَا خُلِقَ لَهُ » وذكَرَ تَمامَ الحديث. متفقٌ عليه .

945. Hazrat Ali (R.A.A.) says: 'We were (once) in the cemetry of Baqia in connection with a funeral. In the meantime the Holy Prophet (S.A.W.) came and sat down there. We also took our seats around him. At that time he (S.A.W.) had a pointed walking stick in his hand. He bent down his head (in a pensive mood) and began scratching the ground with his stick, and said: 'Among you there is none who has not had his place already marked in the Hell or in Heaven.' The companions asked:

'O Messenger of Allah! Then let us rest content with what has already been earmarked for each of us?' He answered: 'Continue your efforts. For everybody that thing has been made easy which has been previously destined for him.' He (S.A.W.) then narrated the remaining part of the tradition. *(Bukhari and Muslim)*

* * * * * * *

CHAPTER 161

PRAYING FOR THE DECEASED AFTER BURIAL AND TO STAY NEAR THE GRAVE FOR PRAYERS AND RECITATION OF THE HOLY QURAN

٩٤٦ – عن أبي عَمْرو – وقيل: أبو عبد الله ، وقيل: أبو لَيْلى عُثْمانُ بن عَفَّانَ – رضي الله عنه قال : كانَ النَّبيُّ صلَّى اللهُ عليه وسلَّمَ إذا فَرَغَ من دَفنِ المَيِّتِ وقَفَ علَيه ، وقال : «استَغفِرُوا لأَخيكُم وسَلُوا لَهُ التَّثْبيتَ ، فَإنَّهُ الآن يُسأَلُ » رواه أبو داود

946. Hazrat Abu Amr called as **Abu Abdullah** (his Kunniyat is also Abu Laila) reports from Hazrat Usman ibn Affan (R.A.A.) that after having buried a deceased person, the Holy Prophet (S.A.W.) used to stay near the grave for a while and therefore urge upon the gathering there. 'Seek Allah's forgiveness for your (deceased) brother and pray for his steadfastness because he is now being interrogated.' *(Abu Daud)*

٩٤٧ – وعن عمرو بن العاص رضي الله عنه قال : إذا دَفنتمُوني ، فأقيمُوا حوْلَ قَبرِي قَدْرَ مَا تُنحرُ جزُورٌ ، وَيُقَسَّمُ لحمُها حتى أَستأْنِسَ بِكم ، وَأَعلمَ مَاذا أُرَاجِعُ بِهِ رُسُلَ رَبِّي . رواه مسلم . وقد سبق بطولِه .

قال الشَّافِعِيُّ رَحِمَهُ الله : وَيُسْتَحَبُّ أَن يُقرَأَ عِنْدَهُ شيءٌ مِنَ القُرآنِ ، وَإن ختَمُوا القُرآن عِنْدَهُ كانَ حَسَناً .

947. This Hadis is part of No. 711 of Chapter 95.

Imam Sh'afie said that it is better to recite Quran near the grave. It would be still better if all join in completing the recitation of the Holy Quran.

* * * * * * *

CHAPTER 162

GIVING OF ALMS ON BEHALF OF A DECEASED PERSON AND PRAYING FOR HIS SALVATION

قال الله تعالى : وَالَّذِينَ جَاؤُوا مِنْ بَعْدِهِمْ يَقُولُونَ : رَبَّنَا اغْفِرْ لَنَا وَلإِخْوَانِنَا الَّذِينَ سَبَقُونَا بِالإِيمَانِ [الحشر : ١٠] .

Allah, The Exalted has said:

278. And those who came (into the faith) after that say: Our Lord! Forgive us and our brethren who were before us in the faith. (59:10)

٩٤٨ — وعَنْ عَائِشَةَ رَضِيَ اللهُ عَنْهَا أَنَّ رَجُلاً قال للنَّبِيِّ صلَّى الله عَلَيْهِ وسَلَّمَ : إنَّ أُمِّي افتُلِتَتْ نَفْسُهَا وأُرَاهَا لوتَكَلَّمَتْ ، تَصَدَّقَتْ، فَهَلْ لَهَا أَجْرٌ إن تصَدَّقْتُ عَنْهَا ؟ قال : « نَعَمْ » متفقٌ عليه

948. **Hazrat Ayesha** (R.A.A.) says that a man enquired from the Holy Prophet (S.A.W.), 'My mother met with a sudden death. I think that if she had a chance to speak, she would have given away something in charity. Would it be accounted for as virtuous on her part, if I give some charity on her behalf?' He (S.A.W.) answered: 'Yes.'

(Bukhari and Muslim)

٩٤٩ — وعن أَبي هُرَيْرَةَ رَضِيَ اللهُ عَنْهُ أَنَّ رَسُولَ اللهِ صلَّى اللهُ عَلَيْهِ وَسَلَّمَ قَالَ : « إذا مَاتَ الإنسَانُ انقَطَعَ عَمَلُهُ إلاَّ مِنْ ثَلاثٍ : صَدَقَةٍ جَارِيَةٍ ، أَوْ عِلمٍ يُنْتَفَعُ بِهِ ، أَوْ وَلَدٍ صَالِحٍ يَدعُو له » رواه مسلم

949. **Hazrat Abu Hurairah** (R.A.A.) relates that the Holy Prophet (S.A.W.) said: After the death of a person his actions stop, save three things: that he leaves behind: First continuous charity, second a knowledge from which some benefit may be obtained, and then a virtuous son who prays for him.' *(Muslim)*

* * * * * * *

CHAPTER 163

PRAISING A DEAD PERSON

٩٥٠ — عن أنسٍ رضي الله عنه قال : مَرُّوا بِجَنَازَةٍ ، فَأَثْنَوا عَلَيْهَا خَيْراً ، فقال النبيُّ صلَّى اللهُ عَلَيْهِ وسَلَّمَ : « وَجَبَتْ » ، ثم مَرُّوا بِأُخْرَى ،

فَأَثْنَوْا عليها شَرّاً ، فَقَالَ النَّبيُّ صَلَّى اللهُ عَلَيْهِ وَسَلَّمَ : « وَجَبَتْ » فَقَالَ عُمَرُ بنُ الخَطَّابِ رَضِيَ اللهُ عَنْهُ : ما وَجَبَتْ ؟ قَالَ : « هذا أَثْنَيْتُم عَلَيْهِ خيراً ، فَوَجَبَتْ لَهُ الجَنَّةُ ، وهذا أَثْنَيْتُم عليه شَرّاً ، فَوَجَبَتْ لَهُ النَّارُ ، أَنتُم شُهَدَاءُ اللهِ في الأَرضِ » متفقٌ عليه .

950. Hazrat Anas (R.A.A.) relates that some companions of the Holy Prophet (S.A.W.) happen to pass a funeral procession and praised the deceased upon which the Holy Prophet (S.A.W.) said: 'It has (now) become incumbent.' Soon after they passed by another person's funeral and spoke ill of him. On this the Holy Prophet (S.A.W.) remarked: It has now become incumbent Hazrat Umar Bin Khattab (R.A.A.) inquired from the Holy Prophet (S.A.W.), 'O Messenger of Allah, what has become incumbent?' He (S.A.W.) answered: The one whom you have praised is definitely entitled to heaven, and the person you have spoken ill, is certainly entitled to hell. You are the witnesses of Allah upon the earth.'

(Bukhari and Muslim)

٩٥١ – وعن أبي الأَسودِ قال : قَدِمْتُ المَدِينَةَ ، فَجَلَسْتُ إلى عُمَرَ ابنِ الخَطَّابِ رَضِيَ اللهُ عَنْهُ فَمَرَّتْ بِهِم جَنَازَةٌ ، فَأُثني عَلى صَاحِبِها خَيْراً فقال عُمَرُ : وجَبَت ، ثم مُرَّ بِأُخرَى ، فَأُثني على صَاحِبِها خيراً . فَقَالَ عُمَرُ : وجَبَت ، ثم مُرَّ بِالثَّالِثَةِ ، فَأُثني عَلى صَاحِبِها شَرّاً ، فَقَالَ عُمَرُ : وَجَبَتْ : قَالَ أَبُو الأَسْوَدِ : فَقُلْتُ : وما وجَبَتْ يَا أَميرَ المُؤْمِنِينَ ؟ قال : قُلْتُ كما قَالَ النَّبيُّ صَلَّى اللهُ عَلَيْهِ وَسَلَّمَ : « أَيُّمَا مُسلِم شَهِدَ لهُ أَربعَةٌ بِخَير ، أَدخَلَهُ اللهُ الجَنَّةَ » فَقُلنَا : وثَلاثَةٌ ؟ قال : « وثَلاثَةٌ » فقلنا : واثنَانِ ؟ قال : « واثنَانِ » ثُمَّ لَم نَسأَلْهُ عَنِ الواحِدِ . رواه البخاري

951. Hazrat Abu Aswad (R.A.A.) relates; Once I visited Medina and was sitting with Hazrat Umar bin Khattab (R.A.A.) when a funeral procession passed by and those present there praised the deceased for his virtues. On this Hazrat Umar (R.A.A.) remarked: 'It has (now) become incumbent! Then another funeral procession passed by and those present (on the spot) eulogised the deceased. Hazrat Umar (R.A.A.) repeated his remark that it has (now) become incumbent.' Then a third procession passed and those present condemned the deceased for his wickedness. This time also Hazrat Umar (R.A.A.) said: 'It has (now) become incumbent.' On this Hazrat Abu Aswad inquired: 'O Commander of the Faithfuls! 'What is that thing which has become incumbent?' He answered: I had simply repeated what the Holy Prophet (S.A.W.) had said, that is: "Allah will admit a Muslim into heaven whose good deeds are affirmed by four persons:. We asked: 'If there be only three such persons' He answered: 'Even if there may be only three persons'. Then we asked: 'If there be only two such persons?' He answered: 'Even if there may be only two'. We, however, avoided from asking him about one person. *(Bukhari)*

* * * * * * *

CHAPTER 164

VIRTUES FOR ONE WHO LOSES SMALL CHILDREN

٩٥٢ – عن أنسٍ رضي اللهُ عنهُ قالَ : قالَ رَسُولُ اللهِ صلّى اللهُ عَلَيْهِ وسلَّم : « مَامِنْ مُسلِمٍ يَمُوتُ له ثلاثةٌ لم يبلغُوا الحِنْثَ إلَّا أدخلَهُ اللهُ الجَنَّةَ بِفَضْلِ رَحْمَتِهِ إيَّاهُمْ » متفقٌ عليه

952. Hazrat Anas (R.A.A.) relates that the Holy Prophet (S.A.W.) said. 'When three children of a Muslim die before attaining maturity, Allah will enter him in paradise by His grace on account of these children. *(Bukhari and Muslim)*

٩٥٣ – وعن أبي هُرَيْرَةَ رَضِيَ اللهُ عَنْهُ قالَ : قالَ رَسُولُ اللهِ صلّى اللهُ عليهِ وسلَّم : « لا يَمُوتُ لأَحَدٍ مِنَ المُسْلِمِينَ ثلاثةٌ مِنَ الوَلَدِ لاتَمَسُّهُ النَّارُ إلاَّ تَحِلَّةَ القَسَمِ » متفقٌ عليه

953. Hazrat Abu Hurairah (R.A.A.) says that the Holy Prophet (S.A.W.) said: The fire (of Hell) will not touch a Muslim, three of whose children have died, except as a token for the fulfilment of oath. *(Bukhari and Muslim)*

« وَتَحِلَّةُ القَسَمِ » قولُ اللهِ تعالى : (وَإِنْ مِنْكُمْ إلاَّ وَارِدُهَا) وَالوُرُودُ : هُوَ العُبُورُ عَلَى الصِّرَاطِ ، وَهُوَ جِسْرٌ مَنْصُوبٌ عَلَى ظَهْرِ جَهَنَّمَ . عَافَانَا اللهُ مِنْهَا .

Note.- As a token for the fulfilment of oath is a reference to the command of Allah, the Exalted, that there is not one of you but shall approach it (hell) (19:17).

But another tradition of the Holy Prophet (S.A.W.) says that all the virtuous persons will pass through the bridge over hell but the sinners will fall down in the fire of Hell below.

٩٥٤ ـ وعن أبي سعيد الخُدْرِيِّ رَضِيَ اللهُ عَنْهُ قَالَ : جاءَتِ امرأةٌ إلى رَسُولِ اللهِ صلّى اللهُ عليه وسلّم ، فَقَالَتْ: يا رَسُولَ اللهِ ذَهَبَ الرِّجالُ بِحَدِيثِكَ ، فاجْعَلْ لَنَا مِنْ نَفْسِكَ يَوماً نَأتيكَ فيه تُعَلِّمُنَا مِمَّا عَلَّمَكَ اللهُ ، قَالَ : « اجْتَمِعْنَ يوم كذا وكذا » فاجْتَمَعْنَ ، فَأَتَاهُنَّ النبيُّ صَلَّى اللهُ عَلَيْهِ وسَلَّمَ فَعَلَّمَهُنَّ مِمَّا عَلَّمَهُ اللهُ ، ثُمَّ قَالَ : « مامِنْكُنَّ مِنِ امْرَأَةٍ تُقَدِّمُ ثَلاثَةً مِنَ الوَلَدِ إلاَّ كانُوا لَهَا حِجَاباً مِنَ النَّارِ » فَقَالَتِ امْرَأَةٌ : واثْنَيْنِ ؟ فَقَالَ رَسُولُ اللهِ صلّى اللهُ عَلَيْهِ وَسَلَّمَ « واثْنَيْنِ » متفقٌ عليه

954. Hazrat Abu Sa'eed Khudri (R.A.A.) relates that a woman came to the Holy Prophet (S.A.W.) and said: 'O Messenger of Allah ! The men relate your traditions (which they hear from you). Please, therefore, fix a day for us as well, when we may come to learn from you the thing which Allah has taught you. The Holy Prophet (S.A.W.) fixed a day for this purpose. Accordingly, women assembled on the appointed day, when the Holy Prophet (S.A.W.) came to them and taught them what he had learnt from Allah. He also told them: Any one of you, who has lost three children, for her these children will be a shield from the fire of Hell. A women asked: If somebody has lost only two. The Holy Prophet (S.A.W.) said: "Even two," (such children will shield her from the fire of Hell). *(Bukhari and Muslim)*

* * * * * * *

CHAPTER 165

EXPRESSION OF FEAR AND LAMENTATION OVER THE GRAVES OF TYRANTS, SUBMISSIVENESS TO ALLAH AND ADMONITION AGAINST FAILURE TO DO SO.

٩٥٥ ـ عَنِ ابْنِ عُمَرَ رَضِيَ اللهُ عَنْهُمَا أنَّ رَسُولَ اللهِ صلّى اللهُ عَلَيْهِ وَسَلَّمَ قَالَ لأَصْحَابِهِ ـ يَعْني لَمَّا وَصَلُوا الحِجْرَ : دِيَارَ ثَمُودَ ـ: « لاتَدْخُلُوا عَلَى هَؤُلاءِ المُعَذَّبِينَ إلاَّ أَنْ تَكُونُوا بَاكِينَ ، فَإنْ لَمْ تَكُونُوا بَاكِينَ ، فَلا تَدْخُلُوا عَلَيْهِمْ ؛ لا يُصِيبُكُمْ مَا أَصَابَهُمْ » متفقٌ عليه .

وفي روايةٍ قال : لَمَّا مَرَّ رَسُولُ اللهِ صَلَّى اللهُ عَلَيْهِ وسَلَّمَ بِالحِجْرِ قال : « لا تَدْخُلُوا مَسَاكِنَ الَّذِينَ ظَلَمُوا أَنْفُسَهُمْ أَنْ يُصِيبَكُمْ

مَا أَصَابَهُمْ إلاَّ أَنْ تَكُونُوا بَاكِينَ » ثُمَّ قَنَّعَ رَسُولُ اللهِ صَلَّى الله عليه وَسَلَّمَ رَأْسَهُ وَأَسْرَعَ السَّيْرَ حَتَّى أَجَازَ الوَادِي .

955. Hazrat Ibn Umar (R.A.A.) relates that when the Holy Prophet (S.A.W.) reached the hoary remains in Hijr, the land of Samud, he admonished his companions: 'Do not enter these ill-fated places of the condemned people, without tears (by way of expressing grief and fear) and if you cannot do so, do not pass through them, otherwise you may meet the same fate.' *(Bukhari and Muslim)*

Another version says: When the Holy Prophet (S.A.W.) passed through Hijr, he cautioned his companions: 'Do not enter the houses of the people who had wronged themselves except with tears in your eyes, lest you meet the same fate. Therefore the Holy Prophet (S.A.W.) wrapped his head (with a cloth) and accelerated the pace of his mount and passed hastily from the cursed valley.

* * * * * * *

BOOK OF ETIQUETTE OF JOURNEY

CHAPTER 166

EXCELLENCE OF JOURNEY ON THURSDAY IN THE EARLY MORNING

٩٥٦ – عن كعبِ بن مالكٍ ، رَضيَ اللهُ عنهُ ،أنّ النبيَّ ، صلّى اللهُ عليه وسلّم خرجَ في غزوةِ تبوكَ يومَ الخميسِ ،وكانَ يحبُّ أنْ يخرجَ يومَ الخميسِ. متفقٌ عليه .

وفي رواية في « الصحيحين » لقلّما كانَ رسُولُ الله ، صلّى اللهُ عليهِ وسلّم يخرُجُ إلاّ في يومِ الخميسِ

956. This Hadis has already been covered in the last paragraph of No. 21 of Chapter 2.

٩٥٧ – وعن صَخْرِ بنِ وَدَاعَةَ الغامِديِّ الصّحابيِّ رَضيَ اللهُ عَنْهُ :أنّ رَسُولَ اللهِ صَلّى اللهُ عَلَيْهِ وَسَلّمَ قَالَ : « اللّهُمَّ بَارِكْ لأُمّتي في بكُورها » وكانَ إذا بعَثَ سَرِيّةً أوْ جيشاً بعَثَهُم مِنْ أوّلِ النّهَارِ . وكان صَخْرٌ تاجِراً ، فكانَ يبعَثُ تِجارَتَهُ أوّلَ النّهارِ ، فأثرَى وكَثُرَ مالُهُ ، رواه أبو داود والترمذيُّ وقال : حديثٌ حسن .

957. Hazrat Sakh'r ibn Wad'ah Ghamidi As Sahabi (R.A.A.) relates that the Holy Prophet (S.A.W.) supplicated: *Allahumma Barik Li-Ummati Fi Bukureha :* 'O Allah bless the mornings of my people.' Whenever he despatched a small or big army, he despatched it early in the morning. Hazrat Sakh'r (R.A.A.) was a merchant. He always despatched his goods in the early part of the day and as such his business flourished and his wealth increased. *(Abu Daud and Tirmizi).*

* * * * * * *

CHAPTER 167

EXCELLENCE OF TRAVELLING IN COMPANY UNDER A LEADER AND OBEYING HIM

٩٥٨ – عَن ابنِ عُمَرَ رَضيَ اللهُ عَنهُمَا قَالَ : قَالَ رَسُولُ اللهِ صلّى اللهُ عَلَيْهِ وَسَلّمَ : « لَوْ أنّ النّاسَ يَعلَمُونَ مِنَ الوَحْدَةِ ما أعلَمُ ماسَارَ رَاكِبٌ بِلَيْلٍ وَحْدَهُ » رواه البخاري

958. Hazrat Ibn Umar (R.A.A.) relates that the Holy Prophet (S.A.W.) said: 'If people could know what I know of the hazards of travelling alone, no rider would set forth on a journey alone at night.'

(Bukhari)

٩٥٩ – وعن عمرِو بن شُعَيْبٍ ، عن أبيه ، عن جَدِّهِ رَضِيَ اللهُ عَنْهُ قَالَ : قَالَ رَسُولُ اللهِ صَلَّى اللهُ عَلَيْهِ وَسَلَّمَ : « الرَّاكِبُ شَيطَانٌ ، والرَّاكِبَانِ شَيطَانَانِ ، وَالثَّلاثَةُ رَكْبٌ »

رواه أبو داود ، والترمذي ، والنسائي بأسانيد صحيحة ، وقال الترمذي : حديثٌ حسن .

959. Hazrat ʿAmr ibn Shuaib (R.A.A.) relates on the authority of his father and grandfather that the Holy Prophet (S.A.W.) said: One rider is a Satan, two riders are two Satans and three riders make a caravan (as they will be immune from the hazards of travelling alone).

(Abu Daud, Tirmizi and Nisai)

٩٦٠ – وعن أبي سعيدٍ وأبي هُرَيرةَ رَضِيَ اللهُ عَنْهُما قَالا : قَالَ رسولُ اللهِ صَلَّى اللهُ عليهِ وسلَّم : « إذا خَرَجَ ثَلاثَةٌ في سَفَرٍ فَلْيُؤَمِّرُوا أَحَدَهم »

حديث حسن ، رواه أبو داود بإسنادٍ حسن .

960. Hazrat Abu Saʿeed Khudri (R.A.A.) and **Hazrat Abu Hurairah** (R.A.A.) relate that the Holy Prophet (S.A.W.) said: When three people set out on a journey they should appoint one of them as a leader.

(Abu Daud)

٩٦١ – وعَنِ ابْنِ عَبَّاسٍ رَضِيَ اللهُ عَنْهُما عن النَّبيِّ صَلَّى اللهُ عَلَيْهِ وَسَلَّمَ قَالَ : « خَيرُ الصَّحَابَةِ أَرْبَعَةٌ ، وَخَيرُ السَّرَايَا أَرْبَعُمائَةٍ ، وَخَيرُ الجُيُوشِ أَرْبَعَةُ آلافٍ ، وَلَن يُغْلَبَ اثْنَا عشَرَ أَلفاً عَنْ قِلَّةٍ »

رواه أبو داود والترمذي وقال : حديث حسن .

961. Hazrat Ibn Abbas (R.A.A.) relates that the Holy Prophet (S.A.W.) said: The best company is four, the best scouting party is four hundred and the best army is four thousand; and an army of twelve thousand will not be overpowered for want of numbers.

(Abu Daud and Tirmizi)

* * * * * * *

CHAPTER 168

ETTIQUETTE OF TRAVELLING, ALIGHTING, PASSING THE NIGHT AND SLEEPING IN THE NIGHT, TRAVELLING IN THE NIGHT AND TREATING THE ANIMALS KINDLY, AND KEEPING THEIR NEEDS IN VIEW. CALLING UPON ONE WHO FAILS IN DISCHARGING HIS DUTIES IN THIS BEHALF TO CARRY OUT HIS OBLIGATIONS. JUSTIFICATION FOR HAVING ANOTHER PERSON'S SHARE ON THE MOUNT IF IT BE STRONG ENOUGH.

٩٦٢ – عن أبي هُرَيْرَةَ رَضِيَ اللهُ عَنْهُ قَالَ : قَالَ رَسُولُ اللهِ صَلَّى اللهُ عَلَيْهِ وَسَلَّمَ : « إذا سَافَرْتم في الخِصْبِ فَأَعْطُوا الإبِلَ حَظَّهَا مِنَ الأَرْضِ ، وإذا سَافَرْتُمْ في الجَدْبِ ، فَأَسْرِعُوا عَلَيْهَا السَّيْرَ . وبَادِروا بِهَا نِقْيَهَا ، وإذا عَرَّسْتُم ، فَاجْتَنِبُوا الطَّرِيقَ ، فَإنَّهَا طُرُقُ الدَّوَابِّ ، وَمَأْوَى الهَوَامِّ بِاللَّيْلِ » رواه مسلم .

962. Hazrat Abu Hurairah (R.A.A.) relates that the Holy Prophet (S.A.W.) said: 'When you travel through fertile land, give the camels their share from the (vegetation of the) land and when you travel through barren tracts, hasten your pace and thus conserve their energy; and when you halt for the night, leave the track unoccupied, for it is also the passage for the beasts and the haunt of insects and reptiles during the night.' *(Muslim)*

٩٦٣ – وعن أبي قتَادَةَ ، رَضِيَ اللهُ عنهُ ، قَالَ : كانَ رسولُ اللهِ . صلَّى اللهُ عليهِ وسلَّم ، إذا كانَ في سَفَرٍ ، فعَرَّسَ بليْلٍ اضْطَجَعَ علَى يَمينِه وَإذا عَرَّسَ قُبيْلَ الصُّبْحِ نَصَبَ ذِرَاعَهُ ، ووَضَعَ رَأْسَهُ عَلى كَفِّهِ . رواه مسلم

963. Hazrat Abu Qatadah (R.A.A.) says that when in the course of a journey, the Holy Prophet (S.A.W.) used to halt in the latter part of the night, he would lie down on his right side. And if halted a little before dawn, he would stretch out, raising his arm and resting his head on his palm. *(Muslim)*

Note:- This he would do so that he may not fall asleep and miss or delay his morning prayers.

٩٦٤ – عن أنسٍ ، رَضِيَ اللهُ عنهُ ، قَالَ : قَالَ رسولُ اللهِ ، صلَّى اللهُ عليهِ وسلَّم : « عَلَيْكُم بِالدُّلْجَةِ ، فَإنَّ الأَرْضَ تُطْوَى بِاللَّيْلِ »

رواه أبو داود بإسناد حسن .

964. Hazrat Anas (R.A.A.) relates that the Holy Prophet (S.A.W.) asked us: You should always journey by night because the earth is shortened during night.' *(Abu Daud)*

٩٦٥ — وعن أبي ثَعْلَبَةَ الخُشَنيِّ ، رَضِيَ اللهُ عنهُ ، قالَ : كانَ النَّاس إذا نَزَلُوا مَنْزِلاً تَفَرَّقُوا في الشِّعَابِ وَالأَوْدِيَةِ . فقالَ رسول الله ، صلَّى الله عليه وسلَّم : « إنَّ تَفَرُّقَكُمْ في هذهِ الشِّعَابِ وَالأَوْدِيَةِ إنَّمَا ذلكُمْ منَ الشَّيْطَانِ ! » فَلَمْ يَنْزِلُوا بَعْدَ ذلكَ مَنْزِلاً إلاَّ انْضَمَّ بَعْضُهُمْ إلى بَعْضٍ . رواه أبو داود بإسناد حسن .

965. Hazrat Abu Salabah Khushanie (R.A.A.) says that when (we) halted in the course of a journey (we) used to disperse in the valleys and dales. The Holy Prophet (S.A.W.) noticing this would remark: 'Your dispersing in the hills and valleys is (due to the instigation) from Satan.' Thereafter whenever the companions made a camp they used to be close to one another. *(Abu Daud)*

٩٦٦ — وعَنْ سَهْلِ بنِ عمرٍو — وَقيلَ سَهْلِ بن الرَّبيعِ بنِ عَمْرٍو الأَنْصَاريِّ المَعْروفِ بابنِ الحَنْظَلِيَّةِ ، وَهُوَ منْ أَهْلِ بَيْعَةِ الرِّضْوَانِ ، رَضِيَ الله عنه ، قالَ : مرَّ رسول اللهِ ، صلَّى الله عليهِ وسلَّم ، ببَعيرٍ قَدْ لَحِقَ ظَهْرُهُ ببَطْنِهِ ، فقال : « اتَّقُوا اللهَ في هذه البَهائِمِ المُعْجَمَةِ ، فَارْكَبُوها صَالِحَةً ، وكُلُوها صَالِحَةً » رواه أبو داود بإسناد صحيح .

966. Hazrat Sahl ibn 'Amr (R.A.A.) who is also called as Sahl bin Rabi' bin 'Amr Al-Ansari and known as Ibn Hanzalia who was one of those who took the oath of Ridwan at Hudaibiya relates that the Holy Prophet (S.A.W.) once passed by a camel whose belly was sticking to his back (due to weakness). On this he remarked, 'Fear Allah as regards these inarticulate animals. Ride on them while they are healthy and similarly eat their meat when they are in good health. *(Abu Daud)*

٩٦٧ — وعَنْ أبي جعفرٍ عبدِ اللهِ بنِ جعفرٍ ، رَضِيَ الله عنهما ، قالَ : أَرْدَفني رسول اللهِ ، صلَّى الله عليه وسلَّم ، ذاتَ يَوْمٍ خَلْفَه ، وَأَسَرَّ إليَّ حَديثاً لاأُحَدِّث بهِ أَحَداً منَ النَّاسِ ، وكانَ أَحَبَّ مَا اسْتَتَرَ بهِ رسول الله ، صلَّى اللهُ عليهِ وسلَّم ، لِحاجَتِهِ هَدَفٌ أَوْ حَائِشُ نَخلٍ . يَعْني :

حَائِطَ نَخْلٍ . رواه مسلم هكذا مختصراً .

وزاد فيهِ البَرْقاني بإسناد مسلم بعد قوله : حَائِشُ نَخْلٍ : فَدَخَلَ حَائطاً لِرَجُلٍ مِنَ الأنصارِ ، فإذا فيهِ جَمَلٌ ، فلَمَّا رَأى رسولَ الله ، صلى اللهُ عليهِ وسلَّمَ ، جَرْجَرَ وَذَرَفَتْ عَيْناهُ ، فأتاهُ النبيُّ ، صلّى اللهُ عليه وسلّم ،فَمَسَحَ سَرَاتَهُ ــ أي : سنامَهُ ــ وَذِفْرَاهُ فَسَكَنَ ؛ فقال : « مَنْ رَبُّ هذا الجَمَلِ ، لِمَنْ هَذا الجَمَلُ ؟ » فَجاءَ فَتىً مِنَ الأنصارِ فقالَ : هذا لي يا رسولَ اللهِ . فقالَ : « أفَلا تَتَّقِي اللهَ في هذهِ البَهيمَةِ التي مَلَّكَكَ اللهُ إيّاهَا ؟ فإنَّهُ يَشْكُو إليَّ أنَّكَ تُجيعُهُ وَتُدْئِبُهُ »

ورواه أبو داود كروايةِ البَرْقاني .

967. Hazrat Abu Ja'far Abdullah ibn Ja'far (R.A.A.) says. Once the Holy Prophet (S.A.W.) made me sit behind him on the pillion seat and said something in confidence to me which I shall not tell to anyone. I feel pride that he did not screen himself from me (while answering the call of nature) behind a wall or a date palm tree. *(Muslim).* To this *Imam Barqani* has added: 'Thereafter the Holy Prophet (S.A.W.) entered a garden belonging to an Ansari and by chance saw there a camel which, on seeing the Holy Prophet (S.A.W.) groaned and started weeping. The Holy Prophet (S.A.W.) went to the camel and patted it on the hump and the upper portion of its head, thereby the camel felt comforted. The Holy Prophet (S.A.W.) then wanted to know as to who was the owner of this camel. One of the Ansari youths stepped forward and said, 'O Messenger of Allah! This camel belongs to me. He said. 'Do you not fear Allah regarding the maintenance of these animals of which He has made you the owner? This camel complains that you do not feed it well, and load it heavily.' *(Abu Daud)*

٩٦٨ ــ وعن أنسٍ ، رَضِيَ اللهُ عنهُ ، قال : كُنَّا إذا نَزَلْنا مَنْزِلاً ، لانُسَبِّحُ حتَّى نَحُلَّ الرِّحَالَ . رواه أبو داود بإسناد على شرط مسلم .

وقوله : « لانُسَبِّحُ » : أيْ لا نُصَلِّي النَّافلَةَ ، ومعناه : أنَّا ــ مَعَ حِرْصِنا عَلى الصَّلاةِ ــ لانُقَدِّمُها عَلى حَطِّ الرِّحالِ وَإراحَةِ الدَّوابِّ .

968. Hazrat Anas (R.A.A.) relates: When we used to make a camp, we would first take off the saddle from our animals, and then said our obligatory prayers.

* * * * * * *

CHAPTER 169

HELPING A COMPANION WHILE ON JOURNEY

٩٦٩ – وعن أبي سعيدٍ الخُدْرِيِّ ، رَضيَ اللهُ عنهُ ، قال : بَيْنَما نَحْنُ في سَفَرٍ إذ جَاءَ رَجُلٌ عَلى رَاحِلةٍ لهُ ، فَجَعَلَ يَصْرِفُ بَصَرَهُ يَميناً وَشِمَالاً ، فقالَ رسولُ الله ، صلَّى اللهُ عليهِ وسلَّم : « مَنْ كانَ معهُ فَضْلُ ظَهرٍ ؛ فَلْيَعُدْ بهِ عَلى مَنْ لاظَهرَ له ، وَمنْ كانَ له فَضلُ زَادٍ ؛ فَلْيَعُدْ بهِ عَلى مَنْ لا زَادَ له » فَذَكَرَ مِنْ أَصْناف المال ماذَكَرَهُ ، حتى رَأَينا : أنَّهُ لاحَقَّ لأحَدٍ منا في فضْلٍ . رواه مسلم

969. This Hadis is the same as No. 566 of Chapter 62.

٩٧٠ – وعَنْ جابرٍ رضيَ اللهُ عنهُ ، عَنْ رسولِ اللهِ ، صلَّى اللهُ عليهِ وسلَّم ، أنَّهُ أَرَادَ أَنْ يَغْزُوَ ، فقال : يَامَعْشَرَ المُهَاجِرِينَ والأنصَارِ ! إنَّ مِنْ إخوَانِكُمْ قَوْماً ، لَيسَ لهمْ مَالٌ ، وَلا عَشِيرَةٌ ، فَلْيَضُمَّ أَحَدكم إليْهِ الرَّجُلَيْنِ ، أَوِ الثَّلاثَةَ ، فَما لِأحَدِنَا منْ ظهرٍ يَحْمِلُهُ إلا عُقْبَةٌ ١٩٣ كَعُقْبَةِ ، يَعْني أحَدهمْ . قال : فَضَمَمْتُ إليَّ اثْنَيْنِ أَوْ ثَلاثَةً مَا لي إلاَّ عُقْبَةٌ كعقبَةِ أَحَدهمْ مِنْ جَملي . رواه أبو داود

970. Hazrat Jabir (R.A.A.) relates that when the Holy Prophet (S.A.W.) was preparing for a campaign he (S.A.W.) addressed us 'O ye the gathering of emigrants and helpers! There are among you persons who have no money and nor they belong to any tribe; then let everyone of you should let two or three of them join with him because due to shortage of transport animals, everybody will have to ride on animal turn by turn. As such I associated two or three (such persons) with me and I shared my camel turn by turn equally with them. *(Abu Daud)*

٩٧١ – وعنه قال : كانَ رسولُ اللهِ ، صلَّى الله عليهِ وسلَّم ، يتَخلَّف في المَسيرِ ، فيُزْجِي الضَّعيفَ ويُرْدِف ويَدعُوا له . رواه أبو داود بإسناد حسن .

971. Hazrat Jabir (R.A.A.) relates that the Holy Prohet (S.A.W.) always used .to be in the rear in order to help in driving the weaker animals and to give a lift to those who had no mount, and were walking on foot and to pray for them. *(Abu Daud)*

* * * * * * *

CHAPTER 170

SUPPLICATION WHEN RIDING A MOUNT ON A JOURNEY

قالَ الله تعالى : وَجَعَلَ لَكُم مِنَ الفُلْكِ والأَنْعامِ ماتَرْكَبُونَ .
لِتَسْتَوُوا عَلَى ظُهورِهِ ثُمَّ تَذْكُرُوا نِعْمَةَ رَبِّكُمْ إذا اسْتَوَيْتُمْ عَلَيْه وتَقولوا :
سُبْحَانَ الَّذي سَخَّرَ لَنا هذا وَما كُنَّا لَهُ مُقرنِينَ . وَإنَّا إلى رَبِّنَا لَمُنْقَلِبونَ
[الزخرف : ١٢ ، ١٤]

Allah, the Exalted has said:

279. He who created all the pairs, and appointed for you ships and cattle whereupon ye ride. That ye may mount upon their backs, and may remember your Lord's favour when ye mount thereon, and may say: Glorified be He, who hath subdued these unto us, and we were not capable (of subduing them), and lo! unto our Lord we are returning.
(43.12-14)

٩٧٢ — وعن ابنِ عمرَ ، رَضيَ الله عنهما ، أَنَّ رسولَ الله ، صلّى الله
عليهِ وسلَّم ، كانَ إذا استَوَى عَلى بَعيرِهِ خَارجاً إلى سَفَرٍ ؛ كَبَّرَ ثَلاثاً ،
ثمَّ قالَ : « سُبْحَانَ الذي سَخَّرَ لَنَا هذا وَما كنَّاله مُقرنِينَ ، وَإنَّا إلى رَبِّنَا
لمُنقَلِبُونَ . اللَّهُمَّ إنَّا نَسْأَلُكَ في سَفَرِنَا هذا البِرَّ وَالتَّقوَى ، وَمِنَ العَمَلِ
ماتَرْضى . اللَّهُمَّ هَوِّنْ عَلَيْنَا سَفَرَنَا هذا وَاطْوِ عَنَّا بُعْدَهُ . اللَّهُمَّ أَنتَ
الصَّاحِبُ في السَّفَرِ ، وَالخَلِيفَةُ في الأَهْلِ . اللَّهُمَّ إنِّي أَعوذُ بِكَ مِنْ وَعْثَاءِ
السَّفَرِ ، وكَآبَةِ المَنظَرِ ، وَسُوءِ المُنْقَلَبِ في المَالِ وَالأَهلِ وَالوَلَدِ » وَإذا
رَجَعَ قَالَهُنَّ وزَادَ فِيهِنَّ : « آيِبونَ تَائِبونَ عَابِدُونَ لِرَبِّنَا حَامِدُونَ »
رواه مسلم

972. Hazrat Ibn 'Umar (R.A.A.) relates that when the Holy Prophet (S.A.W.) rode a camel while starting on a journey he used to recite: *Allah-o-Akbar:* (Allah is Great) three times, and would then supplicate: Glorified be He who has subdued these unto us, and we were not able to subdue them, and Lo unto our Lord we are returning. Allah, we request Thee for virtue and piety and such deed in this journey as may please Thee O Allah, make this journey comfortable for us and fold up (shorten) its length for our sake. O Allah, Thou art our Protector in this journey and the Guardian of our families we left behind. O Allah! I solicit Thy help from the hardships and difficulties of our journey and I pray that I may not encounter any grief on my return regarding my assets and my family.'

On his return he used to repeat the same supplication and would add:

We are returning from journey in safety, turning to our Lord seeking His forgiveness, worshipping Him and praising Him. *(Muslim)*

٩٧٣ – وعن عبد الله بن سَرْجِسَ ، رَضِيَ اللهُ عنهُ قالَ :كانَ رسولُ اللهِ صلَّى اللهُ عليهِ وسلَّم إذا سافرَ يتعوَّذُ مِنْ وَعْثاءِ السفَرِ ، وكآبَةِ المُنْقلَبِ ، وَالحَوْرِ بَعْدَ الكَوْنِ ، ودَعْوَةِ المَظْلُومِ . وَسُوءِ المَنْظَرِ في الأَهْلِ وَالمَالِ . رواه مسلم . هكذا هو في صحيحِ مسلمِ : الحورِ بَعْدَ الكوْنِ ، بالنون،وكذا رواه الترمذيُّ ، والنسائيُّ . قال الترمذي : ويروى « الكَوْرُ » بالراء ، وكِلاهُما لهُ وَجْهٌ .

973. **Hazrat Abdullah bin Sarjis** (R.A.A.) says that when the Holy Prophet (S.A.W.) started on a journey he used to pray seeking Allah's help against the hardships and difficulties of the journey, and returning in a distressed condition, and suffering loss after gain and with the curse of an oppressed person and witnessing anything unpleasant and horrible relating to property and family.' *(Muslim)*

Note: The two words "*Haur*" and "*Kaun*" used in this tradition mean to return (from a journey) stability or abundance to (with) some defect and shortage (loss)

٩٧٤ – وعن عَلِيِّ بن رَبيعَة قال : شَهِدْتُ عليَّ بنَ أبي طالب رَضِيَ اللهُ عنهُ أُتِيَ بِدَابَّةٍ لِيَرْكَبَها ، فلَمَّا وَضَعَ رِجْلَهُ في الرِّكابِ قال : بِسْمِ اللهِ ، فلَمَّا استَوَى علَى ظَهْرِها قال الحَمْدُ للهِ الذي سَخَّرَ لنَا هذا ، وَما كُنَّا لَهُ مُقْرِنينَ ، وَإنَّا إلى رَبِّنا لمُنْقَلِبُونَ ، ثُمَّ قالَ:الحَمْدُ للهِ ، ثَلاثَ مرَّاتٍ ، ثُمَّ قال:اللهُ أكبَرُ، ثَلاثَ مرَّاتٍ ، ثُمَّ قال : سُبْحانَكَ إنِّي ظَلَمْتُ نَفْسي فَاغْفِرْ لي إنَّهُ لايَغْفِرُ الذُّنُوبَ إلاَّ أَنْتَ ، ثُمَّ ضَحِكَ ، فَقِيلَ : يا أميرَ المُؤْمِنِينَ ، مِنْ أيِّ شَيْءٍ ضَحِكْتَ ؟ قال : رَأَيْتُ النبيَّ صلَّى اللهُ عليهِ وسلَّم فعَلَ كما فعَلْتُ ، ثُمَّ ضَحِكَ ، فقلتُ : يا رسولَ اللهِ مِنْ أيِّ شَيْءٍ ضَحِكْتَ ؟ قال : « إنَّ رَبَّكَ سُبْحانَهُ يَعْجَبُ مِنْ عَبْدِه إذا قال : اغْفِرْ

لي ذنوبي ، يَعْلَمُ أَنَّهُ لا يَغْفِرُ الذُّنُوبَ غَيْرِي » . رواه أبو داود ، والترمذي

وقال : حديثٌ حسنٌ ، وفي بعض النسخ : حسنٌ صحيحٌ . وهذا لفظ أبي داود .

974. **Hazrat Ali ibn Rabia** relates: Once I went to see **Hazrat Ali bin Abu Talib** when an animal was brought for him to ride. When he inserted his foot in the stirrup he said: '*Bismillah*' (in the name of Allah), and when he had fully settled down on the saddle, he affirmed:

Alhamdo Lilla-hil-lazi sakh-khara lana haaza Wama kunna Lahu Muq-re-neena wa inna ila rab-bina La-Mun-qaleboon. Sub-hanaka inni zalam-ṭu naf si fagh-fir-li in-nahu la yagh-fir uz-zunooba illa anta.

'Praised be He, Who hath subdued these unto us, and we were not capable of subduing them and Lo! unto our Lord weare returning,'

Then he recited three times: *Al-hamdo-lil-lah* (All praise is due to Allah) and thereafter he said three times: *Allah-o Akbar* (Allah is Great) and then he affirmed:

Holy art Thou. I have wronged my soul, do Thou forgive me, for none forgives sins save Thyself:

and then he smiled. Somebody asked: 'O Ruler of the Muslims, why did you smile.' He replied: I have seen the Holy Prophet (S.A.W.) doing like this, and when I asked him, 'O Messenger of Allah, why did you smile ?' He said, 'Your Holy and Exalted Sustainer expresses His pleasure with that servant who asks for his forgiveness believing that there is none except Him who can forgive sins. *(Abu Daud and Tirmizi)*

* * * * * * *

CHAPTER 171

THE TRAVELLER SHOULD SAY TAKBIR WHEN ASCENDING AND TO SAY SUBHAN ALLAH WHILE DESCENDING AND PROHIBITION OF RECITING TAKBIR IN A LOUDER TONE.

٩٧٥ — عن جابرٍ رَضيَ اللهُ عنهُ قال : كُنَّا إذا صَعِدْنَا كَبَّرْنَا ، وَإذا نَزَلْنَا سَبَّحْنا . رواه البخاري

975. **Hazrat Jabir** relates. When we ascended a height we used to say *Allah-o-Akbar* (Allah is Great) and when we descended from a height we used to say '*Subhan Allah*' (Holy is Allah). *(Bukhari)*

٩٧٦ — وعنِ ابنِ عُمرَ رَضيَ اللهُ عنهما قال : كانَ النبيُّ صلّى اللهُ عليهِ وسلّم وَجيُوشُهُ إذا عَلَوُا الثَّنَايَا كَبَّرُوا ، وَإذا هَبَطُوا سَبَّحوا .

رواه أبوداود بإسناد صحيح .

976. Hazrat Ibn 'Umar (R.A.A.) relates that when the Holy Prophet (S.A.W.) and his army climbed a height they used to say Takbir *(Allah-o-Akbar)* i.e. Allah is Great, and when they came down they would say *Subhan Allah* i.e. Allah is Holy. *(Abu Daud* has quoted this tradition with sound chain).

٩٧٧ – وعنهُ قال : كانَ النَّبيُّ صلَّى اللهُ عليهِ وسلَّمَ إذا قَفَلَ مِنَ الحَجِّ أو العُمْرَةِ كُلَّمَا أوفى على ثَنِيَّةٍ أوْ فَدْفَدٍ كَبَّرَ ثَلاثاً ، ثُمَّ قال : « لاإلهَ إلاَّ اللهُ وَحْدَهُ لاشَرِيكَ لهُ ، لَهُ المُلْكُ وَلَهُ الحَمْدُ ، وَهُوَ عَلى كلِّ شَيْءٍ قَدِيرٌ . آيِبُونَ تَائِبُونَ عَابِدونَ سَاجِدُونَ لِرَبِّنَا حَامِدُونَ . صَدَقَ اللهُ وَعْدَهُ ، وَنَصَرَ عَبْدَهُ ، وَهَزَمَ الأَحْزابَ وَحْدَهُ » متفقٌ عليه

وفي روايةٍ لمسلم : إذا قَفَلَ مِنَ الجيُوشِ أوِ السَّرَايَا أو الحَجِّ أَو العُمْرَةِ .

977. Hazrat Ibn 'Umar (R.A.A.) relates that when the Holy Prophet (S.A.W.) used to return from Hajj or Umra and had to climb a height *en route* he would recite Takbir *Allah-o-Akbar* i.e. Allah is Great, three times, and would then say, 'There is none worthy of worship save Allah, the only One, without any associate. Sovereignty belongs to Him, and all praise is for Him, and He has power over all the things. We are returning in safety, repentant for our sins, worshipping Him, prostrating ourselves before Him and eulogising our Sustainer, Allah has fulfilled His promise, and has helped His servant and has singly defeated the armies (of enemies). *(Bukhari and Muslim)*

Imam Muslim adds: When he returned from an engagement or an expedition, Hajj,or Umra.

٩٧٨ – وعن أبي هُرَيرَةَ رَضِيَ اللهُ عنهُ أنَّ رَجلاً قال : يا رسولَ اللهِ ، إنِي أُرِيدُ أن أُسافرَ فَأَوْصِنِي ، قال : « عَلَيْكَ بِتَقوى اللهِ ، وَالتَّكبِيرِ عَلى كلِّ شَرَفٍ » فَلَمَّا وَلَّى الرَّجُلُ قالَ : « اللَّهمَّ اطْوِ لهُ البُعْدَ ، وَهَوِّنْ عَلَيْهِ السَّفَرَ » رواه الترمذي وقال : حديث حسن .

978. Hazrat Abu Hurairah (R.A.A.) says that a person submitted to the Holy Prophet: 'O Messenger of Allah, I intend to proceed on a journey, kindly advise me'. The Holy Prophet (S.A.W.) advised him 'Hold fast to piety (as directed by Allah), and while ascending a height say Takbir i.e. *Allah-o-Akbar.* When the said man had already started, the Holy Prophet (S.A.W.) prayed for him thus:

Alla-hum-mat-wil-hul-bu'da wa hawiwan 'alaihis-safar.
'O Allah! shorten the length of the journey for him and make it easy for him.' *(Tirmizi)*

٩٧٩ — وعن أبي موسى الأشعري رضي الله عنه قال : كنّا مع النبي صلّى الله عليه وسلم في سفرٍ ، فكنّا إذا أشرفنا على وادٍ هلّلنا وكبّرنا وارتفعت أصواتنا ، فقال النبيُّ صلّى الله عليه وسلّم : « يا أيُّها الناس اربعُوا على أنفُسكم فإنّكم لا تدعون أصمّ ولا غائباً . إنّه معكم ، إنّه سميعٌ قريبٌ» متفقٌ عليه .

979. Hazrat Abu Musa Ash'ari (R.A.A.) relates: 'Once we accompanied the Holy Prophet (S.A.W.) on a journey and when we had to climb a height we used to say loudly: *La Ilaha illallah* and *Allaho Akbar.* There is none worthy of worship save Allah and Allah is Great. On this the Holy Prophet (S.A.W.) cautioned us: 'O people, do not tax yourself so much. You are not calling the One who is deaf and non-existent. He is (always) close with you, undoubtedly He is All-hearing and close.''
(Bukhari and Muslim)

* * * * * * *

CHAPTER 172

VIRTUE OF PRAYING WHILE IN JOURNEY

٩٨٠ — عن أبي هُريرة رضي الله عنه قال : قال رسولُ الله صلّى الله عليه وسلّم : « ثلاثُ دعواتٍ مُستجاباتٌ لا شكّ فيهنّ : دعوةُ المظلومِ ، ودعوةُ المسافرِ . ودعوةُ الوالدِ على ولدِهِ » رواه أبو داود . والترمذي وقال : حديث حسن . وليس في رواية أبي داود : « على ولدِهِ » .

980. Hazrat Abu Hurairah (R.A.A.) says that the Holy Prophet (S.A.W.) said: Three kinds of prayers are to be granted without an iota of doubt: the prayer of an oppressed person, the prayer of a traveller and the prayer of a father for his son. *(Abu Daud and Tirmizi)*

* * * * * * *

CHAPTER 173

WHAT TO PRAY WHEN FEARING MEN OR SOMETHING ELSE

٩٨١ – عن أبي موسى الأشعَرِيِّ رَضِيَ اللهُ عنهُ أنَّ رسولَ اللهِ صلَّى اللهُ عَليهِ وسلَّمَ كانَ إذا خافَ قَوْماً قال : « اللَّهُمَّ إنَّا نَجعَلُكَ في نُحورِهِمْ ، وَنعُوذُ بِكَ مِنْ شُرُورِهِمْ » رواه أبو داود ، والنسائي بإسنادٍ صحيحٍ .

981. Hazrat Abu Musa Ash'ari (R.A.A.) relates that when the Holy Prophet (S.A.W.) anticipated some danger or mischief from a people, he used to pray thus: *'Alla--humma inna naj'aluka fee nuh re-him Wa na'oozo bika min shuroore-him.* 'O Allah! We seek Thy help against them and solicit Thy shield to thwart their mischief.'

(Abu Daud and Nasai)

* * * * * * *

CHAPTER 174

WHAT TO PRAY ON ARRIVING AT A PLACE

٩٨٢ – عن خَولَةَ بنتِ حَكيمٍ رَضِيَ اللهُ عنها قالتْ : سَمِعْتُ رسولَ اللهِ صلَّى اللهُ عليهِ وسلَّم يقولُ : « مَنْ نَزَلَ مَنزِلاً ثُمَّ قال : أعُوذُ بِكَلِماتِ اللهِ التَّامَّاتِ مِنْ شَرِّ مَا خَلَقَ : لَمْ يَضرُّهُ شَيْءٌ حتَّى يَرْتَحِلَ مِنْ مَنزِلِهِ ذلكَ » رواه مسلم

982. Hazrat Khaulah bint Hakim (R.A.A.) relates that she heard the Holy Prophet (S.A.W.) say: A person who breaks journey at a place and then prays: *A'oozo be-kalematil-la-hittam-matemin Sharrema khalaq.* 'I solicit Allah's protection with the help of His words (prayers) against the mischief of the things which he has created.' Such a person will then remain immune from the harm of those things till he departs from there.

(Muslim)

٩٨٣ – [عن] ابنِ عمرَ رَضِيَ اللهُ عَنهمَا قال : كانَ رسولُ اللهِ صلَّى اللهُ عَليهِ وسلَّمَ إذا سافَرَ فَأقبَلَ اللَّيْلُ قال : « يا أرْضُ ، رَبِّي وَرَبُّكِ اللهُ ، أعُوذُ باللهِ مِنْ شَرِّكِ وَشَرِّ مَا فيكِ ، وَشَرِّ مَا خلقَ فيكِ ، وَشَرِّ مَا يدبُّ عليكِ أعوذ باللهِ مِنْ شَرِّ أسَدٍ وَأسْوَدٍ ، وَمِنَ الحَيَّةِ وَالعَقرَبِ ، وَمِنْ سَاكِنِ البلَدِ ، وَمِنْ وَالِدٍ وَمَا وَلَدَ » رواه أبو داود

983. Hazrat Ibn 'Umar (R.A.A.) relates that whenever in the course of a journey the Holy Prophet (S.A.W.) met with night-fall he would say:

'O earth, Allah is my Sustainer as well as thine. I solicit Allah's protection from thy mischief, and the mischief of that thing which is inside thee, and the mischief of that evil which has been created in thee, and the harm of that creature which walks over thee. I seek Allah's protection against the mischief of a lion, a black cobra and snakes, a scorpion and the mischief from the dwellers of the town, the breeder and which it breeds. *(Abu Daud)*

Note: According to Imam Khattabi, by dwellers of towns is meant genies or evil spirits who dwell on earth.

* * * * * * *

CHAPTER 175

VIRTUE OF EARLY RETURN OF THE TRAVELLER TO HOME AFTER COMPLETION OF HIS MISSION

٩٨٤ — عن أبي هُرَيْرَةَ رَضِيَ اللهُ عنهُ أنَّ رسولَ اللهِ صلَّى اللهُ عليهِ وسلَّمَ قالَ : « السَّفَرُ قِطْعَةٌ مِنَ العَذَابِ ؛ يَمْنَعُ أحَدَكُم طَعَامَهُ ، وشَرَابَهُ وَنَوْمَهُ ، فإذا قَضَى أحَدُكُمْ نَهْمَتَهُ مِنْ سَفَرِهِ ، فَلْيُعَجِّلْ إلى أهْلِهِ» متفقٌ عليه

984. **Hazrat Abu Hurairah** (R.A.A.) relates that the Holy Prophet (S.A.W.) said: A journey is a part of chastisement. Each of you (who undertakes a journey) is deprived of facilities of eating, drinking and sleeping. Therefore, when you have completed the purpose of your journey you should return home quickly. *(Bukhari and Muslim)*

* * * * * * *

CHAPTER 176

PREFERENCE OF RETURNING HOME BY DAYLIGHT AND ABHORRENCE OF RETURNING HOME BY NIGHT WHEN NOT NECESSARY

٩٨٥ — عن جابرٍ رَضِيَ اللهُ عنهُ أنَّ رسولَ اللهِ صلَّى اللهُ عَليهِ وسلَّمَ قال: « إذا أطالَ أحَدُكُمْ الغَيْبَةَ فَلايَطْرُقَنَّ أهْلَهُ لَيْلاً » .

وفي روايةٍ أنَّ رسولَ اللهِ صلَّى اللهُ عَليهِ وسلَّمَ نَهَى أنْ يَطْرُقَ الرَّجُلُ أهْلَهُ لَيْلاً . متفقٌ عليه

985. Hazrat Jabir (R.A.A.) relates that the Holy Prophet (S.A.W.) said, 'When anyone of you has been absent from home for sometime, he should avoid returning home after nightfall.

Another version says that Holy Prophet (S.A.W.) has prohibited a person returning home by night. *(Bukhari and Muslim)*

٩٨٦ – وعن أنسٍ رَضيَ اللهُ عنهُ قَالَ : كانَ رسولُ اللهِ صلّى اللهُ عليهِ وسلّمَ لايطرُقُ أهْلَهُ ليْلاً ، وكانَ يأْتيهم غُدْوَةً أوْ عَشيَّةً . متفقٌ عليه

986. Hazrat Anas (R.A.A.) relates that the Holy Prophet (S.A.W.) avoided returning home from a journey by night. He used to come home in the morning or in afternoon. *(Bukhari and Muslim)*

* * * * * * *

CHAPTER 177

WHAT TO SUPPLICATE ON RETURN FROM JOURNEY AND ON SIGHTING ONE'S HOME TOWN

فيهِ حديثُ ابْنِ عُمَرَ السَّابقُ في باب تكبيرِ المسافرِ إذا صَعِدَ الثَّنَايَا .

On this topic one tradition quoted by *Hazrat Ibn Umar* (R.A.A.) has been mentioned earlier in Chapter 171.

٩٨٧ – وعن أنسٍ رَضيَ اللهُ عنهُ قال : أقْبَلْنَا معَ النَّبيِّ صلّى اللهُ عليهِ وسلّم ، حتّى إذا كُنَّا بظَهْرِ المَدينَةِ قال : « آيبُونَ ، تائبُونَ ، عابدونَ ، لربِّنا حامدُونَ » فلَمْ يزَلْ يقُولُ ذلكَ حتّى قدمْنا المَدينَةَ ، رواه مسلم

987. Hazrat Anas (R.A.A.) relates: 'Once, we along with the Holy Prophet (S.A.W.) were returning from a journey, and when we reached a point from where Madina became visible, the Holy Prophet (S.A.W.) said: *Aye-buna, tai-buna 'abi-duna, li-rab-bina Hami-Dun.* 'We are returning from journey, we are repentant, worshipping our Lord and praising Him;

and he (S.A.W.) kept on repeating these sentences till we reached Madina. *(Muslim)*

* * * * * * *

CHAPTER 178

PREFERENCE OF VISITING THE MOHALLAH MOSQUE FIRST AND OFFER TWO RAKATS OF NAF'L THERE AFTER RETURNING FROM JOURNEY

٩٨٨ – عن كعب بن مالك رضي الله عنه أن رسول الله صلى الله عليه وسلم كان إذا قدم من سفر بدأ بالمسجد فركع فيه ركعتين . متفق عليه

988. Hazrat Ka'b Ibn Malik (R.A.A.) says that when the Holy Prophet (S.A.W.) returned from a journey he used to visit a mosque first and offer there two raka'ats of Naf'l prayer. *(Bukhari and Muslim)*

* * * * * * *

CHAPTER 179

PROHIBITION OF WOMAN TRAVELLING ALONE

٩٨٩ – عن أبي هريرة رضي الله عنه قال : قال رسول الله صلى الله عليه وسلم : « لا يحل لامرأة تؤمن بالله واليوم الآخر تسافر مسيرة يوم وليلة إلا مع ذي محرم عليها » متفق عليه

989. Hazrat Abu Hurairah (R.A.A.) relates that the Holy Prophet (S.A.W.) said: It is not lawful for a woman who believes in Allah and the Day of Judgment to go on a journey lasting for a day and night without accompanying a person who is related to her within the prohibited degrees (i.e. with whom marriage is unlawful). *(Bukhari and Muslim)*

٩٩٠ – وعن ابن عباس رضي الله عنهما أنه سمع النبي صلى الله عليه وسلم يقول : « لا يخلون رجل بامرأة إلا ومعها ذو محرم ، ولا تسافر المرأة إلا مع ذي محرم » فقال له رجل : يا رسول الله إن امرأتي خرجت حاجة ، وإني اكتتبت في غزوة كذا وكذا ؟ قال : « انطلق فحج مع امرأتك » متفق عليه

990. Hazrat Ibn Abbas (R.A.A.) says that he heard from the Holy Prophet (S.A.W.) saying that no man should remain with a woman in loneliness unless there is present some one who is related to her within the prohibited degrees, nor should she travel except in the company of such a relative. A person asked: "O Messenger of Allah, my wife is to go out for Haj and I have been entrusted for such and such expedition." He (S.A.W.) told him: 'Go and perform Haj along with your wife.'

(Bukhari and Muslim)

* * * * * * *

BOOK OF MERITS AND EXCELLENCES OF HOLY QURAN

CHAPTER 180

VIRTUES OF READING THE HOLY QURAN

٩٩١ ــ عن أبي أُمَامَةَ رضي اللهُ عنهُ قالَ : سَمِعتُ رسولَ اللهِ صلّى اللهُ عليهِ وسلَّمَ يقولُ : « اقرَؤُوا القُرآنَ فَإِنَّهُ يَأْتي يَوْمَ القِيامَةِ شَفيعاً لأَصْحَابِهِ » رواه مسلم .

991. Hazrat Abu Umamah (R.A.A.) relates that he heard the Holy Prophet (S.A.W.) say: 'Study the Quran (regularly) for it will act as an intercessor and entreat for its readers on the Day of Judgement. *(Muslim)*

٩٩٢ ــ وعَن النَّوَّاسِ بن سَمعَانَ رضيَ اللهُ عنهُ قالَ : سَمِعتُ رسولَ اللهِ صلَّى اللهُ عليهِ وسلَّمَ يقولُ : « يُؤْتَى يَوْمَ القِيامَةِ بالقُرآنِ وَأَهْلِه الذين كانُوا يَعْمَلُونَ بهِ في الدُّنيا تَقدُمهُ سورَةُ البَقَرَةِ وَآلِ عِمرَانَ ، تُحَاجَّانِ عن صاحِبِهِمَا» رواه مسلم .

992. Hazrat Nawwas bin Sam'an (R.A.A.) says that he heard the Holy Prophet say: On the Day of Judgement the Quran will also be brought along with those who acted upon it in the world. But before it, Surahs *Al-Baqarah* and *Al-e-Imran* will lead them and plead the cause of those persons who read these Surahs in this life. *(Muslim)*

٩٩٣ ــ وعن عثمانَ بنِ عفانَ رضيَ اللهُ عنهُ قال : قالَ رسولُ اللهِ صلَّى اللهُ عليهِ وسلَّم : « خَيرُكُم مَنْ تَعَلَّمَ القرآنَ وَعَلَّمَهُ » رواه البخاري

993. Hazrat Usman bin 'Affan (R.A.A.) relates that the Holy Prophet (S.A.W.) said: 'The best among you are those who have learnt the Quran and teach (to others). *(Bukhari)*

٩٩٤ ــ وعن عائشةَ رضيَ اللهُ عنهَا قالتْ : قالَ رسولُ اللهِ صلَّى اللهُ عليهِ وسلَّم : « الَّذي يَقرَأُ القُرآنَ وَهُوَ ماهِرٌ بهِ مع السَّفَرَةِ الكِرَامِ البَرَرَةِ ، وَالذي يَقرَأُ القُرآنَ وَيَتَتَعتَعُ فيهِ وَهُوَ عليهِ شَاقٌّ له أَجْرَان » متفقٌ عليه

994. Hazrat Ayesha (R.A.A.) says that the Holy Prophet (S.A.W.) said: "A person who recites the Quran, and reads it fluently, will be in the company of the obedient and noble angels, and he who reads the Quran haltingly and with difficulty will have a double recompense".
(Bukhari and Muslim)

٩٩٥ – وعن أبي موسى الأشعَريّ رضيَ اللهُ عنهُ قالَ : قالَ رسولُ الله صلى اللهُ عليهِ وسلّمَ : « مَثَلُ المُؤمنِ الّذي يقْرأُ القرآنَ مثلُ الأُترجّةِ : ريحها طيّبٌ وطَعمُها طيّبٌ ، ومثلُ المؤمنِ الّذي لايقرأُ القرآنَ كمثلِ التّمرةِ : لاريح لها وطعمُها حلْوٌ ، ومثلُ المُنافقِ الذي يقرأُ القرآنَ كمثلِ الرّيحانةِ : ريحها طيّبٌ وطعمُها مرٌّ ، ومَثَلُ المُنافقِ الذي لايقرأُ القرآنَ كمثلِ الحنظلةِ : ليْسَ لها ريحٌ وطعمُها مُرٌّ » متفقٌ عليه

995. Hazrat Abu Musa Ash'ari (R.A.A.) relates that the Holy Prophet (S.A.W.) said: "The case of a Muslim who studies the Holy Quran is like the orange which is aromatic and delicious, and the example of a Muslim who does not recite the Holy Quran is like a dried date which has no aroma but is sweet; and the case of an hypocrite who recites the Holy Quran is like the fruit which is although scented yet it tastes bitter; and the case of a hypocrite who does not recite the Holy Quran is like the fruit which has no aroma and is bitter in taste."
(Bukhari and Muslim)

٩٩٦ – وعن عمرَ بنِ الخطابِ رضيَ اللهُ عنهُ أنَّ النّبيَّ صلّى اللهُ عليهِ وسلّمَ قال : « إنّ اللهَ يرفعُ بهذا الكتابِ أقواماً ويضعُ بهِ آخرين »

رواه مسلم

996. Hazrat Umar bin Khattab (R.A.A.) relates that the Holy Prophet (S.A.W.) said: Allah will elevate some nations through this book (the Holy Quran) and degrade others with it. *(Muslim)*

٩٩٧ – وعنِ ابنِ عمرَ رضيَ اللهُ عنهما عنِ النّبيّ صلّى اللهُ عليهِ وسلّم قال : « لا حسَدَ إلاّ في اثنتيْنِ : رجلٌ آتاهُ اللهُ القرآنَ ، فهوَ يقومُ بهِ آناءَ اللّيلِ وآناءَ النّهارِ ، ورجلٌ آتاهُ اللهُ مالاً ، فهوَ ينفقهُ آناءَ اللّيلِ وآناءَ النهارِ » متفقٌ عليه

997. This Hadis is the same as No. 572 of Chapter 64.

٩٩٨– وعن البراءِ بن عازبٍ رضيَ اللهُ عنهما قال : كانَ رجلٌ يقرأُ سورةَ الكهفِ، وعندَه فرسٌ مربوطٌ بشطنينِ ، فتغشته سحابةٌ(٤) فجعلت تدنو ، وجعلَ فرسُه ينفِرُ منها . فلمَّا أصبحَ أتى النبيَّ صلى اللهُ عليهِ وسلَّمَ ، فذكرَ ذلكَ لهُ فقالَ : « تلكَ السَّكينةُ تنزَّلتْ للقرآنِ » متفقٌ عليهِ .

998. Hazrat Bra'a ibn 'Aazib (R.A.A.) states that a person was reading *Surah Al-Kahf* (Chapter 18) and his horse was tied near him with two ropes. It so happened that a patch of cloud reached the horse and covered it. The animal whereupon began jumping. Next day in the morning the man went to the Holy Prophet (S.A.W.) and related the incident to him. (S.A.W.) The Holy Prophet (S.A.W.) said: This was 'sakeenat' (mental and spiritual peace and satisfaction) that came down as a result of the recitation of the Holy Quran.

(Bukhari and Muslim)

٩٩٩ – وعن ابنِ مسعودٍ رضيَ اللهُ عنهُ قالَ : قالَ رسولُ اللهِ صلَّى اللهُ عليهِ وسلَّم : « مَنْ قرأَ حرْفاً مِنْ كتابِ اللهِ فلَهُ حسنَةٌ ، والحسنَةُ بعشرِ أمثالِها لا أقول : ألم حرفٌ ، ولكنِ : ألفٌ حرْفٌ ، ولامٌ حرْفٌ وميمٌ حرْفٌ » رواه الترمذي وقال : حديث حسن صحيح .

999. Hazrat Abdullah bin Mas'ud (R.A.A.) relates that the Holy Prophet (S.A.W.) said that when somebody recites one letter from the Holy Quran he will get one good deed in recompense and this one recompense will be equal to ten good deeds. I do not say that Alif Lam Meem is a letter, but A is a letter, L is a Letter and M is a letter i.e. it is equal to 3 letters. *(Tirmizi)*

١٠٠٠– وعن ابنِ عباسٍ رضيَ اللهُ عنهما قال : قالَ رسولُ اللهِ صلى اللهُ عليهِ وسلَّم : « إنَّ الَّذي ليسَ في جوْفِهِ شيْءٌ مِنَ القرآنِ كالبيتِ الخرِبِ » رواه الترمذي وقال : حديث حسن صحيح .

1000. Hazrat Ibn 'Abbas (R.A.A.) relates that the Holy Prophet (S.A.W.) said: 'One whose heart does not contain anything from the Holy Quran, is like a deserted house.' *(Tirmizi and said it is sound)*

١٠٠١ – وعن عبد الله بن عمرو بن العاص رضي الله عنهما عن النبي صلى الله عليه وسلم قال: «يقال لصاحب القرآن: اقرأ وارتق ورتل كما كنت ترتل في الدنيا، فإن منزلتك عند آخر آية تقرؤها» رواه أبو داود، والترمذي وقال: حسن صحيح.

1001. Hazrat Abdullah bin 'Amr bin A'as (R.A.A.) reports from the Holy Prophet (S.A.W.) that he (S.A.W.) said: 'A reader of the Holy Quran will be called upon on the Day of Judgement: 'Start reading the Holy Quran and ascend the (high) stages of the Heaven, and recite slowly as you had been reading in the world, as thy abode will be where the last verse of thy recitation will end. *(Abu Daud and Trimizi)*

* * * * * *

CHAPTER 181
CARE OF THE HOLY QURAN, ITS REGULAR RECITATION AND PRESERVATION IN MEMORY

١٠٠٢ – عن أبي موسى رضي الله عنه عن النبي صلى الله عليه وسلم قال: «تعاهدوا هذا القرآن فوالذي نفس محمد بيده لهو أشد تفلتاً من الإبل في عقلها» متفق عليه

1002. Hazrat Abu Musa Ash'ari (R.A.A.) relates that the Holy Prophet (S.A.W.) said: Preserve the Holy Quran in your hearts, by Allah in whose hands lies the life of Muhammad (S.A.W.) it goes out of memory faster than a camel escapes from its rope.

(Bukhari and Muslim)

١٠٠٣ – وعن ابن عمر رضي الله عنهما أن رسول الله صلى الله عليه وسلم قال: «إنما مثل صاحب القرآن كمثل الإبل المعقلة، إن عاهد عليها، أمسكها، وإن أطلقها، ذهبت» متفق عليه

1003. Hazrat Ibn 'Umar (R.A.A.) says that the Holy Prophet (S.A.W.) said: The example of a Hafiz (a person who has learnt the Holy Quran by heart) is like that of a person who has secured a camel by rope. If he looks after it, he holds it and if neglects it, it goes away. *(Bukahri and Muslim)*

* * * * * * *

CHAPTER 182

PREFERENCE OF MELODIOUS RECITATION OF THE HOLY QURAN AND TO GET IT RECITED MELODIOUSLY AND TO LISTEN TO IT

١٠٠٤ – عَنْ أَبِي هُرَيْرَةَ رَضِيَ اللهُ عنهُ قال : سمعتُ رسولَ اللهِ صلَّى اللهُ عليه وسلَّمَ يقولُ : « مَا أَذِنَ اللهُ لِشَيْءٍ مَا أَذِنَ لِنَبِيٍّ حَسَنِ الصَّوْتِ يَتَغَنَّى بِالقُرْآنِ يَجْهَرُ بِهِ » متفقٌ عليه .

1004. Hazrat Abu Hurairah (R.A.A.) relates that he heard the Holy Prophet (S.A.W.) say: 'Allah lends not His ears so attentively to anything as He does to the recitation of the Holy Quran by a Prophet who recites well, audibly and with a good tune.

(Bukhari and Muslim)

١٠٠٥ – وعن أَبِي موسى الأَشْعَرِيِّ رضيَ اللهُ عنهُ أنَّ رسولَ اللهِ صلَّى اللهُ عليهِ وسلَّمَ قالَ لهُ : « لَقَدْ أُوتِيتَ مِزْمَاراً مِنْ مَزَامِيرِ آلِ دَاوُدَ » متفقٌ عليه .

وفي روايةٍ لمسلمٍ : أنَّ رسولَ اللهِ صلَّى اللهُ عليهِ وسلَّمَ قالَ لهُ : « لَوْ رَأَيْتَنِي وَأَنَا أَسْتَمِعُ لِقِرَاءَتِكَ البَارِحَةَ » .

1005. Hazrat Abu Musa Ash'ari (R.A.A.) reports that the Holy Prophet (S.A.W.) said to him: 'You have been bestowed with one of the tunes of Hazrat Daud' (Prophet David). *(Bukhari and Muslim)*

Muslim has added: You would have been much pleased, had you seen me when I was listening to your reciting the Holy Quran last night.

١٠٠٦ – وعنِ البَرَاءِ بنِ عَازِبٍ رضيَ اللهُ عنهمَا قالَ : سَمِعْتُ النبيَّ صلَّى اللهُ عليهِ وسلَّمَ قَرَأَ في العِشَاءِ بِالتِّينِ والزَّيْتُونِ ، فَمَا سَمِعْتُ أَحَداً أَحْسَنَ صَوْتاً مِنْهُ . متفقٌ عليه

1006. Hazrat Bra'a bin 'Aazib (R.A.A.) relates (once) I had a chance to listen the Holy Prophet (S.A.W.) recite Sura At-Tin (Chapter 95) during Isha prayers (prayer offered at early night) : I have not heard anyone reciting in a more charming voice than his (S.A.W.).

(Bukahri and Muslim)

١٠٠٧ – وعنْ أبي لُبَابَةَ بَشِيرِ بنِ عبدِ المُنْذرِ رضيَ اللهُ عنهُ ، أنَّ النبيَّ صلَّى اللهُ عليهِ وسلَّمَ قال : « مَنْ لَمْ يَتَغَنَّ بِالقُرْآنِ فَلَيْسَ مِنَّا » رواه أبو داود بإسنادٍ جيد .

1007. Hazrat Abu Lubaba Bashir bin Abdul Munzir (R.A.A.) says that the Holy Prophet (S.A.W.) said: One who does not read Holy Quran melodiously is not from us. *(Abu Daud)*

١٠٠٨ –وعنِ ابنِ مسعودٍ رضيَ اللهُ عنهُ قَالَ : قَالَ لي النَّبيُّ صلَّى اللهُ عليهِ وسلَّمَ : « اقْرَأْ عَلَيَّ القُرْآنَ » ، فَقُلْتُ : يا رَسُولَ اللهِ ، أَقْرَأُ عَلَيْكَ وَعَلَيْكَ أُنْزِلَ ؟! قال : « إنِّي أُحِبُّ أَنْ أَسْمَعَهُ مِنْ غَيْرِي » فقَرَأْتُ عَلَيْهِ سُورَةَ النِّسَاءِ حَتَّى جِئْتُ إلى هذه الآيَة : (فَكَيْفَ إذا جِئْنَا مِنْ كُلِّ أُمَّةٍ بِشَهِيدٍ وَجِئْنَا بِكَ عَلى هؤُلاءِ شَهِيدا) قال : « حَسْبُكَ الآنَ » فَالْتَفَتُّ إلَيْهِ ، فَإذا عَيْنَاهُ تَذْرِفَان . متفقٌ عليه

1008. This Hadis is the same as No. 446 of Chapter 54.

* * * * * * *

CHAPTER 183

ENCOURAGING RECITATION OF SOME PARTICULAR CHAPTERS AND VERSES

١٠٠٩ – عن أبي سعيدٍ رافعِ بنِ المُعَلَّى رضيَ اللهُ عَنْهُ قَالَ : قَالَ لي رسولُ اللهِ صَلَّى اللهُ عَلَيْهِ وسلَّمَ : « ألا أُعَلِّمُكَ أَعْظَمَ سُورَةٍ في القُرْآنِ قَبْلَ أنْ تَخْرُجَ مِنَ المَسْجِدِ ؟ فَأَخذَ بِيَدِي ، فَلَمَّا أَرَدْنَا أَنْ نَخْرُجَ قُلْتُ : يا رَسُولَ اللهِ إنَّكَ قُلْتَ : لأُعَلِّمَنَّكَ أَعْظَمَ سُورَةٍ في القُرْآنِ ؟ قال : « الحَمْدُ لِلهِ رَبِّ العَالمِينَ هِيَ السَّبْعُ المَثَاني وَالقُرْآنُ العَظِيمُ الَّذي أُوتِيتُهُ » رواه البخاري

1009. Hazrat Abu Sa'eed Rafai' bin Al-Mualla relates: The Holy Prophet (S.A.W.) (Once) said to me: Before you go out of the mosque, may I tell you which is the greatest (most important) Surah of the Holy Quran? and thereafter he grasped my hand. When we were just going out of the mosque I submitted: 'O' Messenger of Allah, you had just promised to tell me as to which is the greatest Surah of the Holy Quran.' He said. "It is the Surah *Al-Fateha*' seven verses which are so frequently used in prayers, and the glorious Quran which has been revealed upon me." *(Bukhari)*

١٠١٠ – وعن أبي سعيدٍ الخُدْرِيِّ رضيَ اللهُ عنهُ أنَّ رسولَ اللهِ صلَّى اللهُ عليهِ وسلَّمَ قالَ في : قُلْ هُوَ اللهُ أَحَدٌ : « وَالَّذي نَفْسي بِيَدِهِ ، إنَّهَا لَتَعْدِلُ ثُلُثَ القُرْآنِ » .

وفي روايةٍ : أنَّ رسولَ اللهِ صلَّى اللهُ عليهِ وسلَّمَ قالَ لأَصْحَابِهِ : « أَيَعْجِزُ أَحَدُكُمْ أنْ يَقْرَأَ بِثُلُثِ القُرْآنِ في لَيْلَةٍ » فَشَقَّ ذلكَ عَلَيْهِمْ ، وَقَالُوا : أَيُّنَا يُطِيقُ ذلكَ يا رسولَ اللهِ : فقالَ : « قُلْ هُوَ اللهُ أَحَدٌ ، اللهُ الصَّمَدُ : ثُلُثُ القُرْآنِ » رواه البخاري

1010. **Hazrat Abu Sa'eed Khudri** (R.A.A.) states that about the recitation of Surah *Al-Ikhlas* (Chapter 112) the Holy Prophet (S.A.W.) said. By Allah in whose possession is my life, undoubtedly this Surah is equal to one third of the Quran.

According to another version (Once) the Holy Prophet (S.A.W.) enquired from his companions if one of them was unable to read one-third of the Holy Quran in one night? The Companions thought it difficult to do so and submitted: 'O' Messenger of Allah! who has got the capacity to do so.' He (S.A.W.) said.:Surah *Al-Ikhlas* (Chapter 112) is equal to one third of the Holy Quran. *(Bukhari)*

١٠١١ – وعَنْهُ أنَّ رَجُلاً سَمِعَ رَجُلاً يَقْرَأُ : « قُلْ هُوَ اللهُ أَحَدٌ » يُرَدِّدُهَا فَلَمَّا أَصْبَحَ جَاءَ إلى رسولِ اللهِ صلَّى اللهُ عليهِ وسلَّمَ ، فَذَكَرَ ذلكَ لَهُ وَكَانَ الرَّجُلُ يَتَقَالُّهَا فَقَالَ رسولُ اللهِ صلَّى اللهُ عليهِ وسلَّمَ : « وَالَّذي نَفْسي بِيَدِهِ ، إنَّهَا لَتَعْدِلُ ثُلُثَ القُرْآنِ » رواه البخاري .

1011. It is reported by **Hazrat Abu Sa'eed Khudri** (R.A.A.) that a man heard another recite Surah *Al-Ikhlas* (Chapter 112) repeatedly. Next morning he came to Holy Prophet (S.A.W.) and reported this to him (S.A.W.) considering the same as of small value. The Holy Prophet (S.A.W.) said: By Allah in Whose possession is my life, this Surah is equal to one third of the Quran. *(Bukhari)*

١٠١٢ – وعن أبي هريرةَ رضيَ اللهُ عنهُ أنَّ رسولَ اللهِ صلّى اللهُ عليهِ وسلّمَ قال في : قُلْ هُوَ اللهُ أَحَدٌ : « إنَّهَا تَعْدِلُ ثُلُثَ القُرْآنِ » رواه مسلم

1012. Hazrat Abu Hurairah (R.A.A.) **says that the Holy Prophet** (S.A.W.) said that the Surah Al-Ikhlas is equal to one third of the Holy Quran. *(Muslim)*

١٠١٣ – وعنْ أنسٍ رضي اللهُ عنهُ أنَّ رَجُلاً قال : يارسولَ اللهِ إني أُحِبُّ هذهِ السُّورَةَ : قُلْ هُوَ اللهُ أَحَدٌ ، قال : «إنَّ حُبَّهَا أَدْخَلَكَ الجَنَّةَ » رواه الترمذي وقال : حديثٌ حسن . ورواه البخاري في صحيحه تعليقاً :

1013. Hazrat Anas (R.A.A.) relates that a man said to the Holy Prophet (S.A.W.) 'O' Messenger of Allah! I love Surah ***Al-Ikhlas.*** **He (S.A.W.) informed him: Verily its love will enable you enter into** Paradise. *(Tirmizi)*

١٠١٤ – وعن عُقْبَةَ بنِ عامِرٍ رَضِيَ اللهُ عنهُ أنَّ رسولَ اللهِ صلّى اللهُ عليهِ وسلّمَ قال : « أَلَمْ تَرَ آياتٍ أُنْزِلَتْ هذهِ اللَّيْلَةَ لَمْ يُرَ مِثْلُهُنَّ قَطُّ ؟ قُلْ أَعُوذُ بِرَبِّ الفَلَقِ ، وَقُلْ أَعُوذُ بِرَبِّ النَّاسِ » رواه مسلم

1014. Hazrat Uqbah bin Aamir (R.A.A.) says that the Holy Prophet (S.A.W.) once said: Do you not know that last night some verses were revealed (to me), the like of which has not been seen before. These are Surah *Al-Falaq* and Surah *An-Nas.* (Chapter 113 and 114). *(Muslim)*

١٠١٥ – وعن أبي سَعيدٍ الخُدْرِيِّ رَضِيَ اللهُ عنهُ قال : كانَ رسولُ اللهِ صلّى اللهُ عليهِ وسلّمَ يَتَعَوَّذُ مِنَ الجَانِّ ، وَعَيْنِ الإِنْسَانِ ، حَتَّى نَزَلَتِ المُعَوِّذَتَانِ ، فَلَمَّا نَزَلَتَا ، أَخَذَ بِهِما وَتَرَكَ مَا سِوَاهُمَا .

رواه الترمذي وقال : حديث حسن .

1015. Hazrat Abu Sa'eed Khudri (R.A.A.) reports that the Holy Prophet (S.A.W.) used to seek (Allah's) protection against the genii and the evil eyes of human beings when Surahs *Al-Falaq* and *An-Nas* were revealed, he (S.A.W.) adopted them (to ward off the evil effects) and discarded everything else. *(Tirmizi)*

١٠١٦ — عن أبي هريرةَ رضيَ اللهُ عنهُ أنَّ رسولَ اللهِ صلَّى اللهُ عليهِ وسلَّمَ قالَ : « مِنَ القُرْآنِ سُورَةٌ ثَلاثُونَ آيَةً شَفَعَتْ لِرَجُلٍ حَتَّى غُفِرَ لَهُ ، وَهِيَ : تَبَارَكَ الذي بِيَدِهِ المُلْكُ »

رواه أبو داود والترمذي وقال : حديث حسن .

وفي رواية أبي داود : « تَشْفَعُ »

1016. Hazrat Abu Hurairah (R.A.A.) relates that the Holy Prophet (S.A.W.) said. there is a Surah in Holy Quran. It contains thirty verses. These verses continue to intercede for a person till Allah forgives him, this is Surah *Al-Mulk*. (Chapter 67).

(Abu Daud and Tirmizi)

١٠١٧ — وعن أبي مسعودٍ البَدْرِيِّ رضيَ اللهُ عنهُ عنِ النبيِّ صلَّى اللهُ عليهِ وسلَّمَ قال : « مَنْ قَرَأَ بِالآيَتَيْنِ مِنْ آخِرِ سُورَةِ البَقَرَةِ في لَيْلَةٍ كَفَتَاهُ » متفقٌ عليه

قيلَ : كَفَتَاهُ المَكْرُوهَ تِلْكَ اللَّيْلَةَ ، وَقِيلَ : كَفَتَاهُ مِنْ قِيَامِ اللَّيْلِ .

1017. Abu Mas'ud Badri (R.A.A.) relates that the Holy Prophet (S.A.W.) said: If a person recites the last two verses of Surah *Al-Baqarah* (Chapter 2) in night, they will suffice him (for his welfare). Imam Nawawi further elucidates that these two verses will save him from all vices or for the prayers at night. *(Bukhari and Muslim)*

١٠١٨ — وعن أبي هريرةَ رضيَ اللهُ عنهُ أنَّ رسولَ اللهِ صلَّى اللهُ عليهِ وسلَّمَ قال : « لا تَجْعَلُوا بُيُوتَكُمْ مَقَابِرَ ، إنَّ الشَّيْطَانَ يَنْفِرُ مِنَ البَيْتِ الَّذي تُقْرَأُ فِيهِ سُورَةُ البَقَرَةِ » رواه مسلم .

1018. Hazrat Abu Hurairah (R.A.A.) relates that the Holy Prophet (S.A.W.) cautioned us: Do not allow your houses to become graves. The Satan flees away from a house in which Surah *Al-Baqarah* (Chapter 2) is read. *(Muslim)*

١٠١٩ — وعن أُبَيِّ بنِ كَعْبٍ رَضيَ اللهُ عَنْهُ قَالَ : قَالَ رسولُ اللهِ صلَّى اللهُ عَلَيْهِ وسلَّمَ : « يا أَبا المُنْذِرِ أَتَدْرِي أَيُّ آيَةٍ مِنْ كِتَابِ اللهِ مَعَكَ

أَعْظَمُ ؟ قُلْتُ : اللهُ لا إلهَ إلاَّ هُوَ الحَيُّ القَيُّومُ ، فَضَرَبَ في صَدْرِي وَقَالَ : « لِيَهْنِكَ العِلْمُ أَبَا المُنْذِرِ » رواه مسلم .

1019. Hazrat Ubayy ibn Ka'b (R.A.A.) says: Once the Holy Prophet (S.A.W.) asked me: O' Abu Munzir, do you know which verse of the Holy Quran with you is the most magnificent? I submitted: *Allah-o-la ilaha illa huwal—haiyyul Qaiyyum)* (2. 256). He (S.A.W.) thumped my chest as a gesture of appreciation and said: Congratulations on your knowledge (of the Holy Quran) O Abu Munzir.

(Muslim)

١٠٢٠ ـ وعن أَبي هريرةَ رضيَ اللهُ عنهُ قال: وَكَّلَنِي رسولُ اللهِ صلَّى اللهُ عليهِ وسلَّمَ بِحِفْظِ زَكَاةِ رَمَضَانَ ، فَأَتَانِي آتٍ ، فَجَعَلَ يَحْثُو مِنَ الطَّعَامِ . فَأَخَذْتُهُ فَقُلْتُ : لأَرْفَعَنَّكَ إلى رَسُولِ اللهِ صَلَّى اللهُ عَلَيْهِ وسلَّمَ ، قَالَ : إنِّي مُحْتَاجٌ ، وَعَلَيَّ عِيَالٌ ، وَبِي حَاجَةٌ شَدِيدَةٌ ، فَخَلَّيْتُ عَنْهُ ، فَأَصْبَحْتُ ، فَقَالَ رَسُولُ اللهِ صَلَّى اللهُ عَلَيْهِ وآلهِ وسَلَّمَ : « يَا أَبَا هُرَيرةَ ، مَافعَلَ أَسيرُكَ البَارِحَةَ ؟ » قُلْتُ : يَارَسُولَ اللهِ شَكَا حَاجَةً وَعِيَالاً ، فَرَحِمْتُهُ . فَخَلَّيْتُ سَبِيلَهُ . فَقَالَ : « أَمَا إنَّهُ قَدْ كَذَبَكَ وَسَيَعُودُ » فَعَرَفْتُ أَنَّهُ سَيَعُودُ لِقَوْلِ رَسُولِ اللهِ صَلَّى اللهُ عَلَيْهِ وسلَّمَ فَرَصَدْتُهُ ، فَجَاءَ يَحْثُو مِنَ الطَّعَامِ ، فَقُلْتُ: لأَرْفَعَنَّكَ إلى رَسُولِ اللهِ صَلَّى اللهُ عَلَيْهِ وَسَلَّمَ ، قَالَ : دَعْنِي فَإنِّي مُحْتَاجٌ ، وَعَلَيَّ عِيَالٌ لاأَعُودُ ، فَرَحِمْتُهُ فَخَلَّيْتُ سَبِيلَهُ ، فَأَصْبَحْتُ فَقَالَ لِي رَسُولُ اللهِ صَلَّى اللهُ عَلَيْهِ وَسَلَّمَ : « يَا أَبَا هُرَيْرَةَ ، مافعَلَ أَسِيرُكَ البَارِحَةَ ؟ » قُلْتُ : يَارَسُولَ اللهِ شَكَا حَاجَةً وَعِيَالاً فَرَحِمْتُهُ ، فَخَلَّيْتُ سَبِيلَهُ ، فَقَالَ : « إنَّهُ قَدْ كَذَبَكَ وَسَيَعُودُ » فَرَصَدْتُهُ الثَّالِثَةَ . فَجَاءَ يَحْثُو مِنَ الطَّعَامِ ، فَأَخَذْتُهُ ، فقلتُ : لأَرْفَعَنَّكَ إلى رَسُولِ اللهِ صلَّى اللهُ عَلَيْهِ وسَلَّمَ ، وَهذا آخِرُ ثَلاثِ مَرَّاتٍ أَنَّكَ تَزْعُمُ أَنَّكَ لاتَعُودُ ، ثُمَّ تَعُودُ ! فقال : دَعْنِي فَإنِّي أُعَلِّمُكَ كَلِمَاتٍ يَنْفَعُكَ اللهُ بِهَا ، قلتُ : مَاهُنَّ ؟ قال : إذا أَوَيْتَ إلى فِرَاشِكَ فَاقْرَأْ آيَةَ الكُرْسِيِّ ، فَإنَّهُ لَنْ يَزَالَ عَلَيْكَ

مِنَ اللهِ حَافِظٌ ، وَلا يَقْرَبُكَ شَيْطَانٌ حَتَّى تُصْبِحَ ، فَخَلَّيْتُ سَبِيلَه

فَأَصْبَحْتُ ، فَقَالَ لِي رَسُولُ اللهِ صَلَّى اللهُ عَلَيْهِ وَسَلَّمَ : « مَافَعَلَ

أَسِيرُكَ الْبَارِحَةَ ؟ » قُلْتُ : يَارَسُولَ اللهِ زَعَمَ أَنَّهُ يُعَلِّمُنِي كَلِمَاتٍ

يَنْفَعُنِي اللهُ بِهَا ، فَخَلَّيْتُ سَبِيلَه . قَالَ : « مَاهِيَ ؟ » قلت : قَالَ لِي :

إذا أَوَيْتَ إِلى فِرَاشِكَ فَاقْرَأْ آيَةَ الْكُرْسِيِّ مِنْ أَوَّلِهَا حَتَّى تَخْتِمَ الآيَةَ :

(اللهُ لا إلهَ إِلاَّ هُوَ الحَيُّ الْقَيُّومُ) وقالَ لي : لايَزَال عَلَيْكَ مِنَ اللهِ حَافِظٌ ،

وَلَنْ يَقْرَبَكَ شَيْطَانٌ حَتَّى تُصْبِحَ . فقالَ النبيُّ صلَّى الله عليهِ وسلَّمَ :

« أَمَا إِنَّه قَدْ صَدَقَكَ وَهُوَ كَذُوبٌ ، تَعْلَمُ مَنْ تُخَاطِبُ مُنْذُ ثَلاثٍ

يَا أَبَا هُرَيْرَةَ » ؟ قلت : لا ، قال : « ذَاكَ شَيْطَانٌ » رواه البخاري

1020. Hazrat Abu Hurairah (R.A.A.) relates: 'The Holy Prophet (S.A.W.) appointed me to guard the *Sadqa Fitr* (alms given during Ramazan before Eid). One night an intruder came and started collecting the food. I caught hold of him and said: I will produce you before the Holy Prophet (S.A.W.) but the intruder pleaded: I am a poor man and have number of children to support. I am badly in need of help and succour. On hearing his woeful tale I let him go. In the morning the Holy Prophet (S.A.W.) asked me. 'Abu Hurairah, what happened to your thief last night?' I answered: 'O' Messenger of Allah! he pleaded his dire necessity and complained about his large family. As such I felt pity for him and let him go. The Holy Prophet (S.A.W.) remarked: He has lied, he will come back again. As such I was sure that he would come again as the Holy Prophet (S.A.W.) had said, and therefore I kept watch and waited for him. The thief did come again and started gathering food. I caught him again and said that I would definitely take him to the Holy Prophet (S.A.W.). On this he requested that he was a needy person and had a large family to support, and that he may be let off and promised that he would not come back. Hazrat Abu Hurairah (R.A.A.) felt pity for him once more and let him go. Next morning the Holy Prophet (S.A.W.) said to him: Abu Hurairah what about your prisoner of last night? He answered: 'O' Messenger of Allah, he pleaded his dire necessity and the fact that he had a large family, and therefore I felt pity for him and let him go. He (S.A.W.) said: He told you lie and will come back again.' So I maintained a watch for him a third time. He did come to steel food (from the alms store). Hazrat Abu Hurairah says: 'I caught hold of him and said: I shall certainly take you to the Holy Prophet (S.A.W.) and this is the last of the three times you promised that you will not come back, (but you have broken your promise and come back). He pleaded: Please let me go, and I will in return teach you some phrases which will bring benefit and mercy to you from Allah. I asked him: What are those? He said: When you go to bed (during night) recite the verse *(Ayatul Kursi)* (2.256). (As a result of its blessings) Allah will appoint a guard to protect you, and Satan will not be able to come near you till morning. So I allowed him to go. Next morning when I visited the Holy Prophet (S.A.W.) he asked me: What did you do with your prisoner last night? I said 'O' Messenger of Allah, he said that he would teach me some such phrases through which I would receive benefit and mercy of Allah. On this I let him go" He (S.A.W.) asked me. What are those phrases. I answered: He told me: when you go to your bed for sleep, recite the verse *'Ayatul Kursi'* from beginning to end, and told me that Allah would post a guard on me and Satan would not be able to come near me till the morning. The Holy Prophet (S.A.W.) observed: This time he told you the truth although he is a liar. Abu Hurairah, do you know with whom you were speaking during these three nights? I answered: 'no' The Holy Prophet (S.A.W.) said: It was Satan (the devil). *(Bukhari)*

١٠٢١ – وعن أبي الدَّرْدَاءِ رَضِيَ اللهُ عَنْهُ أَنَّ رَسُولَ اللهِ صلَّى اللهُ عَلَيْهِ وسلَّمَ قال: «مَنْ حَفِظَ عَشْرَ آيَاتٍ مِنْ أَوَّلِ سُورَةِ الْكَهْفِ، عُصِمَ مِنَ الدَّجَّالِ». وفي رواية: «مِنْ آخِرِ سُورَةِ الكهْفِ» رواهما مسلم .

1021. **Hazrat Abu Darda** (R.A.A.) relates that the Holy Prophet (S.A.W.) said: One who memorises the first ten verses of Surah *Al-Kahf* (Chapter 18) will be secure against *Dajjal* (Anti-Christ). Another version says: One who commits to his memory last ten verses of this Sura will remain immune from *Dajjal* (Anti-Christ). *(Muslim)*

١٠٢٢ – وعَنِ ابْنِ عَبَّاسٍ رَضِيَ اللهُ عَنْهُمَا قَالَ: بَيْنَمَا جِبْرِيلُ عليهِ السَّلام قاعِدٌ عِندَ النَّبِيِّ صلَّى اللهُ عليهِ وسَلَّمَ سَمِعَ نَقِيضاً مِنْ فَوْقِهِ، فَرَفَعَ رَأْسَهُ فَقَالَ: هذا بَابٌ مِنَ السَّمَاءِ فُتِحَ اليَوْمَ، وَلَمْ يُفْتَحْ قَطُّ إلاَّ اليَوْمَ، فَنَزَلَ مِنه مَلَكٌ فقالَ: هذا مَلَكٌ نَزَلَ إلى الأرْضِ لمْ ينزِلْ قَطُّ إلاَّ اليَوْمَ، فَسَلَّمَ وقال: أَبْشِرْ بِنُورَيْنِ أُوتِيتَهُمَا، لَمْ يُؤْتَهُمَا نَبِيٌّ قَبْلَكَ: فَاتِحَةِ الكِتَابِ، وخَوَاتِيمِ سُورَةِ البَقَرَةِ، لَن تَقرَأَ بِحَرْفٍ منها إلاَّ أُعْطِيتَهُ» رواه مسلم .

1022. **Hazrat Ibn Abbas** (R.A.A.) relates: Once while Hazrat Jibrail (Gabriel) was sitting with the Holy Prophet (S.A.W.), a sound was heard from above (the sky)—Angel Gabriel looked up and said.

A door has been opened for the first time from heaven which had not been opened till this day. Thereafter an angel came down from this door and angel Gabriel said: This angel has also descended to the earth for the first time and had not descended before this. He (the angel) had saluted you (the Holy Prophet) (S.A.W.) and said: Please receive the glad tidings (congratulations) of the two lights that have been bestowed upon you and which had not been bestowed upon any prophet before you: The first is the Surah *Fateha* (the opening chapter of the Holy Quran), and next are concluding verses of Surah *Al-Baqarah* (Chapter 2). Even if you recite a word from these verses you will receive due recompense. *(Muslim)*

* * * * * * *

CHAPTER 184

VIRTUES OF GATHERING FOR RECITATION OF THE HOLY QURAN

١٠٢٣ ـ وعَنْ أبي هُرَيْرَةَ رَضِيَ اللهُ عَنْه قَالَ : قَالَ رَسُول الله صَلّى الله عَلَيْهِ وَسَلّمَ : « ومَا اجْتَمَعَ قَوْمٌ في بَيْتٍ من بُيوت الله يَتْلُونَ كِتَابَ الله ، ويَتَدَارَسُونه بَيْنَهُمْ ، إلاّ نَزَلَتْ عَلَيهِم السَّكِينَة ، وغَشِيَتْهُمُ الرَّحْمَة ، وَحَفَّتْهُم المَلائِكَة ، وذَكَرَهُم الله فِيمَنْ عِنْدَه » رواه مسلم .

1023. Hazrat Abu Hurairah (R.A.A.) reports that the Holy Prophet (S.A.W.) said: when the people gather in one of the houses of Allah (mosques) to recite the Book of Allah and teach it to each other, tranquility and peace descend upon the gathering, (Allah's) mercy covers them, angels spread their wings over them and Allah mentions them among those who are around Him. *(Muslim)*

* * * * * * *

CHAPTER 185

VIRTUES OF ABLUTION

قَالَ الله تَعالى :(يَا أَيُّهَا الَّذِينَ آمَنوا إذا قُمْتُمْ إلى الصَّلاةِ فَاغْسِلُوا وجُوهَكُم)إلى قوله تعالى : (مَا يُرِيدُ اللهُ لِيَجْعَلَ عَلَيكم مِنْ حَرَجٍ ،

ولكنْ يُرِيدُ لِيُطَهِّرَكُمْ ، ولِيُتِمَّ نِعْمَتَهُ عَلَيْكُمْ لَعَلَّكُمْ تَشْكُرُونَ ﴾
[المائدة : ٦] .

Allah, the Exalted, has said:

280. 'O ye who believe! When ye rise up for prayer, wash your faces, and your hands up to the elbows, and lightly rub your heads and (wash) your feet up to the ankles; and if ye are unclean, purify yourselves. And if ye are sick or on a journey or one of you cometh from the closet or ye have had contact with women, and ye find no water, then go to clean and high ground and rub your faces and your hands with some of it. Allah would not place a burden on you, but He would purify you and would perfect His grace upon you, that ye may give thanks. (5:6)

١٠٢٤ — وَعَنْ أَبِي هُرَيْرَةَ رَضِيَ اللهُ عَنْهُ قَالَ : سَمِعْتُ رَسُولَ اللهِ صلَّى اللهُ عَلَيْهِ وسَلَّمَ يَقُولُ : « إنَّ أُمَّتِي يُدْعَوْنَ يَوْمَ القِيامَةِ غُرّاً مُحَجَّلِينَ مِنْ آثَارِ الوضوءِ فَمَنِ اسْتَطاعَ مِنْكُم أَنْ يُطِيلَ غُرَّتَه ، فَلْيَفْعَلْ » متفقٌ عليه .

1024. Hazrat Abu Hurairah (R.A.A.) states that he heard the Holy Prophet (S.A.W.) say: 'My Ummah (followers) will be called on the Day of Judgment as a people with bright faces and limbs, this being the effect of their practice of ablution. Therefore any one of you who wish to increase his brightness, he should do so (by making longer ablutions). *(Bukhari and Muslim)*

١٠٢٥ — وعنه قالَ : سَمِعْتُ خَلِيلي صلَّى اللهُ عليهِ وسلَّمَ يقولُ : « تَبْلُغُ الحِلْيَةُ مِنَ المؤمِنِ حَيْثُ يَبْلُغُ الوُضوءُ » رواه مسلم .

1025. Hazrat Abu Hurairah (R.A.A.) relates: I heard my firend (the Holy Prophet (S.A.W.) saying: The elegance of a Muslim in Paradise, will extend as far as the water with which he performs his ablution, goes. *(Muslim)*

١٠٢٦ — وعن عثمانَ بن عفانَ رضيَ اللهُ عنهُ قالَ : قالَ رسولُ اللهِ صلَّى اللهُ عليهِ وسلَّمَ : « مَنْ تَوَضَّأَ فَأَحْسَنَ الوُضوءَ ، خرجَتْ خَطَايَاهُ مِنْ جسَدِهِ حَتَّى تَخْرُجَ مِنْ تَحْتِ أَظفارِهِ » رواه مسلم .

1026. Hazrat Usman bin 'Affan (R.A.A.) relates 'The Holy Prophet (S.A.W.) said: 'A person who makes ablution thoroughly, will have his sins removed from his body, so much so that even from inside his nails. *(Muslim)*

١٠٢٧ — وعنه قال : رَأَيْتُ رَسُولَ اللهِ صلّى اللهُ عليهِ وسلّمَ تَوَضّأَ مثلَ وُضوئي هذا ثمَّ قال : « مَنْ تَوَضَّأَ هكذا ، غُفِرَ لَهُ ما تَقَدَّمَ مِنْ ذَنْبِهِ ، وكانَتْ صلاتُهُ وَمَشْيُهُ إلى المَسْجِدِ نَافِلَةً » رواه مسلم .

1027. Hazrat Usman bin 'Affan (R.A.A.) says: 'I saw the Holy Prophet (S.A.W.) make ablution as I did and remarked: Anybody. who performs his ablution like this, will have his past sins remitted; and his prayers and going to mosque will be treated as nafil. (i.e. will earn additional recompense.) *(Muslim)*

١٠٢٨ — وعن أبي هريرة رَضِيَ اللهُ عنهُ أنَّ رسولَ الله صلّى الله عليه وسلّمَ قال : « إذا تَوَضَّأَ العَبْدُ المُسْلِمُ — أو المُؤْمِنُ — فَغَسَلَ وَجْهَهُ . خَرَجَ مِنْ وَجْهِهِ كلُّ خَطيئَةٍ نَظَرَ إلَيْها بِعَيْنَيْهِ مَعَ الماءِ ، أوْ مع آخِرِ قَطْرِ الماءِ ، فإذا غَسَلَ يَدَيهِ . خَرَجَ مِنْ يَدَيهِ كُلُّ خَطيئَةٍ كانَ بَطَشَتْها يَدَاهُ مَعَ الماءِ ، أوْ مَعَ آخِرِ قَطْرِ الماءِ ، فإذا غَسَلَ رِجلَيْهِ ، خَرَجَتْ كُلُّ خَطيئَةٍ مَشَتْها رجلاه مَعَ الماءِ ، أوْ مَعَ آخِرِ قَطر الماءِ ، حتى يَخْرُجَ نَقِيّاً مِنَ الذُّنُوبِ » رواه مسلم .

1028. This Hadis has already been covered in item No. 129 of Chapter 13.

١٠٢٩ — وعَنْهُ أنَّ رَسُولَ اللهِ صلّى اللهُ عَلَيْهِ وسلّمَ أتى المَقبُرَةَ فَقالَ : « السَّلامُ عَلَيْكُمْ دَارَ قَوْمٍ مُؤْمِنينَ ، وَإنّا إنْ شاءَ اللهُ بِكُمْ لاحِقُونَ ، وَدِدْتُ أنّا قَدْ رَأَيْنا إخْوانَنا » قالُوا : أوَلَسْنا إخْوانَكَ يارَسُولَ اللهِ ؟ قالَ : « أنْتُمْ أصْحابي ، وإخْوانُنا الَّذينَ لَمْ يَأْتُوا بَعْدُ » قالُوا : كَيْفَ تَعْرِفُ مَنْ لَمْ يَأْتِ بَعْدُ مِنْ أُمَّتِكَ يارَسُولَ اللهِ ؟ فَقالَ : « أرَأَيْتَ لَوْ أنَّ رَجُلاً لَهُ خَيْلٌ غُرٌّ مُحَجَّلَةٌ بَيْنَ ظَهْرَيْ خَيْلٍ دُهْمٍ بُهْمٍ ، ألا يَعْرِفُ خَيْلَهُ ؟ ». قالُوا : بَلى يارَسُولَ اللهِ ، قالَ : « فَإنَّهُمْ يَأْتُونَ غُرّاً مُحَجَّلينَ مِنَ الوُضُوءِ ، وأنا فَرَطُهُمْ عَلى الحَوْضِ » رواه مسلم .

1029. Hazrat Abu Hurairah (R.A.A.) relates that once the Holy Prophet (S.A.W.) visited the graveyard of *Jannat-ul-Baqi* (in Madina) and said. *'Assalum-e-Alaikum Dara qaumin momneena wa inna insha Allaho bikum laheqoon.*

Peace be on you the inhabitants of this town of the Muslims. We shall, if Allah wills, join you"

It was my earnest desire to have seen our brethren.

Some companions present on the occasion submitted: O Messenger of Allah, Are we not your brethren? He (S.A.W.) answered: You are my companions, and those who have not yet come in this world are my brethren. He (S.A.W.) was further asked. O Messenger of Allah, how will you recognize your followers, who have yet to come? He (S.A.W.) answered. Let me know if a man has horses with white foreheads and tufts of hair on their hoofs and they intermingled with pure black horses. Will that man not be able to distinguish his animals? The companions answered: Why not, O Messenger of Allah. He (S.A.W.) said: 'Then my followers will come with brilliant faces and shining hands and feet as a result of their ablutions: and I shall reach the tank (Al-Kausar) ahead of them. *(Muslim)*

١٠٣٠ – وعَنْهُ أنَّ رَسُولَ اللهِ صَلَّى اللهُ عَلَيْهِ وَسَلَّمَ قَالَ : « ألا أدُلُّكُمْ عَلى ما يَمْحُو اللهُ بِهِ الخَطَايَا ، وَيَرْفَعُ بِهِ الدَّرَجَاتِ ؟ قَالُوا : بَلَى يارَسُولَ اللهِ ، قَالَ : إسْبَاغُ الوُضُوءِ عَلى المَكَارِهِ ، وَكَثْرَةُ الخُطَا إلى المَسَاجِدِ ، وَانْتِظَارُ الصَّلاةِ بَعْدَ الصَّلاةِ ؛ فَذلِكُمُ الرِّبَاطُ ؛ فَذلِكُمُ الرِّبَاطُ » رواه مسلم .

1030. This Hadis is the same as No. 131 of Chapter 13.

١٠٣١ – وعَنْ أبي مَالِكٍ الأشْعَرِيِّ رَضِيَ اللهُ عَنْهُ قَالَ : قَالَ رَسُولُ اللهِ صَلَّى اللهُ عَلَيْهِ وَسَلَّمَ : « الطُّهُورُ شَطْرُ الإيمَانِ » رواه مسلم
وقد سبقَ بِطولِهِ في بابِ الصبرِ .

وفي البابِ حديثُ عمرو بْنِ عَبَسَةَ رَضِيَ اللهُ عَنْهُ السَّابِقُ في آخرِ بَابِ الرَّجاء . وَهُوَ حَدِيثٌ عظيمٌ ؛ مُشْتَمِلٌ عَلى جُمَلٍ من الخيرات .

1031. This Hadis has been covered in the first part of S. No. 25 of Chapter 3.

١٠٣٢ – وَعَنْ عُمَرَ بْنِ الخَطَّابِ رَضِيَ اللهُ عَنْهُ عَنِ النَّبِيِّ صَلَّى اللهُ عَلَيْهِ وَسَلَّمَ قَالَ: «مَامِنْكُمْ مِنْ أَحَدٍ يَتَوَضَّأُ فَيُبْلِغُ – أَوْ فَيُسْبِغُ الوُضُوءَ – ثُمَّ قَالَ: أَشْهَدُ أَنْ لا إِلٰهَ إِلاَّ اللهُ وَحْدَهُ لاشَرِيكَ لَهُ، وَأَشْهَدُ أَنَّ مُحَمَّداً عَبْدُهُ وَرَسُولُهُ؛ إِلاَّ فُتِحَتْ لَهُ أَبْوَابُ الجَنَّةِ الثَّمَانِيَةُ يَدْخُلُ مِنْ أَيِّهَا شَاءَ» رواه مسلم.

وَزَادَ التِرمذي: «اللَّهُمَّ اجْعَلْنِي مِنَ التَّوَّابِينَ وَاجْعَلْنِي مِنَ المُتَطَهِّرِينَ»

1032. Hazrat 'Umar bin Khattab (R.A.A.) states that the Holy Prophet (S.A.W.) said: When anyone of you perform his ablution carefully and then affirms:

Ash'hado Al-la Ilaha illal-la-ho wah'dahu la sharika lahu wa Ash' hado anna Muhammadan 'abduhu Wa rasuluhu.

I bear witness that there is none worthy of worship except Allah, the only One and Who has no associate; and I bear witness that Muhammad is His Servant and Messenger, will find all the eight gates of the Paradise open for him. He can enter there by any gate he likes.' *(Muslim)*
Imam Tirmizi has added this supplication:

'Allah make me one of those who turn to Thee in repentence and seek Thy forgiveness and include me among those who are pure (pious).'

CHAPTER 186

VIRTUES OF AZAN

١٠٣٣ – عَنْ أَبِي هُرَيْرَةَ رَضِيَ اللهُ عَنْهُ أَنَّ رَسُولَ اللهِ صَلَّى اللهُ عَلَيْهِ وَسَلَّمَ قَالَ: «لَوْ يَعْلَمُ النَّاسُ مَا فِي النِّدَاءِ والصَّفِّ الأَوَّلِ. ثُمَّ لَمْ يَجِدُوا إِلاَّ أَنْ يَسْتَهِمُوا عَلَيْهِ لاسْتَهَمُوا عَلَيْهِ، وَلَوْ يَعْلَمُونَ مَا فِي التَّهْجِيرِ لاسْتَبَقُوا إِلَيْهِ، وَلَوْ يَعْلَمُونَ مَا فِي العَتَمَةِ والصُّبْحِ لأَتَوْهُمَا وَلَوْ حَبْواً» متفقٌ عليه.

1033. Hazrat Abu Hurairah (R.A.A.) relates that the Holy Prophet (S.A.W.) said: If people could know the magnitude of recompense of calling the Azan (the call for prayer) and taking position in the first row of prayers, they would draw lots to secure such a place if necessary; and if they knew the virtues of coming early to the mosque for

prayer, they would hasten to reach there anyway; if they realised the value and merit of the Fajr (early morning) and Isha (late evening) prayers, they would come to them even if they had to drag themselves.
(Bukhari and Muslim)

١٠٣٤ – وَعَنْ مُعَاوِيَةَ رَضِيَ اللهُ عَنْهُ قَالَ : سَمِعْتُ رَسُولَ اللهِ صَلَّى اللهُ عَلَيْهِ وَسَلَّمَ يَقُولُ : « الْمُؤَذِّنُونَ أَطْوَلُ النَّاسِ أَعْنَاقاً يَوْمَ الْقِيَامَةِ » رواه مسلم .

1034. Hazrat Amir Mu'awiah (R.A.A.) says that he heard the Holy Prophet (S.A.W.) say: The Muezzins (Persons who call the Muslims to mosque for prayers) will have the longest necks on the Day of Judgment (which fact will reflect their exclusive eminence).
(Muslim)

١٠٣٥ – وَعَنْ عَبْدِ اللهِ بْنِ عَبْدِ الرَّحْمَنِ بْنِ أَبِي صَعْصَعَةَ أَنَّ أَبَا سَعِيدٍ الْخُدْرِيَّ رَضِيَ اللهُ عَنْهُ قَالَ لَهُ : « إِنِّي أَرَاكَ تُحِبُّ الْغَنَمَ وَالْبَادِيَةَ فَإِذَا كُنْتَ فِي غَنَمِكَ – أَوْ بَادِيَتِكَ – فَأَذَّنْتَ لِلصَّلَاةِ ، فَارْفَعْ صَوْتَكَ بِالنِّدَاءِ ، فَإِنَّهُ لَا يَسْمَعُ مَدَى صَوْتِ الْمُؤَذِّنِ جِنٌّ ، وَلَا إِنْسٌ ، وَلَا شَيْءٌ ، إِلَّا شَهِدَ لَهُ يَوْمَ الْقِيَامَةِ » قال أبو سعيدٍ : سَمِعْتُهُ مِنْ رَسُولِ اللهِ صَلَّى اللهُ عَلَيْهِ وَسَلَّمَ . رواه البخاري

1035. Hazrat Abdullah bin Abdur Rahman bin Abi Sa'sa relates that Hazrat Abu Sa'eed Khudri (R.A.A.) told him: 'I see that you people are interested in goats and the jungle. As such when you happen to be in a jungle and your goats grazing and you had to pronounce Azan, (the call for prayer) do it loudly, because anybody, whether genii, human beings or anything else, who hears the most distant voice of the Muezzin, shall be a witness to it on the Day of Judgment. This I heard from the Holy Prophet (S.A.W.).
(Bukhari)

١٠٣٦ – وَعَنْ أَبِي هُرَيْرَةَ رَضِيَ اللهُ عَنْهُ قَالَ : قَالَ رَسُولُ اللهِ صَلَّى اللهُ عَلَيْهِ وَسَلَّمَ : « إِذَا نُودِيَ بِالصَّلَاةِ ، أَدْبَرَ الشَّيْطَانُ ، لَهُ ضُرَاطٌ حَتَّى لَا يَسْمَعَ التَّأْذِينَ ، فَإِذَا قُضِيَ النِّدَاءُ أَقْبَلَ ، حَتَّى إِذَا ثُوِّبَ لِلصَّلَاةِ أَدْبَرَ ، حَتَّى إِذَا قُضِيَ التَّثْوِيبُ أَقْبَلَ ، حَتَّى يَخْطِرَ بَيْنَ الْمَرْءِ وَنَفْسِهِ يَقُولُ : اذْكُرْ كَذَا ، وَاذْكُرْ كَذَا – لِمَا لَمْ يَذْكُرْ مِنْ قَبْلُ –

حَتَّى يَظَلَّ الرَّجُلُ مَايَدْرِي كَمْ صَلَّى » متفقٌ عليه

1036. Hazrat Abu Hurairah (R.A.A.) states that the Holy Prophet (S.A.W.) said: When Azan is pronounced the Satan turns back and runs away so much so that he does not hear even the words of Azan: and returns after the Azan is over. He again bolts away when the Iqamah is called and returns again when the same is finished, and starts hinting to the worshipper 'Remember such and such thing.' Putting into his mind irrelevant matters which were out of the mind of the worshipper, till he forgets how many raka'ats he offered.

(Bukhari and Muslim)

١٠٣٧ — وَعَنْ عَبْدِ اللهِ بْنِ عَمْرِو بْنِ العَاصِ رَضِيَ اللهُ عَنْهُمَا أنه سَمِعَ رَسُولَ اللهِ صَلَّى اللهُ عَلَيْهِ وَسَلَّمَ يَقُولُ : « إذا سَمِعْتُمُ النِّدَاءَ فَقُولُوا مِثْلَ مَا يَقُولُ ، ثُمَّ صَلُّوا عَلَيَّ ، فَإِنَّهُ مَنْ صَلَّى عَلَيَّ صَلاةً صَلَّى اللهُ عَلَيْهِ بِهَا عَشْراً ، ثُمَّ سَلُوا اللهَ لِيَ الْوَسِيلَةَ ، فَإِنَّهَا مَنْزِلَةٌ في الجَنَّةِ لا تَنْبَغِي إلاَّ لِعَبْدٍ مِنْ عِبَادِ اللهِ وَأَرْجُوا أَنْ أَكُونَ أَنَا هُوَ ، فَمَنْ سَأَلَ لِيَ الْوَسِيلَةَ حَلَّتْ لَهُ الشَّفَاعَةُ » رواه مسلم .

1037. Hazrat Abdullah bin 'Amr bin Al'Aas (R.A.A.) says that he heard the Holy Prophet (S.A.W.) say: When your hear the Azan, repeat its words after the Muezzin, and then recite salat i.e. Allah's blessings on me, for a person who recites salat or Allah's blessings on me, Allah bestows ten fold blessings on him in return.

Thereafter request Allah for *'Waselah'* for me: this is a place in paradise reserved for a servant of Allah, and I am sanguine that I shall be that person. Therefore, whoever requests for *'Waselah'* for me, it becomes necessary for me to intercede for him for his redemption.

(Muslim)

١٠٣٨ — وَعَنْ أَبِي سَعِيدٍ الخُدْرِيِّ رَضِيَ اللهُ عَنْهُ أَنَّ رَسُولَ اللهِ صَلَّى اللهُ عَلَيْهِ وَسَلَّمَ قَالَ : « إذا سَمِعْتُمُ النِّدَاءَ ، فَقُولُوا كَمَا يَقُولُ المُؤَذِّنُ » متفقٌ عليه .

1038. Hazrat Abu Sa'eed Khudri (R.A.A.) states that the Holy Prophet (S.A.W.) said: when you hear the Azan (the call for prayer), repeat the words which the Muezzin says. *(Bukhari and Muslim)*

١٠٣٩ ـ وَعَنْ جَابِرٍ رَضِيَ اللهُ عَنْهُ أَنَّ رَسُولَ اللهِ صَلَّى اللهُ عَلَيْهِ وَسَلَّمَ قَالَ : « مَنْ قَالَ حِينَ يَسْمَعُ النِّدَاءَ : اللَّهُمَّ رَبَّ هٰذِهِ الدَّعْوَةِ التَّامَّةِ ، وَالصَّلاةِ الْقَائِمَةِ ، آتِ مُحَمَّداً الْوَسِيلَةَ ، وَالْفَضِيلَةَ ، وَابْعَثْهُ مَقَاماً مَحْمُوداً الَّذِي وَعَدْتَه ، حَلَّتْ لَهُ شَفَاعَتِي يَوْمَ الْقِيَامَةِ »

رواه البخاري .

1039. **Hazrat Jabir** (R.A.A.) **relates** that the Holy Prophet (S.A.W.) said: Any person who on hearing the Azan supplicates:

Allah, the Lord of this perfect call and of the prayer going to be held bestow on Muhammad (S.A.W.) '*Waselah*' and exultation and raise him to the praiseworthy station which Thou hast promised him;' then it becomes obligatory for me to intercede for him on the Day of Judgment. *(Bukhari)*

١٠٤٠ ـ وَعَنْ سَعْدِ بْنِ أَبِي وَقَّاصٍ رَضِيَ اللهُ عَنْهُ عَنِ النَّبِيِّ صَلَّى اللهُ عَلَيْهِ وَسَلَّمَ أَنَّهُ قَالَ : مَنْ قَالَ حِينَ يَسْمَعُ المُؤَذِّنَ : أَشْهَدُ أَنْ لا إِلٰهَ إِلاَّ اللهُ وَحْدَهُ لاشَرِيكَ لَهُ ، وَأَنَّ مُحَمَّداً عَبْدُهُ وَرَسُولُهُ ، رَضِيتُ بِاللهِ رَبّاً ، وَبِمُحَمَّدٍ رَسُولاً ، وَبِالإِسْلامِ دِيناً ، غُفِرَ لَهُ ذَنْبُهُ »

رواه مسلم

1040. **Hazrat Sa'd bin Abi Waqqas** (R.A.A.) relates that the Holy Prophet (S.A.W.) said: Anybody who, after hearing the Azan, supplicate.

'I bear witness that there is none worthy of worship save Allah, the One, without any associate and that Muhammad (S.A.W.) is his servant and Messenger; I wilfully accept Allah as my Sustainer and Muhammad (S.A.W.) as His Messenger, and Islam as my faith,'

Will have his sins remitted. *(Muslim)*

١٠٤١ ـ وَعَنْ أَنَسٍ رَضِيَ اللهُ عَنْهُ قَالَ : قَالَ رَسُولُ اللهِ صَلَّى اللهُ عَلَيْهِ وَسَلَّمَ : « الدُّعَاءُ لايُرَدُّ بَيْنَ الأَذانِ وَالإِقَامَةِ »

رواه أبو داود والترمذي وقال : حديث حسن .

1041. **Hazrat Anas** (R.A.A.) relates that the Holy Prophet (S.A.W.) said: Any supplication between Azan and the first *takbir* of *Iqamah* will not be rejected. *(Abu Daud and Tirmizi)*

CHAPTER 187

VIRTUES AND BENEFITS OF THE SALAT (PRESCRIBED PRAYER)

قَالَ اللهُ تَعَالَى : إِنَّ الصَّلَاةَ تَنْهَى عَنِ الْفَحْشَاءِ وَالْمُنْكَرِ [العنكبوت : ٤٥]

Allah the Exalted has said:

281. Lo! Salat preserveth from lewdness and inequity. (29:45)

١٠٤٢ – وعَنْ أَبِي هُرَيْرَةَ رَضِيَ اللهُ عَنْهُ قَالَ : سَمِعْتُ رَسُولَ اللهِ صَلَّى اللهُ عَلَيْهِ وَسَلَّمَ يَقُولُ : « أَرَأَيْتُمْ لَوْ أَنَّ نَهْراً بِبَابِ أَحَدِكُمْ يَغْتَسِلُ مِنه كُلَّ يَوْمٍ خَمْسَ مَرَّاتٍ : هَلْ يَبْقَى مِنْ دَرَنِهِ شَيْءٌ ؟ » قَالُوا : لايَبْقَى مِنْ دَرَنِهِ شَيْءٌ ؛ قَالَ : « فَذلكَ مَثَلُ الصَّلَوَاتِ الخَمْسِ ، يَمْحُو اللهُ بِهِنَّ الخَطَايَا » متفقٌ عليه

1042. Hazrat Abu Hurairah (R.A.A.) states that he heard the Holy Prophet (S.A.W.) say: Suppose if one of you had a running canal at his door and he takes bath in it five times every day, then would any dirt be left on his person. The companions submitted: In such a case no dirt would be left on his person. The Holy Prophet (S.A.W.) remarked: Similar is the case of the five obligatory prayers. Allah remits all sins in consideration of these prayers.

(Bukhari and Muslim)

١٠٤٣ – وَعَنْ جَابِرٍ رَضِيَ اللهُ عَنْهُ قَالَ : قَالَ رَسُولُ اللهِ صَلَّى اللهُ عَلَيْهِ وَسَلَّمَ : « مَثَلُ الصَّلَوَاتِ الخَمْسِ كَمَثَلِ نَهْرٍ جَارٍ غَمْرٍ عَلَى بَابِ أَحَدِكُم يَغْتَسِلُ مِنْهُ كُلَّ يَوْمٍ خَمْسَ مَرَّاتٍ » رواه مسلم

1043. This Hadis is the same as already covered in No. 432 of Chapter 51.

١٠٤٤ – وَعَنِ ابْنِ مَسْعُودٍ رَضِيَ اللهُ عَنْهُ أَنَّ رَجُلاً أَصَابَ مِنِ امْرَأَةٍ قُبْلَةً . فَأَتَى النَّبِيَّ صَلَّى اللهُ عَلَيْهِ وسلّمَ فَأَخبرَهُ فَأَنزلَ اللهُ تعالى : (أَقِمِ الصَّلَاةَ طَرَفَيِ النَّهَارِ وَزُلَفاً مِنَ اللَّيْلِ ، إِنَّ الحَسَنَاتِ يُذْهِبْنَ السَّيِّئَاتِ) فقالَ الرَّجُلُ : أَلِيَ هذا ؟ قال : « لِجَمِيعِ أُمَّتِي كلهِمْ » متفقٌ عليه

1044. This Hadis is the same as No. 429 of Chapter 51.

١٠٤٥ - عن أبي هريرة رضي الله عنه أن رسول الله صلى الله عليه وسلم قال : « الصلوات الخمس . والجمعة إلى الجمعة ، كفارة لما بينهن . ما لم تغش الكبائر » رواه مسلم .

1045. This Hadis has been covered earlier in No. 130 of Chap..13.

١٠٤٦ - وعن عثمان بن عفان رضي الله عنه قال : سمعت رسول الله صلى الله عليه سلم يقول : « ما من امرىء مسلم تحضره صلاة مكتوبة فيحسن وضوءها ، وخشوعها ، وركوعها ، إلا كانت كفارة لما قبلها من الذنوب ما لم تؤت كبيرة ، وذلك الدهر كله » رواه مسلم

1046. **Hazrat Usman bin 'Affan** (R.A.A.) says that he heard the Holy Prophet (S.A.W.) say: When, on the approach of the time of an obligatory prayer, a Muslim makes his ablution nicely and then bows (goes into ruku) and offers prayer with humbleness and fearfulness. it serves as an expiation for his previous sins, so long as he avoids committing any major sins; and this privilege is for all times to come. *(Muslim)*

Note: Considering the above traditions and Quranic verses, the august Muslim theologians (Ulema) have declared that by virtue of prayers and his good deeds and obedience to Allah, one gets his minor sins condoned.

* * * * * * *

CHAPTER 188

VIRTUE OF THE DAWN AND AFTERNOON PRAYERS

١٠٤٧ - عن أبي موسى رضي الله عنه أن رسول الله صلى الله عليه وسلم قال : « من صلى البردين دخل الجنة » متفق عليه .

1047. **Hazrat Abu Musa** (R.A.A.) relates that the **Holy Prophet** (S.A.W.) said: One who has offered two cool (time) **prayers i.e. Fajr** (Dawn) and Asr (afternoon) prayers shall enter paradise. *(Bukhari and Muslim)*

١٠٤٨ - وعن أبي زهير عمارة بن رويبة رضي الله عنه قال: سمعت سول الله صلى الله عليه وسلم يقول : « لن يلج النار أحد صلى قبل

طُلوعِ الشَّمْسِ وَقَبْلَ غُرُوبِهَا » يَعْنِي الفَجْرَ . وَالعَصْرَ . رواه مسلم

1048. Hazrat Abu Zuhair Amarah bin Ruwaibah (R.A.A.) states that he heard the Holy Prophet (S.A.W.) say: That a person will not be sent to Hell, who has offered his pre-sunrise *(Fajr)* and the before sunset *(Asr)* prayers. *(Muslim)*

١٠٤٩ – وعن جُنْدُبِ بن سُفيانَ رضيَ اللهُ عنهُ قالَ : قالَ رسولُ اللهِ صلّى اللهُ عليه وسلَّمَ : « مَنْ صَلَّى الصُّبْحَ فَهُوَ في ذِمَّةِ اللهِ فانْظُرْ يا ابنَ آدمَ ، لا يُطْلُبَنَّكَ اللهُ مِنْ ذِمَّتِهِ بِشيءٍ » رواه مسلم .

1049. This Hadis is the same as No. 389 of Chapte·· 49.

١٠٥٠ – وعن أبي هُرَيرةَ رضيَ اللهُ عنهُ قالَ : قالَ رسولُ اللهِ صلّى اللهُ عليهِ وسلَّمَ : « يَتَعاقَبُونَ فيكم مَلائِكَةٌ بِاللَّيْلِ ، وَمَلائِكَةٌ بِالنَّهارِ ، وَيَجْتَمِعُونَ في صَلاةِ الصُّبْحِ وَصَلاةِ العَصْرِ ، ثُمَّ يَعْرُجُ الَّذِينَ بَاتُوا فيكم ؛ فَيَسْأَلُهُمُ اللهُ – وَهُوَ أَعْلَمُ بِهِمْ – : كَيْفَ تَرَكْتُمْ عِبادِي ؟ فَيَقُولُونَ : تَرَكْناهُمْ وَهُمْ يُصَلُّونَ ، وَأَتَيْناهُمْ وَهُمْ يُصَلُّونَ » متفقٌ عليه .

1050. Hazrat Abu Hurairah (R.A.A.) relates that the Holy Prophet (S.A.W.) said: A number of night and day angels continue visiting you throughout the day and night; but they all assemble during the dawn *(Fajr)* and the afternoon *(Asr)* prayers. Then those of the angels who had spent the night among you ascend to heaven and their Lord enquires from them (though He knows better than they), as to in what condition did they leave His servants? They submit: 'They were offering salat when we left them and they were praying when we met them. *(Muslim and Bukhari)*

١٠٥١ – وعن جَرِيرِ بنِ عبدِ اللهِ البَجَلِيِّ رضيَ اللهُ عنهُ قال : كنا عِندَ النبيِّ صلّى اللهُ عليهِ وسلَّمَ ، فَنَظَرَ إلى القَمَرِ لَيْلَةَ البَدْرِ فقال : إنَّكُمْ سَتَرَوْنَ رَبَّكُمْ كما تَرَوْنَ هذا القَمَرَ ، لا تُضَامُونَ [٢٠٧] في رُؤْيَتِهِ ، فإنِ اسْتَطَعْتُمْ أنْ لا تُغْلَبُوا على صَلاةٍ قَبْلَ طُلُوعِ الشَّمْسِ ، وَقَبْلَ غُرُوبِها فافْعَلُوا » متفقٌ عليه .

وفي روايةٍ : « فَنَظَرَ إلى القَمَرِ لَيْلَةَ أَرْبَعَ عَشْرَةَ » .

1051. Hazrat Jarir bin Abdullah Bajali (R.A.A.) relates: Once we were sitting with the Holy Prophet (S.A.W.) one night when the moon was full. He looked at it and remarked: You will see your Lord (on the day of judgement) as you are seeing this moon, and you will not feel any fatigue thereby provided you ensure that you do not miss the prayers before sunrise and before sunset, and persevere in the same.

According to another tradition it was the 14th night moon which the Holy Prophet (S.A.W.) saw. *(Bukahri and Muslim)*

١٠٥٢ ــ وعن بُرَيْدَةَ رضيَ اللهُ عنه قالَ : قالَ رسولُ اللهِ صلَّى اللهُ عليه وسلَّمَ : « مَنْ تَرَكَ صَلاةَ العَصْرِ فَقَدْ حَبِطَ عَمَلُهُ » رواه البخاري .

1052. Hazrat Buraidah (R.A.A.) states that the Holy Prophet (S.A.W.) said: One who misses the afternoon prayer (Asr prayer) renders his good deeds void *(Bukhari)*

* * * * * * *

CHAPTER 189

VIRTUES OF GOING TO THE MOSQUE

١٠٥٣ ــ عن أبي هريرةَ رضيَ اللهُ عنهُ أنَّ النبيَّ صلَّى اللهُ عليهِ وسلَّم قالَ : « مَنْ غَدَا إلى المسْجِدِ أوْ رَاحَ ، أعَدَّ اللهُ لهُ في الجَنَّةِ نُزُلاً كُلَّما غَدَا أوْ رَاحَ » متفقٌ عليه .

1053. Hazrat Abu Hurairah (R.A.A.) relates that the Holy Prophet (S.A.W.) said: A person who goes to a mosque in the morning or evening (for prayers) Allah arranges a feast for him in Paradise every time he visits a mosque in the morning or evening.

(Bukhari and Muslim)

١٠٥٤ ــ وعنهُ أنَّ النَّبيَّ صلَّى اللهُ عليهِ وسلَّمَ قالَ : « مَنْ تَطَهَّرَ في بَيْتِهِ ، ثُمَّ مَضَى إلى بَيْتٍ مِنْ بُيُوتِ اللهِ ؛ لِيَقْضِيَ فَرِيضَةً مِنْ فَرَائِضِ اللهِ ؛ كانَتْ خُطُوَاتُهُ ، إحْدَاها تَحُطُّ خَطِيئَةً ، والأُخْرى تَرفَعُ دَرَجَةً » رواه مسلم

1054. Hazrat Abu Hurairah (R.A.A.) relates that the Holy Prophet (S.A.W.) said: One who purifies himself (makes his ablution) at home and then goes to one of the houses of Allah (mosque) to discharge his duty to Allah (to offer obligatory prayers) his one step towards a mosque wipes out a sin and another step raises his status. *(Muslim)*

١٠٥٥ – وعن أبيِّ بن كعبٍ رضيَ اللهُ عنه قالَ : كانَ رَجُلٌ مِنَ الأَنصارِ لا أعلَم أحداً أبعدَ مِنَ المسجِدِ مِنه ، وكانَتْ لا تُخطِئُهُ صَلاةٌ ! فَقيلَ له : لو اشترَيتَ حِماراً تَرْكَبُهُ في الظَّلْماءِ وَفي الرَّمْضاءِ قالَ : ما يَسُرُّني أنَّ مَنزِلي إلى جَنبِ المسْجِدِ ، إنّي أُريدُ أنْ يُكتَبَ لي مَمْشايَ إلى المسْجِدِ ، ورَجُوعي إذا رَجَعْتُ إلى أهْلي . فقالَ رسولُ اللهِ صلّى اللهُ عليه وسلَّمَ : « قَدْ جَمَعَ اللهُ لكَ ذلكَ كُلَّه » رواه مسلم .

1055. This Hadis is the same as covered in No. 137 of Chap. 13.

١٠٥٦ – وعن جابرٍ رضيَ اللهُ عنهُ قال : خَلَتِ البِقاعُ حَوْلَ المسْجِدِ ، فأرادَ بَنُو سَلِمَةَ أنْ يَنتَقِلُوا قُرْبَ المَسْجِدِ ، فَبَلَغَ ذلكَ النبيَّ صلّى اللهُ عليهِ وسلَّمَ فقالَ لهم : « بَلَغَني أنَّكُمْ تُريدُونَ أن تَنْتَقِلُوا قُرْبَ المَسْجِدِ؟! قالوا . نعم يارسولَ اللهِ قَدْ أَرَدْنَا ذلكَ ، فقالَ : « بَني سَلِمَةَ دِيارَكُمْ تُكْتَبْ آثارُكُمْ ، دِيارَكُمْ تُكْتَبْ آثارُكُمْ » فقالوا : مايَسُرُّنَا أنَّا كُنَّا تَحَوَّلْنَا . رواه مسلم ، وروى البخاري معناه من رواية أنس .

1056. This Hadis is the same as covered in No. 136 of Chap. 13.

١٠٥٧ – وعنْ أبي موسى رضيَ اللهُ عنهُ قالَ : قالَ رسولُ اللهِ صلّى اللهُ عليهِ وسلَّمَ « إنَّ أعْظَمَ النَّاسِ أجراً في الصَّلاةِ أبْعَدُهُمْ إلَيْها مَمْشىً ، فَأبْعَدُهُمْ . والَّذي يَنْتَظِرُ الصَّلاةَ حَتَّى يُصلِّيها مَعَ الإمامِ أعْظَمُ أجراً مِنَ الَّذي يُصَلِّي ثُمَّ يَنامُ » متفقٌ عليه

1057. Hazrat Abu Musa Ash'ari (R.A.A.) relates that the Holy Prophet (S.A.W.) said. A person, who comes to offer prayer from a long distance, gets highest reward; and he who waits so that he might say his prayer along with the Imam (in congregation) has a higher recompense than the one who prays all alone, and thereafter goes to sleep *(Bukahri and Muslim)*

١٠٥٨ – وعن بُرَيْدَةَ رضيَ اللهُ عنهُ عنِ النبيِّ صلّى اللهُ عليهِ وسلَّمَ قال: « بشِّروا المَشّائينَ في الظُّلَمِ إلى المساجِدِ بالنور التامِّ يَوْمَ القِيامةِ » رواه أبو داود ، والترمذي .

1058. Hazrat Buraidah (R.A.A.) says that the Holy Prophet (S.A.W.), said: Convey happy news of full brilliant light on the Day of Judgement to such persons who go to a mosque (to offer prayers) even in dark night. *(Abu Daud and Tirmizi)*

١٠٥٩ – وعن أبي هريرةَ رضيَ اللهُ عنهُ أنَّ رسولَ اللهِ صلَّى اللهُ عليه وسلَّمَ قالَ : « ألا أدُلُّكُمْ عَلى مَا يَمْحُو اللهُ بِهِ الخَطَايَا ، وَيَرْفَعُ بِهِ الدَّرَجَاتِ ؟ قَالُوا : بَلَى يارسولَ اللهِ . قالَ : « إسْبَاغُ الْوُضُوءِ عَلى المَكَارِهِ ، وَكَثْرَةُ الخُطَا إلى المَسَاجِدِ ، وَانْتِظَارُ الصَّلاةِ بَعْدَ الصَّلاةِ ، فَذلِكُمُ الرِّبَاطُ ، فَذلِكُمُ الرِّبَاطُ » رواه مسلم .

1059. This Hadis has been covered by No. 131 Chap. 13.

١٠٦٠ – وعن أبي سعيدٍ الخدْرِيِّ رضيَ اللهُ عنهُ عنِ النبيِّ صلَّى اللهُ عليهِ وسلَّمَ قال : « إذا رَأَيْتُمُ الرَّجُلَ يَعْتَادُ المَسَاجِدَ فَاشْهَدُوا لَهُ بِالإيمَانِ . قَالَ اللهُ عزَّ وجلَّ : (إنَّمَا يَعْمُرُ مَسَاجِدَ اللهِ مَنْ آمَنَ بِاللهِ وَالْيَوْمِ الآخِرِ) » الآية . رواه الترمذي وقال : حديث حسن .

1060. Hazrat Abu Sa'eed Khudri (R.A.A.) relates that the Holy Prophet (S.A.W.) said: When you notice a person regularly visiting a mosque, testify to his faith (his being a believer) for Allah, the Master of Honour and Glory said: He only shall attend Allah's mosques who believeth in Allah and the Last Day." (9: 18) *(Tirmizi)*

* * * * * * *

CHAPTER 190

VIRTUES OF WAITING FOR PRAYER

١٠٦١ – وعنْ أبي هريرةَ رضيَ اللهُ عنهُ أنَّ رسولَ اللهِ صلَّى اللهُ عليهِ وسلَّمَ قالَ : « لايَزَالُ أحَدُكُمْ في صَلاةٍ مَادَامَتِ الصَّلاةُ تَحْبِسُهُ : لايَمْنَعُهُ أنْ يَنْقَلِبَ إلى أهْلِهِ إلاَّ الصَّلاةُ » متفقٌ عليه

1061. Hazrat Abu Hurairah (R.A.A.) states that the Holy Prophet (S.A.W.) said: As long as you stay in a mosque waiting for prayer (congregation), and are held up there only for the sake of prayer, and only this thing prevents you from returning home, you will be treated as continuously in prayer. *(Bukhari and Muslim)*

١٠٦٢ — وعنه أنَّ رسولَ اللهِ صلى اللهُ عليهِ وسلَّمَ قال : « المَلائكَةُ تُصلّي على أحدِكُمْ مادامَ في مُصلاّهُ الّذي صلّى فيه ، مالَمْ يُحْدِثْ ، تَقُولُ : اللّهُمَّ اغفِرْ لَهُ ، اللّهُمَّ ارْحَمْهُ » رواه البخاري .

1062. Hazrat Abu Hurairah (R.A.A.) relates that the Holy Prophet (S.A.W.) said: "When one of you continues sitting on prayer-carpet, after prayer is over, and he remains with ablutions, the angels beseech Allah for His blessings upon him, and pray, "Allah ! grant him salvation; Allah have mercy on him." *(Bukhari)*

١٠٦٣ — وعن أنسٍ رضيَ اللهُ عنهُ أنَّ رسولَ اللهِ صلّى اللهُ عليهِ وسلّمْ أخّرَ ليْلَةً صلاةَ الْعِشاءِ إلى شَطْرِ اللّيْلِ ثُمَّ أقْبلَ علَيْنا بِوجْهِهِ بَعْدَ ما صلّى فقال : « صلّى النّاسُ ورَقَدُوا ولَمْ تزَالُوا في صلاةٍ مُنْذُ انْتَظَرْتُمُوها » . رواه البخاري .

1063. Hazrat Anas bin Malik (R.A.A.) states: "Once the Holy Prophet (S.A.W.) was late in coming to the mosque to lead the *'Isha* congregation till midnight. (By this time some people had offered their prayers and went to their homes to sleep). After the Holy Prophet (S.A.W.) had finished the prayer, he addressed the gathering and said, "some persons said their prayers and (went) to sleep; but those, who waited (for the congregation), were treated as if they remained engaged in prayer throughout. *(Bukhari)*

* * * * * * *

CHAPTER 191

VIRTUES OF CONGREGATIONAL PRAYER

١٠٦٤ — عن ابنِ عمرَ رضيَ اللهُ عنهما أنَّ رسولَ اللهِ صلّى اللهُ عليهِ وسلّمَ قال : « صَلاةُ الجَماعَةِ أفضَلُ مِنْ صَلاةِ الْفَذِّ بِسَبْعٍ وعِشْرينَ دَرَجَةً » . متفقٌ عليه .

1064. Hazrat Ibn 'Umar (R.A.A.) relates that the Holy Prophet (S.A.W.) said: "Recompense for prayer offered along with the congregation is twenty seven times more than the prayer offered in home or bazar. *(Bukhari and Muslim)*

١٠٦٥ — وعن أبي هريرةَ رضيَ اللهُ عنهُ قال : قالَ رسولُ اللهِ صلَّى اللهُ عليهِ وسلَّمَ : « صَلاةُ الرَّجُلِ في جَماعَةٍ تُضعَّفُ على صَلاتِهِ في بَيْتِهِ وَفي سُوقِهِ خمْساً وَعِشْرِينَ ضِعفاً ، وَذلكَ أنَّهُ إذا تَوَضَّأَ فَأَحْسَنَ الوُضُوءَ ، ثُمَّ خَرَجَ إلى المَسْجِدِ ، لا يُخرِجُه إلاَّ الصَّلاةُ ، لَمْ يَخْطُ خَطْوَةً إلاَّ رُفِعَتْ لَه بهَا دَرَجَةٌ ، وَحُطَّتْ عَنْه بهَا خَطيئَةٌ ، فَإذا صَلَّى لَمْ تَزَلِ المَلائِكَة تُصَلِّي عَلَيْهِ مَادامَ في مُصَلاَّه ، مَا لَمْ يُحْدِثْ ، تَقُولُ : اللَّهُمَّ صَلِّ عَلَيْهِ ، اللَّهُمَّ ارحَمْهُ . وَلا يَزَالُ في صَلاةٍ مَا انْتَظرَ الصَّلاةَ » متفقٌ عليه وهذا لفظ البخاري .

1065. Hazrat Abu Hurairah (R.A.A.) says that the Holy Prophet (S.A.W.) said: Reward for the prayer of a male person said in congregation (in mosque) is twenty five times more than the prayer offered at home or in bazaar. This is so because when he has carried out his ablution thoroughly, and goes to mosque with the intention of offering prayer, then for each step he takes, his position is upgraded by one stage, and gets one sin remitted; and when he is engaged in praying, the angels continue praying for mercy for him, and this goes on as long as he stays on prayer carpet, and remains with ablution. Angels pray: Allah shower blessings on him; Allah have mercy on him. And as long as he waits for congregational prayer, he is considered as in prayer. *(Bukhari and Muslim)*

١٠٦٦ — وعنهُ قالَ : أَتَى النبيَّ صلَّى اللهُ عليهِ وسلَّمَ رَجُلٌ أعمى ، فقال : يا رسولَ اللهِ ، لَيْسَ لي قَائِدٌ يَقُودُني إلى المَسْجِدِ ، فَسَأَلَ رسولَ اللهِ صلَّى اللهُ عليهِ وسلَّمَ أن يُرَخِّصَ لَهُ فَيُصَلِّي في بَيْتِهِ ؛ فَرَخَّصَ لَهُ ، فلَمَّا وَلَّى دَعاهُ فقالَ لهُ : « هَلْ تَسْمَعُ النِّداءَ بِالصَّلاةِ ؟ » قال : نَعَمْ ، قال : « فَأَجِبْ » رواه مسلم

1066. Hazrat Abu Hurairah (R.A.A.) relates that once a blind person (Hazrat Ibn Umm Maktum) came to Holy Prophet (S.A.W.) and submitted: O Messenger of Allah, I have nobody to lead me to mosque, and then he sought his permission to say his prayers at home. The Holy Prophet (S.A.W.) gave him the permission but when he was going back, the Holy Prophet (S.A.W.) called him and asked, 'Do you hear the call for prayer?' He answered: 'Yes, Sir.' The Holy Prophet (S.A.W.) then said: 'Therefore respond to it.' *(Muslim)*

١٠٦٧ – وعن عبدِ اللهِ – وقيلَ : عَمْرو بنِ قيسٍ المعروفِ بابنِ أمِّ مكتومٍ المؤذِّنِ رضيَ اللهُ عنه أنه قالَ : يا رسولَ اللهِ إنَّ المدينةَ كثيرةُ الهوامِّ والسِّباعِ . فقالَ رسولُ اللهِ صلّى اللهُ عليهِ وسلَّمَ : « تسمعُ حيَّ على الصَّلاةِ ، حيَّ على الفلاحِ ؛ فحيَّهلاً »

رواه أبو داود بإسناد حسنٍ .

1067. Hazrat Ibn Umm Maktum, the Muezzin (R.A.A.) (his real name is Abdullah and also ‘Amr bin Qais) relates that he requested the Holy Prophet (S.A.W.), ‘O Messenger of Allah ! In Madina there are large number of reptiles and dangerous animals and I am blind. As such I cannot see my way or things there and therefore please permit me to say prayers my house. He (S.A.W.) said if you can hear the words of Azan: *"Haiya ‘Alas Salah Haiya ‘Alal Falah,"* come to prayer; Come to salvation’, then come to mosque for prayer. *(Imam Abu Daud quoted this Hadis with sound chains.)*

١٠٦٨ – وعن أبي هريرةَ رضيَ اللهُ عنه أنَّ رسولَ اللهِ صلّى اللهُ عليه وسلَّمَ قالَ : « والَّذي نفسي بيدِه ، لقدْ هممتُ أنْ آمُرَ بحطبٍ فيُحتطبَ ، ثمَّ آمُرَ بالصَّلاةِ فيُؤذَّنَ لها ، ثمَّ آمُرَ رجلاً فيؤمَّ النَّاسَ ، ثمَّ أخالِفَ إلى رجالٍ فأُحرِّقَ عليهِم بيوتَهمْ » متفقٌ عليه

1068. Hazrat Abu Hurairah (R.A.A.) relates that the Holy Prophet (S.A.W.) said: By Allah in Whose possession is my life, sometimes I feel that I should ask for firewood to be gathered, and order for the holding of prayers and the call for prayer *(Azan)* to be announced, and then ask some one to lead the prayer. Then I may go after those who failed to join the congregation (prayer) and set fire to their houses in their presence. *(Bukahri and Muslim)*

Note. - This tradition proves that a pious ruler (Imam-i-Adil and the ruling Caliph) has the powers to punish those persons who fail to join the congregational prayers in mosque and to compel them to join the same.

١٠٦٩ – وعنِ ابنِ مسعودٍ رضيَ اللهُ عنه قالَ : مَن سرَّه أن يلقَى اللهَ تعالى غداً مسلماً ، فليُحافظْ على هؤلاءِ الصَّلَواتِ ، حيثُ يُنادى بهنَّ . فإنَّ اللهَ شرعَ لنبيِّكم صلّى اللهُ عليهِ وسلَّمَ سُننَ الهُدى ، وإنَّهنَّ من

سُنَنِ الهُدى ، وَلَو أَنَّكُم صَلَّيتُم في بُيوتِكم كما يُصَلِّي هذا المُتَخَلِّفُ في بَيتِهِ لَتَرَكتُم سُنَّةَ نَبِيِّكم ، وَلَو تَرَكتُم سُنَّةَ نَبِيِّكم لَضَلَلتُم ، ولَقَد رَأَيتُنا وما يَتَخَلَّفُ عَنها إلاَّ مُنافِقٌ مَعلُومُ النِّفاقِ ، ولَقَد كانَ الرَّجُلُ يُؤتى بِهِ ، يُهادَى بينَ الرَّجُلَينِ حَتى يُقامَ في الصَّفِّ . رواه مسلم .

وفي رِوايةٍ له قال : إنَّ رسولَ اللهِ صلَّى الله عليهِ وسلَّمَ عَلَّمَنا سُنَنَ الهُدَى ؛ وَإنَّ مِن سُنَنِ الهُدَى الصَّلاةَ في المَسجدِ الَّذي يُؤَذَّنُ فيه .

1069. Hazrat Abdullah bin Mas'ud (R.A.A.) said: A person who likes to meet Allah tomorrow (on the Day of Judgement) as a true Muslim, he should then take care of those prayers where (and when) he is summoned for them. This is necessary as Allah has laid down some practices and rules for us to follow (which have reached us) through our Prophet (S.A.W.) and these prayers (salat) are among them. If you offer prayers at your house as this good for nothing person is doing, you will be guilty of neglecting the way of your Prophet (S.A.W.) then you go astray. I have seen the people in a condition when only known hypocrites used to be out of the lines of congregation. Some of us used to be brought to the mosque with the help of two men on account of their weakness or illness, till they could stand in line.

(Muslim)

According to another version Hazrat Abdullah bin Masud (R.A.A.) said: The Messenger of Allah (S.A.W.) has taught us the (good) ways of guidance, and one of them is to pray in mosque from which the Azan is called.

١٠٧٠ - وعن أَبي الدرداءِ رضيَ الله عنه قال : سَمعت رسولَ اللهِ صلَّى الله عليهِ وسلَّمَ يقول : « ما مِن ثَلاثَةٍ في قَرْيَةٍ وَلا بَدْوٍ لا تُقامُ فيهِمُ الصَّلاةُ إلاَّ قَدِ استَحوَذَ عَلَيهِمُ الشَّيطانُ . فَعَلَيْكُمْ بِالجَماعَةِ ؛ فَإنَّما يَأكُلُ الذِّئبُ مِنَ الغَنَمِ القاصِيَةَ » رواه أَبو داود بإسناد حسن .

1070. Hazrat Abu Darda (R.A.A.) relates that he heard the Holy Prophet (S.A.W.) say: If there happens to be (even) three persons in a village, desert or jungle and they do not pray in congregation, Satan would surely dominate them. So make it obligatory to offer prayers in congregation, for a wolf devours a lone sheep. *(Imam Abu Daud has quoted this with good chains.)*

CHAPTER 192

VIRTUES OF OFFERING DAWN AND NIGHT PRAYERS IN CONGREGATION

١٠٧١ – عن عثمانَ بنِ عفانَ رضيَ اللهُ عنه قالَ : سمعتُ رسولَ الله صلّى اللهُ عليهِ وسلّمَ يقولُ : « مَنْ صلّى العِشاءَ في جَماعةٍ . فكأنّما قامَ نِصْفَ اللّيلِ ، ومَنْ صلّى الصبحَ في جَماعةٍ ، فكأنّما صلّى اللّيلَ كُلَّهُ » رواه مسلم .

وفي روايةِ الترمذيِّ عن عثمانَ بنِ عفانَ رضيَ اللهُ عنه قالَ : قالَ رسولُ الله صلّى اللهُ عليهِ وسلّمَ : « مَنْ شهِدَ العِشاءَ في جَماعةٍ كانَ لهُ قِيامُ نِصفِ ليلةٍ ، ومَنْ صلّى العِشاءَ والفَجْرَ في جَماعةٍ ، كانَ لهُ كقِيامِ ليلةٍ » قال الترمذيّ : حديثٌ حسنٌ صحيحٌ .

1071. Hazrat Usman bin Affan (R.A.A.) says that he heard the Holy Prophet (S.A.W.) say: 'A person who offers night (Isha) prayer in congregation is deemed to have spent half the night in optional prayer and one who joins the dawn (Fajr) prayer in congregation, is considered to have spent the whole night in optional prayer. *(Muslim)*

Imam Tirmizi says that the Holy Prophet (S.A.W.) said: One who offers night prayer in congregation is like having spent half the night in (optional) prayer, and one who offers night and dawn prayers in congregation, is like a person who had spent the whole night in optional prayer. Imam Tirmizi classified this Hadis as good and authentic.

١٠٧٢ – وعن أبي هُريرةَ رضيَ اللهُ عنهُ أنّ رسولَ اللهِ صلى اللهُ عليه وسلّمَ قالَ : « ولَوْ يَعْلَمُونَ مَا في العَتَمةِ والصُّبْحِ لأتَوْهُما ولَو حَبْواً » متفق عليه

1072. Hazrat Abu Hurairah (R.A.A.) reports that the Holy Prophet (S.A.W.) said: "If they (hypocrites) could know the virtues of dawn and night prayers, they would have certainly joined them even if they had to go (to the mosque) crawling.

(Bukhari and Muslim)

١٠٧٣ – وعنهُ قالَ : قالَ رسولُ اللهِ صلّى اللهُ عليهِ وسلّمَ : « ليسَ صَلاةٌ أثقلَ على المُنافِقينَ مِنْ صَلاةِ الفَجْرِ والعِشاءِ ولَوْ يَعْلَمُونَ مَا فيهما

لَا تَوْهُما وَلَوْ حَبْواً »ٌ. متفقٌ عليه

1073. Hazrat Abu Hurairah (R.A.A.) relates that the Holy Prophet (S.A.W.) said: 'The hypocrites find dawn (Fajr) and night (Isha) prayers in congregation as very oppressive. If they could know the virtues of these two prayers, they would certainly join them, even if they had to go crawling. *(Bukhari and Muslim)*

* * * * * * *

CHAPTER 193

ADHERENCE TO THE OBLIGATORY PRAYERS AND SEVERE ADMONITION FOR NEGLECTING THEM

قال الله تعالى : حَافِظُوا عَلَى الصَّلَوَاتِ وَالصَّلَاةِ الوُسْطَى [البقرة:٢٣٨]

وقال تعالى : فَإِنْ تَابُوا وَأَقَامُوا الصَّلَاةَ وَآتَوُا الزَّكَاةَ فَخَلُّوا سَبِيلَهُمْ

[التوبة : ٥].

Allah, the Exalted, has said :

282 Be guardians of your prayers, and of the midmost prayer. (2: 238).

283 But if they repent and establish prayer and pay the poor due, then leave their way free. (9: 5)

١٠٧٤ – وعن ابن مسعودٍ رضيَ اللهُ عنهُ قالَ : سألتُ رسولَ اللهِ صلّى اللهُ عليهِ وسلّمَ : أيُّ الأعمَالِ أفضَلُ ؟ قال : « الصَّلاةُ عَلى وَقْتِها » قلتُ : ثمَّ أيٌّ ؟ قال : « بِرُّ الوَالِدَيْنِ » قلتُ : ثمَّ أيٌّ ؟ قال : « الجِهادُ في سَبيلِ اللهِ » متفقٌ عليه

1074. This Hadis has already been covered in No. 312 of Chapter 40.

١٠٧٥ – وعن ابنِ عمرَ رضيَ اللهُ عنهما قالَ : قالَ رسولُ اللهِ صلّى اللهُ عليهِ وسلّم : « بُنِيَ الإسلامُ عَلى خَمْسٍ : شَهادَةِ أنْ لا إلهَ إلاّ اللهُ ، وَأنَّ مُحَمّداً رسولُ اللهِ ، وإقامِ الصَّلاةِ ، وَإيتاءِ الزَّكاةِ ، وَحَجِّ البَيْتِ ، وَصَوْمِ رَمَضانَ » متفقٌ عليه

1075. Hazrat Abdullah bin Umar (R.A.A.) relates that the Holy Prophet (S.A.W.) said: Islam is founded on pillars. First of all bearing witness that there is no god except Allah and that Muhammad (S.A.W.) is the Messenger of Allah (2) establishing prayer (3) paying the poor due (zakat) (4) Going on pilgrimage to the House of Allah (in Mecca) (5) and observing the Fast of Ramazan..

(Bukahri and Muslim)

١٠٧٦ — وعنهُ قال : قالَ رسولُ اللهِ صلّى اللهُ عليهِ وسلَّمَ : « أُمِرْتُ أنْ أُقاتِلَ النّاسَ حتّى يَشْهَدُوا أنْ لا إلهَ إلاّ اللهُ وأنَّ مُحَمَّداً رسولُ اللهِ ، وَيُقيمُوا الصَّلاةَ ، ويُؤْتُوا الزَّكاةَ . فإذا فعَلُوا ذلكَ ، عَصَمُوا مِنِّي دِماءَهُمْ وأمْوالَهُمْ إلاّ بحَقِّ الإسْلامِ . وَحِسابُهُمْ علَى اللهِ » متفقٌ عليه

1076. This Hadis is the same as No. 390 of Chapter 49.

١٠٧٧ — وعن معاذٍ رضيَ اللهُ عنهُ قالَ : بعثَني رسولُ اللهِ صلّى اللهُ عليهِ وسلَّمَ إلى اليمَنِ فقال : « إنَّكَ تأْتي قَوْماً من أهْلِ الكتابِ ، فادْعُهُمْ إلى شَهادَةِ أنْ لا إلهَ إلاّ اللهُ ، وأنّي رسولُ اللهِ . فإنْ أطاعُوا لِذلكَ ، فأعْلِمْهُمْ أنَّ اللهَ تعالى افترَضَ علَيْهِمْ خمْسَ صَلواتٍ في كلِّ يَوْمٍ ولَيْلَةٍ . فإنْ هُمْ أطاعُوا لِذلكَ . فأعْلِمْهُمْ أنَّ اللهَ تعالى افتَرَضَ علَيْهِمْ صَدَقَةً تُؤْخَذُ مِنْ أغْنيائِهِمْ فَتُرَدُّ علَى فُقَرائِهِمْ . فإنْ هُمْ أطاعُوا لِذلكَ . فإيّاكَ وكَرائِمَ أمْوالِهِمْ واتَّقِ دَعْوَةَ المَظْلُومِ ، فإنَّهُ لَيْسَ بيْنَها وبَيْنَ اللهِ حِجابٌ » متفقٌ عليه

1077. This Hadis is the same as No. 208 of Chapter 26.

١٠٧٨ — وعن جابرٍ رضيَ اللهُ عنهُ قال : سمعتُ رسولَ اللهِ صلّى اللهُ عليهِ وسلَّمَ يقولُ : « إنَّ بَيْنَ الرَّجُلِ وبَيْنَ الشِّرْكِ والكُفْرِ ترْكُ الصَّلاةِ » رواه مسلم

1078. Hazrat Jabir (R.A.A.) relates that he heard the Holy Prophet (S.A.W.) say : The line of demarcation between a man (Muslim) and polytheist and blasphemy is the giving up of Salat.

(Muslim)

١٠٧٩ — وعن بُرَيْدَةَ رضيَ اللهُ عنهُ عنِ النبيِّ صلّى اللهُ عليهِ وسلَّمَ قال : « العَهْدُ الّذي بيْننَا وبَيْنَهُمُ الصَّلاةُ ، فمَنْ ترَكَها فقَدْ كَفَرَ »

رواه الترمذي وقال : حديثٌ حسنٌ صحيحٌ

1079. Hazrat Buraidah (R.A.A.) says that Holy Prophet (S.A.W.) said. The thing which distinguishes us from the hypocrites is our attachment to Salat. Therefore one who gives it up becomes guilty of blasphemy. **(Tirmizi)**

١٠٨٠ ـ وعن شقيقِ بنِ عبدِ اللهِ التابعيِّ المُتَّفَقِ عَلى جَلالتهِ رَحِمَهُ اللهُ قال : كانَ أصْحابُ مُحَمَّدٍ صلّى اللهُ عليهِ وسلَّمَ لايَرَوْنَ شَيْئاً مِنَ الأعْمالِ تَرْكُهُ كُفْرٌ غَيْرَ الصَّلاةِ . رواه الترمذي في كتابِ الإيمانِ بإسنادٍ صحيحٍ .

1080. Hazrat Shaqiq bin Abdullah at-Tabie (R.A.) (his all comprehensive knowledge is acclaimed by all the learned ulema) relates that the companions of the Holy Prophet (S.A.W.) did not consider neglecting of any obligation as amounting to disbelief except neglect of prayer. *Imam Tirmizi* has quoted this Hadis with sound chain in Kitabul Imam).

NOTE :— From these traditions it appears that neglecting five daily prayers is a major sin. These traditions indicate that a person who neglects prayers is nearly a Kafir. (infidel.) According to As'hab-i-Zawahir such a person is kafir, and Imam Malik and Shafie consider that the beheading of such a person is necessary. Imam Abu Hanifa thinks that imprisoning and beating of such a person is necessary and essential till he repents and starts offering prayers.

١٠٨١ ـ وعن أبي هُرَيْرَةَ رضيَ اللهُ عنهُ قالَ : قالَ رسولُ اللهِ صلّى اللهُ عليهِ وسلَّمَ : « إنَّ أوَّلَ ما يُحاسَبُ بهِ العَبْدُ يَوْمَ القيامَةِ مِنْ عَمَلِهِ صَلاتُهُ ، فإنْ صَلَحَتْ ، فقدْ أفْلَحَ وأنْجَحَ ، وإنْ فَسَدَتْ ، فقدْ خابَ وخَسِرَ ، فإنِ انْتَقَصَ مِنْ فَريضَتِهِ شَيْئاً ، قالَ الرَّبُّ ، عَزَّ وَجَلَّ : انظُروا هَلْ لِعَبْدي مِنْ تَطَوُّعٍ ، فَيُكَمَّلُ منها ما انْتَقَصَ مِنَ الفَريضَةِ ؟ ثُمَّ يَكونُ سائِرُ أعمالهِ عَلى هذا » رواه الترمذي وقال حديث حسن .

1081. Hazrat Abu Hurairah (R.A.A.) relates that the Holy Prophet (S.A.W.) said: The first thing about which a person shall be questioned on the Day of Judgement will be prayer *(Salat)*. If his prayer *(Salat)* is found in order, he would be considered as successful, and would achieve his objective. If there would be some defect or deficiency in the same, he would be ruined and a loser. If some shortcomings are found in his obligations which are *Farz* and obligatory, Allah, the Master of Honour and Glory, will say: 'See if my servant has got some optional prayers in his account that may make up the shortcomings in respect of his Farz prayers. All his actions will then be examined in this way. *(Imam Tirmizi* has quoted this tradition and has called it as good.)

* * * * * * *

CHAPTER 194

VIRTUES OF THE FIRST ROW AND ORDER FOR COMPLETING THE FRONT ROWS AND STANDING CLOSELY

١٠٨٢ — عَنْ جابِرِ بْنِ سَمُرَةَ ، رَضِيَ اللهُ عَنْهُمَا ، قَالَ : خَرَجَ عَلَيْنَا رَسُولُ اللهِ ، صَلَّى اللهُ عليه وسَلَّمَ ، فَقَالَ : أَلا تَصُفُّونَ كما تَصُفُّ المَلائِكَةُ عِنْدَ رَبِّهَا ؟ » فَقُلْنَا : يَارَسُولَ اللهِ وكَيْفَ تَصُفُّ المَلائِكَةُ عِنْدَ رَبِّها ؟ قال : « يُتِمُّونَ الصُّفُوفَ الأُوَلَ ، وَيَتَرَاصُّونَ في الصَّفِّ » رواه مسلم

1082. Hazrat Jabir bin Samurah (R.A.A.) says: The Holy Prophet (S.A.W.) once came to us and said: Why do you not make your lines (in prayer) as do the angels before their Lord? We submitted: O Messenger of Allah how do the angels stand before their Lord. He (S.A.W.) answered: They complete the front rows first and stand close to each other. *(Muslim)*

١٠٨٣ — وعن أَبي هُرَيْرَةَ ، رَضِيَ اللهُ عنهُ ، أَنَّ رَسُولَ اللهِ ، صَلَّى اللهُ عَلَيْهِ وَسَلَّمَ ، قَالَ : « لوْ يَعلَمُ النَّاسُ مَا في النِّدَاءِ وَالصَّفِّ الأَوَّلِ ، ثُمَّ لَمْ يَجِدُوا إِلاَّ أَنْ يَسْتَهِمُوا عَلَيْهِ لاسْتَهَمُوا » متفقٌ عليه

1083. This Hadis has been included in item No. 1033 Chapter 206.

١٠٨٤ — وعَنْهُ قَالَ : قَالَ رَسُولُ اللهِ ، صَلَّى اللهُ عَلَيْهِ وَسَلَّمَ : « خيرُ صُفُوفِ الرِّجَالِ أَوَّلُها ، وَشرُّها آخرُها ، وَخيرُ صُفوفِ النِّسَاءِ آخرُها ، وَشرُّها أَوَّلُهَا » رواه مسلم

1084. Hazrat Abu Hurairah (R.A.A.) relates that the Holy Prophet (S.A.W.) said: The best rows of the males in prayer in (congregational prayer) are the first ones and the worst are the last ones, and the best rows among females in prayer are the last ones and the worst are the first ones." *(Muslim)*

١٠٨٥ – وعن أبي سَعيدٍ الخُدْرِيِّ ، رضيَ اللهُ عَنْهُ ، أنَّ رَسُولَ اللهِ صلَّى اللهُ عليهِ وسلَّمَ ، رَأى في أَصْحَابِهِ تأخُّراً ، فَقَالَ لَهُمْ : « تقَدَّمُوا فَأْتَمُّوا بي . ولْيَأْتَمَّ بِكُمْ مَنْ بعْدَكُم ، لايَزالُ قومٌ يتَأخَّرُونَ حتى يُؤخِّرَهُمُ اللهُ » رواه مسلم

1085. Hazrat Abu Sa'eed Khudri (R.A.A.) relates that the Holy Prophet (S.A.W.) noticing a tendency among his companions to stand in the back rows, said to them: Come forward and close to me and let those who came afterwards stand behind you. If a person starts lagging behind, Allah puts them behind. *(Muslim)*

١٠٨٦ – وعن أبي مسعودٍ ، رضيَ اللهُ عَنْهُ ، قال : كانَ رسولُ اللهِ ، صَلَّى اللهُ عَليهِ وسَلَّمَ ، يَمْسَحُ مَناكِبَنا في الصَّلاةِ ، ويَقُولُ : « اسْتَوُوا ولا تختلِفوا فتَخْتَلِفَ قُلُوبُكُمْ ، لِيَلِنِي مِنْكُمْ أولُوا الأَحْلامِ وَالنُّهَى ، ثمَّ الَّذينَ يَلُونَهم ، ثمَّ الَّذينَ يَلُونَهم » رواه مسلم .

1086. This Hadis has been covered in item No. 350 of Chapter 44.

١٠٨٧ – وعن أنسٍ ، رضيَ اللهُ عَنْهُ ، قالَ : قالَ رَسُولُ اللهِ ، صلَّى اللهُ عَلَيهِ وسَلَّم : « سَوُّوا صُفُوفَكُمْ ؛ فَإنَّ تَسْوِيَةَ الصَّفِّ مِنْ تَمامِ الصَّلاةِ » متفقٌ عليه .

وفي روايةِ البخاري : « فإنَّ تَسْوِيَةَ الصُّفُوفِ مِنْ إقَامَةِ الصَّلاةِ » .

1087. Hazrat Anas (R.A.A.) quoted by Hazrat Uqbah bin Amr relates that the Holy Prophet (S.A.W.) said: Keep your lines straight, for keeping them straight is the part of the proper observance of prayer. *(Bukhari and Muslim)*

Imam Bukhari's another report says: keeping the line straight is a part of establishing the prayer.

١٠٨٨ – وَعَنْهُ قال : أُقيمَتِ الصَّلاة ؛ فأقبلَ عَلينا رَسُولُ اللهِ ، صَلَّى اللهُ عَليهِ وَسَلَّم ، بِوَجْهِهِ فقَالَ : « أَقيمُوا صُفُوفَكُمْ وتَرَاصُّوا ، فإنِّي أرَاكُمْ مِنْ وَرَاءِ ظَهْرِي » رَوَاهُ البُخَاري بِلَفْظِهِ ، ومُسْلِمٌ بمَعْنَاهُ .

وفي رِوَايةٍ للبُخَاري : وكَانَ أحَدُنَا يُلْزِقُ مَنكِبَهُ بِمَنْكِبِ صَاحِبِهِ وقَدَمَهُ بِقَدَمِهِ » .

1088. Hazrat Anas (R.A.A.) says Once we lined up for prayer, and then the Holy Prophet (S.A.W.) turning towards us said. 'Correct your lines (straighten them) and stand close to each other for I see you from my back. *(Bukhari and Muslim)*

Imam Bukhari has reported this word for word and Imam Muslim has given its meaning.

Bukhari adds: We used to stand closely shoulder to shoulder and foot to foot after this.

١٠٨٩ – وعَنِ النُّعْمَانِ بنِ بشيرٍ ، رضي اللهُ عنهما ، قال : سمعتُ رسولَ الله ، صلَّى الله عليه وسلَّم ، يقولُ : « لَتُسَوُّنَّ صُفُوفَكُمْ ، أَوْ لَيُخَالِفَنَّ اللهُ بَيْنَ وجُوهِكُمْ » مُتَّفَقٌ عَلَيهِ

وفي روايةٍ لمسلِمٍ : أَنَّ رسولَ اللهِ ، صلَّى اللهُ عليهِ وسلَّم ، كانَ يُسَوِّي صُفُوفَنَا ، حتَّى كَأَنَّمَا يُسَوِّي بِهَا القِدَاحَ ، حتَّى رَأَى أَنَّا قد عَقَلْنَا عَنْهُ . ثُمَّ خَرَجَ يَوْماً فَقَامَ حتَّى كَادَ يُكَبِّرُ ، فرَأَى رَجُلاً بَادِياً صَدْرُهُ مِنَ الصَّفِّ ؛ فقالَ : « عِبَادَ اللهِ ، لَتُسَوُّنَّ صُفُوفَكُمْ ، أَوْ لَيُخَالِفَنَّ اللهُ بَيْنَ وجُوهِكُمْ » .

1089. This Hadis is the same as No. 160 of Chapter 16.

١٠٩٠ – وعَنِ البَرَاءِ بنِ عازِبٍ ، رضيَ اللهُ عنهما ، قالَ : كانَ رسولُ اللهِ ، صلَّى اللهُ عليهِ وسلَّم ، يتَخَلَّلُ الصَّفَّ مِنْ نَاحِيَةٍ إلى نَاحِيَةٍ يَمسَحُ صُدُورَنَا ، ومَنَاكِبَنَا ، ويقولُ : « لا تَختَلِفُوا فتَختَلِفَ قُلُوبُكُمْ » وكانَ يَقولُ : « إنَّ اللهَ ومَلائِكَتَهُ يُصَلُّونَ عَلَى الصُّفُوفِ الأُوَلِ »

رواه أبو داود بإسنادٍ حَسَنٍ .

1090. Hazrat Bra'a ibn 'Aazib (R.A.A.) relates: The Holy Prophet (S.A.W.) used to pass between the lines (in congregation) from one end to the other adjusting our chests and shoulders straightening them in line saying 'Do'nt be out of line, otherwise your hearts will be diversed': and would further remark: 'Allah, and His angels send down blessings on the first lines.' *(Imam Abu Daud has cited this tradition with good chain).*

١٠٩١ – وعَنِ ابنِ عُمَرَ ، رضيَ اللهُ عنهما ، أنَّ رسولَ اللهِ ، صلَّى اللهُ عليهِ وسلَّم ، قالَ : « أقيمُوا الصُّفُوفَ ، وحَاذُوا بَيْنَ المَنَاكِبِ ، وسُدُّوا

الخلَلَ : وَلِينوا بِأَيْدي إخْوَانِكُمْ ، وَلا تَذَرُوا فُرُجَاتٍ للشيْطانِ ، ومَنْ وصَلَ صَفاً وَصَلَهُ اللهُ ، وَمَنْ قَطَعَ صَفاً قَطَعَهُ اللهُ »

رواه أبو داود بإسنادٍ صحيحٍ .

1091. **Hazrat Ibn Umar** (R.A.A.) says that the Holy Prophet (S.A.W.) said: Arrange your lines, and adjust your shoulders filling the gaps between your ranks, be lenient on the arms of your brethren, and do not leave gaps (between you and your colleague) for the Satan. One who joins in a row closer Allah will join him close, and he who disturbs a row Allah will cut him off. *(Abu Daud)*

١٠٩٢- وعَنْ أنسٍ ، رضيَ اللهُ عَنْهُ ، أنَّ رَسولَ اللهِ ، صلَّى اللهُ عليهِ وسلَّم ، قالَ : « رُصُّوا صُفُوفَكُمْ ، وَقَارِبُوا بَيْنَها ، وَحَاذُوابِالأعْناقِ فوَالَّذِي نَفْسِي بيَدِهِ إنِّي لأرَى الشَّيْطَانَ يَدْخُلُ منْ خلَلِ الصَّفِّ ، كأنَّها الحَذَفُ » حديث صحيح رواه أبو داود بإسنادٍ على شرط مسلم .

1092. **Hazrat Anas** (R.A.A.) relates that the Holy Prophet (S.A.W.) directed: Close your ranks, be nearer to each other, and put your necks in line, I swear by Allah in whose possession lies my life, I see the Satan intruding through the gaps in the rows like the kid of a goat. *(Abu Daud has quoted this on the condition of Imam Muslim.)*

١٠٩٣ — وعنهُ ، أنَّ رسولَ اللهِ ، صلَّى اللهُ عليهِ وسلَّم ، قال « أتِمُّوا الصَّفَّ المقدَّمَ ، ثُمَّ الَّذي يَليهِ ؛ فمَا كَانَ مِنْ نَقْصٍ فَلْيَكُنْ في الصَّفِّ المُؤَخَّرِ » رواه ابو داود بإسنادٍ حسن .

1093. **Hazrat Anas** (R.A.A.) relates that the Holy Prophet (S.A.W.) directed: Complete the first row first, then the second nearer to it. If there be any shortage, it should be in the last row. *(Abu Daud quoted this with good chain).*

١٠٩٤ — وعن عائشةَ ، رضيَ اللهُ عنها ، قالتْ : قالَ رسولُ اللهِ ، صلَّى اللهُ عليهِ وسلَّم : « إنَّ اللهَ وَمَلائِكَتَهُ يُصَلُّونَ عَلى مَيَامِنِ الصفوفِ » رواه أبو داود بإسنادٍ عَلى شَرْطِ مُسْلِمٍ ، وفيه رجلٌ مُخْتَلَفٌ في تَوْثيقِهِ .

1094. Hazrat Ayesha (R.A.A.) says that the Holy Prophet (S.A.W.) said: Allah, and His angels send down blessings on the right wing of the rows. *(Imam Abu Daud has cited this on the terms of Imam Muslim)*

١٠٩٥ – وعَنِ البَرَاءِ ، رضيَ اللهُ عَنْهُ ، قالَ : « كُنَّا إذا صَلَّيْنَا خَلْفَ رسولِ اللهِ ، صلَّى اللهُ عليه وسلَّم ، أحْبَبْنا أنْ نَكُونَ عَنْ يَمِينِه ؛ يُقْبِلُ عَلَيْنا بِوَجْهِهِ ، فَسَمِعْتُهُ يقول : « رَبِّ قِنِي عَذَابَكَ يَوْمَ تَبْعَثُ – أوْ تَجْمَعُ – عِبَادَكَ » رواه مسلم .

1095. Hazrat Bra'a bin 'Aazib (R.A.A.) relates: When we used to pray under the leadership of the Holy Prophet (S.A.W.) we preferred to stand on his right so that at the end of the prayer, when he would be seated, he may face us. Once I heard him pray:

Rabbe qini 'azabaka yauma tab'aso au tajmao ibadaka

'O My Lord . protect me from Thy chastisement on the day on which Thou wilt raise Thy servants', or he said: When Thou wilt gather Thy servants. *(Muslim)*

١٠٩٦ – وعَنْ أبي هُرَيْرَةَ ، رَضِيَ اللهُ عَنْهُ ، قالَ : قالَ رسولُ اللهِ ، صلَّى اللهُ عليه وسلَّمَ : « وَسِّطُوا الإمَامَ ، وَسُدُّوا الخَلَلَ » رواه أبو داود .

1096. Hazrat Abu Hurairah (R.A.A.) says that the Holy Prophet (S.A.W.) said: Let the Imam stand in the middle and close the gaps in the rows. *(Abu Daud)*

Note.-- Both the actions and statements of the Holy Prophet (S.A.W.) amply prove the necessity and importance of straightening and levelling the lines of worshippers in the mosque, as will be evident from the above and other scores of traditions on this subject.

* * * * * * *

CHAPTER 195

١٠٩٧ – عَنْ أمِّ المؤمِنِينَ أمِّ حَبِيبَةَ رَمْلَةَ بِنتِ أبي سُفيانَ ، رضيَ اللهُ عنهما ، قَالَتْ : سَمِعْتُ رسولَ اللهِ ، صلَّى اللهُ عليهِ وسلَّمَ ، يقولُ : مَا مِنْ عَبْدٍ مُسْلِمٍ يُصَلِّي لِلهِ تَعَالى كُلَّ يَوْمٍ ثِنْتَيْ عَشْرَةَ رَكْعَةً تَطَوعاً غَيْرَ الفَرِيضَةِ ، إلاَّ بَنَى اللهُ لَهُ بَيْتاً في الجَنَّةِ ! أوْ : إلاَّ بُنِيَ لَهُ بَيْتٌ في

الجَنَّةِ » رواه مسلم

1097. The mother of the faithfuls Hazrat Umm Habibah Ramilah bint Abu Sufyan (R.A.A.) relates that she heard the Holy Prophet (S.A.W.) say: Allah the Most High prepares or has prepared a house in Paradise for every Muslim who offers twelve extra raka'ts of optional prayers over and obove the Farz (compulsory) prayers every day simply for the sake of Allah. *(Muslim)*

Note : These extra 12 rakats of optional prayers, according to Imam Nisai and Tirmizi are — 2 rakats before the Farz prayer of early morning (Fajr) 4 Rakats before and 2 Rakats after the Farz of Mid-day (Zuhr) 2 rakats after Farz of early evening (Maghrib) 2 rakats after four Farz of night (Isha) prayers.

١٠٩٨ — وعَنِ ابنِ عُمَرَ رَضِيَ اللهُ عَنْهُما ، قالَ : صَلَّيْتُ مَعَ رَسُولِ اللهِ ، صلَّى اللهُ عليهِ وسَلَّم ، رَكْعَتَيْنِ قَبْلَ الظُّهْرِ ، ورَكْعَتَيْنِ بَعْدَهَا ، ورَكْعَتَيْنِ بَعْدَ الجُمْعَةِ ، ورَكْعَتَيْنِ بَعْدَ المَغرِبِ ، ورَكْعَتَيْنِ بعْدَ العِشَاءِ . متفقٌ عليه .

1098. **Hazrat Ibn Umar** (R.A.A.) relates : I have offered along with the Holy Prophet (S.A.W.) two rakats of voluntary prayer before the noon prayer and two rakats after it; and two rakats after Friday prayer, and two after the sunset (Maghrib) prayer and two after the night (Isha) prayer. *(Bukhari and Muslim)*

Note : This offering of 2 *rakats* instead of 4 of optional prayers before midday prayers does not rule out the offering of 4 before Midday prayers. There is overwhelming evidence in support of offering 4 *rakats* after *Zohr* prayer .

١٠٩٩ — وعنْ عبدِ اللهِ بنِ مُغَفَّلٍ ، رَضِيَ اللهُ عنهُ ، قالَ : قالَ رسولُ اللهِ ، صلَّى اللهُ عليهِ وسلَّم : « بيْنَ كلِّ أذَانَيْنِ صَلاةٌ ، بيْنَ كلِّ أذَانَيْنِ صَلاةٌ ، بَيْنَ كلِّ أذَانَيْنِ صَلاةٌ » قالَ في الثَّالثَةِ : « لمَنْ شاءَ » متفقٌ عليهِ

المُرَادُ بالأَذَانَيْنِ : الأَذَانُ وَالإقَامَةُ .

1099. **Hazrat Abdullah bin Mughaffal** (R.A.A.) says that the **Holy** Prophet (S.A.W.) said: Between every two Azans there is a prayer **for** one who desire. *(Bukahri and Muslim)*

Note : Between two Azans means between Azan and Iqamat.

CHAPTER 196

IMPORTANCE OF OFFERING TWO RAKA'ATS (SUNNAT) BEFORE DAWN PRAYER

١١٠٠ – عن عائشةَ ، رَضِيَ اللهُ عَنْهَا ، أنَّ النَّبيَّ ، صلَّى اللهُ عليهِ وسلَّم ، كانَ لايَدَعُ أربَعاً قبلَ الظُّهْرِ ، ورَكعَتَيْنِ قبلَ الغدَاةِ .
رواه البخاري

1100. Hazrat Ayesha (R.A.A.) relates that the Holy Prophet (S.A.W.) never omitted four raka'ats before midday prayer and two raka'ats before the dawn prayer. *(Bukhari)*

١١٠١ – وعَنْها قالَتْ : لمْ يكنِ النَّبيُّ ، صلَّى اللهُ عليهِ وسلَّم ، عَلَى شيءٍ مِنَ النوافِلِ أشَدَّ تعَاهُداً مِنْه عَلى رَكْعَتَي الفَجْرِ . مُتَّفَقٌ عَلَيهِ

1101. Hazrat Ayesha (R.A.A.) says that the Holy Prophet (S.A.W.) did not attach much importance to any optional prayer than the two raka'ats before dawn prayer. *(Muslim)*

١١٠٢ – وعَنْها عَنِ النبيِّ ، صلَّى اللهُ عليهِ وسلَّمَ . قالَ : « رَكْعَتا الفجْرِ خيْرٌ مِنَ الدُّنيا ومَا فيها » رواه مسلم

وفي روايةٍ : « لَهُمَا أحبُّ إليَّ مِنَ الدُّنْيا جَميعاً »

1102. Hazrat Ayesha (R.A.A.) relates that the Holy Prophet (S.A.W.). said: The two raka'ats before dawn prayer are better than the world and all that it contains. *(Muslim)*

Another version of *Muslim* says : These two raka'ats are dearer to me than the whole world.

١١٠٣ – وعَنْ أبي عبدِ اللهِ بِلالِ بنِ رَبَاحٍ ، رضيَ اللهُ عَنْهُ ، مُؤَذِّنِ رسولِ اللهِ ، صلَّى اللهُ عليهِ وسلَّم . أنَّهُ أتَى رَسُولَ اللهِ ، صلَّى اللهُ عليهِ وسلَّم ، ليُؤذِنه بِصَلاةِ الغدَاةِ ، فَشَغَلَتْ عَائشَةُ بِلالاً بِأمْرٍ سَألَتْهُ عَنْهُ ، حتَى أصبحَ جِداً ، فَقَامَ بِلالٌ فَآذَنَهُ بِالصَّلاةِ ، وتَابَعَ أذَانَهُ ، فلَمْ يَخرُج رَسُولُ اللهِ ، صَلَّى اللهُ عليهِ وسلَّم ، فلما خرَج صَلَّى بِالنَّاسِ ، فَأخبَرَهُ أنَّ عَائشَةَ شَغَلَتْهُ بِأمْرٍ سَألَتهُ عَنْهُ حتى أصبحَ جِداً ، وأنَّهُ

أبطَأَ عَلَيه بِالخُروجِ ، فَقَالَ - يَعْني النَّبيَّ ، صلَّى اللهُ عليه وسلَّم - : « إني كُنْتُ رَكَعتُ رَكْعَتَي الفَجرِ » فقال : يا رسولَ الله إنكَ أَصْبَحْتَ جِداً ! قَالَ : « لوْ أصبَحتُ أكثَرَ مما أصبَحتُ ، لرَكعتُهُما ، وَأَحْسَنْتُهُمَا . وَأَجمَلْتُهُمَا » رواه أبو داود بإسناد حسن

1103. Hazrat Abu Abdullah Bilal bin Ribah, the Muezzin of the Holy Prophet (S.A.W.) says that once he went to inform him of the advent of the time of Fajr prayer but Hazrat Ayesha (R.A.A.) replying to a question from him, diverted his attention and kept him busy. When light started to become visible, Hazrat Bilal rose and informed the Holy Prophet (S.A.W.) that the congregation was ready, and then reminded him (S.A.W.). But the Holy Prophet (S.A.W.) did not come out. However when he came out he led the prayer. Then Hazrat Bilal (R.A,A.) told him that how he was diverted in connection with his query to Hazrat Ayesha (R.A.A.) which delayed him in informing the Holy Prophet (S.A.W.) of the time of prayer till it began to be light, and the Holy Prophet (S.A.W.) took some time in coming out. The Holy Prophet (S.A.W.) said, I was offering two raka'ats of Sunnah. Hazrat Bilal (R.A.A.) said: 'Messenger of Allah, you took so much time that the light appeared.' Holy Prophet (S.A.W.) replied: 'even if the light had appeared more than this I would have certainly offered two rakats well and adequately.' (Abu Daud has cited this with good chain)

* * * * * * *

CHAPTER 197

LIGHT READING OF SUNNAH PRAYERS AT DAWN AND ITS TIME AND WHAT TO BE RECITED

١١٠٤ - عَنْ عائشةَ رَضِيَ اللهُ عَنْها أنَّ النَّبيَّ ، صلَّى اللهُ عليه وَسلَّم ، كانَ يُصَلي رَكْعَتَيْنِ خَفِيفتَيْنِ بَيْنَ النِّداءِ وَالإقامَةِ مِن صَلاةِ الصُّبْحِ . مُتَّفَقٌ عَليه

وفي روايةٍ لهمَا : يُصَلِّي رَكعتَي الفَجرِ ،إذَا سَمِعَ الأذَانَ فَيُخَفِّفُهمَا حتى أقولَ : هَل قرَأَ فيهما بِأُمِّ القُرْآنِ !

وفي روايةٍ لمُسْلِمٍ : كانَ يُصَلِّي رَكعتَي الفَجرِ إذا سَمِعَ الأَذَانَ وَيُخَفِّفُهمَا . وفي روايةٍ : إذا طَلَعَ الفَجْرُ .

1104. **Hazrat Ayesha** (R.A.A.) says that the Holy Prophet (S.A.W.) used to offer two brief rakats between the Azan and Iqamah of the Fajr (dawn) prayer. *(Bukhari and Muslim)*

Another version of these two traditionists says "He offered the two raka'ats of (Sunnah) so much shortening them that I thought whether he had recited the opening Surah *Fateha* or not.

Muslim's another version says: He (S.A.W.) would offer the two raka'ats when he heard the *Azan* and made them brief.

Still another version says the words are that when the light of the dawn was visible.

١١٠٥ — وعَنْ حَفصَةَ رَضِيَ اللهُ عَنْها أنَّ رسولَ اللهِ ، صَلَّى اللهُ عليه وسلَّم ، كانَ إذا أذَّنَ المُؤَذِّنُ للصُّبحِ ، وَبَدَا الصُّبحُ ، صَلَّى رَكعتَيْنِ خَفيفَتَيْنِ . متفقٌ عليه

وفي روايةٍ لمسلمٍ : كانَ رسولُ اللهِ ، صَلَّى اللهُ عليهِ وسلَّم ، إذا طَلَعَ صلى الفَجرَ لايُصَلّي إلاَّ رَكعتَيْنِ خَفيفتَيْنِ .

1105. **Hazrat Hafsah** (R.A.A.) reports that the Holy Prophet (S.A.W.) used to offer two brief rakats after the Muazzin had called Azan for the Fajr prayer, and it started to dawn. *(Bukhari and Muslim)*

Muslim's version is . After it used to become light the Holy Prophet (S.A.W.) did not offer anything but two brief raka'ats of sunnah.

١١٠٦ — وعَنِ ابنِ عُمَرَ رَضِيَ اللهُ عَنهُما قالَ : كانَ رسولُ اللهِ ، صلَّى اللهُ عليهِ وسلَّم ، يُصَلّي مِنَ اللَّيْلِ مَثنَى مَثنَى ، وَيُوتِرُ بِرَكعةٍ مِن آخِرِ اللَّيْلِ ، ويُصَلّي الرَّكعتَيْنِ قَبْلَ صَلاةِ الغَدَاةِ ، وكأنَّ الأذانَ بِأُذُنَيْهِ . متفقٌ عليه .

1106. **Hazrat Ibn Umar** (R.A.A.) relates that the Holy Prophet (S.A.W.) used to offer his midnight voluntary prayer two raka'ats and at the end would turn these raka'ats into odd number by adding one *rakat of witr.* Then he would offer two raka'ats before Fajr (dawn) prayer so brief that as if he could hear the Iqamah being called. *(Bukhari and Muslim)*

١١٠٧ — وعَنِ ابنِ عباسٍ رَضِيَ اللهُ عَنهما أنَّ رَسُولَ اللهِ ، صَلَّى اللهُ عليهِ وَسَلَّم ، كانَ يَقرَأُ في رَكعَتَي الفَجرِ في الأُولى مِنهُمَا : (قُولُوا آمَنَّا بِاللهِ وَمَا أُنزِلَ إلَيْنَا) الآيةُ التي في البقرة ، وفي الآخرةِ منهما : (آمَنَّا

بِاللهِ وَاشْهَدْ بِأَنَّا مُسْلِمُونَ) .

وفي روايةٍ : في الآخرةِ التي في آلِ عِمرانَ : (تَعَالَوْا إلى كَلِمَةٍ سَوَاءٍ بَيْنَنَا وَبَيْنَكُمْ) رواهما مسلم .

1107. Hazrat Ibn Abbas (R.A.A.) says that occasionally in his two raka'ats before Fajr prayer, the Holy Prophet (S.A.W.) recited the verse :

'Say (O' Muslims). We believe in Allah and that which is revealed unto us. (2 : 136) in the first *raka'at* and the verse

We believe in Allah, and bear thou witness that we have surrendered (3 : 52) in the second *raka'at*.

According to another version the Holy Prophet (S.A.W.) in the second raka'at read the verse :

Come to an agreement between us and you. (3 : 64) *(Muslim)*

١١٠٨ – وَعَنْ أَبي هُرَيرةَ رَضِيَ اللهُ عَنْهُ أَنَّ رسولَ اللهِ ، صَلَّى اللهُ عليهِ وسلَّم ، قَرَأَ في رَكْعَتَي الْفَجْرِ : (قُلْ يَا أَيُّهَا الْكَافِرُونَ) و (قُلْ هُوَ اللهُ أَحَدٌ) رواه مسلم .

1108. Hazrat Abu Hurairah (R.A.A.) relates that the Holy Prophet (S.A.W.) recited Surah *Al-Kafirun* (Chap. 109) in the first raka'at and Sura *Al-Ikhlas* (Chap. 112) in the second before Fajr (dawn) prayer. *(Muslim)*

١١٠٩ – وَعَنِ ابنِ عمرَ ، رَضِيَ اللهُ عنهُما ، قالَ : رَمَقْتُ النَّبيَّ ، صلَّى اللهُ عليهِ وسلَّم ، شَهْراً وكان يَقْرَأُ في الرَّكْعَتَيْنِ قَبْلَ الْفَجْرِ : (قُلْ يَا أَيُّهَا الْكَافِرُونَ) ، و : (قل هُوَ اللهُ أَحَدٌ) . رَوَاهُ الترمذي وقالَ : حديثٌ حَسَنٌ .

1109. Hazrat Ibn 'Umar (R.A.A.) says: I observed the Holy Prophet (S.A.W.) for a month reading Surahs *Al-Kafirun* (Chap. 109) and *Al-Ikhlas* (Chap. 112) in two raka'ats before Fajr prayer.

(Tirmizi)

* * * * * * *

CHAPTER 198

VIRTUES OF LYING ON THE RIGHT SIDE AFTER OFFERING TWO RAKA'TS OF SUNNAT PRAYERS AND INDUCEMENT FOR THE SAME WHETHER TAHAJJUD PRAYERS WERE OFFERED DURING NIGHT OR NOT

١١١٠ — عَنْ عائشَةَ ، رَضِيَ اللهُ عَنْهَا قَالَتْ : كانَ النَّبيُّ ، صلَّى اللهُ عليهِ وسلَّم ، إذا صلَّى رَكْعَتَي الْفَجْرِ ، اضْطَجَعَ عَلَى شِقِّهِ الأَيْمَنِ . رواه البخاري

1110. Hazrat Ayesha (R.A.A.) relates that after offering his two sunnat optional raka'as of morning prayers, the Holy Prophet (S.A.W.) used to lie down on his right side. *(Bukhari)*

١١١١ — وَعَنْهَا قَالَتْ : كَانَ النبيُّ ، صلَّى اللهُ عليهِ وسلَّم ، يُصَلِّي فيمَا بَيْنَ أَنْ يَفْرُغَ مِنْ صَلاةِ الْعِشَاءِ إلى الْفَجْرِ إحْدَى عَشْرَةَ رَكْعَةً ، يُسَلِّمُ بَيْنَ كُلِّ رَكْعَتَيْنِ ، وَيُوتِرُ بِوَاحِدَةٍ ، فَإذا سَكَتَ المُؤَذِّنُ مِن صَلاةِ الْفَجْرِ ، وَتَبَيَّنَ لَهُ الْفَجْرُ ، وَجَاءَهُ المُؤَذِّنُ ، قَامَ فَرَكَعَ رَكْعَتَيْنِ خَفِيفَتَيْنِ ، ثُمَّ اضْطَجَعَ عَلَى شِقِّهِ الأَيْمَنِ ، هكذا حَتَّى يَأْتِيَهُ المُؤَذِّنُ لِلإقَامَةِ . رَوَاه مُسْلِمٌ .

قَوْلُهَا : « يُسَلِّمُ بَيْنَ كُلِّ رَكْعَتَيْنِ » هكذا هو في مسلمٍ ومعناه: بَعْدَ كُلِّ رَكْعَتَيْنِ .

1111. Hazrat Ayesha (R.A.A.) says that between the night (Isha) and dawn prayers Holy Prophet (S.A.W.) used to offer eleven raka'ats i.e. Tahajjud prayer and after every two raka'ats he (S.A.W.) would turn his face right and left reciting salam: and with one more raka'at he used to convert all these raka'ats into *witr* (odd number), and when the Muazzin had finished the call for Fajr (prayer) and it became brighter, he would come to apprise the Holy Prophet (S.A.W.) of the time of prayer, he (S.A.W.) would then get up and offer two brief raka'ats, and then lie down on his right side till the Muazzin would again come to inform him (S.A.W.) that the congregation was ready, and then the Holy Prophet (S.A.W.) would proceed to lead the prayer. *(Muslim)*

١١١٢ـ وَعَنْ أبي هُرَيرةَ ، رضيَ اللهُ عنهُ ، قالَ : قالَ رسولُ اللهِ ، صَلَّى اللهُ عَلَيْهِ وسلَّمَ : « إذا صَلَّى أحَدُكُمْ رَكْعَتَي الفَجْرِ، فَلْيَضْطَجِعْ عَلَى يَمِينِهِ » .

رَوَاه أبو داود ، والترمذي بأسانيدَ صحيحةٍ . قالَ الترمذي : حديثٌ حَسَنٌ صَحِيحٌ

1112. Hazrat Abu Hurairah (R.A.A.) relates that the Holy Prophet (S.A.W.) said: When anyone of you has offered two raka'ats (of sunnat) prayer of the Fajr, then he should lie down on his right side. *(Abu Daud and Tirmizi* have cited this with sound chain of narrators).

* * * * * * *

CHAPTER 199

THE SUNNAHS OF THE ZUHR (NOON) PRAYER

١١١٣ ـ عَنِ ابنِ عُمَرَ ، رَضِيَ اللهُ عَنْهُمَا ، قالَ : صلَّيْتُ مَعَ رسولِ اللهِ ، صلَّى اللهُ عليهِ وسلَّم ، رَكْعَتَيْنِ قَبْلَ الظُّهْرِ ، وَرَكْعَتَيْنِ بَعْدَهَا متفقٌ عليه .

1113. Hazrat Ibn 'Umar (R.A.A.) says. I offered two raka'ats of sunnat prayer before Zuhr (noon) prayer and two after it, along with the Holy Prophet (S.A.W.). *(Bukhari and Muslim)*

١١١٤ ـ وَعَنْ عائِشَةَ ، رَضِيَ اللهُ عَنْهَا ، أنَّ النَّبِيَّ ، صلَّى اللهُ عَليهِ وسلَّم ، كانَ لا يدَعُ أرْبَعاً قَبْلَ الظُّهْرِ ، رَوَاه البخاريُّ

1114. Hazrat Ayesha (R.A.A.) relates that the Holy Prophet (S.A.W.) never missed four (sunnah) raka'ats before Zuhr (noon) prayers. *(Bukhari)*

Note : This and earlier traditions prove that the four raka'ats before and two *raka'ats* after the *Zuhr* prayers are sunnat *Mu'akkada* i.e. much pressed.

١١١٥ ـ وَعَنْهَا قَالَتْ : كانَ النبيُّ ، صلَّى اللهُ عَليهِ وسلَّم ، يُصَلِّي في بَيْتي قَبْلَ الظُّهْرِ أرْبَعاً ، ثُمَّ يَخْرُجُ ، فَيُصَلِّي بِالنَّاسِ ، ثُمَّ يَدْخُلُ فَيُصَلِّي رَكْعَتَيْنِ ، وَكانَ يُصَلِّي بِالنَّاسِ المَغْرِبَ ، ثُمَّ يَدْخُلُ

فَيُصَلِّي رَكْعَتَيْنِ ، وَيُصَلِّي بِالنَّاسِ العِشَاءَ، وَيَدْخُلُ بَيْتِي ، فَيُصَلِّي رَكْعَتَيْنِ . رواه مسلم .

1115. Hazrat Ayesha (R.A.A,) says: When Holy Prophet (S.A.W.) used to be in my house, he would offer four sunnat raka'ats before Zuhr, then go and lead the congregation, and thereafter return home and offer two sunnat raka'ats. Similarly, he (S.A.W.) would lead Maghrib prayer in the congregation and come back and offer two sunnat raka'ats. Likewise after having led the Isha prayer, he (S.A.W.) would come back to my apartment and offer two *sunnat raka'ats*''. *(Muslim)*

١١١٦ ـ وعن أمِّ حَبيبَةَ ، رَضِيَ اللهُ عَنْهَا قَالَتْ : قالَ رسولُ اللهِ ، صلَّى الله عليهِ وسلَّم : « مَنْ حَافَظَ عَلى أَرْبَعِ رَكَعَاتٍ قَبْلَ الظُّهْرِ ، وَأَرْبَعٍ بَعْدَهَا ، حَرَّمَهُ اللهُ عَلَى النَّارِ » .

رواه أبو داود ، والترمذي وقال : حديثٌ حسنٌ صحيحٌ .

1116. Hazrat Umm Habiba (R.A.A.) says that Holy Prophet (S.A.W.) said: One who adheres to four sunnat raka'ats before Zuhr and four *sunnat raka'ats* after it, Allah has forbidden fire of Hell for him.
(Abu Daud and Tirmizi have reported this and Imam Tirmizi had called it good.)

Note : In this tradition there is an inducement for four sunnat raka'ats before and four sunnat raka'ats after Zuhr prayer. Of total eight such raka'ats, six are sunnat Muakkada, as is evident from other traditions; the remaining two are considered as Nafil. (voluntary).

١١١٧ – وَعَنْ عبدِ اللهِ بنِ السائبِ ، رَضِيَ اللهُ عَنْهُ ، أَنَّ رسولَ اللهِ ، صلَّى اللهُ عليهِ وسلَّمَ ، كانَ يُصَلِّي أَرْبعاً بعْدَ أن تَزولَ الشَّمسُ قَبْلَ الظُّهْرِ ، وقالَ : « إنَّهَا ساعَةٌ تُفْتَحُ فيهَا أبوابُ السَّمَاءِ ، فأُحِبُّ أن يَصعَدَ لي فيها عَمَلٌ صَالِحٌ » رواه الترمذي وَقَالَ : حديثٌ حسنٌ .

1117 Hazrat Abdullah bin Sa'ib relates that the Holy Prophet (S.A.W.) used to offer four (sunnat) raka'ats after the sun had declined and before the Zuhr noon prayer, and said: This is the time when doors of the heaven are thrown open and as such I like some good deeds on my part may rise to heaven during this hour. *(Imam Tirmizi has cited this and said that it is good).*

١١١٨ – وعَنْ عائِشَةَ ، رَضِيَ اللهُ عَنْهَا ، أَنَّ النَّبِيَّ ، صلَّى اللهُ عليهِ وسلَّم ، كانَ إذا لَمْ يُصَلِّ أَرْبعاً قبْلَ الظهْرِ ، صَلَّاهُنَّ بعْدَها .

رَوَاهُ الترمذي وقَالَ : حديثٌ حَسَنٌ .

1118. **Hazrat Ayesha** (R.A.A.) says that when the Holy Prophet (S.A.W.) could not offer four sunnat raka'ats before the Zuhr prayer then he (S.A.W.) would offer them after Zuhr. *(Tirmizi has cited this and called it as good).*

* * * * * * *

CHAPTER 200

THE SUNNAHS OF 'ASR (Afternoon) PRAYER

١١١٩ – عَنْ عليٍّ بنِ أَبي طَالبٍ ، رضيَ اللهُ عَنْهُ ، قالَ : كانَ النبي ، صلَّى اللهُ عَليهِ وسلَّم ، يُصَلِّي قَبْلَ العَصْرِ أَرْبعَ ركعَاتٍ ، يَفْصِلُ بَيْنَهُنَّ بالتَّسْليمِ عَلى المَلائِكَةِ المقرَّبينَ ، وَمَنْ تَبِعَهُمْ مِنَ المسْلِمينَ وَالمؤْمِنينَ .

رواه الترمذي وقَالَ : حديثٌ حَسَنٌ .

1119. **Hazrat Ali bin Abu Talib** (R.A.A.) relates that the Holy Prophet (S.A.W.) occasionally offered four sunnat raka'ats before Asr prayer; he (S.A.W.) would bifurcate them with the usual salutation on right and left to the angels closer to him (S.A.W.) and those who are immediately after or under them, the believers and the Muslims. *(Tirmizi has cited this and called it as good).*

١١٢٠ – وَعنِ ابنِ عُمَرَ ، رَضِيَ اللهُ عَنْهُمَا ، عَنِ النَّبِيِّ ، صلَّى اللهُ عليهِ وسلَّم ، قالَ : « رَحِمَ اللهُ امْرَأً صلَّى قبْلَ العَصْرِ أَرْبعاً »

رَوَاهُ أبو داود ، والترمذي وقالَ : حديثٌ حَسَنٌ .

1120. **Hazrat Ibn-i-Umar** (R.A.A.) says that the Holy Prophet (S.A.W.) said: May Allah have mercy on the person who offers four raka'ats before 'Asr prayer'. *(Abu Daud and Tirmizi have cited this tradition and have called it as good.*

١١٢١ – وعنْ عليٍّ بنِ أَبي طالبٍ ، رَضِيَ اللهُ عنهُ ، أَنَّ النبيَّ صلَّى اللهُ عليهِ وسلَّم ، كانَ يُصلِّي قبْلَ العَصرِ ركْعَتَيْنِ .

رَوَاهُ أبو داود بإسنادٍ صحيحٍ .

1121. Hazrat Ali bin Abu Talib (R.A.A.) relates that the Holy Prophet (S.A.W.) occasionally offered two raka'ats before Asr prayer. *(Imam Abu Daud has cited this with sound chain)*

Note : This tradition established the virtues of four or two *sunnat raka'ats* before Asr prayer.

* * * * * * *

CHAPTER 201

THE SUNNAHS BEFORE AND AFTER MAGHRIB (SUNSET) PRAYER

١١٢٢ — وَعَنْ عَبْدِ اللهِ بنِ مُغَفَّلٍ ، رَضِيَ اللهُ عنه ، عَنِ النَّبِيِّ ، صلّى اللهُ عَليهِ وسلّم ، قالَ : « صَلُّوا قَبلَ المَغربِ » قالَ في الثَّالثَة : « لِمَنْ شاءَ »
رواه البخاري

1122. Hazrat Abdullah bin Mughaffal (R.A.A.) relates that the Holy Prophet (S.A.W.) asked us: Offer two (sunnat) raka'ats before Maghrib (sunset) prayer and he repeated this direction twice. On the third time he added: One who likes may do so (so that people may not take this direction as muakkadah (essential). *(Bukhari)*

١١٢٣ — وعن أنسٍ ، رَضِيَ اللهُ عَنْه ، قالَ : لَقَدْ رَأَيتُ كِبارَ أصحابِ رسولِ اللهِ ، صلّى اللهُ عليهِ وَسلّم ، يَبْتَدِرُونَ السَّوَارِيَ عندَ المغربِ .
رواه البخاري

1123. Hazrat Anas bin Malik (R.A.A.) relates: I noticed leading companions of Holy Prophet (S.A.W.) hastening towards the pillars of the mosque at the time of *Maghrib* (to offer *sunnats*). *(Bukhari)*

١١٢٤ — وعَنْهُ قَالَ : كُنَّا نُصَلّي عَلى عَهدِ رسولِ اللهِ ، صلّى اللهُ عَليهِ وسلّم ، رَكعَتَيْنِ بعدَ غُروبِ الشَّمس قَبلَ المَغرِبِ ، فقيلَ : أكَانَ رسولُ اللهِ ، صَلّى اللهُ عليهِ وسلّم ، صلاَّهُمَا ؟ قال : كانَ يَرانا نُصَلّيهِما فلَمْ يَأمُرْنَا وَلَم يَنْهَنا . رَوَاه مُسْلِم

1124. Hazrat Anas bin Malik reports. During the days of the Holy Prophet (S.A.W.) we used to offer two (sunnat) raka'ats after sunset but before Maghrib. He was asked. Did Holy Prophet (S.A.W.) too offer these (sunnat) raka'ats. He (Hazrat Anas R.A.A.)

replied: He used to see us offer them; but he neither asked us to offer nor forbade us. *(Muslim)*

١١٢٥ ـ وعنه قَالَ : كُنَّا بِالمَدِينَةِ فإذا أَذَّنَ المُؤَذِّنُ لِصَلاةِ المَغرِبِ، ابْتَدَرُوا السَّوَارِيَ، فَرَكَعُوا رَكعَتَيْنِ ، حَتى إنَّ الرَّجُلَ الغَرِيبَ لَيَدخُلُ المَسجِدَ فَيَحْسَبُ أَنَّ الصَّلاةَ قَدْ صُلِّيَتْ من كَثْرَةِ مَنْ يُصَلِّيهِمَا . رَوَاه مُسْلِمٌ

1125. **Hazrat Anas bin Malik** (R.A.A.) relates: while we were in Madina and Muazzin called the Azan for maghrib prayer, we used to hasten towards the pillars in the mosque and offered two raka'ats. At times it so happened that travellers (late comers) noticing so many of us offering prayers separately would sometimes think that the congregational prayer was already over. *(Muslim)*

* * * * * * *

CHAPTER 202

SUNNAH (RAKA 'ATS) BEFORE AND AFTER ISHA (NIGHT) PRAYER

فيهِ حديثُ ابنِ عُمَرَ السَّابِقُ : صَلَّيْتُ مَعَ النَّبيِّ ، صلّى اللهُ عليهِ وسَلَّم ، رَكعَتينِ بَعْدَ العِشَاءِ ، وحديثُ عبدِ اللهِ بنِ مُغَفَّل : « بَيْنَ كلِّ أَذَانَيْنِ صَلاةٌ » مُتَّفَقٌ عَليهِ . كما سَبَقَ .

IMAM NAWAWI elucidating this topic recalls that "Hazrat Ibn-e-'Umar (R.A.A.) stated that he offered two sunnat raka'ats after Isha prayers along with Holy Prophet (S.A.W.) (See S. No. 1089 Chap. 196). And Hazrat Abdullah bin Mughaffal (R.A.A.) quoted a tradition stating that Holy Prophet (S.A.W.) has said that between the two calls for prayers, i.e. between Azan and Iqama there is a sunnat prayer. (See S. No. 1099 of Chapter 195).

* * * * * * *

CHAPTER 203

SUNNAT RAKA'ATS OF FRIDAY

فِيهِ حديثُ ابنِ عُمَرَ السَّابِقُ أنَّهُ صَلَّى مَعَ النَّبيِّ ، صَلَّى اللهُ عَليهِ وسلَّم ، رَكعَتَيْنِ بَعْدَ الجُمُعَةِ . متفقٌ عليه .

Imam Nawawi here recalls the Hadis quoted bv Hazrat Ibn-i-Umar (R.A.A.) (No. 1098 of Chapter 195).

١١٢٦ — وعَنْ أبي هُريرَةَ ، رَضِيَ اللهُ عَنْهُ قالَ : قالَ رسولُ اللهَ ، صَلّى اللهُ عليهِ وسلَّم : « إذا صَلّى أحَدُكُمُ الجُمُعَةَ ، فَلْيُصَلِّ بعْدَها أرْبَعاً» رواه مسلم .

1126. Hazrat Abu Hurairah (R.A.A.) says that Holy Prophet (S.A.W.) directed us After you have finished Friday (obligatory) prayer, offer four sunnat raka'ats as well. *(Muslim)*

١١٢٧ — وعَنِ ابنِ عُمَرَ ، رَضِيَ اللهُ عَنهُما ، أنَّ النَّبيَّ ، صَلّى اللهُ عليهِ وسلَّم ، كانَ لا يُصَلّي بعْدَ الجُمُعَةِ حتّى يَنْصَرِفَ ، فيُصَلّي رَكْعتَيْنِ في بَيْتِهِ . رواه مسلم .

1127. Hazrat Ibn Umar (R.A.A.) relates that aft Holy Prophet (S.A.W.) had offered Friday (obligatory) prayers, he did not offer any sunnat prayer in the mosque but he used to go to his house and offer there two (sunnat) raka'ats.

Note . This establishes that four sunnat prayers before Friday prayers are sunnat Muakkadha. Other traditions also prove that four sunnat prayers after Friday are merely sunnat.

* * * * * * *

CHAPTER 204

PREFERENCE OF OFFERING VOLUNTARY PRAYERS AT HOME WHETHER MUAKKADAH OR NON-MUAKKADAH, AND TO CHANGE PLACE FOR OFFERING SUNNAT (VOLUNTARY) PRAYERS OR SEPARATING COMPULSORY PRAYERS FROM VOLUNTARY PRAYERS BY TALKING.

١١٢٨ — عَنْ زيدِ بنِ ثابتٍ ، رَضِيَ اللهُ عنْهُ ، أنَّ النَّبيَّ ، صلّى اللهُ عليهِ وسلَّمَ قالَ : « صَلّوا أيُّها النّاسُ في بُيُوتِكُم ؛ فإنَّ أفْضَلَ الصَّلاةِ صَلاةُ المَرْءِ في بَيْتِهِ إلاّ المَكْتُوبَةَ » متفقٌ عليه .

1128. Hazrat Zaid bin Sabit (R.A.A.) relates that Holy Prophet (S.A.W.) said: O people offer your optional prayers in your homes for, with the exception of Farz (compulsory) prayers, the best prayer is that which is offered at home *(Bukhari and Muslim)*

١١٢٩ – وَعَنِ ابنِ عُمَرَ رَضِيَ اللهُ عَنْهُمَا عَنِ النَّبِيِّ ، صلَّى اللهُ عليهِ وَسَلَّم ، قالَ : « اجْعَلُوا مِنْ صَلاتِكُمْ في بُيُوتِكُمْ ، وَلا تَتَّخِذُوهَا قُبُوراً » متفقٌ عليه .

1129. **Hazrat Ibn Umar** (R.A.A.) says that the Holy Prophet (S.A.W.) said: you should offer some (voluntary) prayer at your home also. Do not turn your homes into graves. (i.e. Don't make your abodes void of prayers like graves). *(Bukhari and Muslim)*

١١٣٠ – وعَنْ جابرٍ ، رَضِيَ اللهُ عَنْهُ ، قالَ : قَالَ رسولُ اللهِ ، صلَّى اللهُ عَليهِ وسَلَّم : « إذا قَضَى أَحَدُكُمْ صَلاتَهُ في مَسْجِدِهِ ؛ فَلْيَجْعَلْ لِبَيْتِهِ نَصِيباً مِنْ صَلاتِهِ ؛ فَإِنَّ اللهَ جَاعِلٌ في بَيْتِهِ مِنْ صَلاتِهِ خَيْراً » رواه مسلم .

1130. **Hazrat Jabir** (R.A.A.) relates that Holy Prophet (S.A.W.) said: when you have finished your Farz prayer in mosque, you should earmark some portion of your prayer (voluntary) at home, for Allah will bless your home on account of this. *(Muslim)*

١١٣١ – وَعَنْ عُمَرَ بْنِ عَطَاءٍ أَنَّ نَافِعَ بْنَ جُبَيْرٍ أَرْسَلَهُ إلى السَّائِبِ ابنِ أُخْتِ نَمِرٍ يَسْأَلُهُ عَنْ شَيْءٍ رَآهُ مِنْهُ مُعَاوِيَةُ في الصَّلاةِ فَقَالَ : نَعَمْ صَلَّيْتُ مَعَهُ الجُمُعَةَ في المَقْصُورَةِ ، فَلَمَّا سَلَّمَ الإمامُ ،قُمتُ في مَقَامِي ، فَصَلَّيْتُ ، فَلَمَّا دَخَلَ أَرْسَلَ إليَّ فقال : لاتَعُدْ لِمَا فَعَلْتَ : إذا صَلَّيْتَ الجُمُعَةَ ،فَلا تَصِلْهَا بِصَلاةٍ حَتَّى تَتَكَلَّمَ أَوْ تَخْرُجَ؛فَإِنَّ رسولَ اللهِ ، صلَّى اللهُ عليهِ وسلَّم ، أَمَرَنَا بِذلِكَ ، أَنْ لانُوصِلَ صَلاةً بِصَلاةٍ حَتَّى نَتَكَلَّمَ أَوْ نَخْرُجَ . رواه مسلم .

1131. **Hazrat Umar Ibn Ata** (R.A.A.) says that Hazrat Nafa'i bin Jubair (R.A.A.) sent him to Hazrat Sa'ib bin Ukht Nami (R.A.A.) to enquire from him as to whether what Hazrat Amir Mu'awiah had seen about his prayer is correct. Hazrat Sa'ib (R.A.A.) said: Yes, I offered Friday prayer within the cordoned area of the mosque with him and when the Imam had finishedd prayer and offered salams to right and left, I stood up in my place and offered sunnat prayer. When Amir Mu'awiah went into retirement he sent for me and cautioned me: Never do such thing again. After you have finished (obligatory) Friday prayer, do not continue with sunnat prayers unless you have spoken to someone or have shifted your place, for Holy Prophet (S.A.W.) directed us that we should not follow up the congregational prayer with sunnat prayers unless we had talked to some one or had changed our place. *(Muslim)*

* * * * * * *

CHAPTER 205

THE IMPORTANCE AND TIME OF WITR PRAYER AND THAT IT IS OBLIGATORY

١١٣٢ – عَنْ عَلِيٍّ ، رَضِيَ اللهُ عَنْهُ قالَ : الوِترُ لَيْسَ بِحَتْمٍ كَصَلاةِ المَكْتُوبَةِ ، وَلَكِنْ سَنَّ رسولُ اللهِ ، صَلَّى اللهُ عَليهِ وَسَلَّمَ ، قالَ : « إنَّ اللهَ وِترٌ يُحِبُّ الوِتْرَ ، فَأَوْتِرُوا يا أَهْلَ القُرْآنِ » .

رواه أبو داود والترمذي وقالَ : حديثٌ حسنٌ .

1132. Hazrat Ali (R.A.A.) said: Witr (odd) prayer is not compulsory like the prescribed(farz) because the order about farz (compulsory) prayers is quite clear and definite and the witr are not like that) but the Holy Prophet (S.A.W.) offered witr regularly and said: 'Allah is one and loves witr. Therefore O' people who believe in Quran offer witr prayers. *(Abu Daud and Tirmizi)*

Note : Witr literally means an odd number.

١١٣٣ – وَعَنْ عائِشَةَ ، رَضِيَ اللهُ عَنْها ، قالَتْ : مِنْ كُلِّ اللَّيْلِ قَدْ أَوْتَرَ رسولُ اللهِ ، صلَّى اللهُ عَليهِ وَسَلَّم ، مِنْ أَوَّلِ اللَّيْلِ ، وَمِن أَوْسَطِهِ ، وَمِنْ آخِرِهِ . وَانْتَهى وِتْرُهُ إلى السَّحَرِ » متفقٌ عليهِ .

1133. Hazrat Ayesha (R.A.A.) relates: 'The Holy Prophet (S.A.W.) offered witr prayers in all the later part of the night in which case his witr prayers used to be finished by about dawn. *(Bukhari and Muslim)*

١١٣٤ – وعَنِ ابنِ عُمَرَ رَضِيَ اللهُ عَنْهُما ، عَنِ النَّبِيِّ صَلَّى اللهُ عَليهِ وَسَلَّمَ قالَ : « اجْعَلوا آخِرَ صَلاتِكُمْ بِاللَّيْلِ وِتْراً » متفقٌ عليه .

1134. Hazrat Ibn Umar (R.A.A.) says that Holy Prophet (S.A.W.) said: make your last voluntary prayer of night as witr (that is) offer your witr after Tahajjud prayer. *(Bukhari and Muslim)*

١١٣٥ — وَعَنْ أَبِي سَعِيدٍ الخُدْرِيِّ ، رَضِيَ اللهُ عَنْهُ ، أَنَّ النَّبِيَّ صَلَّى اللهُ عَلَيهِ وَسَلَّمَ قالَ : « أَوْتِرُوا قَبْلَ أَنْ تُصْبِحُوا » رواه مسلم

1135. **Hazrat Abu Sa'id Khudri** (R.A.A.) relates that Holy Prophet (S.A.W.) asked us: Offer your witr prayer before dawn.

(Muslim)

١١٣٦ — وعن عائشةَ ، رضيَ اللهُ عَنْهَا ، أنَّ النَّبيَّ ، صَلَّى اللهُ عليهِ وسلَّم ، كانَ يُصَلِّي صَلاتَهُ بِاللَّيْلِ ، وَهِيَ مُعْتَرِضَةٌ بينَ يَدَيهِ ، فَإذا بَقِيَ الوِتْرُ ، أيقَظَهَا فَأَوْتَرتْ . رواه مسلم .

وفي روايةٍ له : فَإذا بَقِيَ الوترُ قالَ : « قُومِي فَأَوْتِري يَاعَائشَةُ » .

1136. **Hazrat Ayesha** (R.A.A.) says that when Holy Prophet (S.A.W.) used to offer night (voluntary) prayer, she used to be sleeping in front of him (nearby) and when the time would come for his witr prayer, he used to wake her up and she would offer her witr prayer.

(Muslim)

Another report from Imam Muslim says: 'When the time for witr prayer would come, he would say to Ayesha, get up and offer your witr prayer.'

١١٣٧ — وعَنِ ابنِ عُمَرَ رَضِيَ اللهُ عَنْهُمَا ، أنَّ النَّبيَّ ، صلَّى اللهُ عليهِ وسلَّم ، قالَ : « بَادِرُوا الصُّبْحَ بالوِتْرِ » .

رَوَاه أبو داود ، والترمذي وقالَ : حديثٌ حسنٌ صحيحٌ

1137. **Hazrat Ibn 'Umar** (R.A.A.) relates that Holy Prophet (S.A.W.) said: You should prefer offering witr prayer by the dawn.

(Abu Daud and Tirmizi, the latter called it as sound and good).

١١٣٨ — وَعَنْ جابرٍ ، رَضِيَ اللهُ عَنْهُ ، قالَ : قالَ رسولُ اللهِ ، صلَّى اللهُ عليهِ وسلَّم : « مَنْ خَافَ أَنْ لايَقُومَ مِنْ آخرِ اللَّيْلِ ،فَلْيُوتِرْ أَوَّلَهُ ، وَمَنْ طَمِعَ أَنْ يَقُومَ آخِرَهُ ، فَلْيوتِرْ آخرَ اللَّيْلِ ، فإنَّ صَلاةَ آخرِ اللَّيْلِ مَشْهُودَةٌ ، وَذلكَ أَفضَلُ » رواه مسلم .

1138. **Hazrat Jabir** (R.A.A.) reports that Holy Prophet (S.A.W.) said: A person who apprehends that he might not be able to get up in latter part of the night (for Tahajjud), then he should offer his witr prayer in the beginning of night; but the person who likes to get up for Tahajjud prayer in the later part of night, should offer witr prayer at the last end of night, for prayer in the later part of night is presented before Allah and it is superior. *(Muslim)*

* * * * * * *

CHAPTER 206

VIRTUES OF ISHRAQ (AFTER SUNRISE) VOLUNTARY PRAYER AND CHASHT FORENOON PRAYERS AND EXPLAINING THEIR MINIMUM, MAXIMUM, AND MIDDLE NUMBER AND INDUCEMENT TO STICK TO IT

١١٣٩ – عَنْ أَبي هُرَيرَةَ ، رَضِيَ اللهُ عَنْهُ ، قالَ : أَوْصَاني خَليلي ، صلَّى اللهُ عليهِ وسلَّم ، بصِيَامِ ثَلاثَةِ أَيَّامٍ مِنْ كُلِّ شَهرٍ ، ورَكْعَتَي الضُّحَى ، وأَنْ أُوتِرَ قَبلَ أَنْ أَرْقُدَ » متفقٌ عليه .

والإِيتَارُ قَبلَ النَّومِ إِنَّمَا يُستَحَبُّ لِمَنْ لايَثِقُ بِالاستيقَاظِ آخِرَ اللَّيلِ ، فَإِنْ وَثِقَ ، فَآخِرُ اللَّيْلِ أَفْضَلُ .

1139. **Hazrat Abu Hurairah** (R.A.A.) relates: My friend (benefactor and well-wisher) Holy Prophet (S.A.W.) directed me to observe fast for three days in every month and to offer two raka'ats voluntary prayers of *chasht* (forenoon) and offer witr prayers before going to bed. *(Bukhari and Muslim)*

Note :— Offering of *witr* prayers before going to sleep is better for one who apprehends he may not be able to get up in the later part of night. If one is confident of his capability to get up in later part of night then he should offer witr in that part of night.

١١٤٠ – وعَنْ أَبي ذَرٍّ رَضِيَ اللهُ عَنْهُ ، عنِ النَّبيِّ ، صلَّى اللهُ عليه وسلَّم ، قالَ : « يُصْبِحُ عَلى كُلِّ سُلامَى مِنْ أَحَدِكُمْ صدَقَةٌ : فَكُلُّ تَسبيحَةٍ صَدَقَةٌ ، وكُلُّ تَحميدَةٍ صَدقَةٌ ، وكُلُّ تَهليلَةٍ صَدَقَةٌ ، وكُلُّ تَكبيرَةٍ صَدَقَةٌ ، وأَمرٌ بالمعرُوفِ صَدَقَةٌ ، ونَهْيٌ عَنِ المُنْكَرِ صدَقَةٌ ، ويُجزِىءُ مِنْ ذلكَ رَكعَتَانِ يَركَعُهُما مِنَ الضُّحَى » رواه مسلم .

1140. This Hadis is the same as No. 118 of Chapter 13.

١١٤١ – وعَنْ عائشةَ رَضِيَ اللهُ عَنْهَا ، قالتْ : كانَ رسولُ اللهِ ، صلَّى اللهُ عليهِ وسلَّم ، يُصَلِّي الضُّحَى أَرْبَعاً ، وَيَزِيدُ مَاشاءَ اللهُ . رواه مسلم .

1141. Hazrat Ayesha (R.A.A.) says that Holy Prophet (S.A.W.) used to offer four sunnat raka'ats at sunrise and added to them whatever Allah wished. *(Muslim)*

١١٤٢ – وعنْ أُمِّ هَانِئٍ فاخِتةَ بنتِ أبي طالبٍ ، رَضِيَ اللهُ عَنْها ، قَالتْ: ذهَبْتُ إلى رسولِ اللهِ ، صلَّى اللهُ عليهِ وسلَّم ، عامَ الفَتْحِ فَوَجَدْتُهُ يَغْتَسِلُ ، فَلَمَّا فَرَغَ مِنْ غُسْلِهِ ، صَلَّى ثَمَانِيَ رَكعَاتٍ ، وَذلكَ ضُحَى » متفقٌ عليه . وهذا مختصر لفظِ إحدى روايات مسلم .

1142. Hazrat Umm Hani Fakhita bint Abu Talib relates: I went to Holy Prophet (S.A.W.) on the day of the conquest of Mecca, and he was then taking a bath. When he (S.A.W.) had finished bath he (S.A.W.) offered eight raka'ats of voluntary prayers. This was after sunrise (chasht or Ishraq) prayer. *(Bukhari and Muslim)*

Note :— These traditions establish the virtues of Ishraq and Chasht prayers.

* * * * * * *

CHAPTER 207

THE BEST WAY OF OFFERING CHASHT PRAYER IS TO OFFER WHEN SUN STARTS RISING TILL NOON (ZAWAL TIME) WHEN IT IS EXTREMELY HOT

١١٤٣ – عن زيدِ بنِ أَرْقَمٍ ، رَضِيَ اللهُ عَنْهُ ، أَنَّهُ رَأَى قَوْماً يُصَلُّون مِنَ الضُّحَى ، فقالَ : أَمَا لَقَدْ عَلِمُوا أَنَّ الصَّلاةَ في غَيْرِ هذهِ السَّاعَةِ أفْضَلُ ، إنَّ رسولَ اللهِ ، صلَّى اللهُ عليهِ وسلَّم ، قالَ : « صَلاةُ الأَوَّابِينَ حِينَ تَرْمَضُ الفِصَالُ » رواه مسلم .

1143. Hazrat Zaid bin Arqam (R.A.A.) says that he noticed some people offering *chasht* prayer and remarked: These people know that the better time for this voluntary prayer is a bit later than this for Holy Prophet (S.A.W.) said: for those devoteeswho are fully devoted to Allah, the time for prayer is that when kids of camels get warmed that is when the sun has risen fairly high." *(Muslim)*

* * * * * * *

CHAPTER 208

TAHYATUL MASJID PRAYER (RESPECT OF MOSQUE PRAYER)– A VOLUNTARY PRAYER ON ENTERING A MOSQUE – THE REPUGNANCE OF NOT OFFERING TWO RAKA'ATS OF PRAYER BEFORE SITTING, WHETHER THESE TWO RAKA'ATS ARE OFFERED AS A TAḤYYATUL MASAJID (NAFL) OR FARZ OR SUNNAT MUAKKADAH OR SUNNAT GHAIR MUAKKADAH, IT MAKES NO DIFFERENCE.

١١٤٤ — وعن أبي قتادةَ ، رَضِيَ اللهُ عَنْهُ ، قالَ : قالَ رسولُ الله ، صلَّى اللهُ عليهِ وسَلَّم : « إذا دَخَلَ أَحَدُكُمُ المَسْجِدَ، فلا يَجْلِسْ حتَّى يُصَلِّيَ رَكْعَتَيْنِ » متفقٌ عليه .

1144. Hazrat Abu Qatadah (R.A.A.) relates that Holy Prophet (S.A.W.) said: When any of you enters a mosque, he should not sit down till he has offered two raka'ats of voluntary prayer (tahyatul Masjid). *(Bukhari and Muslim)*

١١٤٥ — وعن جابرٍ ، رَضِيَ اللهُ عَنْهُ قالَ : أَتَيْتُ النَّبيَّ ، صلَّى اللهُ عليه وسلَّم ، وهوَ في المَسْجدِ ، فقَالَ : « صَلِّ رَكعتَيْنِ » متفقٌ عليه .

1145. Hazrat Jabir (R.A.A.) says: Once I came to Holy Prophet (S.A.W.) when he was sitting in a mosque. He (S.A.W.) said to me: Offer two raka'ats (Tahyatul Masjid). *(Bukhari and Muslim)*

* * * * * * *

CHAPTER 209

VIRTUES OF OFFERING TWO RAKA'ATS AFTER ABLUTION (WUDU)

١١٤٦ — عن أبي هُريرَةَ ، رَضِيَ اللهُ عَنْهُ أنَّ رَسُولَ اللهِ ، صلَّى اللهُ عَليهِ وسلَّم ، قالَ لِبلالٍ : « يَابِلالُ حَدِّثْني بِأَرْجَى عَمَلٍ عَمِلْتَهُ في الإسْلامِ ، فإنِّي سَمِعْتُ دَفَّ نَعْلَيْكَ بَيْنَ يَدَيَّ في الجَنَّةِ ، قالَ :

مَاعَمِلْتُ عَمَلاً أَرْجَى عِنْدِي مِنْ أَنِّي لَمْ أَتَطَهَّرْ طُهُوراً فِي سَاعَةٍ مِنْ لَيْلٍ أَوْ نَهارٍ إِلَّا صَلَّيْتُ بِذلكَ الطُّهُورِ ما كُتِبَ لي أَنْ أُصَلِّيَ .

متفقٌ عليه . وهذا لفظُ البخاري .

1146. Hazrat Abu Hurairah (R.A.A.) relates that Holy Prophet (S.A.W.) said to Hazrat Bilal (R.A.A.): O Bilal! Tell me, which of your act is most auspicious (meritorious) after you had accepted Islam, for I have heard the sound of your shoes in Paradise ahead of me. Hazrat Bilal (R.A.A.) replied: I do not have any action of mine more auspicious (meritorious) than that whenever I have cleaned myself (washed, bathed or performed ablution) during the day or night, I have each time offered prayer, as much as Allah had destined for me. *(Bukhari and Muslim)*

* * * * * * *

CHAPTER 210

VIRTUES OF FRIDAY PRAYERS AND ITS ESSENTIALITY; TO HAVE A BATH, APPLY PERFUME AND TO GO (TO MOSQUE) EARLY. TO SUPPLICATE AND TO RECITE SALAT ON HOLY PROPHET (S.A.W.) ON FRIDAY. THE TIME FOR ACCEPTANCE OF SUPPLICATIONS AND THE MERIT OF PROFUSELY REMEMBERING ALLAH.

قالَ اللهُ تعالى : فإذا قُضِيَتِ الصَّلاةُ فَانْتَشِرُوا في الأَرْضِ ، وَابْتَغُوا مِنْ فَضْلِ اللهِ ، وَاذْكُرُوا اللهَ كَثِيراً لَعَلَّكُمْ تُفْلِحُونَ [الجمعة : ١٠] .

284. And when prayer is ended, then disperse in the land and seek Allah's bounty, and remember Allah much, that ye may be successful. (62:10).

١١٤٧ — وعَنْ أبي هُرَيرَةَ ، رَضِيَ اللهُ عَنْهُ ، قالَ : قالَ رسولُ اللهِ ، صلَّى الله عليهِ وسلَّم : « خَيْرُ يَوْمٍ طَلَعَتْ عَلَيْهِ الشَّمْسُ يَوْمُ الجُمُعَةِ : فيهِ خُلِقَ آدم ، وَفيه أُدْخِلَ الجَنَّةَ ، وَفيه أُخْرِجَ مِنْهَا » رواه مسلم .

1147. Hazrat Abu Hurairah (R.A.A.) relates that Holy Prophet (S.A.W.) said: The best day among the days on which the sun rises, is Friday; this is the day when Hazrat Adam (A.S.) was created; on that day he was admitted into the Paradise and on that very day he was sent down from the heaven. *(Muslim)*

١١٤٨ – وَعَنْهُ قَالَ: قَالَ رَسُولُ اللهِ، صلّى الله عليه وسلّم: «مَنْ تَوَضَّأَ فَأَحْسَنَ الوُضُوءَ ثُمَّ أَتَى الجُمُعَةَ، فاستَمَعَ وَأَنْصَتَ، غُفِرَ له ما بَيْنَه وَبَيْنَ الجُمُعَةِ وَزِيَادة ثلاثةِ أيَّامٍ، وَمَنْ مَسَّ الحَصَى، فقد لَغَا» رواه مسلم.

1148. This Hadis has already been covered in No. 128 of Chapter 13.

١١٤٩ – وَعَنْهُ عَنِ النَّبِيِّ، صلّى الله عَلَيهِ وسلّم، قالَ «الصَّلَوَاتُ الخَمْسُ وَالجُمُعَةُ إلى الجُمُعَةِ، ورَمَضَانُ إلى رَمَضَانَ، مُكَفِّرَاتٌ ما بَيْنَهُنَّ إذا اجْتُنِبَتِ الكَبَائِرُ» رواه مسلم.

1149. Hazrat Abu Hurairah (R.A.A.) reports that Holy Prophet (S.A.W.) said: The five daily (obligatory) prayers and Friday Prayer to next Friday prayer and keeping of fast from one Ramadhan to the observance of next Remadhan atone for all minor sins during this period so long as major sins are avoided. *(Muslim)*

١١٥٠ – وَعَنْهُ وعَنِ ابْنِ عُمَرَ، رَضِيَ اللهُ عَنْهُمْ، أَنَّهُما سَمِعَا رسولَ اللهِ، صلّى اللهُ عليه وسلّم، يقولُ عَلَى أَعْوَادِ مِنْبَرِهِ: «لَيَنْتَهِيَنَّ أَقْوَامٌ عَنْ وَدْعِهِمُ الجُمُعَاتِ، أَوْ لَيَخْتِمَنَّ اللهُ عَلَى قُلُوبِهِمْ، ثُمَّ لَيَكُونُنَّ مِنَ الغَافِلِينَ» رواه مسلم.

1150. Hazrat Abu Hurairah (R.A.A.) and **Hazrat Ibn Umar** (R.A.A.) relate that they heard Holy Prophet (S.A.W.) say from his wooden pulpit. The people should not neglect Friday prayer, otherwise Allah will seal their hearts, and they will be counted among the negligent ones. *(Muslim)*

١١٥١ – وَعَنِ ابنِ عُمَرَ رَضِيَ اللهُ عَنْهُمَا، أَنَّ رَسولَ اللهِ صَلَّى اللهُ عَلَيهِ وسلّم، قالَ: «إذا جَاءَ أَحَدُكُمُ الجُمُعَةَ، فَلْيَغْتَسِلْ» متفقٌ عليه.

1151. Hazrat Ibn 'Umar (R.A.A.) says that Holy Prophet (S.A.W.) said: when anyone of you comes for Friday prayer, he should take a bath. *(Bukhari and Muslim)*

١١٥٢ – وعن أبي سعيدٍ الخُدْرِيِّ، رَضِيَ اللهُ عَنْهُ، أَنَّ رسولَ اللهِ، صلّى اللهُ عليهِ وسلّم، قالَ: «غُسْلُ يَوْمِ الجُمُعَةِ وَاجِبٌ عَلى كلِّ مُحْتَلِمٍ» متفقٌ عليه.

1152. **Hazrat Abu Sa'eed Khudri** (R.A.A.) relates that Holy Prophet said: Bath on Friday is incumbent upon every adult person. *(Bukhari and Muslim)*

١١٥٣ ــ وَعَنْ سَمُرَةَ ، رَضِيَ اللهُ عَنْهُ قالَ : قالَ رَسُولُ اللهِ . صلّى اللهُ عليهِ وسلّم : « مَنْ تَوَضَّأَ يَوْمَ الجُمُعَةِ . فبِها وَنِعْمَتْ وَمَنْ اغْتَسَلَ فَالغُسْلُ أَفْضَلُ » رواهُ أبو داود . والترمذي وقالَ حديثٌ حسنٌ .

1153. **Hazrat Samurah bin Jundab** (R.A.A.) relates that Holy Prophet (S.A.W.) said: He who performs his ablution for Friday prayer and adopts the easier course and it is good, and one who takes bath then this bath is superior. *(Abu Daud and Tirmizi)* Imam *Tirmizi* called it as sound.

١١٥٤ ــ وَعَنْ سَلمَانَ ، رَضِيَ اللهُ عَنْهُ ، قالَ : قَالَ رَسُولُ اللهِ . صلّى اللهُ عليهِ وسلّم : « لا يَغْتَسِلُ رَجُلٌ يَوْمَ الجُمُعَةِ ، وَيَتَطَهَّرُ ما استَطَاعَ مِنْ طُهْرٍ ، وَيَدَّهِنُ مِنْ دُهْنِهِ ، أو يَمَسُّ مِن طيبِ بَيْتِهِ . ثُمَّ يَخْرُجُ فَلا يُفَرِّقُ بَيْنَ اثنَيْنِ ، ثُمَّ يُصَلِّي مَا كُتِبَ لَهُ ، ثُمَّ يُنصِتُ إذا تَكَلَّمَ الإمَامُ ، إلاَّ غُفِرَ لهُ ما بَيْنَهُ وَبَيْنَ الجُمُعَةِ الأخرَى » .

رواه البخاري .

1154. This Hadis is contained in No. 828 of Chapter 128.

١١٥٥ ــ وَعَنْ أبي هُرَيرَةَ . رَضِيَ اللهُ عَنْهُ ، أنَّ رسولَ اللهِ ، صلّى اللهُ عَليهِ وسلّم ، قالَ : « مَنِ اغْتَسَلَ يَوْمَ الجُمُعَةِ غُسْلَ الجَنَابَةِ ، ثُمَّ رَاحَ في الساعة الأولى ، فَكَأَنَّما قرَّبَ بَدَنَةً ، وَمَنْ رَاحَ في السَّاعَةِ الثَّانِيَةِ ، فَكَأَنَّما قَرَّبَ بَقَرَةً ، وَمَنْ رَاحَ في السَّاعَةِ الثَّالِثَةِ ، فَكَأَنَّمَا قَرَّبَ كَبْشاً أقرَنَ ، وَمَنْ رَاحَ في السَّاعَةِ الرَّابِعَةِ ، فَكَأَنَّما قَرَّبَ دَجَاجَةً ، وَمَنْ رَاحَ في السَّاعَةِ الخَامِسَةِ ، فَكَأَنَّمَا قَرَّبَ بَيْضَةً ، فَإذا خرجَ الإمامُ ، حَضَرَتِ المَلائكَةُ يَسْتَمِعُونَ الذِّكْرَ » متفقٌ عليه .

قوله : « غُسلَ الجَنَابَةِ » ؛ أي : غُسلاً كَغُسل الجَنابَةِ في الصِّفَةِ .

1155. **Hazrat Abu Hurairah** (R.A.A.) says that Holy Prophet (S.A.W.) said: A person who takes full bath for purification after having intercourse on Friday and reaches mosque early is as meritorious as if he had sacrificed a camel for the sake of Allah; and one who reaches mosque after him, is as if he had sacrificed a cow; and the person who goes subsequently, is as if he had sacrificed a full grown sheep; and the person who goes afterwards is as if he had sacrificed a hen; and the person who reaches the mosque in the fifth turn is like one who has sacrificed an egg. At last when the Imam comes for Friday sermon, the angels at the gates of mosque leave the gates to listen to the Imam's sermon and the names of the late comers are left out.

(Bukahri and Muslim)

١١٥٦ — وَعَنْهُ أَنَّ رَسُولَ اللهِ ، صَلَّى اللهُ عليه وسلَّم ، ذَكَرَ يَوْمَ الجُمُعَةِ ، فَقَالَ : « فِيهَا سَاعَةٌ لا يُوَافِقُهَا عَبْدٌ مُسْلِمٌ ، وَهُوَ قَائِمٌ يُصَلِّي يَسْأَلُ اللهَ شَيْئاً ، إلاَّ أَعْطَاهُ إِيَّاهُ » وَأَشَارَ بِيَدِهِ يُقَلِّلُهَا ، متفقٌ عليه .

1156. Hazrat Abu Hurairah (R.A.A.) relates that the Holy Prophet (S.A.W.) referring to the (sanctity) of Friday said: On this day there is such (an auspicious) spell of time which if a Muslim could get and he supplicates after his prayers and asks for a boon from Allah, he gets it. The Holy Prophet (S.A.W.) indicated the shortage of this spell with a movement of his (S.A.W.) hand. *(Bukhari and Muslim)*

١١٥٧ — وَعَنْ أَبِي بُرْدَةَ بْنِ أَبِي مُوسَى الأَشْعَرِيِّ ، رَضِيَ اللهُ عَنْهُ ، قَالَ : قَالَ عَبْدُ اللهِ بنِ عُمَرَ رَضِيَ اللهُ عَنْهُمَا : أَسَمِعْتَ أَبَاكَ يُحَدِّثُ عَنْ رَسُولِ اللهِ ، صلَّى اللهُ عَلَيهِ وسلَّم ، فِي شَأْنِ سَاعَةِ الجُمُعَةِ ؟ قَالَ : قلتُ : نعم ، سَمِعْتُهُ يَقُولُ : سَمِعْتُ رَسُولَ اللهِ ، صلَّى اللهُ عَلَيهِ وَسلَّم ، يَقُولُ : « هِيَ مَا بَيْنَ أَنْ يَجْلِسَ الإمامُ إلى أَنْ تُقْضَى الصَّلاةُ » رواه مسلم .

1157. Hazrat Abu Burdah bin Abu Musa Al-Ash'ari (R.A.A.) says: Hazrat Abdullah bin Umar (R.A.A.) asked me: Did you hear your father relate anything from the Holy Prophet (S.A.W.) regarding the moment of acceptance of prayers in the course of the Friday prayer? I said: Yes, I learnt from him say that he heard the Holy Prophet (S.A.W.) as saying that this moment takes place from the moment the Imam ascends the pulpit and lasts till the prayer ends. *(Muslim)*

Note : From the traditions it appears that the duration of the time for the acceptance or grant of requests or supplication, is very short. As regards its exact location there are many different vrsions. However, majority of them fix the same between '*Asr* and *Maghrib* prayers'.

١١٥٨ — وَعَنْ أَوْسِ بنِ أَوْسٍ ، رَضِيَ اللهُ عَنْهُ ، قَالَ : قَالَ رَسُولُ اللهِ ، صَلَّى اللهُ عَلَيهِ وسَلَّم : « إِنَّ مِنْ أَفْضَلِ أَيَّامِكُمْ يَوْمَ الجُمُعَةِ ،

فأكثِرُوا عَلَيَّ مِنَ الصَّلاةِ فِيهِ ؛ فَإنَّ صَلاتَكُمْ مَعْرُوضَةٌ عَلَيَّ » .

رواه أبوداود بإسناد صحيح .

1158. Hazrat Aus bin Aus (R.A.A.) relates that the Holy Prophet (S.A.W.) said. 'Among your days the best day is Friday; as such you should recite *Salat* (Invoking Allah's benediction) on me, for your blessings are communicated to me. *(Abu Daud has cited this with sound chains).*

* * * * * *

CHAPTER 211

PROSTRATION IN GRATITUDE TO ALLAH FOR THE GRANT OF UNEXPECTED FAVOURS AND PASSING AWAY OF SOME MISFORTUNE

١١٥٩ - عَنْ سَعْدِ بنِ أبي وَقَّاصٍ ، رَضِيَ اللهُ عَنْهُ ، قَالَ : خَرَجْنا مَعَ رَسُولِ اللهِ صَلَّى اللهُ عَلَيهِ وَسلَّم ، مِن مَكَّةَ نُرِيدُ المَدِينَةَ ، فَلَمَّا كُنَّا قَرِيباً مِن عَزْوَرَاءَ نَزَلَ ثُمَّ رَفَعَ يَدَيْهِ ، فَدَعَا اللهَ سَاعَةً ، ثُمَّ خَرَّ سَاجِداً ، فَمَكَثَ طَوِيلاً ، ثُمَّ قَامَ فَرَفَعَ يَدَيْهِ سَاعَةً ، ثُمَّ خَرَّ ساجِداً - فعَلَهُ ثَلاثاً - وَقَالَ : إنِّي سَأَلْتُ رَبِّي . وَشَفَعْتُ لأُمَّتي ، فَأعْطَانِي ثُلُثَ أُمَّتِي . فَخَرَرتُ ساجِداً لِرَبِّي شُكْراً ، ثُمَّ رَفَعْتُ رَأْسِي ، فَسَأَلْتُ رَبِّي لأُمَّتي : فأَعْطَاني ثُلُثَ أُمَّتي . فَخَرَرتُ ساجِداً لِرَبِّي شُكْراً . ثُمَّ رَفَعْتُ رَأْسِي . فَسَأَلْتُ رَبِّي لأُمَّتي ، فَأعْطَانِي الثُّلُثَ الآخَرَ ، فَخَرَرتُ ساجِداً لِرَبِّي » رَوَاهُ أبو داودَ .

1159. Hazrat Sa'ad bin Abi Waqqas (R.A.A.) says: (Once) we along with the Holy Prophet (S.A.W.) started from Mecca for Medina. When we reached Azwara, a place near Mecca, the Holy Prophet (S.A.W.) descended and raising his hands supplicated for some time and fell into prostration and remained in this position for a long time; then he raised his head and stretched his hands and prayed and stood for some time and then again went into prostration. He (S.A.W.) did this thrice. And (then turning to us) said : 'I prayed to my Lord and requested for the redemption of my Ummah, on this Allah granted me one third of my Ummah (i.e. redeemed one third of them). I therefore fell into prostration before my Allah to express my thanks to Him.

Thereafter I raised my head again and supplicated Allah for my Ummah; who granted me another third of my Ummah (i.e. He redeemed another third), whereupon I fell into prostration before my Allah (once more) for thanking Him.

I raised my head again and prayed and requested my Lord for the redemption of my Ummah, and He granted me the remaining one third of my Ummah (i.e. He redeemed the remaining one third of them). On this too I prostrated myself before my Lord, to thank him.

(Abu Daud)

* * * * * * *

CHAPTER 212

THE VIRTUES OF TAHAJJUD PRAYER AT MIDNIGHT

قالَ اللهُ تعَالى : وَمِنَ اللَّيْلِ فتَهجَّد بهِ نَافِلَةً لَكَ ، عَسَى أن يَبْعَثَكَ رَبُّكَ مَقاماً محمُوداً [الإسراء : ٧٩] . وقَالَ تعَالى : تَتَجافَى جُنُوبهُم عَنِ المضَاجِعِ [السجدة : ١٦] . وقَالَ تعَالى : كَانُوا قَليلاً مِنَ اللَّيْلِ ما يَهْجَعُونَ [الذاريات : ١٧] .

Allah the Exalted, has said :

285. And some part of the night awake for it, a largess for thee. It may be that thy Lord will raise thee to a praised estate.

(17:79)

286. Who forsake their beds. (32:16).

287. They used to sleep but little of the night. (51:17).

١١٦٠ — وعَن عائِشةَ ، رَضِيَ اللهُ عَنْهَا . قَالَتْ : كَانَ النَّبيُّ ، صَلَّى اللهُ عَليهِ وسلَّم ، يَقُومُ مِنَ اللَّيلِ حَتى تَتَفطَّرَ قَدَماه ، فَقُلْتُ لَهُ : لِمَ تَصنَعُ هذا ، يا رَسُولَ اللهِ ، وَقد غُفِرَ لَكَ ما تَقَدَّمَ مِن ذَنبكَ وَما تأخَّرَ ؟ قَالَ : « أفَلا أكُونُ عَبْداً شَكُوراً ! » .

متفقٌ عليه . وعَنِ المغيرَةِ بنِ شعبةَ نحوهُ ، متفقٌ عليه

1160. This has already been covered in S.No. 98 of Chapter 11.

١١٦١ — وَعَنْ عَلِيٍّ ، رَضِيَ اللهُ عَنْهُ ، أَنَّ النَّبِيَّ ، صَلَّى اللهُ عَلَيهِ وَسَلَّمَ ، طَرَقَهُ وَفاطِمَةَ لَيْلاً ، فَقَالَ : « أَلا تُصَلِّيَانِ ؟ » متفقٌ عليه .

1161. Hazrat Ali (R.A.A.) relates that Holy Prophet (S.A.W.) (once) visited him and his wife Hazrat Fatimah (R.A.A.) one night, and inquired from them: Do you not offer Salat-ul-lail (prayer of night)? *(Bukhari and Muslim)*

١١٦٢ — وَعَنْ سالِمِ بنِ عبدِ اللهِ بنِ عُمَرَ بنِ الخَطَّابِ ، رَضِيَ اللهُ عَنْهُم ، عَنْ أَبِيهِ : أَنَّ رسولَ اللهِ ، صلَّى اللهُ عَلَيهِ وسلَّم ، قَالَ : « نِعْمَ الرَّجلُ عَبْدُ اللهِ لَو كَانَ يُصَلِّي مِنَ اللَّيْلِ » قالَ سالِمٌ : فَكَانَ عَبْدُ اللهِ بعْدَ ذلكَ لايَنَامُ مِنَ اللَّيْلِ إلاَّ قَليلاً . متفقٌ عليه .

1162. Hazrat Salim bin Abdullah bin 'Umar bin Khattab (R.A.A.) reports on the auhority of his father, that Holy Prophet (S.A.W.) said: Abdullah is an excellent man if he continues to offer voluntary prayer at night. Hazrat Salim (R.A.A.) says that hereafter Hazrat Abdullah (R.A.A.) slept but little at night. *(Bukhari and Muslim)*

١١٦٣ — وَعَن عبدِ اللهِ بنِ عَمْرِو بنِ العاصِ ، رَضِيَ اللهُ عَنْهُمَا قالَ : قَالَ رَسُولُ اللهِ صَلَّى اللهُ عليهِ وسلَّم : « يَاعَبْدَ اللهِ لا تكن مِثْلَ فُلانٍ : كانَ يَقُومُ اللَّيْلَ فَتَرَكَ قِيَامَ اللَّيْلِ » متفقٌ عليه .

1163. This Hadis is the same as No. 154 of Chapter 15.

١١٦٤ — وعنِ ابنِ مَسْعُودٍ ، رَضِيَ اللهُ عَنْهُ ، قَالَ : ذُكِرَ عِنْدَ النَّبِيِّ ، صلَّى اللهُ عَلَيهِ وسَلَّمَ رَجُلٌ نَامَ لَيْلَةً حَتى أَصبحَ ! قالَ : « ذاكَ رَجُلٌ بَالَ الشَّيْطَانُ في أُذُنَيْهِ — أو قال : في أُذنِهِ — » متفقٌ عليه .

1164. Hazrat Abdullah bin Mas'ud (R.A.A.) says that a person was named before Holy Prophet (S.A.W.) that he continued to sleep throughout the night till dawn (i.e. he missed his Tahajjud prayer), on which he (S.A.W.) remarked: He is a man in whose ears the Satan has urinated; or he (S.A.W.) said in one of his ears the Satan has urinated. *(Bukahri and Muslim)*

١١٦٥— وعَن أَبي هُريرَةَ ، رَضِيَ اللهُ عَنْهُ ، أَنَّ رَسُولَ اللهِ ، صَلَّى اللهُ عليهِ وسلَّمَ ، قالَ : « يَعْقِدُ الشَّيْطَانُ عَلى قافِيَةِ رَأْسِ أَحَدِكُم ، إذا هُوَ نَامَ ، ثَلاثَ عُقَدٍ ، يَضْرِبُ عَلى كل عُقْدَةٍ : عَلَيْكَ لَيلٌ طَوِيلٌ

فَارْقُدْ ، فَإِنِ اسْتَيْقَظَ ، فَذَكَرَ اللهَ تَعَالَى انْحَلَّتْ عُقْدَةٌ ، فَإِنْ تَوَضَّأَ ، انْحَلَّتْ عُقْدَةٌ ، فَإِنْ صَلَّى ، انْحَلَّتْ عُقَدُهُ ، فَأَصْبَحَ نَشِيطاً طَيِّبَ النَّفْسِ ، وَإِلَّا أَصْبَحَ خَبِيثَ النَّفْسِ كَسْلَانَ » متفقٌ عليه .

1165, Hazrat Abu Hurairah (R.A.A.) relates that the Holy Prophet (S.A.W.) said: When a person goes under sound sleep the Satan ties three knots at the nape of his neck (where it touches the head) reciting some spell over each of these knots i.e. there is enough of the night, go on sleeping. If he wakes up and remembers Allah, one of the knots is untied. Then if he gets up and makes his ablution, another one is loosened. If he offers his prayer, then the remaining third knot is loosened. Thus he faces his morning quite fresh and is in a cheerful mood. Otherwise he gets up in unpleasant, dull and lethargic mood.
(Bukhari and Muslim)

١١٦٦ — وَعَنْ عبدِ اللهِ بنِ سلام ، رَضِيَ اللهُ عَنْهُ ، أَنَّ النَّبِيَّ ، صلَّى اللهُ عَلَيهِ وَسَلَّمَ قالَ : « أَيُّهَا النَّاسُ أَفْشُوا السَّلَامَ ، وَأَطْعِمُوا الطَّعَامَ ، وَصَلُّوا بِاللَّيْلِ وَالنَّاسُ نِيَامٌ ، تَدْخُلُوا الجَنَّةَ بِسَلَامٍ » .

رواهُ الترمذيُّ وقالَ : حديثٌ حسنٌ صحيحٌ .

1166. **This Hadis is the same as No. 849 of Chapter 131.**

١١٦٧ — وَعَنْ أَبِي هُرَيْرَةَ ، رَضِيَ اللهُ عَنْهُ قالَ : قَالَ رَسُولُ اللهِ ، صلَّى اللهُ عَليهِ وسَلَّمَ : « أَفْضَلُ الصِّيَامِ بَعْدَ رَمَضَانَ شَهْرُ اللهِ المُحَرَّمُ ، وَأَفْضَلُ الصَّلَاةِ بَعْدَ الفَرِيضَةِ صَلَاةُ اللَّيْلِ » رواه مُسلِمٌ .

1167. Hazrat Abu Hurairah (R.A.A.) relates that the Holy Prophet (S.A.W.) said: the best month for fasting after Ramazan is the month of Muharram, and the best salat *(Prayer)* after the prescribed (compulsory) salat is the Tahajjud (voluntary prayer of mid-night). *(Muslim)*

١١٦٨ — وَعَنِ ابنِ عُمَرَ ، رَضِيَ اللهُ عَنْهُمَا ، أَنَّ النَّبِيَّ ، صَلَّى اللهُ عَليهِ وَسَلَّمَ ، قَالَ : « صَلَاةُ اللَّيْلِ مَثْنَى مَثْنَى ، فَإِذَا خِفْتَ الصُّبْحَ فَأَوْتِرْ بِوَاحِدَةٍ » متفقٌ عليه .

1168. **Hazrat Abdullah bin Umar** (R.A.A.) says that the Holy Prophet (S.A.W.) said: Night prayer *(Tahajjud)* is offered in a series of two raka'as at a time, and when you anticipate the advent of dawn, add a single raka'at to make the total an odd number *(Witr)*.
(Bukhari and Muslim)

١١٦٩ ــ وَعَنْهُ قَالَ : كانَ النَّبِيُّ ، صلَّى اللهُ عَلَيهِ وَسَلَّمَ ، يُصَلِّي مِنَ اللَّيْلِ مَثْنَى مَثْنَى ، وَيُوتِرُ بِرَكْعَةٍ . متفقٌ عليه .

1169. **Hazrat Abdullah bin 'Umar** (R.A.A.) relates that the Holy Prophet (S.A.W.) used to offer prayer in succession of two raka'ats at night followed by a single raka'at to make the total an odd number (i.e. Witr) *(Bukhari and Muslim)*

١١٧٠ ــ وَعَنْ أَنَسٍ ، رَضِيَ اللهُ عَنْهُ ، قَالَ : كَانَ رَسُولُ اللهِ ، صلَّى اللهُ عَلَيهِ وسَلَّم ، يُفطِرُ مِنَ الشَّهْرِ حَتَّى نَظُنَّ أَنْ لا يَصُومَ مِنْهُ ، وَيَصُومُ حَتَّى نَظُنَّ أَنْ لايُفْطِرَ مِنْهُ شَيْئاً ؛ وكَانَ لا تَشَاءُ أَنْ تَرَاهُ مِنَ اللَّيْلِ مُصَلِّياً إِلا رَأَيْتَهُ ، وَلا نَائِماً إِلا رَأَيْتَهُ . رواهُ البخاريُّ .

1170. **Hazrat Anas** (R.A.A.) says that when the Holy Prophet (S.A.W.) used to omit fasting during a month, we used to think that he (S.A.W.) would not fast at all in this month, and when he would go on fasting we used to think that he would continue fasting throughout the month. If you like to see him offering prayer at night, you could see that and if you desire to see him sleeping at night you could do that. *(Bukahri)*

١١٧١ ــ وَعَنْ عَائِشَةَ ، رَضِيَ اللهُ عَنْهَا ، أَنَّ رَسولَ اللهِ ، صَلَّى اللهُ عَليهِ وسلَّم ، كَانَ يُصَلِّي إِحْدَى عَشْرَةَ رَكْعَةً ــ تَعْنِي فِي اللَّيْلِ ــ يَسْجُدُ السَّجْدَةَ مِنْ ذلكَ قَدْرَ مَايَقْرَأُ أَحَدُكُمْ خَمْسِينَ آيَةً قَبْلَ أن يَرْفَعَ رَأْسَهُ ، وَيَرْكَعُ رَكْعَتَيْنِ قَبْلَ صَلاةِ الفَجْرِ ، ثُمَّ يَضْطَجِعُ عَلَى شِقِّهِ الأَيْمَنِ حَتَّى يَأْتِيَهُ المُنَادِي للصَّلاة ، رواه البخاري .

1171. **It is reported by Hazrat Ayesha** (R.A.A.) that the Holy Prophet (S.A.W.) used to offer eleven raka'ats at night *(in Tahajjud)*; in this session his (S.A.W.) prostration used to be prolonged so much that in this time some of you could recite fifty verses. Thereafter he (S.A.W.) would offer two raka'ats before the Fajr (early dawn) prayer, and then recline on his (S.A.W.) right side till the Muezzin would come to call him for the congregation *(Fajr prayer)*. *(Bukhari)*

١١٧٢ ــ وَعَنْهَا قَالَتْ : ماكانَ رَسُولُ اللهِ ، صلَّى اللهُ عَليهِ وسلَّم ، يَزِيدُ ــ فِي رَمَضانَ وَلا فِي غَيْرِهِ ــ عَلَى إِحْدَى عَشْرَةَ رَكْعَةً : يُصَلِّي أَرْبعاً فَلا تَسْأَلْ عَنْ حُسْنِهِنَّ وَطولِهِنَّ ! ثُمَّ يُصَلِّي أَرْبعاً فَلا تَسْأَلْ عَنْ

حُسْنِهِنَّ وَطولِهِنَّ ! ثُمَّ يُصَلِّي ثَلاثاً . فَقُلْتُ : يا رَسُولَ اللهِ أَتَنَامُ قَبْلَ أَنْ تُوتِرَ !؟ فقال : « يَا عائِشَةُ إنَّ عَيْنَيَّ تَنَامانِ وَلايَنَامُ قَلْبِي » متفقٌ عليه

1172. **Hazrat Ayesha** (R.A.A.) reports that the Holy Prophet (S.A.W.) offered only eleven raka'ats at night *(Tahajjud prayer)* during the month of *Ramadhan* or any other month. First of all he (S.A.W.) used to offer four raka'ats. But don't ask as to how fine, perfect and lengthy these raka'ats used to be. These were followed by another, but do not ask as to how fine, decent and lengthy these raka'ats used to be. I asked him, O Messenger of Allah ! Do you go to sleep before offering Witr prayer? He (S.A.W.) answered: 'Ayesha! Only my eyes sleep but by heart does not.' *(Bukhari and Muslim)*

١١٧٣ ــ وَعَنْها أنَّ النَّبيَّ ، صلَّى اللهُ عَليهِ وَسَلَّم ، كانَ يَنامُ أَوَّلَ اللَّيْلِ ، وَيقومُ آخِرَهُ فَيُصَلِّي . متفقٌ عليه .

1173. **Hazrat Ayesha** (R.A.A.) says that the Holy Prophet (S.A.W.) used to sleep in the early part of the night and would get up in the latter part and prayed. *(Bukhari and Muslim)*

١١٧٤ ــ وَعَنِ ابنِ مَسْعُودٍ ، رَضِيَ اللهُ عَنْهُ ، قالَ : صَلَّيْتُ مَعَ النَّبيِّ ، صَلَّى اللهُ عَليه وَسلَّمَ لَيْلَةً ، فَلَمْ يَزَلْ قائماً حتَّى هَمَمْتُ بِأَمْرِ سُوءٍ . قِيل : مَاهَمَمْتَ ؟ قالَ : هَمَمْتُ أَنْ أَجْلِسَ وَأَدَعَهُ .

متفق عليه

1174. This Hadis is the same as No. 103 of Chapter 11.

١١٧٥ ــ وَعَنْ حُذَيفَةَ ، رَضِيَ اللهُ عَنْهُ ، قَالَ : صَلَّيْتُ مَعَ النَّبيِّ ، صلَّى اللهُ عَلَيهِ وَسَلَّمَ ، ذاتَ لَيْلَةٍ فَافْتَتَحَ البَقَرَةَ ، فقلتُ : يَرْكَعُ عِنْدَ المِائَةِ ، ثُمَّ مَضَى ، فقلتُ : يُصَلِّي بها في رَكْعَةٍ ، فَمَضَى ، فَقُلْتُ : يَرْكَعُ بها ، ثُمَّ افْتَتَحَ النِّسَاءَ فَقَرَأَها ، ثُمَّ افْتَتَحَ آلَ عِمْرَانَ ، فَقَرَأَها ، يَقْرَأُ مُتَرَسِّلاً . إذا مَرَّ بِآيَةٍ فِيها تَسْبِيحٌ ، سَبَّحَ ، وَإذا مَرَّ بِسُؤَالٍ ، سَأَلَ ، وَإذا مَرَّ بِتَعَوُّذٍ ، تَعَوَّذَ ، ثُمَّ رَكَعَ ، فَجَعَلَ يَقُولُ : سُبْحَانَ رَبِّي العَظِيمِ ، فَكَانَ رُكُوعُهُ نَحْواً مِنْ قِيَامِهِ ، ثُمَّ قالَ : سَمِعَ اللهُ لِمَنْ حَمِدَهُ ، رَبَّنَا لكَ الحَمْدُ ، ثُمَّ قامَ طَوِيلاً قَرِيباً مِمَّا رَكَعَ ، ثُمَّ سَجَدَ فَقَالَ : سُبْحَانَ رَبِّيَ الأَعْلَى ، فَكَانَ سُجُودُهُ قَرِيباً مِنْ قِيَامِهِ . رواه مسلم

1175. This Hadis is the same as No. 102 of Chapter 11.

١١٧٦ – وَعَنْ جَابِرٍ ، رَضِيَ اللهُ عَنْهُ قَالَ : سُئِلَ رَسُولُ اللهِ ، صلَّى اللهُ عليهِ وَسَلَّمَ : أيُّ الصَّلاةِ أفْضَلُ ؟ قالَ : « طُولُ القُنُوتِ » رواه مسلم .

1176. Hazrat Jabir (R.A.A.) relates that the Holy Prophet (S.A.W.) was asked: Which Salat *(prayer)* is better? He (S.A.W.) said: The one in which the Qunut (the standing position) of the worshipper is of a longer duration. *(Muslim)*

١١٧٧. – وَعَنْ عبدِ اللهِ بنِ عَمْرِو بنِ العَاصِ ، رَضِيَ اللهُ عَنْهُمَا ، أنَّ رَسُولَ اللهِ ، صَلَّى اللهُ عَليهِ وسلَّم ، قالَ : « أحَبُّ الصَّلاةِ إلى اللهِ صَلاةُ دَاوُدَ ، وَأحَبُّ الصيامِ إلى اللهِ صِيَامُ دَاوُدَ ، كانَ يَنَامُ نِصْفَ اللَّيْلِ وَيقُومُ ثُلُثَهُ وَيَنَامُ سُدُسَهُ وَيصومُ يَوماً وَيفطِرُ يَوماً » متفقٌ عليه .

1177. This Hadis has been covered in No. 150 of Chapter 14.

١١٧٨ – وَعَنْ جَابِرٍ ، رَضِيَ اللهُ عَنْهُ قَالَ : سَمِعْتُ رَسُولَ اللهِ ، صَلَّى اللهُ عَليهِ وَسَلَّمَ ، يَقُولُ : « إنَّ في اللَّيْلِ لَسَاعَةً ، لايُوافِقُهَا رَجُلٌ مُسلِمٌ يَسْألُ اللهَ تعالى خيْراً مِن أمْرِ الدُّنيا وَالآخِرَةِ ، إلاَّ أعْطَاهُ إيَّاهُ ، وَذلكَ كلَّ لَيْلَةٍ » رواه مسلم .

1178. Hazrat Jabir (R.A.A.) says that he heard from the Holy Prophet (S.A.W.) as saying: The night has got a short spell of time for the grant of prayers, during which, if a Muslim prays for anything beneficial to his life in this world or the next, the same will be granted by Allah; and this time occurs every night. *(Muslim)*

١١٧٩ – وَعَنْ أبي هُرَيرَةَ ، رَضِيَ اللهُ عَنْهُ ، أنَّ النَّبيَّ ، صلَّى اللهُ عَليهِ وسلَّم ، قَالَ : إذا قامَ أحَدُكُم مِنَ اللَّيْلِ فَليَفتَتِحِ الصَّلاةَ بِركعتَيْنِ خَفيفتَيْنِ » رواهُ مُسْلِمٌ

1179. Hazrat Abu Hurairah (R.A.A.) reports that the Holy Prophet (S.A.W.) said: When anyone of you who gets up for the night prayer *(Tahajjud)*, he should start the same with two brief raka'ats. *(Muslim)*

١١٨٠ — وعَنْ عائِشةَ ، رَضِيَ اللهُ عَنها ، قالَتْ : كانَ رَسُولُ اللهِ ، صلّى اللهُ عليه وسَلَّمَ . إذا قامَ مِنَ اللَّيْلِ افتتَحَ صَلاتَهُ بِرَكْعَتَيْنِ خفيفَتَيْنِ ، رواه مسلم

1180. Hazrat Ayesha (R.A.A.) relates that when the Holy Prophet (S.A.W.) used to get up for his night prayer *(Tahajjud)*, he would start with two brief raka'ats. *(Muslim)*

١١٨١ — وعَنها ، رَضِيَ اللهُ عَنها ، قالَتْ : كانَ رَسُولُ اللهِ ، صَلّى اللهُ عَليه وسلّم ، إذا فاتَتْهُ الصَّلاةُ من اللّيل مِنْ وَجَعٍ أوْ غَيْرِهِ ، صَلّى مِنَ النَّهارِ ثِنتَي عَشْرَةَ رَكْعَةً . رواه مسلم .

1181. Hazrat Ayesha (R.A.A.) says that if the Holy Prophet (S.A.W.) missed his night prayer due to pain or some unavoidable circumstances, he (S.A.W.) would offer twelve extra raka'ats (of voluntary prayers) during the day. *(Muslim)*

١١٨٢ — وعَنْ عُمَرَ بنِ الخطّابِ ، رَضِيَ اللهُ عَنْهُ ، قالَ : قالَ رَسُولُ اللهِ ، صَلّى اللهُ عَليهِ وَسَلَّم : « مَنْ نامَ عَنْ حِزْبِهِ ، أوْ عَنْ شَيْءٍ مِنْهُ ، فقرَأهُ فيما بَيْنَ صَلاةِ الفَجْرِ وَصَلاةِ الظُّهْرِ ، كُتِبَ له كأنَّما قرَأهُ مِنَ اللَّيْلِ » رواهُ مُسْلِمٌ .

1182. Hazrat Umar bin Khattab (R.A.A.) relates that the Holy Prophet has said. If a person has forgotten to recite his usual religious chants or anything like this, and went to sleep, and then he recites the same at any time between Fajr and Zuhr prayers, it is accounted for him as if he had offered it during the night. *(Muslim)*

١١٨٣ — وعَنْ أبي هُرَيرَةَ ، رَضِيَ اللهُ عَنْهُ ، قالَ : قالَ رَسُولُ اللهِ ، صَلّى اللهُ عَليهِ وَسَلَّم : « رَحِمَ اللهُ رَجُلاً قامَ مِنَ اللَّيْلِ ، فَصَلّى وَأيْقَظَ امرَأتَهُ ، فإنْ أبَتْ نَضَحَ في وَجْهِها المَاءَ ، رَحِمَ اللهُ امرَأةً قامَتْ مِنَ اللَّيْلِ فَصَلَّتْ ، وَأيْقَظَتْ زَوْجَها فإنْ أبى نَضَحَتْ في وَجْهِهِ الماءَ » رواهُ أبو داود . بإسنادٍ صحيحٍ .

1183. Hazrat Abu Hurairah (R.A.A.) reports that the Holy Prophet (S.A.W.) said: May Allah have mercy on a person who got up at night, offered his voluntary prayer *(Tahajjud)*, and awoke his wife for the same purpose, and if she hesitated, he splashed some water over her face to enable her to get up, similarly, may Allah have the mercy and be much pleased with a woman who gets up at night to offer voluntary prayer *(Tahajjud)* and awakens her husband for the same purpose, and if he hesitates, sprinkles water on his face to make him get up. *(Imam Abu Daud reported this with sound chains).*

١١٨٤ ـ وَعَنْهُ وَعَنْ أَبِي سَعِيدٍ ، رَضِيَ اللهُ عَنْهُمَا ، قَالا : قالَ رسولُ اللهِ صَلَّى اللهُ عَلَيهِ وسَلَّم : « إذا أيقظَ الرَّجُلُ أهْلَهُ مِنَ اللَّيْلِ فَصَلَّيَا ـ أوْ صَلَّى رَكعتَيْنِ جَمِيعاً ، كُتِبَ في الذَّاكِرِينَ وَالذَّاكِرَاتِ » رواهُ أبو داود بإسنادٍ صحيحٍ .

1184. Hazrat Abu Hurairah and Hazrat Abu Sa'eed (R.A.A.) say that the Holy Prophet (S.A.W.) has said: If a man awakens his wife at night for the *Tahajjud* (night prayers) and both offer prayer or offer two raka'ats, they are recorded among those who remember Allah (very much) *(Zakiran wa zakirat* as described in Quran Chapter 33 : 35). *(Abu Daud)*

١١٨٥ ـ وعَنْ عَائِشَةَ ، رَضِيَ اللهُ عَنْهَا ، أنَّ النَّبيَّ صَلَّى اللهُ عَليهِ وسلَّمَ ، قَالَ : « إذا نَعَسَ أحَدُكُمْ في الصَّلاةِ ، فَلْيَرْقُدْ حتى يَذهَبَ عَنْهُ النَّومُ ، فإنَّ أحدَكُمْ إذا صَلَّى وَهو نَاعِسٌ ، لَعَلَّهُ يَذهَبُ يَستَغفِرُ فَيَسُبَّ نَفسَهُ » متفقٌ عليهِ .

1185. This Hadis is the same as No. 147 of Chapter 14.

١١٨٦ ـ وَعَنْ أبي هُرَيرَةَ ، رَضِيَ اللهُ عَنْهُ قَالَ : قَالَ رَسُولُ اللهِ ، صَلَّى اللهُ عَليهِ وَسَلَّمَ : « إذا قَامَ أحَدُكُمْ ، مِنَ اللَّيْلِ فَاستَعجَمَ القُرآنُ على لِسَانِهِ ، فَلَمْ يَدرِ ما يَقُولُ ، فَلْيَضْطَجِعْ » رَواهُ مُسْلِمٌ .

1186. Hazrat Abu Hurairah (R.A.A.) relates that the Holy Prophet (S.A.W.) said: If one of you stands up for *Tahajjud* prayer at night, and finds it difficult to pronounce the verses from the Holy Quran accurately, and may not know as to what he is saying, he should lie down to sleep. *(Muslim)*

* * * * * * *

CHAPTER 213

VIRTUES OF TARAVIH (VOLUNTARY PRAYER) DURING RAMADHAN

١١٨٧ — عَنْ أبي هُرَيرَةَ ، رَضِيَ اللهُ عَنهُ أنَّ رَسُولَ اللهِ صَلّى الله عليهِ وَسلّمَ قالَ : «مَنْ قامَ رَمَضَانَ إيماناً واحتِساباً غُفِرَ لَهُ مَا تَقَدَّمَ مِنْ ذَنْبِهِ » متفقٌ عليهِ .

1187 **Hazrat Abu Hurairah** (R A.A.) relates that the Holy Prophet (S.A.W.) said. Anybody who gets up to offer voluntary prayer during the month of *Ramadhan* with deep sense of belief and self scrutiny will have his previous sins remitted.

(Bukhari and Muslim)

١١٨٨ — وَعَنْهُ ، رَضِيَ اللهُ عَنْهُ ، قَالَ : كانَ رَسُولُ اللهِ ، صَلّى اللهُ عليهِ وَسَلّمَ ، يرَغِّبُ في قِيَامِ رَمَضَانَ مِنْ غَيْرِ أنْ يَأْمُرَهُمْ فيهِ بِعَزِيمَةٍ ، فيقولُ : «مَنْ قامَ رَمَضَانَ إيمَاناً وَاحتِسَاباً غُفِرَ لَهُ مَاتَقَدَّمَ مِنْ ذَنْبِهِ » رَوَاهُ مُسْلِمٌ .

1188 **Hazrat Abu Hurairah** (R.A.A.) relates that the Holy Prophet (S.A.W.) only used to persuade people to offer voluntary prayer during the month of *Ramadhan* but would not order for its observance (so that this may not become an obligatory prayer). He said: One who gets up for voluntary prayer during *Ramadhan* with deep sense for his faith and self scrutiny, will have his past sins remitted.

(Muslim)

Note. The virtues and importance of extra voluntary prayers *(Taravih)* during the month of *Ramadhan*, are established from the sayings and actions of the Holy Prophet (S.A.W.). But during his (S A W) life time its observance as *Taravih* was not enforced so that the same may not become an obligatory duty. But after his (S.A.W.) passing away when there was no danger of its becoming a *farz* compulsory act Hazrat Umar Farooq with the agreement of pious companions introduced it as a voluntary prayer

* * * * * * *

CHAPTER 214

VIRTUES OF PRAYERS DURING THE BLESSED NIGHTS AND AN ACCOUNT OF ITS NIGHTS OF FULL OF HOPES

قالَ اللهُ تعَالى: إنَّا أنزَلْنَاهُ فِي لَيْلَةِ القَدْرِ [القدر : ١] إلى آخرِ السورة

وقال تعالى : إنَّا أنزَلْناهُ في لَيْلَةٍ مُبارَكَةٍ .. الآيات [الدخان : ٣]

Allah the Exalted has said:

288. Lo! We revealed it on the Night of Power. Ah, what will convey unto thee what the Night of Power is ! The Night of Power is better than a thousand months The angels and the Spirit descend therein by the permission of their Lord, with all decrees (That night is) Peace until the rising of the dawn. (97.1 5)

289 Lo ! We revealed it on a blessed night (44.3).

١١٨٩ – وَعَنْ أبي هُرَيرَةَ ، رَضِيَ اللهُ عَنْهُ ، عَنِ النَّبيِّ ، صلَّى اللهُ عَليهِ وَسَلَّمَ قَالَ : « مَنْ قامَ لَيْلَةَ القَدْرِ إيماناً وَاحتِساباً ، غُفِرَ لَهُ مَا تَقَدَّمَ مِنْ ذَنْبِهِ » . مُتفقٌ عليه .

1189. Hazrat Abu Hurairah (R.A.A.) reports the Holy prophet (S.A.W.) as having said that: Anybody who gets up to offer Nafl (voluntary prayer) on the Bleassed Night due to deep sense of his faith and with self scrutiny will have his past sins remitted.

(Bukhari and Muslim)

١١٩٠ – وَعَنِ ابنِ عُمَرَ رَضِيَ اللهُ عَنهُمَا أنَّ رِجالاً مِنْ أصْحابِ النَّبيِّ ، صَلَّى اللهُ عليهِ وسلَّم ، أُرُوا لَيْلَةَ القَدْرِ في المَنامِ في السَّبْعِ الأوَاخِرِ ، فَقَالَ رَسُولُ اللهِ ، صَلَّى اللهُ عَليهِ وَسَلَّمَ : « أرَى رُؤْيَاكُمْ قَدْ تَوَاطَأتْ في السَّبْعِ الأوَاخِرِ ، فَمَنْ كانَ مُتَحَرِّيهَا ، فَلْيَتَحَرَّهَا في السَّبْعِ الأوَاخِرِ » مُتفقٌ عليهِ .

1190 Hazrat Ibn Umar (R.A.A.) states that some companions of the Holy Prophet (S.A.W.) were able to see the Blessed Night among the last seven nights of the month of *Ramadhan* in dream. On this the Holy Prophet (S.A.W.) remarked. Your dreams have confirmed the existence of the Blessed Night among the last seven nights (of *Rama-*

dhan). Therefore anybody who seeks the Blessed Night should look for it among the last seven nights of the month of *Ramadhan.*

(Bukhari and Muslim)

١١٩١ – وعن عائشة رضي الله عنها ، قالت : كان رسول الله ، صلّى الله عليه وسلّم يجاور في العشر الأواخر من رمضان ، ويقول : « تحرّوا ليلة القدر في العشر الأواخر من رمضان » متفق عليه .

1191. **Hazrat Ayesha** (R.A.A.) relates that the Holy Prophet (S.A.W.) used to retire to the mosque for *Itikaf* during the last ten days of *Ramadhan* and say: Search for the Blessed Night among the last ten nights of the month of *Ramadhan.* *(Bukhari and Muslim)*

١١٩٢ – وعنها ، رضي الله عنها ، أنّ رسول الله ، صلّى الله عليه وسلّم ، قال : « تحرّوا ليلة القدر في الوتر من العشر الأواخر من رمضان » رواه البخاري .

1192. **Hazrat Ayesha** (R.A.A.) states that the Holy Prophet (S.A.W.) said: Look for the Blessed Night among the odd nights (i.e. 21st, 23rd, 25th, 27th and 29th) of the last ten nights of *Ramadhan.*

(Bukhari)

١١٩٣ – وعنها ، رضي الله عنها ، قالت : كان رسول الله صلّى الله عليه وسلّم : « إذا دخل العشر الأواخر من رمضان ، أحيا الليل ، وأيقظ أهله ، وجدّ وشدّ المئزر » متفق عليه .

1193. **Hazrat Ayesha** (R.A.A.) relates that when the last ten days of the month of *Ramadhan* began, the Holy Prophet (S.A.W.) used to keep himself awake the whole night, and would also awaken his family members and lighten his belts i.e. he was most assiduous in praying to Allah. *(Bukhari and Muslim)*

١١٩٤ – وعنها قالت : كان رسول الله صلّى الله عليه وسلّم ، يجتهد في رمضان ما لا يجتهد في غيره . وفي العشر الأواخر منه ، ما لا يجتهد في غيره » رواه مسلم .

1194. **Hazrat Ayesha** (R.A.A.) says that the Holy Prophet (S.A.W.) used to endeavour (in worshipping) during the month of *Ramadhan* more than he strove in any other month, and he prayed harder and more earnestly in the last ten days of the month of *Ramadhan* more than he did in the first twenty days of this month.

(Muslim)

١١٩٥ ـ وعَنْهَا قَالَتْ : قُلْتُ : يا رَسُولَ اللهِ أَرَأَيْتَ إن عَلِمْتُ أيَّ لَيْلَةٍ لَيْلَةُ القَدْرِ مَا أقُولُ فيها ؟ قَالَ : « قُولي : اللّهُمّ إنَّكَ عَفُوٌّ تُحِبُّ العَفْوَ فاعْفُ عنّي » رواهُ التِرْمذيُّ وقالَ : حديثٌ حسنٌ صحيحٌ .

1195. Hazrat Ayesha (R.A.A.) says that she asked the Holy Prophet (S.A.W.) : 'O' Messenger of Allah, if I come to locate the Blessed Night then how should I pray in this night? The Holy Prophet (S.A.W.) said: Say, *Alla-humma In-nakaafuwun, tuhibbul'af-wa fa'fo 'an-ni.* (Allah Thous art Most Forgiving and loveth forgiveness then do thou forgive me). *(Tirmizi)*

* * * * * * *

CHAPTER 215

VIRTUES OF CLEANING (BRUSHING) TEETH WITH MISWAK BEING THE NATURAL HABITS

١١٩٦ ـ عَنْ أبي هُرَيرَةَ رَضِيَ اللهُ عَنْهُ ، أنَّ رَسُولَ اللهِ صلّى اللهُ عليهِ وسلَّم ، قَالَ : « لَوْلا أنْ أَشُقَّ عَلَى أُمَّتِي ـ أوْ عَلَى النَّاس ـ لأمَرْتُهُمْ بالسِّوَاكِ مَعَ كلِّ صَلاةٍ » مُتفقٌ عليهِ .

1196. Hazrat Abu Hurairah (R.A.A.) relates that the Holy Prophet (S.A.W.) remarked: Had I not feared that it would cause inconvenience to my Ummah (or people) then I would have prescribed the brushing of teeth with a *miswak* before every prayer. *(Bukhari and Muslim)*

١١٩٧ ـ وعَنْ حُذيفةَ رَضِيَ اللهُ عَنْهُ ، قالَ : كَانَ رَسُولُ اللهِ ، صَلَّى اللهُ عَليهِ وَسلَّم ، إذا قَامَ مِنَ النَّومِ يَشُوصُ فَاهُ بالسِّوَاكِ . متفقٌ عليه .

1197. Hazrat Huzaifah (R.A.A.) says that when the Holy Prophet (S.A.W.) used to get up from sleep he rubbed (brushed) his mouth (teeth) with a twig of a tree. *(Bukhari and Muslim)*

١١٩٨ ـ وعَنْ عَائشةَ رَضِيَ اللهُ عَنْهَا قَالَتْ : كُنَّا نُعِدُّ لرَسُولِ اللهِ صَلَّى اللهُ عليهِ وسلَّم ، سِوَاكَهُ وَطَهُورَهُ ، فَيَبْعَثُهُ اللهُ مَاشَاءَ أنْ يَبعثَهُ مِنَ اللَّيْلِ ، فَيتسَوَّكُ ، وَيَتَوضَّأُ وَيُصَلّي » رَوَاهُ مُسلمٌ .

1198. **Hazrat Ayesha** (R.A.A.) states that before the Holy Prophet (S.A.W) would wake up .we used to keep ready *miswak* (toothbrush) and the water for ablution, so that whenever Allah awakened him during the night, he, (S.A.W.) would first brush his teeth (with *a miswak)* and make his ablution and then offer prayer. *(Muslim)*

١١٩٩ — وعَنْ أنس ، رَضِيَ اللهُ عَنْهُ ، قَالَ : قَالَ رَسُولُ اللهِ ، صَلَّى اللهُ عليه وسلَّمَ : « أَكثرتُ عليكُم في السِّوَاكِ » رواهُ البُخاريُّ .

1199. **Hazrat Anas** (R.A.A.) relates that the Holy Prophet (S.A.W.) said. I have very much impressed upon you about the *miswak* (the importance and utility of brushing your teeth with a *miswak). (Bukhari)*

١٢٠٠ — وعَنْ شُرَيحِ بنِ هانِىءٍ قالَ : قُلْتُ لِعَائِشَةَ ، رَضِيَ اللهُ عَنهَا : بأيِّ شيءٍ كانَ يَبْدَأُ النَّبِيُّ ، صلَّى اللهُ عَليهِ وسَلَّم ، إذا دَخَلَ بَيْتَهُ . قَالَتْ : بِالسِّوَاكِ ، رَوَاهُ مُسْلِمٌ .

1200. **Hazrat Shuraih bin Hani** (R.A.A.) says. I asked Hazrat Ayesha (R.A.A.) what was the first thing that the Holy Prophet (S.A.W.) did on reaching his house? she said. He used to brush his teeth'. *(Muslim)*

١٢٠١ — وعَنْ أبي مُوسَى الأشعَرِيِّ ، رَضِيَ اللهُ عَنْهُ ، قَالَ : دَخَلْتُ عَلى النَّبيِّ صلَّى اللهُ عليهِ وسلَّم ، وَطَرَفُ السِّوَاكِ على لِسانِهِ . مُتَّفَقٌ عَلَيهِ ، وهذا لَفْظُ مُسْلِمٍ .

1201. **Hazrat Abu Musa Ash'ari** (R.A.A.) relates: (Once) I went to the Holy Prophet (S.A.W.) and saw that he held the end of a *miswak* with his tongue. *(Bukhari and Muslim)*

١٢٠٢ — وعَنْ عَائِشَةَ ، رَضِيَ اللهُ عَنْها ، أنَّ النَّبيَّ صلَّى اللهُ عليهِ وسلَّم ، قَالَ : « السِّوَاكُ مَطْهَرَةٌ للفَمِ مَرْضَاةٌ للرَّبِّ » رَوَاهُ النَّسائيُّ ، وابنُ خُزَيْمَةَ في صحيحِهِ بأسانيدَ صحيحةٍ .

1202. **Hazrat Ayesha** (R.A.A.) relates that the Holy Prophet (S.A.W.) said. The *miswak* cleanses the mouth, and pleases the Lord. *(Nisai and Ibn Khuzaimah)*

١٢٠٣ — وَعَنْ أبي هُرَيرَةَ ، رَضِيَ اللهُ عَنْهُ ، عَنِ النَّبيِّ ، صلَّى اللهُ عَليهِ وَسَلَّم ، قَالَ : « الفِطرَةُ خَمْسٌ ، أوْ خَمْسٌ مِنَ الفِطرَةِ : الخِتان ، وَالاسْتِحْدَادُ ، وَتقليمُ الأَظفَارِ ، وَنَتفُ الإبطِ ، وَقَصُّ الشَّارِبِ » مُتفقٌ عليهِ .

1203. **Hazrat Abu Hurairah** (R.A.A.) relates that the Holy Prophet (S.A.W.) said: Five acts are natural or the demands of nature: namely Circumcision, removal of hair which grow around private parts after puberty, impairing of nails, removal of the hair on the lips (moustaches) *(Bukhari and Muslim)*

١٢٠٤ — وَعَنْ عَائِشَةَ رَضِيَ اللهُ عَنْهَا قَالَتْ : قالَ رَسُولُ اللهِ ، صَلَّى اللهُ عليهِ وسلَّم : « عَشْرٌ مِنَ الفِطرَةِ : قَصُّ الشَّارِبِ ، وَإعْفَاءُ اللِّحْيَةِ ، وَالسِّوَاكُ ، واسْتِنشَاقُ المَاءِ ، وَقَصُّ الأَظفَارِ ، وغَسْلُ البَرَاجِمِ ، وَنَتفُ الإبطِ ، وَحَلقُ العَانَةِ ، وانتِقاصُ المَاءِ » قال الرَّاوِي : وَنَسِيتُ العَاشِرَةَ إلاَّ أن تَكونَ المَضمَضَةُ ؛ قالَ وَكيعٌ — وَهُوَ أحَدُ رُوَاتِهِ — : انتِقَاصُ الماءِ ؛ يَعْنِي : الاسْتِنْجَاءَ . رَوَاهُ مُسلِمٌ .

1204. **Hazrat Ayesha** (R.A.A.) relates that the Holy Prophet (S.A.W.) said. There are ten demands of nature (or the true religion—Islam). namely cutting the hair close on the lips (moustaches), letting the beard grow, brushing the teeth (with *Miswak)*, cleaning the nose with water impairing of nails, washing the base of the fingers, removal of the hair in the armpits, and the shaving of hair which grow around private parts after puberty, washing the affected parts after call of nature. The narrator of the Hadis says that he has forgotten the tenth, and says that it might possibly be the rinsing of the mouth. *(Muslim)*

١٢٠٥ — وَعَنِ ابنِ عُمَرَ رَضِيَ اللهُ عَنهُمَا ، عَنِ النَّبيِّ ، صلَّى اللهُ عَليهِ وسلَّم، قالَ : « أحْفُوا الشَّوَارِبَ وأعْفُوا اللِّحَى » مُتفقٌ عليهِ .

1205. **Hazrat Ibn Umar** (R.A.A.) relates that the Holy Prophet (S.A.W.) said: Cut down the hair of the moustache and let the beard grow. *(Bukhari and Muslim)*

* * * * * * *

CHAPTER 216

IMPORTANCE AND VIRTUES OF ZAKAT AND THE RELATED MATTER

قَالَ اللهُ تَعَالَى : (وَأَقِيمُوا الصَّلاةَ . وَآتُوا الزَّكَاةَ) [البقرة : ٤٣] .

وقالَ تَعالى : (وَمَا أُمِرُوا إلاَّ لِيَعْبُدُوا اللهَ مُخلِصِينَ لَهُ الدِّينَ حُنفَاءَ وَيُقِيمُوا الصَّلاةَ وَيُؤْتُوا الزَّكَاةَ . وَذلكَ دِينُ القَيِّمَةِ) [البينة : ٥] .

وقَالَ تَعَالى : (خُذْ مِنْ أَمْوَالِهِمْ صَدَقَةً تُطَهِّرُهُمْ وَتُزَكِّيهِمْ بها) [التوبة : ١٠٣] .

Allah the Exalted has said:

290. Establish worship, pay the Zakat (2: 43)

291. And they are ordered naught else than to serve Allah, keeping religion pure for Him, as men by nature are upright, and to establish prayer and to pay *Zakat*. That is true religion. (98:5)

292. Take alms of their wealth, wherewith thou mayest purify them and mayest make them grow. (9. 103)

١٢٠٦ – وعَنِ ابْنِ عُمَرَ ، رَضِيَ اللهُ عَنْهُمَا ، أَنَّ رَسُولَ اللهِ ، صلَّى اللهُ عَلَيهِ وسَلَّم ، قَالَ : بُنِيَ الإسْلامُ عَلى خَمْسٍ : شَهَادَةِ أَنْ لاإلهَ إلاَّ اللهُ ، وَأَنَّ مُحَمَّداً عَبْدُهُ وَرَسُولُه ، وَإقامِ الصَّلاةِ ، وَإيتاءِ الزَّكَاةِ ، وَحَجِّ البَيْتِ ، وَصَوْمِ رَمَضَانَ . متفقٌ عليه

1206. This Hadith has already been covered in No. 1075 Chapter 193.

١٢٠٧ – وعن طَلْحَةَ بنِ عُبَيْدِ اللهِ ، رَضِيَ اللهُ عَنْهُ ، قالَ : جاءَ رَجُلٌ إلى رَسُولِ اللهِ ، صَلَّى اللهُ عَليهِ وسلَّم ، مِنْ أَهْلِ نَجْدٍ ثَائِرُ الرَّأْسِ نَسْمَعُ دَوِيَّ صَوْتِهِ ، ولانَفْقَهُ ما يقُولُ ، حتى دَنَا مِنْ رَسُولِ اللهِ ، صلَّى اللهُ عَليهِ وسَلَّم ، فإذا هُوَ يَسْأَلُ عَنِ الإسْلامِ ، فَقَالَ رَسُولُ اللهِ ، صَلَّى اللهُ عَليهِ وسَلَّم : «خَمْسُ صَلَوَاتٍ في اليَوْمِ وَاللَّيْلَةِ » قالَ : هَلْ عَلَيَّ غَيْرُهُنَّ؟ قال : « لا ، إلّا أَنْ تَطَوَّعَ » فَقَالَ رَسُولُ اللهِ ، صَلَّى اللهُ عَليه

وسَلَّم : « وصِيامُ شَهرِ رَمَضَانَ » قَالَ : هَلْ عَلَيَّ غَيْرُهُ ؟ قَالَ : « لا ، إلَّا أنْ تَطَوَّعَ » قَالَ : وذَكَرَ لَهُ رَسُولُ اللهِ ، صَلَّى اللهُ عَليه وَسَلَّمَ ، الزَّكَاةَ فَقَالَ : هَلْ عَلَيَّ غَيْرُهَا ؟ قَالَ : « لا ، إلَّا أنْ تَطَوَّعَ » فَأَدْبَرَ الرَّجُلُ وهُوَ يَقُولُ : وَاللهِ لا أَزِيدُ عَلى هَذا ولا أَنْقُصُ مِنْهُ ، فَقَالَ رَسُولُ اللهِ ، صَلَّى اللهُ عَليهِ وسَلَّم : « أَفْلَحَ إنْ صَدَقَ » مُتفقٌ عليهِ

1207. Hazrat Talha bin Ubaidullah (R.A.A.) says: A man from Najd with dishavelled hair came to the Holy Prophet (S.A.W.). We did hear his voice but we could not follow him. When he reached nearer to the Holy Prophet (S.A.W.) we came to know that he was making enquiries about Islam. Replying him the Holy Prophet (S.A.W.) said: There are five obligatory prayers *(Salat)* in a day and night. The man then asked: Are there any more prayers in a day than these ? Holy Prophet (S.A.W.) replied. No, except your voluntary prayers. The Holy Prophet (S.A.W.) further told him: Then there is the fasting of month of Ramadhan. The man asked: Is there any more than that? The Holy Prophet (S.A.W.) Said: No, except voluntary (fasts). Hazrat Talha continuing his report says: Thereafter the Holy Prophet (S.A.W. mentioned to him about the *Zakat*, and the man made the same inquiry as to whether he had to pay anything more, (as compulsory contribution). The Holy Prophet (S.A.W.) said: No, except voluntary contribution. The man then turned away saying: Allah is my witness that I shall not add anything to this nor shall I deduct anything from it. On this the Holy Prophet (S.A.W.) remarked: He succeeded if he is true.

(Bukhari and Muslim)

١٢٠٨ – وَعَنِ ابنِ عَبَّاسٍ ، رَضِيَ اللهُ عَنْهُ ، أَنَّ النَّبِيَّ ، صَلَّى اللهُ عليهِ وسلَّم ، بَعَثَ مُعَاذاً رَضِيَ اللهُ عَنْهُ ، إلى اليَمَنِ فَقَالَ : « ادْعُهُم إلى شَهَادَةِ أَنْ لا إلهَ إلاّ اللهُ وَأَنِّي رَسُولُ اللهِ ، فإنْ هُمْ أَطَاعُوا لِذلكَ ، فَأَعْلِمْهُم أَنَّ اللهَ ، تعَالى ، افترَضَ عَليهِم خَمسَ صَلواتٍ في كُلِّ يَوْمٍ وَلَيلةٍ ، فَإن هُمْ أطاعُوا لِذلكَ فَأَعْلِمْهُمْ أَنَّ اللهَ افترَضَ عَليهم صَدَقَةً تُؤخَذُ مِنْ أَغنِيَائِهِمْ ، وَتُرَدُّ عَلى فُقَرائِهِم » مُتَّفَقٌ عليهِ .

1208 This Hadis has been covered in No. 208 of Chapter 26.

١٢٠٩ – وَعَنِ ابنِ عُمَرَ ، رَضِيَ اللهُ عَنهُمَا ، قَالَ : قَالَ رَسُولُ اللهِ ، صَلَّى اللهُ عَليهِ وسَلَّم : « أُمِرْتُ أَنْ أُقاتِلَ النَّاسَ حتى يَشهدُوا أَنْ

لاإلهَ إلاَّ اللهُ وأنَّ مُحمَّداً رَسُولُ اللهِ ، وَيُقِيمُوا الصَّلاةَ ، وَيُؤْتُوا الزَّكاةَ ، فَإذا فَعَلوا ذلكَ ، عَصَمُوا مِنِّي دِماءَهُم وَأَمْوالَهُمْ إلاَّ بحَقِّ الإسْلامِ ، وَحِسابُهُم عَلى اللهِ » مُتفقٌ عليه .

1209 This Hadis is the same as No. 390 of Chapter 49.

١٢١٠ – وَعنْ أبي هُريرَةَ ، رَضِيَ اللهُ عَنْهُ ، قَالَ : لَمَّا تُوُفِّيَ رَسُولُ اللهِ ، صَلَّى اللهُ عَليه وسَلَّم ، وَكانَ أبُو بَكْرٍ ، رَضِيَ اللهُ عَنْهُ ، وكَفَرَ مَنْ كَفَرَ مِنَ العَرَبِ ، فَقَالَ عُمَرُ رَضِيَ اللهُ عَنْهُ : كيفَ تُقَاتِلُ النَّاسَ وقدْ قَالَ رَسُولُ اللهِ ، صلَّى اللهُ عَليه وسَلَّم : « أُمِرتُ أنْ أُقاتِلَ النَّاسَ حَتَّى يَقُولُوا لا إلهَ إلاَّ اللهُ ، فَمَنْ قالَهَا ، فَقَدْ عَصَمَ مِني مَالَهُ وَنَفْسَهُ إلاَّ بحَقِّهِ ، وَحِسَابُهُ عَلى اللهِ » ؟! فَقَالَ أبُو بَكْرٍ : واللهِ لأُقَاتِلَنَّ مَنْ فَرَّقَ بَيْنَ الصَّلاةِ وَالزَّكاةِ ، فإنَّ الزَّكَاةَ حَقُّ المَالِ . واللهِ لَو مَنَعُوني عِقَالاً كَانُوا يُؤَدُّونَهُ إلى رَسُولِ اللهِ ، صَلَّى اللهُ عَليهِ وَسَلَّمَ ، لَقَاتَلْتُهُمْ عَلى مَنعِه . قَالَ عُمَرُ ، رَضِيَ اللهُ عَنْهُ : فَوَاللهِ مَا هُوَ إلاَّ أنْ رَأيْتُ اللهُ قَدْ شَرَحَ صَدْرَ أبي بَكْرٍ للقِتَالِ ، فَعَرَفْتُ أنَّهُ الحَقُّ . مُتفقٌ عليهِ .

1210. Hazrat Abu Hurairah (R.A.A.) relates: When the Holy Prophet (S.A.W.) passed away and Hazrat Abu Bakr (R.A.A.) became *Khalifa* (Caliph), and some of the Arabs turned heretics, (Hazrat Abu Bakr (R.A.A.) resolved to fight against them. Hazrat Umar (R.A.A.) said to him: How will you fight against them while the Holy Prophet (S.A.W.) has said. I have been commanded to wage war against them till they declare that there is no god save Allah Then one who affirmed this, he made his life and property secure from me except to the extent of his obligations, and he is accountable to Allah (for his faith). Hazrat Abu Bakr (R.A.A.) said: By Allah, I shall certainly fight that person who discriminates between Salat *(Prayer)* and *Zakat* (the poor due). *Zakat* is (Allah's) right in a person's wealth. By Allah! If they hold back from me even equal to a piece of rope of a camel which they paid during the days of the Holy Prophet (S.A.W.), then I shall fight against them for holding this piece of rope back.

Hazrat Umar (R.A.A.) then said: After this I realised that Allah has made the matter of fighting the renegades for the recovery of

Zakat, quite clear to Hazrat Abu Bakr (R.A.A.), and appreciated that Hazrat Abu Bakr (R.A.A.) was right. *(Bukhari and Muslim)*

١٢١١ – وَعَنْ أَبِي أَيوبَ رَضِيَ اللهُ عَنْهُ ، أَنَّ رَجُلاً قَالَ لِلنَّبِيِّ ، صَلَّى اللهُ عَلَيهِ وسَلَّم : أَخْبِرْنِي بِعَمَلٍ يُدْخِلُنِي الجَنَّةَ ، قَالَ : « تَعْبُدُ اللهَ لاتُشْرِكُ بِهِ شَيْئاً ، وَتُقِيمُ الصَّلاةَ ، وَتُؤْتِي الزَّكاةَ ، وَتَصِلُ الرَّحِمَ » مُتَّفَقٌ عليه .

1211. Hazrat Abu Ayub (R.A.A.) reports that a man requested the Holy Prophet (S.A.W.) : Please let me know the act which would entitle me for admission into the paradise. He (S.A.W.) said: Worship Allah, do not associate anything (partner) with Him, establish (observe) salat, pay *zakat*, and treat well blood relations.

(Bukhari and Muslim)

١٢١٢ – وَعَنْ أَبِي هُرِيرَةَ ، رَضِيَ اللهُ عَنْهُ ، أَنَّ أَعرَابِياً أَتَى النَّبِيَّ ، صَلَّى اللهُ عَلَيهِ وسَلَّم فَقَالَ : يا رَسُولَ اللهِ دُلَّنِي عَلى عَمَلٍ إذا عَمِلْتُهُ ، دَخَلْتُ الجَنَّةَ . قَالَ : « تَعْبُدُ اللهَ لا تُشْرِكُ بِهِ شَيْئاً ، وَتُقِيمُ الصَّلاةَ ، وَتُؤْتِي الزَّكاةَ المَفْرُوضَةَ ، وَتَصُومُ رَمَضَانَ » قَالَ : وَالذي نَفْسِي بِيَدِهِ ، لا أَزِيدُ عَلى هذا . فَلَمَّا وَلَّى ، قالَ النَّبِيُّ ، صلَّى اللهُ عَليهِ وسَلَّم ، « مَنْ سَرَّهُ أَنْ يَنْظُرَ إلى رَجُلٍ مِنْ أَهْلِ الجَنَّةِ فَلْيَنْظُرْ إلى هذا » مُتفقٌ عليهِ .

1212. Hazrat Abu Hurairah (R.A.A.) says: Once a village folk came to the Holy Prophet (S.A.W.) and submitted "O' Messenger of Allah, please let me know the act which would lead me into paradise. He (S.A.W.) told him: Worship Allah without associating anything with Him, establish salat, pay the prescribed *zakat* and observe the fast of *Ramadhan*. The man said: By Him in Whose Hands is my life,I will not do more than this. When he went away the Holy Prophet (S.A.W.) addressing his companions said: Anybody who wants to see a dweller of paradise, should see this man. *(Bukhari and Muslim)*

١٢١٣ – وَعَنْ جَرِيرِ بنِ عبدِ اللهِ ، رَضِيَ اللهُ عَنْهُ ، قَالَ : بَايَعْتُ النَّبِيَّ . صلَّى اللهُ عَليهِ وسَلَّم . عَلى إقَامِ الصَّلاةِ ، وَإِيتَاءِ الزَّكاةِ ، والنُّصْحِ لِكُلِّ مُسْلِمٍ . مُتَّفَقٌ عَلَيهِ

1213. Hazrat Jarir bin Abdullah (R.A.A.) states: I have taken a pledge with the Holy Prophet (S.A.W.) to observe salat *(prayer)*, pay the *Zakat* (poor due) and to be sincere and well wisher to every Muslim.

(Bukhari and Muslim)

١٢١٤ — وعَنْ أبي هريرةَ رَضِيَ اللهُ عنْهُ قالَ : قَالَ رسولُ اللهِ ، صَلَّى اللهُ علَيهِ وسلَّمَ : « مَامِنْ صَاحِبِ ذهَبٍ ، ولا فِضَّةٍ ، لايُؤدِّي مِنْهَا حقَّهَا إلاَّ إذاكَانَ يَوْمُ القِيَامَةِ صُفِّحَتْ لهُ صَفَائِحُ مِنْ نَارٍ ، فَأُحْمِيَ علَيْهَا في نارِ جهَنَّمَ ، فيُكْوَى بهَا جَنْبُهُ ، وجَبِينُهُ ، وظَهْرُهُ ، كُلَّمَا بَرَدَتْ أُعِيدَتْ لهُ في يَوْمٍ كَانَ مِقْدَارُهُ خَمْسِينَ أَلْفَ سَنَةٍ ، حتَّى يُقْضَى بَيْنَ العِبَادِ فيُرَى سَبِيلُهُ ، إمَّا إلى الجنَّةِ ، وإمَّا إلى النَّارِ » قِيلَ : يا رَسُولَ اللهِ فَالإبلُ ؟ قَالَ : « ولا صاحِبِ إبلٍ لايُؤدِّي مِنْهَا حقَّهَا : ومِنْ حقِّهَا حلَبُهَا يَوْمَ وِرْدِها ، إلاَّ إذا كانَ يَوْمُ القِيامَةِ بُطِحَ لهَا بِقَاعٍ قَرْقَرٍ أوْفَرَ ماكَانَتْ ، لا يَفْقِدُ مِنْهَا فَصِيلاً واحِداً ، تَطَؤُهُ بأَخْفَافِهَا ، وتَعَضُّهُ بِأَفْوَاهِها ، كُلَّمَا مرَّ علَيْهِ أُولاها ، رُدَّ علَيْهِ أُخْرَاها ، في يومٍ كانَ مِقْدارُه خَمْسِينَ أَلْفَ سَنةٍ ، حتَّى يُقْضَى بَيْنَ العِبَادِ ، فيُرَى سَبِيلُه ، إمَّا إلى الجنَّةِ وإمَّا إلى النارِ » .

قِيلَ : يَا رسولَ اللهِ فَالبَقَرُ والغَنَمُ ؟ قالَ : « ولا صَاحِبِ بقَرٍ ولا غَنَمٍ لايُؤدِّي مِنْها حقَّهَا ، إلاَّ إذا كانَ يَوْمُ القِيامَةِ ، بُطِحَ لهَا بقَاعٍ قَرْقَرٍ ، لايَفْقِد مِنْهَا شَيْئاً ، لَيْسَ فِيها عَقْصَاءُ ، ولا جَلْحَاءُ ، ولا عَضْبَاءُ ، تَنْطَحُهُ بِقُرُونِهَا ، وتَطَؤُهُ بِأَظْلافِهَا ، كُلَّمَا مرَّ علَيْهِ أُولاها ، رُدَّ علَيْهِ أُخْرَاها ، في يَومٍ كانَ مِقْدَارُهُ خَمْسِينَ أَلْفَ سَنَةٍ حتَّى يُقْضَى بَيْنَ العِبَادِ ، فيُرَى سَبِيلُهُ إمَّا إلى الجنَّةِ وإمَّا إلى النَّارِ » .

قِيلَ : يارَسُولَ اللهِ فالخَيْلُ ؟ قَالَ : « الخَيْلُ ثَلاثَةٌ : هِيَ لِرَجُلٍ وِزْرٌ ، وهِيَ لِرجُلٍ سِتْرٌ ، وهِيَ لِرجُلٍ أَجْرٌ ، فَأمَّا التي هِيَ لهُ وِزْرٌ فَرَجُلٌ رَبَطَهَا رِيَاءً وفَخْراً ونِواءً على أَهْلِ الإسْلامِ ، فَهِيَ لَهُ وِزْرٌ ، وأَمَّا التي هِيَ لَهُ سِتْرٌ ، فَرَجُلٌ رَبَطَهَا فِي سبِيلِ اللهِ ، ثُمَّ لَمْ يَنْسَ حَقَّ اللهِ في ظُهُورِها ، ولا رِقابِهَا ؛ فهِيَ لَهُ سِتْرٌ ، وأَمَّا التي هِيَ لَهُ أَجْرٌ ، فرَجُلٌ رَبَطَهَا في سَبِيلِ اللهِ لأَهْلِ الإسْلامِ في مَرْجٍ ، أو رَوْضَةٍ ، فمَا أَكَلَتْ

مِن ذلكَ المَرجِ أوِ الرَّوضَةِ مِن شَيءٍ إلاَّ كُتِبَ لَهُ عَدَدَ مَا أكَلَتْ حَسَنَاتٌ، وَكُتِبَ لَهُ عَدَدَ أروَاثِهَا وَأبوَالِهَا حَسَنَاتٌ، وَلاتَقطَعُ طِوَلَهَا فاستَنَّتْ شَرَفاً أو شَرَفَينِ إلاَّ كَتَبَ اللهُ لَهُ عَدَدَ آثَارِهَا، وأروَاثِهَا حَسَنَاتٍ، وَلامَرَّ بِهَا صَاحِبُهَا عَلَى نَهرٍ، فَشَرِبَت مِنهُ، وَلايُرِيدُ أن يَسقِيَهَا إلاَّ كَتَبَ اللهُ لَهُ عَدَدَ مَاشَرِبَت حَسَنَاتٍ » .

قِيلَ : يا رسولَ اللهِ فالحُمُرُ؟ قالَ : « مَا أُنزِلَ عَلَيَّ فِي الحُمُرِ شَيءٌ إلاَّ هذهِ الآيَةُ الفَاذَّةُ الجَامِعَةُ : (فَمَن يَعمَل مِثقَالَ ذَرَّةٍ خَيراً يَرَهُ . وَمَن يَعمَل مِثقَالَ ذَرَّةٍ شَرّاً يَرَهُ) .

مُتَّفَقٌ عَلَيهِ . وهذا لفظُ مُسلِمٍ .

1214. Hazrat Abu Hurairah (R.A.A.) says that the Holy Prophet (S.A.W.) said: A wealthy person who has got gold and silver, but does not pay the *Zakat* due on the same, (should know that) his gold and silver will be melted on the Day of Judgement and converted into slabs which will then be heated in the fire of Hell, and then his sides, his forehead, and his back will be branded therewith. When these slabs will get cold, they will be heated up once more in the furnace of the Hell, the branding will be continued throughout the day, the duration of which will be equal to fifty thousand years, and the cases of all the people will have been decided by this time and they will be shown their way either to the Hell or to Paradise.

The Companions submitted: 'O Messenger of Allah, what about camels? He (S.A.W.) said: In the same way, the owner of camels who does not pay the *Zakat* which is due in respect of them, and apart from *zakat* the milk of the camels which the day she is given water, is to be given in charity, and if he fails to do so then such a person will be thrown on his face in a wide and level plain on the Day of Judgement to be trampled upon by the camels. These camels will be very sturdy and fat and not one from among them, or even a baby camel will be missing. They will trample him under their feet, and will tear him apart with their teeth. When the last of them will have passed over him, the first of them will begin the operation once again throughout a day the length of which will be equal to fifty thousand years, till all men have been judged and they will be shown their way either to Paradise or to the Hell (as the case may be).

Then he was asked: 'O Messenger of Allah, what are the orders as regards cows and goats? He (S.A.W.) answered: Similarly if a person owning cows and goats does not pay the *Zakat* due on account of these animals, will on the Day of Judgement, be thrown on his face, in a wide level plain, when none of the animals will be missing and none will be without horns. They will tear him with their horns, and trample him under their hoofs, and when one side has finished, the other side will begin, throughout a day, the length of which will be equal to fifty thousand years, and by this time all persons would have been judged and each of them shown his way either to paradise or to the Hell. (according to the nature of his case). The Holy Prophet (S.A.W.) was then asked: 'O Messenger of Allah, what about (those persons who own) horses? He (S.A.W.) said: Horses are divided into three categories, firstly which are a burden for their owner, secondly those which are a cover for him, and thirdly those which make their owner worthy of reward. As regards those who are a burden for their owner, they are the ones, who are reared for show or for pride or for causing aggression on the Muslims. They will be a cause of torment for their owner. Those which cover for their owner are those that are reared by him for service in the cause of Allah *(Jihad)* and he does not forget that which is due to Allah in respect of their backs and their necks. They are his cover. Those which will earn reward for their owner, are those which are reared in meadows and gardens (on green and fresh grass) for being used in the cause of Allah *(Jihad)* by the Muslims. For each straw or blade of grass they eat from these meadows, will be written down one virtue for their owner, and whenever they drop their droppings and urine etc., all these acts are counted for an equal number of virtue for him. Every piece of rope which is used (and broken) in their jumping, and every hillock from which they jump, and for every sound of the animals's feet or hoof mark, an equal number of virtues is recorded for him. And when their owner takes them through water (retreat, pond etc.) and they drink water from it, whether their owner intended them to do so or not, every mouthful of water they take counts as a virtue for him.

The people then asked the Holy Prophet (S.A.W.) : O Messenger of Allah, what are the orders about donkeys? He (S.A.W.) said: no particular orders have been revealed to me about them, but there is a comprehensive and valuable verse (worth consideration in this connection) : 'whoso will have done the smallest, And whose doeto good an atom's weight, will see it then, and whoso doeth ill an atom's weight will see it then. (99:7—8).

(Bukhari and Muslim; this wording is quoted from Muslim)

* * * * * * *

CHAPTER 217

OBLIGATORY NATURE OF FASTING DURING RAMADHAN, ITS VIRTUES AND RELATED TOPICS

قَالَ اللهُ تَعَالَى : يَا أَيُّهَا الَّذِينَ آمَنُوا كُتِبَ عَلَيْكُمُ الصِّيَامُ كَمَا كُتِبَ عَلَى الَّذِينَ مِنْ قَبْلِكُمْ إلى قوله تعالى : شَهْرُ رَمَضَانَ الَّذِي أُنْزِلَ فِيهِ الْقُرْآنُ هُدىً لِلنَّاسِ ، وَبَيِّنَاتٍ مِنَ الْهُدَى وَالْفُرْقَانِ فَمَنْ شَهِدَ مِنْكُمُ الشَّهْرَ فَلْيَصُمْهُ ، وَمَنْ كَانَ مَرِيضاً ، أَوْ عَلَى سَفَرٍ ، فَعِدَّةٌ مِنْ أَيَّامٍ أُخَرَ . الآية [البقرة : ١٨٣-١٨٥] .

Allah, the Exalted, has said:

293. 'O' ye who believe ! Fasting is prescribed for you, even as it was prescribed for those before you, that ye may ward off (evil); (fast) a certain number of days; and (for him who is sick among you, or on a journey, (the same) number of other days; and for those who can afford it there is a ransom the feeding of a man in need — But whoso doeth good of his own accord, it is better for him: and that ye fast is better for you if ye did but know. The month of Ramadhan in which was revealed the Quran, a guidance for mankind, and clear proofs of the guidance, and the criterion (of right and wrong). And whosoever of you is present, let him fast the month and whosoever of you is sick or on a journey (let him fast the same) number of other days. (2 : 183—185)

١٢١٥ — وَعَنْ أَبِي هُرَيْرَةَ رَضِيَ اللهُ عَنْهُ ، قَالَ :

قالَ رَسُولُ اللهِ صَلَّى اللهُ عَلَيْهِ وَسَلَّم : « قَالَ اللهُ عَزَّ وَجَلَّ : كُلُّ عَمَلِ ابْنِ آدَمَ لَهُ إلاَّ الصِّيَامَ ، فَإِنَّهُ لِي وَأَنَا أَجْزِي بِهِ . وَالصِّيَامُ جُنَّةٌ ؛ فَإِذَا كَانَ يَوْمُ صَوْمِ أَحَدِكُمْ فَلا يَرْفُثْ وَلا يَصْخَبْ ، فَإِنْ سَابَّهُ أَحَدٌ أَوْ قَاتَلَهُ ، فَلْيَقُلْ : إنِّي صَائِمٌ . وَالَّذِي نَفْسُ مُحَمَّدٍ بِيَدِهِ لَخُلُوفُ فَمِ الصَّائِمِ أَطْيَبُ عِنْدَ اللهِ مِنْ رِيحِ الْمِسْكِ . لِلصَّائِمِ فَرْحَتَانِ يَفْرَحُهُمَا : إذاأَفْطَرَ فَرِحَ بِفِطْرِهِ ،وَإذالَقِيَ رَبَّهُ فَرِحَ بِصَوْمِهِ » متفقٌ عليه

وهذا لفظ روايةِ الْبُخَارِي . وفي روايةٍ له : « يَتْرُكُ طَعَامَهُ ، وَشَرَابَهُ ، وَشَهْوَتَهُ ، مِنْ أَجْلِي ، الصِّيَامُ لِي وَأَنَا أَجْزِي بِهِ ، وَالْحَسَنَةُ بِعَشْرِ

أمْثَالِهَا .

وفي روايةٍ لمسلمٍ : « كُلُّ عَمَلِ ابْنِ آدَمَ يُضَاعَفُ : الحَسَنَةُ بِعَشْرِ أمْثَالِهَا إلى سَبْعِمائة ضِعْفٍ . قال الله تعالى : « إلاَّ الصَّوْمَ فَإنَّهُ لي وَأنَا أجْزِي بِهِ : يَدَعُ شَهْوَتَهُ وَطَعَامَهُ مِنْ أجْلي . لِلصَّائِمِ فَرْحَتَانِ : فَرْحَةٌ عِنْدَ فِطْرِهِ ، وَفَرْحَةٌ عِنْدَ لِقَاءِ رَبِّهِ . ولَخُلُوفُ فيه أطْيَبُ عِنْدَ اللهِ مِنْ رِيحِ المِسْكِ » .

1215. Hazrat Abu Hurairah (R.A.A.) says that the Holy Prophet (S.A.W.) said: Allah, the Almighty and Master of Honour says : All other actions of a person are for himself, except the case of his fasting which is exclusively for Me and I shall pay (recompense) for him for the same. The fast is a shield (against vice and the fire of Hell). Therefore when anyone of you is fasting he should abstain from loose talk and avoid verbosity and noisy exchange of words. If somebody starts abusing him or picks up a quarrel with him, he should tell him that 'I am observing a fast.' By Allah in whose hands is the life of Muhammad (S.A.W.), the breath of the mouth of one who is fasting is more pleasant in the sight of Allah than the fragrance of musk. A fasting person gets two kinds of pleasure: firstly he feels pleasure when he breaks his fast, and secondly he will be joyful by virtue of his fast, when he meets his sustainer. *(Bukhari and Muslim)*

This is the wording of *Bukhari.*

Another version of *Bukhari* adds: Allah says: The fasting person abstains from food, drink and from satisfying his passion simply for My sake; as such a fast is undertaken for My sake, I shall grant him the recompense for this. Other virtuous deeds (done in the month of Ramadhan) are rewarded ten times.

Imam Muslim's version says: A man's good acts are recompensed many times, from ten times to seven hundred times. Allah the Exalted says: But a fast is an exception because it is undertaken simply for My sake, (i.e. there is no limit for its recompenses.) I, Alone, shall bestow the reward for it. (The person who observes a fast), gives up his food, drink and sensual desires for My sake. For a fasting person there are two pleasures; firstly a joy when he breaks his fast and secondly another joy when he meets his Lord. His breath is more pleasant in the sight of Allah than the fragrance of musk.

١٢١٦ – وعنهُ أنَّ رسولَ اللهِ صَلَّى اللهُ عليهِ وسلَّمَ قالَ : « مَنْ أنْفَقَ زَوْجَيْنِ في سَبِيلِ اللهِ نُودِيَ مِنْ أبْوابِ الجَنَّةِ : يَا عَبْدَ اللهِ هذا خَيْرٌ ،

فَمَنْ كَانَ مِنْ أَهْلِ الصَّلاةِ دُعِيَ مِنْ بَابِ الصَّلاةِ ، وَمَنْ كانَ مِنْ أَهْلِ الجِهَادِ دُعِيَ مِنْ بَابِ الجِهَادِ ، وَمَنْ كَانَ مِنْ أَهْلِ الصِّيَامِ دُعِيَ مِنْ بَابِ الرَّيَّانِ ، وَمَنْ كَانَ مِنْ أَهْلِ الصَّدَقَة دُعِيَ مِنْ بَابِ الصَّدَقَةِ » قال أبو بكرٍ ، رَضِيَ اللهُ عَنهُ : بِأَبِي أَنتَ وَأُمِّي يارسولَ اللهِ ! ما عَلَى مَنْ دُعِيَ مِنْ تِلكَ الأَبْوابِ مِنْ ضَرُورَةٍ ، فهلْ يدعَى أَحَدٌ مِنْ تِلكَ الأَبْوابِ كلِّهَا ؟ قال : « نَعَم وَأَرْجُو أَنْ تكونَ مِنهم » متفقٌ عليه .

1216. Hazrat Abu Hurairah (R.A.A.) relates that the Holy Prophet (S.A.W.) said: A person who spends a pair of anything for the sake of Allah, will be called from the gates of Paradise thus: 'O Servant of Allah, this gate is better for thee. Thus a person who is regular in offering Salat (prayer) will be called from the gate of Salat and those persons who undertake Jihad for the sake of Allah, will be called (to enter into heaven) from the gate of Raiyan i.e. the gate of freshness. The person who gives alms, will be called (to enter paradise from the gate of charity). Hazrat Abu Bakr (R.A.A.) said, 'O Messenger of Allah ! May my parents be sacrificed for you, although a person who is called (to enter heaven) from any of these gates, does not need this, yet will any one be called from all these gates? He (S.A.W.) answered: Yes, and I hope that you will be one of them?

(Bukhari and Muslim)

١٢١٧ - وعنْ سهلِ بنِ سعدٍ رضيَ اللهُ عنهُ عنِ النَّبيِّ ، صَلَّى اللهُ عَلَيهِ وسلَّمَ ، قالَ : « إنَّ في الجَنَّةِ بَاباً يُقَالُ لهُ : الرَّيَّانُ ، يَدْخُلُ مِنهُ الصَّائِمُونَ يَومَ القِيامةِ ، لايدخلُ مِنْهُ أَحَدٌ غيرهم ، يقالُ : أَينَ الصَّائِمُونَ ؟ فَيَقومونَ لايدخلُ مِنهُ أَحَدٌ غيرهم ، فَإِذا دَخَلوا أُغلِقَ فَلَم يَدخلَ مِنْهُ أَحَدٌ » متفقٌ عليه .

1217. Hazrat Sahl bin Sa'd (R.A.A.) says that the Holy Prophet (S.A.W.) said: There is a gate in Paradise known as 'Ar-Raiyan' through which only fasting persons will enter on the Day of Judgement, and no one else. It will be said: where are the fasting persons? They will come forward. No one will enter it except them. After they shall have entered, the gate will be closed and no one else will enter thereafter.

(Bukhari and Muslim)

١٢١٨ - وعَنْ أبي سَعيدِ الخُدْرِيِّ ، رضيَ اللهُ عنهُ ، قالَ : قالَ رَسولُ اللهِ ، صَلَّى اللهُ عليهِ وسلَّم : « مَا مِنْ عَبْدٍ يصُومُ يَوماً في سَبيلِ اللهِ إلاَّ

بَاعَدَ اللهُ بِذلكَ اليَومِ وَجهَهُ عَنِ النَّارِ سَبعِينَ خَرِيفاً » متفقٌ عليه

1218. **Hazrat Abu Sa'eed Khudri** (R.A.A.) reports that the Holy Prophet (S,A.W.) said: when a person fasts for a day, for the sake of Allah, then Allah drives away the Hell from him to a distance of seventy years of travelling. *(Bukhari and Muslim)*

١٢١٩ – وعنْ أبي هُرَيْرَةَ ، رضِيَ اللهُ عَنْهُ ، عَنِ النَّبِيِّ ، صَلَّى اللهُ عَلَيْهِ وَسَلَّمَ ، قالَ : « مَنْ صَامَ رَمَضَانَ إيمَاناً واحْتِسَاباً ، غفِرَ لهُ ما تَقَدَّمَ مِنْ ذنْبِهِ » متفقٌ عليه .

1219. **Hazrat Abu Hurairah** (R.A.A.) says that the Holy Prophet (S.A.W.) said: A person who fasts during the month of Ramadhan with faith self scrutiny, will have his past sins remitted. *(Bukhari and Muslim)*

١٢٢٠ – وعنهُ ، رضيَ اللهُ عنهُ ، أنَّ رسولَ اللهِ ، صَلَّى اللهُ عليهِ وسلَّمَ . قالَ : « إذا جَاءَ رَمَضَانُ ، فُتِّحتْ أبْوَابُ الجنَّةِ ، وَغُلِّقَتْ أبْوَابُ النَّارِ ، وصُفِّدَتِ الشَّيَاطِينُ » متفقٌ عليه .

1220. **Hazrat Abu Hurairah** (R.A.A.) relates that the Holy Prophet (S.A.W.) said: When the month of Ramadhan arrives the gates of the Paradise are opened, and those of the Hell are closed up, and the Satans are imprisoned. *(Bukhari and Muslim)*

١٢٢١ – وعنهُ أنَّ رسولَ اللهِ ، صلَّى اللهُ عليهِ وسلَّمَ ، قالَ : صُومُوا لِرُؤْيَتِهِ ، وَأفْطِرُوا لِرُؤْيَتِهِ ، فإن غَبِيَ عَليكم ، فَأكْمِلُوا عِدَّةَ شَعْبَانَ ثَلاثِينَ » متفقٌ عليه وهذا لفظ البخاري .

وفي روايةِ مسلم : « فَإنْ غُمَّ عَليكم فَصُومُوا ثَلاثِينَ يَوْماً » .

1221. **Hazrat Abu Hurairah** (R.A.A.) says that the Holy Prophet (S.A.W.) said: Start fasting on seeing the new moon and stop fasting also on observing the same. If you are unable to spot it due to the sky being cloudy then treat the month of Shaban as of 30 days. *(Bukhari and Muslim)*

Another version of Imam Muslim adds: Similarly, if the new moon is invisible (due to clouds) at the end of Ramadhan, then fast for 30 days.

* * * * * * *

CHAPTER 218

INCREASED GENEROSITY AND VIRTUOUS DEEDS DURING THE MONTH OF RAMADHAN PARTICULARLY IN ITS LAST TEN DAYS

١٢٢٢ – وعن ابنِ عباسٍ ، رضيَ اللهُ عنهما ، قالَ : كانَ رَسُولُ اللهِ ، صَلَّى اللهُ عَلَيْهِ وَسَلَّمَ ، أجودَ النَّاسِ ، وكانَ أجْوَدَ ما يكُونُ في رَمضانَ حينَ يلْقاهُ جبريلُ ، وكانَ جبريلُ يلقاهُ في كُلِّ ليلةٍ مِنْ رَمَضَانَ فيُدارِسُهُ القرآنَ ، فلَرسُولُ اللهِ ، صلَّى اللهُ عليهِ وسلَّمَ ، حينَ يلقاهُ جبريلُ أجْوَدُ بالخيْرِ مِنَ الرِّيحِ المُرْسَلَةِ » متفقٌ عليه .

1222. Hazrat Ibn Abbas (R.A.A.) says that the Holy Prophet(S.A.W.) was the most generous person among all the men, particularly during the month of Ramadhan he (S.A.W.) used to be extraordinarily benevolent and generous when he met Gabriel. And during this month Angel Gabriel used to visit him every night and recite the Holy Quran to him. At this time the normal generosity of the Holy Prophet (S.A.W.) used to be very much increased, faster than the rain-bearing wind.

(Bukhari and Muslim)

١٢٢٣ – وعَنْ عائشةَ رضيَ اللهُ عنها قالَتْ : « كانَ رَسُولُ اللهِ ، صَلَّى اللهُ عَلَيْهِ وسلَّمَ ، إذا دَخَلَ العَشرُ أحيا اللَّيْلَ ، وأيقَظَ أهْلَهُ ، وشَدَّ المئزرَ » متفقٌ عليه .

1223. This Hadis has been covered in No. 1193 of Chapter 214.

* * * * * * *

CHAPTER 219

PROHIBITION OF FASTING BEFORE A DAY OR TWO OF RAMADHAN AND THE SECOND FORTNIGHT OF SHABAN EXCEPT ONE WHO IS ACCUSTOMED TO KEEPING FAST ON MONDAYS AND THURSDAYS

١٢٢٤ – عن أبي هُريرةَ ، رضيَ اللهُ عَنْهُ ، عنِ النبيِّ ، صلَّى اللهُ عليهِ وآلهِ وسلَّمَ ، قال : « لايتَقَدَّمَنَّ أحَدُكم رَمَضَانَ بِصَومِ يَومٍ أوْ يومَيْنِ ، إلاّ أنْ يكونَ رَجُلٌ كَانَ يَصُومُ صَوْمَهُ ، فَلْيَصُمْ ذلكَ اليَوْمَ » متّفقٌ عليه .

1224. **Hazrat Abu Hurairah** (R.A.A.) relates that the Holy Prophet (S.A.W.) said: None of you should observe the fast on one or two days just before the month of Ramadhan except in the case of a person who is accustomed to fasting on these days, so he may fast on that day. *(Bukhari and Muslim)*

١٢٢٥ – وعن ابنِ عباسٍ ، رضيَ اللهُ عنهما ، قال : قالَ رسولُ اللهِ ، صلّى اللهُ عَلَيْهِ وسلَّم : « لاتَصُومُوا قَبْلَ رَمَضَانَ ، صُومُوا لِرُؤْيَتِهِ ، وَأَفْطِرُوا لِرُؤْيَتِهِ ، فَإِنْ حَالَتْ دُونَهُ غَيَايَةٌ فَأَكْمِلُوا ثَلاثِينَ يَوماً » رواه الترمذي وقال : حديث حسنٌ صحيحٌ .

1225. **Hazrat Ibn Abbas** (R.A.A.) reports that the Holy Prophet (S.A.W.) said: Do not observe fasting before the month of Ramadhan, rather you should start your fast after sighting the new moon and terminate it after sighting the (next) new moon. If the weather be cloudy, let the month of (Shaban or Ramadhan) be of thirty days. *(Tirmizi)*

١٢٢٦ – وعنْ أبي هُرَيْرَةَ ، رَضِيَ اللهُ عَنْهُ قالَ : قالَ رسولُ اللهِ ، صلّى اللهُ عليهِ وسلم : « إذا بَقِيَ نِصْفٌ مِنْ شَعْبَانَ فَلا تَصُومُوا » رواه الترمذي وقال : حديثٌ حَسَنٌ صَحِيح .

1226. **Hazrat Abu Hurairah** (R.A.A.) relates that the Holy Prophet (S.A.W.) said: You should not fast when the second half of Shaban starts. *(Imam Tirmizi* who has quoted this tradition, says that it is sound).

١٢٢٧ – وَعَنْ أبي اليَقظانِ عمارِ بنِ ياسرٍ ، رضيَ اللهُ عَنْهما ، قالَ : « مَن صَامَ اليَوْمَ الّذي يُشَكُّ فيهِ فَقَدْ عَصَى أَبَا القَاسِمِ ، صلّى اللهُ عَلَيْهِ وَسَلَّمَ » رواه أبو داود ، والترمذي وقالَ : حديثٌ حَسَنٌ صَحِيحٌ .

1227. **Hazrat Abu Yaqzan 'Ammar bin Yasir** (R.A.A.) said. One who observes fast on a doubtful day (i.e. non visibility of moon due to clouds) disobeys the Holy Prophet,Abul Qasim (Hazrat Muhammad S.A.W.). *(Abu Daud and Tirmizi*, Latter said it is sound).

* * * * * * *

CHAPTER 220

WHAT TO SUPPLICATE ON SIGHTING THE NEW MOON

١٢٢٨ – عَنْ طَلْحَةَ بنِ عُبَيْدِ اللهِ ، رَضِيَ اللهُ عَنْهُ ، أَنَّ النبيَّ ، صلَّى اللهُ عليهِ وسلَّم ، كانَ إذا رَأى الهِلالَ قالَ : « اللهُمَّ أهِلَّهُ عَلَيْنَا بِالأَمنِ والإيمَانِ ، وَالسَّلامَةِ والإسْلامِ ، رَبِّي وَرَبُّكَ اللهُ ، هِلالُ رُشْدٍ وخَيْرٍ » رواه الترمذي وقالَ : حديثٌ حَسَنٌ .

1228. Hazrat Talha bin 'Ubaidullah (R.A.A.) says that on sighting a new moon, the Holy Prophet (S.A.W.) used to pray thus:

Allahumma Ahillahu'Alaina Bil Am'ne Wal Imane Was-salam 'e Wal Islam Rabbi wa Rabbukal-lah. Hilal-o-rush'din wa Khairin.

'O' Allah, do let the appearance of this moon be a forerunner of peace, faith, safety and Islam for us. (O moon) mine and your Lord is Allah. May this be a moon of (right) guidance and virtue *(Imam Tirmizi* called this as sound).

* * * * * * *

CHAPTER 221

VIRTUE OF TAKING FOOD BEFORE DAWN (SAHRI) IN THE LAST HOURS OF NIGHT (DURING RAMADHAN) AS LONG AS APPEARANCE OF DAWN IS NOT FEARED

١٢٢٩ – عَنْ أنسٍ ، رَضِيَ اللهُ عَنْهُ ، قالَ : قالَ رسولُ اللهِ ، صلَّى اللهَ عَليهِ وسلَّم : « تَسَحَّرُوا ؛ فَإنَّ في السُّحُورِ بَرَكَةً » متفقٌ عليه .

1229. Hazrat Anas bin Malik (R.A.A.) relates that the Holy Prophet (S.A.W.) said: Take *sahri* (i.e. breakfast before dawn and commencement of the fast) because, there is blessing in this breakfast. *(Bukhari and Muslim)*

١٢٣٠– وعن زيدِ بنِ ثابتٍ ، رَضِيَ اللهُ عَنْهُ قالَ : تَسَحَّرْنَا مَعَ رسولِ اللهِ ، صلَّى اللهُ عليهِ وسلَّم ، ثُمَّ قُمْنَا إلى الصَّلاةِ . قِيلَ : كَمْ كانَ بَيْنَهُمَا ؟ قالَ : قَدْرُ خَمْسِينَ آيَةً . متفقٌ عليه .

1230. Hazrat Zaid bin Sabit (R.A.A.) says Once we ate *'Sahri'* (breakfast before dawn during Ramadhan) with the Holy Prophet

(S.A.W.) and then stood up for the morning salat. He was asked as to what was the interval between the two. He said: The time required for the recital of fifty verses (Of the Holy Quran).
(Bukhari and Muslim)

١٢٣١ — وَعَنِ ابنِ عُمَرَ رَضِيَ اللهُ عَنهُمَا ، قالَ : كانَ لرسولِ اللهِ ، صلّى اللهُ عليهِ وسلَّم مُؤَذِّنَانِ : بِلالٌ . وَابْنُ أُمِّ مَكْتُومٍ . فقَالَ رسولُ اللهِ ، صلّى اللهُ عليهِ وسلَّم : « إنَّ بِلالاً يُؤَذِّنُ بِلَيْلٍ ؛ فَكُلُوا وَاشْرَبُوا حَتّى يُؤَذِّنَ ابْنُ أُمِّ مَكْتُومٍ » قالَ وَلَمْ يَكُنْ بَيْنَهُمَا إلاَّ أَنْ يَنْزِلَ هذا وَيَرْقَى هذا ، متفقٌ عليه .

1231. Hazrat Ibn 'Umar (R.A.A.) relates that the Holy Prophet (S.A.W.) had two Muezzins (Callers for prayers). One was Hazrat Bilal (R.A.A.) and the other was Hazrat Ibn Ume Maktum (R.A.A.). The Holy Prophet (S.A.W.) said: Bilal (R.A.A.) calls the Azan (a bit earlier) when it is still night. Therefore, continue eating and drinking till Ibn Umm Maktum (R.A.A.) calls it. He said, there was in fact only a brief interval between the two when one descended and the other ascended (the high platform). *(Bukhari and Muslim)*

١٢٣٢ — وَعَنْ عَمْرِو بنِ العاصِ رَضِيَ اللهُ عَنهُ أَنَّ رسولَ اللهِ ، صلّى اللهُ عليهِ وسلَّم ، قالَ : « فَصْلُ ما بَيْنَ صِيَامِنا وَصِيَامِ أَهْلِ الكِتابِ أَكْلَةُ السَّحَرِ » رواهُ مسلم .

1232. Hazrat 'Amr bin Al-Aas (R.A.A.) says that the Holy Prophet (S.A.W.) said: Only distinguishing factor between our fasting and that of the other people of the Book is Sahri, (that is Christians and Jews who do not eat pre-dawn breakfast). *(Muslim)*

CHAPTER 222

VIRTUES HASTENING THE BREAKING OF THE FASTS, AND THE THING WITH WHICH TO BREAK AND WHAT TO PRAY AFTER BREAKING THE FAST

١٢٣٣ — عَنْ سَهْلِ بنِ سَعْدٍ ، رَضِيَ اللهُ عَنهُ ، أَنَّ رَسُولَ اللهِ ، صلّى اللهُ عَلَيْهِ وسلَّم ، قَالَ : « لايَزالُ النَّاسُ بخَيْرٍ مَا عَجَّلُوا الفِطْرَ » متفقٌ عليه .

1233. Sahl bin Sa'd (R.A.A.) relates that the Holy Prophet (S.A.W.) said: The people (Muslims) will remain on the right path as long as they make haste in breaking the fast (immediately after the sun has set and the time to pray after breaking of fast has arrived).

(Bukhari and Muslim)

١٢٣٤ – وَعَنْ أَبِي عَطِيَّةَ قَالَ : دَخَلْتُ أَنَا وَمَسْرُوقٌ عَلى عائشةَ ، رَضِيَ اللهُ عَنْها فَقَالَ لَهَا مَسْرُوقٌ : رَجُلانِ مِنْ أَصْحَابِ مُحَمَّدٍ ، صلّى اللهُ عَلَيهِ وسلَّم ، كِلاهُمَا لايَأْلُو عَنِ الخَيْرِ : أَحَدُهُمَا يُعَجِّلُ المَغْرِبَ وَالإفْطَارَ ، والآخرُ يُؤَخِّرُ المغربَ وَالإفطَارَ ؟ فَقَالَتْ : مَنْ يُعَجِّلُ المَغْرِبَ وَالإفْطَارَ ؟ قالَ : عَبْدُ اللهِ – يعني ابنَ مَسْعودٍ – فَقَالَتْ : هكَذَا كَانَ رَسُولُ اللهِ ، صلّى اللهُ عَليهِ وسَلَّم ، يَصْنَعُ .رواه مسلم .

1234. Hazrat Abu Atiya (R.A.A.) relates: I and Hazrat Masrooq went to see Hazrat Ayesha. Hazrat Masrooq said to her: Of the companions of the Holy Prophet (S.A.W.) there are two persons, both of them do not lack to earn goodness, but one of them hastens in breaking his fast and offering Maghrib (evening prayers)and the other delays a bit both these functions. Hazrat Ayesha (R.A.A.) asked: Who is the person who hastens in breaking his fast and offering Maghrib Salat (prayers). He answered: Abdullah ibn Mas'ud'. She remarked. The Holy·Prophet (S.A.W.) also did the same. *(Muslim)*

١٢٣٥ – وَعَنْ أَبِي هُرَيرَةَ رَضِيَ اللهُ عَنْهُ قالَ : قالَ رَسُولُ اللهِ ، صلّى اللهُ عَليهِ وسلَّم ، قالَ اللهُ عَزَّ وَجَلَّ : « أَحَبُّ عِبَادِي إليَّ أَعْجَلُهُمْ فِطْراً » رواه الترمذي وقالَ : حَديثٌ حَسَنٌ .

1235. Hazrat Abu Hurairah (R.A.A.) reports that the Holy Prophet (S.A.W.) said: Allah the Almighty and Master of Glory says: Among My servants I like most the person who hastens in breaking his fast. (*Tirmizi* called it sound)

١٢٣٦– وَعَنْ عُمَرَ بنِ الخَطَّابِ ، رَضِيَ اللهُ عَنْهُ ، قالَ : قالَ رَسُولُ اللهِ ، صلّى اللهُ عَليهِ وسَلَّم : « إذا أَقبَلَ اللَّيْلُ مِنْ ههُنَا وَأَدْبَرَ النَّهَارُ مِنْ ههُنَا ، وَغَرَبَتِ الشَّمْسُ ، فَقَدْ أَفطَرَ الصَّائمُ » متفقٌ عليه .

1236. Hazrat Umar bin Khattab (R.A.A.) relates that the Holy Prophet (S.A.W.) said: When the night has approached from this side (East) and the day has retired beyond this (the West) and the sun has set, then the one observing the fast ought to break it.

(Bukhari and Muslim)

١٢٣٧ – وَعَنْ أبي إبراهيمَ عبدِ اللهِ بنِ أبي أوفى ، رَضِيَ اللهُ عَنْهُمَا ، قالَ : سِرْنَا مَعَ رسولِ اللهِ ، صلّى اللهُ عليهِ وسلّم ، وَهُوَ صَائِمٌ ، فَلَمّ غَرَبَتِ الشّمْسُ ، قالَ لِبَعْضِ القَوْمِ : « يافُلانُ انزِلْ فَاجْدَحْ لَنا ، فَقَالَ : يا رَسُولَ اللهِ لَوْ أمْسَيْتَ ؟ قالَ : « انزِلْ فَاجْدَحْ لَنَا » قال : إنّ عَلَيْكَ نَهاراً ، قال : « انزِلْ فَاجْدَحْ لنا » قَالَ : فَنَزَلَ فَجَدَحَ لَهُمْ فَشَرِبَ رَسُولُ اللهِ ، صلّى اللهُ عليهِ وسَلّم، ثُمّ قالَ : « إذا رَأَيْتُمُ اللّيْلَ قَدْ أقْبَلَ مِنْ ههُنَا ، فَقَدْ أفْطَرَ الصّائِمُ » وأشارَ بِيَدِهِ قِبَلَ المَشْرِقِ . متفقٌ عليهِ .

1237. Hazrat Abu Ibrahim Abdullah bin Aufi (R.A.A.) relates: Once we accompanied the Holy Prophet (S.A.W.) on a journey, and he was fasting. When the sun had set, He (S.A.W.) asked some-one from amongst the party,' 'So and so, please get down and prepare the syrup from the roasted barley flour for us. The man submitted: 'O' Messenger of Allah ! Please let the evening be dark. He (S.A.W.) repeated: 'Get down and prepare the barley syrup. The man submitted: 'There is still daylight'. The Holy Prophet (S.A.W.) said a third time: 'Get down and prepare the barley syrup for us'. Hazrat Abdullah bin Aufi (R.A.A.) says: The man dismounted and prepared the syrup for him. (S.A.W.) The Holy Prophet (S.A.W.) drank it and pointing towards the east said: 'When you see the night approaching from that direction (East) the person observing the fast should break it.

(Bukhari and Muslim)

١٢٣٨ – وَعَنْ سَلْمَانَ بنِ عَامِرٍ الضّبّيّ الصّحَابيّ ، رَضِيَ اللهُ عَنْهُ ، عَنِ النّبيّ صلّى اللهُ عَليهِ وَسَلّمَ قَالَ : « إذا أفْطَرَ أحَدُكُمْ ، فَلْيُفْطِرْ عَلى تَمْرٍ ، فإنْ لَمْ يَجِدْ ، فَلْيُفْطِرْ عَلى ماءٍ فإنّهُ طَهُورٌ »
رَوَاهُ أبو دَاودَ، والترمذي وقالَ : حديثٌ حَسَنٌ صَحيحٌ .

1238. Hazrat Sal'man bin 'Amir Zabai as Sahabi (R.A.A.) relates that the Holy Prophet (S.A.W.) said. When somebody breaks his fast then he should do so with a date. If he does not get it, then with water for it is pure and purifies others. *(Abu Daud and Tirmizi have narrated this and latter called it as sound).*

١٢٣٩ – وَعَنْ أَنَسٍ ، رَضِيَ اللهُ عَنْهُ ، قالَ : كانَ رَسُولُ اللهِ صلّى اللهُ عَلَيهِ وسَلَّم ، يُفْطِرُ قَبْلَ أنْ يُصَلِّيَ عَلى رُطَبَاتٍ ، فَإنْ لَمْ تَكُنْ رُطَبَاتٌ فَتُمَيْرَاتٌ ، فَإنْ لَمْ تَكُنْ تُمَيْرَاتٌ حَسَا حَسَوَاتٍ مِنْ ماءٍ رواه أبو داود ، والترمذي وقال : حديثٌ حَسَنٌ .

1239. Hazrat Anas bin Malik (R.A.A.) relates: Holy Prophet (S.A.W.) used to break his fast before offering Maghrib (evening) salat with some pieces of fresh dates, failing which, with dry dates, and failing that too, he (S.A.W.) would drink a few mouthfuls of water. *(Abu Daud and Tirmizi cited this and latter called it sound)*

* * * * * * *

CHAPTER 223

A FASTING PERSON SHOULD GUARD HIS TONGUE FR M ABUSES, TAUNTS AND QUARRELS

١٢٤٠ – عنْ أبي هُرَيرةَ رضيَ اللهُ عنهُ قالَ : قالَ رسولُ اللهِ ، صلّى اللهُ عليهِ وسلَّم : « إذا كَانَ يَوْمُ صَوْمِ أحدِكُمْ ، فَلا يَرْفُثْ وَلا يَصْخَبْ ، فَإنْ سَابَّهُ أَحَدٌ ، أَوْ قاتَلَهُ ، فَلْيَقُلْ : إنّي صائمٌ » متفقٌ عليه .

1240. This Hadis has been covered in No. 1215 of Chapter 217.

١٢٤١ – وعنهُ قالَ : قالَ النبيُّ ، صلّى اللهُ عليهِ وسَلَّم : « مَنْ لَمْ يَدَعْ قَوْلَ الزُّورِ والعَمَلَ بِهِ فَلَيْسَ للهِ حاجَةٌ في أنْ يَدَعَ طَعَامَهُ وَشَرَابَهُ » رواه البخاري .

1241. Hazrat Abu Hurairah (R.A.A.) relates that the Holy Prophet (S.A.W.) said: If a person does not refrain from lying and indecent activities, Allah, does not want that he should abstain from eating and drinking. *(Bukhari)*

Note : The idea behind these traditions is that back-biting, lying and indecent activities while fasting lessen the recompense of the fast and decreases its radiance. Therefore one should shun these things while fasting.

* * * * * * *

CHAPTER 224

SOME MISCELLANEOUS TOPICS ABOUT FASTING

١٢٤٢ – عَنْ أبي هريرةَ ، رَضِيَ اللهُ عَنْهُ ، عَنِ النبيِّ ، صَلَّى اللهُ عليهِ وسلَّم ، قالَ : « إذا نَسِيَ أَحَدُكُمْ ، فَأَكَلَ ، أوْ شَرِبَ ، فَلْيُتِمَّ صَوْمَهُ ؛ فإنَّما أَطْعَمَهُ اللهُ وَسَقَاهُ » . متفقٌ عليه .

1242. **Hazrat Abu Hurairah** (R.A.A.) says that the Holy Prophet (S.A.W.) said: When anyone of you eats or drinks accidentally forgetting his fast, he should continue his fast till the end (because his eating and drinking through mistake) means that Allah has fed him and given him to drink. *(Bukhari and Muslim)*

١٢٤٣ – وعن لَقيطِ بنِ صَبِرَةَ ، رَضِيَ اللهُ عَنْهُ ، قالَ : قلتُ : يارسولَ اللهِ أخبِرْني عَنِ الوُضُوءِ ؟ قالَ : « أَسْبِغِ الوضوءَ ، وَخَلِّلْ بَيْنَ الأَصَابِعِ ، وَبَالِغْ في الاسْتِنْشَاقِ ، إلَّا أنْ تَكُونَ صَائماً » رواه أبو داود ، والترمذي وقالَ : حديثٌ حَسَنٌ صَحيحٌ .

1243. **Hazrat Laqit bin Sabarah** (R.A.A.) states that once I presented myself before the Holy Prophet (S.A.W.) and requested him to inform me about the ablutions. He (S.A.W.) said: Perform the ablutions thoroughly and completely and clean the base of your fingers where the two fingers meet by rubbing on with opposite fingers and wash out your nostrils well, but if you are fasting then be careful in this respect (lest some water gets into nostrils. *(Abu Daud and Tirmizi* quoted and latter said it is sound).

١٢٤٤ – وعنْ عائشةَ ، رَضِيَ اللهُ عَنْها ، قالَتْ : كانَ رَسُولُ اللهِ ، صَلَّى اللهُ عليهِ وسلَّم ، يدْرِكُهُ الفَجْرُ وَهُوَ جُنُبٌ مِنْ أَهْلِهِ ، ثُمَّ يَغْتَسِلُ وَيَصُومُ . متفقٌ عليه .

1244. **Hazrat Ayesha** (R.A.A.) relates: If the Holy Prophet (S.A.W.) got dawn in a state he had consorted with a wife, he would take bath and observe the fast as usual. *(Bukhari and Muslim)*

١٢٤٥ – وعنْ عائشةَ وأمِّ سَلَمَةَ ، رَضِيَ اللهُ عَنْهُمَا ، قَالَتَا : كانَ رسولُ اللهِ ، صَلَّى اللهُ عليهِ وسلَّمَ ، يُصْبِحُ جُنُباً مِنْ غَيْرِ حُلُمٍ ، ثُمَّ يَصُومُ » متفقٌ عليهِ .

1245. Hazrat Ayesha (R.A.A.) and Hazrat Umm Salamah (R.A.A.) relate: Whenever the Holy Prophet (S.A.W.) found the dawn in a state of inpurity, (consorting with a wife and not of night discharge) he (S.A.W.) took bath and observed fast. *(Bukhari and Muslim)*

* * * * * * *

CHAPTER 225

VIRTUES OF FASTING IN THE MONTHS OF MUHARRAM, SHA'BAN AND THE SACRED MONTHS

١٢٤٦ – عَنْ أبي هُرَيْرَةَ ، رضيَ اللهُ عَنْهُ ، قَالَ : قَالَ رَسُولُ اللهِ ، صَلَّى اللهُ عليهِ وسَلَّمَ : « أَفْضَلُ الصِّيَامِ بعْدَ رَمَضَانَ : شَهْرُ اللهِ المحَرَّمُ : وَأَفْضَلُ الصَّلاةِ بَعْدَ الفَرِيضَةِ : صَلاةُ اللَّيْلِ » رواه مسلمٌ .

1246. This Hadis has been covered in No. 1167 of Chapter 2.

١٢٤٧ – عَنْ عائشةَ ، رَضِيَ اللهُ عَنْها ، قَالتْ : لَمْ يَكُنِ النبيُّ ، صَلَّى اللهُ عليهِ وسَلَّمَ ، يَصُوم مِنْ شَهْرٍ أَكْثَرَ مِنْ شَعْبَانَ ، فإنَّه كَانَ يَصُوم شَعْبَانَ كلَّه . وفي روايةٍ : كَانَ يَصُومُ شَعبانَ إلاَّ قَلِيلاً . متفقٌ عليهِ .

1247. Hazrat Ayesha (R.A.A.) relates: 'The Holy Prophet (S.A.W.) did not use to observe the optional fasts very much in the month of Shaban but he (S.A.W.) observed the fast throughout the month of Sha'ban. Another version says: He (S.A.W.) used to observe the fast during the month of Sha'ban but for a few days only.

(Bukhari and Muslim)

١٢٤٨ – وعن مجيبةَ البَاهِلِيَّةِ عَنْ أَبِيهَا أَوْ عمِّها ، أنَّهُ أَتَى رَسُولَ اللهِ ، صلَّى اللهُ عليهِ وسَلَّم ، ثمَّ انطَلَقَ فَأَتَاه بعدَ سَنَةٍ ، وَقَد تَغَيَّرَتْ حَالهُ وَهَيْئَتهُ ، فَقَالَ : يا رَسُولَ اللهِ أَمَا تَعْرِفُنِي ؟ قَالَ : « وَمَنْ أَنتَ ؟» قالَ : أَنَا البَاهِلِيُّ الذي جِئتكَ عامَ الأَوَّلِ . قَالَ : « فَمَا غَيَّرَكَ ، وَقد كنتَ حَسَنَ الهَيئةِ ؟ » قالَ : ما أكلتُ طعَاماً منذ فَارَقْتكَ إلاَّ بِلَيْلٍ . فَقَالَ رَسولُ اللهِ ، صَلَّى اللهُ عليهِ وسَلَّم :« عَذَّبتَ نَفسَكَ ! » ثُمَّ قَالَ : « صُمْ شَهرَ الصَّبرِ ، وَيَوماً مِنْ كلِّ شَهرٍ » قال : زِدْني ، فإنَّ بي قوَّةً ، قَالَ : « صُمْ يَومينِ » قالَ : زِدْني ، قالَ : « صُمْ ثلاثَةَ أَيَّامٍ » قالَ : زِدْني ، قالَ :

« صُمْ مِنَ الحُرُمِ وَاتْرُكْ ، صُمْ مِنَ الحرمِ وَاترُكْ . صُمْ مِنَ الحرمِ وَاتْرُكْ » وقالَ بِأَصَابِعِهِ الثَّلاثِ فَضَمَّهَا ، ثُمَّ أَرْسَلَهَا . رواه أبو داود .

1248. Hazrat Mujiba Al-Bahiliyah (R.A.A.) states on the authority of her father or uncle that her father or uncle once visited the Holy Prophet (S.A.W.) and went back. He visited the Holy Prophet (S.A.W.) again after the lapse of one year. During this period his appearance and condition had undergone considerable change. He asked the Holy Prophet (S.A.W.) : O ! Messenger of Allah, do you recognize me? The Holy Prophet (S.A.W.) inquired: 'Who are you?' He submitted: I am that person of the Bahili tribe who visited you last year. The Holy Prophet (S.A.W.) further asked: 'Why this change in you? Although you were quite handsome? He (Bahili) answered: Since I left you last time I have not eaten except at night (that is for the whole year he fasted). The Holy Prophet (S.A.W.) remarked: You tortured yourself. The Holy Prophet (S.A.W.) then told him: You should observe the fast during the month of Patience (Ramadhan) and on one day in every other month The man requested: Permit me to observe fasting a little more for I am strong enough. The Holy Prophet (S.A.W.) said: Then keep the fast on two days in every month. The Bahili again submitted: Please add a little more. The Holy Prophet (S.A.W.) said: Then fast on three days in every month: The man pleaded for more. The Holy Prophet (S.A.W.) said: That is all, and during the sacred months fast and abstain from fasting. The Holy Prophet (S.A.W.) said this thrice, and then he explained this by joining his (S.A.W.) three fingers and then released them, thereby meaning that he should fast for three days and then abstain from fasting for three days. *(Abu Daud)*

* * * * * * *

CHAPTER 226

VIRTUES OF FASTING AND DOING OTHER GOOD THINGS IN THE FIRST TEN DAYS OF ZIL HIJJ

١٢٤٩ — عنِ ابنِ عبَّاسٍ ، رَضِيَ اللهُ عَنْهمَا ، قالَ : قالَ رسولُ اللهِ ، صَلَّى اللهُ عليهِ وسَلَّمَ : « مَا مِنْ أَيامٍ العَمَلُ الصَّالِحُ فِيها أَحبُّ إلى اللهِ مِنْ هذهِ الأَيَّامِ » يعني : أيامَ العشرِ ، قالوا : يارسولَ اللهِ وَلا الجهادُ في سبيلِ اللهِ ؟ قالَ : « وَلا الجهادُ في سَبيلِ اللهِ ، إلاَّ رَجلٌ خَرَجَ بِنَفْسِهِ ، وَمَالِهِ ، فَلَم يَرجِعْ مِنْ ذلكَ بِشَيْءٍ » رواه البخاريُّ .

1249. Hazrat Ibn Abbas (R.A.A.) relates that the Holy Prophet (S.A.W.) said: There are no other days during which virtuous action is so pleasing to Allah, as the first ten days of Zilhij. The Companions submitted: 'O' Messenger of Allah, not even fighting (carrying on Jihad) in the cause of Allah? He (S.A.W.) answered: Yes! not even Jihad in the cause of Allah except in the case of a person who goes on Jihad along with his life and his property and does not come back with either (i.e. he is martyred in the Jihad). *(Bukhari)*

* * * * * * *

CHAPTER 227

VIRTUES OF FASTING ON THE DAY OF ARAFA AND THE NINTH AND TENTH DAY OF MUHARRAM

١٢٥٠ – عَنْ أَبِي قَتَادَةَ ، رَضِيَ اللهُ عَنْهُ . قَالَ : سُئِلَ رَسُولُ اللهِ ، صَلَّى اللهُ عَلَيهِ وسَلَّم : عَنْ صَوْمِ يَوْمِ عَرَفَةَ ؟ قَالَ : « يُكَفِّرُ السَّنَةَ المَاضِيَةَ وَالبَاقِيَةَ » رواه مسلمٌ .

1250. Hazrat Abu Qatadah (R.A.A.) relates. (Once) the Holy Prophet (S.A.W.) was asked about observing the fast on the day of Arafa (Hajj) He (S.A.W.) replied: It makes amends for the sins (committed) during past year and the subsequent year. *(Muslim)*

١٢٥١ – وعَنْ ابنِ عباسٍ رضيَ اللهُ عنهما ، أنَّ رَسولَ اللهِ ، صَلَّى اللهُ عليهِ وسلَّمَ ، صَامَ يَوْمَ عاشوراءَ ، وَأَمَرَ بِصِيَامِهِ . متفقٌ عليهِ .

1251. Hazrat Ibn Abbas (R.A.A.) says that the Holy Prophet (S.A.W.) himself observed the fast on the Day of Aashoora (tenth day of Muharram), and he exhorted others to fast on that day. *(Bukhari and Muslim)*

١٢٥٢ – وعنْ أبي قَتَادَةَ . رَضِيَ اللهُ عَنْهُ . أنَّ رسولَ اللهِ ، صلَّى اللهُ عليهِ وسَلَّمَ ، سُئِلَ عَنْ صِيَامِ يَوْمِ عَاشُورَاءَ . فَقَالَ : « يُكَفِّرُ السَّنَةَ المَاضِيَةَ » رواهُ مُسْلِمٌ .

1252. Hazrat Abu Qatadah (R.A.A.) relates that the Holy Prophet (S.A.W.) was asked about fasting on the Day of Aashoora (tenth Day of Muharram). He (S.A.W.) answered: It atones for the sins of the preceding year. *(Muslim)*

١٢٥٣– وعَنِ ابنِ عبَّاسٍ ، رَضيَ اللهُ عنهما ، قالَ : قالَ رسُول اللهِ ، صَلَّى اللهُ عليه وسلَّم : « لَئِنْ بَقِيتُ إلى قابِلٍ لأَصُومَنَّ التَّاسِعَ » رواه مُسْلِمٌ

1253. Hazrat Ibn Abbas (R.A.A.) relates that the Holy Prophet (S.A.W.) said: If I survive till the next year, I shall fast on the ninth day (of Muharram). *(Muslim)*

* * * * * * *

CHAPTER 228

VIRTUES OF FASTING IN THE SIX DAYS OF SHAWWAL

١٢٥٤– عَنْ أبي أيوبَ ، رَضِيَ اللهُ عَنْهُ ، أنَّ رسولَ اللهِ ، صلَّى اللهُ عليهِ وسلَّم ، قالَ : « مَنْ صامَ رَمَضانَ ، ثمَّ أتبعَهُ سِتاً مِنْ شَوَّالٍ ، كانَ كصِيَامِ الدَّهْرِ » رواهُ مُسْلِمٌ .

1254. Hazrat Abu Ayub (R.A.A.) states that the Holy Prophet (S.A.W.) said: One who observes the fast throughout the month of Ramadhan then followed by fasting on the six days of Shawwal, is as good as if he observed the fast throughout the Year. *(Muslim)*

* * * * * * *

CHAPTER 229

VIRTUES OF FASTING ON MONDAYS AND THURSDAYS

١٢٥٥– عن أبي قَتَادَةَ ، رَضِيَ اللهُ عَنْهُ ، أنَّ رسولَ اللهِ ، صلَّى اللهُ عليهِ وسلَّم ، سُئِلَ عَنْ صَوْمِ يَوْمِ الاثْنَيْنِ فقَالَ : « ذلكَ يَوْمٌ وُلِدْتُ فيهِ ، ويَوْمٌ بُعِثْتُ ، أوْ أُنزِلَ عَلَيَّ فيهِ » رواه مسلمٌ

1255. Hazrat Abu Qatadah (R.A.A.) relates that the Holy Prophet (S.A.W.) was asked about fasting on Monday; he (S.A.W.) said: This (Monday) is the day on which I was born, and the day on which I was commissioned for prophethood; or he (S.A.W.) said the day on which I received the first call. *(Muslim)*

١٢٥٦ – وعَنْ أبي هُرَيْرَةَ ، رَضِيَ اللهُ عنه ، عَنْ رسولِ اللهِ ، صَلَّى اللهُ عَلَيهِ وسلَّم ، قالَ : « تُعْرَضُ الأعْمَالُ يَوْمَ الاثنَيْنِ والخَميسِ ، فَأحِبُّ أنْ يُعْرَضَ عَملي وَأنَا صَائمٌ » رَوَاهُ التِرْمِذِيُّ وقالَ : حديثٌ حَسَنٌ . ورواهُ مُسلمٌ بغيرِ ذِكرِ الصَوْم .

1256. Hazrat Abu Hurairah (R.A.A.) relates that the Holy Prophet (S.A.W.) said: On Mondays and Thursdays a report on man's actions is presented and as such I wish that when my deeds are reported I should be fasting. *(Tirmizi)* *Muslim* reported it without the word fasting.

١٢٥٧ – وَعَنْ عائشةَ ، رَضِيَ اللهُ عَنْها ، قَالَتْ : كانَ رسولُ اللهِ ، صلَّى اللهُ عليهِ وسَلَّم ، يَتَحَرَّى صَوْمَ الاثنَيْنِ وَالخَميسِ . رواهالترمذيُّ وقالَ : حديثٌ حسنٌ .

1257. Hazrat Ayesha (R.A.A.) says that the Holy Prophet (S.A.W.) was very particular about fasting on Mondays and Thursdays. *(Tirmizi)*

* * * * * * *

CHAPTER 230

DESIRABILITY OF FASTING ON THREE DAYS IN EVERY MONTH

والأفضلُ صومُها في الأيامِ البيضِ ، وهيَ : الثالثَ عشرَ ، والرابعَ عشرَ والخامسَ عشرَ . وقيلَ : الثاني عشرَ ، والثالثَ عشرَ ، والرابعَ عشَرَ ، والصحيحُ المَشهُورُ هوَ الأوَّلُ .

Note :— According to Imam Nawavi the suitable days for fasting in the month other than Ramadhan are the bright (moon light) dates of 13th, 14th and 15th of the lunar month. In this respect 12th, 13th and 14th dates have also been mentioned; but the former dates are well known and considered authentic.

١٢٥٨ – وعن أبي هُريرةَ ، رَضِيَ اللهُ عَنْهُ ، قالَ : أوْصاني خليلي ، صَلَّى اللهُ عَليهِ وسلَّم ، بِثلاثٍ : صيامِ ثَلاثَةِ أيَّامٍ مِن كلِّ شَهرٍ ، ورَكعتَيِ الضُّحَى ، وَأن أُوتِرَ قبلَ أنْ أنَامَ . مُتفقٌ عليهِ .

1258. This Hadis has already been covered in No. 1139 of Chapter 206.

١٢٥٩ – وعَنْ أبي الدَرْدَاء ، رَضِيَ اللهُ عنهُ ، قالَ : أوْصَاني حَبيبي ، صَلَّى اللهُ عليهِ وسلَّم بثلاثٍ لَنْ أدَعَهُنَّ ما عِشْتُ : بِصِيامِ ثلاثةِ أيَّامٍ مِن كُلِّ شَهرٍ ، وَصَلاةِ الضحى ، وبِأنْ لا أنامَ حتى أوتِرَ . رواهُ مُسلِمٌ

1259. Hazrat Abu Darda (R.A.A.) relates that 'My dearest friend (the Holy Prophet) (S.A.W.) has advised me for three things, which I will not leave till I live. Firstly to fast for three days in each month (other than Ramadhan), Secondly to offer two rakats of prayer for (chast) after sun rise and lastly not to sleep till I'offer witr prayer. *(Muslim)*

١٢٦٠ – وعَنْ عبدِ اللهِ بنِ عَمْرِو بنِ العاصِ . رَضِيَ اللهُ عنهُما ، قالَ : قالَ رسولُ اللهِ صَلَّى اللهُ عليهِ وسلَّمَ : « صومُ ثلاثةِ أيَّامٍ مِنْ كلِّ شهرٍ صومُ الدهرِ كُلِّهُ » مُتَّفقٌ عليهِ .

1260. This hadis has already been dealt with in Hadis No. 150 of Chapter 14.

١٢٦١ – وعنْ مُعَاذةَ العَدَوِيَّةِ أنَّها سَألَتْ عائشةَ ، رَضِيَ اللهُ عَنْها : أكانَ رَسُولُ اللهِ صَلَّى اللهُ عليهِ وسلَّمَ ، يصومُ مِن كُلِّ شهرٍ ثلاثةَ أيَّامٍ قالَتْ : نَعمْ . فَقُلْتُ : مِنْ أيِّ الشَّهرِ كانَ يَصُومُ ؟ قالَتْ : لَمْ يَكُنْ يُبَالي مِنْ أيِّ الشَّهْرِ يَصُومُ . رواهُ مسلمٌ

1261. Hazrat Mu'azah Al-'Adawiah (R.A.A.) relates that she asked Ayesha (R.A.A.) 'Did the Holy Prophet (S.A.W.) observe fast on three days in each month (other than Ramadhan)? She said Yes. I further asked: In which part of the month he (S.A.W.) used to fast. He was not particular about this, and would fast in any part of the month. *(Muslim)*

١٢٦٢ – وعَنْ أبي ذرٍّ ، رَضِيَ اللهُ عنهُ . قالَ قالَ : رسولُ اللهِ ، صلَّى اللهُ عليهِ وسلَّمَ : « إذا صُمْتَ مِنَ الشَّهرِ ثلاثاً ، فَصُمْ ثلاثَ عَشْرَةَ ، وأرْبعَ عَشْرَةَ ، وَخَمسَ عَشْرَةَ » رواهُ الترمِذيُّ وقالَ : حديثٌ حسنٌ .

1262. Hazrat Abu Zarr (R.A.A.) says that the Holy Prophet (S.A.W.) said: When you fast for three days in a month, then let these days be the 13th, 14th and 15th (moonlit nights of the lunar month). *(Tirmizi, and said this is good)*

١٢٦٣ – وعنْ قتادةَ بنِ ملحانَ ، رَضِيَ اللهُ عَنْهُ ، قالَ : كانَ رَسولُ اللهِ ، صَلّى اللهُ عليهِ وسلّم ، يأمُرُنا بصِيامِ أيّامِ البيضِ : ثلاثَ عشْرَةَ ، وأربعَ عشْرَةَ ، وخمسَ عشْرَةَ . رواهُ أبو داودَ .

1263. Hazrat Qatadah bin Milhan (R.A.A.) relates: The Holy Prophet (S.A.W.) ordained us to fast on the three shining days (of every month) that is the 13th, 14th and 15th (of the lunar month).

(Abu Daud)

١٢٦٤ – وعنْ ابنِ عبّاسٍ ، رَضِيَ اللهُ عَنْهُما ، قالَ : كانَ رسولُ اللهِ ، صَلّى اللهُ عليهِ وسلّمَ ، « لا يُفْطِرُ أيّامَ البِيضِ في حَضَرٍ ولا سَفَرٍ » رواهُ النَّسائي بإسنادٍ حَسَنٍ .

1264. Hazrat Ibn Abbas (R.A.A.) reports that the Holy Prophet (S.A.W.) never missed observing fast on white days (i.e. during the moonlit Three nights of the lunar month) whether at home or on a journey. *(Nasai* quoted this on sound authority)

* * * * * * *

CHAPTER 231

VIRTUES OF PROVIDING FOR THE BREAKING OF THE FAST AND EXCELLENCE OF THE HOST IN WHOSE PRESENCE THE GUEST EATS AND SUPPLICATES FOR HIM

١٢٦٥ – عنْ زَيدِ بنِ خالدٍ الجُهَنيِّ ، رَضِيَ اللهُ عَنْهُ عَنِ النبيِّ ، صَلّى اللهُ عليهِ وسلّم ، قالَ : « مَنْ فَطّرَ صائماً ، كانَ لهُ مِثلُ أجْرِهِ غيرَ أنّهُ لا يَنْقُصُ مِنْ أجْرِ الصّائمِ شيءٌ »

رواهُ الترمذيُّ وقالَ : حديثٌ حسنٌ صحيحٌ .

1265. Hazrat Zaid bin Khalid Al-Juhani (R.A.A.) relates that the Holy Prophet (S.A.W.) said: Anybody who offers meal for the breakking of the fast of another person, earns the same merit as the one who was observing the fast without diminishing in any way the recompense of the fasting person. *(Tirmizi* and said this is sound and good)

١٢٦٦ – وعَنْ أمِّ عُمارَةَ الأنصاريّةِ ، رَضِيَ اللهُ عَنْها ، أنَّ النبيَّ ، صَلّى اللهُ عليهِ وسلّم . دَخلَ عليْها ، فقدّمتْ إليْهِ طعاماً ، فقالَ

« كُلِي » فَقَالَتْ . إِنِّي صَائِمَةٌ ، فقالَ رسولُ اللهِ ، صلَّى اللهُ عليهِ وسلَّمَ : « إنَّ الصَّائِمَ تُصَلِّي عَلَيْهِ المَلائِكَةُ إذا أُكِلَ عِنْدَهُ حَتَّى يَفْرُغُوا » وَرُبَّما قالَ : « حَتَّى يَشْبَعُوا » رواهُ الترمذيُّ وقالَ : حديثٌ حسنٌ .

1266. Hazrat Umm 'Ammarah Al-Ansaria (R.A.A.) relates that once the Holy Prophet (S.A.W.) visited her when she placed some food before him. He (S.A.W.) asked her to eat also. Thereupon she said: I am fasting today. On this he (S.A.W.) remarked when non-fasting persons eat before a fasting person the angels call for Allah's mercies upon him till they have finished or he said, till they have eaten to their satisfaction. *(Tirmizi* reported this and said it good).

١٢٦٧ – وعَنْ أنسٍ ، رَضِيَ اللهُ عنهُ ، أنَّ النبيَّ ، صَلَّى اللهُ عليهِ وسلَّم ، جَاءَ إلى سَعْدِ ابْنِ عُبَادَةَ ، رَضِيَ اللهُ عنهُ ، فَجَاءَ بِخُبْزٍ وَزَيْتٍ ، فَأَكَلَ ، ثُمَّ قالَ النبيُّ ، صلَّى اللهُ عليهِ وسلَّم : « أَفْطَرَ عِنْدَكُمُ الصَّائِمُونَ ، وَأَكَلَ طَعَامَكُمُ الأَبْرَارُ وَصَلَّتْ عَلَيْكُمُ المَلائِكَةُ »

رواهُ أبو داود بإسنادٍ صحيحٍ .

1267. Hazrat Anas (R.A.A.) says that once the Holy Prophet (S.A.W.) visited Hazrat Sa'ad bin Ubadah (R.A.A.). The latter brought bread and olive oil for him (S.A.W.). The Holy Prophet (S.A.W.) ate it and then said:

'Aftara 'Ind-akumu-Saimoona wa Akala Ta'ama-kumul-Abrar wa sallat 'Alaikumul-malaikato'

'The fasting people have broken their fast with you and virtuous persons have eaten food provided by you while the angels have supplicated for you'. *(Abu Daud* reported this on sound authorities).

* * * * * * *

BOOK OF I'TIKAF

(TO RETIRE TO MOSQUE FOR WORSHIP)

CHAPTER 232

١٢٦٨ – عَنِ ابنِ عُمَرَ، رَضِيَ اللهُ عَنْهُمَا ، قالَ : كانَ رسولُ اللهِ ، صلَّى اللهُ عليهِ وسلَّمَ يَعْتَكِفُ العَشْرَ الأَوَاخِرَ مِنْ رَمَضانَ . مُتفقٌ عليهِ

1268. Hazrat Ibn Umar (R.A.A.) states that the Holy Prophet (S.A.W.) used to retire to mosque for devotion and abstention during the last ten days of the month of Ramadhan. *(Bukhari and Muslim)*

١٢٦٩ – وعنْ عائشةَ ، رَضِيَ اللهُ عَنْها ، أنَّ النبيَّ ، صَلَّى اللهُ عليهِ وسلَّمَ ، كانَ يَعْتَكِفُ العَشْرَ الأَوَاخِرَ مِنْ رَمَضانَ ، حتَّى تَوَفَّاهُ اللهُ تعالى ، ثُمَّ اعتَكَفَ أزْوَاجُهُ مِنْ بَعْدِهِ . متفقٌ عَليهِ .

1269. Ummul Momineen Hazrat Ayesha Siddiqa (R.A.A.) relates that the Holy Prophet (S.A.W.) was regular in retiring to the mosque for prayers during the last ten days of Ramadhan up to the last days of his life. After his (S.A.W.) demise his (S.A.W.) wives continued the practice. *(Bukhari and Muslim)*

١٢٧٠ – وعَنْ أبي هُرَيرةَ ، رَضِيَ اللهُ عنهُ ، قالَ : كانَ النبيُّ : صَلَّى اللهُ عليهِ وَسَلَّمَ يَعْتَكِفُ في كُلِّ رَمَضَانَ عَشْرَةَ أيَّامٍ ، فلَمَّا كَانَ العَامُ الَّذِي قُبِضَ فِيهِ اعتَكَفَ عِشْرِينَ يَوْماً . رواه البخاريُّ .

1270. Hazrat Abu Hurairah (R.A.A.) says that the Holy Prophet (S.A.W.) retired to the mosque for ten days every year in the month of Ramadhan, but in the last year of his life he retired to the mosque for twenty days. *(Bukhari)*

* * * * * * *

BOOK OF HAJJ (PILGRIMAGE)

CHAPTER 233

قَالَ اللهُ تَعَالى : وَلِلهِ عَلى النَّاسِ حِجُّ البَيْتِ مَنِ اسْتَطَاعَ إِلَيْهِ سَبِيلاً وَمَنْ كَفَرَ فَإِنَّ اللهَ غَنِيٌّ عَنِ الْعَالَمِينَ » [آل عمران : ٩٧] .

Allah the Exalted, has said:

294. And pilgrimage to the House of Allah is a duty unto Allah for mankind, for him who can find a way thither. As for him who disbelieveth (let him know that) lo! Allah is independent of (all) creatures. (3:97)

١٢٧١ – وَعَنِ ابْنِ عُمَرَ، رَضِيَ اللهُ عَنْهُمَا ، أَنَّ رَسُولَ اللهِ ، صَلَّى اللهُ عليهِ وسَلَّمَ ، قَالَ : بُنِيَ الإِسْلامُ عَلَى خَمْسٍ : شَهَادَةِ أَنْ لا إِلهَ إِلاَّ اللهُ وَأَنَّ مُحَمَّداً رسولُ اللهِ ، وإِقَامِ الصَّلاةِ وإِيتَاءِ الزَّكَاةِ ، وَحَجِّ البَيْتِ ، وَصَوْمِ رَمَضَانَ » متفقٌ عليهِ .

1271. This Hadis has already been mentioned as No. 1075 of Chapter 193.

١٢٧٢ – وعَنْ أبي هُرَيْرَةَ ، رَضِيَ اللهُ عنهُ ، قالَ : خَطَبَنَا رسولُ اللهِ صلَّى اللهُ عليهِ وسَلَّمَ فَقَالَ : « يَا أَيُّهَا النَّاسُ قَدْ فَرَضَ اللهَ عَلَيْكُمُ الحَجَّ فَحُجُّوا » فَقَالَ رَجُلٌ : أَكُلَّ عَامٍ يا رسولَ اللهِ ؟ فَسَكَتَ ، حَتَّى قَالَهَا ثَلاثاً . فَقَالَ رَسُولُ اللهِ ، صَلَّى اللهُ عَلَيهِ وسَلَّم ، : « لَوْ قُلْتُ نَعَمْ لَوَجَبَتْ ، وَلَمَا اسْتَطَعْتُمْ » ثُمَّ قالَ : « ذَرُونِي مَا تَرَكْتُكُمْ ؛ فَإِنَّمَا هَلَكَ مَنْ كَانَ قَبْلَكُمْ بِكَثْرَةِ سُؤَالِهِمْ ، وَاخْتِلافِهِمْ عَلى أَنْبِيَائِهِمْ ، فإِذَا أَمَرْتُكُمْ بِشَيءٍ فَأْتُوا مِنْهُ مَا اسْتَطَعْتُم ، وَإِذا نَهَيْتُكُم عَن شَيءٍ فَدَعُوهُ » رواهُ مسلمٌ .

1272. **Hazrat Abu Hurairah** (R.A.A.) says: The Holy Prophet (S.A.W.) once delivered a sermon and addressing us said : 'O people Allah has made it obligatory for you to perform Hajj (the pilgrimage), and as such you should perform it. A man asked: O Messenger of Allah, should we perform Hajj every year? The Holy Prophet (S.A.W.) kept quiet, till the man repeated his question thrice. Then the Holy Prophet (S.A.W.) said: Had I said 'yes' then this Hajj would have become an yearly obligatory duty, and this you could not have afforded. The Holy Prophet (S.A.W.) further said: Leave me when I omit something for you (i.e.) don't pester me with such questions, when I am not imposing anything on you. Some people who lived before you, used to ask too many unnecessary questions, and would disagree with their prophets. On this account they were destroyed. As such when I call upon you to do something, you must obey and carry out my direction as far as it may be within your capacity, and when I forbid you to refrain from anything then avoid it. *(Muslim)*

١٢٧٣ — وَعَنْهُ قَالَ : سُئِلَ النَّبِيُّ ، صَلَّى اللهُ عليه وسَلَّمَ ، أيُّ العَمَلِ أفضَلُ ؟ قال : « إيمَانٌ بِاللهِ وَرَسُولِهِ » قِيلَ : ثُمَّ مَاذَا ؟ قال : « الجِهَادُ في سَبِيلِ اللهِ » قِيلَ : ثُمَّ مَاذَا ؟ قَالَ : « حَجٌّ مَبْرُورٌ » متفقٌ عليه .

1273. Hazrat Abu Hurairah (R.A.A.) says that the Holy Prophet (S.A.W.) was once asked: Which action is the best of all? He (S.A.W.) said: To believe in Allah and his Messenger (S.A.W.) He (S.A.W.) was further asked: And what next? He (S.A.W.) said: Jihad (fighting) in the cause of Allah. He (S.A.W.) was asked again. And what after that? He (S.A.W.) answered. The Pilgrimage free from vices and defects. *(Bukhari and Muslim)*

١٢٧٤ — وَعَنْهُ قالَ : سَمِعْتُ رسُولَ اللهِ ، صَلَّى اللهُ عليهِ وَسلَّمَ يقولُ : « مَنْ حَجَّ ، فَلَمْ يَرْفُثْ ، وَلَمْ يَفسُقْ ، رَجَعَ كَيَومَ وَلَدَتهُ أُمُّهُ » متفقٌ عليه

1274. Hazrat Abu Hurairah (R.A.A.) reports that he heard the Holy Prophet (S.A.W.) said: A person who performs the pilgrimage during which he neither indulges in lewdness nor abuses, such a person returns (from the pilgrimage duly purified) as if born by his mother on that very day. *(Bukhari and Muslim)*

١٢٧٥ — وعَنْه أنَّ رسولَ اللهِ ، صلَّى الله عليهِ وسلَّم ، قالَ : « العُمْرَةِ إلى العُمرَةِ كَفَّارَةٌ لِمَا بَيْنَهُمَا ، والحَجُّ المَبْرُورُ لَيسَ لَهُ جَزَاءٌ إلاَّ الجَنَّةَ » متفقٌ عليهِ

1275. It is also reported by **Hazrat Abu Hurairah** (R.A.A.) that the Holy Prophet (S.A.W.) said: 'Umrah followed by another Umrah atones for the sins committed between the two. The recompense for a pilgrimage (free from vice) is nothing but the paradise.

(Bukhari and Muslim)

١٢٧٦ـ وعن عائشة، رضي الله عنها، قالت: قلت يا رسول الله، نرى الجهاد أفضل العمل، أفلا نجاهد؟ فقال: «لكن أفضل الجهاد حج مبرور» رواه البخاري.

1276. Hazrat Ayesha (R.A.A.) relates: 'I once requested the Holy Prophet (S.A.W.) O' Messenger of Allah (S.A.W.), we, (the women folk) consider that Jihad (fighting) in the cause of Allah is the best deed, then may we not go forth fighting in the cause of Allah? He (S.A.W.) said: The best form of Jihad in the cause of Allah for you is the pilgrimage, free from all vices and defects. *(Bukhari)*

١٢٧٧ـ وعنها أن رسول الله، صلى الله عليه وسلم، قال: «ما من يوم أكثر من أن يعتق الله فيه عبداً من النار من يوم عرفة» رواه مسلم.

1277. Hazrat Ayesha (R.A.A.) relates that the Holy Prophet (S.A.W.) said: There is no other day on which Allah frees the largest number of his bondsmen from the fire of Hell than the Day of Arafath. *(Muslim)*

١٢٧٨ـ وعن ابن عباس، رضي الله عنهما، أن النبي، صلى الله عليه وسلم، قال: «عمرة في رمضان تعدل حجة ـ أو حجة معي» متفق عليه.

1278. Hazrat Ibn Abbas (R.A.A.) says that the Holy Prophet (S.A.W.) said: Umrah performed during the month of Ramadhan is equivalent to a pilgrimage or equals to the pilgrimage performed in my company. *(Bukhari and Muslim)*

١٢٧٩ ـ وعنه أن امرأة قالت: يا رسول الله، إن فريضة الله على عباده في الحج، أدركت أبي شيخاً كبيراً، لا يثبت على الراحلة، أفأحج عنه؟ قال: «نعم». متفق عليه.

1279. Hazrat Ibn Abbas (R.A.A.) relates: A woman asked the Holy Prophet (S.A.W.) : 'O Messenger of Allah, the pilgrimage has been made obligatory duty by Allah on his servants at a time when my father has reached old age and has not strength to ride an animal. Can I perform the pilgrimage on his behalf? He (S.A.W.) answered, 'Yes! *(Bukhari and Muslim)*

١٢٨٠ – وعن لَقِيطِ بنِ عامرٍ ، رَضِيَ اللهُ عنهُ ، أنَّهُ أتى النَّبيَّ ، صلَّى اللهُ عليهِ وسلَّم ، فقَالَ : إنَّ أبي شَيخٌ كَبيرٌ لايَستَطِيعُ الحَجَّ ، وَلاالعُمرَةَ ، وَلا الظَّعنَ ؟ قالَ : « حُجَّ عَنْ أبيكَ وَاعتَمِرْ »

رواهُ أبو داودَ . والترمذيُّ وقالَ : حديثٌ حسنٌ صحيحٌ .

1280. Hazrat Laqit bin 'Aamir (R.A.A.) says that once he visited the Holy Prophet (S.A.W.) and submitted: My father has grown very old and is not strong enough to undertake the journey to perform the pilgrimage or Umrah. The Holy Prophet (S.A.W.) said: You perform the Hajj and Umrah on behalf of your father.' *(Abu Daud and Tirmizi Imam Tirmiżi* said it is sound and good)

١٢٨١ – وعَنِ السائبِ بنِ يزيدَ ، رَضِيَ اللهُ عنهُ ، قالَ : حُجَّ بي معَ رسولِ اللهِ ، صلَّى اللهُ عليهِ وسلَّمَ ، في حَجةِ الوَدَاعِ ، وَأنَا ابنُ سَبعِ سِنِينَ . رواه البخاريُّ .

1281. Hazrat Saib bin Yazid (R.A.A.) relates: I was seven years old and I accompanied the Holy Prophet (S.A.W.) in his last pilgrimage. *(Bukhari)*

١٢٨٢ – وعَنِ ابنِ عبَّاسٍ ، رَضِيَ اللهُ عَنهُمَا ، أنَّ النبيَّ ، صلَّى اللهُ عليهِ وسلَّم ، لَقِيَ رَكباً بِالرَّوحَاءِ ، فقَالَ : « مَنِ القَومُ ؟ » قَالُوا : المسلِمُونَ . قَالُوا : مَنْ أنتَ ؟ قَالَ : « رسولُ اللهِ » فرَفَعَتِ امرَأةٌ صَبِيّاً فَقَالَتْ : ألِهَذا حَجٌّ ؟ قَالَ : « نعَمْ وَلكِ أجرٌ » رواهُ مُسلمٌ .

1282. This Hadis has been covered in item No. 179 of Chapter 21.

١٢٨٣ – وعَنْ أنسٍ ، رَضِيَ اللهُ عنهُ ، أنَّ رسولَ اللهِ ، صلَّى اللهُ عليهِ وسلَّمَ ، حَجَّ على رَحْلٍ ، وَكانتْ زامِلتَهُ . رواهُ البخاريُّ .

1283. Hazrat Anas bin Malik (R.A.A.) relates that the Holy Prophet (S.A.W.) performed the pilgrimage on a camel which also carried his provisions and there was no separate animal to carry it. *(Bukhari)*

١٢٨٤ – وعَنِ ابنِ عبَّاسٍ ، رَضِيَ اللهُ عَنهُمَا ، قَالَ : كَانَتْ عُكاظُ وَمِجَنَّةُ ، وَذو المَجَازِ أسوَاقاً في الجَاهِلِيَّةِ ، فتَأثَّمُوا أن يَتَّجِرُوا في

الموَاسِمِ ، فنزلَتْ : (ليسَ عليكُمْ جُناحٌ أن تبتغُوا فضلاً مِن رَبِّكُم) [البقرة : ١٩٨] في مواسِمِ الحَجِّ . رواهُ البخاريُّ ٢٥٩ .

1284. **Hazrat Ibn Abbas** (R.A.A.) relates: 'Ukaz, Majinnah and Zul-majaz were markets (seasonal marketing places) during the days of Jahillia (Pre-Islamic days). After the advent of Islam some people thought that it might be sinful to carry on trade and commerce in these markets during the season of pilgrimage. On this the following verse was revealed:

'It is no sin for you that ye seek the bounty of your Lord (by trading in Hajj season).' (2 : 198) *(Bukhari)*

* * * * * * *

BOOK OF JIHAD

CHAPTER 234

VIRTUES OF JIHAD AND ITS IMPORTANCE

قَالَ اللهُ تَعَالَى : وَقَاتِلُوا الْمُشْرِكِينَ كَافَّةً كَمَا يُقَاتِلُونَكُمْ كَافَّةً . وَاعْلَمُوا أَنَّ اللهَ مَعَ الْمُتَّقِينَ [التوبة : ٣٦] وقَالَ تَعَالَى : كُتِبَ عَلَيْكُمُ الْقِتَالُ وَهُوَ كُرْهٌ لَكُمْ ، وَعَسَى أَن تَكْرَهُوا شَيْئاً وَهُوَ خَيْرٌ لَكُمْ ، وَعَسَى أَنْ تُحِبُّوا شَيْئاً وَهُوَ شَرٌّ لَكُمْ . وَاللهُ يَعْلَمُ وَأَنْتُمْ لَاتَعْلَمُونَ . [البقرة : ٢١٦] وقَالَ تَعَالَى : انفِرُوا خِفَافاً وَثِقَالاً ، وجَاهِدُوا بِأَمْوَالِكُمْ وَأَنْفُسِكُمْ فِي سَبِيلِ اللهِ [التوبة : ٤١] وقَالَ تَعَالَى : إِنَّ اللهَ اشْتَرَى مِنَ الْمُؤْمِنِينَ أَنْفُسَهُمْ وَأَمْوَالَهُم بِأَنَّ لَهُمُ الْجَنَّةَ يُقَاتِلُونَ فِي سَبِيلِ اللهِ فَيَقْتُلُونَ وَيُقْتَلُونَ ، وَعْداً عَلَيْهِ حَقّاً فِي التَّوْرَاةِ وَالإِنجِيلِ وَالقُرْآنِ . وَمَنْ أَوْفَى بِعَهْدِهِ مِنَ اللهِ ، فَاسْتَبْشِرُوا بِبَيْعِكُمُ الَّذِي بَايَعْتُمْ بِهِ . وَذَلِكَ هُوَ الْفَوْزُ الْعَظِيمُ [التوبة : ١١١] وقَالَ اللهُ تَعَالَى : لَايَسْتَوِي الْقَاعِدُونَ مِنَ الْمُؤْمِنِينَ غَيْرُ أُولِي الضَّرَرِ ، وَالْمُجَاهِدُونَ فِي سَبِيلِ اللهِ بِأَمْوَالِهِمْ وَأَنْفُسِهِمْ . فَضَّلَ اللهُ الْمُجَاهِدِينَ بِأَمْوَالِهِمْ وَأَنْفُسِهِمْ عَلَى الْقَاعِدِينَ دَرَجَةً ، وَكُلاً وَعَدَ اللهُ الْحُسْنَى ، وَفَضَّلَ اللهُ الْمُجَاهِدِينَ عَلَى الْقَاعِدِينَ أَجْراً عَظِيماً . دَرَجَاتٍ مِنْهُ ، وَمَغْفِرَةً ، وَرَحْمَةً . وَكَانَ اللهُ غَفُوراً رَحِيماً . [النساء : ٩٥] . وقَالَ تَعَالَى : يَا أَيُّهَا الَّذِينَ آمَنُوا هَلْ أَدُلُّكُمْ عَلَى تِجَارَةٍ تُنجِيكُمْ مِنْ عَذَابٍ أَلِيمٍ ؟ تُؤْمِنُونَ بِاللهِ وَرَسُولِهِ ، وَتُجَاهِدُونَ فِي سَبِيلِ اللهِ بِأَمْوَالِكُم وَأَنفُسِكُم . ذَلِكُم خَيْرٌ لَكُم إِنْ كُنتُم تَعْلَمُونَ ، يَغْفِرْ لَكُم ذُنُوبَكُمْ ، وَيُدْخِلْكُمْ جَنَّاتٍ تَجْرِي مِنْ تَحْتِهَا الأَنْهَارُ ، وَمَسَاكِنَ طَيِّبَةً فِي جَنَّاتِ عَدْنٍ ، ذَلِكَ الْفَوْزُ الْعَظِيمُ ، وَأُخْرَى تُحِبُّونَهَا نَصْرٌ مِنَ اللهِ وَفَتْحٌ قَرِيبٌ . وَبَشِّرِ الْمُؤْمِنِينَ [الصف : ١٠ — ١٣]

Allah the Exalted has said:

295. And wage war on all the idolators as they are waging war on all of you. And know that Allah is with those who keep their duty (Unto Him) (9: 36).

296. Warfare is ordained for you, though it is hateful unto you, but it may happen that ye hate a thing which is good for you, and it may happen that ye love a thing which is bad for you. Allah knoweth, ye know not (2: 216).

297. Go forth, light-armed and heavy armed, and strive
with your wealth and with your lives in the way of Allah! (9:41)

298. Lo! Allah hath bought from the believers their lives and their wealth because th Gardens will be theirs. They shall fight in the way of Allah and shall slay and shall be slain. It is a promise which is binding on Him in the Torah and the Gospel and the Quran. Who fulfilleth His covenant better than Allah? Rejoice then in your bargain that ye have made, for that is the supreme triumph (9:111)

299. Those of the believers who sit still, other than those who have a (disabling) hurt are not on an equality with those who strive in the way of Allah with their wealth and lives. Allah hath conferred on those who strive with their wealth and lives, a rank above the sedentary. Unto each Allah hath promised good but He hath bestowed on those who strive for a great reward above the sedentary. Degrees of rank from Him, and forgiveness and mercy. Allah is ever Forgiving, Merciful. (4.95-96)

300. O ye who believe! shall I show you a commerce that will save you from a painful doom? Ye should believe in Allah and His messenger, and should strive for the cause of Allah with your wealth and your lives. That is better for you, if ye did but know. He will forgive you your sins and bring you into Gardens underneath which rivers flow, and pleasant dwellings in Gardens of Eden. That is the supreme triumph. And (He wil give you) another blessing which ye love: help from Allah and present victory: Give good tidings (O' Muhammad) to believers. (61:10-13)

١٢٨٥ – عَنْ أبي هُرَيرَةَ ، رَضِيَ اللهُ عَنْهُ ، قالَ : سُئِلَ رسولُ اللهِ ، صَلّى اللهُ عَليهِ وسلَّمَ : أيُّ الأعمالِ أفْضَلُ ؟ قالَ : « إيمانٌ باللهِ ورَسولِهِ » قيلَ : ثمَّ ماذَا ؟ قالَ : « الجهادُ في سبيلِ اللهِ » قيلَ : ثمَّ ماذا ؟ قالَ : « حَجٌّ مَبرُورٌ » متفقٌ عليهِ .

1285. This Hadis is the same as No. 1273 of Chapter 238.

١٢٨٦ – وَعَنِ ابنِ مَسْعُودٍ ، رَضِيَ اللهُ عَنْهُ ، قَالَ : قُلْتُ يارَسُولَ اللهِ ، أيُّ العَمَلِ أَحَبُّ إلى اللهِ تَعَالى ؟ قَالَ : « الصَّلاةُ عَلى وَقْتِها » قُلْتُ ثُمَّ أيٌّ ؟ قالَ : « بِرُّ الوَالدَيْنِ » قُلْتُ : ثُمَّ أيٌّ ؟ قَالَ : « الجِهَادُ في سَبيلِ اللهِ » متفقٌ عليهِ .

1286. This Hadis has been covered in No. 312 of Chapter 40.

١٢٨٧ – وَعَنْ أبي ذَرٍّ ، رَضِيَ اللهُ عنهُ ، قَالَ : قُلْتُ يارَسُولَ اللهِ أيُّ العَمَلِ أفضَلُ ؟ قَالَ : « الإيمَانُ باللهِ ، وَالجِهَادُ في سَبيلِهِ » مُتفقٌ عليهِ

1287. This Hhas been included in No. 1273 of Chapter 233.

١٢٨٨ – وَعَنْ أَنَسٍ ، رَضِيَ اللهُ عنهُ ، أنَّ رَسُولَ اللهِ ، صَلَّى اللهُ عليهِ وسلَّم ، قَالَ : « لَغَدْوَةٌ في سَبيلِ اللهِ ، أَوْ رَوْحَةٌ ، خَيْرٌ مِنَ الدُّنْيَا وَمَا فيها » متفقٌ عليهِ .

1288. **Hazrat Anas bin Malik** (R.A.A.) relates that the Holy Prophet (S.A.W.) said: 'To spend one morning or evening (i.e. carrying Jihad) in the cause of Allah is better than the world and whatever is in the world. *(Bukhari and Muslim)*

١٢٨٩ – وَعَنْ أبي سَعيدٍ الخُدْرِيِّ ، رَضِيَ اللهُ عَنْهُ قَالَ : أتى رَجُلٌ رَسُولَ اللهِ ، صَلَّى اللهُ عَليهِ وسلَّمَ ، فَقَالَ : أيُّ النَّاسِ أَفْضَلُ ؟ قَالَ : « مُؤْمِنٌ يُجَاهِدُ بِنَفْسِهِ وَمَالِهِ في سَبيلِ اللهِ » قال : ثُمَّ مَنْ ؟ قَالَ : « مُؤْمِنٌ في شِعْبٍ مِنَ الشِّعَابِ يَعْبُدُ اللهَ ، وَيَدَعُ النَّاسَ مِنْ شَرِّهِ » متفقٌ عليهِ .

1289. **Hazrat Abu Sa'eed Khudri** (R.A.A.) relates that a man visited the Holy Prophet (S.A.W.) and submitted: O Messenger of Allah, who is the best person (among all the human beings)? The Holy Prophet (S.A.W.) replied: A believer who carries on Jihad with his life and wealth for the sake of Allah. The man again asked: 'And who after him? He (S.A.W.) said. A Muslim who retires to one of the valleys and prays to Allah and does not harm the people.

(Bukhari and Muslim)

١٢٩٠ – وعَنْ سَهْلِ بنِ سَعْدٍ ، رَضِيَ اللهُ عَنْهُ ، أنَّ رَسُولَ اللهِ ، صَلَّى اللهُ عليهِ وَسَلَّمَ ، قَالَ : « رِباطُ يَوْمٍ في سَبِيلِ اللهِ خَيْرٌ مِنَ الدُّنْيَا وَمَا عَلَيْهَا ، وَمَوْضِعُ سَوْطِ أَحَدِكُمْ مِنَ الجَنَّةِ خَيْرٌ مِنَ الدُّنْيَا وَمَا عَلَيْهَا ، والرَّوْحَةُ يَرُوحُهَا العَبْدُ في سَبِيلِ اللهِ ، تَعالى ، أو الغَدْوَةُ ، خَيْرٌ مِنَ الدُّنْيَا وَمَا عَلَيْهَا » متفقٌ عليه

1290. Hazrat Sahl bin Sa'd (R.A.A.) states that the Holy Prophet (S.A.W.) said: Guarding the border land (even) for a day is better than the world and all that it contains; and the smallest piece of land in Paradise equal to even your whip, is better than the world and all that it contains. For a person to go on Jihad (fighting or striving) for the sake of Allah for a morning or an evening, is better than the world and all that it contains. *(Bukhari and Muslim)*

١٢٩١ – وعَنْ سَلْمَانَ ، رَضِيَ اللهُ عَنْهُ ، قالَ : سَمِعْتُ رَسُولَ اللهِ ، صلَّى اللهُ عليهِ وسلَّمَ يَقُولُ : « رِباطُ يَوْمٍ وَلَيْلَةٍ خَيْرٌ مِنْ صِيامِ شَهْرٍ وَقِيامِه ، وإنْ ماتَ فيه جرَى عَلَيْهِ عَمَلُهُ الَّذي كانَ يَعْمَلُ ، وأُجْرِيَ عَلَيْهِ رِزْقُهُ ، وأَمِنَ الفَتَّانَ » رواه مُسلم .

1291. Hazrat Salman (R.A.A.) relates that he heard the Holy Prophet (S.A.W.) say: Guarding the frontiers of an Islamic State for a day and a night is better than a month's fasting and praying at night; and if anybody dies (while guarding the frontiers), the work which he was performing, will be continued, similarly his subsistence will be maintained and he will be protected against trials and mischiefs (of the grave). *(Muslim)*

١٢٩٢ – وعَنْ فَضالَةَ بنِ عُبَيْدٍ ، رَضِيَ اللهُ عَنْهُ ، أنَّ رَسُولَ اللهِ ، صَلَّى اللهُ عليهِ وسلَّمَ ، قَالَ : « كُلُّ مَيِّتٍ يُخْتَمُ عَلى عَمَلِهِ إلاَّ المُرابِطَ في سَبِيلِ اللهِ ، فَإنَّهُ يَنْمِي لهُ عَمَلُهُ إلى يَوْمِ القِيامَةِ ، وَيُؤَمَّنُ مِن فِتْنَةِ القَبْرِ » رواهُ أبو داودَ ، والترمذيُّ وَقَالَ : حديثٌ حَسَنٌ صحيحٌ .

1292. Hazrat Fudalah bin 'Ubaid (R.A.A.) relates that the Holy Prophet (S.A.W.) said: Death terminates all actions except in the case of a person who guards the frontiers of an Islamic State for the sake of Allah; the activities of such person continues to multiply till the day of judgement, and he is protected against the treats (horrors or torments) of grave. *(Abu Daud and Tirmizi*, latter said it is sound and good)

١٢٩٣ - وَعَنْ عُثْمَانَ ، رَضِيَ اللهُ عَنْهُ ، قَالَ : سَمِعْتُ رَسُولَ اللهِ صَلَّى اللهُ عَلَيهِ وسَلَّمَ ، يَقُولُ : « رِباطُ يَوْمٍ في سَبِيلِ اللهِ خَيْرٌ مِنْ أَلْفِ يَوْمٍ فِيما سِوَاهُ مِنَ المَنَازِلِ » رواهُ التِرمذيُّ وقالَ : حديثٌ حَسَنٌ صَحيحٌ .

1293. Hazrat 'Usman (R.A.A.) relates that he heard the Holy Prophet (S.A.W.) say: Guarding the frontiers of an Islamic State for a day for the sake of Allah, is better than a thousand days of other good works. *(Tirmizi)*

١٢٩٤ - وَعَنْ أَبِي هُرَيرةَ ، رَضِيَ اللهُ عَنْهُ ، قَالَ : قَالَ رسولُ اللهِ ، صَلَّى اللهُ عليه وَسَلَّم : « تَضَمَّنَ اللهُ لِمَنْ خَرَجَ في سَبِيلِهِ ، لا يُخْرِجُهُ إلاَّ جِهَادٌ في سَبِيلي ، وَإيمَانٌ بي وَتَصْدِيقٌ بِرُسُلي ؛ فَهوَ ضَامِنٌ أنْ أُدْخِلَهُ الجَنَّةَ ، أوْ أُرْجِعَهُ إلى مَنْزِلِهِ الَّذي خَرَجَ مِنْهُ بما نَالَ مِنْ أَجْرٍ ، أوْ غَنِيمَةٍ . وَالَّذي نَفْسُ مُحمَّدٍ بِيَدِهِ ما مِنْ كَلْمٍ يُكْلَمُ في سَبيلِ اللهِ إلاَّ جاءَ يَوْمَ القِيَامةِ كَهَيْئَتِهِ يَوْمَ كُلِمَ ؛ لَوْنُهُ لَوْنُ دَمٍ ، وَرِيحُهُ رِيحُ مِسْكٍ . وَالَّذي نَفْسُ مُحَمَّدٍ بِيَدِهِ لَوْلا أنْ أَشُقَّ عَلَى المُسْلِمِينَ ما قَعَدْتُ خِلافَ سَرِيَّةٍ تَغزُو في سَبيلِ اللهِ أبَداً ، وَلَكِنْ لاأَجِدُ سَعَةً فأَحْمِلَهمْ وَلا يَجِدُونَ سَعَةً ، وَيَشُقُّ عَلَيْهِمْ أن يَتَخَلَّفُوا عَنِّي . وَالَّذي نَفسُ مُحَمَّدٍ بِيَدِهِ ، لَوَدِدْتُ أن أغزوَ في سَبِيلِ اللهِ ، فَأُقْتَلَ ، ثُمَّ أغزو ، فَأُقتلَ ، ثُمَّ أغزو ؛ فَأُقتلَ ، رواهُ مُسلمٌ وروى البخاريُّ بَعْضَهُ .

1294. Hazrat Abu Hurairah (R.A.A.) relates that the Holy Prophet (S.A.W.) said: A person who proceeds on Jihad for the sake of Allah, impelled only by his faith in Allah and by his affirmation of the truth of Allah's prophets, Allah the Exalted guarantees that he will be either admitted into paradise (if he is martyred) or bring him back to his place from which he started on Jihad, along with the recompense or spoils achieved by him. By Allah in whose hands is the life of Muhammad (S.A.W.), such a person will suffer no injury for the sake of Allah but that he will appear on the Day of Judgement in the same condition in which he was on the day when he was injured, its colour will be the colour of blood but it will smell like the fragrance of musk. By Allah in whose hands is the life of Muhammad (S.A.W.), had it been not hard upon the Muslims, I would not lag behind any army that goes on jihad to fight for the sake of Allah: but neither I have the means to provide conveyance to them (soldiers) nor have the Muslims such means and the Muslims would never like that they may stand behind while I go on jihad. By Allah in whose hands is my life, undoubtedly I long to fight in the cause of Allah and be martyred, and to fight again and be martyred and to fight again and be martyred. *(Muslim. Bukhari* reported some parts of it.)

١٢٩٥ – وَعَنْهُ قَالَ: قَالَ رَسُولُ اللهِ، صَلَّى اللهُ عليه وسلَّم: «ما مِنْ مَكلومٍ يُكْلَمُ في سَبيلِ اللهِ إلاَّ جاءَ يَوْمَ القِيامَةِ، وكَلْمُهُ يَدْمَى: اللوْنُ لونُ دَمٍ، والريحُ رِيحُ مِسْكٍ» متفقٌ عليه.

1295. Hazrat Abu Hurairah (R.A.A.) says that the Holy Prophet (S.A.W.) said a person who is injured in the cause of Allah (jihad) will appear on the Day of Judgement with his wounds bleeding, its colour will be the colour of blood, but its smell will be like the fragrance of musk. *(Bukhari and Muslim)*

١٢٩٦ – وَعَنْ مُعَاذٍ رَضِيَ اللهُ عَنْهُ، عَنِ النَّبي صلَّى اللهُ عليهِ وسلَّم، قَالَ: «مَنْ قاتَلَ في سَبيلِ اللهِ مِن رَجلٍ مُسلِمٍ فُواقَ نَاقةٍ وَجَبَتْ له الجَنَّةُ. وَمَنْ جُرِحَ جُرْحاً في سَبيلِ اللهِ أَوْ نُكِبَ نَكبةً؛ فإنَّهَا تجيءُ يَوْمَ القِيامَةِ كأغْزَرِ ماكانَتْ: لَوْنُها الزَّعفَرَانُ، ورِيحُهَا كالمِسكِ» رواهُ أبو داودَ، والترمذيُّ وقَالَ: حديثٌ حَسَنٌ صحيحٌ.

1296. Hazrat Mu'az bin Jabal (R.A.A.) relates that the Holy Prophet (S.A.W.) said: For a man amongst the Muslims who fights for the cause of Allah (carries on Jihad) for (the shortest time) during which a she camel is milked, he is entitled to go to heaven; and one who receives a wound or even a bruise in fighting in the cause of Allah (Jihad) will appear on the Day of Judgement, quite fresh as it was (when he received it); its colour will be that of saffron and its smell like the fragrance of musk. *(Abu Daud and Tirmizi* and the latter said it is good and sound).

١٢٩٧ – وَعَنْ أَبي هُرَيرةَ، رَضِيَ اللهُ عَنْهُ، قَالَ: مَرَّ رَجُلٌ مِنْ أَصْحَابِ رَسُولِ اللهِ صَلَّى اللهُ عَليهِ وَسلَّم، بِشِعْبٍ فيه عُيَيْنَةٌ مِن مَاءٍ عَذبَةٍ؛ فأَعجبَتهُ، فقَالَ: لو اعتزَلتُ النَّاسَ فأقَمْتُ في هذا الشِّعبِ، ولَنْ أفعَلَ حتى أستأذِنَ رَسُولَ اللهِ، صَلَّى اللهُ عليه وَسلَّم، فذكرَ ذلكَ لِرسُولِ اللهِ صَلَّى اللهُ عليهِ وَسلَّم؛ فقَالَ: «لا تفعلْ، فإنَّ مُقامَ أحدِكُمْ في سَبيلِ

اللهِ أفضَلُ مِنْ صَلاتِهِ في بَيْتِهِ سَبْعِينَ عَاماً ، ألا تُحِبُّونَ أنْ يَغْفِرَ اللهُ لكُمْ وَيُدْخِلَكُمُ الجنَّةَ ؟ أغزُوا في سبيلِ اللهِ ، مَنْ قَاتَلَ في سَبيلِ اللهِ فُوَاقَ نَاقَةٍ وَجَبَتْ له الجنَّةُ » رواهُ الترمذيُّ وقَالَ : حديثٌ حَسَنٌ .

1297. Hazrat Abu Hurairah (R.A.A.) states that a companion of the Holy Prophet (S.A.W.) passed through a valley, where there was a small spring of sweet water. He liked the spring very much. He said to himself: I wish I could withdraw from the people and live in this valley; but I shall do so only with the approval of the Holy Prophet (S.A.W.); at last he mentioned this to the Holy Prophet (S.A.W.) who said to him: Do not do this (retire from the world), for any one of you who stands ready for the cause of Allah, is better than his praying in his home for seventy years. Do you not like that Allah the Most High may forgive you and admit you in the paradise? (If you want this) then fight (carry on Jihad) in the cause of Allah. Paradise becomes certain for him who fights (carries on Jihad) in the cause of Allah, the Most High even for the shortest spell during which a she-camel is milked twice. *(Tirmizi)*

١٢٩٨ – وعَنْهُ قَالَ قِيلَ : يا رَسُولَ اللهِ ، ما يَعْدِلُ الجِهَادَ في سَبيلِ اللهِ ؟ قَالَ : « لاتَسْتَطِيعُونَهُ » فَأعَادُوا عليهِ مرَّتَيْنِ أو ثَلاثاً كُلُّ ذلكَ يقول : « لاتَسْتَطِيعُونَه ! » ثُمَّ قالَ : « مَثَلُ المُجَاهدِ في سَبيلِ اللهِ كَمَثَلِ الصَّائمِ القَائمِ القَانِتِ بآياتِ اللهِ لا يَفْتُرُ : مِنْ صَلاةٍ ، ولا صِيامٍ ، حتَى يَرجِعَ المجَاهِدُ في سَبيلِ اللهِ » متفقٌ عليه . وهذا لفظُ مسلِمٍ .

وفي روايةِ البخاريِّ ، أنَّ رَجلاً قَالَ : يا رَسُولَ اللهِ دُلَّني عَلى عَمَلٍ يَعْدِلُ الجِهَادَ ؟ قالَ : « لا أجِدهُ » ثُمَّ قال : « هَلْ تَستَطِيعُ إذا خَرَجَ المُجَاهِدُ أن تَدخُلَ مَسجِدَكَ فَتَقُومَ وَلا تَفتُرَ ، وتَصُومَ ولا تُفطِرَ ؟ » فَقَالَ : ومَنْ يستطيعُ ذَلكَ ؟ !

1298. Hazrat Abu Hurairah (R.A.A.) relates that the Holy Prophet (S.A.W.) was asked: O Messenger of Allah (S.A.W.), what other good act is equivalent to the recompense for Jihad (fighting in the cause of Allah)? He (S.A.W.) answered: you do not have the strength to carry it out. The Companions repeated twice or thrice the same question, and each time he (S.A.W.) answered: you do not have the strength to carry it out. He then added: The case of one who strives (carries out Jihad) for the sake of Allah is like that of a person who observes the fast and the *salat* (prayers) and reads the Holy Quran with fervour and devotion, and he continues his prayers till the return of the person fighting for the sake of Allah from Jihad, and does not forsake his prayers. (This is *Muslims* wording).

Bukhari's version says: A man asked the Holy Prophet (S.A.W.): O Messenger of Allah (S.A.W.), please let me know some action which may be equal to Jihad in its recompense. He (S.A.W.) answered : I am not aware of any such action. The Holy Prophet (S.A.W.) further added: When a person goes on Jihad for the sake of Allah, can you enter a mosque and continue praying there without interruption, and go on fasting without breaking it, till the Mujahid returns from Jihad? The said man replied: who can have so much power for this? (meaning that this is an almost impossible job).

١٢٩٩ – وَعَنْهُ أنَّ رَسُولَ اللهِ ، صَلَّى اللهُ عليه وَسَلَّم ، قَالَ : « مِن خَيرِ مَعَاشِ النَّاسِ لَهُم رجُلٌ مُمسِكٌ بِعنَانِ فَرَسِهِ في سَبيلِ اللهِ ، يَطِيرُ عَلَى مَتنِهِ كُلَّمَا سَمِعَ هَيعةً ، أوْ فَزعَةً طَارَ عَلى مَتنِهِ ، يَبتَغِي القتلَ أو المَوتَ مَظَانَّهُ أو رَجُلٌ في غُنَيْمَةٍ أو شَعَفَةٍ مِن هذا الشُّعَفِ أو بَطنِ وادٍ من هذهِ الأودِيَةِ يُقِيمُ الصَّلاةَ ، وَيُؤتِي الزَّكَاةَ ، وَيَعبُدُ رَبَّهُ حَتَّى يَأتِيَهُ اليَقِينُ لَيسَ مِنَ النَّاسِ إلاَّ في خَيرٍ » رواهُ مسلم .

1299. Hazrat Abu Hurairah (R.A.A.) relates that the Holy Prophet (S.A.W.) said: 'The best life is that of a person who is always ready and alert holding the reins of his horse, for the cause of Allah. As soon as he hears anything about some danger, he runs to the affected spot on the back of his horse seeking to kill the (enemy) or get himself killed, or the life of that person who lives on the top of a hill or in a valley with some goats, prays, pays the zakat (the poor due) and continues worshipping Allah till his death, and does not have any concern with the affairs of anyone except the welfare of the humanity.
(Muslim)

١٣٠٠ – وَعَنْهُ ، أنَّ رسولَ اللهِ ، صلَّى اللهُ عليهِ وسَلَّم ، قالَ : « إنَّ في الجنَّةِ مائَةَ دَرَجَةٍ أعَدَّهَا اللهُ للمُجَاهِدِينَ في سَبِيلِ اللهِ ما بَيْنَ الدَّرَجَتَيْنِ كَمَا بَيْنَ السَّمَاءِ وَالأرْضِ » رواهُ البخاريُّ .

1300. Hazrat Abu Hurairah (R.A.A.) says that the Holy Prophet (S.A.W.) said: There are one hundred stages in the Paradise which Allah, the Exalted, has prepared for those persons who carry on Jihad (fighting or struggle) in the cause of Allah. The distance between any two of these stages is equal to the distance between the earth and the sky.
(Bukhari)

١٣٠١ – وعَنْ أبي سَعيدٍ الخُدْرِيِّ ، رضِيَ اللهُ عَنْهُ ، أنَّ رسُولَ اللهِ ، صلَّى اللهُ عليهِ وسلَّم ، قَالَ : « مَنْ رَضِيَ بِاللهِ رَبّاً ، وَبالإسْلامِ دِيناً ، وبِمُحَمَّدٍ رَسُولاً . وَجَبَتْ لَهُ الجَنَّةُ » فَعَجِبَ لها أبو سَعيدٍ ، فقَالَ أَعِدْها عَلَيَّ يا رَسولَ اللهِ . فَأَعَادَهَا عَلَيْهِ ، ثُمَّ قَالَ : « وأُخْرَى يرْفَعُ اللهُ بِها العَبْدَ مِائَةَ دَرَجَةٍ في الجَنَّةِ ، ما بيْنَ كُلِّ دَرَجَتَيْنِ كَمَا بَيْنَ السَّماءِ وَالأَرْضِ » قالَ : وما هِيَ يا رسولَ اللهِ ؟ قال : « الجِهادُ في سَبيلِ اللهِ ، الجِهادُ في سَبيلِ اللهِ » رواهُ مُسلمٌ .

1301. Hazrat Abu Sa'eed Khudri (R.A.A.) reports that the Holy Prophet (S.A.W.) said: For a person who has accepted and becomes contented with it that Allah is his Sustainer, Islam is his Religion and Muhammad (S.A.W.) is the Prophet of Allah, the heaven has become certain for him. Hazrat Abu Sa'eed (R.A.A.) was very much surprised on this, and therefore he requested the Holy Prophet (S.A.W.) who stated it once more and further said: There is yet another thing by which Allah will upgrade His servant by one hundred grades in Paradise, and the distance between any two stages is equal to the distance between the earth and the sky. Hazrat Abu Sa'eed (R.A.A.) submitted. O Messenger of Allah! What is that thing? He answered. Jihad in the cause of Allah. *(Muslim)*

١٣٠٢ – وعَنْ أبي بَكْرِ بنِ أبي مُوسى الأشْعَرِيِّ ، قَالَ : سَمِعْتُ أبي ، رضِيَ اللهُ عَنْه ، وَهُو بِحَضْرَةِ العَدُوِّ ، يقول : قَالَ رَسُولُ اللهِ ، صلَّى اللهُ عليهِ وسلَّم : « إنَّ أَبْوَابَ الجَنَّةِ تَحْتَ ظِلالِ السُّيُوفِ » فَقامَ رَجُلٌ رَثُّ الهَيْئَةِ فَقَالَ : يَا أَبَا مُوسَى أأنْتَ سمِعْتَ رسولَ اللهِ ، صلَّى اللهُ عليهِ وسلَّم ، يقول هذا ؟ قالَ : نَعَمْ ، فرَجَعَ إلى أصْحَابِهِ ، فَقَالَ : « أَقْرَأُ عَلَيْكُمُ السَّلامَ » ثُمَّ كَسَرَ جَفْنَ[٢٦٣] سَيْفِهِ فَألْقَاه ، ثُمَّ مَشَى بسَيْفِهِ إلى العَدُوِّ فَضَرَبَ بِهِ حَتَّى قُتِلَ » رواه مسلمٌ .

1302. Hazrat Abu Bakr bin Abu Musa Al-Ash'ari (R.A.A.) relates that he heard his father say in the presence of an enemy: The Holy Prophet (S.A.W.) said: That the gates of Paradise lie under the shadow of swords. On this a man who was in ugly appearance stood up and enquired: O Abu Musa, was it you who heard the Holy Prophet (S.A.W.) say this? He answered: Yes. The man then came back towards his companions and said: 'I offer my (Last) salute, saying this he saluted them in farewell, broke the scabbard of his sword and threw it away, and walked with his sword towards the enemy and fought till he was martyred. *(Muslim)*

١٣٠٣ – وعَنْ أبي عَبْسٍ عبدِ الرَّحمنِ بنِ جَبْرٍ ، رَضِيَ اللهُ عنه ، قالَ : قالَ رَسُولُ الله ، صلَّى اللهُ عليه وسلَّمَ : « ما اغبرَّتْ قَدَمَا عَبْدٍ في سَبِيلِ الله فتَمَسَّهُ النَّارُ » رواهُ البُخاريُّ .

1303. Hazrat Abu 'Abs Abdur Rahman bin Jub'r (R.A.A.) relates that the Holy Prophet (S.A.W.) said: The fire of Hell will not touch the feet of a person which are covered with dust in the struggle (Jihad), for the cause of Allah. *(Bukhari)*

١٣٠٤ – وعَنْ أبي هُرَيرَةَ ، رَضِيَ اللهُ عَنْهُ ، قالَ : قالَ رَسُولُ الله ، صلَّى اللهُ عليهِ وسلَّم . « لا يَلِجُ النَّارَ رَجُلٌ بَكَى مِنْ خَشْيَةِ الله حتَّى يَعُودَ اللَّبَنُ في الضَّرعِ ، ولا يَجْتَمِعُ عَلى عَبْدٍ غُبارٌ في سَبِيلِ الله ودُخَانُ جَهَنَّمَ » رواه التِّرمذيُّ وقالَ : حديثٌ حسنٌ صحيحٌ .

1304. This Hadis has already been mentioned vide No. 448 of Chapter 54.

١٣٠٥ – وعَنِ ابنِ عبَّاسٍ ، رَضِيَ الله عَنْهُما . قالَ : سَمِعْتُ رَسُولَ اللهِ ، صلَّى الله عليهِ وسلَّم ، يَقُولُ : « عَيْنَانِ لا تَمَسُّهُما النَّار : عَيْنٌ بَكَتْ مِنْ خَشْيَةِ اللهِ ، وعَيْنٌ بَاتَتْ تَحْرُسُ في سَبِيلِ اللهِ » رواه التِّرمذيُّ وقالَ : حديثٌ حسنٌ .

1305. Hazrat Ibn-Abbas (R.A.A.) says that he heard the Holy Prophet (S.A.W.) say: The fire of Hell will not touch two pairs of eyes: one that sheds tears out of fear of Allah and the other that keeps watch through the night in the cause of Allah. *(Tirmizi)*

١٣٠٦ – وعن زَيدِ بنِ خالدٍ ، رضِيَ الله عَنه ، أنَّ رَسُولَ اللهِ ، صلَّى الله عليهِ وسلَّم ، قالَ « مَن جهَّزَ غازِياً في سَبِيلِ اللهِ فقَدْ غزَا ، ومَنْ خلَفَ غازِياً في أهلِهِ بخيرٍ فقَدْ غزَا » متفقٌ عليه .

1306. This Hadith is the same as No. 177 of Chapter 21.

١٣٠٧ – وَعَنْ أبي أُمَامَةَ ، رَضِيَ اللهُ عَنْهُ قَالَ : قَالَ رَسُولُ اللهِ ، صَلَّى اللهُ عَلَيهِ وسَلَّمَ : « أَفْضَلُ الصَّدَقَاتِ ظِلُّ فُسْطَاطٍ[٢٦٣] في سَبِيلِ اللهِ وَمَنِيحَةُ خادِمٍ فِي سَبِيلِ اللهِ ، أَو طَرُوقَةُ فَحْلٍ في سبيلِ اللهِ » رواه الترمذي وقالَ : حديثٌ حَسَنٌ صحيحٌ .

1307. Hazrat Abu Ummah (R.A.A.) relates that the Holy Prophet (S.A.W.) said: 'The best charity is providing a tent for protection against the heat in the cause of Allah, or providing a servant to a person who strives in the cause of Allah (carries on Jihad), or providing a young she-camel to a mujahid (fighter) in the cause of Allah.

(Tirmizi. He said it is sound and good)

١٣٠٨ – وَعَن أَنَسٍ ، رَضِيَ اللهُ عَنْه ، أَنَّ فَتىً مِن أَسْلَمَ قَالَ : يا رسولَ اللهِ إنِّي أُرِيد الغَزْوَ وَلَيْسَ مَعِي ما أَتَجَهَّزُ بِهِ ، قَالَ : « ائْتِ فُلاناً ، فَإِنَّه كانَ قَدْ تَجَهَّزَ فَمَرِضَ » فَأَتاه فَقَالَ : إنَّ رَسُولَ اللهِ ، صلَّى اللهُ عليهِ وسلَّم ، يَقْرِئكَ السَّلامَ ويقولُ : أَعْطِني الذي تَجَهَّزتَ بِهِ . قَالَ : يَا فُلانَةُ . أَعْطِيهِ الذي كُنْتُ تَجَهَّزْتُ بِهِ ، وَلا تَحْبِسِي عَنْهُ شَيْئاً . فَوَاللهِ لا تَحْبِسِي مِنْه شَيْئاً فَيُبَارَكَ لَكِ فيهِ . رَوَاه مسلمٌ .

1308. This Hadith is the same as No. 176 of Chapter 20.

١٣٠٩ – وَعَن أَبي سَعِيدٍ الخُدْرِيِّ ، رَضِيَ اللهُ عَنْهُ ، أَنَّ رَسُولَ اللهِ ، صَلَّى اللهُ عليهِ وسلَّم ، بَعَثَ إلى بَنِي لَحيَانَ ، فَقَالَ : « لِيَنْبَعِثْ مِنْ كُلِّ رَجُلَيْنِ أَحَدُهُما . وَالأَجْرُ بَيْنَهُما » رَوَاهُ مسلمٌ .

وفي روايةٍ لهُ : « لِيَخْرُجْ مِنْ كُلِّ رَجُلَيْنِ رَجُلٌ » ثُمَّ قالَ لِلقاعِدِ : « أَيُّكُمْ خَلَفَ الخارِجَ فِي أَهْلِهِ وَمالِهِ بِخَيْرٍ كانَ لهُ مِثْلُ نِصْفِ أَجرِ الخارِجِ » .

1309. Hazrat Abu Sa'eed Khudri (R.A.A.) relates that the Holy Prophet (S.A.W.) proposed to send a force towards Bani Lahyan tribe for Jihad and directed that out of every two men one should join the force (for Jihad) and further said that the recompense of both will be equal. *(Muslim)*

Another version of Muslim says: The Holy Prophet (S.A.W.) said: Let one out of two men should go forth for Jihad and then addressing those who stayed behind he (S.A.W.) said: Those of you who look after the family and property of those who have joined the force shall have his recompense equal to half of the recompense of the Mujahid (Fighter).

١٣١٠ – وعَنِ البَراءِ ، رضي اللهُ عَنْهُ ، قالَ : أتى النّبيَّ ، صلّى الله عليه وسلّمَ ، رَجلٌ مُقَنَّعٌ بالحَديد . فقال : يا رَسُولَ الله أقاتِلُ أوْ أُسْلِمُ ؟ قالَ : « أَسْلِمْ، ثُمَّ قاتِلْ » فأَسْلَمَ ، ثمّ قاتَلَ فقُتِلَ . فقالَ رسولُ الله ، صَلّى اللهُ عليه وسلّمَ : « عَمِلَ قليلاً وأُجِرَ كثيراً »

متفقٌ عليهِ . وهذا لفظُ البخاريّ .

1310. Hazrat Bra'a bin 'Aazib (R.A.A.) relates: A man fully armed came to the Holy Prophet (S.A.W.) and said: O Messenger of Allah, shall I go on Jihad first or I should embrace Islam first? He (S.A.W.) answered: Embrace Islam first and then go on Jihad. Accordingly he embraced Islam and thereafter he fought and was martyred. On this the Holy Prophet (S.A.W.) said: He did a little, but was recompensed much. *(Bukhari and Muslim.* This is the wording of *Bukhari)*

١٣١١ – وعَنْ أنَسٍ ، رَضِيَ الله عَنه ، أنَّ النّبيَّ ، صلّى الله عَليهِ وسلّم ، قالَ : « ما أحَدٌ يَدْخُلُ الجَنّةَ يُحِبُّ أنْ يَرْجِعَ إلى الدُّنْيا ولَه ما عَلى الأرْضِ مِنْ شَيْءٍ إلّا الشّهيد ، يَتَمَنّى أنْ يَرْجِعَ إلى الدُّنْيا ، فيُقْتَلَ عَشْرَ مَرّاتٍ ؛ لِما يَرَى مِنَ الكَرامَةِ » .

وفي روايةٍ : « لِمَا يَرَى مِنْ فَضْلِ الشّهادَةِ » مُتفقٌ عليهِ .

1311. Hazrat Anas (R.A.A.) relates that the Holy Prophet (S.A.W.) said: No person who has entered paradise, would like to come back to this world, even if he may be given all that the world contains; but a martyr, yearns that he may return to the world and be slain ten times for the sake of Allah on account of the honour that he experienced by virtue of his martyrdom.

According to another version: (Of course) when a martyr sees the honour and esteem of martyrdom, he desires to return to this world. *(Bukhari and Muslim)*

١٣١٢ – وعَنْ عَبدِ اللهِ بنِ عَمروِ بنِ العاصِ ، رَضِيَ اللهُ عَنهما ، أنّ رَسُولَ اللهِ ، صَلّى الله عليهِ وسلّم ، قالَ : « يَغْفِرُ اللهُ للشّهيدِ كُلَّ ذَنْبٍ إلّا الدَّيْنَ » رواه مسلمٌ .

وفي رواية له : « القَتْلُ في سَبِيلِ اللهِ يُكَفِّرُ كُلَّ شَيْءٍ إلاَّ الدَّيْنَ » .

1312. Hazrat Abdullah bin 'Amr bin Al'Aas (R.A.A.) relates that the Holy Prophet (S.A.W.) said: Allah forgives all sins of a martyr except his debt.
(Muslim)

Another version says: Being slain in the cause of Allah is enough to atone for everything except debt.
(Muslim)

١٣١٣– وعَنْ أبي قَتَادَةَ ، رَضِيَ اللهُ عَنْه ، أنَّ رَسُولَ اللهِ ، صَلَّى اللهُ عَليهِ وَسَلَّمَ ، قَامَ فيهمْ فَذَكَرَ أنَّ الجِهادَ في سَبيلِ اللهِ ، وَالإيمانَ باللهِ ، أفضَلُ الأَعْمَالِ . فقَامَ رَجُلٌ ، فقَالَ : يا رَسُولَ اللهِ أرَأَيْتَ إنْ قُتِلْتُ في سَبيلِ اللهِ أتُكَفَّرُ عَنِّي خَطَايَايَ ؟ فقَالَ لَهُ رَسولُ اللهِ ، صَلَّى اللهُ عَليهِ وسلَّمَ : « نَعَمْ إنْ قُتِلْتَ في سَبيلِ اللهِ وَأَنْتَ صَابِرٌ ، مُحْتَسِبٌ مُقبِلٌ غيرُ مُدْبِرٍ » ثُمَّ قَالَ رَسُولُ اللهِ صَلَّى اللهُ عَليهِ وسلَّمَ : « كَيْفَ قُلْتَ ؟ » قالَ : أرَأَيْتَ إنْ قُتِلْتُ في سَبيلِ اللهِ أتُكَفَّرُ عَنِّي خَطَايَايَ ؟ فقَالَ رَسُولُ اللهِ ، صَلَّى اللهُ عَليهِ وسلَّمَ : « نَعَمْ وَأَنْتَ صَابِرٌ مُحْتَسِبٌ ، مُقْبِلٌ غَيْرُ مُدْبِرٍ ، إلاَّ الدَّيْنَ ، فَإنَّ جِبْرِيلَ عليهِ السلامَ قالَ لي ذلكَ » رواهُ مسلمٌ .

1313. This Hadith has been covered in No. 218 of Chapter 26.

١٣١٤ – وعَنْ جابرٍ رَضِيَ اللهُ عَنْهُ ، قالَ : قالَ رَجُلٌ : أينَ أنَا يا رَسُولَ اللهِ إنْ قُتِلتُ ؟ قالَ : « في الجَنَّةِ » فَألقَى تَمَرَاتٍ كُنَّ في يَدِهِ ، ثُمَّ قاتَلَ حتَّى قُتِلَ ، رَواهُ مسلم .

1314. This Hadith has been covered in No. 89 of Chapter 10.

١٣١٥ – وعَنْ أَنَسٍ رَضِيَ اللهُ عَنْهُ ، قالَ انْطَلَقَ رَسُولُ اللهِ ، صَلَّى اللهُ عَلَيْهِ وسَلَّمَ وَأَصْحَابُهُ حَتَّى سَبَقُوا المشركِينَ إلى بَدرٍ ، وَجَاءَ المُشرِكونَ ، فقالَ رسولُ اللهِ صَلَّى اللهُ عَلَيْهِ وسلَّم : « لا يَقْدَمَنَّ أَحَدٌ مِنْكُمْ إلى شَيْءٍ حتَّى أكُونَ أنا دُونَهُ » فَدَنَا المُشرِكونَ ، فقَالَ رَسُولُ اللهِ صَلَّى اللهُ عَلَيْهِ وسَلَّم : « قُومُوا إلى جَنَّةٍ عَرْضُهَا السَّموَاتُ وَالأَرْضُ »

قال : يَقولُ عُمَيْرُ بنُ الحُمَامِ الأنصارِيُّ رضيَ اللهُ عَنْهُ : يا رسولَ اللهِ جَنَّةٌ عرْضُهَا السَّموات والأرضُ ؟ قال : « نعَم » قال : بَخٍ بَخٍ ! فقالَ رَسُولُ اللهِ صَلَّى اللهُ عَلَيْهِ وَسَلَّمَ : « ما يَحْمِلُكَ على قَولِكَ بَخٍ بَخٍ ؟ » قالَ : لا واللهِ يا رَسُولَ اللهِ إلاَّ رَجاءَ أنْ أكُونَ مِنْ أهْلِها ، قال : « فإنَّكَ مِنْ أهْلِهَا » فأَخرجَ تَمرَاتٍ مِنْ قَرَنِهِ ، فجعَلَ يأْكُلُ منْهُنَّ ، ثم قالَ لئِنْ أنا حَيِيتُ حتى آكُلَ تَمرَاتي هذهِ إنَّهَا لحياةٌ طَويلَةٌ ! فرمَى بما كانَ معَهُ مِنَ التَّمرِ ، ثم قاتَلَهُمْ حتَّى قُتِلَ . رواهُ مسلمٌ .

1315. **Hazrat Anas** (R.A.A.) describing the incident of Badr says: The Holy Prophet (S.A.W.) went forth along with his companions and reached Badr ahead of the non-believers who arrived there later. The Holy Prophet (S.A.W.) directed: Nobody should march forward towards anything unless I do so. When the non-believers came nearer the Holy Prophet (S.A.W.) said: Now stand up (to enter) the Paradise whose extent covers the heaven and the earth; on this Hazrat 'Umair bin Al-Humam Al-Ansari (R.A.A.) enquired: O Messenger of Allah, is the space of paradise as wide as the heavens and the earth?' He (S.A.W.) answered: Yes, it is so wide. On this Hazrat 'Umair exclaimed: "Excellent". The Holy Prophet (S.A.W.) asked him. what has made you say so? He answered: By Allah, Messenger of Allah, I simply uttered these words to express my desire that I too might become one of the dwellers of Paradise. The Holy Prophet (S.A.W.) told him: You are one of the dwellers of paradise. Hearing this Hazrat 'Umair took out some dates from his quiver and started eating them and then he said: Were I to survive till I finish (eating) these dates, that would be too late. So saying he threw away the remaining dates and rushed into the fighting till he was slain. *(Muslim)*

١٣١٦ – وعنه قال : جاءَ ناسٌ إلى النَّبيِّ صَلَّى اللهُ عَلَيْهِ وَسَلَّمَ أنِ ابْعَثْ معَنا رِجالاً يُعَلِّمُونَا القُرآنَ والسُّنَّةَ ، فَبَعَثَ إليهِم سَبعينَ رَجُلاً مِنَ الأنْصارِ يُقَالُ لَهُمْ : القُرَّاءُ ، فيهِم خَالي حرَامٌ ، يَقرؤُونَ القُرآنَ ، ويَتَدارَسُونَ بالليْلِ يتَعلَّمُونَ ، وكانُوا بالنَّهارِ يَجيئُونَ بالمَاءِ ، فيَضَعُونَه في المَسجِدِ ، ويَحْتَطِبُونَ فَيَبيعُونَه ، ويَشتَرُونَ بهِ الطَّعَامَ لأهلِ الصُّفَّةِ ، ولِلفُقَرَاءِ ، فَبَعَثَهم النَّبيُّ صَلَّى اللهُ عليهِ وَسَلَّمَ ، فعَرَضُوا لهم فقَتَلُوهُمْ

قبلَ أنْ يَبلُغُوا المَكانَ ، فَقَالُوا : اللَّهُمَّ بَلِّغ عَنَّا نَبِيَّنَا أنَّا قَد لَقِينَاكَ فَرَضِينَا عَنْكَ وَرَضِيتَ عَنَّا ، وَأَتى رجُلٌ حَرَاماً خالَ أَنَسٍ مِنْ خَلفِهِ ، فَطَعَنَهُ بِرُمحٍ حتى أنفَذَهُ ، فَقَالَ حَرَامٌ : فُزتُ وربِّ الكَعْبَةِ ، فقالَ رسولُ اللهِ صلَّى اللهُ عليهِ وسلَّم : « إنَّ إخْوَانَكم قَد قُتِلُوا وإنَّهم قَالُوا : اللَّهُمَّ بَلِّغ عَنَّا نَبِيَّنَا أنَّا قَد لَقِينَاكَ فَرَضِينَا عَنكَ وَرَضِيتَ عَنَّا »

متفقٌ عليه ، وهذا لفظ مسلم .

1316. Hazrat Anas (R.A.A.) relates that some people came to the Holy Prophet (S.A.W.) and requested that he (S.A.W.) may depute some persons to go with them to teach them the Holy Quran and the Sunnah. (Accordingly) he (S.A.W.) sent with them seventy men of the Ansar who were called as Qurraa (reciters of the Holy Quran); among them was my maternal uncle, Haraam (R.A.A.). These people used to recite the Holy Quran and occupied themselves at night with teaching and learning the Holy Quran. During the day, they used to bring water to the mosque, and gather wood for fuel which they sold, and with its sale proceeds, they would purchase food for As-haab-us-suffa (those poor persons who remained in attendance in the mosque) and other poor persons. The seventy Ansar were sent by the Holy Prophet (S.A.W.) with those visitors who had asked for them but the Ansar were slaughtered treacherously before reaching their destination. While they were being killed, they prayed: 'O' Allah, convey our message to our Prophet (S.A.W.) that we have reached thee, and are pleased with thee, and thou art pleased with us. It is reported that a man approached Hazrat Haram (R.A.A.) the maternal uncle of Hazrat Anas from his back and thrust his spear which pierced through his body, whereupon Hazrat Haram (R.A.A.) exclaimed: 'By the Lord of the Kaaba I have achieved my object.' The Holy Prophet (S.A.W.) informed (his companion): Your brethren have been slain, and they prayed to Allah to convey from them to their Prophet (S.A.W.) that they had reached him, and that they were pleased with thee and that he was pleased with them. *(Bukhari and Muslim)*

١٣١٧ — وعنْهُ قالَ : غَابَ عَمِّي أنسُ بنُ النَّضْرِ رَضِيَ اللهُ عَنْهُ عن قِتَالِ بَدرٍ ، فقال : يارسولَ اللهِ غِبتُ عن أوَّلِ قِتَالٍ قَاتَلتَ المُشرِكِينَ ، لَئِنِ اللهُ أشْهَدَني قِتَالَ المُشرِكِينَ لَيُرِيَنَّ اللهُ ما أصنَعُ . فَلَمَّا كانَ يَومُ أُحُدٍ انكَشَفَ المُسلِمُونَ ، فقالَ : اللَّهُمَّ إنِّي أعتَذِرُ إليكَ مِمَّا صَنَعَ هؤُلاءِ — يَعني أصْحَابَهُ — وَأبرَأُ إليكَ مِمَّا صَنَعَ هؤُلاءِ — يعني المُشرِكِينَ —

ثم تقدَّمَ فاستقبله سعدُ بنُ معاذ فقال : يَاسعدَ بنَ مُعاذٍ الجنَّةَ وَربِّ النَّضرِ ، إنِّي أجِدُ رِيحَهَا مِنْ دُونِ أُحُدٍ ! قالَ سعدٌ : فما استطعتُ يارَسُولَ اللهِ مَاصَنَعَ ! قالَ أنسٌ : فوَجدْنَا بِهِ بِضعاً وثَمانِينَ ضَربَةً بالسَّيفِ ، أوْ طَعنَةً بِرُمحٍ أوْ رَميةً بِسَهمٍ ، ووَجدْنَاهُ قد قُتِلَ وَمثَّلَ بِهِ المُشرِكون ، فما عرفَهُ أحدٌ إلاَّ أُختُهُ بِبنَانِهِ . قال أنسٌ : كُنَّا نُرَى ـ أوْ نَظُنُّ ـ أنَّ هذهِ الآية نَزلَتْ فِيهِ وَفِي أشباهِهِ : (مِنَ المُؤمنينَ رِجَالٌ صَدَقُوا مَاعَاهَدُوا اللهَ عَلَيْهِ فَمِنهُم مَنْ قَضَى نَحْبَهُ) إلى آخرها [الأحزاب : ٢٣]. متفقٌ عليه .

1317. This Hadith is the same as No. 109 of Chapter 11.

١٣١٨ ــ وعَنْ سَمُرَةَ رَضِيَ اللهُ عَنْهُ قالَ : قالَ رَسُولُ اللهِ صَلَّى اللهُ عليهِ وسلَّمَ : « رَأيتُ اللَّيلَةَ رَجُلَيْنِ أتَيانِي ، فَصَعِدَا بِي الشَّجَرَةَ ، فَأدْخلانِي دَاراً هِيَ أحْسَنُ وَأفْضَلُ ، لَمْ أرَ قَطُّ أحْسَنَ مِنها ، قالا : أمَّا هذهِ الدَّارُ فَدارُ الشُّهَدَاءِ » رواه البخاري وهو بعضٌ من حديثٍ طويلٍ فيه أنواع العلم سيأتي في باب تحريم الكذب إنْ شاءَ اللهُ تعالى .

1318. Hazrat Samurah bin Jundub (R.A.A.) reports that the Holy Prophet (S.A.W.) once, said that 'Last night I saw two persons (in dream). They came to me and taking me along with them climbed a tree, then took me inside a house, which was more beautiful than this one. The two persons told me,' Remember this is the house of martyrs. *(Bukhari)*

This tradition is part of a long tradition which will be found in S. No. 1544 of Chapter 247.

١٣١٩ــ وعنْ أنسٍ رَضِيَ اللهُ عَنْهُ أنَّ أُمَّ الرُّبَيِّعِ بِنْتَ البَراءِ وَهِيَ أُمُّ حارثَةَ بنِ سُراقَةَ ، أتَتِ النَّبيَّ صلَّى اللهُ عليهِ وسلَّمَ فَقالَتْ : يا رَسُولَ اللهِ ألا تُحدِّثُني عَنْ حارثَةَ . وكَانَ قُتِلَ يَومَ بَدرٍ ؛ فإنْ كانَ في الجنَّةِ صَبرتُ ، وإنْ كانَ غيرَ ذلكَ اجتَهَدْتُ عليهِ في البُكاءِ ، فقال : « يا أُمَّ حارثَةَ إنَّهَا جِنانٌ في الجنَّةِ ، وإنَّ ابنَكِ أصابَ الفِردَوسَ الأعْلَى » رواه البخاري .

1319. Hazrat Anas (R.A.A.) relates that Ummur-Rubaie bint Al-Bara'a (and he was mother of Harisa bin Suraqah) went to the Holy Prophet (S.A.W.) and said: O Messenger of Allah, will you not tell me something about Harisa, who was martyred on the day of Badar? If he is in heaven I must endure it with patience and if otherwise, I shall weep bitterly. The Holy Prophet (S.A.W.) said to her: 'O Umm-Harisa, there are many types pf paradise and your son has achieved Firdous, the best type. *(Bukhari)*

١٣٢٠ – وعَنْ جابرِ بنِ عبدِ اللهِ رضيَ اللهُ عَنْهُما قالَ : جيءَ بِأبي إلى النَّبيِّ صَلّى اللهُ عليهِ وسَلَّمَ قَدْ مُثِّلَ بِهِ ، فوُضعَ بيْنَ يدَيْه ، فذَهَبْتَ أكْشِفُ عَنْ وَجْهِهِ فنَهاني قَوْمٌ فقالَ النبيُّ صَلّى اللهُ عليهِ وسلَّم : « ما زَالَتِ المَلائِكَةُ تُظِلُّهُ بِأجْنِحَتِها » متفقٌ عليه .

1320. Hazrat Jabir bin Abdullah (R.A.A.) relates: The mutilated dead body of my martyred father was brought and placed before the Holy Prophet (S.A.W.). I was going to uncover his face but the members of my community stopped me from doing so, the Holy Prophet (S.A.W.) remarked: The angels continued to cover and protect him with their wings. *(Bukhari and Muslim)*

١٣٢١ – وعَنْ سهلِ بنِ حُنَيْفٍ رَضِيَ اللهُ عنه أنَّ رَسُولَ اللهِ صَلّى اللهُ عَلَيْهِ وسَلَّمَ قال : « مَنْ سَألَ اللهَ تَعالى الشَّهادَةَ بِصِدْقٍ بَلَّغَهُ اللهُ مَنازِلَ الشُّهَداءِ وإنْ مَاتَ عَلى فِراشِهِ » رواه مسلم .

1321. This Hadith has already been given in S. No. 57 of Chapter 4.

١٣٢٢ – وعَنْ أنَسٍ رَضِيَ اللهُ عَنْهُ قالَ : قالَ رَسُولُ اللهِ صَلّى اللهُ عليْهِ وسَلَّمَ : « مَنْ طَلَبَ الشَّهادَةَ صادِقاً أُعطِيَها ولو لم تُصِبْهُ » رواه مسلم .

1322. Hazrat Anas bin Malik (R.A.A.) relates that the Holy Prophet (S.A.W.) said: If a person prays sincerely for martyrdom, it is granted even though he is not hurt. *(Muslim)*

١٣٢٣ – وعَنْ أبي هُرَيْرَةَ رضيَ اللهُ عنهُ قالَ : قالَ رسُولُ اللهِ صَلّى اللهُ عليْهِ وسَلَّمَ : « مَا يَجِدُ الشَّهيدُ مِنْ مَسِّ القَتْلِ إلاَّ كما يَجِدُ أحَدُكُمْ مِنْ مَسِّ القَرْصَةِ » رواه الترمذي وقال : حديثٌ حَسَنٌ صحيحٌ .

1323. Hazrat Abu Hurairah (R.A.A.) relates that the Holy Prophet (S.A.W.) said: A martyr does not suffer any pain when he is slain, more than any one of you feel from our biting.

(*Tirmizi*, and said it is sound and good)

١٣٢٤ – وعن عبد الله بن أبي أوفى رضي الله عنهما أن رسول الله صلى الله عليه وسلم في بعض أيامه التي لقي فيها العدو وانتظر حتى مالت الشمس، ثم قام في الناس فقال: «أيها الناس، لا تتمنوا لقاء العدو، وسلوا الله العافية، فإذا لقيتموهم فاصبروا، واعلموا أن الجنة تحت ظلال السيوف». ثم قال: «اللهم منزل الكتاب ومجري السحاب، وهازم الأحزاب اهزمهم وانصرنا عليهم» متفق عليه.

1324. Hazrat Abdullah bin Abu Aufa (R.A.A.) relates. Once when the Holy Prophet (S.A.W.) was facing the enemy and was waiting for the setting of the sun, he (S.A.W.) stood up and addressed the people saying: O' People! Do not desire a combat with the enemy, but pray to Allah for safety. But when you are face to face with the enemy, be steadfast and remember that Paradise lies under the shadow of swords. Then he supplicated: '*Allahumma Munzilal Kitabe wa mujreas sahabe wa hazimal Ahzaba Ahzim hum wansurna alaihim*'

'O' Allah! Revealer of the book, Driver of the clouds, Vanquisher of hosts, destroy them and help us over them. (*Bukhari and Muslim*)

١٣٢٥ – وعن سهل بن سعد رضي الله عنه قال: قال رسول الله صلى الله عليه وسلم «ثنتان لا تردان، أو قلما تردان: الدعاء عند النداء وعند البأس حين يلحم بعضهم بعضاً»

رواه أبو داود بإسناد صحيح.

1325. Hazrat Sahl bin Sa'ad (R.A.A.) relates that the Holy Prophet (S.A.W.) said: "There are two moments when supplications are not turned down or are rarely turned down; a supplication while the azan is being called and a supplication during battle when the fighting is severe. (*Abu Daud* quoted with sound chains)

١٣٢٦ – وعن أنس رضي الله عنه قال: كان رسول الله صلى الله عليه وسلم إذا غزا قال: «اللهم أنت عضدي ونصيري، بك أحول، وبك أصول، وبك أقاتل» رواه أبو داود، والترمذي وقال: حديث حسن.

1326. Hazrat Anas (R.A.A.) relates: When the Holy Prophet (S.A.W.) used to go on Jihad, he would supplicate: *Allahumma ańta adudi wa naseeri bika ahulo wa bika asulo bika uqatilo.* Allah! Thou art my only support and Thou art my only Hepler. I turn to Thee alone and from Thee I get the strength and with Thy (help) I fight with. *(Abu Daud and Tirmizi)*

١٣٢٧ – وعَنْ أبي مُوسَى ، رَضِيَ اللهُ عَنْهُ ، أنَّ النَّبِيَّ ، صَلَّى اللهُ عَلَيْهِ وسَلَّم ، كانَ إذا خَافَ قَوماً قالَ : اللَّهُمَّ إنَّا نَجعَلُكَ في نُحُورِهِم ، وَنَعُوذُ بِكَ مِنْ شُرورِهِم » رواه أبو داود بإسنادٍ صحيحٍ .

1327. This hadith has already been given in S. No. 981 of Chapter 173.

١٣٢٨ – وعَنْ ابنِ عُمَرَ ، رَضِيَ اللهُ عَنْهُمَا ، أنَّ رَسُولَ اللهِ ، صَلَّى اللهُ عَلَيْهِ وَسَلَّمَ ، قالَ : « الخَيْلُ مَعْقُودٌ في نَوَاصِيْها الخَيرُ إلى يَوْمِ القِيَامَةِ » متفقٌ عليه .

1328. Hazrat Ibn Umar (R.A.A.) states that the Holy Prophet (S.A.W.) said: There is good in the forehead of horses till the Day of Judgement. *(Bukhari and Muslim)*

١٣٢٩ – وعَنْ عُرْوَةَ البَارِقِيِّ ، رَضِيَ اللهُ عَنْهُ ، أنَّ النبيَّ ، صَلَّى اللهُ عليهِ وسَلَّمَ ، قالَ : « الخَيْلُ مَعقُودٌ في نَوَاصِيْهَا الخَيرُ إلى يَوْمِ القِيَامَةِ : الأَجرُ ، والمَغنَمُ » متفقٌ عليه .

1329. Hazrat 'Urwatul Bariqi (R.A.A.) says that the Holy Prophet (S.A.W.) said. There is good in the forehead of horses till the Day of Judgement, and (also) reward and spoils. *(Bukhari and Muslim)*

١٣٣٠ – وعَنْ أبي هُرَيْرَةَ ، رَضِيَ اللهُ عَنْهُ ، قالَ : قالَ رَسُولُ اللهِ ، صَلَّى اللهُ عَلَيْهِ وسَلَّمَ : « مَنِ احتَبَسَ فَرَساً في سَبيلِ اللهِ ، إيمَاناً باللهِ ، وَتَصدِيقاً بِوَعْدِهِ ، فإنَّ شِبَعَهُ ، وَرِيَّهُ وَرَوْثَهُ ، وَبَولَهُ في مِيزَانِهِ يَومَ القِيَامَةِ » رواه البخاريُّ .

1330. Hazrat Abu Hurairah (R.A.A.) relates that the Holy Prophet (S.A.W.) said: A person, believing in Allah and relying on his promise, reares a horse for Jihad for the sake of Allah, he will find that its fodder drink droppings and urine will all be credited to him in the scales on the Day of Judgement. *(Bukhari)*

Note :— This tradition does not mean that the fodder and water taken by the horse and his droppings and urine will be placed in the scales in his favour, but this means that on account of his sincere actions and motives, all these things will become good deeds and credited to his account.

١٣٣١— وعَنْ أبي مَسْعُودٍ ، رَضِيَ اللهُ عَنْهُ ، قالَ : جاءَ رَجُلٌ إلى النَّبِيِّ ، صَلَّى اللهُ علَيْهِ وسَلَّم ، بِناقَةٍ مَخْطُومَةٍ فقالَ هذهِ في سَبيلِ اللهِ ، فقالَ رسُولُ اللهِ ، صَلَّى اللهُ علَيْهِ وسَلَّمَ : « لكَ بِها يَوْمَ القِيامَةِ سَبْعُمِائَةِ ناقَةٍ كُلُّها مَخْطُومَةٌ » رواهُ مسلم .

1331. Hazrat Abu Mas'ud (R.A.A.) relates: A man came to the Holy Prophet (S.A.W.) with a thorough bred she-camel wearing a noze string and said: This is for the sake of Allah. The Holy Prophet (S.A.W.) said to him: You will get seven Hundred such she-camels for it on the Day of Judgement. *(Muslim)*

١٣٣٢— وعن أبي حَمّادٍ — ويُقال : أبو سُعاد ، ويُقالُ : أبو أَسَدٍ ، ويقال : أبو عامِرٍ ، ويقالُ : أبو عَمْرو ، ويقالُ : أبو الأسْودِ ، ويقالُ : أبو عَبْسٍ — عُقْبَةَ بن عامرٍ الجُهَنيِّ ، رَضِيَ اللهُ عَنْهُ ، قالَ : سَمِعْتُ رَسُولَ اللهِ صَلَّى اللهُ عليهِ وَسَلَّمَ وَهُوَ عَلى المِنْبَرِ يقولُ : « وَأَعِدُّوا لهُم ما اسْتَطَعْتُم من قُوَّةٍ ، ألا إنَّ القُوَّةَ الرَّمْيُ ، ألا إنَّ القُوَّةَ الرَّمْيُ ، ألا إنَّ القوَّةَ الرَّمْيُ » رواه مسلم

1332. Hazrat Abu Hammad (R.A.A.) (He is also known by his other adopted names such as Abu Su'aad, or Abu Asad or Abu 'Aamir or Abu 'Amr, Abu Aswad or Abu 'Abs) Uqbah bin 'Amir Juhani (R.A.A.) relates that he heard the Holy Prophet (S.A.W.) recite from the pulpit a verse:

'Make ready for them all thou canst of armed force (8 : 60)

He (S.A.W.) elucidating this point said: that armed force means archery; beware armed strength means archery beware armed strength means archery. *(Muslim)*

١٣٣٣ — وَعَنْهُ قالَ : سمِعْتُ رَسُولَ اللهِ ، صَلَّى اللهُ عَلَيْهِ وسَلَّمَ ، يقولُ : « سَتُفْتَحُ عَلَيكُم أَرَضُونَ ، ويَكفِيكُمُ اللهُ ، فَلا يَعْجِزُ أَحَدُكُم أَنْ يَلْهُوَ بِأَسْهُمِهِ » رواه مسلم .

1333. Hazrat 'Uqbah bin 'Amir Juhani (R.A.A.) relates that he heard the Holy Prophet (S.A.W.) say: In the near future many lands (countries) will be conquered by you, and Allah will help you, so let no one from you lag behind in archery. *(Muslim)*

١٣٣٤ــ وعَنْهُ أنَّهُ قالَ : قالَ رَسُولُ اللهِ ، صَلَّى اللهُ عليه وسلَّمَ : « مَنْ عُلِّمَ الرَّمْيَ ، ثمَّ تَرَكَهُ ، فلَيْسَ مِنَّا ، أوْ فقدْ عَصَى » رواه مسلم .

1334. Hazrat 'Uqbah bin 'Amir Juhani (R.A.A.) relates that the Holy Prophet (S.A.W.) said: A person who received training in archery, but has abandoned it, is not one of us, he is guilty of disobedience. *(Muslim)*

١٣٣٥ــ وعنهُ ، رضيَ اللهُ عَنْهُ ، قالَ : سَمِعْتُ رَسُولَ اللهِ ، صَلَّى اللهُ عليْهِ وَسَلَّمَ ، يقولُ : « إنَّ اللهَ يُدخِلُ بالسَّهمِ الوَاحِدِ ثلاثَةَ نَفَرٍ الجنَّةَ : صَانِعَهُ يحتَسِبُ في صَنْعَتِهِ الخيرَ ، وَالرَّامِي بِهِ ، وَمُنْبِلَهُ . وَارْمُوا وَارْكَبُوا ، وَأنْ تَرمُوا أحَبُّ إليَّ مِنْ أنْ تَرْكَبُوا . ومَنْ تَرَكَ الرَّمْيَ بَعْدَ ما عُلِّمَهُ رَغبَةً عنه ، فإنَّها نِعمَةٌ تَرَكَهَا » أوْ قال : « كَفَرَهَا » رواهُ أبو داودَ .

1335. Hazrat 'Uqbah bin 'Aamir Juhani (R.A.A.) says that he heard the Holy Prophet (S.A.W.) say: Allah will admit three persons to paradise on account of one arrow. firstly the person who manufactures it with the best perfection, secondly the man who shoots it, and, thirdly the person who picks and hands it up to the archer. So, O People! learn archery and horse riding. I prefer that you should learn archery rather than riding. The person who having learnt archery, loses interest in it and gives it up, forsakes a heavenly bounty or he (S.A.W.) said: he has been ungrateful. *(Abu Daud)*

١٣٣٦ــ وعَنْ سَلَمَةَ بنِ الأكوَعِ ، رَضِيَ اللهُ عَنْهُ ، قالَ : مَرَّ النَّبيُّ ، صَلَّى اللهُ عَلَيْهِ وسَلَّمَ ، على نَفَرٍ يَنْتَضِلُونَ ، فقَالَ : « ارْمُوا بَنِي إسْماعيلَ فإنَّ أبَاكم كانَ رَامِياً » رواهُ البخاري .

1336. Hazrat Salama b n Al-Akwa' (R.A.A.) relates: (Once) The Holy Prophet (S.A.W.) passed by a party of some persons who were practising archery. The Holy Prophet (S.A.W.) said to them: O the Children of Ismail, practise archery, for your ancestor (Prophet Ismail) was also an archer. *(Bukhari)*

١٣٣٧– وعَنْ عَمْرِو بنِ عَبسَةَ ، رَضِيَ اللهُ عَنْهُ قال : سَمِعْتُ رَسُولَ اللهِ ، صَلَّى اللهُ عليهِ وسلَّمَ ، يَقُولُ : « مَنْ رَمَى بِسَهمٍ في سَبيلِ اللهِ فَهُوَ لَهُ عِدْلُ مُحرَّرةٍ »

رواهُ أبو داودَ ، والترمذي وقال : حديثٌ حسنٌ صحيحٌ .

1337. Hazrat 'Amr bin Abasa (R.A.A.) relates that he heard the Holy Prophet (S.A.W.) say: The person who shoots an arrow in the cause of Allah, earns recompense equal to freeing a slave.

(Abu Daud and Tirmizi, latter said this tradition is sound and good)

Note .— These traditions enumerate the virtues and advantages of archery. This was an important weapon of warfare during the days of Holy Prophet (S.A.W.). But this weapon is no more useful in the modern warfare, its place has been taken over by the modern weapons like guns, rifles, missiles, bombs etc. Therefore to acquire skill in the manufacture and use of weapons has the same recompense and advantages.

١٣٣٨ – وعَنْ أبي يحيى خُرَيْم بنِ فاتِكٍ ، رَضِيَ اللهُ عَنْهُ ، قالَ : قالَ رَسُولُ اللهِ ، صَلَّى اللهُ عليهِ وَسَلَّمَ : « مَنْ أَنْفَقَ نَفَقَةً في سَبيلِ اللهِ كُتِبَ لَهُ سَبْعُمِائةِ ضِعْفٍ » رواهُ الترمذي وقالَ : حديثٌ حَسَنٌ .

1338. Hazrat Abu Yayha Khuraim bin Fatik (R.A.A.) says that the Holy Prophet (S.A.A.) said: A person who spends in the cause of Allah (for Jihad) has his recompense seven hundred times.

(Tirmizi and said this tradition is good)

١٣٣٩ – وعَنْ أبي سَعيدٍ ، رَضِيَ اللهُ عَنْهُ . قالَ : قالَ رَسُولُ اللهِ ، صَلَّى اللهُ عَلَيْهِ وَسَلَّمَ : « مَامِنْ عَبْدٍ يَصُومُ يَوْماً في سَبيلِ اللهِ إلاَّ بَاعَدَ اللهُ بِذلكَ اليَوْمِ وَجْهَهُ عَنِ النَّارِ سَبْعينَ خَريفاً » متفقٌ عليه

1339. This Hadis has already been covered in S. No. 1218 of Chapter 217.

١٣٤٠ – وعَنْ أبي أُمَامَةَ ، رَضِيَ اللهُ عَنْهُ ، عَنِ النبيِّ ، صَلَّى اللهُ عَلَيْهِ وسَلَّمَ ، قالَ : « مَنْ صَامَ يَوْماً في سَبيلِ اللهِ جَعَلَ اللهُ بَيْنَهُ وَبَيْنَ النَّارِ خَنْدَقاً كَمَا بَيْنَ السَّماءِ وَالأَرْضِ » رواهُ الترمذي وقالَ : حديثٌ حسنٌ صحيحٌ .

1340. Hazrat Abu Umamah (R.A.A.) reports that the Holy Prophet (S.A.W.) said. A person who observes the fast for one day during Jihad for the sake of Allah, Allah will dig a ditch between him and the Fire of Hell as wide as the distance between heaven and earth. *(Tirmizi*, and said it is sound and good)

١٣٤١ – وعَنْ أبي هُرَيْرَةَ ، رَضِيَ اللهُ عنهُ ، قالَ : قالَ رَسُولُ اللهِ ، صَلَّى اللهُ عَلَيْهِ وَسَلَّمَ : « مَنْ ماتَ وَلَمْ يَغْزُ ، وَلَمْ يُحَدِّثْ نَفْسَه بِغَزْوٍ ، ماتَ عَلى شُعْبَةٍ مِنَ النِّفَاقِ » رواهُ مسلمٌ .

1341. Hazrat Abu Hurairah (R.A.A.) relates that the Holy Prophet (S.A.W.) said: A person who dies without having fought in a Jihad (for the sake of Allah) and not having any longing to do so, dies with one aspect of hypocrisy. *(Muslim)*

١٣٤٢ – وعَنْ جابرٍ ، رَضِيَ اللهُ عَنْهُ ، قالَ : كنّا مَعَ النَّبيِّ ، صَلَّى اللهُ عَلَيْهِ وَسَلَّمَ ، في غَزَاةٍ فقالَ : « إنَّ بِالمَدِينَةِ لَرِجَالاً ماسِرْتُمْ مَسِيراً ، وَلا قَطَعْتُمْ وَادياً إلاَّ كانُوا مَعَكُمْ ، حَبَسَهُمُ المَرَضُ » .

وفي روايةٍ : « حَبَسَهُمُ العُذْرُ » . وفي روايةٍ : « إلاَّ شَرَكُوكُمْ في الأَجْرِ » رواهُ البخاري من روايةِ أنسٍ ، وَرواهُ مُسلمٌ من روايةِ جابرٍ واللفظ له .

1342. Hazrat Jabir (R.A.A.) relates: Once we accompanied the Holy Prophet (S.A.W.) in an expedition for Jihad when he (S.A.W.) said: There are in Madina people who are with you (in their hearts) so far as merit is concerned, wherever you travel and whatever valley you cross. they have only been prevented by illness.

According to another version, 'due to some other cause from being with you.'

According to yet another version, 'they are your partners in recompense.' *(Bukhari and Muslim*, this is wording of Muslim)

١٣٤٣ – وعنْ أبي مُوسى ، رَضِيَ اللهُ عَنْهُ ، أنَّ أعْرَابِيّاً أتَى النبيَّ ، صَلَّى اللهُ عَلَيْهِ وسَلَّمَ ، فَقَالَ : يا رسولَ اللهِ ، الرَّجُلُ يُقَاتِلُ لِلْمَغْنَمِ ، وَالرَّجُلُ يُقَاتِلُ لِيُذْكَرَ ، وَالرَّجُلُ يُقَاتِلُ لِيُرَى مَكانُهُ ؟

وفي روايةٍ : يُقَاتِلُ شَجَاعَةً ، وَيُقَاتِلُ حَمِيَّةً .

وفي رواية : وَيُقَاتِلُ غَضَباً ، فَمَنْ في سَبيلِ اللهِ ؟ فَقَالَ رسولُ اللهِ ، صَلَّى اللهُ عليهِ وسلَّم : « مَنْ قَاتَلَ لِتَكُونَ كَلِمَةُ اللهِ هِيَ العُلْيَا ، فَهُوَ في سَبيلِ اللهِ » متفقٌ عليه .

1343. This Hadis has been covered by S. No. 8 of Chapter 1 of Vol. I.

١٣٤٤ ــ وعنْ عبدِ اللهِ بنِ عَمرِو بنِ العاصِ ، رَضِيَ اللهُ عَنهُمَا ، قالَ : قالَ رَسُولُ اللهِ ، صَلَّى اللهُ عَلَيْهِ وسلَّمَ : « مَا مِنْ غَازِيَةٍ ، أَوْ سَرِيَّةٍ تَغْزُو ، فَتَغْنَمُ وَتَسْلَمُ ، إلاَّ كَانُوا قَدْ تَعَجَّلُوا ثُلُثَيْ أُجورِهِمْ ، وَمَا مِنْ غَازِيَةٍ أَوْ سَرِيَّةٍ تُخْفِقُ وَتُصَابُ إلاَّ تَمَّ أُجورُهُمْ » . رواهُ مسلم .

1344. Hazrat Abdullah bin 'Amr bin Al'Aas (R.A.A.) states that the Holy Prophet (S.A.W.) said: There is no army or battalian which carries on Jihad for the sake of Allah and collects booty and is intact and safe but has received two-thirds of its recompense promptly. Similarly there is no army or battalian which is defeated and is harmed but that its full recompense remains in reserve and will be given on the Day of Judgement. *(Muslim)*

١٣٤٥ ــ وعنْ أَبي أُمَامَةَ ، رَضِيَ اللهُ عَنْهُ ، أَنَّ رَجُلاً قالَ : يارسولَ اللهِ ائْذَنْ لي في السِّيَاحَةِ ، فَقَالَ النَّبيُّ ، صلَّى اللهُ عليهِ وسلَّم : « إنَّ سِيَاحَةَ أُمَّتي الجِهادُ في سَبيلِ اللهِ ، عزَّ وجلَّ » رواهُ أبو داود بإسنادٍ جيِّدٍ .

1345. Hazrat Abu Umamah (R.A.A.) relates that a man sought permission of the Holy Prophet (S.A.W.) to adopt reclusion. The Holy Prophet (S.A.W.) told him. The reclusion for my Ummah is Jihad in the cause of Allah, the Lord of honour and glory.

(*Abu Daud* quoted this with good chains)

١٣٤٦ ــ وعَنْ عبدِ اللهِ بنِ عَمْرِو بنِ العاصِ ، رَضِيَ اللهُ عَنهُمَا ، عَنِ النَّبيِّ ، صَلَّى اللهُ عليْهِ وَسَلَّمَ ، قَالَ : « قَفْلَةٌ كَغَزْوَةٍ » رواهُ أبوداود بإسنادٍ جيدٍ .

1346. Hazrat Abdullah bin 'Amr bin Al'Aas (R.A.A.) says that the Holy Prophet (S.A.W.) said: The return from an expedition of Jihad (after it is over) is as meritorious as the Jihad itself.

(*Abu Daud* cited this with good chains)

١٣٤٧ – وعن السائب بن يزيد ، رضي الله عنه ، قال : لمّا قدم النبيُّ ، صلّى الله عليه وسلّم ، من غزوة تبوك تلقّاه الناس ، فتلقّيته مع الصبيان على ثنيّة الوداع . رواه أبو داود بإسناد صحيح بهذا اللفظ ، ورواه البخاري قال : ذهبنا نتلقّى رسول الله ، صلّى الله عليه وسلّم ، مع الصبيان إلى ثنيّة الوداع .

1347. Hazrat Sa'ib bin Yazid (R.A.A.) relates: When the Holy Prophet (S.A.W.) returned from the battle of Tabuk, people came out from Madina and went ahead to meet him (S.A.W.). Accordingly I also went ahead and met him along with children at Saniyya al- Wada' *(Abu Daud)*

Imam Bukhari says that: Hazrat Sa'ib says we went to Saniyyah-al-Wada with other boys to receive the Holy Prophet (S.A.W.).

١٣٤٨ – وعن أبي أمامة ، رضي الله عنه ، عن النبيّ ، صلّى الله عليه وسلّم ، قال : « من لم يغزُ ، أو يجهّز غازياً ، أو يخلف غازياً في أهله بخير ، أصابه الله بقارعة قبل يوم القيامة » رواه أبو داود بإسناد صحيح .

1348. Hazrat Abu Umamah (R.A.A.) says that the Holy Prophet (S.A.W.) said: A person who did not take part in Jihad (fighting) or failed to equip a fighter, or did not look well after the family of a fighter, would be severely punished by Allah before the Day of Judgement. *(Abu Daud* quoted with sound chains)

١٣٤٩ – وعن أنس ، رضي الله عنه ، أنّ النبيّ ، صلّى الله عليه وسلّم ، قال : « جاهدوا المشركين بأموالكم وأنفسكم وألسنتكم » رواه أبو داود بإسناد صحيح .

1349. Hazrat Anas (R.A.A.) says that the Holy Prophet (S.A.W.) said: Carry on Jihad against the non-believers with your wealth, your person and your tongues. *(Abu Daud* quoted this with sound chains)

١٣٥٠ – وعن أبي عمرو . ويقال : أبو حكيم النعمان بن مقرّن رضي الله عنه قال : شهدت رسول الله ، صلّى الله عليه وسلّم ، إذا لم يقاتل من أوّل النهار أخّر القتال حتّى تزول الشمس ، وتهبّ الرياح ، وينزل النصر .

رواهُ أبو داود ، والترمذي ، وقالَ : حديثٌ حَسَنٌ صحيحٌ .

1350. Hazrat Abu 'Amr (R.A.A.) also known as Abu Hakeem Nu'man bin Muaqarrin (R.A.A.) relates: Once I accompanied the Holy Prophet (S.A.W.) on Jihad. I noticed that if the Holy Prophet (S.A.W.) did not go on fighting in the early part of the day, he used to postpon it till the sun declined, the breeze started and help from Allah the Exalted had come.

(Abu Daud and Tirmizi and the latter called it as sound and good)

١٣٥١ — وعنْ أبي هُرَيْرَةَ ، رَضِيَ اللهُ عنهُ ، قالَ : قالَ رَسولُ اللهِ ، صلّى اللهُ عليهِ وسلّم ، « لاتَتَمَنَّوْا لِقاءَ العَدُوِّ ، وَاسْألوا اللهَ العافِيَةَ ، فإذا لَقيتُموهم ، فاصبِروُا » متفقٌ عليه .

1351. Hazrat Abu Hurairah (R.A.A.) reports that the Holy Prophet (S.A.W.) said: Do not seek an engagement with the enemy, but when you come into clash with the enemy then be firm.

(Bukhari and Muslim)

١٣٥٢ — وعَنْهُ وعَنْ جابِرٍ ، رَضِيَ اللهُ عَنْهُما ، أنَّ النبيَّ ، صلّى اللهُ عليْهِ وسلّم ، قالَ : « الحَرْبُ خَدْعَةٌ » متفقٌ عليه .

1352. Hazrat Abu Hurairah (R.A.A.) and Hazrat Jabir (R.A.A.) relate that the Holy Prophet (S.A.W.) said: War is the name of strategum and cleverness. *(Bukhari and Muslim)*

Note . The word 'Jihad' comes from the Arabic root 'Jahada (meaning with the utmost power and ability). It is one of the basic principles of Islam, and is based on three principles, namely, intensifaction of Islamic doctrines and practices in our day to day life, and eradiction of evil and expansion of the Commands of Allah all over the world through wisdom and advice.

"Call thou to the way of thy Lord with wisdom and good admonition"

* * * * * * *

CHAPTER 235

A CLASS OF MARTYR FROM THE POINT OF VIEW OF RECOMPENSE IN THE HEREAFTER, WHICH WILL BE GIVEN A BATH AND A FUNERAL PRAYER OFFERED CONTRARY TO THOSE WHO FOUGHT WITH THE INFIDELS AND WERE MARTYRED IN BATTLE

١٣٥٣ – عَنْ أَبي هُرَيْرَةَ ، رَضِيَ اللهُ عَنْهُ ، قالَ : قالَ رَسُولُ اللهِ ، صَلَّى اللهُ عَلَيْهِ وسَلَّمَ : « الشُّهَدَاءُ خَمسَةٌ : المَطعُونُ وَالمَبْطُونُ ، وَالغَرِيقُ ، وَصاحِبُ الهَدْمِ ، وَالشَّهِيدُ في سَبيلِ اللهِ » متفقٌ عليهِ .

1353. Hazrat Abu Hurairah (R.A.A.) reports that the Holy Prophet (S.A.W.) said: There are five classes of Martyrs; (1) One who dies in plague (2) One who dies of diseases of stomach. (3) One who dies due to drowning (4) One who is crushed under a wall. and (5) one who is killed while fighting in the cause of Allah .

(Bukhari and Muslim)

١٣٥٤ – وعنهُ قالَ : قالَ رسولُ اللهُ ، صَلَّى اللهُ عليهِ وسَلَّمَ : « ما تَعُدُّونَ الشُّهَدَاءَ فيكُم ؟ قالُوا : يارَسُولَ اللهِ مَنْ قُتِلَ في سَبيلِ اللهِ ،فَهُوَ شهيدٌ . قال : « إنَّ شُهَدَاءَ أُمَّتي إذاً لَقَليلٌ ! » قالُوا : فَمَنْ يارَسُولَ اللهِ ؟ قالَ : « مَنْ قُتِلَ في سَبيلِ اللهِ فَهُوَ شَهيدٌ ، وَمَنْ ماتَ في سَبيلِ اللهِ فَهُوَ شَهيدٌ ، وَمَنْ مَاتَ في الطَّاعُونِ فَهُوَ شَهيدٌ ، وَمَنْ مَاتَ في البَطنِ فَهُوَ شَهيدٌ ، وَالغَرِيقُ شَهيدٌ » رواهُ مُسْلمٌ .

1354. Hazrat Abu Hurairah (R.A.A.) relates that the Holy Prophet (S.A.W.) asked his companions as to whom they consider a martyr? They said: O Messenger of Allah, a person who is slain in the cause of Allah, He (S.A.W.) said: Then there will be very few martyrs among my Ummah. The Companions asked: O Messenger of Allah! then who are the martyrs? He (S.A.W.) answered: He, who is slain in the cause of Allah is of course a martyr; One who dies a natural death in the way of Allah is a martyr; one who dies of plague is a martyr; one who dies of the stomach disease is a martyr; and one who dies due to drowning is a martyr. *(Muslim)*

١٣٥٥ – وعَنْ عبدِ اللهِ بنِ عَمْرِو بنِ العاصِ ، رَضِيَ اللهُ عَنْهُما ، قالَ : قالَ رسولُ اللهِ ، صَلَّى اللهُ عليهِ وسَلَّمَ : «مَنْ قُتِلَ دُونَ مالِهِ ،فَهُوَ شَهيدٌ » متفقٌ عليهِ .

1355. Hazrat Abdullah bin 'Amr bin Al-'Aas (R.A.A.) says that the Holy Prophet (S.A.W.) said: A person who is killed while protecting his property is also a martyr. (Bukhari and Muslim)

١٣٥٦ – وعَنْ أبي الأعْوَرِ سَعيدِ بنِ زَيْدِ بنِ عمروِ بنِ نُفَيْلٍ ، أحَدِ العَشَرَةِ المَشْهُودِ لهُمْ بالجَنَّةِ ، رَضِيَ اللهُ عَنْهُمْ ، قالَ : سَمِعْتُ رسُولَ اللهِ ، صلَّى اللهُ عَلَيْهِ وسلَّم ، يقولُ : « مَنْ قُتِلَ دُونَ مالِهِ فَهُوَ شَهِيدٌ ، وَمَنْ قُتِلَ دُونَ دَمِهِ فَهُوَ شَهِيدٌ ، وَمَنْ قُتِلَ دُونَ دِينِهِ فَهُوَ شَهِيدٌ ، وَمَنْ قُتِلَ دُونَ أَهْلِهِ فَهُوَ شَهِيدٌ »

رواهُ أبو داودَ ، والترمذي وقال : حديثٌ حسنٌ صحيحٌ .

1356. Hazrat Abul A'awar Sa'eed bin Zaid bin Nufail (R.A.A.) (He is one of those ten (10) persons who have been given good news of having been ear-marked for paradise while they were alive in this world). relates that he heard the Holy Prophet (S.A.W.) say: One who dies while defending his property, is a martyr; one who dies in his own defence is a martyr; one who dies defending his religion is a martyr; and one who is killed while protecting his family members is a martyr. (*Abu Daud and Tirmizi*, said it is sound and good)

١٣٥٧ – وعنْ أبي هُريرةَ ، رَضِيَ اللهُ عَنْهُ ، قالَ : جاءَ رَجُلٌ إلى رسولِ اللهِ ، صلَّى اللهُ عليهِ وسلَّمَ ، فقَالَ : يارسولَ اللهِ أرَأَيْتَ إنْ جاءَ رَجُلٌ يُرِيدُ أخْذَ مَالي ؟ قالَ : « فَلا تُعْطِهِ مَالَكَ » قال: أرَأَيْتَ إنْ قَاتَلَني ؟ قال : « قَاتِلْهُ » قالَ : أرَأَيْتَ إنْ قَتَلَني ؟ قالَ : « فَأَنْتَ شَهِيدٌ » قال : أرَأَيْتَ إنْ قَتَلْتُهُ ؟ : قال : « هُوَ في النَّارِ » رواهُ مسلمٌ .

1357. Hazrat Abu Hurairah (R.A.A.) relates: a man came to the Holy Prophet (S.A.W.) and asked: O Messenger of Allah! Please tell me if a person comes with the intention of robbing my property then what should I do? He (S.A.W.) answered: Do not allow him to take away your property. Then man submitted: Very well, if he starts fighting with me? The Holy Prophet (S.A.W.) said: Then you should also fight with him; the man asked: If he should kill me? Then the Holy Prophet (S.A.W.) said. Then you will be a martyr. The man asked. 'If I succeed in killing him? The Holy Prophet (S.A.W.) answered: He will go to Hell. *(Muslim)*

* * * * * * *

CHAPTER 236

VIRTUES OF FREEING SLAVES

قال اللهُ تعالى : فَلا اقْتَحَمَ الْعَقَبَةَ • وَمَا أَدْرَاكَ مَا الْعَقَبَةُ
فَكُّ رَقَبَةٍ [البلد : ١١ – ١٣] .

Allah, the Exalted, has said:

301. But he hath not attempted the ascent—Ah, What will convey unto thee what the Ascent is! (It is) to free a slave (90: 11-13)

١٣٥٨ – وعَنْ أبي هُريرةَ ، رَضِيَ اللهُ عنهُ ، قَالَ : قَالَ لي رَسولُ اللهِ ، صَلَّى اللهُ عليهِ وسلَّم : « مَنْ أَعْتَقَ رَقَبَةً مُسْلِمَةً أَعْتَقَ اللهُ بِكُلِّ عُضْوٍ مِنْهُ عُضْواً مِنْهُ مِنَ النَّارِ حتى فَرْجَهُ بِفَرْجِهِ » متفقٌ عليهِ .

1358. Hazrat Abu Hurairah (R.A.A.) relates that the Holy Prophet (S.A.W.) said: A person who frees a Muslim slave, Allah will deliver every one of his limbs from the fire of Hell in return for each of the limbs of the slave, even his private organs for the sake of the freed slaves' organs.

١٣٥٩ – وعَنْ أبي ذَرٍّ ، رَضِيَ اللهُ عَنْهُ ، قَالَ : قُلْتُ يا رَسُولَ اللهِ ، أيُّ الأعْمَالِ أفضَلُ ؟ قَالَ : « الإيمَانُ باللهِ ، وَالجِهَادُ في سَبيلِ اللهِ » قَالَ : قُلْتُ : أيُّ الرِّقَابِ أفْضَلُ ؟ قَالَ : « أنفَسُهَا عِنْدَ أهْلِهَا ، وَأكثَرُهَا ثَمَناً » مُتَّفَقٌ عَلَيهِ

1359. This Hadis is included in S. No. 117 of Chapter 13.

CHAPTER 237

VIRTUES OF KIND TREATMENT OF THE SLAVES

قَالَ اللهُ تَعَالَى : وَاعْبُدُوا اللهَ وَلا تُشْرِكُوا بِهِ شَيْئاً وَبالوَالِدَيْنِ إحْسَاناً ، وَبِذِي القُرْبَى ، وَاليَتَامَى ، وَالمَسَاكِينِ ، وَالجَارِ ذِي القُرْبَى ، وَالجَارِ الجُنُبِ وَالصَّاحِبِ بالجَنْبِ ، وَابْنِ السَّبيلِ ، وَمَا مَلَكَتْ أيْمَانُكُمْ [النساء : ٣٦] .

Allah, the Exalted, has said :—

302. and serve Allah. Ascribe nothing as partner unto Him. Show kindness unto parents, and unto near kindred and orphans and the needy, and unto the neighbour who is of kin (unto you) and the neighbour who is not of kin, and the fellow-traveller and the way farer and the salves whom your right hand possesses. (4: 36)

١٣٦٠ – وَعَنِ المَعْرُورِ بنِ سُوَيْدٍ قَالَ : رَأَيْتُ أَبَا ذَرٍّ ، رَضِيَ اللهُ عَنْهُ ، وعليه حُلَّةٌ ، وعلى غلامِهِ مِثْلُهَا ، فَسَأَلْتُهُ عَنْ ذلكَ ، فَذَكَرَ أَنَّهُ سَابَّ رَجُلاً عَلَى عَهْدِ رَسُولِ اللهِ ، صَلَّى اللهُ عليهِ وسلَّم ، فَعَيَّرَهُ بِأُمِّهِ ، فَقَالَ النَّبِيُّ ، صلَّى اللهُ عليهِ وسلَّم : « إِنَّكَ امْرُؤٌ فِيكَ جَاهِلِيَّةٌ » : هُمْ إِخْوَانُكُمْ ، وَخَوَلُكُمْ جَعَلَهُمُ اللهُ تَحْتَ أَيْدِيكُمْ ، فَمَنْ كَانَ أَخُوهُ تَحْتَ يَدِهِ ؛ فَلْيُطْعِمْهُ مِمَّا يَأْكُلُ ، وَلْيُلْبِسْهُ مِمَّا يَلْبَسُ ، وَلا تُكَلِّفُوهُمْ مَا يَغْلِبُهُمْ ، فَإِنْ كَلَّفْتُمُوهُمْ فَأَعِينُوهُمْ » . متفقٌ عليهِ .

1360. Hazrat Ma'rur bin Suwaid (R.A.A.) relates: I saw Hazrat Abu Zarr (R.A.A.) wearing a suit and his slave was also wearing a similar dress. I enquired from him about this, and he explained that during the days of the Holy Prophet (S.A.W.) he had an altercation with a man and humiliated him by making a reference to his mother (because his mother was an Iranian). Thereupon the Holy Prophet (S.A.W.) said to me: You still have traces of pre-Islamic Culture in your behaviour. Your servants are your brothers whom Allah the Most High has placed under your authority. Therefore, a person who has a brother under his authority, should feed him out of that which he eats himself and should dress him with the same kind of clothes which he wears clothes himself; he should not assign work to him which is beyond his capacity, and if you do so, then help him in his work. *(Bukhari and Muslim)*

١٣٦١ – وَعَنْ أَبِي هُرَيْرَةَ ، رَضِيَ اللهُ عَنْهُ ، عَنِ النَّبِيِّ ، صَلَّى اللهُ عَلَيهِ وَسَلَّم : قالَ : « إذا أتى أَحَدَكم خادِمُهُ بِطَعَامِهِ ، فَإِنْ لم يُجْلِسْهُ مَعَهُ ، فَلْيُنَاوِلْهُ لُقْمَةً أَوْ لُقْمَتَيْنِ أَوْ أُكْلَةً أَوْ أُكْلَتَيْنِ ؛ فَإِنَّهُ وَلِيَ عِلاجَهُ » رواه البخاري .

1361. Hazrat Abu Hurairah (R.A.A.) relates that the Holy Prophet (S.A.W.) said: When a servant of one of you brings him his food, and if he does not ask him to sit down with him, he should at least give him a morsel or two out of it, for he has laboured in preparing it. *(Bukhari)*

* * * * * * *

CHAPTER 238

VIRTUE OF A SLAVE WHO DISCHARGES HIS DUTY TO ALLAH AND HIS DUTY TO HIS MASTER

١٣٦٢ – عَنِ ابنِ عُمَرَ ، رَضِيَ اللهُ عَنْهُما ، أنَّ رَسُولَ اللهِ ، صَلَّى اللهُ عليهِ وسَلَّم ، قالَ : « إنَّ العَبْدَ إذا نَصَحَ لِسَيِّدِهِ ، وَأَحْسَنَ عِبادَةَ اللهِ ، فَلَهُ أَجْرُهُ مرَّتَيْنِ » مُتَّفَقٌ عَلَيهِ .

1362. Hazrat Abdullah bin 'Umar (R.A.A.) relates that the Holy Prophet (S.A.W.) said: A slave who serves his master well and then prays to Allah well, will have a double recompense.

(Bukhari and Muslim)

١٣٦٣ – وَعَنْ أبي هُرَيرَةَ ، رَضِيَ اللهُ عَنْهُ ، قَالَ : قَالَ رَسُولُ اللهِ ، صَلَّى اللهُ عَلَيهِ وسَلَّم : « لِلْعَبْدِ المَمْلُوكِ المُصْلِحِ أَجْرَانِ ، وَالَّذي نَفسُ أَبي هُرَيرَةَ بِيَدِهِ لَوْلا الجِهَادُ في سَبيلِ اللهِ ، وَالحَجُّ ، وَبِرُّ أُمِّي ، لأَحْبَبْتُ أنْ أَمُوتَ وَأَنَا مَمْلوكٌ » مُتَّفَقٌ عليهِ .

1363. Hazrat Abu Hurairah (R.A.A.) reports that the Holy Prophet (S.A.W.) said: A virtuous (faithful to his master and worshipper) slave is entitled to double recompense. Hazrat Abu Hurairah (R.A.A.) further added. By Allah in whose possession is Abu Hurairah's life, had there been no obligations of Jihad in the cause of Allah, performance of Hajj and obedience of mother, I would have preferred to die as a slave. *(Bukhari and Muslim)*

١٣٦٤ – وَعَنْ أبي مُوسَى الأشْعَرِيِّ ، رَضِيَ اللهُ عَنْهُ ، قَالَ : قَالَ رَسُولُ اللهِ ، صَلَّى اللهُ عَلَيهِ وسَلَّم : « المَمْلُوكُ الَّذي يُحْسِنُ عِبَادَةَ رَبِّهِ ، وَيُؤَدِّي إلى سَيِّدِهِ الذي عليهِ مِنَ الحَقِّ ، وَالنَّصيحَةِ ، وَالطَّاعَةِ ، لهُ أَجْرَانِ » رواهُ البخاريُّ .

1364. Hazrat Abu Musa Ash'ari (R.A.A.) relates that the Holy Prophet (S.A.W.) said: A slave who worships his Sustainer (Allah) well, and discharges diligently, sincerely and obediently his duties which he owes to his master, will have a double recompense. *(Bukhari)*

١٣٦٥ – وَعَنْهُ قَالَ : قَالَ رَسُولُ اللهِ ، صَلَّى اللهُ عَليهِ وسَلَّم : « ثلاثةٌ لَهُمْ أَجْرَانِ : رَجُلٌ مِنْ أَهْلِ الكِتابِ آمَنَ بِنَبيِّهِ ، وَآمَنَ

بِمُحَمَّدٍ ، وَالعَبْدُ المَمْلُوكُ إذا أدّى حقَّ اللهِ ، وَحقَّ مَوَالِيهِ . ورَجُلٌ
كانَتْ لَهُ أمَةٌ فَأدَّبَها فأحْسَنَ تَأدِيبَها ، وعَلَّمَها فأحْسَنَ تعْلِيمَها ،
ثُمَّ أعتَقَها فتَزَوَّجَها ؛ فَلَهُ أجْرانِ » مُتَّفَقٌ عَليهِ .

1365. Hazart Abu Musa Ash'ari (R.A.A.) reports that the Holy Prophet (S.A.W.) has said: 'There are three persons who are entitled to double recompense. One, a man believing in a revealed Book and in his prophet, and also believing in Muhammad (S.A.W.); two, a slave who discharges satisfactorily the duties he owes to Allah, and the duties he owes to his master, and three, a man who owns a female slave and teachers her good manners and educates her well, and then frees her and marries her. *(Bukhari and Muslim)*

* * * * * * *

CHAPTER 239

VIRTUES OF PRAYERS DURING LAWLESSNESS AND CHAOS

١٣٦٦ – عَنْ مَعْقِلِ بنِ يسارٍ ، رَضِيَ اللهُ عَنْهُ ، قَالَ : قَالَ رَسُولُ
اللهِ ، صَلّى اللهُ عليهِ وسَلَّمَ : « العِبادَةُ في الهَرْجِ كَهِجْرَةٍ إليَّ »
رواهُ مُسْلِمٌ .

1366. Hazrat Ma'qil bin Yasar (R.A.A.) relates that the Holy Prophet (S.A.W.) has said: To pray during the period of lawlessness and disorder is equal to emigration towards me. *(Muslim)*

* * * * * * *

CHAPTER 240

VIRTUES OF BENEVOLENCE AND FAIR DEALING IN BUSINESS, DISCHARGING OBLIGATIONS AND RECEIVING DUES; FAIRNESS IN MEASUREMENT AND PROHIBITION OF SHORTAGE IN THE SAME AND VIRTUES OF AFFORDING RELIEF TO BOTH THE RICH AND THE POOR AND TO GRANT REMISSION

قَالَ اللهُ تَعَالَى : وَمَا تَفْعَلُوا مِنْ خَيْرٍ فإنَّ اللهَ بِهِ عَلِيمٌ [البقرة: ٢١٥]
وَقَالَ تَعَالَى : وَيَاقَوْمِ أَوْفُوا المِكْيَالَ وَالمِيزَانَ بالقِسْطِ وَلَاتَبْخَسُوا

النَّاسَ أَشْيَاءَهُمْ [هود : ٨٥] وقَالَ تَعَالَى : وَيْلٌ لِلْمُطَفِّفِينَ الَّذِينَ
إِذَا اكْتَالُوا عَلَى النَّاسِ يَسْتَوْفُونَ ، وَإِذَا كَالُوهُمْ أَوْ وَزَنُوهُمْ يُخْسِرُونَ ،
أَلا يَظُنُّ أُولَئِكَ أَنَّهُمْ مَبْعُوثُونَ لِيَوْمٍ عَظِيمٍ ، يَوْمَ يَقُومُ النَّاسُ لِرَبِّ
الْعَالَمِينَ [المطففين : ١] .

Allah, the Exalted, has said:

303. And whatsoever good ye do, Lo! Allah is aware of it. (2.215)

304. O my people! Give full measure and full weight in justice, and wrong not people in respect of their goods. (11: 85)

305. Woe unto the defrauders: Those who when they take the measure from mankind demand it full, but if they measure unto them or weigh for them, they cause them loss. Do such (men) not consider that they will be raised again unto an awful Day, the day when all mankind stand before the Lord of the worlds? (83:1-6)

١٣٦٧ – وَعَنْ أَبِي هُرَيْرَةَ ، رَضِيَ اللهُ عَنْهُ ، أَنَّ رَجُلاً أَتَى النَّبِيَّ ،
صَلَّى اللهُ عَلَيهِ وسلَّم يَتَقَاضَاهُ فَأَغْلَظَ لَهُ ، فَهَمَّ بِهِ أَصْحَابُهُ ، فَقَالَ
رَسُولُ اللهِ ، صَلَّى اللهُ عَلَيهِ وسلَّم : « دَعُوهُ فَإِنَّ لِصَاحِبِ الْحَقِّ مَقَالاً »
ثُمَّ قَالَ : « أَعْطُوهُ سِنّاً مِثْلَ سِنِّهِ » قالوا : يارسولَ اللهِ لاَ نَجِدُ إِلاَّ أَمْثَلَ
مِنْ سِنِّهِ . قال : « أَعْطُوهُ فَإِنَّ خَيْرَكُمْ أَحْسَنُكُمْ قَضَاءً »
مُتَّفَقٌ عَلَيهِ .

1367. Hazrat Abu Hurairah (R.A.A.) relates that a man came to the Holy Prophet (S.A.W.) and was vehement in demanding the return of his loan. The companions of the Holy Prophet (S.A.W.) wanted to catch hold and rebuke him, when the Holy Prophet (S.A.W.) said: Leave him alone, because a person having a right is entitled to speak rudely, and he (S.A.W.) added: Give him a camel of the same age as the camel that is due to him. (The Holy Prophet (S.A.W.) had taken a camel on loan from him). He (S.A.W.) was told that only a better camel than the one due to the said person was available. The Holy Prophet (S.A.W.) said: 'Well, let him have the better one, for the best of you are those who repay their debts in better way.

(Bukhari and Muslim)

١٣٦٨ – وَعَنْ جَابِرٍ ، رَضِيَ اللهُ عَنْهُ ، أَنَّ رَسُولَ اللهِ ، صَلَّى اللهُ عَلَيهِ وَسَلَّمَ ، قَالَ : « رَحِمَ اللهُ رَجُلاً سَمْحاً إذا بَاعَ ، وَإذا اشْتَرَى ، وَإذا اقْتَضَى » رواهُ البخاريُّ .

1368. Hazrat Jabir (R.A.A.) says that the Holy Prophet (S.A.W.) said: May Allah have mercy on a person who is easy and courteous when he sells, buys or asks for the payment of his dues. *(Bukhari)*

١٣٦٩ – وَعَنْ أَبي قَتَادَةَ ، رَضِيَ اللهُ عَنْهُ ، قَالَ : سَمِعْتُ رَسُولَ اللهِ ، صَلَّى اللهُ عَلَيهِ وَسَلَّمَ يَقُولُ : « مَنْ سَرَّهُ أَنْ يُنَجِّيَهُ اللهُ مِن كُرَبِ يَوْمِ القِيامَةِ ، فَلْيُنَفِّسْ عَنْ مُعْسِرٍ أَوْ يَضَعْ عَنْهُ » رواهُ مسلمٌ .

1369. Hazrat Abu Qatadah (R.A.A.) says that he heard the Holy Prophet (S.A.W.) say: A person who desires that Allah may keep him immune from the hardships of the Day of Judgment, he should grant respite to one who is in straitened circumstances or should remit the debt. *(Muslim)*

١٣٧٠ – وَعَنْ أَبي هُرَيرَةَ ، رَضِيَ اللهُ عَنْهُ ، أَنَّ رَسُولَ اللهِ ، صَلَّى اللهُ عَلَيهِ وَسَلَّمَ ، قَالَ : « كَانَ رَجُلٌ يُدَايِنُ النَّاسَ ، وَكَانَ يَقُولُ لِفَتَاهُ : إذا أَتَيْتَ مُعْسِراً فَتَجَاوَزْ عَنْهُ ، لَعَلَّ اللهَ أَنْ يَتَجَاوَزَ عَنَّا ، فَلَقِيَ اللهَ فَتَجَاوَزَ عَنْهُ » مُتَّفَقٌ عَلَيهِ .

1370. Hazrat Abu Hurairah (R.A.A.) relates that the Holy Prophet (S.A.W.) said: A man had monetary dealings with the people, had instructed his servant When you go to a person who is in straitened circumstances, forbear; perchance Allah may forbear us when we go to His presence. Accordingly, when he met Allah after his death, Allah remitted his sins. *(Bukhari and Muslim)*

١٣٧١ – وَعَنْ أَبي مَسْعُودٍ البَدْرِيِّ ، رَضِيَ اللهُ عَنْهُ ، قَالَ : قَالَ رَسُولُ اللهِ ، صَلَّى اللهُ عَلَيهِ وَسَلَّمَ : « حُوسِبَ رَجُلٌ مِمَّنْ كَانَ قَبْلَكُمْ ، فَلَمْ يُوجَدْ لَهُ مِنَ الخَيْرِ شَيْءٌ ، إلاَّ أَنَّهُ كَانَ يُخَالِطُ النَّاسَ ، وَكَانَ مُوسِراً ، وَكَانَ يَأْمُرُ غِلْمَانَهُ أَنْ يَتَجَاوَزُوا عَنِ المُعْسِرِ . قَالَ اللهُ ، عَزَّ وَجَلَّ : « نَحْنُ أَحَقُّ بِذلكَ مِنْهُ ؛ تَجَاوَزُوا عَنْهُ » رواهُ مسلمٌ .

1371. Hazrat Abu Mas'ud-al Badri (R.A.A.) relates that the Holy Prophet (S.A.W.) said: A man who lived before you was (after his death) called upon to give account, but there was nothing good in his account. The only thing was that when he had dealings with the people, and was himself in easy circumstances, he instructed his servants that they should forbear in the case of those who happen to be in straitened circumstances, Allah, the Exalted and Supreme said. I am more worthy of this quality, and asked (the angels) to forbear from him. *(Muslim)*

١٣٧٢ – وَعَنْ حُذَيْفَةَ ، رَضِيَ اللهُ عَنْهُ . قَالَ : أُتِيَ اللهُ . تَعَالَى . بِعَبْدٍ مِنْ عِبَادِهِ آتَاهُ اللهُ مَالاً ، فَقَالَ لَهُ : مَاذَا عَمِلْتَ فِي الدُّنْيَا ؟ قَالَ : – وَلا يَكْتُمُونَ اللهَ حَدِيثاً – قَالَ : يَارَبِّ آتَيْتَنِي مالَكَ ، فَكُنْتُ أُبَايِعُ النَّاسَ ، وَكَانَ مِنْ خُلُقِي الجَوَازُ ، فَكُنْتُ أَتَيَسَّرُ عَلَى المُوسِرِ ، وَأُنْظِرُ المُعْسِرَ . فَقَالَ اللهُ تَعَالَى : « أَنَا أَحَقُّ بِذا مِنْكَ تَجَاوَزُوا عَنْ عَبْدِي » فَقَالَ عُقْبَةُ بنُ عَامِرٍ ، وأَبو مَسْعُودٍ الأنصاريُّ ، رَضِيَ اللهُ عَنْهُمَا : هكذَا سَمِعْنَاهُ مِنْ فِي رَسولِ اللهِ ، صَلَّى اللهُ عليهِ وَسَلَّم .

رواهُ مسلمٌ .

1372. Hazrat Huzaifah (R.A.A.) relates that when a man upon whom Allah had bestowed wealth, was brought before Him, He asked him: What did you do in the world? He answered: Though it is not possible to conceal anything from Allah, O my Lord whatever thou had bestowed, with that I carried on business with the people, and it was my habit to forbear, I was easy with one who was in easy circumstances and granted remission to one who was in straitened circumstances. Thereupon Allah the Exalted, said: I am more worthy of these qualities than you are; and he commanded: Forbear against this servant of Mine. Hearing this tradition, Hazrat 'Utbah bin 'Aamir (R.A.A.) and Hazrat Abu Mas'ud Ansari (R.A.A.) said: That they too had heard this from the Holy Prophet (S.A.W.). *(Muslim)*

١٣٧٣ – وَعَنْ أَبِي هُرَيرَةَ ، رَضِيَ اللهُ عَنْهُ ، قَالَ : قَالَ رَسُولُ اللهِ صَلَّى اللهُ عَلَيهِ وَسَلَّم ، « مَنْ أَنْظَرَ مُعْسِراً ، أَوْ وَضَعَ لَهُ ، أَظَلَّهُ اللهُ يَوْمَ القِيَامَةِ تَحْتَ ظِلِّ عَرْشِهِ يَوْمَ لا ظِلَّ إلاَّ ظِلُّهُ »

رواهُ التِّرمذيُّ وقَالَ : حديثٌ حسنٌ صحيحٌ .

1373. Hazrat Abu Hurairah (R.A.A.) relates that the Holy Prophet (S.A.W.) said: A person who grants respite to a debtor who is in straintened circumstances, or remits his claim against him, will be given shelter by Allah under the shadow of His throne, on the Day of Judgement, when there will be no other shelter. *(Tirmizi* said this is sound and good).

١٣٧٤ — وعَنْ جابرٍ ، رَضِيَ اللهُ عَنْهُ ، أنَّ النَّبِيَّ ، صَلَّى اللهُ عليهِ وَسلَّم ، اشْتَرَى مِنْهُ بَعِيراً ، فوزَنَ لَهُ ، فأرْجَحَ . مُتَّفَقٌ عليهِ .

1374. Hazrat Jabir (R.A.A.) says that the Holy Prophet (S.A.W.) purchased a camel from him and paid him the animal's price after weighment more than its original price. *(Bukahri and Muslim)*

١٣٧٥ — وعَنْ أبي صَفْوانَ سُوَيْدِ بنِ قَيْسٍ ، رَضِيَ اللهُ عَنْهُ ، قالَ : جَلَبْتُ أنا وَمَخْرَمَةُ العَبْدِيُّ بَزّاً مِنْ هَجَرَ ، فَجاءَنا النَّبِيُّ ، صَلَّى اللهُ عليهِ وسلَّم ، فَسَاوَمَنا بِسَراويلَ ، وَعِنْدِي وَزَّانٌ يَزِنُ بالأجْرِ ، فَقالَ النبيُّ ، صلَّى اللهُ عليهِ وسلَّم ، لِلْوَزَّانِ : « زِنْ وَأرْجِحْ » رواهُ أبوداودَ ، والترمذيُّ وقالَ : حديثٌ حسنٌ صحيحٌ .

1375. Hazrat Abu Safwan Suwaid bin Qais (R.A.A.) relates that once he and Mukhramah Al-'Ab'di brought some drapery for sale from Hajar. On learning about this, the Holy Prophet (S.A.W.) went to them, and purchased a pair of trousers. They had a person who used to weigh coins (gold or silver). The Holy Prophet (S.A.W.) said to him Weigh it for its price and add a little over it.' *(Abu Daud and Tirmizi,* latter said it is sound and good).

* * * * * * *

BOOK OF KNOWLEDGE

CHAPTER 241

قَالَ اللهُ تَعَالَى : وَقُلْ رَبِّ زِدْنِي عِلْماً [طه : ١١٤] وقَالَ تَعَالَى :

قُلْ هَلْ يَسْتَوِي الَّذِينَ يَعْلَمُونَ وَالَّذِينَ لا يَعْلَمُونَ [الزمر : ٩]

وَقَالَ تَعَالَى : يَرْفَعِ اللهُ الَّذِينَ آمَنُوا مِنْكُمْ وَالَّذِينَ أُوتُوا العِلْمَ

دَرَجَاتٍ [المجادلة : ١١] وَقَالَ تَعَالَى : إِنَّمَا يَخْشَى اللهَ مِنْ عِبَادِهِ

العُلَمَاءُ [فاطر : ٢٨] .

Allah, the Exalted, has said :

306. And say: My Lord! Increase me in knowledge (20:114)

307. Say (Unto them, O Muhammad): Are those who know equal with those who know not? (39:9)

308. Allah will exalt those who believe among you, and those who have knowledge, to high ranks. (58:11)

309. The erudite among his bondsmen fear Allah alone. (35:28)

١٣٧٦ – وَعَنْ مُعَاوِيَةَ ، رَضِيَ اللهُ عَنْهُ ، قَالَ : قَالَ رَسُولُ اللهِ ،

صَلَّى اللهُ عَلَيهِ وسَلَّم : « مَنْ يُرِدِ اللهُ بِهِ خَيْراً يُفَقِّهْهُ فِي الدِّينِ »

مُتَّفَقٌ عَلَيه .

1376. Hazrat Mu'awiah (R.A.A.) relates that the Holy Prophet (S.A.W.) said: Upon a person whom Allah desires good, He bestows the knowledge of Faith. *(Bukhari and Muslim)*

١٣٧٧ – وَعَنْ ابنِ مَسْعُودٍ ، رَضِيَ اللهُ عَنْهُ ، قَالَ : قَالَ رَسُولُ

اللهِ ، صَلَّى اللهُ عَلَيهِ وسَلَّم : « لاحَسَدَ إِلاَّ فِي اثْنَتَيْنِ : رَجُلٌ آتَاهُ اللهُ

مَالاً فَسَلَّطَهُ عَلَى هَلَكَتِهِ فِي الحَقِّ ، وَرَجُلٌ آتَاهُ اللهُ الحِكْمَةَ فَهُوَ

يَقْضِي بِهَا ، وَيُعَلِّمُهَا » مُتَّفَقٌ عَلَيه .

1377. This Hadith has already been covered in the Hadith vide No. 544 of Chapter 60.

١٣٧٨ – وَعَنْ أبي مُوسَى ، رَضِيَ اللهُ عَنْهُ ، قَالَ : قَالَ النَّبِيُّ ، صَلَّى اللهُ عَلَيهِ وسَلَّم : « مَثَلُ مَا بَعَثَنِي اللهُ بِهِ مِنَ الهُدَى والعِلْمِ كَمَثَلِ غَيْثٍ أصَابَ أرْضاً ؛ فكَانَتْ مِنْهَا طَائِفَةٌ طَيِّبَةٌ قَبِلَتِ المَاءَ فَأنْبَتَتْ الكَلأَ ، والعُشْبَ الكَثِيرَ ، وكَانَ مِنْهَا أجَادِبُ أمسَكَتِ المَاءَ ، فَنَفَعَ اللهُ بِهَا النَّاسَ ؛ فَشَرِبُوا مِنْهَا وَسَقَوْا وزَرَعُوا ، وأصَابَ طَائِفَةً مِنْهَا أُخْرَى إنَّمَا هِيَ قِيعَانٌ ، لا تُمْسِكُ مَاءً ، ولا تُنْبِتُ كَلأً ، فذَلِكَ مَثَلُ مَنْ فَقُهَ في دِينِ اللهِ ، وَنَفَعَهُ مابَعَثَنِي اللهُ بِهِ ، فَعَلِمَ وَعَلَّمَ ، وَمَثَلُ مَنْ لَمْ يَرفَعْ بِذلكَ رَأْساً ، وَلَمْ يَقبَلْ هُدَى اللهِ الَّذي أُرْسِلْتُ بِهِ » . مُتفقٌ عليه .

1378. This Hadith has already been covered in Hadith No. 162 of Chapter 16.

١٣٧٩ – وَعَنْ سَهْلِ بنِ سَعْدٍ ، رَضِيَ اللهُ عَنْهُ ، أنَّ النَّبِيَّ صَلَّى اللهُ عليهِ وَسَلَّم ، قَالَ لِعَلِيٍّ ، رَضِيَ اللهُ عَنْهُ : « فواللهِ لأنْ يَهْدِيَ اللهُ بِكَ رَجُلاً وَاحِداً خَيْرٌ لكَ مِن حُمْرِ النَّعَمِ » مُتَّفَقٌ عليه .

1379. This Hadith is contained in the last sentence of S. No. 175 of Chapter 20.

١٣٨٠ – وَعَنْ عبدِ اللهِ بنِ عمرِو بنِ العاصِ ، رَضِيَ اللهُ عَنْهُمَا ، أنَّ النَّبِيَّ ، صَلَّى اللهُ عَلَيهِ وسلَّم قَالَ : « بَلِّغُوا عَنِّي وَلَوْ آيَةً ، وَحَدِّثُوا عَنْ بَنِي إسْرَائِيلَ وَلا حَرَجَ ، وَمَنْ كَذَبَ عَلَيَّ مُتَعَمِّداً فَلْيَتَبَوَّأْ مَقْعَدَهُ مِنَ النَّارِ » رواه البخاريُّ .

1380. Hazrat Abdullah bin 'Amr bin Al-'Aas (R.A.A.) says that the Holy Prophet (S.A.W.) said: Convey from me to the people though it may be only one verse; and you may narrate events from the accounts of Bani Israil, there is no harm in doing so. But a person who deliberately attributes to me something which is not true, should find out his abode in Hell. *(Bukhari)*

١٣٨١ – وَعَنْ أبي هُرَيرَةَ ، رَضِيَ اللهُ عَنْهُ ، أنَّ رَسُولَ اللهِ ، صَلَّى اللهُ عليهِ وسلَّم . قَالَ : « وَمَنْ سَلَكَ طَرِيقاً يَلْتَمِسُ فِيهِ عِلْماً ، سَهَّلَ

اللهُ لَهُ بِهِ طَرِيقاً إلى الجَنَّةِ » رواهُ مسلمٌ

1381. **Hazrat Abu Hurairah** (R.A.A.) relates that the Holy Prophet (S.A.W.) said: A person who follows a path for acquiring knowledge, Allah, will make easy the passage for Paradise for him. *(Muslim)*

١٣٨٢ – وعَنْهُ ، أيضاً ، رَضِيَ اللهُ عَنْهُ ، أنَّ رَسُولَ اللهِ ، صَلَّى اللهُ عليهِ وسلَّم ، قَالَ : « مَنْ دَعَا إلى هُدىً كانَ لَهُ مِنَ الأجْرِ مِثلُ أُجُورِ مَنْ تبعَهُ لايَنْقُصُ ذلكَ مِنْ أُجُورِهِم شَيْئاً » رواهُ مسلمٌ .

1382. **Hazrat Abu Hurairah** (R.A.A.) reports that the Holy Prophet (S.A.W.) said: A person who invited (somebody) towards righteousness have a recompense equal to the recompense of one who receives guidance from him, without reducing the recompense of either of them. *(Muslim)*

١٣٨٣ – وعَنْهُ قَالَ : قَالَ رَسُولُ اللهِ ، صَلَّى اللهُ عليهِ وسلَّم : « إذَا مَاتَ ابْنُ آدَمَ انْقَطَعَ عَمَلُهُ إلاَّ مِنْ ثَلاثٍ : صَدَقَةٍ جَارِيَةٍ ، أوْ عِلمٍ يُنْتَفَعُ بِهِ ، أوْ وَلَدٍ صَالِحٍ يَدْعُو لَهُ » رواهُ مسلمٌ .

1383. This Hadis has already been dealt with as No. 940 of Chapter 162.

١٣٨٤ – وعَنْهُ قَالَ : سَمِعْتُ رَسُولَ اللهِ ، صَلَّى اللهُ عليهِ وسلَّم ، يَقُولُ : « الدُّنْيَا مَلعُونَةٌ ، مَلْعُونٌ ما فِيهَا ، إلاَّ ذِكْرَ اللهِ تَعَالى ، وَمَا والاهُ ، وَعَالِماً ، أوْ مُتَعَلِماً » رواهُ الترمذيُّ وقَالَ : حديثٌ حسنٌ .

1384. This Hadis is the same as No. 478 of Chapter 55.

١٣٨٥ – وعَنْ أنسٍ ، رَضِيَ اللهُ عَنْهُ قَالَ : قَالَ رَسُولُ اللهِ ، صَلَّى اللهُ عليهِ وسَلَّمَ : « مَنْ خرَجَ في طَلَبِ العِلمِ ، فهو في سَبِيلِ اللهِ حتى يَرجِعَ » رواهُ التِرمِذيُّ وقَالَ : حديثٌ حَسَنٌ .

1385. **Hazrat Anas** (R.A.A.) relates that the Holy Prophet (S.A.W.) said: A person who goes (out of his house) in search of knowledge, he is on Allah's way and he remains so till he returns. *(Tirmizi said it is good)*

١٣٨٦ – وعَنْ أبي سَعِيدٍ الخدْرِيَّ ، رَضِيَ اللهُ عَنْهُ ، عَنْ رَسُولِ اللهِ ، صَلَّى اللهُ عَليهِ وَسَلَّم ، قَالَ : « لَنْ يَشبَعَ مُؤمِنٌ مِنْ خَيْرٍ حتى يكونَ

مُنْتَهَاهُ الجَنَّةَ » رواهُ التِرمذيُّ وَقَالَ : حديثٌ حَسَنٌ .

1386. Hazrat Abu Sa'eed Khudri (R.A.A.) relates that the Holy Prophet (S.A.W.) said: A Muslim is never satiated in his quest for good (knowledge) till it ends in paradise. *(Tirmizi* said this Hadis is good)

١٣٨٧— وَعَنْ أبي أُمامَةَ ، رَضِيَ اللهُ عَنْهُ ، أَنَّ رَسُولَ اللهِ ، صَلَّى اللهُ عليهِ وسَلَّمَ ، قَالَ : « فَضْلُ العَالِمِ عَلَى العَابِدِ كَفَضْلِي عَلى أَدْنَاكُمْ » ثُمَّ قالَ رَسُولُ اللهِ ، صَلَّى اللهُ عليهِ وسَلَّمَ : « إنَّ اللهَ وَمَلائِكَتَهُ وَأَهْلَ السَّمواتِ وَالأَرْضِ حَتَّى النَّمْلَةَ في جُحْرِهَا وَحَتَّى الحُوتَ لَيُصَلُّونَ عَلى مُعَلِّمِي النَّاسِ الخَيْرَ » رواهُ التِرمذيُّ وقَالَ : حَديثٌ حَسَنٌ .

1387. Hazrat Abu Umamah (R.A.A.) reports that the Holy Prophet (S.A W.) said. An'Aalim (learned person or theologian) is as much superior to an 'A abid (worshipper) as I am superior to an ordinary Muslim among you; the Holy Prophet (S.A.W.) further added: Allah, His angels and all those who live in the heavens and the earth, even the ants in their holes and the fish supplicate for those who instruct people in virtuous knowledge. *(Tirmizi* and said this Hadis is good)

١٣٨٨— وَعَنْ أبي الدَّرْدَاءِ ، رَضِيَ اللهُ عَنْهُ ، قَالَ : سَمِعْتُ رَسُولَ اللهِ ، صَلَّى اللهُ عليهِ وسلَّمَ ، يَقُولُ : « مَنْ سَلَكَ طَرِيقاً يَبْتَغِي فِيهِ عِلْماً سَهَّلَ اللهُ لَهُ طَرِيقاً إلى الجَنَّةِ ، وَإنَّ المَلائِكَةَ لَتَضَعُ أَجْنِحَتَهَا لِطَالِبِ العِلْمِ رِضاً بِمَا يَصْنَعُ ، وَإنَّ العَالِمَ لَيَسْتَغْفِرُ لَهُ مَنْ في السَّمواتِ وَمَنْ في الأَرْضِ حَتَّى الحِيتَانُ في المَاءِ ، وَفَضْلُ العَالِمِ عَلَى العَابِدِ كَفَضْلِ القَمَرِ عَلى سَائِرِ الكَوَاكِبِ ، وَإنَّ العُلَمَاءَ وَرَثَةُ الأَنْبِيَاءِ ، وَإنَّ الأَنْبِيَاءَ لَمْ يُوَرِّثُوا دِينَاراً وَلا دِرْهَماً وَإنَّمَا وَرَّثُوا العِلْمَ . فَمَنْ أَخَذَهُ أَخَذَ بِحَظٍّ وَافِرٍ » رَوَاهُ أبو داودَ والترمذيُّ .

1388. Hazrat Abu Darda (R.A.A.) relates that he heard the Holy Prophet (S.A.W.) say: A person who starts his journey to acquire knowledge, Allah eases his passage to paradise, and angels to express their appreciation on his acts, spread their wings and all the creatures that are in the heavens and on the earth, including the fish in the water, ask for forgiveness for an 'Aalim (learned person). A learned person is superior to a worshipper as the full moon is superior to all the stars.

The learned are heirs of the prophets and, the prophets do not leave any inheritence in the shape of dirhams and dinars (wealth), but they do leave knowledge as their legacy. As such a person who acquires knowledge, acquires his full share. *(Abu Daud and Tirmizi)*

١٣٨٩ – وَعَنِ ابنِ مَسْعُودٍ ، رَضِيَ اللهُ عَنْهُ ، قَالَ : سَمِعْتُ رَسُولَ اللهِ ، صَلَّى اللهُ عليهِ وَسَلَّمَ يَقُولُ : « نَضَّرَ اللهُ امْرَءاً سَمِعَ مِنَّا شَيْئاً ، فَبَلَّغَهُ كَمَا سَمِعَهُ ، فَرُبَّ مُبَلَّغٍ أَوْعَى مِنْ سَامِعٍ » رواهُ التِرمذيُّ وقَالَ : حديثٌ حَسَنٌ صحيحٌ .

1389. Hazrat Ibn Mas'ud (R.A.A.) relates that he heard the Holy Prophet (S.A.W.) say: May Allah, keep the person happy who hears something from us and conveys it to others, what he has heard, for sometimes the people who hear from others remember it better than the first hearer himself. *(Tirmizi)*

١٣٩٠ – وَعَنْ أبي هُرَيرَةَ ، رَضِيَ اللهُ عَنْهُ ، قَالَ : قَالَ رَسُولُ اللهِ صَلَّى اللهُ عليهِ وسلَّم : « مَنْ سُئِلَ عَنْ عِلمٍ فَكَتَمَهُ ، أُلجِمَ يَوْمَ القِيَامَةِ بِلِجَامٍ مِنْ نَارٍ » رَوَاهُ أبو داودَ والترمذيُّ وقَالَ : حديثٌ حَسَنٌ .

1390. Hazrat Abu Hurairah (R.A.A.) reports that the Holy Prophet (S.A.W.) said: A learned person who is asked about something (about the religion) and he conceals it, such a person will be bridled on the Day of Judgement with a bridle of fire.

(Abu Daud and Tirmizi)

١٣٩١ – وعنهُ قالَ : قالَ رسولُ اللهِ صلَّى اللهُ عليهِ وسلَّم : « مَنْ تَعَلَّمَ عِلماً مِمَّا يُبْتَغى بِهِ وَجْهُ اللهِ عَزَّ وَجَلَّ لا يَتَعَلَّمُهُ إلا لِيُصِيبَ بِهِ عَرَضاً مِنَ الدُّنْيَا لَمْ يَجِدْ عَرْفَ الجَنَّةِ يَوْمَ القِيَامَةِ » يَعْني : رِيحَها . رواهُ أبو داودَ بإسنادٍ صَحيحٍ .

1391. Hazrat Abu Hurairah (R.A.A.) relates that the Holy Prophet (S.A.W.) said: A person who acquires knowledge, which is being sought for the pleasure of Allah, with the intention to attain some worldly gains, such a person will not get even the fragrance of paradise on the Day of Judgement. *(Abu Daud* quoted with sound chains).

١٣٩٢ – وعَنْ عبدِ اللهِ بنِ عَمرِو بنِ العاصِ رَضيَ اللهُ عَنهُمَا قالَ : سَمِعْتُ رسولَ اللهِ صلَّى اللهُ عَلَيْهِ وسَلَّمَ يقولُ : « إنَّ اللهَ لايَقْبِضُ

العِلْمَ انتِزَاعاً يَنْتَزِعُهُ مِنَ النَّاسِ ، وَلَكِنْ يَقْبِضُ العِلْمَ بِقَبْضِ
العُلَمَاءِ ، حَتَّى إذا لَمْ يُبْقِ عالِماً ، اتَّخَذَ النَّاسُ رُؤوساً جُهَّالاً .
فَسُئِلُوا ، فَأَفْتَوا بِغَيْرِ عِلْمٍ ، فَضَلُّوا وَأَضَلُّوا » متفق عليه .

1392. Hazrat Abdullah bin 'Amr bin Al-'Aas (R.A.A.) relates that he heard the Holy Prophet (S.A.W.) say: Allah will not withdraw knowledge by snatching it away from people, but it will be withdrawn as a result of the death of learned persons (divines), as such when there will be no learned person, people will appoint ignorant persons as their leaders and will ask them for guidance in religious matters, and they will issue edicts (Fatawas) without knowledge. Thus they will go astray themselves, and will lead others astray. *(Bukhari and Muslim)*

* * * * * * *

BOOK OF EULOGIZING AND THANKING ALLAH, THE EXALTED

CHAPTER 242

قَالَ اللهُ تَعَالَى : فَاذْكُرُونِي أَذْكُرْكُمْ ، وَاشْكُرُوا لِي وَلَا تَكْفُرُونِ [البقرة : ١٥٢] وقَالَ تَعَالَى : لَئِنْ شَكَرْتُمْ لَأَزِيدَنَّكُمْ [إبراهيم : ٧] وقَالَ تَعَالَى : وَقُلِ الحَمْدُ لِلهِ [الإسراء : ١١١] وقَالَ تَعَالَى : وَآخِرُ دَعْوَاهُمْ أَنِ الحَمْدُ لِلهِ رَبِّ العَالَمِينَ [يونس: ١٠-١١] .

Allah, the Exalted, has siad:

310. Therefore remember, I will remember you. Give thanks to and reject not. (2: 152)

311. If ye give thanks, I will give you more. (14.7)

312. And say: Praise be to Allah (17:111)

313. And the conclusion of their prayer will be: Praise be to Allah, Lord of the worlds! (10:11)

١٣٩٣ – وعَنْ أَبي هُرَيْرَةَ ، رَضِيَ اللهُ عَنْهُ ، أَنَّ النبيَّ صلَّى اللهُ عليه وسلَّمَ أُتِيَ لَيْلَةَ أُسْرِيَ بِهِ بِقَدَحَيْنِ مِنْ خَمْرٍ وَلَبَنٍ . فَنَظَرَ إِلَيْهِمَا فَأَخَذَ اللَّبَنَ . فَقَالَ جبريلُ صلَّى اللهُ عليهِ وسلَّم : « الحَمْدُ لِلهِ الَّذي هَدَاكَ لِلفِطْرَةِ لَوْ أَخَذْتَ الخَمْرَ غَوَتْ أُمَّتُكَ » رواهُ مسلم .

1393. Hazrat Abu Hurairah (R.A.A.) relates that on the Night of Ascension, the Holy Prophet (S.A.W.) was presented with two cups, one containing liquor and the other containing milk. He glanced at them and took the one containing milk. Thereupon the Angel Gabriel, remarked: All praise be to Allah, Allah has guided you to nature. Had you selected the cup containing liquor, your Ummah would have gone astray. *(Muslim)*

١٣٩٤ – وعَنْهُ عَنْ رسولِ اللهِ صَلَّى اللهُ عليْهِ وَسَلَّمَ قالَ : « كُلُّ أَمْرٍ ذِي بَالٍ لايُبْدَأُ فيهِ بِـ: الحَمْدُ لِلهِ فَهُوَ أَقْطَعُ » حديثٌ حَسَنٌ ، رواهُ أَبو داود وغيرُهُ .

1394. Hazrat Abu Hurairah (R.A.A.) relates that the Holy Prophet (S.A.W.) said: Every magnificent and important project not begun with the praise of Allah, remains defective. *(Abu Daud)*

١٣٩٥ – وعَنْ أبي موسى الأَشعريِّ رضيَ اللهُ عنهُ . أنَّ رَسُولَ اللهِ صَلَّى اللهُ عليْهِ وسلَّم قالَ : « إذا ماتَ وَلَدُ العبْدِ قالَ اللهُ تعالى لِملائكته : قَبَضْتُمْ وَلَدَ عبْدي ؟ فيقولُونَ : نعَمْ . فيَقُولُ : قبَضْتُمْ ثمرَةَ فؤادِهِ ؟ فيقولون : نعَمْ ، فيقولُ : فماذا قالَ عبْدي ؟ فيقولون : حمِدَكَ واسْتَرْجَعَ فيَقُولُ اللهُ تعالى : ابْنُوا لعبْدي بيْتاً في الجنَّةِ ، وسمُّوهُ بيْتَ الحمْدِ » رواهُ الترمذي وقالَ : حديثٌ حسنٌ .

1395. This Hadis is the same as No. 922 of Chapter 152

١٣٩٦ – وعنْ أنسٍ رضيَ اللهُ عنْهُ قالَ : قالَ رسُولُ اللهِ صَلَّى اللهُ عليهِ وسلَّمَ : « إنَّ اللهَ ليَرْضَى عنِ العبْدِ يأْكُلُ الأَكْلَةَ فيَحْمَدُهُ عليْهَا ، ويَشْرَبُ الشَّرْبَةَ ، فيَحْمَدُهُ عليْهَا » رواهُ مسلم

1396. This Hadis is the same as No. 140 of Chapter 13.

* * * * * * *

BOOK OF INVOKING ALLAH'S BLESSINGS AND MERCIES ON THE HOLY PROPHET (S.A.W.)

CHAPTER 243

قَالَ اللهُ تَعَالَى : إِنَّ اللهَ وَمَلائِكَتَهُ يُصَلُّونَ عَلَى النَّبِيِّ ، يَا أَيُّهَا الَّذِينَ آمَنُوا صَلُّوا عَلَيْهِ وَسَلِّمُوا تَسْلِيماً [الأحزاب : ٥٦] .

Allah, the Exalted, has said:

314. Lo! Allah and His Angels shower blessings on the Prophet. O ye who believe ! Ask blessings on him and salute him with a worthy salutation. (33:56)

١٣٩٧ – وعنْ عَبْدِ اللهِ بنِ عَمرو بنِ العاصِ ، رَضيَ اللهُ عَنْهُما أنَّهُ سَمِعَ رَسُولَ اللهِ صلّى اللهُ عَلَيْهِ وَسَلَّمَ يقُولُ : « مَنْ صَلَّى عَلَيَّ صَلاةً ، صَلَّى اللهُ عَلَيْهِ بِهَا عَشْراً » رواهُ مسلم .

1397. Hazrat Abdullah bin 'Amr bin Al-'Aas (R.A.A.) says that he heard the Holy Prophet (S.A.W.) say. A person who calls for blessings on me, (recites Salat) once, Allah sends down mercies on him ten times. *(Muslim)*

١٣٩٨ – وعنِ ابنِ مَسْعُودٍ رَضِيَ اللهُ عَنْهُ أنَّ رَسُولَ اللهِ صَلَّى اللهُ عَلَيْهِ وسَلَّمَ قالَ : « أَوْلى النَّاسِ بِي يَوْمَ الْقِيامَةِ أَكْثَرُهُمْ عَلَيَّ صَلاةً » رواه الترمذي وقالَ : حديثٌ حسنٌ .

1398. Hazrat Abdullah bin Mas'ud (R.A.A.) relates that the Holy Prophet (S.A.W.) said. On the Day of Judgement the nearest to me will be the person from among you who invokes Allah's blessings (Salat) on me most. *(Tirmizi,* and said this tradition as good)

١٣٩٩ – وعنْ أَوسِ بنِ أوسٍ ، رضيَ اللهُ عَنْهُ قالَ : قالَ رسُولُ اللهِ صَلَّى اللهُ عليهِ وسَلَّمَ : « إنَّ مِنْ أَفضَلِ أَيَّامِكُمْ يَوْمَ الجُمُعَةِ ، فَأَكْثِرُوا عَلَيَّ مِنَ الصَّلاةِ فِيهِ ، فَإِنَّ صَلاتَكُمْ مَعْرُوضَةٌ عَلَيَّ » فقالوا : يا رسُولَ اللهِ ، وكَيْفَ تُعْرَضُ صَلاتُنا عَلَيْكَ وَقَدْ أَرِمْتَ ؟! قالَ : يقولُ : بَلِيتَ ، قالَ : « إنَّ اللهَ حَرَّمَ عَلَى الأَرْضِ أَجْسَادَ الأَنْبِياءِ » .

رواهُ أبو داود بإسنادٍ صَحيحٍ .

1399. Hazrat Aus bin Aus (R.A.A.) reports that the Holy Prophet (S.A.W.) said: Friday is the best day among your days. Therefore, send Salat (invoke Allah's blessings and mercies) upon me as much as you can on that day, for your Salat is conveyed to me. The companions submitted: O Messenger of Allah, how will our invocation (containing Salat) be conveyed to you, when you having buried in the earth, will be resting (there). He (S.A.W.) answered: Allah has forbidden the earth (from damaging) the bodies of prophets. *(Abu Daud* with sound chains)

١٤٠٠– وعَنْ أبي هُرَيْرَةَ رَضيَ اللهَ عنه قالَ : قالَ رسُولُ اللهِ صَلّى اللهُ عليه وسَلّمَ : « رَغِمَ أنْفُ رَجُلٍ ذُكِرتُ عِنْدَهُ فلَمْ يُصَلِّ عَلَيَّ » رواه الترمذي وقالَ : حديثٌ حسنٌ .

1400. Hazrat Abu Hurairah (R.A.A.) relates that the Holy Prophet (S.A.W.) said. May that person be humbled in whose presence my name is mentioned but he does not invoke Salat (blessings) upon *(Tirmizi)*

١٤٠١– وعَنهُ رَضِيَ اللهُ عَنْهُ قالَ : قالَ رَسُولُ اللهِ صَلّى اللهُ عليهِ وسلّمَ : « لا تجعَلُوا قبْري عِيداً ، وصَلّوا عليّ ؛ فإنّ صَلاتَكُمْ تبلُغُني حَيْثُ كُنْتُمْ » رواهُ أبوداود بإسنادٍ صحيحٍ .

1401. Hazrat Abu Hurairah (R.A.A.) relates that the Holy Prophet (S.A.W.) said: Do not make my grave a place of festivity and merry-making (but) invoke blessings upon me (by reciting Salat) for your blessings (Salat) will reach me, wherever you may be.

(Abu Daud has cited with sound chains)

١٤٠٢ – وعنه أنّ رسُولَ اللهِ صَلّى اللهُ عليهِ وسَلّمَ قالَ : « مَامِن أحَدٍ يُسَلّمُ عَلَيَّ إلاّ رَدّ اللهُ عَلَيّ رُوحِي حتّى أرُدّ عَلَيْهِ السّلامَ » رواهُ أبو داود بإسنادٍ صحيحٍ .

1402. Hazrat Abu Hurairah (R.A.A.) relates that the Holy Prophet (S.A.W.) said: Whenever anyone sends Salam to me (invokes blessings upon me) Allah will restore my soul to me, till I respond to his invocation. *(Abu Daud* with sound chains)

١٤٠٣ – وعن عَليٍّ رضيَ اللهُ عَنْهُ قالَ : قالَ رسُولُ اللهِ صَلّى اللهُ علَيْهِ وسَلّمَ : «البَخيلُ مَنْ ذُكِرتُ عِنْدَهُ ،فلَمْ يُصَلِّ عَلَيَّ » رواهُ الترمذي وقالَ : حديثٌ حَسَنٌ صحيحٌ .

1403. Hazrat Ali (R.A.A.) relates that the Holy Prophet (S.A.W.) said: A miser is a person who does not invoke blessings upon me (by reciting Salat) when my name is taken in his presence.

(*Tirmizi*, and said this as sound and good)

١٤٠٤ – وعَنْ فَضَالَةَ بنِ عُبَيْدٍ ، رضيَ اللهُ عَنْهُ ، قالَ : سَمِعَ رسولُ اللهِ صَلَّى اللهُ عَلَيْهِ وسلَّم رَجُلاً يَدْعُو في صَلاتِهِ لَمْ يُمَجِّدِ اللهَ تَعَالى ، وَلَمْ يُصَلِّ عَلَى النبيِّ صَلَّى اللهُ عليهِ وسلَّم ، فقالَ رسولُ اللهِ ، صلَّى اللهُ عليهِ وسلَّم : « عَجِلَ هذا » ثُمَّ دَعَاهُ فقالَ لهُ – أوْ لِغَيْرِهِ – : « إذا صَلَّى أحَدُكُمْ فَلْيَبْدَأْ بِتَحْمِيدِ رَبِّهِ سُبْحَانَهُ ، وَالثَّنَاءِ عليهِ ، ثُمَّ يُصَلِّي عَلى النبيِّ ، صَلَّى اللهُ عليهِ وسلَّم ، ثُمَّ يَدْعُو بَعدُ بِمَا شَاءَ »

رواهُ أبو داودَ والترمذي وقال : حديثٌ حسن صحيحٌ .

1404. Hazrat Fazala bin Ubaid (R.A.A.) relates; The Holy Prophet (S.A.W.) heard a person supplicating in his Salat (prayer) without eulogising Allah, the Exalted and without invoking Allah's mercies and blessings (reciting Salat) upon the Holy Prophet (S.A.W.). The Holy Prophet (S.A.W.) remarked: That person made haste. The Holy Prophet (S.A.W.) then said to him, or to somebody else that 'when one of you offers prayer he should begin with the eulogy of his Lord, the Glorious and Praise Him! and then invoke the mercies and blessings of Allah (recite Salat) on the Prophet (S.A.W.) and then supplicate as he may like. (*Abu Daud and Tirmizi.* Latter said that it is good and sound).

١٤٠٥ – وعَنْ أبي محمدٍ كَعْبِ بنِ عُجْرَةَ ، رضِيَ اللهُ عَنْهُ ، قالَ : خرَجَ عَلَيْنَا النبيُّ صَلَّى اللهُ عليهِ وسَلَّمَ فقُلْنا : يارسولَ اللهِ : قَدْ عَلِمْنَا كَيْفَ نُسَلِّمُ عَلَيْكَ ، فَكَيْفَ نُصَلِّي عَلَيْكَ ؟ قال : « قُولُوا : اللَّهُمَّ صَلِّ عَلى مُحَمَّدٍ ، وَعَلى آلِ مُحَمَّدٍ ، كَمَا صَلَّيْتَ عَلى آلِ إبْرَاهِيمَ ، إنَّكَ حَمِيدٌ مَجِيدٌ . اللَّهُمَّ بَارِكْ عَلى مُحَمَّدٍ ، وَعَلى آلِ مُحَمَّدٍ ، كَمَا بَارَكْتَ عَلى آلِ إبْرَاهِيمَ ، إنَّكَ حَمِيدٌ مَجِيدٌ » متفقٌ عليهِ .

1405. Hazrat Abu Muhammad Ka'b bin 'Ujrah (R.A.A.) says: (Once) the Holy Prophet (S.A.W.) visited us, then we submitted: 'O Messenger of Allah, we have now understood as to how to invoke peace upon you, now please let us know how shall we invoke Allah's blessings upon you? He (S.A.W.) answered. Say these words:

Alla-humma sal-le 'Ala Muham-madim Wa 'ala Aale Muham-madin Kama Sal-laita 'ala Ibrahima In-naka Hamidum Majeed. Alla-humma Barik 'ala Muham-madim Wa 'ala Ale Muham-madin Kama Barak-ta 'ala Aale Ibrahima In-naka Hamiddum Majeed.
O Allah, send thy blessings on Muhammad (S.A.W.) as Thou didst send Thy blessings on the Prophet Ibraham and his children. Thou art indeed pariseworthy, the Glorious. O Allah, bless Muhammad (S.A.W.) and the children of Muhammad (S.A.W.) as Thou didst bless the children of Abraham, for Thou art undoubtedly the Praiseworthy, the Glorious. *(Bukhari and Muslim)*

١٤٠٦ – وعَنْ أبي مَسْعُودٍ البَدْرِيِّ ، رضيَ اللهُ عَنْهُ ، قالَ : أتانا
رَسُولُ اللهِ صَلَّى اللهُ عليهِ وسَلَّم ، ونَحْنُ في مَجْلِسِ سعدِ بنِ عُبَادَةَ
رضيَ اللهُ عنهُ ، فقالَ لهُ بَشِيرُ بْنُ سعدٍ : أَمَرَنا اللهُ أنْ نُصَلِّيَ عَلَيْكَ
يا رسولَ اللهِ ، فكَيْفَ نُصَلِّي عَلَيْكَ ؟ فسَكَتَ رسولُ اللهِ ، صَلَّى اللهُ عليهِ
وسلَّم ، حتى تَمَنَّيْنَا أنَّهُ لمْ يَسْأَلْهُ ، ثمَّ قالَ رسولُ اللهِ ، صلَّى اللهُ عليه
وسلَّم ، «قولُوا : اللَّهُمَّ صَلِّ على مُحَمَّدٍ ، وعلى آلِ مُحَمَّدٍ ، كما صَلَّيْتَ
على إبْراهيمَ ، وبَارِكْ على مُحَمَّدٍ ، وعلى آلِ مُحَمَّدٍ ، كما باركْتَ على
إبراهيمَ ، إنَّكَ حَمِيدٌ مَجِيدٌ ؛ والسلامُ كما قدْ عَلِمتمْ» رواهُ مسلمٌ .

1406. Hazrat Abu Mas'ud Badri (R.A.A.) relates: (Once) we, were sitting with Hazrat Sa'd bin Ubadah when the Holy Prophet (S.A.W.) came to us. Hazrat Bashir ibn Sa'ad (R.A.A.) asked the Holy Prophet (S.A.W.) O Messenger of Allah, 'we have been commanded by Allah to invoke blessings on you by reciting Salat, then how shall we do this? The Holy Prophet (S.A.W.) kept quiet for sometime, so much so that we wished that Bashir bin Sa'ad (R.A.A.) had not asked this question from the Holy Prophet (S.A.W.). After sometime the Holy Prophet (S.A.W.) said: Say these words:

Alla-humma Sal-le 'Ala Muham-madimwa 'ala Aale Muham-madin Kama Sal-laita 'ala Ibrahima Wa barik 'ala Muham-medimwa 'ala Aale Muham-madin Kama barak-ta 'ala Ibrahima, In-naka Hamidum Majeed.

'O Allah, send Thy blessings on Muhammad (S.A.W.) and on the children of Muhammad (S.A:W.) as Thou didst send Thy blessings on Abraham, and bless Muhammad (S.A.W.) and the children of Muhammad (S.A.W.) as Thou didst bless Abraham. Indeed Thou art the praiseworthy, the Glorious'. Continuing the Holy Prophet (S.A.W.) said: and the salutation is already known to you. *(Muslim)*

١٤٠٧ – وَعَنْ أبي حُمَيْدٍ السَّاعِدِيِّ ، رضيَ اللهُ عنهُ ، قالَ : قَالُوا يا رسولَ اللهِ كيْفَ نُصَلِّي عَلَيكَ ؟ قالَ : «قولُوا : اللَّهُمَّ صَلِّ عَلى مُحَمَّدٍ ، وَعَلى أَزْوَاجِهِ وَذُرِّيَّتِهِ ، كما صَلَّيْتَ عَلى إبْرَاهِيمَ ، وَبَارِكْ عَلى مُحَمَّدٍ ، وَعَلى أَزْوَاجِهِ وَذُرِّيَّتِهِ ، كما بَارَكْتَ عَلى إبْرَاهِيمَ ، إنَّكَ حَمِيدٌ مَجِيدٌ» متفقٌ عليهِ .

1407. **Hazrat Abu Humaid As-Sa'di** (R.A.A.) relates. The Holy Prophet (S.A.W.) was asked by the Companions 'How shall we invoke blessings on you? He (S.A.W.) answered: Say these words:

Alla-humma Sal-le 'ala Muham-madim wa 'ala azwaji-hi wa Zur-riyate-hi Kama Sal-laita 'ala Ibrahima Wa barik 'ala Muhammadim wa 'ala azwaji-hi wa zur-riyate-hi Kama barak-ta 'ala Ibrahima innaka hamidum Majeed

O' Allah, send Thy blessings on Muhammad (S.A.W.) and on his wives and on his progeny as Thou didst send down Thy blessings on Abraham and bless Muhammad (S.A.W.) and his wives and his progeny as Thou didst bless Abraham. Indeed Thou art the Praiseworthy, the Glorious. *(Bukhari and Muslim)*

* * * * * * *

BOOK OF REMEMBERING ALLAH

CHAPTER 244

VIRTUES OF GLORIFICATION AND REMEMBRANCE OF ALLAH

قالَ اللهُ تعَالى : (ولَذِكرُ اللهِ أكبَرُ) [العنكبوت : ٤٥] وقالَ تعَالى: (فاذكرُوني أذكرْكُمْ) [البقرة : ١٥٢] وقالَ تعَالى : (واذكرْ ربَّكَ في نفسِكَ تضرُّعاً وخيفةً ودُونَ الجهرِ مِنَ القولِ بالغُدُوِّ والآصالِ، ولا تكُنْ مِنَ الغافلِينَ) [الأعراف : ٢٠٥] وقالَ تعَالى : (واذكُروا اللهَ كثيراً لعَلَّكم تُفلِحونَ) [الجمعة : ١٠] وقالَ تعَالى : إنَّ المُسْلِمِينَ والمُسْلِمَاتِ إلى قوله تعالى : والذّاكِرِينَ اللهَ كثيراً والذّاكِراتِ أعدَّ اللهُ لَهُمْ مَغفِرَةً وأجراً عظيماً [الأحزاب : ٣٥] . وقالَ تعَالى : يا أيُّها الّذينَ آمَنُوا اذكُرُوا اللهَ ذِكراً كثيراً ، وسَبِّحُوهُ بُكرةً وأصِيلاً [الأحزاب:٤١-٤٢]

Allah, the Exalted has said:

315. But verily rememberance of Allah is more important. (29 : 45)

316. Therefore remember Me, I will remember you. (2 : 152)

317. And do thou ('O' Muhammad) remember thy Lord within thyself humbly and with awe, below thy breath, at morn and evening. And be thou not of the neglectful. (7 ; 205)

318. And remember Allah much, that ye may be successful. (62 . 10)

319. Lo! men who surrender unto Allah, and women who surrender, and men who believe and women who believe, and men who obey and women who obey, and men who speak the truth and women who speak the truth, and men who persevere (in righteousness) and women who persevere and men who are humble and women who are humble, and men who give alms and women who give alms, and men who fast and women who fast, and men who guard their modesty and women who guard (their modesty), and men who remember Allah much and women who remember—Allah hath prepared for them forgiveness and vast reward. (33 : 35)

320. O ye who believe ! Remember Allah with much remembrance, and glorify Him early and late. (33 : 41—42)

١٤٠٨ – وعَنْ أبي هُرَيْرَةَ ، رضيَ اللهُ عَنْهُ قالَ : قالَ رَسُولُ اللهِ ، صَلّى اللهُ عَلَيْهِ وَسَلَّمَ : « كَلِمَتَانِ خَفِيفَتَانِ عَلى اللِّسانِ . ثَقِيلَتَانِ في المِيزَانِ . حَبِيبَتَانِ إلى الرَّحْمَنِ : سُبْحَانَ اللهِ وَبِحَمْدِهِ : سُبْحَانَ اللهِ العَظِيمِ » متفقٌ عليه .

1408. Hazrat Abu Hurairah (R.A.A.) relates that the Holy Prophet (S.A.W.) said: There are two phrases which are easy and light to say but are heavy and precious in the balance (to weigh the deeds) and are very much liked by Rahman (Most Merciful). These phrases are .

Subha-nal-lahi wa-bi ham-dihi, Subha-nal-lahil 'Azeem.

Glorified be Allah and His is the Praise; Glorified be Allah, the Most Exalted.
(Bukhari and Muslim)

١٤٠٩ وعنهُ رضيَ اللهُ عَنْهُ قال : قالَ رَسُولُ اللهِ صَلّى اللهُ عَلَيْهِ وَسَلَّمَ : لأنْ أقُولَ : سُبْحَانَ اللهِ ، وَالحَمْدُ للهِ ، وَلا إلهَ إلاّ اللهُ ، وَاللهُ أكْبَرُ ، أحَبُّ إليَّ مِمَّا طَلَعَتْ عليهِ الشَّمْسُ » رواه مسلم

1409. Hazrat Abu Hurairah (R.A.A.) reports that the Holy Prophet (S.A.W.) said: For me to recite :

Subha-nal-lah, wal-hamdo-lil-lah wa la-ilaha illal-laho wal-laho Akbar.

Glory be to Allah, and to Allah belongs all Praise and there is no god save Allah, and Allah is the Greatest
is dearer to me than all the things on which the sun rises. *(Muslim)*

١٤١٠ – وعنهُ أنَّ رَسُولَ اللهِ صَلّى اللهُ عَلَيْهِ وسَلَّمَ قالَ : « مَنْ قالَ لاإلهَ إلاّ اللهُ وَحْدَهُ لاشَريكَ لَهُ : لَهُ المُلْكُ ، وَلَهُ الحَمْدُ . وَهُوَ عَلَى كُلِّ شَيْءٍ قَدِيرٌ . في يَوْمٍ مِائَةَ مَرَّةٍ كانَتْ لَهُ عَدْلَ عَشْرِ رِقَابٍ وَكُتِبَتْ لَهُ مِائَةُ حَسَنَةٍ . وَمُحِيَتْ عنهُ مِائَةُ سَيِّئَةٍ ، وَكانت له حِرْزاً مِنَ الشَّيْطَانِ يَوْمَهُ ذَلِكَ حَتّى يُمْسِيَ . وَلَمْ يَأْتِ أحَدٌ بِأفْضَلَ مِمَّا جاءَ بِهِ إلاّ رَجُلٌ عَمِلَ

أكثرَ منه » وقال : « من قالَ سُبْحَانَ اللهِ وبِحَمْدِهِ : في يَوْمٍ مِائَةَ مَرَّةٍ ، حُطَّتْ خَطَايَاهُ . وإنْ كَانَتْ مثلَ زَبَدِ البَحْرِ » متفقٌ عليهِ .

1410. Hazrat Abu Hurairah (R.A.A.) reports that the Holy Prophet (S.A.W.) said: A person who recites:

La Illaha illal-laho wah-dahu la Sha-rika lahu, Lahul-mul-ko wa lahul hamdu wa huwa 'ala Kul-li shai-in Qadeer

There is no God save Allah the One, who has no associate, His is the Kingdom and His is the Praise and He has Power over all things,

a hundred times daily will have recompense equal to that of freeing ten slaves, and one hundred virtuous deeds will be credited to his account, and one hundred of his sins (shortcomings) will be remitted, and on that day he will remain immune from the Satan till the evening; and on the Day of Judgement no one will exceed him in merit except one who has done more virtues (or recites these phrases more often than him).

He also said: All the sins of a person, even if they be like the foam of the sea, will be wiped out if he recites in the day a hundred times the following phrase.

'Subhan Allahe wa Behamdehi'

'Holy is Allah and to Him belongs all praise'. *(Bukhari and Muslim)*

١٤١١ ـ وعَنْ أبي أيوبَ الأنصَارِيِّ رَضِيَ اللهُ عَنْهُ عَنْ النبيِّ صَلَّى اللهُ عَلَيْهِ وسَلَّمَ قال : « مَنْ قالَ لا إلهَ إلاَّ اللهُ وَحْدَهُ لاشَريكَ لَهُ . لَهُ المُلْكُ . ولَهُ الحَمْدُ . وَهُوَ عَلى كُلِّ شيءٍ قَديرٌ . عَشْرَ مرَّاتٍ : كانَ كَمَنْ أعْتَقَ أرْبَعَةَ أنفسٍ مِنَ وَلَدِ إسْمَاعِيلَ » متفقٌ عليهِ .

1411. Hazrat Abu Ayub Ansari (R.A.A.) relates that the Holy Prophet (S.A.W.) said: A person who recites:

La ilaha il-lal-laho wah-dahu La Sha-rika lahu, La-hul Mul-ko wa la-hul hamdo wa hu-wa 'ala kul-li shai-in Qadeer.

There is no god save Allah, the One, Who has no associate, His is the Kingdom and His is the Praise, and He has Power over all things,' ten times,

Then it is like one who sets free four persons from among the descendants of Prophet Ismael. *(Bukhari and Muslim)*

١٤١٢ – وعنْ أبي ذرٍّ رَضيَ اللهُ عنْهُ قالَ : قالَ لي رَسُولُ اللهِ صلّى اللهُ علَيْهِ وَسلَّمَ : « ألا أخبِرُكَ بِأحَبِّ الكَلامِ إلى اللهِ ؟ إنَّ أحَبَّ الكَلامِ إلى اللهِ : سُبْحَانَ اللهِ وَبِحَمْدِهِ » رواه مسلم .

1412. Hazrat Abu Zarr (R.A.A.) relates that once the Holy Prophet (S.A.W.) said to him: May I tell you as to which phrase is most liked by Allah? This phrase is:

Sub-ha-nal-lahi Wa bi Hamde-hi.

'Holy is Allah and worthy of all praise.' *(Muslim)*

١٤١٣ – وعَنْ أبي مالكٍ الأشْعَرِيِّ رَضيَ اللهُ عنْهُ قالَ : قالَ رَسُولُ اللهِ صَلّى اللهُ عَلَيْهِ وَسلَّم : « الطُّهُورُ شَطْرُ الإيمانِ . وَالحمدُ للهِ تَمْلأُ المِيزَانَ . وَسُبْحَانَ اللهِ . وَالحَمْدُ للهِ تَمْلآنِ – أوْ تَمْلأُ – مابَيْنَ السَّمَوات وَالأرْضِ » رواهُ مسلم .

1413. Hazrat Abu Malik Al-Ash'ari (R.A.A.) relates that the Holy Prophet (S.A.W.) said: Cleanliness is half the faith, and the phrase:

Wal-hamdo lil-lah

'All praise belongs to Allah'

fills the balance, and the phrase .

Sub-ha-nal-lahi wal ham-do lil-lah.

Holy is Allah, all praise belongs to Allah,
Both or each of them, fills the space (with recompense) between the heavens and the earth. *(Muslim)*

١٤١٤ – وعنْ سعْدِ بنِ أبي وَقّاصٍ رَضِيَ اللهُ عنْهُ قال : جاءَ أعْرَابيٌّ إلى رَسُولِ اللهِ صَلّى اللهُ عَلَيْهِ وسَلَّم فقالَ : علِّمْني كَلاماً أقولُهُ . قالَ : « قُلْ لاإلهَ إلاَّ اللهُ وَحْدَهُ لاشَرِيكَ لهُ . اللهُ أكْبَرُ كَبيراً . وَالحَمْدُ للهِ كَثيراً . وسُبْحَانَ اللهِ ربِّ العَالَمِينَ . وَلا حَوْلَ وَلا قُوَّةَ إلاَّ باللهِ العَزيزِ الحَكِيمِ » قال : فَهؤُلاءِ لِرَبِّي ، فَمَا لي ؟ قال : « قُلْ : اللّهُمَّ اغْفِرْ لي . وَارْحَمْني . وَاهْدِني ، وَارْزُقْني » رواهُ مسلم .

1414. Hazrat Sa'd bin Abi Waqqas (R.A.A.) relates that a bedouin Arab came to the Holy Prophet (S.A.W.) and requested him to teach him some supplications that he may recite. The Holy Prophet (S.A.W.) told him: Recite:

La ila-ha il-lal-laho wah-da-hu La sha-rika lah. Allah-o Ak-bar Kabira, wal ham-do lil-la-hi Ka-see-ra, wa sub-hanal-la-hi rab-bil 'alamin Wa la hau-la wa la quw-wata il-la bil-lahil-azi-zil Hakeem.

'There is no god save Allah the One, Who has no associate . Allah is the greatest and much praise is due to him. Holy is Allah, the Lord of the worlds, and there is no power to resist the evil, nor power to do good except through Allah, the Mighty, the Wise.'

The man said: All this is for my Lord--Sustainer, what is for me? The Holy Prophet (S.A.W.) said: Recite:

Al-la-hum-magh-fir-li war ham-ni wah-di-ni war-zuq-ni.

'O Allah forgive me and have mercy on me, guide me and provide for me.'

(Muslim)

١٤١٥ – وعَنْ ثوبَانَ رضِيَ اللهُ عَنْهُ قالَ : كانَ رَسُول اللهِ صَلّى اللهُ عَلَيْهِ وسَلّمَ : إذا انْصرَفَ مِنْ صَلاتِهِ اسْتَغْفَرَ ثَلاثاً ، وقالَ : « اللّهُمَّ أنْتَ السّلام ، ومِنْكَ السّلامُ ، تَبارَكْتَ يَاذا الجَلالِ وَالإكْرَامِ » قِيلَ لِلأوْزاعِيّ ، وَهُوَ أحَدُ رُواة الحديث : كَيْفَ الاسْتِغْفَارُ ؟ قال : تقول : أسْتَغْفِرُ الله ، أسْتَغْفِرُ الله . رواهُ مسلمٌ .

1415. Hazrat Sauban (R.A.A.) relates that when the Holy Prophet (S.A.W.) finished his Salat (prayer) he asked forgiveness, three times Istaghfara and recited.

Al-la-hum-maAn-tas Salam wa min-kas ṣalamo taba-rak-ta ya zal- jalale wal ik-ram.

'Allah, Thou art the Peace and from Thee is peace, Blessed art Thou, O Lord of Glory and Honour.'

Imam Auza'ee, one of the narrators of this hadis was asked. what was the form of forgiveness that was recited by the Holy Prophet (S.A.W.). He answered: The Holy Prophet (S.A.W.) used to say:

Astaghfirullaha, astaghfirullaha

'I beseech Allah for forgiveness, I beseech Allah for forgiveness.'

(Muslim)

١٤١٦ – وعَنِ المُغيرَةِ بنِ شُعْبَةَ رضِيَ اللهُ عَنْهُ أنَّ رَسُولَ اللهِ ، صَلّى اللهُ عليْهِ وسَلّمَ ، كَانَ إذا فَرَغَ مِنَ الصَّلاةِ وَسَلّمَ قالَ : « لا إلهَ إلاّ

اللهُ وَحْدَهُ لاشَرِيكَ لَهُ ، لَهُ المُلْكُ وَلَهُ الحَمْدُ ، وَهُوَ عَلى كُلِّ شَيْءٍ
قَديرٌ . اللَّهُمَّ لا مانِعَ لما أعْطَيْتَ ، وَلا مُعْطِيَ لما مَنَعْتَ ، وَلاينْفَعُ ذَا
الجَدِّ مِنْكَ الجَدُّ » متفقٌ عليه .

1416. Hazrat Mughirah bin Shu'bah (R.A.A.) says that when the Holy Prophet (S.A.W.) finished his prayer and had saluted on both sides, he would recite:

la ilaha illal-laho wah-dahu la shari-ka lah, lahul-mul-ko wa la-hul ham-do wa huwa 'ala kul-li shai-in-Qadeer. Al-la-hum-ma la mane 'a lima a-'tai-ta wa la mo'tia li-ma-ma-na'-ta wa la yan-fa o' zal-ja-dde min-kal jadd

'There is no god save Allah, the One, Who has no associate, His is the Sovereignty and His is the Praise and He has power over all things. Allah, none may obstruct what Thou dost bestow and none may bestow what Thou dost hold back and to a man of means his means will avail nothing against Thee.' *(Bukhari and Muslim)*

١٤١٧ — وعَنْ عبدِ اللهِ بنِ الزُّبَيْرِ رَضِيَ اللهُ تَعَالى عَنْهُما أنَّهُ كانَ
يقُولُ دُبُرَ كُلِّ صَلاة . حينَ يُسَلِّمُ : لا إلهَ إلاَّ اللهُ وَحْدَهُ لا شَرِيكَ لَهُ ،
لهُ المُلْكُ ولهُ الحَمْدُ . وَهُوَ عَلى كُلِّ شَيْءٍ قَديرٌ . لاحَوْلَ وَلا قُوَّةَ إلَّا
بِاللهِ . لا إلهَ إلَّا اللهُ . وَلا نَعْبُدُ إلَّا إيَّاهُ . لهُ النِّعْمَةُ ، ولَهُ الفَضْلُ
وَلَهُ الثَّنَاءُ الحَسَنُ . لا إلهَ إلاَّ اللهُ مُخْلِصِينَ لَهُ الدِّينَ وَلَوْ كَرِهَ الكَافِرُونَ .
قالَ ابْنُ الزُّبَيْرِ : وَكَانَ رَسولُ اللهِ . صلَّى اللهُ عليهِ وسلَّم ، يُهَلِّلُ بِهِنَّ
دُبُرَ كُلِّ صَلاةٍ مَكتوبة . رواه مسلم .

1417. Hazrat Abdullah bin Zubair (R.A.A.) used to recite after pronouncing salam at the end of each salat (prayer):

La ila-ha il-lal-laho wah-da-hu La Shari-ka lah, la-hul mul-ko Wa la-hul ham-do wa hu-wa 'ala kul-li Shain'in qadeer. La hau-la wa la quw-wata il--la bil-lah, la ila-ha il-lal lah, wa la na'budu il-la iy-ya-ho la-hun na'ma-to wa la-hul faz-lo wa la-hus sa-naa-ul ha-sa-n La ila-ha il-lal-laho mukh-li-sena la-hud-dina wa lau ka-re-hal ka-fi-roon.

'There is no god save Allah, the One Who has no associate: His is the Kingdom and His is the Praise and He has power over all things. There is no strength (to resist evil) nor power (to do good) except through Allah. There is no god save Allah. We worship none save Him; His is the bounty and the grace and for

Him is all excellent praise; there is no god save Allah. We keep His Deen (religion) exclusively pure for Him though the disbelievers may be displeased.

Ibn Zubáir said the Holy Prophet (S.A.W.) used to call Allah in these words after every prayer. *(Muslim)*

١٤١٨ — وعَنْ أبي هُرَيْرَةَ رضيَ اللهُ عَنْهُ أنَّ فُقَرَاءَ المُهَاجِرِينَ أتَوْا رَسُولَ اللهِ صَلَّى اللهُ عَلَيْهِ وَسَلَّمَ فقالُوا : ذَهَبَ أَهْلُ الدُّثُورِ بِالدَّرَجَاتِ العُلَى ، وَالنَّعِيمِ المُقِيمِ : يُصَلُّونَ كَمَا نُصَلِّي ، وَيَصُومُونَ كَمَا نَصُومُ ، وَلَهُمْ فَضْلٌ مِنْ أَمْوَالٍ : يَحُجُّونَ ، وَيَعْتَمِرُونَ ، وَيُجَاهِدُونَ ، وَيَتَصَدَّقُونَ . فقالَ : « ألا أُعَلِّمُكُمْ شَيْئاً تُدْرِكُونَ بِهِ مَنْ سَبَقَكُمْ ، وَتَسْبِقُونَ بِهِ مَنْ بَعْدَكُمْ ، وَلا يَكُونُ أَحَدٌ أَفْضَلَ مِنْكُمْ إلاَّ مَنْ صَنَعَ مِثْلَ مَا صَنَعْتُمْ ؟ » قالوا : بَلَى يا رسولَ اللهِ ، قالَ : « تُسَبِّحُونَ ، وَتَحْمَدُونَ ، وَتُكَبِّرُونَ ، خَلْفَ كُلِّ صَلاةٍ ثَلاثاً وَثَلاثِينَ » قالَ أبُو صالِحٍ الرَّاوي عَنْ أبي هُرَيْرَةَ ، لَمَّا سُئِلَ عَنْ كَيْفِيَّةِ ذِكْرِهِنَّ ، قال : يقولُ : سُبْحَانَ اللهِ ، وَالحَمْدُ للهِ ، واللهُ أَكْبَرُ ، حَتَّى يَكُونَ مِنْهُنَّ كُلِّهِنَّ ثَلاثاً وَثَلاثِينَ . متفقٌ عليه

وزادَ مُسْلِمٌ في رِوايَتِهِ : فَرَجَعَ فُقَرَاءُ المُهَاجِرِينَ إلى رَسُولِ اللهِ صَلَّى اللهُ عَلَيْهِ وسَلَّمَ ، فقالوا : سَمِعَ إخْوَانُنا أَهْلُ الأَمْوالِ بِمَا فَعَلْنا ، فَفَعَلُوا مِثْلَهُ ؟ فقالَ رَسُولُ اللهِ صلَّى اللهُ عَلَيْه وسَلَّمَ : « ذلكَ فَضْلُ اللهِ يُؤْتِيهِ مَنْ يَشَاءُ » .

1418. This hadis has already been covered in S. No. 573 of Chapter 64.

١٤١٩ — وَعَنْهُ عَنْ رسُولِ اللهِ صَلَّى اللهُ عليهِ وسَلَّمَ قالَ : « مَنْ سَبَّحَ اللهَ في دُبُرِ كُلِّ صَلاةٍ ثَلاثاً وَثَلاثِينَ ، وَحَمِدَ اللهَ ثَلاثاً وثَلاثِينَ ، وكَبَّرَ اللهَ ثَلاثاً وثَلاثِينَ ، وقالَ تَمَامَ المِائَةِ : لاإلهَ إلَّا اللهُ وَحْدَهُ لاشَرِيكَ لَهُ ، لَهُ المُلْكُ وَلَهُ الحَمْدُ ، وَهُوَ عَلى كُلِّ شَيْءٍ قَديرٌ ، غُفِرتَ خَطَايَاهُ

وَإِن كَانَتْ مِثْلَ زَبَدِ الْبَحْرِ » رواه مسلم .

1419. Hazrat Abu Hurairah (R.A.A.) relates that the Holy Prophet (S.A.W.) said: A person who recites after every Salat (prayer): *Sub-han Al-lah* (Holy is Allah) thirty-three times, *Al-ham-do Lil-lah* (All praise belongs to Allah) thirty three times, and *Al-la-ho Akbar* (Allah is Great) thirty three times, and completes the figure of hundred with the recitation of

'La ila-ha il-lal-la-ho wah-da-hu La Sha-ri-ka lahu la-hul mul-ko wa la-hul ham-do wa hu-wa 'ala kul-li Shai'in qadeer.
There is no god save Allah, the One, Who has no associates; His is the sovereignty and His is the praise, and He has power over all things; will have his (minor) sins forgiven, although they may be as much as the foam of the ocean. *(Muslim)*

١٤٢٠ – وعَنْ كَعْبِ بْنِ عُجْرَةَ رَضِيَ اللهُ عَنْهُ عَنْ رسولِ اللهِ صَلَّى اللهُ عَلَيْهِ وسَلَّمَ قالَ : « مُعَقِّبَاتٌ لاَيَخِيبُ قَائِلُهُنَّ – أوْ فَاعِلُهُنَّ – دُبُرَ كُلِّ صَلاةٍ مَكْتُوبَةٍ : ثَلاثاً وَثَلاثِينَ تَسْبِيحَةً ، وَثَلاثاً وَثَلاثِينَ تَحْمِيدَةً ، وَأَرْبَعاً وَثَلاثِينَ تَكْبِيرَةً » رواه مسلم

1420. Hazrat Ka'b bin ' Ujrah (R.A.A.) relates that the Holy Prophet (S.A.W.) said: There are phrases and a person who recites them after every prescribed Salat (prayer) will never be disappointed, that is to say, recitation of Allah's Holiness *(Subhan Al-lah)* thirty three times, His praise *(Al-hamd-o Lil lah)* thirty three times and His Greatness *(Alla-ho Akbar)* Allah is the greatest thirty four times. *(Muslim)*

١٤٢١ – وعَنْ سعدِ بنِ أبي وقاصٍ رضيَ اللهُ عَنْهُ أنَّ رَسُولَ اللهِ صَلَّى اللهُ عَلَيْهِ وسَلَّمَ كانَ يَتَعَوَّذُ دُبُرَ الصَّلَوَاتِ بِهَؤُلاءِ الكَلِمَاتِ : « اللَّهُمَّ إنِّي أعُوذُ بِكَ مِنَ الجُبْنِ وَالبُخلِ ، وَأعُوذُ بِكَ مِنْ أنْ أرَدَّ إلى أرْذَلِ العُمُرِ وَأعُوذُ بِكَ مِنْ فِتْنَةِ الدُّنْيَا ، وَأعُوذُ بِكَ مِنْ فِتْنَةِ القَبرِ » رواه البخاري .

1421. Hazrat Sa'd ibn Abi Waqqas (R.A.A.) says that the Holy Prophet (S.A.W.) used to seek protection of Allah, after his prayers through these phrases :

All-hum-ma in-ni a'oozo-bika minal jub-ne wal bukh-le, wa a'oozo-bika min an arad-da ila arza-lil umo-re wa a'oozo-bika min fitna-ted-dunya wa a'oozo-bika min fitna-til-qabr.

'Allah? I seek Thy protection from cowardice and miserliness and from being rued to worst age (being brought to a state of weakness and helplessness in old age) and seek Thy protection from the trials of this life (sufferings of the present world) and from the trials of the grave. *(Bukhari)*

١٤٢٢– وعن معاذ رضي الله عنه أن رسول الله صلى الله عليه وسلم أخذ بيده وقال: «يامعاذ. والله إني لأحبك» فقال: «أوصيك يامعاذ لاتدعن في دبر كل صلاة تقول: اللهم أعني على ذكرك. وشكرك، وحسن عبادتك» رواه أبو داود بإسناد صحيح

1422. **Hazrat Mu'az** (R.A.A.) relates that one day the Holy Prophet (S.A.W.) caught hold of his hand and said. Mu'az, by Allah I love you, and emphatically advise you, Mu'az, that you should never forget to recite after every salat (prayer):

Alla-hum-ma a'inni 'ala zik-rika wa shuk-rika wa hus-ne 'iba-datika

O Allah, assist me in remembering Thee and being grateful to Thee and performing Thy worship in an excellent manner.'
(*Abu Daud* cited this with good chains)

١٤٢٣– عن أبي هريرة رضي الله عنه أن رسول الله صلى الله عليه سلم قال: «إذا تشهد أحدكم فليستعذ بالله من أربع، يقول: اللهم إني أعوذ بك من عذاب جهنم. ومن عذاب القبر. ومن فتنة المحيا والممات، ومن شر فتنة المسيح الدجال» رواه مسلم

1423. **Hazrat Abu Hurairah** (R.A.A.) relates that the Holy Prophet (S.A.W.) said: When you have recited tashahud (after invoking blessing in the final sitting position), you should seek the protection of Allah from four (evil situations), saying:

Alla-hum-ma in-ni a'oozu 'bika min 'aza-be Jahan-nam wa min 'aza -bil Qab-ri wa min fitna-til-Mah-ya wal ma-mate wa min. Shar-re fitna-til masih-hid-daj-jal.

'O Allah, I seek Thy protection from the torment of Hell, from the torment of the grave, from the trials of life and death, and from the mischief and trials of Masihid-Dajjal (the Anti Christ). *(Muslim)*

١٤٢٤– وعن علي رضي الله عنه قال: كان رسول الله صلى الله عليه وسلم إذا قام إلى الصلاة يكون من آخر ما يقول بين التشهد

وَالتَّسْلِيمِ : « اللَّهُمَّ اغفِرْ لِي مَاقَدَّمتُ وَمَا أَخَّرْتُ . وَمَا أَسْرَرْتُ وَمَا أَعْلَنْتُ ، وما أَسْرَفْتُ . وما أَنتَ أَعْلَمُ بِهِ مِنِّي . أَنْتَ الْمُقَدِّمُ ، وَأَنْتَ الْمُؤَخِّرُ . لاإلهَ إِلاَّ أَنْتَ » رواهُ مسلم

1424. Hazrat Ali (R.A.A.) says that the Holy Prophet (S.A.W.) when praying would supplicate at the end between the recitation of Tashahhud and salutation thus:

Alla-hum-magh-firli ma qad-dam-to wa ma akh-khar-to wa ma as-rar-to wa ma a'lan-to wa ma asraf-to wa ma anta a'lamo bihi min-ni antal mu-qad-damo wa antal mu-akh-kharo La ila-ha illa Anta.

Allah forgive me sins which I have committed in the past and which I have committed thereafter, and which I have committed secretly and which I have committed openly; and that in which I have committed excess, and those of my sins which Thou knowest more than I. Thou first of all and last of all. There is no god save Thee. *(Muslim)*

١٤٢٥ – وعنْ عائشةَ رضيَ اللهُ عَنْهَا قَالَتْ : كانَ النَّبيُّ صَلَّى اللهُ عَلَيْهِ وسَلَّمَ يُكثِرُ أَنْ يقولَ فِي رُكُوعِهِ وَسُجُودِهِ : سُبْحَانَكَ اللَّهُمَّ رَبَّنَا وَبِحَمْدِكَ . اللَّهُمَّ اغْفِرْ لِي » متفقٌ عليه

1425. Haarat Ayesha (R.A.A.) says that the Holy Prophet (S.A.W.) in his bowing *(Ruku)* and prostration *(Sajda)* repeatedly recited

Subha-nak - Alla-hum-ma Rab-bana wa bi-himdi-ka, Alla-hum-magh-firli.

Holy art Thou, O Allah our Sustainer, and Thine is the praise. O Allah Forgive me. *(Bukhari and Muslim)*

١٤٢٦ – وعَنْها أَنَّ رَسُولَ اللهِ صَلَّى اللهُ عَلَيْهِ وسَلَّم كانَ يَقُولُ فِي رُكوعِهِ وَسجودِهِ : « سُبُّوحٌ قُدُّوسٌ رَبُّ الملائكة وَالرُّوحِ » رواه مسلم

1426. Hazrat Ayesha (R.A.A.) says that the Holy Prophet (S.A.W.) recited in his bowings *(Ruku)* and prostrations *(Sajda)* (In optional prayers):

Sub-bu-hun Qud-du-sun, Rab-bul Malai-kate war rooh.

Glorified, The Noblest— free from all defects, Sustainer, (Lord) of the angels and of the spirit ***(Muslim)***

١٤٢٧ـ وعَنِ ابنِ عبّاسٍ رضيَ اللهُ عنهما أنَّ رسولَ اللهِ صلّى اللهُ عليهِ وسلّمَ قالَ : « فأمّا الرّكوعُ فعظِّموا فيهِ الرّبَّ ، وأمّا السُّجودُ فاجتهدوا في الدُّعاءِ ، فقمِنٌ أنْ يُستجابَ لكُم » رواه مسلم

1427. Hazrat Ibn Abbas (R.A.A.) reports that the Holy Prophet (S.A.W.) said: 'While in bowing (Ruku) in Salat exalt thy (Lord) ie say *Subhana Rab-bi-Al-Azeem*. and in prostration exert yourself in supplication (seeking from Allah the Most High what you want). In this way you will ensure the acceptance of your supplications. *(Muslim)*

١٤٢٨ـ وعن أبي هريرةَ رضيَ اللهُ عنهُ أنَّ رسولَ اللهِ صلّى اللهُ عليهِ وسلّمَ قالَ : « أقربُ ما يكونُ العبدُ مِن ربِّه وهوَ ساجدٌ ، فأكثِروا الدُّعاءَ » رواهُ مسلم

1428. Hazrat Abu Hurairah (R.A.A.) relates that the Holy Prophet (S.A.W.) said: A servant is closest to his Sustainer (Lord) when he is in prostration, (while praying) so supplicate profusely while you are in this position. *(Muslim)*

١٤٢٩ـ وعنهُ أنَّ رسولَ اللهِ صلّى اللهُ عليهِ وسلّمَ كانَ يقولُ في سُجودِهِ : اللّهُمَّ اغفرْ لي ذَنبي كُلَّهُ : دِقَّهُ وجِلَّهُ ، وأوّلَه وآخِرَهُ ، وعلانيتَه وسِرَّهُ » رواهُ مسلم .

1429. Hazrat Abu Hurairah (R.A.A.) says that the Holy Prophet (S.A.W.) used to supplicate in his Sajda (Prostration)

Alla-hum-maghi-firli Zambi kul-lahu diq-qahu wa jil-lahu wa aw-wa la-hu wa akhi-rahu wa 'alani-yata wa ser-ra-hu.

'O' Allah, forgive all of my sins, small or big, the first and the last, overt and covert. *(Muslim)*

١٤٣٠ـ وعَنْ عائشةَ رضيَ اللهُ عنها قالَتْ : افتقدْتُ النّبيَّ صلّى اللهُ عليهِ وسلّمَ ذاتَ ليلةٍ ، فتحسَّسْتُ ، فإذا هوَ راكِعٌ ـ أوْ ساجدٌ ـ يقولُ : « سبحانَك وبحمدِكَ ، لاإلهَ إلاّ أنتَ » وفي روايةٍ : فوقعَت يدي على بطنِ قدمَيه ، وهوَ في المسجدِ ، وهما منصوبتانِ ، وهوَ يقولُ : « اللّهُمَّ إنّي أعوذُ برِضاكَ مِنْ سخَطِكَ ، وبمُعافاتِكَ مِنْ عقوبتِكَ ، وأعوذُ بكَ منكَ ، لا أُحصي ثناءً عليكَ أنتَ كما أثنيتَ على نفسِكَ » رواهُ مسلم

1430. Hazrat Ayesha (R.A.A.) ssys: One night I did not find the Holy Prophet (S.A.W.) in his bed, and therefore, I looked around and found that he was either bowing or prostrating and reciting:

Sub-hanaka wa bi-hamdi-ka la ila-ha il-la anta.

Holy art Thou and Thine is the praise and there is no god save Thee. *(Muslim)*

Another version says: 'When I searched forhim(S.A.W.) my hand touched his (S.A.W.) sole of the feet, while he was in prostration and his feet were erect and while in this position he was supplicating:

Al-la-humma in-ni a'oozo bi-raza-ka min Sakha-tika wa bi-mu'afa-tika min'uqoo-bati-ka wa a'oozo bika minka la uh'si sana-an 'alai-ka anta kama as-nai-ta 'ala naf-sika.

O Allah, I seek the protection of Thy pleasure against Thy wrath, and the protection of Thy forgiveness against Thy chastisement and Thy protection with thee. I have not the capacity to enumerate Thy praise. (Indeed) Thou art as Thou hast praised Thyself. *(Mulim)*

١٤٣١- وعَنْ سعدِ بنِ أبي وقاصٍ رَضِيَ اللهُ عَنْهُ قالَ: كُنَّا عِنْدَ رَسُولِ اللهِ صَلَّى اللهُ عليهِ وسَلَّمَ فقال: «أيعجزُ أحَدُكم أنْ يَكْسِبَ في كلِّ يَوْمٍ ألفَ حَسَنَةٍ!» فسَألَهُ سَائِلٌ مِنْ جُلَسَائِهِ: كَيفَ يَكسِبُ ألفَ حَسَنَةٍ؟ قالَ: «يُسَبِّحُ مِائَةَ تَسْبِيحَةٍ، فيُكْتَبُ له ألفُ حَسَنَةٍ، أوْ يُحَطُّ عَنْهُ ألفُ خَطِيئَةٍ» رواه مسلم

قالَ الحُمَيدِيُّ: كذا هوَ في كِتَابِ مسلِمٍ: «أوْ يُحَطُّ» قالَ البَرْقَانِيُّ: ورواهُ شُعْبَةُ، وأبو عَوَانَة، ويَحيَى القَطَّانُ، عَنْ مُوسَى الذي رواه مسلم مِن جِهَتِهِ فقالُوا: «ويُحطُّ» بِغَيْرِ ألِفٍ.

1431. Hazrat Sa'd bin Abi Waqqas (R.A.A.) relates once we were sitting with the Holy Prophet (S.A.W.) when he said: Could any of you have the strength to earn a thousand virtues in a day? One of the audience asked as to how one thousand good deeds be earned? He (S.A.W.) answered: If one glorifies Allah (i.e. recites Subhan Allah) a hundred times he would be credited with a thousand good deeds or a thousand of his sins would be remitted. *(Muslim)*

١٤٣٢- وعَنْ أبي ذَرٍّ رَضِيَ اللهُ عَنْهُ أنَّ رَسُولَ اللهِ صَلَّى اللهُ عَلَيْهِ وَسَلَّمَ قالَ: «يُصْبِحُ عَلَى كُلِّ سُلامَى[٢٨٦] مِنْ أحَدِكُمْ صَدَقَةٌ: فَكُلُّ تَسْبِيحَةٍ صَدَقَةٌ، وكُلُّ تَحْمِيدَةٍ صَدَقَةٌ. وكُلُّ تَهْلِيلَةٍ صَدَقَةٌ،

وَكُلُّ تَكْبِيرَةٍ صَدَقَةٌ ، وَأَمْرٌ بِالمَعْرُوفِ صَدَقَةٌ . وَنَهْيٌ عَنِ المُنْكَرِ صَدَقَةٌ . وَيُجْزِىءُ مِنْ ذَلِكَ رَكْعَتَانِ يَرْكَعُهُمَا مِنَ الضُّحَى » رواه مسلم

1432. This Hadis has already been covered in 118 of Chapter 13.

١٤٣٣–وَعَنْ أُمِّ المُؤْمِنِينَ جُوَيْرِيَةَ بِنْتِ الحَارِثِ رَضِيَ اللهُ عَنْهَا أَنَّ النَّبِيَّ صَلَّى اللهُ عَلَيْهِ وَسَلَّمَ خَرَجَ مِنْ عِنْدِهَا بُكْرَةً حِينَ صَلَّى الصُّبْحَ وَهِيَ فِي مَسْجِدِهَا ، ثُمَّ رَجَعَ بَعْدَ أَنْ أَضْحَى وَهِيَ جَالِسَةٌ ، فَقَالَ : « مَا زِلْتِ عَلَى الحَالِ الَّتِي فَارَقْتُكِ عَلَيْهَا ؟ » قَالَتْ : نَعَمْ : فَقَالَ النَّبِيُّ صَلَّى اللهُ عَلَيْهِ وَسَلَّمَ : « لَقَدْ قُلْتُ بَعْدَكِ أَرْبَعَ كَلِمَاتٍ ثَلَاثَ مَرَّاتٍ ، لَوْ وُزِنَتْ بِمَا قُلْتِ مُنْذُ الْيَوْمِ لَوَزَنَتْهُنَّ : سُبْحَانَ اللهِ وَبِحَمْدِهِ عَدَدَ خَلْقِهِ ، وَرِضَاءَ نَفْسِهِ ، وَزِنَةَ عَرْشِهِ ، وَمِدَادَ كَلِمَاتِهِ » رواه مسلم

وَفِي رِوَايَةٍ لَهُ : « سُبْحَانَ اللهِ عَدَدَ خَلْقِهِ ، سُبْحَانَ اللهِ رِضَاءَ نَفْسِهِ ، سُبْحَانَ اللهِ زِنَةَ عَرْشِهِ ، سُبْحَانَ اللهِ مِدَادَ كَلِمَاتِهِ » .

وَفِي رِوَايَةِ التِّرمِذِي : « أَلَا أُعَلِّمُكِ كَلِمَاتٍ تَقُولِينَهَا ؟ سُبْحَانَ اللهِ عَدَدَ خَلْقِهِ . سُبْحَانَ اللهِ عَدَدَ خَلْقِهِ ، سُبْحَانَ اللهِ عَدَدَ خَلْقِهِ . سُبْحَانَ اللهِ رِضَى نَفْسِهِ ، سُبْحَانَ اللهِ رِضَى نَفْسِهِ ، سُبْحَانَ اللهِ رِضَى نَفْسِهِ ، سُبْحَانَ اللهِ زِنَةَ عَرْشِهِ ، سُبْحَانَ اللهِ زِنَةَ عَرْشِهِ ، سُبْحَانَ اللهِ زِنَةَ عَرْشِهِ ، سُبْحَانَ اللهِ مِدَادَ كَلِمَاتِهِ ، سُبْحَانَ اللهِ مِدَادَ كَلِمَاتِهِ ، سُبْحَانَ اللهِ مِدَادَ كَلِمَاتِهِ » .

1433. Ummul Momineen Hazrat Juwairiah bin Al-Haris (R.A.A.) relates that once the Holy Prophet (S.A.W.) went out of her chamber at the morning Salat (prayer) time when she was offering prayer and when he (S.A.W.) returned after Chasht Prayer, he (S.A.W.) found her still on her prayer carpet. On this he (S.A.W.) said: Are you continuously sitting in the same position in which I left you? I said: yes. He said: After I left you, I have recited four sentences three times; if they could be measured against that which you have said this morning (i.e. your continuous prayer from morning), they would prove weightier. These sentences are:

Sub-ha-nal-lahi riza'a naf-sihi, Sub-ha-nal-lahi riza'a naf-sihi, Sub-ha-nallahi riza'a naf-sihi,
Sub-ha-nal-lahi zinata 'arshe-hi, Sub-ha-nal-lahi zinata 'arshe-ni, Sub-ha-nal-lahi z inata 'arshe-hi,

Sub-ha-nal-lahi mida-da Kali-ma-tihi, Sub-ha-nal-lahi mida-da Kali-ma-tihi, Sub-ha-nal-lahi mida-da Kali-ma-tihi,

Glorified be Allah, as the number of His creation, three times; Glorified be Allah according to His pleasure, three times;
Glorified be Allah corresponding to the weight of His 'Arsh (His Throne) three times,
Glorified be according to the ink of His words, three times.
Sub-ha-nal-lahi wa bi ham-di-hi ada-da Khal-qihi wa riza'a naf-sihi wa zina-ta 'ar-shi-hi wa mida-da Kale-mate-hi.

Glorified be with His praise, as many times as the number of all His creatures, and according to His pleasure and corresponding to the weight of His 'Arsh (throne) and as much as the ink of His words. *(Muslim)*

Another version says these sentences are: Glorified be Allah (as many times or as much) as the number of His creation, Glorified be according to His pleasure, Glorified be Allah corresponding to the weight of His 'Arsh (Throne), Glorified be according to the ink of His words.

Imam Tirmizi's version says: The Holy Prophet (S.A.W.) said: May I not teach you phrases which you might recite? They are.
Sub-ha-nal-lahi 'ada-da Khal-qe-hi , Sub-ha-nal-lahi 'ada-da Khal-qe-hi, Sub-ha-nal-lahi 'ada-da Khal-qe-hi,

١٤٣٤ — وعَنْ أبي مُوسَى الأشعَرِيِّ ، رَضِيَ اللهُ عنهُ ، عنِ النَّبيِّ : صلَّى اللهُ عليهِ وسلَّم ، قالَ : « مَثَلُ الَّذي يَذكُرُ رَبَّهُ وَالَّذي لايَذكُرُهُ ، مَثَلُ الحَيِّ وَالمَيِّتِ » رواهُ البخاري .

ورواه مسلم فقالَ : « مَثَلُ البَيْتِ الَّذي يُذكَرُ اللهُ فيهِ ، وَالبَيتِ الَّذي لايُذْكَرُ اللهُ فيهِ ، مَثَلُ الحَيِّ وَالمَيِّتِ » .

1434. **Hazrat Abu Musa Ash'ari** (R.A.A.) relates that the Holy Prophet (S.A.W.) said: The case of a person who remembers his Lord, and of one who does not remember Him is like that of the living and the dead. *(Bukhari)*

Imam Muslim's version says: The case of a house in which Allah is remembered, and of one in which Allah is not remembered, is like that of the living and the dead.

١٤٣٥ – وعَنْ أبي هُرَيْرَةَ ، رَضِيَ اللهُ عَنْهُ ، أنَّ رَسُولَ اللهِ ، صَلَّى اللهُ عَلَيْهِ وَسَلَّمَ ، قالَ : « يَقُولُ اللهُ تَعالَى : أنا عِنْدَ ظَنِّ عَبْدِي بِي ، وَأنا مَعَهُ إذا ذَكَرَني ؛ فَإنْ ذَكَرَنِي في نَفْسِهِ ، ذَكَرْتُهُ في نَفْسِي ، وَإنْ ذَكَرَنِي في مَلأٍ ، ذَكَرْتُهُ في مَلأٍ خَيْرٍ مِنْهُمْ » متفقٌ عليه .

1435. Hazrat Abu Hurairah (R.A.A.) reports that the Holy Prophet (S.A.W.) said: Allah, the Exalted said, I am to a servant of Mine according to his imagination. I am with him when he remembers Me; if he remembers Me in his mind, I also remember him in My mind; and if he remembers Me in company, I remember him in a better company. *(Bukhari and Muslim)*

١٤٣٦ – وعَنْهُ قالَ : قالَ رَسُولُ اللهِ . صَلَّى اللهُ عليه وَسَلَّمَ : « سَبَقَ المُفَرِّدُونَ » قالوا : وَمَا المُفَرِّدُونَ يارَسُولَ اللهِ ؟ قالَ : « الذَّاكِرُونَ اللهَ كَثِيراً والذَّاكِرَاتُ » رواه مسلم .

روي : « المُفَرَّدُونَ » بتشديد الراء وتخفيفها . وَالمَشْهُورُ الَّذي قَالَهُ الجمْهُورُ : التَّشْديدُ .

1436. Hazrat Abu Hurairah (R.A.A.) relates that the Holy Prophet (S.A.W.) said: The 'Mufarradun' have taken a lead over the rest. The Companions asked him (S.A.W.): O Messenger of Allah, who are the *Mufarradun?* He, (S.A.W.) answered: The men who remember Allah much and the women who remember Allah much. *(Muslim)*

١٤٣٧ – وعَنْ جابرٍ رَضِيَ اللهُ عَنْهُ قالَ : سَمِعْتُ رَسُولَ اللهِ صَلَّى اللهُ عَلَيْهِ وسَلَّم يقولُ : « أفْضَلُ الذِّكْرِ : لا إلهَ إلاَّ اللهُ »

رواه الترمذي وقالَ : حديثٌ حَسَنٌ .

1437. Hazrat Jabir (R.A.A.) relates that he heard the Holy Prophet (S.A.W.) having said: The best rememberance of Allah is *'La ilaha il-lal-laho' i.e.* There is no god but Allah' *(Tirmizi)*

١٤٣٨ – وعنْ عبدِ اللهِ بنِ بُسْرٍ رضيَ اللهُ عَنْهُ أنَّ رَجُلاً قالَ : يارَسُولَ اللهِ ، إنَّ شَرَائِعَ الإسْلامِ قَدْ كَثُرَتْ عَلَيَّ . فَأخبِرْني بِشَيْءٍ أتَشَبَّثُ بهِ قالَ : «لايَزالُ لِسَانُكَ رَطْباً مِنْ ذِكْرِ اللهِ»

رواه الترمذي وقال : حديثٌ حَسَنٌ .

1438. Hazrat Abdullah bin Busr (R.A.A.) says that a man requested the Holy Prophet (S.A.W.): O Messenger of Allah! the Islamic edicts appear to me a bit too much, so kindly tell me something (lighter and easier) which I should hold fast. He (S.A.W.) answered: Let thy tongue remain wet (busy) constantly with the remembrance of Allah. *(Tirmizi*, and said this is good)

١٤٣٩ – وعَنْ جابِرٍ رضِيَ اللهُ عَنْهُ ، عَنِ النبي صَلّى اللهُ عَلَيهِ وسَلّم قالَ : « مَنْ قالَ : سُبْحَانَ اللهِ وبِحَمدِهِ ، غُرِسَتْ لهُ نَخْلَةٌ في الجَنَّةِ » رواه الترمذي وقالَ : حديثٌ حسنٌ .

1439. Hazrat Jabir (R.A.A.) relates that the Holy Prophet (S.A.W.) said: For a person who says:

Sub-ha-nal-lahi wa bi-hamde-hi.

i.e. Holy is Allah and to Him belongs all praise, a date tree is planted for him in Paradise. *(Tirmizi* and said this is good)

١٤٤٠ – وعن ابنِ مَسْعُودٍ رضِيَ اللهُ عَنْهُ قالَ : قالَ رَسُولُ اللهِ صَلّى اللهُ عَلَيْهِ وَسَلّمَ « لَقِيتُ إبْرَاهِيمَ صَلّى اللهُ عَلَيْهِ وَسَلّمَ لَيْلَةَ أُسْرِيَ بي فقالَ : يا مُحَمّدُ أقرِىءْ أُمّتَكَ مِنّي السّلامَ ، وأخبِرْهُمْ أنّ الجَنّةَ طَيِّبَةُ التُّرْبَةِ ، عَذْبَةُ الماءِ ؛ وأنّها قِيعَانٌ وأنّ غِرَاسَهَا : سُبْحَانَ اللهِ ، والحَمْدُ لِلهِ ، ولا إلهَ إلاّ اللهُ ، واللهُ أكبَرُ » رواه الترمذي وقال : حديثٌ حَسَنٌ :

1440. Hazrat Abdullah bin Mas'ud (R.A.A.) relates that the Holy Prophet (S.A.W.) said: On the night of my Ascension when I met Prophet Abraham (A.S.) he told me: O Muhammad (S.A.W.), please convey my Salam to your people *(Ummah)* and tell them that Paradise is a place of fine soil and sweet water, and a vast and spacious place; and that its blooming plants are: *Sub-han Allah* (Holy is Allah) *Alhmdo Lillah* (And all praise is due to Allah) *La-illaha Illal-laho* (There is no god save Allah) and *Allaho Akbar* (Allah is Great).

(Tirmizi and said this is good)

١٤٤١ – وعنْ أبي الدَّرْدَاءِ ، رضِيَ اللهُ عَنْهُ قالَ : قالَ رَسُولُ اللهِ صَلّى اللهُ عَلَيْهِ وَسَلّم : « ألا أُنَبِّئُكُم بخَيْرِ أعْمَالِكُم ، وأزْكَاهَا عِنْدَ مَلِيكِكُم ، وأرْفَعِها في دَرَجَاتِكم ، وخَيْرٌ لَكُمْ مِنْ إنْفَاقِ الذَّهَبِ والفِضّةِ وَخَيْرٌ لَكُمْ مِنْ أنْ تَلْقَوْا عَدُوّكم ، فتَضرِبُوا أعْناقَهُم ؛ ويَضرِبوا

أعناقكم ؟ » قالوا : بلى ، قال : « ذكر الله تعالى »

رواه الترمذي : قال الحاكم أبو عبد الله : إسناده صحيح .

1441. Hazrat Abu Darda (R.A.A.) relates that the Holy Prophet (S.A.W.) said. 'May I not tell you what is the best of your deeds, which is the purest in the estimation of your King, the deeds which are the highest and noblest among your deeds, and are better for you than spending the gold and silver, and are better for you than that you should encounter your enemies and cut off their necks and they be cutting off yours (i.e. you meet them in Jihad). The Companions said: O Messenger of Allah) Do tell us. The Holy Prophet (S.A.W.) said . It is the remembrance of Allah, the Most High. *(Tirmizi)*

Imam Hakim Abu Abdullah said it is sound.

١٤٤٢ — وعن سعد بن أبي وقاص رضي الله عنه أنه دخل مع رسول الله صلّى الله عليه وسلّم على امرأة وبين يديها نوى — أو حصى — تسبح به فقال : « أخبرك بما هو أيسر عليك من هذا — أو أفضل » فقال : « سبحان الله عدد ما خلق في السماء، وسبحان الله عدد ما خلق في الأرض ، وسبحان الله عدد ما بين ذلك ، وسبحان الله عدد ما هو خالق . والله أكبر مثل ذلك ، والحمد لله مثل ذلك ، ولا إله إلا الله مثل ذلك ، ولا حول ولا قوة إلا بالله مثل ذلك » .

رواه الترمذي وقال : حديث حسن .

1442. Hazrat Sa'd bin Abi Waqqas (R.A.A.) relates that he along with the Holy Prophet (S.A.W.) went to a woman who had a heap of date stones or pebbles before her which she used as a rosary to recite the name and glorification of Allah. The Holy Prophet (S.A.W.) told her. May I tell you what is easier or better than this? Recite.

Subhan Al-lahe 'Ada-da Ma Kha-la-qa fis sama'i wa subhan Al-lahi Ada-da ma khala-qa fil arzi, wa subhan-Al-lahi 'Ada-da ma baina Zalika wa subhan-Al-lahi 'Ada-da ma hu-wa khaliqu

(Glorify Allah) the number of those things which He has created in the heaven, and I glorify Allah the number of those things which He has created in the earth and I glorify Allah the number of those things which are between the heaven and the earth, and I glorify Allah the number of those things which He has created and He will create, and then also say.

Wal-laho Akbar (Allah is Great) along with these phrases; Similarly is *Wal Hamdo lil-lahi* (All praise belong to Allah) *Wa La ila-ha il-lal-laho* (There is no god save Allah) and *Wala Haula wala Quw-wata il-la bil-lahi* (There is neither strength nor power except Allah). *(Tirmizi* and said this is good)

١٤٤٣– وعَنْ أبي مُوسى رضيَ اللهُ عَنْهُ قالَ : قالَ لي رَسُولُ اللهِ صَلّى اللهُ عليْهِ وسَلّمَ : « ألا أدُلُّكَ عَلى كَنْزٍ مِنْ كُنُوزِ الجَنَّةِ ؟ » فقلت : بَلى يا رسولَ اللهِ قالَ : « لا حَوْلَ وَلا قُوَّةَ إلاَّ باللهِ » متفقٌ عليه

1443. Hazrat Abu Musa Ash'ari (R.A.A.) relates: The Holy Prophet (S.A.W.) said to me: May I lead you to one of the treasures of Paradise? I said: Of Course, O Messenger of Allah! He (S.A.W.) said: It is:

La Haula wala Quw-wata il-la bil-lah
(there is neither strength nor power except Allah).
(Bukhari and Muslim)

* * * * * * *

CHAPTER 245

ETIQUETTE OF REMEMBERING ALLAH, THE EXALTED WHILE STANDING, SITTING AND LYING DOWN, AND IN A STATE OF POLLUTION, WITHOUT ABLUTION AND DURING THE PERIOD OF MONTHLY COURSE, EXCEPT THE QURAN WHICH IS NOT PERMITTED TO BE READ BY A WOMAN IN MENSES OR MAN IN A STATE OF POLLUTION

قالَ اللهُ تَعَالى : إنَّ في خَلْقِ السَّموَاتِ وَالأرْضِ ، وَاخْتِلافِ اللَّيْلِ وَالنَّهَارِ لآيَاتٍ لأُولي الألْبَابِ ، الَّذينَ يَذْكُرُونَ اللهَ قيَاماً وَقُعُوداً وعَلى جُنُوبهِمْ [آل عمران : ١٩٠-١٩١].

321. Lo! In the creation of Heavens and the earth and in of night and day are tokens (of His sovereignty) for men of understanding, such as remember Allah, in standing, sitting and reclining. (3 : 190-191).

١٤٤٤ – وعَنْ عائشَةَ رضيَ اللهُ عَنْها قالَتْ : كانَ رَسُولُ اللهِ صَلّى اللهُ عَلَيْهِ وَسَلّمَ يَذكُرُ اللهَ تَعالى عَلى كُلِّ أحيَانِهِ . رواه مسلم

1444. Hazrat Ayesha (R.A.A.) says that the Holy Prophet (S.A.W.) remembered Allah the Exalted, at all times. *(Muslim)*

١٤٤٥ — وعن ابن عباس رضي الله عنهما عن النبي ، صلى الله عليه
وسلم قال : « لو أن أحدكم إذا أتى أهله قال : بسم الله ، اللهم
جنبنا الشيطان ، وجنب الشيطان مارزقتنا ، فقضي بينهما ولد ، لم
يضره » متفق عليه .

1445. Hazrat Ibn 'Abbas (R.A.A.) relates that the Holy Prophet (S.A.W.) said. When one of you cohabits with his wife, he should supplicate thus:

In the name of Allah, O Allah keep us away from Satan, and keep Satan away from (the offspring) that which Thou mightest grant us. Then if a child is born out of this union, the same would remain safe (against all harms by Satan). *(Bukhari and Muslim)*

* * * * * * *

CHAPTER 246

WHAT TO SUPPLICATE WHEN GOING TO BED AND ON AWAKENING

١٤٤٦ — عن حذيفة ، وأبي ذر رضي الله عنهما قالا : كان رسول
الله صلى الله عليه وسلم ، إذا أوى إلى فراشه قال : « باسمك اللهم أحيا
وأموت » ،وإذا استيقظ قال : « الحمد لله الذي أحيانا بعد ما أماتنا
وإليه النشور » رواه البخاري

1446. Hazrat Huzaifah (R.A.A.) and **Hazrat Abu Ẕar** (R.A.A.) state that the Holy Prophet (S.A.W.) supplicated on going to sleep at night thus.

Bismi-kal-la-huma Ahya wa Amo-to
With Thy name, O Allah, I expire and return to life,

And when he (S.A.W.) awoke he (S.A.W.) supplicated in this way:
Alhamdo lil-lahil-lazi Ahyana ba'da ma amatana wa ilaihin nushor.
All praise belongs to Allah Who has brought me back to life after He had caused me to die, to Him is the return.

(Bukhari)

* * * * * * *

CHAPTER 247

VIRTUES OF REMEMBERING ALLAH IN CONGREGATION, TO CONTINUE SUCH GATHERINGS AND PROHIBITION OF DIS-ASSOCIATION FROM SUCH ASSEMBLIES WITHOUT EXCUSE

قالَ اللهُ تعالى : وَاصْبِرْ نَفسَكَ مَعَ الَّذِينَ يَدعُونَ رَبَّهُم بِالغَدَاةِ وَالعَشِيِّ يُرِيدُونَ وَجهَهُ ، وَلا تَعْدُ عَيناكَ عَنهُم . [الكهف : ٢٨] .

Allah, the Exalted, has said:

322. Restrain thyself along with those who try unto their Lord at morn and evening, seeking His countenance; and let not thine eyes overlook them: (18:28)

١٤٤٧– وعنْ أبي هُرَيْرَةَ رضيَ اللهُ عنهُ قالَ : قالَ رَسُولُ اللهِ صلَّى اللهُ عليهِ وسلَّم : « إنَّ للهِ تعالى ملائكةً يَطُوفُونَ في الطُّرُقِ يلْتَمِسُونَ أهلَ الذِّكرِ ، فإذا وَجدُوا قوْماً يذكُرُونَ اللهَ عزَّ وجلَّ ، تنادَوْا : هلُمُّوا إلى حاجَتِكُمْ ، فيَحُفُّونَهم بأجنحتِهِم إلى السَّماءِ الدُّنيا ، فيَسألُهم ربُّهم –وهُوَ أعلم–: ما يقولُ عبادي ؟ قال : يقولون : يُسبِّحُونَكَ ويُكبِّرونَكَ ، ويَحمَدُونَكَ ، ويُمَجِّدُونَكَ ، فيقولُ : هل رأوني ؟ فيقولون : لا واللهِ ما رأوْكَ . فيَقُولُ : كيفَ لو رأوني ؟! قالَ : يقُولُونَ لو رأوْكَ كانُوا أشدَّ لكَ عِبادةً ، وأشدَّ لكَ تمجيداً ، وأكثرَ لكَ تسبيحاً . فيَقُولُ : فماذا يسألُونَ ؟ قالَ : يقُولونَ : يسألُونَكَ الجنَّةَ . قالَ : يقولُ : وهل رأوْها ؟ قالَ : يقُولُونَ : لا واللهِ يا ربِّ ما رأوْها . قالَ : يقُولُ : فكيفَ لو رأوْها ؟! قالَ : يقُولُونَ : لو أنَّهم رأوْها كانُوا أشدَّ عليْها حِرصاً ، وأشدَّ لها طلَباً ، وأعظَم فيها رغْبةً . قالَ : فمِمَّ يتعَوَّذُونَ ؟ قالَ : يتعَوَّذُونَ منَ النَّارِ ؛ قالَ : فيقُولُ : وهلْ رأوْها ؟ قالَ : يقولونَ : لا واللهِ ما رأوْها . فيقُولُ : كيفَ لو رأوْها ؟ ! قالَ : يقُولُون : لو رأوها كانُوا أشدَّ منها فِراراً ، وأشدَّ لها مخافةً . قالَ : فيقُولُ : فأُشْهِدُكم

أنّي قَدْ غَفَرْتُ لهم، قالَ: يقولُ مَلَكٌ مِنَ المَلائِكَةِ: فيهم فُلانٌ لَيسَ مِنهم، إنّما جاءَ لِحاجَةٍ، قالَ: هُمُ الجُلَساءُ لا يَشقَى بِهِم جَلِيسُهُم»

متفقٌ عليه

وفي روايةٍ لِمسلمٍ عَنْ أبي هُرَيرةَ رَضيَ اللهُ عَنهُ، عَنِ النبيِّ صَلّى اللهُ عَلَيهِ وسَلَّمَ قالَ: «إنَّ للهِ مَلائِكَةً سَيّارَةً فُضُلاً يَتَتَبَّعُونَ مَجالِسَ الذِّكرِ، فإذا وجَدُوا مَجلِساً فيهِ ذِكرٌ، قَعَدُوا مَعَهُم، وحَفَّ بَعضُهُم بَعضاً بِأجنِحَتِهِم حَتّى يَملَؤُوا ما بَينَهُم وبَينَ السَّماءِ الدُّنيا، فإذا تَفَرَّقُوا عَرَجُوا وصَعِدوا إلى السَّماءِ، فَيَسألُهُمُ اللهُ عَزَّ وجَلَّ — وهُوَ أعلَمُ —: مِنْ أينَ جِئتُم؟ فَيَقُولُونَ: جِئنا مِنْ عِندِ عِبادٍ لَكَ في الأرضِ: يُسَبِّحُونَكَ، ويُكَبِّرُونَكَ، ويُهَلِّلُونَكَ، ويَحمَدُونَكَ، ويَسألُونَكَ. قالَ: وماذا يَسألُوني؟ قالُوا: يَسألُونَكَ جَنَّتَكَ. قالَ: وهَلْ رَأوا جَنَّتي؟ قالُوا: لا، أي رَبِّ: قالَ: فَكَيفَ لَوْ رَأوا جَنَّتي؟! قالُوا: ويَستَجِيرُونَكَ. قال: ومِمَّ يَستَجِيرُوني؟ قالوا: مِنْ نارِكَ يارَبِّ. قالَ: وهَلْ رَأوا نارِي؟ قالوا: لا، قال: فَكَيفَ لَوْ رَأوا نارِي؟! قالُوا: ويَستَغفِرُونَكَ، فيقول: قَدْ غَفَرْتُ لَهُمْ، وأعطَيتُهُمْ ما سَألُوا، وأجَرْتُهُمْ مِمّا استَجارُوا. قال: فَيَقُولُونَ: ربِّ فيهِمْ فُلانٌ عَبْدٌ خَطّاءٌ إنّما مَرَّ، فَجَلَسَ مَعَهُمْ، فيقولُ: ولهُ غَفَرْتُ، هُمُ القَوْمُ لا يَشقَى بِهِمْ جَلِيسُهُمْ».

1447. Hazrat Abu Hurairah (R.A.A.) relates that the Holy Prophet (S.A.W.) said: There is a group of Allah's angels who move about the streets searching for those persons who remember Allah; and when they find a people remembering Allah, the Most Exalted, they call (Their Compainions) 'Come to your object' (i.e, here is the thing you are looking for); and they cover them with their wings right up to the sky. When these angels return, their Lord inquires from them, although He himself knows it the most, as to what His servants were saying. The Holy Prophet (S.A.W.) said: The Angels say: They were proclaiming Thy Holiness and Greatness, and were busy in praising Thee and glorifying Thee, (Allah, the Most High) then inquires: Have they seen Me? Angels reply: By Allah! they have not seen Thee. Allah, the Exalted again inquires. What will be the position, if they could see Me? The Holy Prophet (S.A.W.) said: The angels replied that in that case they would he more assiduous in Thy worship and Thy glorification and in proclaiming Thy Holiness. Then Allah, the Exalted enquires: What did they ask from Me'! The Holy Prophet (S.A.W.) said: The angels replied that they begged for Paradise from Allah. Allah Enquires: Have they seen it? They answer: O by Thee, they have not seen it. Allah further enquires: What would have been the position if they had seen it? The Holy Prophet (S.A.W.) said: The angels answer: Had they seen it, they would desire it more eagerly, and seek it more and yearn more for it. Then Allah enquires: From what thing did they seek protection? The angels answered: They were seeking protection from Hell. The Holy Prophet (S.A.W.) said, Allah Exalted enquires: Have they seen the Hell. They Answer: No, By Allah, they have not seen it. Allah the Exalted then enquires: What would happen if they could see it? The angels answer: if they could see it, they would run from it more and would fear it more. The Holy Prophet (S.A.W.) says that then Allah Exalted declares: Be witness, I have forgiven them! One of the angels then says that among them was so and so, who is not one of them. He had simply come to Thee, for some need. Then Allah the Exalted says: They were sitting together therefore even their associate shall not go unrewarded.

(Bukhari and Muslim)

Imam Muslim's version says: According to a report from Hazrat Abu Hurairah, (R.A.A.) the Holy Prophet (S.A.W.) said that Allah has a party of angels which constantly travels looking for gatherings (of His servants) which assemble for the remembrance (of Allah). Whenever they find such a gathering of rememberance, they too sit with them and cover one another with their wings so that the space between them and the sky is filled. When this gathering, disperses, the angels also get up and fly to the heaven. Allah, the Exalted asks them, although He himself knows well as to from where you are coming? The angels answer: We are coming from some of Thy servants on the earth, who proclaim Thy Holiness and Greatness, and Thy Oneness and praise Thee and beg of Thee. Allah the Exalted enquiries. What do they ask from Me? The angels answer: They ask Thy paradise from Thee. Allah the Exalted again enquires: Have they seen My paradise? They answer: No, O Lord. Then He enquires: What would have been the situation if they could see My paradise? The angels say: They were also seeking Thy protection. He enquires: From what do they seek My protection? They answer: O Lord! From Thy Fire, He enquires: Have they seen My Hell? They say: No. He enquires: What would if they could see My Fire? They said: And they also solicit Thy forgiveness. Allah the Exalted says: I have forgiven them, and bestowed upon them what they ask for and have rewarded them My protection with the thing from which they seek. They say: 'O' Lord, among them there is one, so and so, who is a great sinner'. He was passing by and simply sat down among them. Allah the Exalted says: I have forgiven him also. They are a community of such a virtuous persons whose associates shall not be deprived.

١٤٤٨ـ وعنه عَنْ أبي سعيد رَضِيَ اللهُ عَنْهُمَا قالا : قَالَ رَسُولُ اللهِ صَلَّى اللهُ عليهِ وسَلَّم : « لايَقْعُدُ قَوْمٌ يَذْكُرُونَ اللهَ إلاَّ حَفَّتْهُمُ المَلائِكَةُ ، وَغَشِيَتْهُمُ الرَّحْمَةُ وَنَزَلَتْ عَلَيْهِمُ السَّكِينَةُ ، وَذَكَرَهُمُ اللهُ فِيمن عِنْدَهُ » رواه مسلم .

1448. Hazrat Abu Sa'eed Khudri (R.A.A.) and Hazrat Abu Hurairah (R.A.A.) relate that the Holy Prophet (S.A.W.) said: A people do not gather together for the remembrance of Allah the Exalted but its members are surrounded by angels, and are covered by Allah's mercy, and the mental and spiritual peace descends upon them and Allah speaks of them high to those around Him. *(Muslim)*

١٤٤٩ـ وعن أبي واقِدٍ الحارِثِ بنِ عَوْفٍ رَضِيَ اللهُ عَنْهُ أنَّ رَسُولَ اللهِ ، صَلَّى اللهُ عليه وسلَّم ، بَيْنَما هُوَ جَالِسٌ في المَسْجِدِ ، وَالنَّاسُ مَعَهُ ، إذ أقْبَلَ ثَلاثَةُ نَفَرٍ ، فَأقْبَلَ اثْنَانِ إلى رَسولِ اللهِ ، صَلَّى الله عليه وسلم ، وَذَهَبَ وَاحِدٌ ، فَوَقَفَا عَلى رسول الله صلى الله عليه وسلم . فَأمَّا أحَدُهُما فرأى فُرجَةً في الحَلْقَةِ ، فَجَلَسَ فيها وأمَّا الآخرُ ، فَجَلَسَ خَلْفَهُم ، وَأمَّا الثالثُ فَأدبَرَ ذاهِباً . فَلَمَّا فَرَغَ رسُولُ اللهِ ، صَلَّى اللهُ عَلَيْهِ وسلَّم ، قال : ألاَ أُخْبِرُكم عَنِ النَّفَرِ الثَّلاثَةِ : أمَّا أحَدُهم ، فَأوَى إلى اللهِ ، فَآوَاهُ اللهُ ، وأمَّا الآخرُ فَاسْتَحْيَا فَاسْتَحْيا اللهُ مِنهُ ، وأمَّا الآخرُ ، فَأعْرَضَ ، فَأعرَضَ اللهُ عَنْهُ » متفقٌ عليه

1449. Hazrat Abu Waqid-Al Haris bin Auf (R.A.A.) relates that once when the Holy Prophet (S.A.W.) was seated in the mosque surrounded by persons, suddenly three persons came in. Out of these, two approached him (S.A.W.) and third went away. One of them noticed some space between those who were seated, and took his seat there. The other sat down behind those who were already seated there. The Third one turned away. When the Holy Prophet (S.A.W.) finished his talk, he said: May I tell you something about these three?

One of them sought refuge with Allah the Exalted, and He took him under His cover. The second felt shy (to thrust himself into the crowd) so Allah the Exalted also felt shy for him. The third turned back and went away, so Allah also turned away from him.

(Bukhari and Muslim)

١٤٥٠ – وعن أبي سعيدٍ الخُدْرِيِّ رضيَ اللهُ عَنْهُ قالَ : خرجَ مُعاوِيَةُ رضيَ اللهُ عنهُ علَى حَلْقَةٍ في المَسْجِدِ ، فقال : ما أجْلَسَكُمْ ؟ قالُوا : جلَسْنَا نَذْكُرُ الله . قَالَ آللهِ ما أجْلَسَكُم إلاَّ ذَاكَ ؟ قالوا: ما أجْلَسَنَا إلاَّ ذَاكَ ، قـال : أمَـا إنِّي لم أسْتَحْلِفْكُم تُهْمَةً لَكُم ، ومَـا كانَ أحَدٌ بِمَنْزِلَتِي مِنْ رسُولِ اللهِ صَلَّى اللهُ عَلَيْهِ وسَلَّمَ أقلَّ عَنْهُ حَدِيثاً مِنِّي : إنَّ رَسُولَ اللهِ صَلَّى اللهُ عليه وسَلَّم خَرَجَ علَى حَلْقَةٍ مِن أصحابِه فقال : « ما أجْلَسَكُمْ ؟ » قالوا : جلَسْنا نَذكُرُ الله ، ونَحْمَدُهُ علَى ما هدَانَا لِلإسْلامِ ، ومَنَّ بهِ عَلَيْنا . قَال : « آللهِ ما أجْلَسَكُمْ إلاَّ ذَاكَ ؟ قالوا : والله ما أجْلَسَنَا إلاَّ ذَاكَ . قالَ : « أمَا إنِّي لَمْ أسْتَحْلِفْكُمْ تُهْمَةً لَكُمْ ، ولكِنَّهُ أتَانِي جِبرِيلُ فَأخْبَرَنِي أنَّ الله يُبَاهِي بِكُمُ المَلائكَةَ » : رواهُ مسلمٌ .

1450. Hazrat Abu Sa'eed Khudri (R.A.A.) realtes that once Hazrat Mu'awiyah (R.A.A.) visited the mosque and saw a circle (of reciters). He asked: What has made you sitting? They said: We have assembled here to remember Allah. He said: By Allah you did not sit except for this purpose? They affirmed: We did not sit except for this. Hazrat Mu'awiyah (R.A.A.) then told them, I did not ask you to swear on account of any malice. None of you can match me for scanty narration of Holy Prophet (S.A.W.) (and as such have narrated very few traditions about him (S.A.W.). The Holy Prophet (S.A.W.) once visited a gathering of his (S.A.W.) companions and enquired. What has made you assemble here? They answered: We have gathered together to remember Allah and praise Him for having led us to Islam and granted this favour to us. The Holy Prophet (S.A.W.) enquired: Do you affirm by Allah that it is so? The Holy Prophet's Companions affirmed: By Allah we are sitting here for this purpose only. He (S.A.W.) said: I have not put you on oath on account of any doubt, but angel Gabriel had visited me and told me that Allah felt proud of you among the angels. *(Muslim)*

* * * * * * *

CHAPTER 248

PROCLAIMING (ALLAH'S HOLINESS AND GLORIFICATION) EVERY MORNING AND EVENING

قالَ اللهُ تعالى: وَاذْكُرْ رَبَّكَ فِي نَفْسِكَ تَضَرُّعاً وَخِيفَةً وَدُونَ الْجَهْرِ
مِنَ الْقَوْلِ بِالْغُدُوِّ وَالآصَالِ وَلا تَكُنْ مِنَ الْغَافِلِينَ [الأعراف: ٢٠٥]
وقال تعالى: وَسَبِّحْ بِحَمْدِ رَبِّكَ قَبْلَ طُلُوعِ الشَّمْسِ وَقَبْلَ
غُرُوبِهَا [طه : ١٣٠] وقال تعالى : وَسَبِّحْ بِحَمْدِ رَبِّكَ بِالْعَشِيِّ
وَالإِبْكَارِ [غافر : ٥٥]

وقال تعالى : فِي بُيُوتٍ أَذِنَ اللهُ أَنْ تُرْفَعَ وَيُذْكَرَ
فِيهَا اسْمُهُ : يُسَبِّحُ لَهُ فِيهَا بِالْغُدُوِّ وَالآصَالِ رِجَالٌ لا تُلْهِيهِمْ تِجَارَةٌ
وَلا بَيْعٌ عَنْ ذِكْرِ اللهِ - الآية [النور : ٣٦-٣٧] وقال تعالى : إِنَّا سَخَّرْنَا
الْجِبَالَ مَعَهُ يُسَبِّحْنَ بِالْعَشِيِّ وَالإِشْرَاقِ [ص : ١٩].

Allah the Exalted has said:

323. And do thou (O Muhammad) remember thy Lord within thyself humbly and with awe below thy breath, at morn and evening. And be thou not of the neglectful (7 : 205)

324. And celebrate the praises of thy Lord ere the rising of the sun, and ere the going down thereof. (20 : 130)

325. And hymn the praise of the Lord at the fall of night and in the early hours. (40 . 55)

326. (This lamp is found) in houses which Allah hath allowed to be exalted, and that His name shall be remembered there-in. Therein do offer praise to Him, at morn and evening. Men whom neither merchandise nor sale beguileth from remembrance of Allah. (24 : 36—37)

327. Lo! We subdued the hills to hymn the praises (of their Lord) with him at nightfall and sunrise. (38 : 19)

١٤٥١- وعنْ أبي هريرةَ رضيَ اللهُ عنهُ قالَ : قالَ رَسولُ اللهِ ، صَلّى اللهُ عَلَيْهِ وسلَّمَ : « مَنْ قالَ حينَ يُصْبِحُ وحينَ يُمسي : سُبْحَانَ اللهِ وَبِحَمْدِهِ مِائَةَ مَرَّةٍ ، لَمْ يأتِ أحَدٌ يَوْمَ القِيامَةِ بأفضَلَ مِمّا جاءَ به ، إلّا أحَدٌ قالَ مِثلَ مَا قالَ أوْ زادَ » رواهُ مسلم .

1451. Hazrat Abu Hurairah (R.A.A.) relates that the Holy Prophet (S.A.W.) said: A person who recites both in the morning and evening:

Subha-nal-lahi wa bi Hamdi-hi

Holy is Allah and all praise belongs to Him: One hundred times, will not be surpassed by anyone in good works on the Day of Judgement unless by one who shall have recited the same like him or more. *(Muslim)*

١٤٥٢- وعنهُ قالَ : جاءَ رجُلٌ إلى النَّبيِّ صَلّى اللهُ عليهِ وَسَلَّمَ ، فقالَ : يارسُولَ اللهِ مَالَقيتُ مِنْ عقْرَبٍ لَدَغتني البارِحَةَ ! قال : « أمَا لَوقُلْتَ حينَ أمْسَيْتَ : أعُوذُ بِكَلماتِ اللهِ التّامّاتِ منْ شَرِّ مَا خَلَقَ لم تَضُرّكَ » رواه مسلم .

1452. Hazrat Abu Hurairah (R.A.A.) says: A person came to the Holy Prophet (S.A.W.) and complained: O Messenger of Allah, a scorpion stung me last night which caused sharp pain to me. The Holy Prophet (S.A.W.) said: Had you recited at night:

A'oozo Bikale-ma - til-lahit-tam-maate min Shar-re ma Kha-la-qa.

I seek the protection of the perfect words of Allah from the mischief of whatever He has created: *(Muslim)*

then this scorpion would not have harmed you.

١٤٥٣- وعَنْهُ ،عنِ النبيِّ ، صَلّى اللهُ عليهِ وسَلَّمَ ، أنَّهُ كان يقولُ إذا أصْبَحَ : « اللّهُمَّ بِكَ أصْبَحْنَا ، وبِكَ أمْسَيْنا ، وبِكَ نَحْيا ، وبِكَ نَمُوتُ ، وإليكَ النُّشُورُ » وإذا أمْسَى قال : « اللّهُمَّ بِكَ أمْسَيْنَا ، وبِكَ نَحْيَا ، وبِكَ نَمُوتُ . وإليكَ النُّشُورُ » .

رواه أبو داود ، والترمذي وقال : حديث حسن .

1453. Hazrat Abu Hurairah (R.A.A.) relates that the Holy Prophet (S.A.W.) used to recite in the morning,

Alla-hum-ma bika asbah-na wa bika amsai-na wa bika nah-ya wa bika namulo wa ilai-kan-nu-shor

('O Allah, with thy favour we got the morning, and with Thy favour get the evening, and with thy favour we live and shall die on thy name, and to Thee shall we return):
And in the evening he (S.A.W.) recited.
Alla-hum-ma bika amsai-na wa bika Nah-ya wa bika Namu-to wa ilai-kan na-shoor.

'O Allah, with Thy favour have we got the evening and with Thy favour do we live and we die, and to Thee we shall return).
(*Abu Daud and Tirmizi, Imam Tirmizi,* said it is good).

١٤٥٤ – وعنه أنَّ أبا بكرٍ الصدِّيق ، رضي الله عنه ، قال: يارَسُول الله مُرْني بِكلماتٍ أقولُهنَّ إذا أصبحتُ وإذا أمسيتُ ، قال : قُلْ : اللَّهُمَّ فاطِرَ السمواتِ والأرضِ عالمَ الغيبِ والشهادةِ ، ربَّ كلِّ شيءٍ ومليكه . أشهدُ أن لا إله إلَّا أنتَ ، أعوذُ بكَ من شرِّ نفسي وشرِّ الشيطانِ وشِركه » قال : « قُلْها إذا أصبحتَ ، وإذا أمسيتَ ، وإذا أخذتَ مضجعكَ » رواه أبو داود والترمذي وقال : حديثٌ حسنٌ صحيحٌ .

1454. Hazrat Abu Hurairah (R.A.A.) relates that Hazrat Abu Bakr Siddiq (R.A.A.) requested the Holy Prophet (S.A.W.): O Messenger of Allah, instruct me some supplications for the morning and evening the Holy Prophet (S.A.W.) said: Recite:

Alla-hum-ma Fati-ras sama-wate wal ardhe 'aali-mal-ghai-bi wash-sha-ha-da-te rab-ba kul-le Shai-in wa mali-kahu, Ash-hadu al-la ila-ha il-la anta a'oozu-bika min shar-re nafsi wa shar-rish-shai-tane wa shir-kihi.

('O' Allah, the Creator of the heavens and the earth, Knower of both unseen and the seen), Sustainer and Master of all-things. I testify that there is no god save Thee, and I seek Thy protection from the mischief of my self and the evil of Satan and his (incite-ment tō creat) Thy associates.

The Holy Prophet (S.A.W.) said: Recite these sentences in the morning and in the evening and also on retiring to bed.
(*Abu Daud and Tirmizi.* Later said this is sound and good)

١٤٥٥ – وعَنْ ابنِ مسعودٍ رضي اللهُ عنهُ قالَ : كانَ نبيُّ اللهِ ، صلى الله عليهِ وسلَّمَ ، إذا أمسَى قال أمسَينا وأمسى المُلكُ لله ، والحمدُ لله ، لا إلهَ إلاَّ اللهُ وحدهُ لا شريكَ لهُ » قالَ الراوي : أراهُ قال فيهنَّ : « لهُ المُلكُ ولهُ الحمدُ وهوَ على كلِّ شيءٍ قديرٌ ، ربِّ أسألُكَ خيرَ

مَافي هذهِ اللَّيلَةِ ، وَخيرَ مَا بعدَهَا ، وأعوذُ بِكَ منْ شرِّ مَافي هذهِ اللَّيلَةِ وَشرِّ ما بعدَهَا ، رَبِّ أعوذُ بِكَ منَ الكَسَلِ ، وَسوءِ الكِبَرِ ، أعوذُ بِكَ منْ عذَابٍ في النَّارِ ، وَعذَابٍ في القَبرِ » وَإذا أصبحَ قال ذلكَ أيضاً : « أصبَحنا وَأصبحَ المُلْكُ للهِ » رواه مسلم

1455. Hazrat Abdullah ıbn Mas'ud (R.A.A.) relates that the Holy Prophet (S.A.W.) used to say in the evening:

Am-sai-na wa amsil mulko lil-lahe wal hamdo lil-lahe la ila-ha il-lal-laho wah-dahu La shar-rika Lahu

(We got the evening, and so the country, and the country belongs to Allah, and all praise belongs to Allah, and there is no god save Allah, the One, Who has no associate):

The reporter says: I think that the Holy Prophet (S.A.W.) has also said these sentences in this connection:

Lahul mul-ko wa lahul hamdo wa hu-wa 'Ala kul-le Shai'n Qadeer, Rab-be as'alu-ka Khai-ra mafi hazi-hil lai-late wa khai-ra ma ba'da-ha wa a'oozo bika min shar-re ma fi hazi-hil lai-late wa shar-re ma ba'da-ha, Rab-be a'oozo-bika minal kasa-le wa soo'il kiba-re, a'oozo bika min 'aza-bin fin-nare wa 'aza-bin fill Qabr.

His is the Kingdom and His the Paradise, and He has power over all things. O Allah, I request Thee for all the good of this night and the good of that which will follow it, and solicit Thy protection against the evil of this night and that will follow it. O Allah! I seek Thy protection against laziness and the mischief of old age. And seek Thy protection against the torment in the Hell and torment in the grave).

In the morning he would recite the same sentences substituting the word *(Asbaha wa asbaha al mulka* instead of *amsaina wa amsal-mulka)* (morning for the word evening) *(Muslim)*

١٤٥٦ — وعنْ عبدِ اللهِ بنِ خُبَيْبٍ — بضمِّ الخَاءِ المُعْجَمَةِ — رضي اللهُ عَنْهُ قالَ : قالَ لي رَسُولُ اللهِ ، صلَّى الله عليه وسلم : « اقْرَأْ : قُلْ هوَ اللهُ أحَدٌ ، والمعوِّذَتَيْنِ حينَ تُمْسي وَحينَ تُصْبِحُ ، ثلاثَ مرَّاتٍ تَكْفيكَ مِنْ كلِّ شَيْءٍ » رواهُ أبو داود والترمذي وقال : حديثٌ حسن صحيح .

1456. Hazrat Abdullah bin Khubaib (R.A.A.) relates that the Holy Prophet (S.A.W.) asked him: Recite the *Sura Al-Ikhlas*, *Sura Al Falaq* and *Sura An-Nas* three times, morning and evening, and they will shield thee against all (i.e. troubles mishaps and particularly effects of magic)

(Abu Daud and Tirmizi. Tirmizi said this is good and sound).

١٤٥٧ — وعن عثمان بن عفان رضي الله عنه قال: قال رسول الله صلّى الله عليه وسلّم: «ما من عبد يقول في صباح كل يوم ومساء كل ليلة: بسم الله الذي لا يضرّ مع اسمه شيء في الأرض ولا في السماء وهو السميع العليم، ثلاث مرات، إلا لم يضره شيء»

رواه أبو داود. والترمذي وقال: حديث حسن صحيح.

1457. Hazrat Usman bin 'Affan (R.A.A.) relates that the Holy Prophet (S.A.W.) said. A person who recites the following supplication three times every morning and every evening:

Bis-mil-la-hil-lazee La ya-dur-ro ma'is-mihi, shai un fil ardhe wa la fis-samai wa hu-was-Sami-ul Aleem.

'In the name of Allah, with the blessings of Whose name, there nothing will harm in the earth and in the heaven, and He is the All-Hearing, All-Knowing', will not be harmed by anything.'

(Abu Daud and Tirmizi. Imam Tirmizi, said this tradition is sound and good).

* * * * * * *

CHAPTER 249

WHAT TO SUPPLICATE ON GOING TO SLEEP

قال الله تعالى: إنّ في خلق السموات والأرض واختلاف الليل والنهار، لآيات لأولي الألباب، الذين يذكرون الله قياماً وقعوداً وعلى جنوبهم، ويتفكرون في خلق السموات والأرض الآيات.

[آل عمران: ١٩٠-١٩١].

Allah, the Exalted, has said:

328. Lo! In the creation of the heavens and the earth and (in) the difference of night and day are tokens (of His Sovereignty) for men of understanding, such as remember Allah, standing, sitting, and reclining and ponder on the creation of the heavens and the earth. (3 : 190—191)

١٤٥٨– وعنْ حُذيفةَ وأبي ذرٍّ رضي اللهُ عَنْهما أنَّ رسُولَ اللهِ صَلَّى اللهُ عليه وسلَّمَ كانَ إذَا أوى إلى فِراشِهِ قالَ : « باسْمِكَ اللَّهُمَّ أحْيَا وَأمُوتُ » رواه البخاري .

1458. This Hadis has been covered in S. No. 1446 of Chapter 246.

١٤٥٩ – وعَنْ عليٍّ رضيَ اللهُ عَنْهُ أنَّ رَسُولَ اللهِ صَلَّى اللهُ عَلَيهِ وسلَّمَ قالَ له ولِفاطِمةَ ، رَضِيَ اللهُ عنهما : « إذَا أوَيْتُمَا إلى فِراشِكُمَا ، أوْ : إذَا أخَذْتُمَا مَضَاجِعَكُمَا – فَكَبِّرَا ثَلاثاً وثَلاثِينَ ، وَسَبِّحَا ثَلاثاً وَثَلاثِينَ ، وَاحْمَدَا ثَلاثاً وثَلاثِينَ » وفي رِوايةٍ : التَّسْبِيحُ أرْبعاً وَثَلاثِينَ » وفي رِوايةٍ : « التَّكبيرُ أربَعاً وَثَلاثِينَ » متفقٌ عليه .

1459. Hazrat Ali (R.A.A.) relates that the Holy Prophet (S.A.W.) said to him and Hazrat Fatimah (R.A.A.): When you go to bed or to rest recite: *Al-laho Akbar* (Allah is Great thirty three times). and *Sub-han-al-lah* (Allah is Holy) Thirty three times, and *Al-hamdo-lil-lah* (All praise to Allah) Thirty times.

In another version, *Sub-han-al-lah* (Allah is Holy) has been described as thirty four times,

and yet in another version *Al-laho Akbar* (Allah is Great) has been described thirty four times. *(Bukhari and Muslim)*

١٤٦٠– وعن أبي هُريرةَ ، رَضِيَ الله عنهُ ، قالَ : قالَ رسولُ اللهِ صَلَّى اللهُ عليهِ وسَلَّمَ : « إذا أوى أحَدُكُم إلى فِرَاشِهِ ، فَلْيَنْفُضْ فِرَاشَهُ بِداخِلَةِ إزَارِهِ فإنَّهُ لا يَدْرِي مَا خَلَفَهُ عَلَيْهِ ، ثُمَّ يَقُولُ : بِاسْمِكَ رَبِّي وَضَعْتُ جَنْبِي ،وَبِكَ أرْفَعُهُ ، إنْ أمْسَكْتَ نَفْسِي فَارْحَمْهَا ، وإنْ أرْسَلْتَهَا : فَاحْفَظْهَا بِمَا تَحْفَظُ بِهِ عِبَادَكَ الصَّالِحِينَ » متفقٌ عليه .

1460. Hazrat Abu Hurairah (R.A.A.) says that the Holy Prophet (S.A.W.) said. 'When one of you goes to bed should clear his bed with a part of loin cloth as he does not know on it behind him, and should supplicate:

Bismi-ka rab-bi wada'to jan-bi wa bika arfa'-o-hoo, in am-sak-ta nafsi farham-ha wa in arsal-taha fah-faz-ha bima tah-fazo bihi 'ibada-kas sa-le-heen.

(With Thy name, O my Sustainer, have I laid on my side, and shall raise it only with Thy name what has got. If Thou holds my soul (i.e. takes my life) then, have mercy on it, and if Thou returns it, then protect it with that thing which Thou does guard Thy pious servants). *(Bukahri and Muslim)*

١٤٦١ــ وعنْ عائشةَ ، رضيَ اللهُ عنْها ، أنَّ رسولَ اللهِ ، صلّى اللهُ عليهِ وسلّمَ ، كان إذا أخذَ مضجعَهُ نفثَ في يديْهِ ، وقرأ بالمُعوِّذاتِ ومسحَ بهما جسدَهُ . متفقٌ عليه

وفي رواية لهما : أنّ النبيَّ ، صلّى اللهُ عليهِ وسلّمَ ، كانَ إذا أوَى إلى فراشِهِ كلَّ ليْلةٍ جمعَ كفّيْهِ ، ثُمَّ نفثَ فيهما فقرأ فيهمَا : قُلْ هُوَ اللهُ أحدٌ ، وقُلْ أعوذُ بربِّ الفلَقِ ، وقُلْ أعوذُ بربِّ النّاسِ ، ثُمَّ مسحَ بهما ما استطاعَ مِنْ جسدِهِ ، يبْدأُ بهمَا علَى رأسِهِ ووجهِهِ ، ومَا أقبلَ مِنْ جسدِهِ ، يفْعلُ ذلكَ ثلاثَ مرّاتٍ . متفقٌ عليهِ .

1461. Hazrat Ayesha (R.A.A.) relates that when the Holy Prophet (S.A.W.) used to lie, he would recite *Sura Al-Falaq* and *Sura An Nas* and blow upon his palms, and then wipes them all over his body. *(Bukhari and Muslim)*

Another version of both these authorities says. On every night when the Holy Prophet (S.A.W.) used to go to his bed he would collect his hands and blow upon the palms and recite *Suras Ikhlas, Al Falaq* and *An Nas* into them and then wipe them over his body, as far as they could reach, beginning with his head and face and continuing over the front of his body, repeating this three times.

١٤٦٢ــ وعنِ البرَاءِ بنِ عازبٍ ، رضيَ اللهُ عنهمَا ، قالَ : قالَ لي رسولُ اللهِ ، صلّى اللهُ عليهِ وسلّمَ : « إذا أتيتَ مضجعكَ فتوضّأْ وضوءكَ للصّلاةِ ، ثمّ اضطجعْ على شقّكَ الأيمنِ ، وقلْ : اللّهُمَّ أسلمْتُ نفسي إليكَ ، وفوّضتُ أمري إليْكَ ، وألجأتُ ظهري إليْكَ ، رغبةً ورهبةً إليكَ ، لاملجأَ ولامنجى منكَ إلّا إليْكَ ، آمنتُ بكتابكَ الذي أنزلْتَ ، وبنبيّكَ الذي أرسلتَ . فإنْ متَّ ، متَّ على الفطرةِ ، واجعلْهنّ آخرَ ماتقولُ » متّفقٌ عليه

1462. Hazrat Bra'a bin 'Aazib (R.A.A.) says that the Holy Prophet (S.A.W.) told him, when you go to bed, make your ablution like the one for Salat, and then lying down on your right side, recite:

Alla-hum-ma aslam-to nafsi ilai-ka wa faw-waz-to amri ilai-ka, walija'to zahri ilai-ka ragh-ba-tan wa rah-ba-tan ilai-ka la maljaa wa la manja'a min-ka il-la ilai-ka, aa'manto be -ki-ta-bikal-lazi anzal-ta wa bi-nabi-ye-kal-lazi ars-alta.

O Allah I have surrendered my soul to Thee and entrusted my affairs to Thee, and made my back attentive towards Thee; hoping to get Thy recompense and fearing Thy punishment. There is no refuge and no asylum against Thee save with Thyself. I believe in the Book that Thou has revealed and believe in the Prophet whom Thou has revealed and believe in the Prophet whom Thou has commissioned). Then if you die (in sleep), you will die on the true nature (real faith). Let these words be your last words to speak at night. *(Bukhari and Muslim)*

١٤٦٣ – وَعَنْ أَنَسٍ ، رَضِيَ اللهُ عَنْهُ ، أَنَّ النَّبِيَّ ، صَلَّى اللهُ عليهِ وسلَّم ، كَانَ إذا أوَى إلى فِرَاشِهِ قَالَ : « الحَمْدُ للهِ الَّذي أطْعَمَنَا وسَقَانَا ، وكفَانَا وآوانَا ، فَكَمْ مِمَّنْ لاكافِيَ لَهُ وَلا مُؤْوِيَ » رواهُ مسلمٌ .

1463. Hazrat Anas (R.A.A.) relates that when the Holy Prophet (S.A.W.) went to bed he would recite:

Al-hmdo lil-la-hil lazi at'ama-na wa saqaa-na wa kafa-na wa aaw-na fa-kam mimman-la ka-fia-lahu wa la moo'vi.

All praise belongs to Allah, Who has given us to eat and drink, and has fulfilled our designs and has provided us with shelter, when there are so many others who have not any shelter nor have their sustainer . *(Muslim)*

١٤٦٤ – وَعَنْ حُذَيْفَةَ ، رَضِيَ اللهُ عَنْهُ ، أَنَّ رَسُولَ اللهِ ، صَلَّى اللهُ عَليهِ وَسَلَّم ، كَانَ إذا أرَادَ أَنْ يَرْقُدَ ،وَضَعَ يَدَهُ اليُمنَى تَحْتَ خَدِّهِ ، ثمَّ يَقُولُ : « اللَّهمَّ قِنِي عَذَابَكَ يَوْمَ تَبْعَثُ عِبَادَكَ » رَوَاهُ التِرمِذيُّ وقالَ : حَدِيثٌ حَسَنٌ .

وَرَوَاهُ أبو داودَ مِنْ رِوَايَةِ حَفْصَةَ ، رَضِيَ اللهُ عَنْها ؛ وَفيهِ أنَّهُ كَانَ يَقُولهُ ثَلاثَ مرَّاتٍ .

1464. Hazrat Huzaifah (R.A.A.) says that when the Holy Prophet (S.A.W.) intended to sleep, he used to put his right hand under his cheek and then supplicate.

Alla-hum-ma qini 'aza-baka yauma tab-'aso 'iba-daka.

'O' Allah, save me from Thy torment on the Day when Thou wilt raise up Thy servants . *(Tirmizi)*

Abu Daud related this tradition on the authority of Hazrat Hafsah (R.A.A.) adding: 'He would repeat it three times.'

* * * * * * *

CHAPTER 250

BOOK OF SUPPLICATIONS

قَالَ اللهُ تَعَالَى : (وَقَالَ رَبُّكُم ادْعُونِي أَسْتَجِبْ لَكُمْ).[غافر : ٦٠].
وَقَالَ تَعَالَى : (ادْعُوا رَبَّكُمْ تَضَرُّعاً وَخُفْيَةً إِنَّهُ لا يُحِبُّ المُعْتَدِينَ)
[الأعراف : ٥٥] . وَقَالَ تَعَالَى : (وَإِذا سَأَلَكَ عِبَادِي عَنِّي فَإِنِّي قَرِيبٌ
أُجِيبُ دَعْوَةَ الدَّاعِ إِذا دَعَانِ) الآية [البقرة : ١٨٦] . وَقَالَ تَعَالَى : (أَمَّنْ
يُجِيبُ المُضْطَرَّ إِذا دَعَاهُ وَيَكْشِفُ السُّوءَ) الآية [النمل : ٦٢]

Allah the Exalted, has said:

329. And your Lord hath said: Pray unto Me: and I will hear your prayer. (40 : 60)

330. (O' Mankind!) Call upon your Lord humbly and in secret. Lo! He loveth not aggressors. (7 : 55)

331. And when My servants question thee concerning Me, then surely I am nigh. I answer the prayer of the supplicant when he crieth unto me. (2 : 186)

332. Is not He (best) who answereth the wronged one when he crieth unto Him and removeth the evil. (27 : 62)

١٤٦٥– وَعَنِ النُّعْمانِ بْنِ بَشِيرٍ . رَضِيَ اللهُ عَنْهُمَا ، عَنِ النَّبِيِّ ، صَلَّى اللهُ عَلَيهِ وسَلَّم ، قَالَ : « الدُّعَاءُ هوَ العِبادَةُ » .

رَوَاهُ أَبو دَاودَ ، والترمذيُّ ، وَقَالَ : حديثٌ حَسَنٌ صَحيحٌ .

1465. Hazrat Nu'man bin Bashir (R.A.A.) relates that the Holy Prophet (S.A.W.) said: 'Supplication is the worship' *(Abu Daud and Tirmizi) Imam Tirmizi* said this is sound and good.

١٤٦٦ – وَعَنْ عَائِشَةَ ، رَضِيَ اللهُ عَنْهَا ، قَالَتْ : كَانَ رَسُولُ اللهِ . صَلَّى اللهُ عَلَيهِ وَسَلَّم ، يَسْتَحِبُّ الجَوامِعَ مِنَ الدُّعَاءِ ، وَيَدَعُ مَاسِوَى ذلكَ . رَوَاهُ أَبو دَاودَ بإسْنادٍ جَيِّدٍ .

1466. Hazrat 'Ayesha (R.A.A.) says that from amongst the prayers, the Holy Prophet (S.A.W.) preferred those that were Comprehensive and avoided others.

(Imam Abu Daud has cited this with sound chains).

١٤٦٧ – وَعَنْ أَنَسٍ ، رَضِيَ اللهُ عَنْهُ ، قَالَ : كَانَ أَكْثَرُ دُعَاءِ النَّبِيِّ ، صَلَّى اللهُ عَلَيهِ وسَلَّم : « اللَّهُمَّ آتِنَا في الدُّنْيَا حَسَنَةً ، وَفي الآخِرَةِ حَسَنَةً ، وَقِنَا عَذَابَ النَّارِ » مُتَّفَقٌ عَليهِ .

زادَ مُسلِمٌ في رِوَايَتِهِ قَالَ : وكَانَ أَنَسٌ إذا أَرَادَ أَنْ يَدعُوَ بِدعْوَةٍ دَعَا بِهَا ، وَإذا أَرَادَ أَن يَدعوَ بدُعَاءٍ دَعَا بِهَا فيه .

1467. Hazrat Anas (R.A.A.) relates that the Holy Prophet (S.A.W.) mostly supplicated:

Alla-hum-ma aa-tina fid dun-ya hasa-natan - wa fil aakhi-rati hasa-natan'-wa qina 'azab-an-nar.

(Allah! bestow upon us the best of this world and the best of the next world, and save us from the torments of the Fire of Hell. *(Bukhari and Muslim)*

Imam Muslim has added in his version: When Hazrat Anas bin Malik wanted to pray, he made the same (above mentioned) supplications, and if he made any other, he included this one in it.

١٤٦٨– وَعَنِ ابنِ مَسْعُودٍ ، رَضِيَ اللهُ عَنْهُ ، أنَّ النَّبيَّ ، صَلَّى اللهُ عَليهِ وسلَّم ، كَانَ يَقُولُ : « اللَّهُمَّ إنِّي أَسأَلُكَ الهُدَى ، وَالتُّقَى ، وَالعَفَافَ ، والغِنَى » رَوَاهُ مُسْلِمٌ .

1468. Hazrat Ibn Mas'ud (R.A.A.) reports that the Holy Prophet (S.A.W.) supplicated: O Allah! I beseech Thee for guidance, virtuousness, chastity and unattachment with the world. *(Muslim)*

١٤٦٩ – وَعَنْ طارِقِ بنِ أَشْيَمَ ، رَضِيَ اللهُ عَنْهُ ، قَالَ : كانَ الرَّجلُ إذا أَسْلَمَ عَلَّمَهُ النَّبيُّ ، صَلَّى اللهُ عَليهِ وَسَلَّم ، الصَّلاةَ ، ثُمَّ أَمرَهُ أَنْ يَدعُوَ بهؤُلاءِ الكَلِمَاتِ : « اللَّهُمَّ اغفِرْ لي ، وَارْحَمْني ، وَاهْدِني ، وَعَافِني ، وَارْزُقني » رواهُ مسلمٌ .

وفي رِوَايَةٍ لَهُ عَنْ طارقٍ أنَّهُ سَمِعَ النَّبيَّ ، صَلَّى اللهُ عَليهِ وَسَلَّمَ ، وَأَتاهُ رَجُلٌ ، فَقَالَ : يا رَسُولَ اللهِ . كَيْفَ أَقُولُ حِينَ أَسأَلُ رَبِّي ؟ قَالَ : « قُلْ : اللَّهُمَّ اغفِرْ لي ، وَارحَمْني ، وَعَافِني ، وَارْزُقني ، فَإنَّ هؤُلاءِ تَجْمَعُ لَكَ دُنْيَاكَ وَآخِرَتَكَ » .

1469. Hazrat Tariq bin Ushaim (R.A.A.) says that when a man embraced Islam, the Holy Prophet (S.A.W.) would (first of all) teach him how to pray (Salat) and then ask him to supplicate with these words:

Alla-hum-magh firli war ham-ni wah dini wa 'aafi-ni war zuqni

'O Allah! forgive me and have mercy on me, and guide me and let me be in peace and security, and provide for my livelihood.

(Muslim)

Imam Muslim in another version from Hazrat Tariq (R.A.A.) says: A man came to the Holy Prophet (S.A.W.) and submitted. O Messenger of Allah! what should I say when I supplicate to Allah? He (S.A.W.) answered:

Alla-hum-magh-firli war ham-ni wa aafi-ni war zuq-ni.

Allah forgive me, and have mercy on me, grant me peace, and security, and provide for my living. These sentences will help you gather all the blessings of this world and the hereafter.

١٤٧٠ – وَعَنْ عَبْدِ اللهِ بنِ عمرِو بنِ العاصِ ، رَضِيَ اللهُ عَنْهُمَا ، قَالَ : قَالَ رَسُولُ اللهِ صَلَّى اللهُ عليهِ وَسَلَّمَ : « اللَّهُمَّ مُصَرِّفَ القُلُوبِ صَرِّفْ قُلُوبَنَا عَلَى طَاعَتِكَ » رَوَاهُ مُسْلِمٌ .

1470. Hazrat Abdullah bin 'Amr bin Al-Aas (R.A.A.) relates that (once the Holy Prophet (S.A.W.) supplicated:

Alla-hum-ma mu-sar-rifal Quloo-bi sar-rif quloo-bana 'ala ta'atik.

'O Allah! Conductor of hearts, direct our hearts to Thy obedience.

(Muslim)

١٤٧١ – وَعَنْ أبي هُرَيْرَةَ ، رَضِيَ اللهُ عَنْهُ ، عَنِ النَّبِيِّ ، صَلَّى اللهُ عَليهِ وَسَلَّمَ ، قَالَ : « تَعَوَّذُوا باللهِ مِنْ جَهْدِ البَلاءِ [290] ، وَدَرَكِ الشَّقَاءِ ، وَسُوءِ القَضَاءِ ، وَشَمَاتَةِ الأعْدَاءِ » مُتَّفَقٌ عَلَيهِ .

وفي رِوَايةٍ : قَالَ سُفْيَانُ : أَشُكُّ أنِّي زِدْتُ وَاحِدَةً مِنها .

1471. Hazrat Abu Hurairah (R.A.A.) relates that the Holy Prophet (S.A.W.) said: Seek Allah's refuge against being severely tried, from misfortune and bad luck, and the humiliation by the enemies.

(Bukhari and Muslim)

١٤٧٢ – وَعَنْهُ قَالَ : كَانَ رَسُولُ اللهِ ، صَلَّى اللهُ عَليهِ وَسَلَّمَ ، يَقُولُ : اللَّهُمَّ أَصْلِحْ لي دِيني الَّذي هُوَ عِصْمَةُ أمْرِي (١) ، وَأَصْلِحْ لي

دُنْيَايَ الَّتِي فِيهَا مَعَاشِي ، وَأَصْلِحْ لِي آخِرَتِي الَّتِي فِيهَا مَعَادِي ، وَاجْعَلِ الْحَيَاةَ زِيَادَةً لِي فِي كُلِّ خَيْرٍ ، وَاجْعَلِ الْمَوْتَ رَاحَةً لِي مِنْ كُلِّ شَرٍّ » رَوَاهُ مُسْلِمٌ .

1472. **Hazrat Abu Hurairah** (R.A.A.) reports that the Holy Prophet (S.A.W.) supplicated:

Alla-hum-ma as-leh li deni-yal lazi hu-wa 'is-mato amri wa as-leh li dunya yal-lati fi-ha ma'a-shi wa as-leh li aakhi-rqti-yal-lati fiha ma'adi waj'alil haya-ta ziya-datal-li fi kul-le khai-rin waj-'alil mau-ta rahatal-li min-kul-le shar-ri.

'O' Allah! correct for me my faith which is the guard of my affairs, and make better my world where I have my livelihood; and set right my hereafter where I have to return ultimately, and make my life long in every type of virtue and make my death a comfort against all evils. *(Muslim)*

١٤٧٣ – وَعَنْ عَلِيٍّ ، رَضِيَ اللهُ عَنْهُ ، قَالَ : قَالَ لِي رَسُولُ اللهِ ، صَلَّى اللهُ عَلَيهِ وَسَلَّمَ : « قُلْ : اللَّهُمَّ اهْدِنِي ، وَسَدِّدْنِي » .

وَفِي رِوَايَةٍ : « اللَّهُمَّ إِنِّي أَسْأَلُكَ الْهُدَى ، وَالسَّدَادَ » رَوَاهُ مسلم

1473. **Hazrat Ali** (R.A.A.) relates that the Holy Prophet (S.A.W.) told him: Recite:

Alla-hum-mahdini wa sad-did-ni. Al-la-hum-ma in-ni as'alu-kal huda was-sada-da.

O Allah, guide me and keep me upright.

Another version says:

Alla-hum-ma in-ni as'alu-kal huda was-sadada.

O Allah! I beseech Thee for guidance and straight forwardness. *(Muslim)*

١٤٧٤ – وَعَنْ أَنَسٍ ، رَضِيَ اللهُ عَنْهُ ، قَالَ : كَانَ رَسُولُ اللهِ صَلَّى اللهُ عَلَيهِ وَسَلَّمَ : يَقُولُ : اللَّهُمَّ إِنِّي أَعُوذُ بِكَ مِنَ الْعَجْزِ وَالْكَسَلِ وَالْجُبْنِ وَالْهَرَمِ ، وَالْبُخْلِ ، وَأَعُوذُ بِكَ مِنْ عَذَابِ الْقَبْرِ ، وَأَعُوذُ بِكَ مِنْ فِتْنَةِ الْمَحْيَا وَالْمَمَاتِ » .

٢٩١

وَفِي رِوَايَةٍ : « وَضَلَعِ الدَّيْنِ ، وَغَلَبَةِ الرِّجَالِ » رَوَاهُ مُسْلِمٌ

1474. **Hazrat Anas** (R.A.A.) relates: that the Holy Prophet (S.A.W.) supplicated:

Alla-hum-ma in-ni a'oozo bika minal 'ajze wal kasale, Wal-jub-ne wal hara-me wal bukh-le, wa a'oozo bika min 'aza-bil qabr wa a'oozo bika min fitna-til mah-ya wal ma-mat.

O Allah! I seek Thy refuge against helplessness and lethargy, and against cowardice, (miserable) old age and miserliness; and I solicit Thy refuge against the torture of the grave and the trial of life and death).

According to another version

Wa zala'id-daine wa ghalabatir-rijal.

and from heavy indebtendness and tyranny of people. *(Muslim)*

١٤٧٥ – وَعَن أبي بكرٍ الصِّدِّيقِ ، رَضِيَ اللهُ عَنْهُ ، أنَّهُ قَالَ لِرَسولِ اللهِ ، صَلَّى اللهُ عَلَيهِ وَسَلَّمَ : عَلِّمْنِي دُعَاءً أَدْعُو بِهِ فِي صَلَاتِي ، قَالَ : « قُلْ : اللَّهُمَّ إنِّي ظَلَمْتُ نَفْسِي ظُلْماً كَثِيراً ، وَلا يَغْفِرُ الذُّنُوبَ إِلَّا أَنْتَ ، فَاغْفِرْ لِي مَغْفِرَةً مِنْ عِنْدِكَ ، وَارْحَمْنِي ، إنَّكَ أَنْتَ الْغَفُورُ الرَّحِيمُ » متَّفَقٌ عليهِ

وَفِي رِوَايَةٍ : « وَفِي بَيْتِي » وَرُوِيَ : « ظُلْماً كَثِيراً » وَرُوِيَ « كَبِيراً » بِالثَّاءِ المثلثة وبِالباءِ الموحدة ، فَيَنْبَغِي أن يُجْمَعَ بَيْنَهُمَا ، فَيُقَالُ : كَثِيراً كَبِيراً .

1475. Hazrat Abu Bakr Siddiq (R.A.A.) says: I requested the Holy Prophet (S.A.W.) to teach me some supplication which I might recite in my Salat (prayer). He (S.A.W.) told him: Supplicate.

Alla-hum-ma in-ni zalam-to nafsi zulman kasee-ra wala yagh-firuz-zuno-ba illa anta, fagh-firli magh-fira-tam min 'indi-ka, wa ram-ni in-naka antal Ghafoor-ur-Rahim.

O Allah! I have wronged myself very much, and none can forgive sins, except Thee then grant me forgiveness Thyself, and have mercy on me; indeed Thou art the Most Forgiving, Ever Merciful. *(Bukhari and Muslim)*

١٤٧٦ – وَعَن أبي موسَى ، رَضِيَ اللهُ عَنْهُ ، عَنِ النَّبيِّ ، صَلَّى اللهُ عَلَيهِ وسَلَّمَ ، أنَّهُ كَانَ يَدعُو بِهَذا الدُّعَاءِ : « اللَّهُمَّ اغْفِرْ لِي خَطِيئَتِي وَجَهْلِي ، وَإسْرَافِي فِي أَمْرِي ، وَمَا أَنْتَ أَعْلَمُ بِهِ مِنِّي ، اللَّهُمَّ اغْفِرْ لِي جِدِّي وَهزلِي ، وَخَطَئِي وَعَمْدِي ، وَكلُّ ذلِكَ عِنْدِي ، اللَّهُمَّ اغْفِرْ لِي مَا قَدَّمْتُ وَمَا أَخَّرْتُ ، وَمَا أَسْرَرْتُ وَمَا أَعْلَنْتُ ، وَمَا أَنْتَ أَعْلَمُ بِهِ مِنِّي ، أَنْتَ المُقَدِّمُ ، وَأَنْتَ المُؤَخِّرُ ، وَأَنْتَ عَلَى كُلِّ شَيْءٍ قَدِيرٌ » مُتَّفَقٌ عليه

1476. Abu Musa (R.A.A.) relates that the Holy Prophet (S.A.W.) used to supplicate thus:

Alla-hum-magh-firli Khati-ati wa jah-li wa isra-fi fee amri wama anta a'lamo bi-hi min-ni. Alla-hum-magh-firli jid-di wa haz-li wa khata'ee wa 'amdi wa kul-lo zali-ka 'indi, Alla-hum-magh-firli ma qad-damto wa ma akh-khar to wama as-rar-to wa ma a'lanto wa ma anta a'lamo bihi min-ni Antal Muqad-damo wa antal mo, akh-kharo wa anta 'ala kul-li shai-in Qadeer.

O Allah! forgive me for my mistakes, earlier or later my secret and open sins, and of such defaults which Thou knowest better than me. Thou art the First and Thou art the last, and hast power over all things.' *(Bukhari and Muslim)*

١٤٧٧ــ وَعَنْ عَائِشَةَ ، رَضِيَ اللهُ عَنْهَا ، أَنَّ النَّبِيَّ ، صَلَّى اللهُ عَلَيهِ وَسَلَّمَ ، كَانَ يَقُولُ فِي دُعَائِهِ : « اللَّهُمَّ إِنِّي أَعُوذُ بِكَ مِنْ شَرِّ مَا عَمِلْتُ وَمِنْ شَرِّ مَا لَمْ أَعْمَلْ » رَوَاهُ مُسْلِمٌ .

1477. Hazrat Ayesha (R.A.A.) says that the Holy Prophet (S.A.W.) used to supplicate thus:

Alla-hum-ma in-ni a'oozo bika min shar-ri ma 'amil-to wa min shar-ri ma lum a'a-mal.

O Allah, I seek Thy protection against the evil of that which I have done, and the evil of that which I have not done.' *(Muslim)*

١٤٧٨ــ وَعَنِ ابْنِ عُمَرَ رَضِيَ اللهُ عَنْهُمَا قَالَ : كَانَ مِنْ دُعَاءِ رَسُولِ اللهِ ، صَلَّى اللهُ عَلَيهِ وَسَلَّمَ : « اللَّهُمَّ إِنِّي أَعُوذُ بِكَ مِنْ زَوَالِ نِعْمَتِكَ ، وَتَحَوُّلِ عَافِيَتِكَ ، وَفُجَاءَةِ نِقْمَتِكَ ؛ وَجَمِيعِ سَخَطِكَ » رَوَاهُ مُسْلِمٌ .

1478. Hazrat Ibn Umar (R.A.A.) says that one of the supplications of the Holy Prophet (S.A.W.) was;

Alla-hum-ma in-ni a'oozo bika min zava-le ne 'mat-tika wa ta-haw-wule 'afi-ya-tika wa fujate niq-mate-ka wa jame' sa-kha-tik.

O Allah! I seek Thy refuge against the declining of Thy bounties and the changing of Thy security and the suddenness of Thy wrath and all Thy angers; *(Muslim)*

١٤٧٩ــ وَعَنْ زَيْدِ بْنِ أَرْقَمَ ، رَضِيَ اللهُ عَنْهُ ، قَالَ : كَانَ رَسُولُ اللهِ ، صَلَّى اللهُ عَلَيهِ وَسَلَّمَ ، يَقُولُ : « اللَّهُمَّ إِنِّي أَعُوذُ بِكَ مِنَ العَجْزِ وَالكَسَلِ ، وَالبُخْلِ وَالهَرَمِ ، وَعَذَابِ القَبْرِ ، اللَّهُمَّ آتِ نَفْسِي تَقْوَاهَا ،

وَزَكِّهَا أَنْتَ خَيْرُ مَنْ زَكَّاهَا ، أَنْتَ وَلِيُّهَا وَمَوْلاهَا ، اللَّهُمَّ إِنِّي أَعُوذُ بِكَ مِنْ عِلْمٍ لا يَنْفَعُ ، وَمِنْ قَلْبٍ لاَ يَخْشَعُ ، وَمِنْ نَفْسٍ لا تَشْبَعُ ، وَمِنْ دَعْوَةٍ لا يُسْتَجَابُ لَهَا ، رَوَاهُ مُسْلِمٌ

1479. Hazrat Zaid bin Arqam (R.A.A.) relates that the Holy Prophet (S.A.W.) would supplicate:

Alla-hum-ma in-ni a'oozo bika minal 'aj-ze wal kasali wal bukh-li wal harme wa 'aza bil Qabr, Alla-hum-ma aati nafsi taq-wa-ha wa zak-ka-ha anta khairo man zak-ka-ha, anta wali-yo-ha wa mau-laha, Alla-hum-ma in-ni a'oozo bika min il-mil-la yan-fa'o wa min Qal-bil-la yakh-sha'o wa min nafsil-la tash-ba 'o wa min d'a-watil-la yusta-jabo laha.

'O' Allah! I seek Thy protection against helplessness, lethargy and tardiness; and against miserliness and (evil effects) of old age and the torture of the grave, O' Allah! grant piety to my soul purify it as Thou art the best to purify it and Thou art its Guardian and Master. O Allah! I seek Thy protection against a knowledge which is useless, and a heart which does not fear (Allah), and a soul which is never satiated and a prayer which is not granted. *(Muslim)*

١٤٨٠ – وَعَنِ ابْنِ عَبَّاسٍ رَضِيَ اللهُ عَنْهُمَا ، أَنَّ رَسُولَ اللهِ ، صَلَّى اللهُ عَلَيْهِ وَسَلَّمَ ، كَانَ يَقُولُ : « اللَّهُمَّ لَكَ أَسْلَمْتُ ، وَبِكَ آمَنْتُ ، وَعَلَيْكَ تَوَكَّلْتُ ، وَإِلَيْكَ أَنَبْتُ وَبِكَ خَاصَمْتُ ، وَإِلَيْكَ حَاكَمْتُ. فَاغْفِرْ لِي مَاقَدَّمْتُ ، وَمَا أَخَّرْتُ ، وَمَا أَسْرَرْتُ وَمَا أَعْلَنْتُ ، أَنْتَ الْمُقَدِّمُ ، وَأَنْتَ الْمُؤَخِّرُ ، لا إِلَهَ إِلاَّ أَنْتَ » .

زَادَ بَعْضُ الرُّوَاةِ : « وَلا حَوْلَ وَلا قُوَّةَ إِلاَّ بِاللهِ » مُتَّفَقٌ عَلَيْهِ

1480. Hazrat Ibn Abbas (R.A.A.) relates that the Holy Prophet (S.A.W.) used to supplicate thus:

Alla-hum-ma laka as-lam-to wa bika aa-manto, wa'alai-ka tawak-kalto wa i'lai-ka anabto wa bika kha-sam-to wa ilai-ka ha-kam-to fagh-firli ma qad-damto wama akh-khar-to wa ma as-rar to wa ma a'-lan-to, Antal mu'qad-damo wa Antal Mu'akh-kharo la-ila-ha il-la anta. wa la haula wa la quw-wata il-la bil-lah.

'O Allah! To Thee I surrendered, in Thee I believe, in Thee I confide, and turn to Thee; with Thy help I could contend and from Thee I seek judgement. So, condone my sins which I did in the past and which I may commit in future, and sins which I did covertly and that which I did overtly. Thou art the First and

Thou art the Last. There is no god worthy of worship save Thee.

Some narrators have added. There is no strength and power except through Allah. *(Bukhari and Muslim)*

١٤٨١– وَعَنْ عَائِشَةَ ، رَضِيَ اللهُ عَنْهَا ، أَنَّ النَّبِيَّ ، صَلَّى اللهُ عَلَيه وَسَلَّم ، كَانَ يَدعو بهؤلاء الكَلِمَاتِ : « اللَّهمَّ إني أعوذُ بِكَ مِن فِتْنَةِ النَّارِ ، وعَذَابِ النَّارِ ، وَمِن شَرِّ الغِنى وَالفَقْرِ » .

رَوَاهُ أبو داودَ ، والترمذيُّ وقَالَ : حديثٌ حسَنٌ صحيحٌ ، وهذا لفظُ أبي داودَ .

1481. Hazrat Ayesha (R.A.A.) relates that the Holy Prophet (S.A.W.) used to supplicate in these words:

Alla-hum-ma in-ni a'oozo bika min fitnatin-nare wa 'aza-bin-nare wa min shar-ril ghi-na wal faqr.

'O Allah! I seek Thy protection from the trial of Hell and torment of the Hell, and from the evils of wealth and privation.

(Abu Daud and Tirmizi

Imam Tirmizi said, this is good and sound. This is the wording of *Abu Daud.*

١٤٨٢– وَعَنْ زيادِ بْنِ عِلاقَةَ عن عَمِّهِ ، وهو قُطبَةُ بنُ مالكٍ ، رَضِيَ اللهُ عَنْهُ ، قَالَ : كَانَ النَّبِيُّ ، صَلَّى اللهُ عَليهِ وَسَلَّم ، يقولُ : « اللَّهمَّ إني أعوذُ بِكَ مِن منكَرَاتِ الأخلاقِ ، وَالأعمَالِ ، وَالأهوَاءِ »

رَوَاهُ الترمذيُّ وَقَالَ : حَديثٌ حسَنٌ .

1482. Hazrat Ziad bin 'Ilaqa (R.A.A.) reports from his uncle Hazrat Qut'bah bin Malik (R.A.A.) that the Holy Prophet (S.A.W.) used to supplicate:

Alla-hum-ma in-ni a'oozo bika min mun-kara-til akh-laqe, wal a'amaal, wal ah-waa.

'O Allah, I seek Thy protection against bad manners, bad acts and sensual desires. *(Tirmizi said it is good)*

١٤٨٣– وعن شَكَلِ بنِ حُمَيْدٍ ، رَضِيَ اللهُ عَنْهُ قَالَ : قُلْتُ يا رَسولَ اللهِ : عَلِّمْني دُعَاءً . قَالَ : « قُلْ : اللَّهُمَّ إني أعُوذُ بِكَ مِنْ شَرِّ سَمْعِي ، وَمِن شَرِّ بَصَرِي ، وَمِن شَرِّ لِسَانِي ، وَمِن شَرِّ قَلْبِي ، وَمِن شَرِّ مَنِيِّي » رَوَاهُ أبو داودَ ، والترمذيُّ وقَالَ : حديثٌ حسَنٌ .

1483. Hazrat Shakal bin Humaid (R.A.A.) relates that he requested the Holy Prophet (S.A.W.) to teach him a supplication. He (S.A.W.) said, say,

Alla-hum-ma in-ni a'oozo bika min shar-re sam'ee, wa min shar-re basa-ri, wa min shar-re li-sani wa min shar-re qalbi, wa min shar-re mani'ee.

O Allah! I seek Thy protection from the evil of my hearing and from the evil of my eyes and the evil of my tongue and the evil of my heart and from the evil of my private organs.'

(Abu Daud and Tirmizi), Tirmizi said it is good.

١٤٨٤ – وَعَن أنَس ، رَضِيَ اللهُ عَنهُ ، أنَّ النَّبِيَّ ، صَلَّى اللهُ عَلَيهِ وَسَلَّم ، كَانَ يَقُولُ : « اللَّهُمَّ إنّي أعُوذُ بِكَ مِنَ البَرَص ، وَالجُنُون ، وَالجُذَام ، وَسَيّيءِ الأسْقَام » رَوَاهُ أبو داودَ بإسنادٍ صحيحٍ .

1484. Hazrat Anas bin Malik (R.A.A.) relates that the Holy Prophet (S.A.W.) used to supplicate:

Alla-hum-ma in-ni a'oozo bika minal ba-ras, wal ju-noon, wal ju-zam, wa sai-yil as-qam.

'O Allah! I seek Thy protection against the diseases of leucoderma, lunacy leprosy, and other bad diseases.

(Abu Daud with sound chains)

١٤٨٥ – وَعَن أبي هُرَيرَةَ ، رَضِيَ اللهُ عَنهُ ، قَالَ كَانَ رَسولُ اللهِ ، صَلَّى اللهُ عليهِ وسَلَّم ، يقولُ : اللَّهُمَّ إنّي أعُوذُ بِكَ مِنَ الجُوع ، فإنَّهُ بِئسَ الضَّجِيعُ ، وَأعُوذُ بِكَ من الخِيَانَةِ ، فَإنَّها بِئسَتِ البِطَانَةُ » .

رَوَاهُ أبو داودَ بإسنادٍ صحيحٍ .

1485. Hazrat Abu Hurairah (R.A.A.) says that the Holy Prophet (S.A.W.) used to supplicate:

Alla-hum-ma in-ni a'oozo bika minal ju'e, fa-in-naho bes-adh-dhaji'. wa a'oozo bika minal khiya-nate fa in-naha be' satil bita-nah .

'O Allah! I seek Thy protection against hunger as it is worst of bad fellows, and I solicit Thy protection against misappropriation for it is the worst type of bodily habit.

(Abu Daud with sound chains)

١٤٨٦ – وَعَن عليٍّ ، رَضِيَ اللهُ عَنهُ ، أنَّ مُكَاتَباً جاءَهُ ، فقَالَ : إني عجزتُ عَن كِتَابَتِي . فَأعِنِّي . قَالَ : ألا أعَلِّمُكَ كَلِماتٍ عَلَّمَنِيهِنَّ

رَسُولُ اللهِ ، صَلَّى اللهُ عليهِ وَسَلَّم ، لَو كانَ عَلَيْكَ مِثْلُ جَبَلٍ دَيْناً أَدّاهُ اللهُ عَنْكَ ؟ قُلْ :« اللَّهمَّ اكْفِني بِحَلالِكَ عَن حَرَامِكَ ، وَأَغْنِني بِفَضلِكَ عَمَّن سِوَاكَ ».

رواهُ الترمذيُّ وقَالَ : حديثٌ حَسَنٌ .

1486. Hazrat Ali (R.A.A.) relates that a slave who had settled the terms of his freedom with his master came to him and said: I am not in a position to discharge my instalment of freedom money as per agreement, so help me. Hazrat Ali (R.A.A.) said to him: 'May I not tell you the supplication which the Holy Prophet (S.A.W.) had taught me, whereby Allah will discharge your debt even if it be as heavy as a mountain. Say:

Alla-hum-mak-fini bi-hala-lika 'an hara-mika wa agh-ni-ni bi fadh-lika 'am-man siwak.

'O Allah, make your lawful (bounties) sufficient for me so as to make me independent of that which is unlawful and from Thy grace grant me a sufficiency which may make me independent of all beside Thee. (*Tirmizi* said, this is good)

١٤٨٧ـ وَعَنْ عِمْرَانَ بنِ الحُصَيْنِ ، رَضِيَ اللهُ عَنْهُما ، أَنَّ النَّبيَّ ، صَلَّى اللهُ عليهِ وَسَلَّم ، عَلَّم أَبَاهُ حُصَيْناً كَلِمَتَيْنِ يَدْعُو بهما :« اللَّهُمَّ أَلْهِمْني رُشْدِي ، وَأَعِذْني مِن شَرِّ نفسي ».

رَوَاهُ الترمذيُّ وقَالَ : حديثٌ حَسَنٌ .

1487. Hazrat Imran bin Hussain (R.A.A.) says that the Holy Prophet (S.A.W.) taught his father (Hazrat Hussain (R.A.A.) two phrases of supplication with which he used to pray:

Alla-hum-ma al-him-ni rush-di wa a'iz-ni min shar-re nafsi.

'O Allah, intute me with my guidance and protect me from the evil of causal desire. (*Tirmizi* and said it is good)

١٤٨٨ـ وَعَن أبي الفَضلِ العبَّاسِ بنِ عَبْدِ المُطَّلِبِ ، رَضِيَ اللهُ عَنْهُ ، قَالَ : قُلْتُ يا رَسولَ اللهِ : عَلِّمْني شَيْئاً أَسْأَلُهُ اللهَ تَعالى ، قال :« سَلُوا اللهَ العَافِيَةَ » فَمَكَثْتُ أَيّاماً ، ثُمَّ جِئْتُ فَقُلْتُ : يا رَسولَ اللهِ : عَلِّمْني شَيْئاً أَسْأَلُهُ اللهَ تَعالى ، قَالَ لي :« يا عَبَّاسُ يا عَمَّ رَسولِ اللهِ ، سَلُوا اللهَ العَافِيَةَ في الدُّنْيا وَالآخِرَةِ ». رَوَاهُ الترمذيُّ وقَالَ : حديثٌ حَسَنٌ صَحيحٌ .

1488. Hazrat Abu Fadl Abbas bin Abd Al-Muttalib (R.A.A.) relates: (Once) I asked the Holy Prophet (S.A.W.): O Messenger of Allah! Please teach me a prayer that I may ask from Allah: He (S.A.W.) said: Seek security *(Afiyat)* from Allah. Hazrat Abbas (R.A.A.) waited for some days and then went to him (S.A.W.) again, and once more asked: O Messenger of Allah! Tell me something which I may ask from Allah. He (S.A.W.) said to him: O Abbas, O uncle of the Messenger of Allah, beg Allah for security in this life and in the hereafter. *(Tirmizi* said it is good)

١٤٨٩ ـ وعَنْ شَهْرِ بنِ حَوشَبٍ قَالَ : قُلْتُ لأُمِّ سَلَمَةَ ، رَضِيَ اللهُ عَنْهَا ، يَاأُمَّ المؤمنينَ مَاكَانَ أكثَرُ دُعاءِ رَسُولِ الله ، صَلَّى اللهُ عَليه وَسلَّم ، إذا كَانَ عِندَكِ ؟ قَالَت : كانَ أكثَرُ دُعَائِهِ : « يَامُقَلِّبَ القُلوبِ ثبِّتْ قَلبي عَلَى دِينِكَ » رَوَاهُ الترمذيُّ ، وقَالَ حَدِيثٌ حَسَنٌ .

1489. Hazrat Shahr bin Haushab (R.A.A.) relates I asked Hazrat Umm Salamah (R.A.A.): O Ummul Momeneen! (Mother of the Muslims) what was the supplication most often made by the Holy Prophet (S.A.W.) when he (S.A.W.) used to be in your house? She said. He (S.A.W.) most often used to supplicate 'O Changer of hearts! make my heart firm in Thy faith! *(Imam Tirmizi* said it is good and sound)

١٤٩٠ ـ وعَنْ أبي الدَّرداءِ ، رَضِيَ اللهُ عَنْهُ ، قَالَ : قَالَ رَسولُ اللهِ صَلَّى اللهُ عَلَيهِ وَسلَّم : « كانَ مِن دُعاءِ دَاوُدَ ، صَلَّى اللهُ عَلَيهِ وَسَلَّم : « اللَّهُمَّ إنّي أسألُكَ حُبَّكَ ، وَحُبَّ مَن يُحِبُّكَ ، وَالعَمَلَ الذي يُبَلِّغُني حُبَّكَ ، اللَّهُمَّ اجْعَل حُبَّكَ أحَبَّ إليَّ مِن نَفْسي ، وَأَهْلي ، وَمِنَ المَاءِ البَارِدِ » رَوَاهُ الترمذيُّ وَقَالَ : حديثٌ حَسَنٌ .

1490. Hazrat Abu Darda (R.A.A.) reports that the Holy Prophet (S.A.W.) said: One of the supplications of Prophet David (P.B.U.H.) was:

Alla-hum-ma in-ni as'a luka hub-baka wa hub-ba man yuhib-buka, wal 'amal-al-lazi yu-bal-lighuni hub-bak, Allahum-maj-'al hub-baka a'hub-ba ilai-ya min nafsi wa ahli wa minal ma'el ba-rid.

'O Allah! I beg to Thee for Thy love, and the love of those who love Thee, and the act which may lead me to Thy love. 'O' Allah! make Thy love dearer to me than my soul and my family and dearer than cold water. *(Tirmizi* and said it is good)

١٤٩١ ـ وعَنْ أنَسٍ ، رَضِيَ اللهُ عَنْهُ ، قَالَ : قَالَ رَسُولُ اللهِ ، صَلَّى اللهُ عليهِ وَسَلَّمَ « ألِظُّوا بِيَاذا الجَلالِ وَالإكْرَامِ » .

رواه الترمذي وَرَوَاهُ النَّسَائِيُّ مِن رِوَايَةِ رَبِيعَةَ بنِ عامِرٍ الصَّحَابيِّ ، قَالَ الحاكِمُ : حديثٌ صحيحُ الإِسْنَادِ .

1491. Hazrat Anas (R.A.A.) relates that the Holy Prophet (S.A.W.) said: Recite frequently:

Ya-zal-jalale wal Ikram.

'O Lord of Glory and honour.' *(Tirmizi and Nasai)*

١٤٩٢ – وَعَن أبي أُمَامَةَ ، رَضِيَ اللهُ عَنهُ قَالَ : دَعَا رَسُولُ اللهِ ، صَلَّى اللهُ عَلَيهِ وَسَلَّم ، بِدُعَاءٍ كَثِيرٍ ، لَم نَحفَظْ مِنهُ شَيئاً ؛ قُلنا يارَسُولَ اللهِ دَعَوتَ بِدُعاءٍ كَثيرٍ لم نَحفَظ منهُ شَيئاً ؛ فَقَالَ : « ألا أدُلُّكُم عَلى ما يَجمَعُ ذَلكَ كُلَّهُ ؟ تَقُولُ : « اللَّهُمَّ إنِّي أسألُكَ مِن خَيرِ ما سَألَكَ مِنهُ نَبيُّكَ مُحَمَّدٌ ، صَلَّى اللهُ عَليهِ وسَلَّم ؛ وأعُوذُ بِكَ مِن شَرِّ ما استَعَاذَ مِنهُ نَبيُّكَ مُحَمَّدٌ ، صَلَّى اللهُ عَليهِ وَسَلَّم ، وَأَنتَ المُستَعَانُ ، وَعَلَيكَ البَلاغُ ؛ وَلا حَولَ وَلا قُوَّةَ إلَّا بِاللهِ » رواهُ الترمذيُّ وَقَالَ : حَديثٌ حَسَنٌ

1492. Hazrat Abu Umamah (R.A.A.) says: The Holy Prophet (S.A.W.) used to recite so many supplications that we were not able to retain them in our memories. We therefore submitted to him (S.A.W.): O Messenger of Allah! you have recited so many supplications, that we could not remember them. Then he (S.A.W.) said. May I tell you something which may comprehend all of them? say:

Alla-hum-ma in-ni as'aluka min khai-ri ma sa'laka min-hu nabi-yuka Muham-adun sal-lal-laho 'alai-he wa-sal-lam wa a'oozo bika min shar-re mast'aza min-hu nabi-yuka Muham-madun sal-lal laho 'alai-he wa-sal-lam wa antal musta'an, wa 'alai-kal ba-lagho, wala haula wala quw-wata il-la bil-lah.

'O Allah! I beg of Thee all the good things that Thy Prophet Muhammad (S.A.W.) sought from Thee, and seek Thy protection against all the evils, against which Thy Prophet Muhammad (S.A.W.) sought Thy protection. Thou art the only Helper who is asked for help and it is for Thee to accomplish our prayers. There is no strength nor power except with Allah.'

(Tirmizi, said it is good)

١٤٩٣ – وَعَنِ ابنِ مَسعُودٍ ، رَضِيَ اللهُ عَنهُ ، قَالَ : كَانَ مِن دُعَاءِ رَسُولِ اللهِ ، صَلَّى اللهُ عَلَيهِ وَسَلَّمَ : اللَّهُمَّ إنِّي أسألُكَ مُوجِبَاتِ رَحمَتِكَ ، وَعَزَائِمَ مَغفِرَتِكَ ، وَالسَّلامَةَ مِن كُلِّ إثمٍ ، وَالغَنِيمَةَ

مِن كُلِّ بِرٍ ، وَالفوزَ بِالجنَّةِ ، وَالنَّجَاةَ مِنَ النَّارِ »

رواهُ الحاكِم أبو عبدِ الله ، وقال : حديثٌ صحيحٌ على شرط مسلِم .

1493. Hazrat Ibn Mas'ud (R.A.A.) relates: One of the supplications of the Holy Prophet (S.A.W.) was:

Alla-hum-ma in-ni as'aluka moo-jibati rahmatika wa 'aza-ema magh-fi-ratika was-salama-ta min kul-le ismin, wal ghani-mata min Kul-le bir-rin, wal fauza bil Jannate wan najata minan-nar.

O Allah! I request Thee that which invokes Thy mercy, Thy forgiveness and safety against every sin and treasures of every virtue, and achievement of Paradise and deliverance from the Fire (of Hell).

(Hakim Abu Abdullah said, it is sound according to the standard of *Muslim)*

****

CHAPTER 251

VIRTUES OF SUPPLICATION FOR ABSENTEES

قالَ اللهُ تعالى : وَالَّذِينَ جاءُوا مِنْ بَعْدِهِم يَقُولُونَ : رَبَّنَا اغفِر لَنَاوَلإِخوَانِنَا الَّذِينَ سَبَقُونا بِالإِيمَانِ [الحشر : ١٠] . وقالَ تعَالى : وَاستَغفِر لِذَنبِكَ ، وَلِلمُؤمِنِينَ وَالمُؤمِنَاتِ [محمد : ١٩] . وقالَ تعالى إخباراً عَنْ إبراهِيمَ صلَّى اللهُ عليهِ وسلَّم : رَبَّنَا اغفِرْ لِي ، وَلِوَالِدَيَّ ، وَلِلمُؤمِنِينَ ، يَومَ يَقُومُ الحِسَابُ [إبراهيم : ٤١] .

Allah the Exalted has said:

333. And those who came (into the faith) after them say: Our Lord! Forgive us and our brethren who were before us in the faith. (59 : 10)

334. Ask forgiveness for thy sin and for believing men and believing women.. (47 : 19)

335. Our Lord! Forgive me and my parents and believers on the day when the account is cast. (14 : 41)

١٤٩٤ ـ وَعَن أَبِي الدَّرداءِ رَضِيَ اللهُ عَنهُ أَنَّهُ سَمِعَ رَسُولَ الله صَلَّى اللهُ عَلَيهِ وَسَلَّمَ يَقُولُ : « مَامِن عَبدٍ مُسلِمٍ يَدعُو لأَخِيهِ بِظَهرِ الغَيبِ إلاَّ قَالَ المَلَكُ وَلَكَ بِمِثلٍ » رواه مسلم

1494. Hazrat Abu Darda (R.A.A.) relates that he heard the Holy Prophet (S.A.W.) say: Whenever a Muslim prays for a brother in his absence, an angel repeates: 'May you have also like this and as much. *(Muslim)*

١٤٩٥ – وَعَنْهُ أَنَّ رَسُولَ اللهِ صَلَّى اللهُ عَلَيْهِ وَسَلَّمَ كَانَ يَقُولُ : «دَعْوَةُ المَرْءِ المُسْلِمِ لأَخِيهِ بِظَهْرِ الغَيْبِ مُسْتَجَابَةٌ، عِنْدَ رَأْسِهِ مَلَكٌ مُوَكَّلٌ كُلَّمَا دَعَا لأَخِيهِ بِخَيْرٍ قَالَ المَلَكُ المُوَكَّلُ بِهِ : آمِينَ، وَلَكَ بِمِثْلٍ» رواه مسلم

1495. Hazrat Abu Darda (R.A.A.) says that the Holy Prophet (S.A.W.) was saying: A Muslim's prayer for his brother in his absence, is granted, an angel remains present with him whenever he prays for his brother for goodness, the attendant angel says Amen! the same thing for yourself. *(Muslim)*

* * * * * * *

CHAPTER 252

SOME IMPORTANT POINTS ABOUT SUPPLICATIONS

١٤٩٦ – عَنْ أُسَامَةَ بْنِ زَيْدٍ رَضِيَ اللهُ عَنْهُمَا قَالَ : قَالَ رَسُولُ اللهِ صَلَّى اللهُ عَلَيْهِ وَسَلَّمَ : «مَنْ صُنِعَ إِلَيْهِ مَعْرُوفٌ، فَقَالَ لِفَاعِلِهِ : جَزَاكَ اللهُ خَيْراً، فَقَدْ أَبْلَغَ فِي الثَّنَاءِ»

رواه الترمذي وقَالَ : حَدِيثٌ حَسَنٌ صَحِيحٌ .

1496. Hazrat Usamah bin Zaid (R.A.A.) relates that the Holy Prophet (S.A.W.) said. A person who has received some favour from another and responds to this by saying to his benefactor: May Allah reward thee well. Then the former has adequately praised his benefactor. *(Tirmizi* and said this as sound and good)

١٤٩٧ – وَعَنْ جَابِرٍ رَضِيَ اللهُ عَنْهُ قَالَ : قَالَ رَسُولُ اللهِ صَلَّى اللهُ عَلَيْهِ وَسَلَّمَ : «لاتَدْعُوا عَلَى أَنْفُسِكُم ؛ وَلاتَدْعُوا عَلَى أَوْلادِكُم ، وَلاتَدْعُوا عَلَى أَمْوَالِكُم ، لاتُوَافِقُوا مِنَ اللهِ سَاعَةً يُسْأَلُ فِيهَا عَطَاءً ، فَيَسْتَجِيبَ لَكُم » رواه مسلم

1497. Hazrat Jabir (R.A.A.) relates that the Holy Prophet (S.A.W.) has said: Do not invoke a curse upon yourself or upon your children or upon your property, lest the moment of curse may coincide with the moment of the acceptance of supplications and your malediction might be accepted. *(Muslim)*

١٤٩٨ – وعَن أبي هُريرةَ رضيَ اللهُ عنهْ أنَ رَسولَ الله ، صلَّى اللهُ عليهِ وسلَّمَ قالَ : « أقربُ مايكُونُ العَبْدُ مِن ربِّهِ وهُوَ ساجِدٌ ، فأكثِرُوا الدُّعاءَ » رواه مسلم

1498. This Hadis has already been covered in S. No. 1428 of Chapter 243.

١٤٩٩ – وعنهُ أنَّ رسُولَ الله صلَّى اللهُ علَيْهِ وسلَّمَ قالَ : يُسْتَجابُ لأحَدِكُم مالَم يَعجَل : يقُولُ قد دَعوتُ ربِّي ، فلَم يُسْتَجبْ لي » متفق عليه

وفي رِوايَةٍ لمُسْلِمٍ : « لايزَالُ يُسْتَجابُ للعَبْدِ مالَم يدعُ بإثمٍ ، أوْ قَطيعَةِ رَحِمٍ ، مالَمْ يَسْتَعْجِلْ » قيلَ : يارَسُولَ الله ماالاستعجالُ؟ قالَ : « يقُولُ : قدْ دعوْتُ ، وقدْ دعوْتُ ، فلَم أرَ يَسْتَجيبُ لي ، فيَسْتَحْسِرُ عِندَ ذلكَ ، ويَدعُ الدُّعاءَ » .

1499. Hazrat Abu Hurairah (R.A.A.) reports that the Holy Prophet (S.A.W.) has said. Prayers of all of you are granted provided you do not get impatient and start gumbling that. I prayed to my Lord but He did not grant me. *(Bukhari and Muslim)*

A report from *Imam Muslim* says: A servant's prayer continues to be accepted, so long as he does not ask for something sinful or something that may break the ties of kinship and does not get impatient. Someone asked: O Messenger of Allah! What is meant by impatience? He (S.A.W.) answered: A supplicant saying: I have Prayed, and prayed so many times, but the same was not accepted, and thereafter he may become disappointed and give up praying.

١٥٠٠ – وعَنْ أبي أمامَةَ رَضِيَ اللهُ عَنهُ قالَ : قيلَ لِرَسُولِ اللهِ صلَّى اللهُ علَيْهِ وسَلَّمَ : أيُّ الدُّعاءِ أسْمَعُ ؟ قالَ : « جوْفَ الليْلِ الآخِرِ ، ودُبُرَ الصَّلَوَاتِ المَكتُوبَاتِ » رواه الترمذي وقالَ : حديثٌ حسنٌ .

1500. Hazrat Abu Umamah (R.A.A.) relates that the Holy Prophet (S.A.W.) was asked. Which prayer deserves most to be accepted? The Holy Prophet (S.A.W.) said: A prayer offered in the latter part of the night, and after the *Fard* (compulsory or prescribed) part of Salat (Prayer). (*Tirmizi* and said it is good)

١٥٠١– وَعَنْ عُبَادَةَ بْنِ الصَّامِتِ رَضِيَ اللهُ عَنْهُ أَنَّ رَسُولَ اللهِ صَلَّى اللهُ عَلَيْهِ وَسَلَّمَ قَالَ : « مَا عَلَى الأَرْضِ مُسْلِمٌ يَدْعُو اللهَ تَعَالَى بِدَعْوَةٍ إِلاَّ آتَاهُ اللهُ إِيَّاهَا ، أَوْ صَرَفَ عَنْهُ مِنَ السُّوءِ مِثْلَهَا ، مَا لَمْ يَدْعُ بِإِثْمٍ ، أَوْ قَطِيعَةِ رَحِمٍ » فَقَالَ رَجُلٌ مِنَ القَوْمِ : إِذاً نُكْثِرُ قَالَ : « اللهُ أَكْثَرُ »

رواه الترمذي وقَالَ : حَدِيثٌ حَسَنٌ صَحِيحٌ : وَرَوَاهُ الحَاكِمُ مِنْ رِوَايَةِ أَبِي سَعِيدٍ ، وَزَادَ فِيهِ : « أَوْ يَدَّخِرَ لَهُ مِنَ الأَجْرِ مِثْلَهَا » .

1501. Hazrat 'Ubadah bin Samit (R.A.A.) reports that the Holy Prophet (S.A.W.) said: Whenever a Muslim supplicates to Allah, the Exalted, He grants him the boon he asks for, or averts some equivalent evil from him, provided he does not ask for something sinful or something that would cut off the ties of kinship. (Hearing) this someone said: Then we shall start supplicating much. The Holy Prophet (S.A.W.) said: Allah, is more generous in fulfilling your requests. (*Tirmizi* and said it good and sound)

Hakim narrating from Hazrat Abu Sa'eed, adds: or keeps up a reward equal to his prayer in reserve for him for the Last Day.

Note: Some principles of etiquette of supplications to Allah, the Almighty are enumerated below :—

(1) First of all supplicant should refrain from unlawful, impious or forbidden sources or means of livelihood.

(2) He should only request Allah for the grant of prayers, with utmost humility and due respect to Allah, reciting His holy names, and qualities and keeping his eyes down (i.e. he should not look towards the sky.)

(3) While supplicating he should be neat and clean, having performed ablution and facing the Qibla.

(4) He should praise and eulogise Allah, the Master of Honour and Glory and recite Durud (benediction) for

the Holy Prophet (S.A.W.) both in the beginning and end of the prayer.

(5) He should raise both hands upto his shoulder with palms open facing him.

(6) He should invoke the intercession of Holy Prophet (S.A.W.) and other virtuous and pious personalities between him and Allah the Almighty.

(7) He should confess his mistakes, shortcomings and sins.

(8) He should recite those prayers which were taught us by the Holy Prophet of Islam (S.A.W.).

(9) He should repeat each prayer at least three times.

١٥٠٢ـ وعَن ابنِ عبَّاسٍ رَضِيَ اللهُ عَنهُمَا أنَّ رَسُولَ اللهِ صَلَّى اللهُ عَلَيهِ وَسَلَّمَ كَانَ يَقُولُ عِندَ الكَرْبِ : « لاإلهَ إلاَّ اللهُ العَظِيمُ الحَلِيمُ ، لاإلهَ إلاَّ اللهُ رَبُّ العَرْشِ العَظِيمِ ، لاإلهَ إلاَّ اللهُ رَبُّ السَّموَاتِ ، ورَبُّ الأرْضِ ، ورَبُّ العَرْشِ الكَرِيمِ » متفقٌ عليه .

1502. Hazrat Ibn Abbas (R.A.A.) relates that the Holy Prophet (S.A.W.) at the time of distress used to supplicate:

La-ila-ha il-lal-la-hulAzeem-ul Halim, La ila-ha il-lal-la-hu Rab-bul 'ar-shil Azeem, La ila-ha il-lal-la-hu Rab-bus Sama-wate wa rab-bul ardhe wa rab-bul 'ar-shil Karim.

There is no god except Allah, most venerable and forbearing there is no god except Allah Lord of the Exalted Throne: there is no god except Allah who is the Sustainer of heavens and the earth and the Lord of the honoured throne. *(Bukhari and Muslim)*

* * * * * * *

CHAPTER 253

THE MIRACLES OF THE PIOUS PERSONS (FRIENDS OF ALLAH) AND THEIR VIRTUES

قَالَ اللهُ تَعَالَى: أَلا إنَّ أَوْلِيَاءَ اللهِ لاخَوْفٌ عَلَيْهِمْ وَلا هُمْ يَحْزَنُونَ : الَّذِينَ آمَنُوا وَكَانُوا يَتَّقُونَ ، لَهُمُ البُشْرَى فِي الحَيَاةِ الدُّنيَا وَفِي الآخِرَةِ لاتَبْدِيلَ لِكَلِمَاتِ اللهِ ، ذلكَ هُوَ الفَوْزُ العَظِيمُ [يونس : ٦٢] .

وَقَالَ تَعَالَى : وَهُزِّي إِلَيْكِ بِجِذْعِ النَّخْلَةِ تُسَاقِطْ عَلَيْكِ رُطَباً جَنِيّاً فَكُلِي وَاشْرَبِي [مريم: ٢٥-٢٦] . وقالَ تَعَالَى : كُلَّمَا دَخَلَ عَلَيْهَا زَكَرِيَّا الْمِحْرَابَ وَجَدَ عِنْدَهَا رِزْقاً قَالَ : يَامَرْيَمُ أَنَّى لَكِ هَذَا ؟ قَالَتْ : هُوَ مِنْ عِنْدِ اللهِ ، إِنَّ اللهَ يَرْزُقُ مَنْ يَشَاءُ بِغَيْرِ حِسَابٍ [آل عمران : ٣٧] . وقالَ تَعَالَى : وَإِذِ اعْتَزَلْتُمُوهُمْ وَمَا يَعْبُدُونَ إِلاَّ اللهَ ، فَأْوُوا إِلَى الْكَهْفِ يَنْشُرْ لَكُمْ رَبُّكُمْ مِنْ رَحْمَتِهِ ، وَيُهَيِّىءْ لَكُمْ مِنْ أَمْرِكُمْ مِرْفَقاً ، وَتَرَى الشَّمْسَ إِذَا طَلَعَتْ تَزَاوَرُ عَنْ كَهْفِهِمْ ذَاتَ الْيَمِينِ ، وَإِذَا غَرَبَتْ تَقْرِضُهُمْ ذَاتَ الشِّمَالِ [الكهف : ١٦-١٧].

Allah the Exalted, has said:

336. Lo! Verily the friends of Allah are those on whom fear (cometh) not, nor do they grieve. Those who believe and keep their duty to Allah, theirs are good tidings in the life of the world and in the Hereafter — There is no changing the words of Allah — that is the Supreme Triumph. (10 : 63—65)

337. And shake the trunk of the palm tree towards thee, thou wilt cause ripe dates to fall upon thee. So eat and drink and be consoled. (19 : 25--26)

338. Whenever Zachariah went into the sanctuary, where she was, he found that she had food. He said: O Mary! Whence cometh unto thee this (food)? She answered: It is from Allah, giveth without stint to whom He will. (3 : 37)

339. And When ye withdraw from them and that which they worship except Allah, then seek refuge in the cave: your Lord will spread for you of His mercy and will prepare for you a pillow in your plight. And thou mightest have seen the sun, when it rose, move away from their cave to the right, and when it set, go past them on the left, and they were in the cleft thereof. (18 : 16—17)

١٥٠٣– وَعَنْ أَبِي مُحَمَّدٍ عَبْدِ الرَّحْمَنِ بْنِ أَبِي بَكْرٍ الصِّدِّيقِ رَضِيَ اللهُ عَنْهُمَا أَنَّ أَصْحَابَ الصُّفَّةِ كَانُوا أُنَاساً فُقَرَاءَ وَأَنَّ النَّبِيَّ صَلَّى اللهُ عَلَيْهِ وَسَلَّمَ قَالَ : مَرَّةً «مَنْ كَانَ عِنْدَهُ طَعَامُ اثْنَيْنِ ، فَلْيَذْهَبْ

بِثَالِثٍ، وَمَنْ كَانَ عِنْدَهُ طَعَامُ أَرْبَعَةٍ، فَلْيَذْهَبْ بِخَامِسٍ بِسَادِسٍ » أَوْ كَمَا قَالَ. وأنَّ أَبَا بَكْرٍ رَضِيَ اللهُ عَنْهُ جَاءَ بِثَلَاثَةٍ. وَانْطَلَقَ النَّبِيُّ صَلَّى اللهُ عَلَيْهِ وَسَلَّمَ بِعَشَرَةٍ. وَأَنَّ أَبَا بَكْرٍ تَعَشَّى عِنْدَ النَّبِيِّ صَلَّى اللهُ عَلَيْهِ وَسَلَّمَ. ثُمَّ لَبِثَ حَتَّى صَلَّى العِشَاءَ. ثُمَّ رَجَعَ، فَجَاءَ بَعْدَ مَامَضَى مِنَ اللَّيْلِ مَاشَاءَ اللهُ. قَالَتْ لَهُ امْرَأَتُهُ: مَاحَبَسَكَ عَنْ أَضْيَافِكَ؟ قَالَ: أَوَ مَاعَشَّيْتِهِمْ؟ قَالَتْ: أَبَوْا حَتَّى تَجِيءَ وَقَدْ عَرَضُوا عَلَيْهِمْ قَالَ: فَذَهَبْتُ أَنَا. فَاخْتَبَأْتُ. فَقَالَ: يَا غُنْثَرُ. فَجَدَّعَ وَسَبَّ. وَقَالَ: كُلُوا لاهَنِيئاً. وَاللهِ لاأَطْعَمُهُ أَبَداً. قَالَ: وَايْمُ اللهِ مَاكُنَّا نَأْخُذُ مِنْ لُقْمَةٍ إِلاَّ رَبَا مِنْ أَسْفَلِهَا أَكْثَرُ مِنْهَا حَتَّى شَبِعُوا. وَصَارَتْ أَكْثَرَ مِمَّا كَانَتْ قَبْلَ ذَلِكَ. فَنَظَرَ إِلَيْهَا أَبُو بَكْرٍ فَقَالَ لامْرَأَتِهِ: يَا أُخْتَ بَنِي فِرَاسٍ مَاهَذَا؟ قَالَتْ: لا وَقُرَّةِ عَيْنِي لَهِيَ الآنَ أَكْثَرُ مِنْهَا قَبْلَ ذَلِكَ بِثَلَاثِ مَرَّاتٍ! فَأَكَلَ مِنْهَا أَبُو بَكْرٍ وَقَالَ: إِنَّمَا كَانَ ذَلِكَ مِنَ الشَّيْطَانِ يَعْنِي يَمِينَهُ. ثُمَّ أَكَلَ مِنْهَا لُقْمَةً. ثُمَّ حَمَلَهَا إِلَى النَّبِيِّ صَلَّى اللهُ عَلَيْهِ وَسَلَّمَ فَأَصْبَحَتْ عِنْدَهُ. وَكَانَ بَيْنَنَا وَبَيْنَ قَوْمٍ عَهْدٌ. فَمَضَى الأَجَلُ. فَتَفَرَّقْنَا اثْنَي عَشَرَ رَجُلاً. مَعَ كُلِّ رَجُلٍ مِنْهُمْ أُنَاسٌ. اللهُ أَعْلَمُ كَمْ مَعَ كُلِّ رَجُلٍ. فَأَكَلُوا مِنْهَا أَجْمَعُونَ

وفي رِوَايَةٍ: فَحَلَفَ أَبُوبَكْرٍ لايَطْعَمُهُ. فَحَلَفَتِ المَرْأَةُ لاتَطْعَمُهُ. فَحَلَفَ الضَّيْفُ – أو الأَضْيَافُ – أَنْ لايَطْعَمَهُ، أَوْ يَطْعَمُوهُ حَتَّى يَطْعَمَهُ. فَقَالَ أَبُو بَكْرٍ: هَذِهِ مِنَ الشَّيْطَانِ! فَدَعَا بِالطَّعَامِ. فَأَكَلَ وَأَكَلُوا. فَجَعَلُوا لايَرْفَعُونَ لُقْمَةً إِلاَّ رَبَتْ مِنْ أَسْفَلِهَا أَكْثَرَ مِنْهَا. فَقَالَ: يَا أُخْتَ بَنِي فِرَاسٍ، مَا هَذَا؟ فَقَالَتْ: وَقُرَّةِ عَيْنِي إِنَّهَا الآنَ لأَكْثَرُ مِنْهَا قَبْلَ أَنْ نَأْكُلَ. فَأَكَلُوا. وَبَعَثَ بِهَا إِلَى النَّبِيِّ صَلَّى اللهُ عَلَيْهِ وَسَلَّمَ فَذَكَرَ أَنَّهُ أَكَلَ مِنْهَا.

وفي رِوَايَةٍ: إِنَّ أَبَا بَكْرٍ قَالَ لِعَبْدِ الرَّحْمَنِ: دُونَكَ أَضْيَافَكَ. فَإِنِّي

مُنْطَلِقٌ إِلَى النَّبِيِّ صَلَّى اللهُ عَلَيْهِ وَسَلَّمَ. فَافْرُغْ مِنْ قِرَاهُمْ قَبْلَ أَنْ
أَجِيءَ. فَانْطَلَقَ عَبْدُ الرَّحْمَنِ. فَأَتَاهُم بِمَا عِنْدَهُ. فَقَالَ: اطْعَمُوا،
فَقَالُوا: أَيْنَ رَبُّ مَنْزِلِنَا؟ قَالَ: اطْعَمُوا. قَالُوا: مَا نَحْنُ بِآكِلِينَ
حَتَّى يَجِيءَ رَبُّ مَنْزِلِنَا. قَالَ: اقْبَلُوا عَنَّا قِرَاكُم، فَإِنَّهُ إِنْ جَاءَ وَلَمْ
تَطْعَمُوا، لَنَلْقَيَنَّ مِنْه فَأَبَوْا. فَعَرَفْتُ أَنَّه يَجِدُ عَلَيَّ، فَلَمَّا جَاءَ
تَنَحَّيْتُ عَنْهُ، فَقَالَ: مَاصَنَعْتُم؟ فَأَخْبَرُوه. فَقَالَ: يَاعَبْدَ الرَّحْمَنِ
فَسَكَتُّ، ثُمَّ قَالَ: يَاعَبْدَ الرَّحْمَنِ. فَسَكَتُّ، فَقَالَ: يَاغُنْثَرُ
أَقْسَمْتُ عَلَيْكَ إِنْ كُنْتَ تَسْمَعُ صَوْتِي لَمَّا جِئْتَ! فَخَرَجْتُ، فَقُلْتُ:
سَلْ أَضْيَافَكَ. فَقَالُوا: صَدَقَ. أَتَانَا بِهِ. فَقَالَ: إِنَّمَا انْتَظَرْتُمُونِي وَاللهِ
لا أَطْعَمُهُ اللَّيْلَةَ. فَقَالَ الآخَرُونَ: وَاللهِ لانَطْعَمُه حَتَّى تَطْعَمَه. فَقَالَ:
وَيْلَكُم مَالَكُم لاتَقْبَلُونَ عَنَّا قِرَاكُم؟ هَاتِ طَعَامَكَ، فَجَاءَ بِهِ،
فَوَضَعَ يَدَه، فَقَالَ: بِسْمِ اللهِ. الأُولى مِنَ الشَّيْطَانِ، فَأَكَلَ وَأَكَلُوا.

متفق عليه

1503. Hazrat Abu Muhammad Abdur Rahman bin Abu Bakr Siddiq (R.A.A.) says that *Ashab Suffa* (or the Companions of the platform) were poor people. Once the Holy Prophet (S.A.W.) said: A person who had food for two persons should take with him a third person (from the *Ashab Suffa)* and one who has food for four persons should take with him fifth or sixth person (i.e. from this group and feed them). Accordingly Hazrat Abu Bakr (R.A.A.) took three persons and the Holy Prophet (S.A.W.) took with him ten. But Hazrat Abu Bakr (R.A.A.) took his meal along with the Holy Prophet (S.A.W.) and remained with him till after the *Isha Salat* (night Prayer) and when Hazrat Abu Bakr (R.A.A.) returned home, a part of the night, what Allah willed, had passed and his wife asked him: What detained you behind your guests? He said: Have you not given them food? She answered: They refused to eat till you come back, although it was presented to them. Abdur Rahman (R.A.A.) continues: I went and hid myself out of fear. Hazrat Abu Bakr (R.A.A.) called me in a stern and angry tone and said: Now you eat, and the fare may not prove sufficient for you, by Allah, I shall never eat. (The narrator continues) We started eating and it so happened that for every morsel that we took (from the top) more than its equal would rise from the bottom till every one of us had eaten his fill and the food had increased in quantity more than it was in the beginning. Hazrat Abu Bakr (R.A.A.) looked at the food and said (in amazement) to his wife: O Sister of Bani Firas! What is this? She said: the coolness of my eye! It (the food) has now increased three times of that which it was in the beginning. Hazrat Abu Bakr (R.A.A.) also partook of the food and said about his earlier vow that it was prompted by Satan and then carried it to the Holy Prophet (S.A.W.) where it remained till the morning. At that time the period of truce made with a tribe had expired, and accordingly twelve of us had been appointed as scouts (to watch the movement of the enemy) and each scout had some fixed number of men under him; Allah alone knows as to how many such men were there with these scouts. All of them ate food (to their full satisfaction.)

Another version says: Hazrat Abu Bakr (R.A.A.) had vowed that he would not eat that food, and his wife also vowed that she too would not eat anything, (seeing this) the guests also swore that they would not eat anything, unless he (Abu Bakr R.A.A.) ate, then only they would eat. Then Hazrat Abu Bakr (R.A.A.) said: My oath was instigated by Satan and called for the food. He (Hazrat Abu Bakr R.A.A.) partook the meal along with the guests. When these persons took a morsel, there increased from under more food than the morsel in hand. Hazrat Abu Bakr (R.A.A.) said to his wife. O Sister of Bani Firas! What is this going on? She answered: O coolness of my eye! The food has now increased more than it was when we started eating. Thus they all ate and sent the rest to the Holy Prophet (S.A.W.). It is said that he (S.A.W.) also ate out of it.

Yet another version says: Hazrat Abu Bakr (R.A.A.) said to (his son) Hazrat Abdur Rahman (R.A.A.), as I am going to the Holy Prophet (S.A.W.) you should look after the guests and feed them well before I return from the Holy Prophet (S.A.W.). Accordingly (in the evening) Hazrat Abdur Rahman (R.A.A.) placed before the guests whatever was available with him, and asked them to eat. They asked. Where is the master of the house? He, however, urged them to eat. The guests said: We shall not eat till the master of the house returns. Hazrat Abdur Rahman (R.A.A.) pleaded: please accept our hospitality (and eat the food) for, when he comes and finds that you have not eaten, he will be angry. But the guests remained firm in their refusal. Hazrat Abdur Rahman (R.A.A.) says: I thought that Hazrat Abu Bakr (R.A.A.) would be angry, and as such when he came I went aside. Immediately after his arrival he asked: What you did (with the guests)? He was informed (by the family members) of what had happened. Hazrat Abu Bakr (R.A.A.) called out: O Abdur Rahman, but I kept quiet. He called me once again, Abdur Rahman, but I again kept quiet. He then called out: O stupid fellow, I put you under oath that if you are hearing me then come forth. So I had to come out and said: Just enquire from your guests. They said: It is true. He did bring the food to us. Then Hazrat Abu Bakr (R.A.A.) said.

You unnecessarily waited for me, but by Allah I am not going to take food tonight. The guests said: By Allah we shall also not eat, unless you also join us. Hazrat Abu Bakr (R.A.A.) then said. Very bad of you! Why you are not accepting our hospitality? Take out the food. Accordingly the food was brought and Hazrat Abu Bakr (R.A.A.) reciting *Bismillah* (with the name of Allah) said: My oath was incited by Satan and put forth his hand (on the food), and he and the guests ate the food. *(Bukhari and Muslim)*

١٥٠٤ – وَعَنْ أَبِي هُرَيْرَةَ رَضِيَ اللهُ عَنْهُ قَالَ : قَالَ رَسُولُ اللهِ صَلَّى اللهُ عَلَيْهِ وَسَلَّمَ : « لَقَدْ كَانَ فِيمَا قَبْلَكُمْ مِنَ الأُمَمِ نَاسٌ مُحَدَّثُونَ . فَإِنْ يَكُ فِي أُمَّتِي أَحَدٌ . فَإِنَّهُ عُمَرُ » رواه البخاري ، ورواه مسلم من روايةِ عائشةَ .

1504. Hazrat Abu Hurairah (R.A.A.) relates that the Holy Prophet (S.A.W.) said: There used to be among the people before you '*Muhaddasoon*' (men who were the recepients of indication from Allah). If there be one such person from among my people, it would be 'Umar (R.A.A.). *(Bukhari)*

Imam Muslim has cited this on the authority of Hazrat Ayesha Siddiqa (R.A.A.).

١٥٠٥ – وَعَنْ جَابِرِ بْنِ سَمُرَةَ ، رَضِيَ اللهُ عَنْهُمَا . قَالَ : شَكَا أَهْلُ الكُوفَةِ سَعْداً . يَعْنِي : ابْنَ أَبِي وَقَّاصٍ ، رَضِيَ اللهُ عَنْهُ ، إِلَى عُمَرَ بْنِ الخَطَّابِ ، رَضِيَ اللهُ عَنْهُ . فَعَزَلَهُ وَاسْتَعْمَلَ عَلَيْهِمْ عَمَّاراً . فَشَكَوْا حَتَّى ذَكَرُوا أَنَّهُ لا يُحْسِنُ يُصَلِّي . فَأَرْسَلَ إِلَيْهِ . فَقَالَ : يَا أَبَا إِسْحَاقَ ، إِنَّ هٰؤُلاءِ يَزْعُمُونَ أَنَّكَ لا تُحْسِنُ تُصَلِّي . فَقَالَ : أَمَّا أَنَا وَاللهِ فَإِنِّي كُنْتُ أُصَلِّي بِهِمْ صَلاةَ رَسُولِ اللهِ ، صَلَّى اللهُ عَلَيْهِ وَسَلَّمَ لا أَخْرِمُ عَنْهَا أُصَلِّي صَلاةَ العِشَاءِ فَأَرْكُدُ فِي الأُولَيَيْنِ ، وَأُخِفُّ فِي الأُخْرَيَيْنِ ، قَالَ : ذَلِكَ الظَّنُّ بِكَ يَا أَبَا إِسْحَاقَ ، وَأَرْسَلَ مَعَهُ رَجُلاً – أَوْ رِجَالاً – إِلَى الكُوفَةِ يَسْأَلُ عَنْهُ أَهْلَ الكُوفَةِ ، فَلَمْ يَدَعْ مَسْجِداً إِلاَّ سَأَلَ عَنْهُ . وَيُثْنُونَ مَعْرُوفاً ، حَتَّى دَخَلَ مَسْجِداً لِبَنِي عَبْسٍ ، فَقَامَ رَجُلٌ مِنْهُمْ ، يُقَالُ لَهُ أُسَامَةُ بْنُ قَتَادَةَ . يُكَنَّى أَبَا سَعْدَةَ . فَقَالَ : أَمَا

إذْ نَشَدْتَنَا فَإنَّ سَعْداً كَانَ لايَسِيرُ بِالسَّرِيَّةِ وَلا يَقْسِمُ بِالسَّوِيَّةِ . وَلا يَعْدِلُ في القَضِيَّةِ . قَالَ سَعْدٌ : أمَا وَاللهِ لأدْعُوَنَّ بِثَلاثٍ : اللَّهُمَّ إنْ كَانَ عَبْدُكَ هذا كَاذِباً ، قَامَ رِيَاءً ، وَسُمْعَةً ، فَأطِلْ عُمُرَهُ ، وَأطِلْ فَقْرَهُ ، وَعَرِّضْهُ لِلفِتَنِ . وَكَانَ بَعْدَ ذلكَ إذا سُئِلَ يَقُولُ : شَيْخٌ كَبِيرٌ مَفْتُونٌ ، أصَابَتْنِي دَعْوَةُ سَعْدٍ .

قَالَ عَبْدُ المَلِكِ بْنُ عُمَيْرٍ الرَّاوِي عَنْ جَابِرِ بْنِ سَمُرَةَ : فَأنَا رَأيْتُهُ بَعْدُ قَدْ سَقَطَ حَاجِبَاهُ عَلَى عَيْنَيْهِ مِنَ الكِبَرِ ، وَإنَّهُ لَيَتَعَرَّضُ لِلجَوَارِي في الطُّرُقِ فَيَغْمِزُهُنَّ . متفقٌ عليه .

1505. Hazrat Jabir bin Samurah (R.A.A.) relates that the people of Kufa complained against Hazrat Sa'd bin Abi Waqaas (R.A.A.) to Hazrat 'Umar Farooq (R.A.A.) who expelled Sa'd and appointed Hazrat 'Ammar (R.A.A.) as Amir of Kufa. In their complaint they alleged that he (Sa'd) did not even lead them properly in the prayer. Hazrat Umar (R.A.A.) accordingly summoned Hazrat Sa'd (R.A.A.) to Madina and said to him: O Abu Ishaq! (this is Kunniyat or adopted name) the people of Kufa complain that you do not conduct even the prayers properly. Hazrat Sa'd (R.A.A.) replied: By Allah, I conducted the Salat on the pattern of the Holy Prophet (S.A.W.) without any change in the least. I lead them in the night (Isha) prayer. In this prayer I made the first two raka'ats long and the last two raka'ats short.' Hazrat 'Umar (R.A.A.) said: O Abu Ishaq: This is what I also thought about you; and (thereafter) Hazrat 'Umar sent with him a man (or some men) to Kufa to investigate about the matter from the people of the place. The case was followed up in every mosque and all the people praised him for his good manners and virtues; except in the case of the mosque of Bani 'Abs where a man named Usamah ibn Qatadah whose adopted name was Abu Sa'd, said: Since we have been called upon to say, then I may tell that Hazrat Sa'd (R.A.A.) did not accompany an expedition, nor did he distribute the booty equally and did not do justice in disputes. Hearing this Hazrat Sa'd said: By God! I shall also make three curses (for this man). Hazrat Sa'd, said: O Allah, if this servant of Thine has lied and has stood up seeking to show off and gain notoriety, then do Thou prolong his life and lengthen his poverty, and afflict him with mischief. After this, when this man used to be asked about his condition, he would lament and say. I am a very old man suffering from trials and troubles; I am caught by the curse of Hazrat Sa'd (R.A.A.). About Usamah, the narrator relates from Jabir bin Samurah: I saw this man when his eyebrows, due to extreme old age, had fallen over his eyes, and he roamed the roads cajoling, cuddling and teasing the girls. *(Bukhari and Muslim)*

Note:— Hazrat Sa'd bin Abi Waqqas (R.A.A.) is one of the *Ashra-i-Mubashara* i.e. one of the most virtuous and fortunate persons who, on account of his virtuous deeds, had been foretold for the paradise, while still alive in this world. Anecdotes of his services for Islam and Muslims, sincerity, honesty, fair play, justice and his devotion to the Holy Prophet (S.A.W.) are well-known. The Holy Prophet (S.A.W.) had specially prayed to Allah to make him a (Mustajab-ud-dawat) i.e. one whose supplications may be accepted by Allah, the Almighty. As such the incidents mentioned in the above tradition is the result of his supplications which were granted by Allah.

١٥٠٦ – وَعَنْ عُرْوَةَ بنِ الزُّبَيْرِ أنَّ سَعِيدَ بْنَ زَيْدِ بْنِ عَمْرِو بْنِ نُفَيْلٍ ، رَضِيَ اللهُ عَنْهُ خَاصَمَتْهُ أَرْوَى بِنْتُ أوْسٍ إلى مَرْوَانَ بْنِ الحَكَمِ ، وَادَّعَتْ أنَّهُ أخَذَ شَيْئاً مِنْ أرْضِهَا ، فَقَالَ سَعِيدٌ : أنَا كُنْتُ آخُذُ مِنْ أرْضِهَا شَيْئاً بَعْدَ الَّذِي سَمِعْتُ مِنْ رَسُولِ اللهِ صَلَّى اللهُ عَلَيْهِ وَسَلَّمَ !؟ قَالَ : مَاذا سَمِعْتَ مِنْ رَسُولِ اللهِ صَلَّى اللهُ عَلَيْهِ وَسَلَّمَ ؟ قَالَ : سَمِعْتُ رَسُولَ اللهِ صَلَّى اللهُ عَلَيْهِ وَسَلَّمَ يَقُولُ : « مَنْ أخَذَ شِبْراً مِنَ الأرْضِ ظُلْماً ، طُوِّقَهُ إلى سَبْعِ أرَضِينَ » فَقَالَ لَهُ مَرْوَانُ : لاأسْألُكَ بَيِّنَةً بَعْدَ هذا ، فَقَالَ سَعِيدٌ : اللَّهُمَّ إنْ كانَتْ كاذِبَةً ، فَأعْمِ بَصَرَهَا ، وَاقْتُلْهَا في أرْضِهَا ، قَالَ : فَمَا مَاتَتْ حَتَّى ذَهَبَ بَصَرُهَا ، وَبَيْنَمَا هِيَ تَمْشِي في أرْضِهَا إذْ وَقَعَتْ في حُفْرَةٍ فَمَاتَتْ . متفقٌ عليه .

وفي روايةٍ لمسلمٍ عَنْ مُحَمَّدِ بْنِ زَيْدِ بْنِ عَبْدِ اللهِ بْنِ عُمَرَ بِمَعْنَاهُ وَأنَّهُ رَآهَا عَمْيَاءَ تَلْتَمِسُ الجُدُرَ تَقُولُ : أصَابَتْنِي دَعْوَةُ سَعِيدٍ ، وَأنَّهَا مَرَّتْ عَلَى بِئْرٍ في الدَّارِ الَّتي خَاصَمَتْهُ فيها ، فَوَقَعَتْ فيها ، فَكَانَتْ قَبْرَهَا .

1506. **Hazrat 'Urwah bin Zubair** (R.A.A.) relates that (a woman named) Arwa bint Aus had a dispute with Hazrat Sa'eed bin Zaid (R.A.A.) on a piece of land, and accordingly filed a suit before Marwan bin Hakam, Governor of Madina, alleging that Hazrat Sa'eed bin Zaid had encroached upon a part of her land. Hazrat Sa'eed replied: How could I take her land when I had heard the admonition of the Holy Prophet (S.A.W.)? Marwan asked him as to what he had heard from the Holy Prophet (S.A.W.)? He answered : I heard the Holy Prophet (S.A.W.) say: A person who usurps a hand's breadth of land from anybody unjustly, shall have to wear a necklace made of such seven earths! Marwan said to Hazrat Sa'eed (R.A.A.) : In view of this authority I shall not ask you for any (other) proof. Hazrat Sa'eed then supplicated: Allah! if this woman is a liar then Thou make her blind and cause her death in her very land. It is said that she became blind before her death, and was killed by falling into a pit while she was walking on this land, (about which she had made a false claim) and that pit became her grave. *(Bukhari and Muslim)*

Another version of Muslim narrated by Muhammad bin Zaid bin Abdullah bin 'Umar, (R.A.A.) says that this narrator saw her blind and groping her way along the walls, and used to say: I am afflicted with the curse of (Hazrat) Sa'eed (R.A.A.). One day while she was walking in this way on the disputed land of this house she fell into a well which ultimately became her grave.

١٥٠٧ – وَعَنْ جَابِرِ بْنِ عَبْدِ اللهِ رَضِيَ اللهُ عَنْهُمَا قَالَ : لَمَّا حَضَرَتْ أُحُدٌ دَعَانِي أَبِي مِنَ اللَّيْلِ فَقَالَ : مَا أُرَانِي إِلَّا مَقْتُولاً فِي أَوَّلِ مَنْ يُقْتَلُ مِنْ أَصْحَابِ النَّبِيِّ صَلَّى اللهُ عليهِ وسلَّم ، وَإِنِّي لاَأَتْرُكُ بَعْدِي أَعَزَّ عَلَيَّ مِنْكَ غَيْرَ نَفْسِ رَسُولِ اللهِ ، صَلَّى اللهُ عَلَيْهِ وَسَلَّمَ ، وَإِنَّ عَلَيَّ دَيْناً فَاقْضِ ،وَاسْتَوْصِ بِأَخَوَاتِكَ خَيْراً : فَأَصْبَحْنَا ، فَكَانَ أَوَّلَ قَتِيلٍ ؛ وَدَفَنْتُ مَعَهُ آخَرَ فِي قَبْرِهِ ، ثُمَّ لَمْ تَطِبْ نَفْسِي أَنْ أَتْرُكَهُ مَعَ آخَرَ ، فَاسْتَخْرَجْتُهُ بَعْدَ سِتَّةِ أَشْهُرٍ ،فَإِذَا هُوَ كَيَوْمَ وَضَعْتُهُ غَيْرَ أُذُنِهِ ، فَجَعَلْتُهُ فِي قَبْرٍ عَلَى حِدَةٍ .رواه البخاري .

1507. Hazrat Jabir bin Abdullah (R.A.A.) says: On the eve of the Battle of Uhud my father sent for me at night (before the battle) and said: I think that I might be the first of all the companions of the Holy Prophet (S.A.W.) to be martyred; and since after the Holy Prophet (S.A.W.) you are the dearest to me (I request you) to discharge my debt and do good to your sisters. Next morning when the battle started, he was indeed among the first to be martyred; (and in accordance with the instructions of the Holy Prophet (S.A.W.) I buried him along with another in the same grave. But I did not like that he should lie (in the grave) with somebody else. Therefore I got his body exhumed after six months and found his body in the same condition in which he was buried when martyred, except for a scar in his ear. His body was then buried in a separate grave. *(Bukhari)*

١٥٠٨– وَعَنْ أَنَسٍ رَضِيَ اللهُ عَنْهُ أَنَّ رَجُلَيْنِ مِنْ أَصْحَابِ النَّبِيِّ صَلَّى اللهُ عَلَيْهِ وَسَلَّمَ خَرَجَا مِنْ عِنْدِ النَّبِيِّ صَلَّى اللهُ عَلَيْهِ وسَلَّمَ فِي لَيْلَةٍ مُظْلِمَةٍ وَمَعَهُمَا مِثْلُ المِصْبَاحَيْنِ بيْنَ أَيدِيهِمَا . فَلَمَّا افتَرَقَا ، صَارَ مَعَ كلٍّ وَاحِدٍ مِنهما وَاحِدٌ حَتى أَتَى أَهْلَهُ .

رواه البخاري مِنْ طرُقٍ ؛ وَفِي بعْضِها أَنَّ الرَّجُلَيْنِ أُسَيْدُ بنُ حُضيرٍ ؛ وَعَبَّادُ بنُ بِشرٍ رَضِيَ اللهُ عَنْهُمَا .

1508. Hazrat Anas (R.A.A.) says that two companions of the Holy Prophet (S.A.W.) left the company of the Holy Prophet (S.A.W.) on a pitch dark night and it appeared as if there were two lighted objects like lamps in their hands; and when they separated, each of them had one lamp (in his hand) till they reached their homes. *(Bukhari)*

Imam Bukhari has cited this with various chnins, on some version it is said of these two, one was Hazrat Usaid bin Hudhair (R.A.A.) and the other was Hazrat 'Abbad bin Bish'r.

Yet another version of Bukhari says that the two august companions had over-stayed with the Holy Prophet (S.A.W.) and left for their homes very late in the night both of them had a stick in hand. As it was dark, one of the sticks got alight making the passage clear; and when they separated, the other stick also got lighted up, and thus both of them reached their homes in the light of their sticks.

١٥٠٩ – وَعَنْ أَبِي هُرَيْرَةَ ، رَضِيَ اللهُ عَنْهُ ، قَالَ : بَعَثَ رَسُولُ اللهِ صَلَّى اللهُ عليهِ وسلَّمَ عَشرَةَ رَهْطٍ : عَيْناً سَرِيَّةً ، وَأَمَّرَ عَلَيْهِم عَاصِمَ بنَ ثابِتٍ الأنصَارِيَّ ، رَضِيَ اللهُ عَنْهُ . فَانْطَلَقُوا حَتَّى إذا كَانُوا بِالهَدْأَةِ ، بَيْنَ عُسْفَانَ وَمَكَّةَ ، ذُكِرُوا لِحَيٍّ مِنْ هُذَيْلٍ يُقَالُ لَهُمْ : بَنُو لِحْيَانَ . فَنَفَرُوا لَهُمْ بِقَرِيبٍ مِنْ مِائَةِ رَجُلٍ رَامٍ . فَاقْتَصُّوا آثَارَهُمْ . فَلَمَّا أَحَسَّ بِهِمْ عَاصِمٌ وَأَصحَابُهُ ، لَجَؤُوا إلى مَوْضِعٍ ، فَأَحَاطَ بِهِمُ القَوْمُ . فَقَالُوا انزِلوا ، فَأَعْطُوا بِأَيْدِيكُم وَلَكُمُ العَهْدُ وَالمِيثَاقُ أَنْ لانَقتُلَ مِنكُم أَحَداً . فَقَالَ عَاصِمُ بنُ ثَابِتٍ : أَيُّهَا القَوْمُ أَمَّا أَنَا ، فَلا أَنزِلُ عَلى ذِمَّةِ

كَافِرٍ : اللَّهُمَّ أَخْبِرْ عَنَّا نَبِيَّكَ . صَلَّى اللهُ عَلَيْهِ وَسَلَّمَ ؛ فَرَمَوْهُمْ بِالنَّبْلِ فَقَتَلُوا عَاصِماً . وَنَزَلَ إِلَيْهِمْ ثَلاثَةُ نَفَرٍ عَلَى العَهْدِ وَالمِيثَاقِ ، مِنْهُمْ خُبَيْبٌ . وَزَيْدُ بْنُ الدَّثِنَةِ وَرَجُلٌ آخَرُ . فَلَمَّا اسْتَمْكَنُوا مِنْهُمْ أَطْلَقُوا أَوْتَارَ قِسِيِّهِمْ . فَرَبَطُوهُمْ بِهَا . قَالَ الرَّجُلُ الثَّالِثُ : هذا أَوَّلُ الغَدْرِ واللهِ لاأَصْحَبُكُمْ إِنَّ لِي بِهؤُلاءِ أُسْوَةً ، يُرِيدُ القَتْلَى . فَجَرُّوهُ وَعَالَجُوهُ . فَأَبَى أَنْ يَصْحَبَهُمْ . فَقَتَلُوهُ . وَانْطَلَقُوا بِخُبَيْبٍ ، وَزَيْدِ بْنِ الدَّثِنَةِ . حَتَّى بَاعُوهُمَا بِمَكَّةَ بَعْدَ وَقْعَةِ بَدْرٍ ؛ فَابْتَاعَ بَنُو الحَارِثِ ابْنِ عَامِرِ بْنِ نَوْفَلِ بْنِ عَبْدِ مَنَافٍ خُبَيْباً . وَكَانَ خُبَيْبٌ هُوَ قَتَلَ الحَارِثَ يَوْمَ بَدْرٍ ، فَلَبِثَ خُبَيْبٌ عِنْدَهُمْ أَسِيراً حَتَّى أَجْمَعُوا عَلَى قَتْلِهِ ، فَاسْتَعَارَ مِنْ بَعْضِ بَنَاتِ الحَارِثِ مُوسَى يَسْتَحِدُّ بِهَا فَأَعَارَتْهُ ، فَدَرَجَ بُنَيٌّ لَهَا وَهِيَ غَافِلَةٌ حَتَّى أَتَاهُ ، فَوَجَدَتْهُ مُجْلِسَهُ عَلَى فَخِذِهِ وَالمُوسَى بِيَدِهِ ، فَفَزِعَتْ فَزْعَةً عَرَفَهَا خُبَيْبٌ . فَقَالَ : أَتَخْشَيْنَ أَنْ أَقْتُلَهُ مَاكُنْتُ لأَفْعَلَ ذَلِكَ ! قَالَتْ : وَاللهِ مَا رَأَيْتُ أَسِيراً خَيْراً مِنْ خُبَيْبٍ ، فَوَاللهِ لَقَدْ وَجَدْتُهُ يَوْماً يَأْكُلُ قِطْفاً مِنْ عِنَبٍ فِي يَدِهِ وَإِنَّهُ لَمُوثَقٌ بِالحَدِيدِ وَمَا بِمَكَّةَ مِنْ ثَمَرَةٍ ، وَكَانَتْ تَقُولُ : إِنَّهُ لَرِزْقٌ رَزَقَهُ اللهُ خُبَيْباً. فَلَمَّا خَرَجُو بِهِ مِنَ الحَرَمِ لِيَقْتُلُوهُ فِي الحِلِّ ، قَالَ لَهُمْ خُبَيْبٌ : دَعُونِي أُصَلِّي رَكْعَتَيْنِ ، فَتَرَكُوهُ ، فَرَكَعَ رَكْعَتَيْنِ ، فَقَالَ : وَاللهِ لَوْلا أَنْ تَحْسَبُوا أَنَّ مَابِي جَزَعٌ لَزِدْتُ : اللَّهُمَّ أَحْصِهِمْ عَدَداً . وَاقْتُلْهُمْ بِدَداً . وَلا تُبْقِ مِنْهُمْ أَحَداً ، وَقَالَ :

فَلَسْتُ أُبَالِي حِينَ أُقْتَلُ مُسْلِماً عَلَى أَيِّ جَنْبٍ كَانَ لِلّهِ مَصْرَعِي

وَذَلِكَ فِي ذَاتِ الإِلَهِ وَإِنْ يَشَأْ يُبَارِكْ عَلَى أَوْصَالِ شِلْوٍ مُمَزَّعِ

وَكَانَ خُبَيْبٌ هُوَ سَنَّ لِكُلِّ مُسْلِمٍ قُتِلَ صَبْراً الصَّلاةَ . وَأَخْبَرَ - يَعْنِي النَّبِيَّ صَلَّى اللهُ عَلَيْهِ وَسَلَّمَ - أَصْحَابَهُ يَوْمَ أُصِيبُوا خَبَرَهُمْ . وَبَعَثَ

نَاسٌ مِنْ قُرَيْشٍ إِلى عاصِمِ بْنِ ثَابِتٍ حِينَ حُدِّثُوا أَنَّهُ قُتِلَ أَنْ يُؤْتَوا بِشَيْءٍ مِنْهُ يُعْرَفُ . وَكانَ قَتَلَ رَجُلاً مِنْ عُظَمَائِهِمْ . فَبَعَثَ اللهُ لِعَاصِمٍ مِثْلَ الظُّلَّةِ مِنَ الدَّبْرِ . فَحَمَتْهُ مِنْ رُسُلِهِمْ . فَلَمْ يَقْدِرُوا أَنْ يَقْطَعُوا مِنْهُ شَيْئاً . رواه البخاري .

1509. Hazrat Abu Hurairah (R.A.A.) relates that the Holy Prophet (S.A.W.) once deputed a scouting party of ten persons under the leadership of Hazrat 'Aasim bin Sabit Ansari (R.A.A.). They left for their destination and when they reached Hadat, a place which is between 'Usfan and Mecca, the tribe of Huzail, also called Banu Lihyan, (somehow or other) came to know about them, and the enemy set out in their pursuit with about a hundred archers following them with the help of their footmarks. When Hazrat 'Aasim and his companions learnt that they were being followed by the enemy, they took sheltar on a hillock. The non-believers surrounded them and asked them to come down and surrender, and promised not to kill anyone of them. But Hazrat 'Aasim (R.A.A.) rejecting this offer declared: O my people, I will not get down and surrender to the non-believers. Allah, let our Holy Prophet (S.A.W.) know our position. The enemy then started shooting arrows at them killing Hazrat 'Aasim (R.A.A.). Three of the Muslims Hazrat Khubaib (R.A.A.), Hazrat Zaid bin Dathina and another Muslim, believing the promise of the enemies came down. (The remaining six Muslims had been martyred along with Hazrat 'Aasim (R.A.A.). When the enemy had the above three persons under their control, they took off the chords of their bows with which they tied them up securely. The third man protested: 'This is the first violation of the pledge. By Allah! I will not go with you and shall follow the example set by these martyrs. The nonbelievers pulled him and tried to drag him along with them, but he resisted. So they killed him and carried Hazrat Khubaib (R.A.A.) who was purchased by the children of Haris bin Aamir bin Naufal bin Abd Manaf, and it was Hazrat Khubaib (R.A.A.) who had slain Haris bin Aamir in the battle of Badr. Hazrat Khubaib (R.A.A.) remained a prisoner with them till all the non-believers agreed to kill him. Hazrat Khubaib (R.A.A.) one day borrowed a razor from one of the daughters of Haris. In the meantime a child of this woman strayed up to Hazrat Khubaib (R.A.A.) who seated the baby in his lap while the razor was in his hand and the mother was unaware of the development. When she reached near Hazrat Khubaib (R.A.A.), she saw the child on the lap of Khubaib with a razor in his hand; she was terrified and Hazrat Khubaib (R.A.A.) perceiving her discomfiture said: You fear that I would kill him? I will never do so. Having thus being relieved she used to say about him: I have never seen a prisoner better than Hazrat Khubaib (R.A.A.).

One day, I saw that while in chains, he was eating fresh grapes which he held in his hand; although at that time no grapes were available in Mecca. She used to say: I am convinced that these grapes were provided by Allah to Hazrat Khubaib (R.A.A.). When the non-believers took him out of the *Haram* (sanctuary) to behead him outside the *Haram* limit, Hazrat Khubaib (R.A.A.) asked them. Let me offer two raka'ats of optional prayer. As such they freed him, and he offered two raka'ats of optional prayers. After this he said. I would have made my prayer a bit long, but I thought that you might think that I was afraid to die. He then prayed: O Allah! Count them and kill them all one by one and do not spare any of them.

'He then recited these verses of a poem.

If I am killed while in Islam then I do not mind on which side I fall dead.

This death of mine is for the sake of Allah,
and if He so wills, He would bless the severed parts of my body.

It was Hazrat Khubaib (R.A.A.) who set the example for every Muslim who might be captured and killed for the sake of Allah to be steadfast and offer prayer before execution. The Holy Prophet (S.A.W.) informed his companions of the news of martyrdom of these persons on the day when Hazrat Khubaib (R.A.A.) and his associates were killed. Hazrat 'Aasim bin Sabit (R.A.A.) had slain one of the leading men of the Quraish tribe in the battle of Badr. As such when the said tribe came to know about his death, they deputed some of their men to verify this fact and bring something (some parts of his body) from which he might be identified, but Allah the Most High placed some bees (or wasps) which covered the dead body of Hazrat 'Aasim (R.A.A.) like a cloud and thus saved his corpse from being mutilated by these persons, by cutting away any portion of his body as a token. *(Bukhari)*

١٥١٠ – وَعَنِ ابْنِ عُمَرَ رَضِيَ اللهُ عَنْهُمَا قَالَ : مَا سَمِعْتُ عُمَرَ رَضِيَ اللهُ عَنْهُ يَقُولُ لِشَيْءٍ قَطُّ : إِنِّي لأَظُنُّهُ كَذَا إِلاَّ كَانَ كَمَا يَظُنُّ . رَوَاهُ الْبُخَارِي .

1510. Hazrat Ibn 'Umar (R.A.A.) relates that whenever Hazrat 'Umar (R.A.A.) said about anything: I think that this thing is like this, and that thing used to become as such. *(Bukhari)*

* * * * * * * *

BOOK OF THE PROHIBITED DEEDS

CHAPTER 254

DECLARATION OF BACKBITING AS UNLAWFUL AND DIRECTING TONGUE TO BE GUARDED

قَالَ اللهُ تَعَالَى : وَلَا يَغْتَبْ بَعْضُكُمْ بَعْضاً أَيُحِبُّ أَحَدُكُمْ أَنْ يَأْكُلَ لَحْمَ أَخِيهِ مَيْتاً ؛ فَكَرِهْتُمُوهُ ! وَاتَّقُوا اللهَ إِنَّ اللهَ تَوَّابٌ رَحِيمٌ [الحجرات : ١٢] . وَقَالَ تَعَالَى : وَلَا تَقْفُ مَالَيْسَ لَكَ بِهِ عِلْمٌ . إِنَّ السَّمْعَ . وَالبَصَرَ . وَالفُؤَادَ . كُلُّ أُولئِكَ كَانَ عَنْهُ مَسْئُولاً [الإسراء : ٦٣] . وقَالَ تَعَالَى : مَايَلْفِظُ مِنْ قَوْلٍ إِلَّا لَدَيْهِ رَقِيبٌ عَتِيدٌ [ق : ١٨] .

اِعْلَمْ أَنَّهُ يَنْبَغِي لِكُلِّ مُكَلَّفٍ أَنْ يَحْفَظَ لِسَانَهُ عَنْ جَمِيعِ الكَلَامِ إِلاَّ كَلاماً ظَهَرَتْ فِيهِ المَصْلَحَةُ ، وَمَتَى اسْتَوَى الكَلَامُ وَتَرْكُهُ فِي المَصْلَحَةِ ، فَالسُّنَّةُ الإِمْسَاكُ عَنْهُ ، لأَنَّهُ قَدْ يَنْجَرُّ الكَلَامُ المُبَاحُ إِلَى حَرَامٍ أَوْ مَكْرُوهٍ ، وَذلِكَ كَثِيرٌ فِي العَادَةِ ، وَالسَّلَامَةُ لَايَعْدِلُهَا شَيْءٌ .

340. Neither backbite one another. Would one of you love to eat the flesh of his dead brother? Ye abhor that (so abhor the other)! And keep your duty to (Allah). Lo! Allah is Relenting, Merciful. (49 : 12)

341. (O man), follow not that whereof thou hast no knowledge. Lo! the hearing and the sight and the heart — of each of these it will be asked. (17 : 36)

342. He uttereth no word but there is with him an observer ready. (50 : 18)

Note: Imam Nawawi says that it is incumbent upon every sane and adult person to guard his tongue against all kinds of (unnecessary) talking (i.e. should be very careful in talking).

But in cases of expediency, where speaking or talking both may be equal as a prudent measure, it is better to keep quiet, because often even a lawful talking leads to unlawful and undersirable results; this is a common practice; but there is nothing equivalent to safety.

١٥١١ – وَعَنْ أَبِي هُرَيْرَةَ رَضِيَ اللهُ عَنْهُ عَنِ النَّبِيِّ صَلَّى اللهُ عَلَيْهِ وَسَلَّمَ قَالَ : « مَنْ كَانَ يُؤْمِنُ بِاللهِ وَالْيَوْمِ الآخِرِ . فَلْيَقُلْ خَيْراً . أَوْ لِيَصْمُتْ » متفقٌ عليه .

وَهذا الحَدِيثُ صَرِيحٌ في أَنَّهُ يَنْبَغِي أَنْ لايَتَكَلَّمَ إلاَّ إذا كَانَ الكَلامُ خَيْراً ، وَهُوَ الَّذي ظَهَرَتْ مَصْلَحَتُهُ . وَمَتَى شَكَّ في ظُهُورِ المَصْلَحَةِ فَلا يَتَكَلَّمُ .

1511. This Hadith has been covered in No. 314 of Chapter 40.

١٥١٢ – وَعَنْ أَبِي مُوسَى رَضِيَ اللهُ عَنْهُ قَالَ : قُلْتُ يا رَسُولَ اللهِ أَيُّ المُسْلِمِينَ أَفْضَلُ ؟ قَالَ : « مَنْ سَلِمَ المُسْلِمُونَ مِنْ لِسَانِهِ وَيَدِهِ » متفقٌ عليه .

1512. This Hadith has been covered in No. 211 of Chapter 26.

١٥١٣ – وَعَنْ سَهْلِ بْنِ سَعْدٍ قَالَ : قَالَ رَسُولُ اللهِ صَلَّى اللهُ عَلَيْهِ وَسَلَّمَ : « مَنْ يَضْمَنْ لِي مَابَيْنَ لَحْيَيْهِ وَمَا بَيْنَ رِجْلَيْهِ أَضْمَنْ لَهُ الجَنَّةَ » متفقٌ عليه

1513. Hazrat Sahl bin Sa'd (R.A.A.) says that the Holy Prophet (S.A.W.) has said: a person who gives surety to (safeguard) the thing between the jaws (tongue) and the thing between his two legs (private organs), I guarantee his entrance into Paradise. *(Bukhari and Muslim)*

١٥١٤ – وَعَنْ أَبِي هُرَيْرَةَ رَضِيَ اللهُ عَنْهُ أَنَّهُ سَمِعَ النَّبِيَّ صَلَّى اللهُ عَلَيْهِ وَسَلَّمَ يَقُولُ : « إنَّ العَبْدَ لَيَتَكَلَّمُ بِالكَلِمَةِ مَايَتَبَيَّنُ فيهَا يَزِلُّ بِهَا إلى النَّارِ أَبْعَدَ مِمَّا بَيْنَ المَشْرِقِ وَالمَغْرِبِ » متفقٌ عليه

ومعنى : « يَتَبَيَّنُ » يَتَفَكَّرُ أَنَّهَا خَيْرٌ أَمْ لا

1514. Hazrat Abu Hurairah (R.A.A.) relates that he heard the Holy Prophet say. When a person says something well wishing, with due thinking, he is taken away from the Hell, as far away as the distance between the East and West. *(Bukhari and Muslim)*

١٥١٥ – وَعَنْهُ عَنِ النَّبِيِّ صَلَّى اللهُ عَلَيْهِ وَسَلَّمَ قَالَ : « إنَّ العَبْدَ لَيَتَكَلَّمُ بالكَلَمَةِ مِنْ رِضْوَانِ اللهِ تَعَالَى مَا يُلْقِي لَهَا بَالاً يَرْفَعُهُ اللهُ

بِهَا دَرَجَاتٍ ، وَإِنَّ الْعَبْدَ لَيَتَكَلَّمُ بِالْكَلِمَةِ مِنْ سَخَطِ اللهِ تَعَالَى لَا يُلْقِي لَهَا بَالاً يَهْوِي بِهَا فِي جَهَنَّمَ » رواه البخاري

1515. Hazrat Abu Hurairah (R.A.A.) relates that the Holy Prophet (S.A.W.) said: Sometimes a person says something, which pleases Allah, and in return Allah raises his status, (rewards him); and sometimes a person says something which displeases Allah, it takes him into Hell. *(Bukhari)*

١٥١٦ – وَعَنْ أَبِي عَبْدِ الرَّحمن بِلالِ بْنِ الحَارِثِ المُزَنِيِّ رَضِيَ اللهُ عَنْهُ أَنَّ رَسُولَ اللهِ صَلَّى اللهُ عَلَيْهِ وَسَلَّمَ قَالَ : « إِنَّ الرَّجُلَ لَيَتَكَلَّمُ بِالْكَلِمَةِ مِنْ رِضْوانِ اللهِ تَعَالَى مَا كَانَ يَظُنُّ أَنْ تَبْلُغَ مَا بَلَغَتْ يَكْتُبُ اللهُ لَهُ بِهَا رِضْوَانَهُ إِلَى يَوْمِ يَلْقَاهُ ، وَإِنَّ الرَّجُلَ لَيَتَكَلَّمُ بِالكَلِمَةِ مِنْ سَخَطِ اللهِ مَا كَانَ يَظُنُّ أَن تَبْلُغَ مَا بَلَغَتْ يَكْتُبُ اللهُ لَهُ بِهَا سَخَطَهُ إِلَى يَوْمِ يَلْقَاهُ »

رواهُ مالكٌ في « المُوَطَّأ » والترمذي وقال : حديثٌ حسنٌ صحيحٌ .

1516. Hazrat Abu Abdur Rahman Bilal bin Haris Muzani (R.A.A.) relates that the Holy Prophet (S.A.W.) said: **A man says something without understanding its significance which pleases Allah, in return Allah, the Most High records His pleasure for him till the day when he will meet Him (that is the Day of Judgement); similarly when a person utters something without understanding its significance, which displeases Allah, as a result of which Allah, the Most High records His displeasure for him, till the day when he will meet Him (i.e. the Day of Judgement).** *(Malik and Tirmizi,* latter said this tradition is sound and good).

١٥١٧ – وَعَنْ سُفْيَانَ بْنِ عَبْدِ اللهِ رَضِيَ اللهُ عَنْهُ قَالَ : قُلْتُ يا رَسُولَ اللهِ حَدِّثْنِي بِأَمْرٍ أَعْتَصِمُ بِهِ قَالَ : « قُلْ رَبِّيَ اللهُ ، ثُمَّ اسْتَقِمْ » قُلْتُ : يَا رَسُولَ اللهِ مَا أَخْوَفُ مَا تَخَافُ عَلَيَّ ؟ فَأَخَذَ بِلِسَانِ نَفْسِهِ ، ثُمَّ قَالَ : « هذا » رواه الترمذي وقال : حديثٌ حسنٌ صحيحٌ .

1517. Hazrat Sufyan bin Abdullah (R.A.A.) relates: I requested the Holy Prophet (S.A.W.), O Messenger of Allah! Please tell me something which I may hold fast. He (S.A.W.) said: 'Affirm. 'My Lord and Sustainer is Allah', and then stick to it. I further said: O Messenger of Allah! What it is that thing which you consider as the most injurious to me? He held his tongue and said: 'This'.

(*Tirmizi*, and said that it is sound and good)

١٥١٨ — وَعَنِ ابْنِ عُمَرَ رَضِيَ اللهُ عَنْهُمَا قَالَ : قَالَ رَسُولُ اللهِ صَلَّى اللهُ عَلَيْهِ وَسَلَّمَ : « لاتُكْثِرُوا الكَلامَ بِغَيْرِ ذِكْرِ اللهِ ؛ فَإِنَّ كَثْرَةَ الكَلامِ بِغَيْرِ ذِكْرِ اللهِ تَعالَى قَسْوَةٌ لِلْقَلْبِ ! وَإِنَّ أَبْعَدَ النَّاسِ مِنَ اللهِ القَلْبُ القَاسِي » رواه الترمذي .

1518. Hazrat ibn 'Umar (R.A.A.) relates that the Holy Prophet (S.A.W.) said: Do not indulge in long talks without remembering Allah, the Exalted, for much talk without remembrance of Allah hardens the heart, and the person farthest from Allah will be the one who has a hard heart. *(Tirmizi)*

١٥١٩ — وَعَنْ أَبِي هُرَيْرَةَ رَضِيَ اللهُ عَنْهُ قَالَ : قَالَ رَسُولُ اللهِ صَلَّى اللهُ عَلَيْهِ وَسَلَّمَ : « مَنْ وَقَاهُ اللهُ شَرَّ مَا بَيْنَ لَحْيَيْهِ ، وَشَرَّ مَا بَيْنَ رِجْلَيْهِ دَخَلَ الجَنَّةَ » رَوَاهُ التِّرمِذِي وقالَ : حَدِيثٌ حَسَنٌ .

1519. Hazrat Abu Hurairah (R.A.A.) relates that the Holy Prophet (S.A.W.) said: one whom Allah saved from the mischief of what is between two jaws (tongue) and two thighs, will enter Paradise.

(*Tirmizi* said it is sound)

١٥٢٠ — وَعَنْ عُقْبَةَ بْنِ عَامِرٍ رَضِيَ اللهُ عَنْهُ قَالَ : قُلْتُ يَارَسُولَ اللهِ مَا النَّجَاةُ ؟ قَالَ : « أَمْسِكْ عَلَيْكَ لِسَانَكَ . وَلْيَسَعْكَ بَيْتُكَ ، وَابْكِ عَلَى خَطِيئَتِكَ » رواه الترمذي وقالَ : حديثٌ حسنٌ .

1520. Hazrat Uqbah bin A'mir (R.A.A.) relates: I enquired from the Holy Prophet (S.A.W.): What is the salvation? He (S.A.W.) said. Control your tongue, keep inside your house and weep (be sorry) for your sins. (*Tirmizi*, siad it is good)

١٥٢١ — وَعَنْ أَبِي سَعِيدٍ الخُدْرِيِّ رَضِيَ اللهُ عَنْهُ عَنِ النَّبِيِّ صَلَّى اللهُ عَلَيْهِ وَسَلَّمَ قَالَ : « إذا أَصْبَحَ ابْنُ آدَمَ . فَإِنَّ الأَعْضَاءَ كُلَّهَا تُكَفِّرُ اللِّسَانَ ، تَقُولُ : اتَّقِ اللهَ فينا . فَإِنَّمَا نَحنُ بِكَ : فَإِنِ اسْتَقَمْتَ اسْتَقَمنا وَإِنِ اعْوَجَجْتَ اعْوَجَجْنَا » رواه الترمذي .

معنى « تُكَفِّرُ اللِّسَانَ » : أَيْ تَذِلُّ وَتَخْضَعُ لَهُ .

1521. Hazrat Abu Sa'eed Khudri (R.A.A.) reports that the Holy Prophet (S.A.W.) said: When the son of Adam (a man) gets up in the morning all parts of his body request his tongue saying. Fear Allah regarding us, because we follow you; if you are right we shall also be right, and if you go wrong we shall also go wrong. *(Tirmizi)*

١٥٢٢ – وَعَنْ مُعَاذٍ رَضِيَ اللهُ عَنْهُ قَالَ : قُلْتُ يَارَسُولَ اللهِ أَخْبِرْنِي بِعَمَلٍ يُدْخِلُنِي الجَنَّةَ ، وَيُبَاعِدُنِي مِنَ النَّارِ ؟ قَالَ : « لَقَدْ سَأَلْتَ عَنْ عَظِيمٍ ، وَإِنَّهُ لَيَسِيرٌ عَلَى مَنْ يَسَّرَهُ اللهُ تَعَالَى عَلَيْهِ : تَعْبُدُ اللهَ لاتُشْرِكُ بِهِ شَيْئاً . وَتُقِيمُ الصَّلاةَ . وَتُؤْتِي الزَّكَاةَ . وَتَصُومُ رَمَضَانَ . وَتَحُجُّ البَيْتَ ثُمَّ قَالَ : « أَلا أَدُلُّكَ عَلَى أَبْوَابِ الخَيْرِ ؟ الصَّوْمُ جُنَّةٌ . وَالصَّدَقَةُ تُطْفِيءُ الخَطِيئَةَ كَمَا يُطْفِيءُ المَاءُ النَّارَ . وَصَلاةُ الرَّجُلِ مِنْ جَوْفِ اللَّيْلِ » ثُمَّ تَلا : (تَتَجَافَى جُنُوبُهُمْ عَنِ المَضَاجِعِ) حَتَّى بَلَغَ (يَعْمَلُونَ)[السجدة : ١٦] . ثُمَّ قَالَ : « أَلا أُخْبِرُكَ بِرَأْسِ الأَمْرِ ، وَعَمُودِهِ . وَذِرْوَةِ سَنَامِهِ » قُلْتُ : بَلَى يَارَسُولَ اللهِ . قَالَ : « رَأْسُ الأَمْرِ الإِسْلامُ . وَعَمُودُهُ الصَّلاةُ . وَذِرْوَةُ سَنَامِهِ الجِهَادُ » ثُمَّ قَالَ : « أَلا أُخْبِرُكَ بِمِلاكِ ذلِكَ كُلِّهِ ؟ » قُلْتُ : بَلَى يَارَسُولَ اللهِ . فَأَخَذَ بِلِسَانِهِ قَالَ : « كُفَّ عَلَيْكَ هذا » قُلْتُ : يَارَسُولَ اللهِ وَإِنَّا لَمُؤَاخَذُونَ بِمَا نَتَكَلَّمُ بِهِ ؟ فَقَالَ : ثَكِلَتْكَ أُمُّكَ ! وَهَلْ يَكُبُّ النَّاسَ فِي النَّارِ عَلَى وُجُوهِهِمْ إِلاَّ حَصَائِدُ أَلْسِنَتِهِمْ ؟ » .

رواه الترمذي وقال : حَدِيثٌ حَسَنٌ صَحِيحٌ ، وقد سبق شرحه

1522. Hazrat Mu'az (R.A.A.) relates: I requested the Holy Prophet (S.A.W.): O Messenger of Allah! Please tell me the action which may help me to enter the heaven and keep me away from the Hell. He (S.A.W.) answered. You have asked about a matter of great singificance but it is easy for one for whom Allah makes it easy. Worship Allah and do not associate anything with Him; establish Salat (prayer), pay the Zakat (the poor due), observe the Fast during Ramadhan and perform the pilgrimage of the house (of Allah). Then he (S.A.W.) added: Shall I not tell you something about the passage to excellence and virtue. The fast is a shield, charity (for the sake of Allah) mitigates sins as water extinguishes fire. Similarly the midnight prayer (also wipes out the sins). Then he recited:

Who forsake their beds to cry unto their Lord in fear and hope and spend of what We have bestowed on them. No soul knoweth what is kept hid for them of joy, as a reward for what they used to do. (32 : 16—17)

Then he added: May I not tell you something about the roots (foundation) of the religion and its pillars (mainstay) and of its peak? I said: Certainly O Messenger of Allah. He (S.A.W.) said: The head of the faith is Islam, its support is Salat (prayer) and its peak is Jihad (in the cause of Allah). Then he (S.A.W.) asked: May I not tell you something about a thing which is the controller of all this? I said. Certainly, Messenger of Allah (S.A.W.). Upon this he (S.A.W.) took hold of his tongue and said: Keep this under control. I submitted: O Messenger of Allah! Will we be called to account for what we say? He (S.A.W.) answered: May you be lost to your mother! The people will be thrown with face down, into the Hell only on account of the produce of the tongus (i.e. their talking). *(Tirmizi,* said it is sound and good)

١٥٢٣ – وَعَنْ أَبِي هُرَيْرَةَ رَضِيَ اللهُ عَنْهُ أَنَّ رَسُولَ اللهِ صَلَّى اللهُ عَلَيْهِ وَسَلَّمَ قَالَ : « أَتَدْرُونَ مَا الغِيبَةُ ؟ » قَالُوا : اللهُ وَرَسُولُهُ أَعْلَمُ قَالَ : « ذِكْرُكَ أَخَاكَ بِمَا يَكْرَهُ » قِيلَ : أَفَرَأَيْتَ (٥) إِنْ كَانَ فِي أَخِي مَا أَقُولُ ؟ قَالَ : « إِنْ كَانَ فِيهِ مَا تَقُولُ . فَقَدِ اغْتَبْتَهُ . وَإِنْ لَمْ يَكُنْ فِيهِ مَا تَقُولُ فَقَدْ بَهَتَّهُ » رواه مسلم .

1523. Hazrat Abu Hurairah (R.A.A.) relates that the Holy Prophet (S.A.W.) asked the companions: Do you know what is meant by backbiting? They answered: Allah and His Messenger know better. He (S.A.W.) said: To narrate such things about your brother which he dislikes. One of the audience asked: Even if my brother may be like that? He (S.A.W.) said: If such defects as you say, be present in him, then you have backbited and if he does not have what you say, then you are committing slander. ***(Muslim)***

١٥٢٤ – وَعَنْ أَبِي بَكْرَةَ رَضِيَ اللهُ عَنْهُ أَنَّ رَسُولَ اللهِ صَلَّى اللهُ عَلَيْهِ وَسَلَّمَ قَالَ فِي خُطْبَتِهِ يَوْمَ النَّحْرِ بِمِنى فِي حَجَّةِ الوَدَاعِ : « إِنَّ دِمَاءَكُمْ . وَأَمْوَالَكُمْ ، وَأَعْرَاضَكُمْ . حَرَامٌ عَلَيْكُمْ كَحُرْمَةِ يَوْمِكُمْ هذا . فِي شَهْرِكُمْ هذا . فِي بَلَدِكُمْ هذا . أَلا هَلْ بَلَّغْتُ » متفقٌ عليه

1524. This Hadis has been covered in No. 213 of Chapter 26.

١٥٢٥ ـ وعَنْ عائِشَةَ رَضِيَ اللهُ عَنْهَا قَالَتْ: قُلْتُ لِلنَّبِيِّ صَلَّى اللهُ عَلَيْهِ وَسَلَّمَ حَسْبُكَ مِنْ صَفِيَّةَ كَذَا وَكَذَا. قَالَ بَعْضُ الرُّوَاةِ: تَعْنِي قَصِيرَةً. فَقَالَ: «لَقَدْ قُلْتِ كَلِمَةً لَوْ مُزِجَتْ بِمَاءِ الْبَحْرِ لَمَزَجَتْهُ!» قَالَتْ: وَحَكَيْتُ لَهُ إِنْسَاناً فَقَالَ: «مَا أُحِبُّ أَنِّي حَكَيْتُ إِنْسَاناً وَإِنَّ لِي كَذَا وَكَذَا» رواه أبو داود. والترمذي وقال: حديثٌ حسنٌ صحيحٌ.

1525. Hazrat Ayesha (R.A.A.) relates 'I said to the Holy Prophet (S.A.W.): It is sufficient for you (to know that) she (Hazrat Safia) is such and such (referring to her short stature). The Holy Prophet (S.A.W.) said: You have said a sentence which if mixed in a ocean, it would transform its water to worse. Hazrat Ayesha (R.A.A.) also says. (Once) I said something unpleasant about a person to the Holy Prophet (S.A.W.). He (S.A.W.) said: I do not like to hear anything unpleasant about anyone, even in return for so much and so much. *(Abu Daud and Tirmizi, Imam Tirmizi* says that this tradition is good and sound)

١٥٢٦ ـ وعَنْ أَنَسٍ رَضِيَ اللهُ عَنْهُ قَالَ: قَالَ رَسُولُ اللهِ صَلَّى اللهُ عَلَيْهِ وَسَلَّمَ: «لَمَّا عُرِجَ بِي مَرَرْتُ بِقَوْمٍ لَهُمْ أَظْفَارٌ مِنْ نُحَاسٍ يَخْمِشُونَ وُجُوهَهُمْ وَصُدُورَهُمْ. فَقُلْتُ: مَنْ هَؤُلَاءِ يَا جِبْرِيلُ؟ قَالَ: هَؤُلَاءِ الَّذِينَ يَأْكُلُونَ لُحُومَ النَّاسِ، وَيَقَعُونَ فِي أَعْرَاضِهِمْ!» رواهُ أبو داود

1526. Hazrat Anas (R.A.A.) says that the Holy Prophet (S.A.W.) said: On the night of Ascension I passed by some people who had copper nails and they were clawing their faces and their chests with them. I asked Gabriel: Who are these persons? He said. These are the people who eat the flesh of human beings and disgrace them. *(Abu Daud)*

١٥٢٧ ـ وعَنْ أَبِي هُرَيْرَةَ رَضِيَ اللهُ عَنْهُ أَنَّ رَسُولَ اللهِ صَلَّى اللهُ عَلَيْهِ وَسَلَّمَ قَالَ: «كُلُّ الْمُسْلِمِ عَلَى الْمُسْلِمِ حَرَامٌ: دَمُهُ وعِرْضُه وَمَالُهُ» رواهُ مسلم.

1527. Hazrat Abu Hurairah (R.A.A.) says that the Holy Prophet (S.A.W.) has declared that every things belonging to a Muslim is unlawful for another Muslim; his blood his honour and his property. ***(Muslim)***

* * * * * * *

CHAPTER 255

PROHIBITION OF LISTENING TO BACKBITING, TO DISCOURAGE THE LISTENING OF BACKBITING AND TO CONTRADICT THE BACKBITER. IF HE IS UNABLE TO DO SO OR HIS EXHORTATIONS HAVE NO EFFECT THEN HE SHOULD LEAVE THE COMPANY

قَالَ اللهُ تَعالى : (وَإذا سَمِعُوا اللَّغْوَ (١) أعْرَضُوا عَنْهُ) [القصص : ٥٥]

وقَالَ تَعَالَى : (والَّذِينَ هُمْ عَنِ اللَّغْوِ مُعْرِضُونَ) [المؤمنون : ٣].

وقَالَ تَعالَى : (إنَّ السَّمْعَ وَالبَصرَ وَالفُؤَادَ : كل أولئك كَانَ عَنْهُ مَسْئُولاً) [الإسراء : ٣٦] . وقَالَ تَعالَى : (وإذا رَأَيْتَ الَّذِينَ يَخُوضُونَ في آياتِنَا فَأعْرِضْ عَنْهُمْ حَتَّى يَخُوضُوا في حَدِيثٍ غَيْرِهِ ، وإمَّا يُنْسِيَنَّكَ الشَّيْطَانُ فَلا تَقْعُدْ بَعْدَ الذِّكْرَى مَعَ القَوْمِ الظَّالِمِينَ) . [الأنعام : ٦٨] .

Allah, the Exalted, has said:

343. And when they hear vanity, they withdraw from it. (28:55)

344. And who shun vain conversation. (23:3)

345. Lo! the hearing and the sight and the heart — each of these will be asked. (17:36)

346. And when thou seest those who meddle with our revelations, withdraw from them until they meddle with another topic. And if the devil cause thee to forget, sit not, after the remembrance with the congregation of wrongdoers. (6:68)

١٥٢٨ — وَعَنْ أبي الدَّرْدَاءِ رَضِيَ اللهُ عَنْهُ عَنِ النَّبيِّ صَلَّى اللهُ عَلَيْهِ وَسَلَّمَ قَالَ : « مَنْ رَدَّ عَنْ عِرْضِ أخيهِ ، رَدَّ اللهُ عَنْ وجْهِهِ النَّارَ يَوْمَ القِيَامَةِ » رواه الترمذي وقالَ : حديثٌ حسنٌ .

1528. Hazrat Abu Darda (R.A.A.) relates that the Holy Prophet (S.A.W.) said: A person who avoids dishonouring his brother, Allah will keep his face away from the fire of Hell on the day of judgement. *(Tirmizi* and said this as good)

١٥٢٩– وَعَنْ عِتْبَانَ بْنِ مَالِكٍ رَضِيَ اللهُ عَنْهُ في حَدِيثِهِ الطَّوِيلِ المَشْهُورِ الَّذي تقدَّمَ في بَابِ الرَّجاءِ قَالَ : قَامَ النَّبِيُّ صَلَّى اللهُ عَلَيْهِ وَسَلَّمَ يُصَلِّي فَقَالَ : « أَيْنَ مالِكُ بْنُ الدُّخْشُمِ ؟ » فَقَالَ رجُلٌ : ذَلِكَ مُنافِقٌ لا يُحِبُّ اللهَ وَلا رَسُولَهُ . فَقَالَ النَّبِيُّ صَلَّى اللهُ عَلَيْهِ وَسَلَّمَ : « لا تَقُلْ ذلكَ ألا تَراهُ قدْ قَالَ : لا إلهَ إلاَّ اللهُ يُرِيدُ بِذلكَ وجْهَ اللهِ ! وإنَّ اللهَ قدْ حَرَّمَ على النَّارِ مَنْ قَالَ : لا إلهَ إلاَّ اللهُ يَبْتَغِي بِذلكَ وَجْهَ اللهِ » متفقٌ عليهِ .

1529. This Hadis has been covered in No. 417 of Chapter 51.

١٥٣٠ – وَعَنْ كَعْبِ بْنِ مَالِكٍ رَضِيَ اللهُ عَنْهُ في حَدِيثِهِ الطَّوِيلِ في قصَّةِ تَوْبَتِهِ وقد سَبَقَ في باب التَّوْبَة . قَالَ : قَالَ النَّبيُّ صَلَّى اللهُ عَلَيْهِ وَسَلَّمَ وَهُوَ جَالِسٌ في القَوْمِ بِتَبُوكَ : «مَا فَعَلَ كَعْبُ بْنُ مَالِكٍ ؟ » فَقالَ رَجُلٌ مِنْ بَنِي سَلِمَةَ : يا رَسُولَ اللهِ حَبَسَهُ بُرْداهُ ، والنَّظَرُ في عِطْفَيْهِ . فَقَالَ لَهُ مُعاذُ بنُ جَبَلٍ رَضِيَ اللهُ عَنْهُ : بِئْسَ ما قُلْتَ ، واللهِ يَارَسُولَ اللهِ مَاعَلِمْنَا عَلَيْهِ إلاَّ خَيْراً . فَسَكَتَ رَسُولُ اللهِ صَلَّى اللهُ عَلَيْهِ وَسَلَّمَ . متفقٌ عليهِ .

1530. This Hadis has been covered in No. 21 of Chapter 2.

* * * * * * *

CHAPTER 256

WHEN BACKBITING IS PERMISSIBLE

اِعْلَمْ أنَّ الغِيبَةَ تُباحُ لِغَرَضٍ صَحيحٍ شَرْعِي لا يُمْكِنُ الوُصُولُ إلَيْهِ إلاَّ بِهَا ، وهُوَ سِتَّةُ أَسْبَابٍ :

الأَوَّلُ : التَّظَلُّمُ ، فَيَجُوزُ للمَظْلُومِ أنْ يَتَظَلَّمَ إلى السُّلْطَانِ والقَاضِي وغَيْرِهِمَا مِمَّنْ لَهُ وِلايَةٌ ، أو قُدْرَةٌ عَلى إنْصَافِهِ مِنْ ظَالِمِهِ ، فَيَقُولُ : ظَلَمَني فُلانٌ بكَذا .

الثَّاني : الاستِعانَةُ على تغييرِ المُنكَرِ ، وَرَدُّ العاصي إلى الصَّوابِ ، فيقول لمَنْ يرجو قُدرَتَهُ على إزالةِ المُنكَرِ : فلانٌ يعمَلُ كذا . فازجُرْهُ عنه ونحو ذلكَ . ويَكونُ مقصودُهُ التَوصُّلَ إلى إزالَةِ المُنكَرِ . فإنْ لمْ يقصِدْ ذلكَ كانَ حَراماً .

الثَّالِثُ : الاستِفتاءُ . فيَقولُ للمُفتي : ظَلَمني أبي . أوْ أخي ، أوْ زوجي . أوْ فُلانٌ بكذا . فهَلْ لهُ ذلكَ ؟ وما طَريقي في الخلاصِ منهُ ، وتحصيلِ حقّي . ودَفعِ الظُّلْمِ ؟ ونحو ذلكَ . فهذا جائزٌ للحاجَة . ولكِنَ الأحوَطَ والأفضَلَ أنْ يقولَ : ما تقولُ في رَجُلٍ أوْ شخصٍ . أوْ زوجٍ ، كانَ مِنْ أمرِهِ كذا ؟ فإنَّهُ يحصُلُ بِهِ الغرَضُ مِنْ غيْرِ تعْيِينٍ ومعَ ذلكَ . فالتَّعيِينُ جائزٌ كما سنَذكُرُهُ في حَديثِ هِنْدٍ إنْ شاءَ اللهُ تعالى .

الرَّابِعُ : تحذيرُ المُسلِمينَ مِنَ الشَّرِّ ونَصيحَتُهُمْ . وذلكَ مِنْ وُجُوهٍ :

منها جَرْحُ المَجرُوحينَ مِنَ الرُّوَاةِ والشُّهُودِ ، وَذلكَ جائزٌ بإجْماعِ المُسلِمينَ . بَلْ واجِبٌ للحاجَةِ .

ومنها المُشاوَرَةُ في مُصاهَرَةِ إنْسانٍ . أوْ مُشارَكَتِهِ ، أوْ إيداعِهِ . أوْ مُعامَلَتِهِ ، أوْ غيْرِ ذلكَ . أوْ مجاوَرَتِهِ . ويَجِبُ على المُشاوَرِ أنْ لا يخفي حالَهُ ، بَلْ يذكُرُ المَساوِئَ التي فيه بنيَّةِ النَّصيحَةِ .

ومنها إذا رأى مُتفَقِّهاً يتَرَدَّدُ إلى مُبتَدِعٍ . أو فاسِقٍ يأخُذُ عنهُ العِلْمَ . وخافَ أنْ يتَضرَّرَ المُتفَقِّهُ بذلكَ . فعَلَيْهِ نَصيحَتُهُ ببيانِ حالِه . بشَرْطِ أنْ يَقصِدَ النَّصيحَةَ . وهذا ممَّا يُغلَطُ فيهِ . وقدْ يَحمِلُ المُتكَلِّمَ بذلكَ الحَسدُ ، ويُلَبِّسُ الشَّيطانُ عليهِ ذلكَ . ويُخَيِّلُ إليْهِ أنَّهُ نَصيحَةٌ فلْيَتفَطَّنْ لذلكَ .

ومنها أن يكونَ لهُ وِلايَةٌ لايقومُ بها على وَجْهِها : إمَّا بأنْ لايكونَ صالحاً لها ، وإمَّا بأنْ يكونَ فاسِقاً ، أو مُغفَّلاً . ونحوَ ذلكَ فيَجِبُ ذِكْرُ ذلكَ لمَنْ

له عليه ولاية عامة ليزيله . ويولي من يصلح . أو يعلم ذلك منه ليعامله بمقتضى حاله . ولا يغتر به ، وأن يسعى في أن يحثه على الاستقامة أو يستبدل به .

الخامس : أن يكون مجاهراً بفسقه أو بدعته كالمجاهر بشرب الخمر ، ومصادرة الناس ، وأخذ المكس ، وجباية الأموال ظلماً ، وتولي الأمور الباطلة ، فيجوز ذكره بما يجاهر به ، ويحرم ذكره بغيره من العيوب ، إلا أن يكون لجوازه سبب آخر مما ذكرناه .

السادس : التعريف ، فإذا كان الإنسان معروفاً بلقب ، كالأعمش والأعرج والأصم ، والأعمى ، والأحول ، وغيرهم جاز تعريفهم بذلك ، ويحرم إطلاقه على جهة التنقص ، ولو أمكن تعريفه بغير ذلك كان أولى .

فهذه ستة أسباب ذكرها العلماء وأكثرها مجمع عليه ، ودلائلها من الأحاديث الصحيحة مشهورة . فمن ذلك :

According to Imam Nawawi backbiting or reporting in absence is permissible for some religious purpose, when doing so is indispensable, and this can be done in 6 instances, viz :—

(1) A report for the redress of some injustice, wrong, tyranny or high-handedness. In such case an oppressed person can petition to the King, Qazi or somebody in authority, against a person who has perpetrated such tyranny.

(2) To seek some help to stop some practice or work which may be against the principles of religion.

(3) To seek a ruling *(Fatwa)* on some specific topic from a qualified person in authority.

(4) To caution the Muslims from the evil consequences of some mischief.

(5) If somebody indulges in evil practices openly, as for example openly drinking of liquor, cruel treatment of the people, usurpation of their property and imposition and collection of tax with cruelty.

(6) To introduce somebody, when such a person is already known with such nicknames like lame, deaf, blind, squint eyed. In such a case his introduction with such nickname is permissible. But to use such word in order to humiliate him is forbidden. If he can be introduced in some other way then it is better.

١٥٣١ – عَنْ عَائِشَةَ رَضِيَ اللهُ عَنْهَا أَنَّ رَجُلاً اسْتَأْذَنَ عَلَى النَّبِيِّ صَلَّى اللهُ عَلَيْهِ وَسَلَّمَ فَقَالَ : «ائذَنُوا لَهُ ، بِئسَ أَخُو العَشِيرَةِ ؟» متفقٌ عليهِ .

احتَجَّ بهِ البخاري في جوازِ غيبةِ أهلِ الفسادِ وأهلِ الرِّيَبِ .

1531. **Hazrat Ayesha** (R.A.A.) relates that a man asked for permission to see the Holy Prophet (S.A.W.) whereupon He (S.A.W.) said. He may be permitted to come in; he is rather a bad man in his family. *(Bukhari and Muslim)*

Imam Bukhari has cited this as justification for listening to reports about mischief and mischief mongers.

١٥٣٢ – وَعَنْهَا قَالَتْ : قَالَ رَسُولُ اللهِ صَلَّى اللهُ عَلَيْهِ وَسَلَّمَ : «مَا أَظُنُّ فُلاناً وفُلاناً يَعرِفَانِ مِنْ دِينِنا شَيئاً » . رواه البخاريُّ . قَالَ اللَّيثُ بْنُ سَعْدٍ أَحَدُ رُوَاةِ هَذا الحَدِيثِ : هذَانِ الرَّجُلانِ كَانَا مِنَ المُنَافِقِينَ .

1532. **Hazrat Ayesha** (R.A.A.) relates that the Holy Prophet (S.A.W.) said: I do not think that so and so, and so and so, appreciate (accept) anything of our faith. *(Bukahri)*

Hazrat Lais bin Sa'd (R.A.A.) who is one of the reporters of this tradition says that these two persons were hypocrites.

١٥٣٣ – وَعَنْ فَاطِمَةَ بِنْتِ قَيْسٍ رَضِيَ اللهَ عَنْها قَالَتْ : أَتَيْتُ النَّبِيَّ صَلَّى اللهُ عليهِ وسلَّم ، فقلتُ : إنَّ أبا الجَهْمِ وَمُعَاوِيَةَ خَطَباني ؟ فقالَ رسولُ اللهِ ، صلَّى اللهُ عليهِ وسلَّم : « أَمَّا مُعَاوِيَةُ ، فَصُعْلُوكٌ لامَالَ لَهُ ، وأَمَّا أَبُو الجَهْمِ ، فلا يَضَعُ العَصَا عَنْ عاتِقِهِ » متفقٌ عليه .

وفي روايةٍ لمسلمٍ : « وأَمَّا أَبُو الجَهْمِ فَضَرَّابٌ للنِّسَاءِ » وهو تفسير لرواية: «لا يَضَعُ العَصَا عَنْ عَاتِقِهِ » وقيل : معناه : كثيرُ الأسفارِ .

1533. **Hazrat Fatimah bin Qais** (R.A.A.) relates: I went to the Holy Prophet (S.A.W.) and said: Abul Jahm and Mu'awiah have proposed to marry me. The Holy Prophet (S.A.W.) (by way of information to me) said: As to Mu'awiah, he is poor and has no property, and Abul Jahm, always keeps his stick on his shoulder.

(Bukahri and Muslim)

Imam Muslim's version says: Abul Jahm is a person who beats women very much; and it has also been said that the reference is to his being person with his stick always on his shoulder, and most of the time on journey.

١٥٣٤ – وعنْ زيْدِ بنِ أرْقَمَ رَضِيَ اللهُ عنهُ قالَ : خرَجْنَا معَ رسولِ اللهِ صلّى اللهُ عليهِ وسلَّم في سَفَرٍ أصَابَ النَّاسَ فيهِ شِدَّةٌ ، فقالَ عبدُ اللهِ بنُ أُبَيٍّ : لا تُنْفِقُوا على مَنْ عِنْدَ رسُولِ اللهِ حتى يَنْفَضُّوا وقال : لَئِنْ رَجَعْنَا إلى المَدِينَةِ لَيُخْرِجَنَّ الأعَزُّ مِنْها الأذَلَّ ، فَأتَيْتُ رسولَ اللهِ صَلَّى اللهُ عليْهِ وسَلَّمَ ، فَأخْبَرْتُهُ بِذلكَ ، فأرسلَ إلى عبدِ اللهِ بنِ أُبَيٍّ ، فَاجْتَهَدَ يَمِينَهُ : ما فَعَلَ ، فقالوا : كَذَبَ زيدٌ رسولَ اللهِ ، صَلَّى اللهُ عليهِ وسلَّم ، فَوَقَعَ في نَفْسِي مِمَّا قالوهُ شِدَّةٌ حتى أنزَلَ اللهُ تعالى تَصْدِيقي : (إذا جَاءَكَ المُنَافِقُونَ) ثم دعاهم النبيُّ ، صَلَّى اللهُ عليهِ وسلَّم ، لِيَسْتَغْفِرَ لهم فَلَوَّوْا رُؤُوسَهُمْ . متفقٌ عليه .

1534. Hazrat Zaid bin Arqam (R.A.A.) says. (Once) we went on journey (expedition) with the Holy Prophet (S.A.W.). In this journey we were put to much hardship. Abdullah bin Ubayy (who was with us) said to his associates: Do not spend your provision on those who are with the Messenger of Allah (S.A.W.) so that they may disperse and also said. If we return to Madina the one most honourable will expel the one most mean. I went to the Holy Prophet (S.A.W.) and informed him (S.A.W.) of this and he (S.A.W.) sent for Abdullah bin Ubayy, who denied on oath having said so. People began to say . Zaid has lied before the Holy Prophet (S.A.W.). I was much pained by this till *Sura Al-Munafiqun (Chapter 63)* of the Holy Quran was revealed and Allah the Most High vindicated my position. Then the Holy Prophet (S.A.W.) sent for the hypocrites so that he (S.A.W.) might ask Allah's forgiveness for them, but they turned their heads away due to pride.

(Bukhari and Muslim)

١٥٣٥ – وعن عائشةَ رضيَ اللهُ عنْها قالتْ : قالتْ هِندُ امْرَأةُ أبي سُفْيَانَ للنبيِّ صَلَّى اللهُ علَيْهِ وسلَّم : إنَّ أبا سُفيانَ رجُلٌ شَحِيحٌ ولَيْسَ يُعْطِيني مايَكْفِيني ووَلَدِي إلاَّ ما أخَذْتُ مِنه ، وهوَ لا يَعْلَمُ ؟ قال : «خُذِي ما يَكْفِيكِ ووَلَدَكِ بالمَعْرُوفِ » متفقٌ عليه

1535. Hazrat Ayesha (R.A.A.) says: Hindah, wife of Abu Sufyan, said to the Holy Prophet (S.A.W.): Abu Sufyan is a miser, and does not give me enough (money) which may suffice for me and my children, unless I take something from his money without his knowledge. The Holy Prophet (S.A.W.) said. Take so much (only) which may be sufficient for thee and thy children according to the prevailing practice. *(Bukhari and Muslim)*

* * * * * * *

CHAPTER 257

PROHIBITION OF CARRYING TALES FOR MISCHIEF

قالَ اللهُ تعَالى : هَمَّازٍ مَشَّاءٍ بِنَمِيمٍ [ن : ١١] . وقالَ تعَالى : مَا يَلْفِظُ مِنْ قَوْلٍ إِلَّا لَدَيْهِ رَقِيبٌ عَتِيدٌ [ق : ١٨] .

Allah, the Exalted, said:

347. Detractor, spreader abroad of slanders. (68 : 11)

348. He uttereth no word but there is with him an observer ready. (50 : 18)

١٥٣٦ – وعَنْ حُذَيْفَةَ رضيَ اللهُ عنهُ قالَ : قالَ رسُولُ اللهِ صَلَّى اللهُ عَلَيْهِ وسَلَّمَ : « لايَدْخُلُ الجَنَّةَ نَمَّامٌ » متفقٌ عليه .

1536. Hazrat Huzaifah (R.A.A.) relates that the Holy Prophet (S.A.W.) said. A person who is addicted to carrying tales will not enter Paradise. *(Bukhari and Muslim)*

١٥٣٧ – وَعَنْ ابنِ عبّاسٍ رَضيَ اللهُ عَنهُما أَنَّ رَسُولَ اللهِ صَلَّى اللهُ عَلَيْهِ وَسَلَّمَ : مرَّ بِقَبرَيْنِ فقال : « إنهُمَا يُعَذَّبانِ ، وما يُعَذَّبانِ في كَبيرٍ ! بَلى إنَّهُ كَبيرٌ : أمَّا أحَدُهمَا ،فكَانَ يَمشي بِالنَّميمَةِ ، وَأمَّا الآخَرُ فكَانَ لايَستَتِرُ مِنْ بَولهِ » .

متفقٌ عليه ، وهذا لفظ إحدى روايات البخاري .

1537. Hazrat Ibn Abbas (R.A.A.) says that the Holy Prophet (S.A.W.) once, while passing by two graves, remarked. The (inmates) of these two graves are being tortured not for any serious sin, but in fact they are se ious sins. One of them used to carry tales and the other used to urinate without any cover. *(Bukhari and Muslim)*

١٥٣٨ – وعن ابنِ مَسْعُودٍ رَضِيَ اللهُ عَنْهُ أنَّ النَّبِيَّ صلَّى اللهُ عَلَيْهِ وسَلَّمَ قالَ : « ألا أُنَبِّئُكُمْ ما العَضْهُ ؟ هِيَ النَّمِيمَةُ ، القَالَةُ بَيْنَ النَّاسِ » رواه مسلم .

1538. **Hazrat Ibn Mas'ud** (R.A.A.) relates that the Holy Prophet (S.A.W.) said: May I tell you as to what 'Adha' is? It is carrying tales between people. *(Muslim)*

Note: Allah, the Lord of Honour and Glory has laid down that in order to check the veracity and authenticity of a report (tale) it should first of all be seen as to who is the person carrying this report (tale). If such a person is not a true Muslim, then his report (tale) should not be accepted, lest it is accepted and acted upon,we may have to regret afterwards.

* * * * * * *

CHAPTER 258

PROHIBITION OF REPORTING PEOPLES' TALK TO OFFICERS UNNECESSARILY, SUCH AS FEAR OF DISTURBANCES ETC.

قَالَ اللهُ تَعَالَى : وَلَا تَعَاوَنُوا عَلَى الإِثْمِ وَالْعُدْوَانِ [المائدة : ٢] .

Allah, the Exalted, has said:

349. Help not one another unto sin and transgression. (5 : 2)

١٥٣٩ – وعن ابنِ مَسْعُودٍ رَضِيَ اللهُ عنهُ قالَ : قالَ رَسُولُ اللهِ صَلَّى اللهُ عليهِ وَسَلَّمَ : « لايُبَلِّغْنِي أَحَدٌ من أَصْحابي عَنْ أَحَدٍ شَيْئاً ، فَإِنِّي أُحِبُّ أَنْ أَخْرُجَ إِلَيْكُمْ وأنَا سَلِيمُ الصَّدْرِ » رواهُ أبو داودَ ، والترمذيَ

1539. **Hazrat Ibn Mas'ud** (R.A.A.) relates that the Holy Prophet (S.A.W.) said: No companion of mine should tell me anything bad about another person. For I like that when I meet you my heart should be clean (unbiased). *(Abu Daud and Tirmizi)*

* * * * * * *

CHAPTER 259

CONDEMNATION OF BEING DUPLICITY

قالَ اللهُ تَعالى : يَسْتَخْفُونَ مِنَ النَّاسِ ولا يَسْتَخْفُونَ مِنَ اللهِ وهُوَ مَعَهُم ، إذْ يُبَيِّتُونَ مالا يَرْضَى من القَوْلِ ، وكانَ اللهُ بِمَا يَعْمَلُونَ مُحِيطاً [النساء : ١٠٨] .

Allah, the Exalted, has said:

350. They seek to hide from men and seek not to hide from Allah. He is with them when by night they hold discourse displeasing unto Him. Allah ever surroundeth what they do. (4:108)

١٥٤٠ - وعن أبي هُرَيْرَةَ رَضِيَ اللهُ عَنْهُ قالَ : قالَ رَسُولُ اللهِ صَلَّى اللهُ عَلَيْهِ وَسَلَّم : « تَجِدُونَ النَّاسَ مَعادِنَ : خِيارُهُمْ في الجاهِلِيَّةِ خِيارُهُمْ في الإسْلامِ إذا فَقِهُوا ، وتَجِدُونَ خِيارَ النَّاسِ في هذا الشَّأْنِ أَشَدَّهُم لَهُ كَرَاهِيَةً ، وتَجِدُونَ شَرَّ النَّاسِ ذَا الوَجْهَيْنِ ، الَّذي يَأْتي هؤُلاءِ بِوَجْه ، وهؤُلاءِ بِوَجْه » متفقٌ عليه

1540. Hazrat Abu Hurairah (R.A.A.) reports that the Holy Prophet (S.A.W.) said: You will find (only) such people with good descent who were better among you during the days of (Jahilliya) ignorance. Such people are better if they understand (accept) Islam. And you will find the best people among those in the administration who very much abhor duplicity. You will find double-face person, worst among all the people. He comes to a person with one face and the other with other face.. *(Bukhari and Muslim)*

١٥٤١ - وعنْ محمد بنِ زَيْدٍ أنَّ نَاساً قَالُوا لِجَدِّهِ عبد اللهِ بنِ عُمَرَ رَضِيَ اللهُ عَنْهُما : إنَّا نَدْخُلُ عَلى سَلاطِينِنا فنقولُ لَهُمْ بِخِلافِ ما نَتَكَلَّمُ إذَا خَرَجْنا مِنْ عِنْدِهِمْ قالَ : كُنَّا نَعُدُّ هذا نِفاقاً عَلى عَهْدِ رسولِ اللهِ صَلَّى اللهُ عَلَيْهِ وَسَلَّم . رواه البخاري .

1541. Hazrat Muhammad bin Zaid (R.A.A.) says that some people confessed before his grandfather, Hazrat Abdullah bin 'Umar (R.A.A.) that: When we go to our rulers. We say to them some thing contrary to that which we say when we come out of their courts. Hazrat Abdullah bin Umar (R.A.A.) said: During the days of the Holy Prophet (S.A.W.) we considered this thing as hypocrisy. *(Bukhari)*

Note. According to a tradition reported by Imam Abu Daud the Holy Prophet (S.A.W.) has said that a person indulging in hypocrisy in the World, will have two tongues of fire on the Day of Judgement.

* * * * * * *

CHAPTER 260

SEVERE CONDEMNATION OF FALSEHOOD

قالَ اللهُ تعَالى : وَلا تَقْفُ مَالَيْسَ لَكَ بِهِ عِلْمٌ [الإسراء : ٣٦] .

وقالَ تعَالى : مَايَلْفِظُ مِنْ قَوْلٍ إلّا لَدَيْهِ رَقِيبٌ عَتِيدٌ [ق : ١٨] .

Allah, the Exalted, has said:

351. (O man), follow not that whereof thou hast no knowledge. (17 : 36)

352. He uttereth no word but there is with him an observer ready. (50 : 18)

١٥٤٢ـ وعنْ ابنِ مسعودٍ رَضيَ اللهُ عَنْهُ قالَ : قالَ رَسُولُ اللهِ صلّى اللهُ عَلَيْهِ وَسلّمَ : « إنَّ الصِّدْقَ يَهْدي إلى البِرِّ وَإنَّ البِرَّ يَهْدي إلى الجنّةِ ، وَإنَّ الرَّجُلَ لَيَصْدُقُ حَتّى يُكْتَبَ عِنْدَ اللهِ صِدّيقاً ؛ وَإنَّ الكَذِبَ يَهْدي إلى الفُجُورِ ، وَإنَّ الفُجُورَ يَهْدي إلى النّارِ ، وَإن الرجلَ لَيَكْذِبُ حتّى يُكْتَبَ عِنْدَ اللهِ كَذّاباً » متفقٌ عَلَيْهِ .

1542. This Hadis has already been covered in S. No. 54 of Chapter. 4.

١٥٤٣ـ وعَنْ عبدِ اللهِ بنِ عَمْرو بْنِ العَاصِ رَضيَ اللهُ عَنْهُمَا ، أنَّ النبيَّ صَلّى اللهُ عليهِ وسلّم قال: « أَرْبَعٌ مَنْ كُنَّ فيهِ ، كانَ مُنَافِقاً خالِصاً. وَمَنْ كانَتْ فيه خَصْلَةٌ مِنهُنَّ ، كانَتْ فيهِ خَصْلَةٌ مِنْ نِفاقٍ حتّى يَدَعَهَا: إذا اؤْتُمِنَ خانَ ، وَإذا حَدَّثَ كَذَبَ ، وَإذا عاهَدَ غَدَرَ ،وَإذا خاصَمَ فَجَرَ» متفقٌ عليه

1543. This Hadis has already been covered in S. No. 690 of Chapter 86.

١٥٤٤- وعن ابن عباس رضي اللهُ عنهما عن النبيّ ، صَلّى اللهُ عليهِ وسلَّمَ ، قالَ: «مَنْ تحلَّمَ بِحُلُمٍ لَمْ يَرَهُ ، كُلِّفَ أَنْ يَعقِدَ بينَ شَعيرتينِ وَلَنْ يفعَلَ. وَمَنِ استَمَعَ إلى حَديثِ قَوْمٍ وَهُمْ لَهُ كارِهُونَ ، صُبَّ في أُذُنيهِ الآنُكُ يومَ القيامةِ. وَمَنْ صوَّرَ صورةً عُذِّبَ. وكُلِّفَ أَنْ ينفُخَ فيها الرُّوحَ وليسَ بِنافِخٍ» رواه البخاري

1544. Hazrat Ibn Abbas (R.A.A.) relates that the Holy Prophet (S.A.W.) said: A Person who concocts a false dream which he has not seen will be called upon the Day of Judgement to tie a knot between two grains of barley, which he will not be able to do, and a person who eavesdrops upon a party will have molten lead poured into his ears on the Day of Judgement, and one who paints the portrait of a living being will be punished and called upon to infuse life into it which he will not be able to do. *(Muslim and Bukhari)*

١٥٤٥- وعن ابنِ عُمَرَ رضيَ اللهُ عَنهُما قالَ: قالَ النبيُّ صَلّى اللهُ عَلَيهِ وسلَّمَ: «أفرَى الفِرَى أنْ يُرِيَ الرَّجُلُ عينَيهِ مالَمْ تَرَيا».

رواهُ البخاري . ومعناه: يقولُ: رأيتُ فيما لم يَرَهُ.

1545. Hazrat Ibn 'Umar (R.A.A.) says that the Holy Prophet (S.A.W.) said: The greatest slander is that a person may claim to have seen with his eyes a thing which he has not seen. *(Bukhari).*

That is he speaks a lie that he has seen such a dream, or event which in fact he had not seen at all.

١٥٤٦- وعن سَمُرَةَ بنِ جُندُبٍ رضيَ اللهُ عنهُ قالَ: كانَ رسولُ اللهِ صَلّى اللهُ عليهِ وسلَّمَ مِمّا يُكثِرُ أنْ يقولَ لأصحابِهِ: «هَلْ رأى أحدٌ منكُمْ مِنْ رؤيا؟» فيقُصُّ عليهِ مَنْ شاءَ اللهُ أنْ يقُصَّ ، وإنَّهُ قالَ لنا ذاتَ غَداةٍ: «إنَّهُ أتاني الليلةَ آتيانِ ، وإنَّهما قالا لي: انطلِقْ ، وإنِّي انطلقتُ معهُما ، وإنّا أتينا على رجُلٍ مُضطجِعٍ ، وإذا آخرُ قائمٌ عليهِ بصخرةٍ ، وإذا هوَ يَهوي بالصخرةِ لرأسِهِ ، فيثلَغُ رأسَهُ ، فيتدَهدَهُ الحجرُ ها هُنا ، فيتبَعُ الحجرَ فيأخُذُهُ ، فلا يرجِعُ إليهِ حتّى يَصِحَّ رأسُهُ كما كانَ ، ثُمَّ يعودُ عليهِ ، فيفعَلُ بهِ مِثلَ مافعَلَ

المَرَّةَ الأُولى ! » قال: « قلتُ لهما: سُبْحَانَ اللهِ ! مَا هَذَانِ ؟ قالالي : انْطَلِقْ انْطَلِقْ ، فانْطَلَقْنَا ، فَأَتَيْنَا عَلى رَجُلٍ مُسْتَلْقٍ لِقَفَاه وَإِذا آخَرُ قائمٌ عَلَيْهِ بِكَلُّوبٍ مِنْ حَدِيدٍ ، وإذا هُوَ يَأْتي أحَدَ شِقَّيْ وَجْهِهِ فَيُشَرْشِرُ شِدْقَهُ إلى قَفَاهُ ، وَمَنْخِرَهُ إلى قَفاهُ ، وَعَيْنَهُ إلى قَفاهُ ، ثُمَّ يَتَحَوَّلُ إلى الجانِبِ الآخَرِ ، فَيَفْعَلُ بِهِ مِثْلَ ما فَعَلَ بِالجانِبِ الأَوَّلِ ، فَمَا يَفْرُغُ مِنْ ذلكَ الجانبِ حتَّى يَصِحَّ ذلكَ الجانبُ كما كانَ ، ثمَّ يَعُودُ عليْهِ ، فَيَفْعَلُ مِثْلَ ما فَعَلَ في المَرَّةِ الأُولى » قال: قلتُ: « سُبْحَانَ اللهِ ! ما هذانِ ؟قال: قالا لي : انْطَلِقْ انْطَلِقْ، فَانْطَلَقْنَا . فَأَتَيْنَا عَلى مِثْلِ التَّنُّورِ » فَأَحْسِبُ أنَّهُ قال : « فإذا فيه لَغَطٌ ، وَأَصْوَاتٌ ، فَاطَّلَعْنَا فيهِ فإذا فيه رِجالٌ وَنِساءٌ عُرَاةٌ ، وَإِذا هُمْ يَأْتِيهم لَهَبٌ مِنْ أَسْفَلَ مِنْهُمْ ، فإذا أتَاهُمْ ذلكَ اللَّهَبُ ضَوْضَوْا . قلتُ : ما هؤلاء ؟ قالا لي : انْطَلِقْ انْطَلِقْ ، فَانْطَلَقْنَا فَأَتَيْنَا عَلى نَهرٍ » حَسِبْتُ أنَّهُ كانَ يَقُولُ : «أَحْمَرُ مِثْلُ الدَّمِ ، وإذا في النَّهْرِ رَجُلٌ سَابِحٌ يَسْبَحُ ، وَإِذا عَلى شَطِّ النَّهرِ رَجُلٌ قَدْ جَمَعَ عِنْدَهُ حِجارةً كَثِيرَةً . وإذا ذلكَ السَّابِحُ يَسْبَحُ ما يَسْبَحُ ، ثُمَّ يَأْتي ذلكَ الذي قَدْ جَمَعَ عِنْدَهُ الحِجارَةَ . فَيَفْغَرُ لهُ فاهُ . فَيُلْقِمُهُ حَجَراً ، فَيَنْطَلِقُ فَيَسْبَحُ ، ثُمَّ يَرْجِعُ إليهِ ، كُلَّمَا رَجَعَ إليْهِ .فغرَ لهُ فاهُ .فَأَلْقَمَهُ حَجَراً . قلت لهما : ماهذانِ ؟ قالا لي : انْطَلِقْ انطلِقْ ، فَانْطَلَقْنَا،فَأَتَيْنَا عَلى رَجُلٍ كَرِيهِ المَرْآةِ ، أَوْ كأكرهِ ما أنتَ رَاءٍ رجلاً مَرْأىً ، فإذا هو عِنْدَهُ نَارٌ يَحُشُّها وَيَسْعَى حَوْلَهَا . قلتُ لهما : ما هذا ؟ قالالي : انْطَلِقْ انْطَلِقْ ، فَانْطَلَقْنَا فَأَتَينا على رَوْضَةٍ مُعْتَمَّةٍ فِيها مِنْ كلِّ نَوْرِ الرَّبيعِ ، وإذا بيْنَ ظَهْرَيِ الرَّوْضةِ رَجلٌ طويلٌ لا أكادُ أرى رأْسَهُ طُولاً في السَّماءِ ، وإذا حَوْلَ الرجلِ مِنْ أكثرِ وِلدانٍ رَأَيْتُهُمْ قطُّ ، قُلتُ : ما هذا ؟ وما هؤلاء ؟ قالا لي : انْطَلِقْ انْطَلِقْ ،فَانْطَلَقْنَا،فَأَتَيْنَا إلى دَوْحَةٍ عظيمَةلم أرَ دَوْحَةً قطُّ أعظمَ منها،

ولا أحسنَ ! قالا لي : ارقَ فيها ، فارتقينا فيها إلى مدينةٍ مبنيَّةٍ بلَبِنِ ذهبٍ ولبنِ فضةٍ ، فأتينا بابَ المدينة فاستفتحنا، ففُتِحَ لنا ، فدخلناها، فتلقَّانا رجالٌ شطرٌ من خلقِهم كأحسنِ ما أنت راءٍ ! وشطرٌ منهم كأقبحِ ما أنتَ راءٍ ! قالا لهم : اذهبوا فقعوا في ذلكَ النَّهرِ ، وإذا هوَ نهرٌ معترضٌ يجري كأنَّ ماءَهُ المحضُ في البياضِ ، فذهبُوا فوقعُوا فيه . ثمَّ رجعُوا إلينا قد ذهبَ ذلك السُّوءُ عنهمْ ، فصارُوا في أحسنِ صورةٍ . قال : قالا لي : هذه جنَّةُ عدْنٍ ، وهذاك منزلُكَ ، فسَمَا بصَرِي صعُداً ، فإذا قصرٌ مثلُ الرَّبابَةِ البيضاء . قالا لي : هذاك منزِلكَ ؟ قلتُ لهما : باركَ اللهُ فيكما ، فذراني فأدخلَه . قالا : أما الآن فلا ، وأنتَ داخلُهُ . قلت لهُمَا : فإنِّي رأيتُ منْذُ اللَّيلةَ عجباً ؟ فما هذا الذي رأيتُ ؟ قالا لي : أمَا إنَّا سنخبِرُكَ : أمَّا الرجلُ الأوَّلُ الذي أتيتَ عليه يُثلَغُ رأسُهُ بالحجَرِ ، فإنَّهُ الرَّجلُ يأخُذُ القرآنَ فيرفُضُه ، وينامُ عن الصَّلاةِ المكتُوبَةِ ، وأمَّا الرَّجُلُ الذي أتيتَ عليْهِ يُشرْشرُ شدقُهُ إلى قفَاهُ ، ومَنْخِرُه إلى قفَاهُ ، وعينُه إلى قفاهُ ، فإنه الرَّجلُ يغدُو منْ بيْتِه فيكذِبُ الكذْبَة تبلُغُ الآفاقَ وأمَّا الرِّجالُ والنِّساءُ العُراةُ الذين هُمْ في مِثلِ بِناءِ التَّنُّورِ ، فإنَّهم الزُّناة والزَّواني ، وأما الرجلُ الَّذي أتيْتَ علَيْهِ يَسْبَحُ في النَّهرِ ، ويُلْقَمُ الحِجَارَةَ ، فإنَّهُ آكِلُ الرِّبَا ، وأمَّا الرَّجلُ الكريهُ المرآةِ الذي عندَ النَّارِ يحشُّها ويسْعَى حوْلَهَا ، فإنَّهُ مالِكٌ خازنُ جهنَّمَ ، وأما الرَّجُلُ الطَّويلُ الَّذي في الرَّوْضَةِ ، فإنه إبراهيم ، وأما الوِلدان الذينَ حوْله، فكلُّ مَوْلودٍ ماتَ على الفِطْرَةِ » وفي رواية البَرْقانيِّ : « وُلِدَ على الفِطرَةِ » فقال بعض المسلمينَ : يارسولَ اللهِ ، وأولادُ المشركينَ ؟ فقال رسولُ الله صلَّى الله علَيهِ وسلَّمَ : « وأولادُ المشرِكينَ ، وأما القومُ الذينَ كانُوا شطرٌ منهم حسَنٌ ، وشطرٌ منهمْ قبيحٌ ، فإنهمْ قومٌ خلطُوا عملاً صالحاً وآخرَ سيِّئاً ، تجاوزَ اللهُ عنْهُم » رواه البخاري .

وفي روايةٍ له : « رَأَيتُ اللَّيلَةَ رجلَينِ أتَيَاني فأخرَجاني إلى أرضٍ مُقدَّسةٍ »
ثم ذكَره وقال : « فانطلَقنا إلى نقبٍ مثلِ التَّنُّورِ ، أعلاهُ ضيِّقٌ وأسفَلُهُ
واسعٌ ؛ يتَوقَّدُ تحتَهُ نَاراً ، فإذا ارْتَفَعَت ارتَفعُوا حتى كادُوا أنْ يخرُجوا ،
وإذا خمَدَتْ ؛ رَجَعوا فيها ، وفيها رجالٌ ونساءٌ عراةٌ ، وفيها : حتى أتينا على
نهرٍ من دَمٍ ولم يشكَّ فيه رجُلٌ قائمٌ على وسَطِ النَّهرِ ، وعلى شَطِّ النَّهرِ
رجُلٌ ، وبينَ يدَيهِ حِجارةٌ ، فأقبلَ الرَّجُلُ الذي في النَّهْرِ ، فإذا أرادَ أنْ
يخرُجَ ، رَمَى الرَّجُلُ بحَجرٍ في فيه ، فرَدَّهُ حيثُ كانَ ، فجعَلَ كلَّما
جاءَ ليَخرُجَ جعَلَ يرَمي في فيه بحَجَرٍ ، فيَرْجِعُ كمَا كَانَ . وفيهَا :
« فصعِدَا بي الشَّجرَةَ ، فأدْخلاني دَاراً لَمْ أرَ قطُّ أحْسنَ منْهَا ، فيهَا رجَالٌ
شُيُوخٌ وَشبَابٌ . وفيهَا : الَّذي رَأيتَهُ يُشَقُّ شِدْقُهُ فكَذَّابٌ ، يُحدِّثُ
بالكَذْبَةِ فتُحمَلُ عَنْهُ حتَّى تبلُغَ الآفاقَ ، فيُصْنَعُ به مارَأيتَ إلى يوْمِ القِيامةِ »
وَفيهَا : « الَّذي رَأيتَهُ يُشدَخُ رَأسُهُ فرَجُلٌ علَّمَهُ اللهُ القُرآنَ ، فنامَ عَنْهُ
باللَّيلِ ، ولَمْ يَعمَلْ فيه بالنَّهَارِ ، فيُفعَلُ بِه إلى يوْمِ القِيامَةِ ، وَالدَّارُ
الأُولى الَّتي دَخَلْتَ دَارُ عَامَّةِ المُؤْمنينَ ، وَأمَّا هذه الدَّارُ فدَارُ الشُّهدَاءِ ،
وَأنا جِبريلُ ، وَهذا مِيكَائيلُ ، فارفَعْ رَأسَكَ ، فرَفعتُ رَأسي ، فإذا فوقي
مِثْلُ السَّحَابِ ، قالا : ذاكَ مَنزلُكَ ، قلتُ : دَعاني أدخُلْ مَنزلي ، قالا :
إنَّهُ بَقِيَ لَكَ عُمُرٌ لَم تَستَكمِلهُ ، فلَوْ استَكمَلتَهُ ، أتَيتَ مَنزِلَكَ »
رواه البخاري .

1546. **Hazrat Samurah bin Jundub** (R.A.A.) relates: The Holy Prophet (S.A.W.) occasionally used to inquire from his (S.A.W.) companions: Has any One of you seen a dream? Then, one who has seen a dream would relate his dream, what Allah **willed** to be related. Holy Prophet (S.A.W.) related to us: (Last night) two persons came to me in a dream and asked me to go along with them. Accordingly I accompanied them and we came across a man who was lying flat and another man was standing near him with a boulder in his hand, with which he was striking and crushing his head. After the stone had hit the head of the man, it rolled away to some distance from him. The striker went after the stone and caught it up and returned with it (to strike again). Meanwhile the head of the man on the ground, which was hit, recovered from its previous injury, and the striker hit him again; (and this process continued). I asked my two companions. Holy is Allah! who are these two persons? They said: 'Let us go, let us go. As such we moved onward and met a man lying flat on ground and another man standing near him with a hooked iron bar (whose end was pointed and sharpened) in his hand and coming from one side cut his mouth upto the neck, and then ripped open his nostril upto his neck and tore open his eye also upto his neck, and then turning to his other side repeated the same operation which he did on the first side. By this time the first side of the man's face was restored from its wounds, and the operator returned to the first side and repeated the operation once more. (This process continued in this way). The Holy Prophet (S.A.W.) said, Holy is Allah! What are these two persons doing? They said to me. 'Let us go, let us go.' and we continued going onward and arrived near a hollow ground which looked like an oven. The narrator says that probably the Holy Prophet (S.A.W.) said, 'out of which we could hear some noise of commotion. We looked into it and saw a number of naked men and women who cried out when the flames reached them from below. I asked my companions; 'Who are they'? They said: 'Let us march on, let us march on'; and we proceeded further till we reached a stream, the water of which was red like blood and a man was swimming in it. On the bank of the stream was standing another man with a heap of stones. When the swimmer came towards him, he would strike him with a stone crushing his face, and be would return; and he would start swimming again, and as he approached the bank of the river once more, the man standing on the bank would strike him (again) with a stone which crushed his face. The Holy Prophet (S.A.W.) inquired from the companions. "Who are these two"? They said: 'Let us go, let us go'; and we continued our journey till we came to a frightfully ugly person who was indeed an unsightly person, near a blazing fire which he was circling. The Holy Prophet (S.A.W.) said: I asked my two companions. Who is this'? They said: 'Let us go on, let us go on', and we resumed our journey till we came to a garden which was full of all varieties of spring season flowers, and in the centre of the garden was a man so tall that I could not see his head as if it was touching the sky, and around him were many children whom I had never seen before. I asked my companions: 'Who is this man, and who are these children'? They said to me: 'Let us go ahead, let us go ahead;' and we proceeded and reached a huge tree so big and huge that I had not seen so big and so beautiful a tree before, and my companions asked me to climb the tree and we all climbed and we saw a city which was bullt of gold and silver bricks set by turns. We approached the gate of the city and got it opened; and we entered (the city) and saw there people with half of their body as the most beautiful that one could imagine, and the other half as the most unsightly and ugly, the ugliest that could be imagined. My companions asked (these people) to take a dip in this river, which was flowing through the centre of the city and the water of which was pure and white. They plunged into the river and when they came out their ugliness had disappeared and they had become very beautiful. The Holy Prophet (S.A.W.) continuing said. My two companions informed me: This is the Paradise of Eden and it is meant for your residence. When I raised my eyes I saw a palace as white as a white piece of cloud. Both of them repeated: 'This palace is yours.' I said to them: 'My Allah the Most High bless you both, now please let me enter it.' They said: 'Not today, but (one day) you will surely enter it.' I said to them: To night I have seen many wonderful things. What are these things which I have seen'? They said to me: 'We shall now let you know. The first person near whom you went and whose head was being (repeately) crushed with a stone was one who was in the habit of memorising the Quran and then forgetting it and was careless about the 'Farz Salat' (Compulsory Prayers); The person whose mouth, nostril andeyes were being cut and ripped open upto his neck, was one who issues forth from his home early in the morning spreading forth such lies which get currency all over the world; the men and women burning in the oven, were adulterers and adulteresses; the man you saw swimming in the stream and being stoned was one who earned money through usury. The ugly man who was near the fire was Malik, the keeper of the Hell. The tall man whom you saw in the garden was Prophet Abraham (A.S.) and the children around him were those children who had died on nature. According to Barqani they were born on nature. One of the Muslims requested the Holy Prophet (S.A.W.) 'O Messenger of Allah! Are the children of the non-believers also included among them?' The Holy Prophet (S.A.W.) said: 'Yes, and the children of the non-believers were also there. Those persons who had half of their body handsome and half ugly, were those who had committed virtuous and evil deeds both, and Allah, the Lord of Honour and Glory had forgiven them. *(Bukhari*

According to another version of *Imam Bukhari*, the Holy Prophet (S.A.W.) said: I saw last night that two men took me to the Holy Land and then the narration proceeds as related above and continues: We arrived
then the narration proceeds as related above and continues: We arrived
at a hollow in the ground like an oven, the mouth of which was narrow and the bottom was wide, and fire was burning inside it. As the flames rose higher the inmates also rose, till they were about to come out of the pit, the flames went down, and they also went down with them. These men and women were all naked. Then we came to a stream flowing with blood and there was no doubt about this, and in the middle of this river was standing a man and another one was on the bank with a heap of stones in front of him. The man in the middle of the river wanted to get out of the stream, but when he tried to get out, the one, on the bank, struck him with a stone on his face which made

him go back to the point where he was before. This happened every time the man in the middle of the river tried to get out. This version then says. 'The two (companions) climbed a tree along with me and then made me enter a house. I have never seen a better house than this. In this house there were men, old and young. This narration continues. I was told: The one, you saw with his cheeks ripped open was a liar whose lies were multiplied till they reached all corners of the earth. He will be treated like this till the Day of Judgement. The one you saw whose head was smashed, was a man whom Allah the Most High had taught the Quran, but he went to bed during the night, forgetting it, and did not act upon it during the day. He will be treated like that till the Day of Judgement. The first house you entered was the abode of the believers and this last house is of the martyrs. I am Gabriel and this my colleague, Michael; now please look up; accordingly I raised my head and saw, something like a cloud above me. They told me: This is your house.' I said: 'Leave me to enable me to enter my house. They said: 'Your have still to live some part of your age, which you have not yet completed. When you have completed it, you will enter your house. *(Bukhari)*

* * * * * * *

CHAPTER 261

JUSTIFICATION FOR FALSEHOOD IN SOME CASES

اِعْلَمْ أَنَّ الْكَذِبَ، وَإِنْ كَانَ أَصْلُهُ مُحَرَّماً، فَيَجُوزُ فِي بَعْضِ الأَحْوَالِ بِشُرُوطٍ قد أَوْضَحْتُهَا فِي كِتَاب : « الأَذْكَارِ » ، وَمُخْتَصَرُ ذلك : أَنَّ الكلامَ وسيلةٌ إلى المقاصدِ ، فَكُلُّ مَقْصُودٍ مَحْمُودٍ يُمْكِنُ تَحْصِيلُهُ بغَيْرِ الْكَذِبِ يَحْرُمُ الْكَذِبُ فيه ، وَإِنْ لَمْ يُمكِنْ تَحْصِيلُهُ إلاَّ بالكَذِبِ ، جازَ الْكَذِبُ . ثُمَّ إِنْ كَانَ تَحْصِيلُ ذلك المقصُودِ مُبَاحاً كَانَ الْكَذِبُ مُباحاً ، وَإِنْ كانَ وَاجِباً ، كان الكذِبُ واجِباً . فإذا اخْتَفَى مُسْلِمٌ مِن ظالِمٍ يريد قَتْلَه، أَوْ أَخذَ مالِه ، وَأَخفَى مَالَه ، وَسُئِل إنسانٌ عنه ، وَجَبَ الْكَذِبُ بإخفائِه ، وكذا لو كانَ عِندَهُ وَدِيعَةٌ ، وَأَرَادَ ظالِمٌ أَخْذَهَا ، وَجَبَ الْكَذِبُ بإخفائها . والأَحْوطُ في هذا كُلِّه أَنْ يُوَرِّيَ ، ومعْنَى التَّوْرِيَةِ : أَنْ يَقْصِدَ بِعبَارَتِه مَقْصُوداً صَحِيحاً لَيْسَ هو كاذِباً بالنِّسْبَةِ إليْهِ ، وإنْ كانَ كاذِباً في ظَاهِرِ

اللَّفْظِ ، وَبِالنِّسْبَةِ إلى ما يَفْهَمُهُ المُخَاطَبُ، ولَوْ تَرَكَ التَّوْرِيَةَ وَأَطْلَقَ عِبَارَةَ الكَذِبِ ، فلَيْسَ بِحَرَامٍ في هذا الحَالِ .

وَاسْتَدَلَّ العُلَمَاءُ بِجَوازِ الكَذِبِ في هذا الحَالِ بِحَدِيثِ أُمِّ كُلْثُومٍ رضيَ اللهُ عَنْها أنّها سمعت رسولَ اللهِ صَلَّى اللهُ عليهِ وسلَّمَ يقولُ : « لَيْسَ الكَذَّابُ الَّذي يُصْلِحُ بيْنَ النَّاسِ ،فَيَنْمِي خَيْراً أو يقولُ خَيْراً » متفقٌ عليه

زاد مسلم في رواية : « قالَتْ أُمُّ كُلْثُومٍ : وَلَمْ أَسْمَعْهُ يُرَخِّصُ في شيءٍ مِمَّا يَقُولُ النَّاسُ إلاَّ في ثلاثٍ ؛ تَعْني : الحَرْبَ . وَالإصْلاحَ بَيْنَ النَّاسِ ، وحَدِيثَ الرَّجُلِ امْرَأتَهُ . وحَدِيثَ المَرْأَةِ زَوْجَهَا .

In Islam the severest threat of punishment or "Wa'eed", is "La'nat" i.e. censure or severe condemnation. This means, to be deprived of Allah's mercy. In the Holy Quran this epithet has been used for the Satan. But a Muslim has not been called with this epithet for any lapse, except when he lies. In the Holy Quran, Allah the Lord of Honour and Glory, has permitted to censure and condemn a liar or a person levelling a false allegation on behalf of the Almighty.

(Translator)

Imam Nawawi says:

Although falsehood is basically 'Haram' or unlawful, but in exceptional cases it is permissible under certain circumstances. The learned Imam has described them in his book "Katab-ul-Azkar". The main points are that if telling lie may be the means to achieve a lawful object, and the same could be achieved without resort to lying, then in such a case it is unlawful or 'Haram' to speak a lie; and if the object cannot be achieved without resort to lying, then the same is permissible. And if the achievement of this object be lawful and an act permitted by the Sharia, then to lie to achieve the same is also lawful and an act permitted by the Sharia; and if the achievement of this object be obligatory, it just like a Farz act, but only a little below in status than the Farz act, then in that case it becomes obligatory to lie to achieve this object. As for example, if a Muslim has hidden himself due to fear of some tyrant who may be after his life, or property, then in such a case if a person is asked about him or his property, the said person should speak lie. Similarly, if some body holds another persons property in deposit, and some tyrant is after it, then in order to protect it, the custodian of the property must speak lie. But the best course for him is to employ "Tauriya" while speaking to the tyrant. "Tauriya" means that while speaking, the speaker should speak the truth but in such words which may lead the listner astray and off the mark; if he does not employ "Tauriya" and "Kinaya" or indirect hints, and has spoken in plain falsehood, then this is also lawful. In this connection a tradition of the Holy Prophet (S.A.W.) has been quoted by Imam Bukhari and Muslim from Hazrat Umm Kulsum (R.A.A.) who says she heard from the Holy Prophet (S.A.W.) who said that one who employs better words to make peace between people is not a liar.

Imam Muslim in his version has added the following words. 'Hazrat Umm Kulsum (R.A.A.) says that she never heard the Holy Prophet (S.A.W.) allowing for any equivocation or latitude to any body in talking, except on three occasions such as, to effect peace between peoples, in case of fighting, or talking between husband and wife.

* * * * * * *

CHAPTER 262

DUE ENQUIRY BEFORE RETELLING A STORY

قَالَ اللهُ تَعَالَى : وَلَاتَقْفُ مَا لَيْسَ لَكَ بِهِ عِلْمٌ [الإسراء : ٣٦]

وقالَ تَعَالَى : ما يَلْفِظُ من قَوْلٍ إلاَّ لَدَيْهِ رَقِيبٌ عَتِيدٌ [ق : ١٨] .

Allah, the Exalted, has said:

353. (O man), follow not that whereof thou hast no knowledge. (17 : 36)

354. He uttereth not word but there is with him an observer ready. (50 . 18)

١٥٤٧– وعنْ أبي هُرَيْرَةَ رضيَ اللهُ عَنْهُ أنَّ النبيَّ صَلَّى اللهُ عَلَيْهِ وسَلَّمَ قالَ : « كفى بالمَرءِ كَذِباً أنْ يُحَدِّثَ بِكُلِّ ما سَمِعَ » رواه مسلم .

1547. Hazrat Abu Hurairah (R.A.A.) relates that the Holy **Prophet** (S.A.W.) said: It is sufficient to make a man a liar when he **goes** on circulating (without verification) all that he has heard.

(Muslim)

١٥٤٨ – وعنْ سَمُرَةَ رضيَ اللهُ عَنْهُ قالَ : قالَ رَسُولُ اللهِ صَلَّى اللهُ عَلَيْهِ وسَلَّمَ : « مَنْ حدَّثَ عَنِّي بِحَدِيثٍ يرَى أنَّهُ كَذِبٌ، فَهُوَ أحَدُ الكَاذِبِيْنَ » رواه مسلم .

1548. Hazrat Samurah (R.A.A.) relates that the Holy Prophet (S.A.W.) said: A person who attributes something to me which he believes to be false, is one of the liars. *(Muslim)*

١٥٤٩ — وعنْ أسماءَ رضيَ اللهُ عنْهما أنَّ امرَأةً قالَتْ : يارَسُولَ اللهِ إنَّ لي ضَرَّةً فهل عَلَيَّ جُنَاحٌ إنْ تَشَبَّعْتُ مِن زوجِي غيرَ الذي يُعطِيني ؟ فقال النبيُّ صلَّى اللهُ عليهِ وسلَّم : « المُتَشَبِّعُ بِمَا لم يُعْطَ كَلابِسِ ثَوْبَي زُورٍ » متفقٌ عليه .

1549. Hazrat Asma' (R.A.A.) reports that once a woman came to the Holy Prophet (S.A.W.) and submitted O Messenger of Allah! I have a co-wife. If I say to her that my husband has presented me with such and such thing and which may not be the fact, will it be sinful? The Holy Prophet (S.A.W.) said: A person who pretends having received something, contrary to the fact is like one who wears two cloaks of falsehood. *(Bukhari and Muslim)*

* * * * * * *

CHAPTER 263

PROHIBITION OF TENDERING FALSE EVIDENCE

قَالَ اللهُ تَعَالَى : واجْتَنِبُوا قَوْلَ الزُّورِ [الحج : ٣٠] . وقالَ تَعالَى : ولاتَقْفُ مالَيْسَ لكَ بِهِ عِلمٌ [الإسراء : ٣٦] . وقالَ تَعَالَى : مايَلفِظُ مِنْ قَوْلٍ إلاَّ لدَيْهِ رَقِيبٌ عَتِيدٌ [ق : ١٨] . وقالَ تَعَالَى : إنَّ رَبَّكَ لَبِالمِرصَادِ [الفجر : ١٤] . وقالَ تَعَالَى : والَّذِينَ لا يَشْهَدُونَ الزُّورَ [الفرقان : ٧٢] .

Allah, the Exalted, has said:

355. And shun lying speech. (22 : 30)

356. (O man), follow not that whereof thou hast no knowledge. (17 : 36)

357. He uttereth no word but there is with him an observer ready. (50 . 18)

358. Lo! thy Lord is ever watchful (89 : 14)

359. And those who will not witness vanity. (25 : 72)

١٥٥٠– وعنْ أبي بَكْرَةَ رضيَ اللهُ عَنْهُ قالَ : قالَ رسولُ اللهِ صَلّى اللهُ عَليهِ وسَلّمَ : « ألا أُنَبِّئُكُم بأَكْبَرِ الكَبائِرِ؟ » قُلنا : بَلى يارسولَ اللهِ . قَالَ : « الإشْرَاكُ باللهِ ، وعُقُوقُ الوَالِدَيْنِ » وكانَ مُتَّكِئاً فَجَلَسَ ،فقال : « ألا وقَوْلُ الزُّورِ ! » فما زالَ يُكَرِّرُهَا حتى قلنا : لَيْتَهُ سَكَتَ . متفقٌ عليه .

1550. This Hadith has already been covered in S. No. 336 of Chapter 41.

* * * * * * *

CHAPTER 264

PROHIBITION OF CURSING MAN OR ANIMAL

١٥٥١– عنْ أبي زَيْدٍ ثابتِ بنِ الضَّحاكِ الأنصاريِّ رضيَ اللهُ عَنْهُ ، وهو من أهْلِ بَيْعَةِ الرِّضوان قال : قَالَ رسُولُ اللهِ صَلّى اللهُ عليهِ وسلّمَ : « مَنْ حَلَفَ عَلى يَمِينٍ بِمِلَّةٍ غَيْرِ الإسْلامِ كاذباً مُتَعَمِّداً ، فَهُوَ كَمَا قَالَ ، وَمَنْ قَتَلَ نَفْسَهُ بِشَيْءٍ ، عُذِّبَ بِهِ يَوْمَ القِيامَةِ ،وَلَيْسَ عَلى رَجُلٍ نَذْرٌ فِيما لا يَمْلِكُهُ ، وَلَعْنُ المُؤْمِنِ كَقَتْلِهِ » متفقٌ عليه .

1551. Hazrat Abu Zaid Sabit bin Zahak Al Ansari (R.A.A.) (He is one of the member of the Bait-i-Rizwan Convention), relates that the Holy Prophet (S.A.W.) said: A person who knowingly takes a false oath that if he is not speaking the truth, he might become a follower of a faith other than Islam, then such a person is already as he says. One who kills himself with an instrument, will be tortured on the Day of Judgement by it. A person cannot offer a thing in his vow, which does not belong to him. Cursing a Muslim amounts to his assassination. *(Bukhari and Muslim)*

١٥٥٢ – وعنْ أبي هُرَيْرَةَ رضيَ اللهُ عَنْهُ أنَّ رَسُولَ اللهِ صَلّى اللهُ عَلَيْهِ وسَلّمَ : قال : « لايَنْبَغِي لِصِدِّيقٍ أنْ يَكُونَ لَعّاناً » رواه مسلم .

1552. Hazrat Abu Hurairah (R.A.A.) relates that the Holy Prophet (S.A.W.) said: It does not befit a Siddiq (A true man) that he should opt to cursing. *(Muslim)*

١٥٥٣ – وعنْ أبي الدَّرْداءِ رضِيَ اللهُ عَنْهُ قالَ : قالَ رَسُولُ اللهِ صَلّى

اللهُ عَلَيْهِ وسَلَّمَ : « لايَكُونُ اللَّعَّانُونَ شُفَعَاءَ ، وَلا شُهَدَاءَ يَوْمَ القِيَامَةِ » رواه مسلم .

1553. Hazrat Abu Darda (R.A.A.) says that the Holy Prophet (S.A.W.) said: Those persons who are addicted to cursing too much will neither be inter-cessors nor witnesses on the Day of Judgement. *(Muslim)*

١٥٥٤ – وعَنْ سَمُرَةَ بْنِ جُنْدُبٍ رضيَ اللهُ عَنْهُ قالَ : قالَ رَسُولُ اللهِ صَلَّى اللهُ عَلَيْهِ وسَلَّم : « لاتَلاعَنُوا بلَعْنَةِ الله ، وَلا بِغَضَبِهِ ، وَلا بِالنَّارِ » رواه أبو داودَ ، والترمذيّ وقالا : حديثٌ حَسَنٌ صَحيحٌ .

1554. Hazrat Samurah bin Jundub (R.A.A.) reports that the Holy Prophet (S.A.W.) said. Do not curse anyone among yourself with the curse or wrath of Allah or with the fire of Hell.

(Abu Daud and Tirmizi has said this is sound and good).

١٥٥٥ – وعن ابنِ مسعودٍ رَضِيَ اللهُ عَنْهُ قالَ : قالَ رَسُولُ اللهِ صَلَّى اللهُ عليْهِ وسَلَّمَ : « لَيْسَ المؤمنُ بِالطَّعَّانِ ، وَلا اللَّعَّانِ ، وَلا الفَاحِشِ ، وَلا البَذِيِّ » رواه الترمذي وقالَ : حديثٌ حسنٌ .

1555. Hazrat Abdullah bin Mas'ud (R.A.A.) relates that the Holy Prophet (S.A.W.) said that a perfect Muslim is neither a taunter, curser nor an abuser nor one having a long tongue. *(Tirmizi)*

١٥٥٦ – وعنْ أبي الدَّرْداءِ رَضِيَ اللهُ عنهُ قالَ : قالَ رسُولُ اللهِ صَلَّى اللهُ عَليْهِ وسَلَّمَ : « إنَّ العبْدَ إذا لَعَنَ شَيْئاً ، صَعِدَتِ اللَّعْنَةُ إلى السَّماءِ ، فتُغْلَقُ أبْوابُ السَّماءِ دُونَها ، ثُمَّ تَهبطُ إلى الأرْضِ ، فَتُغْلَقُ أبوابُها دُونَها ، ثُمَّ تَأْخُذُ يَميناً وَشِمالاً ، فَإذا لَمْ تَجِدْ مَسَاغاً ٣٠٣ رَجَعَتْ إلى الذي لُعِنَ ، فَإنْ كانَ أهْلاً لِذَلكَ ، وَإلاَّ رَجَعَتْ إلى قائلِها » رواه أبو داود .

1556. Hazrat Abu Darda (R.A.A.) relates that the Holy Prophet (S.A.W.) said: When a bondsman (person) curses something (or some-body) the curse ascends towards the heaven, then all the gates of heaven are closed against it; thereafter it descends to the earth, and then the gates of the earth are closed against it. After this it turns towards right and left and when it finds no way there too, it turns to the person or the thing which has been cursed and gets attached to him or it, if the same may deserve it, otherwise it returns to the one who uttered it. *(Abu Daud)*

١٥٥٧ – وعن عِمْرَانَ بْنِ الحُصَيْنِ رَضِيَ اللهُ عَنْهُما قالَ : بَيْنَما رَسُولُ اللهِ صَلّى اللهُ عليه وَسَلَّم في بَعْضِ أَسْفَارِه ، وَامرَأَةٌ مِنَ الأنصارِ عَلى نَاقة ، فَضَجِرَتْ ، فَلَعَنَتْهَا . فَسمِعَ ذلكَ رَسُولُ اللهِ صَلَّى اللهُ عليه وسلَّم فقالَ : « خُذُوا ما عَلَيها وَدَعُوها ؛ فإنَّها مَلعُونَةٌ » قالَ عِمرَانُ : فكأَنِّي أَرَاهَا الآنَ تَمشي في النَّاسِ مايَعرِضُ لهَا أَحَدٌ . رواه مسلم .

1557. Hazrat Imran Ibn Husain (R.A.A.) relates. We accompanied the Holy Prophet (S.A.W.) on many journeys. (On such a journey) an Ansari woman accompanied us. She was riding a she-camel, which she rebuked and cursed. The Holy Prophet (S.A.W.) heard this and said: Unload the she-camel and leave it loose for it has been cursed. Hazrat Imran bin Husain (R.A.A.) says: I recollect the panorama that the said she-camel is walking among the people, but nobody takes any notice of the animal. *(Muslim)*

١٥٥٨ – وعن أبي بَرزَةَ نَضلَةَ بنِ عُبَيْدٍ الأسلَمِيِّ رَضِيَ اللهُ عَنْهُ قالَ : بَينَما جارِيَةٌ عَلى نَاقَةٍ عَلَيها بعضُ مَتَاعِ القَوْمِ ، إذْ بَصُرَتْ بالنَّبيِّ ، صَلَّى اللهُ عَلَيْهِ وسلَّمَ . وَتَضَايَقَ بِهِم الجَبَلُ ؛ فقالتْ : حَلْ ، اللَّهُمَّ العَنْهَا . فقالَ النَّبيُّ ، صَلَّى اللهُ عَلَيْهِ وَسَلَّم : « لاتُصَاحِبْنا نَاقَةٌ عَلَيها لَعْنَةٌ » رواه مسلم .

1558. Hazrat Abu Barazah Nadhlah bin 'Ubaid Al-Aslami (R.A.A.) relates: A young woman was riding a she-camel which was also carrying (considerable) load of her tribe, when unexpectedly she saw the Holy Prophet (S.A.W.) and her tribes men became so nervous that the mountain pass became difficult to cross for them. (this was so because they had overloaded the animal). She shouted at her she-camel and goaded her to run faster and cursed it. The Holy Prophet (S.A.W.) (who heard this) said: A she-camel which has been cursed should not accompany us. *(Muslim)*

* * * * * * *

CHAPTER 265

PERMISSION TO CURSE SOME SINNERS WITHOUT NAMING ANYBODY

قالَ اللهُ تَعَالى : أَلا لَعْنَةُ اللهِ عَلى الظَّالِمِينَ [هود : ١٨] . وقالَ تَعَالى : فأَذَّنَ مُؤَذِّنٌ بَيْنَهُمْ أَنْ لَعْنَةُ اللهِ عَلى الظَّالِمِينَ [الأعراف : ٤٤]

وَثَبَتَ فِي الصَّحِيحِ أَنَّ رَسُولَ اللهِ صَلَّى اللهُ عَلَيْهِ وَسَلَّمَ قَالَ: «لَعَنَ اللهُ الْوَاصِلَةَ وَالْمُسْتَوْصِلَةَ» وَأَنَّهُ قَالَ: «لَعَنَ اللهُ آكِلَ الرِّبَا» وَأَنَّهُ لَعَنَ الْمُصَوِّرِينَ، وَأَنَّهُ قَالَ: «لَعَنَ اللهُ مَنْ غَيَّرَ مَنَارَ الأَرْضِ» أَيْ: حُدُودَهَا، وَأَنَّهُ قَالَ: «لَعَنَ اللهُ السَّارِقَ يَسْرِقُ الْبَيْضَةَ» وَأَنَّهُ قَالَ: «لَعَنَ اللهُ مَنْ لَعَنَ وَالِدَيْهِ» «وَلَعَنَ اللهُ مَنْ ذَبَحَ لِغَيْرِ اللهِ» وأَنَّهُ قَالَ: «مَنْ أَحْدَثَ فِيهَا حَدَثاً أَوْ آوَى مُحْدِثاً، فَعَلَيْهِ لَعْنَةُ اللهِ وَالْمَلَائِكَةِ وَالنَّاسِ أَجْمَعِينَ» وأَنَّهُ قَالَ: «اللَّهُمَّ الْعَنْ رِعْلاً، وَذَكْوَانَ وَعُصَيَّةَ؛ عَصَوْا اللهَ وَرَسُولَهُ» وَهذِهِ ثَلاثُ قَبَائِلَ مِنَ الْعَرَبِ وأَنَّهُ قَالَ: «لَعَنَ اللهُ الْيَهُودَ اتَّخَذُوا قُبُورَ أَنْبِيَائِهِمْ مَسَاجِدَ». وَأَنَّهُ «لَعَنَ الْمُتَشَبِّهِينَ مِنَ الرِّجَالِ بِالنِّسَاءِ، وَالْمُتَشَبِّهَاتِ مِنَ النِّسَاءِ بِالرِّجَالِ»

وَجَمِيعُ هذِهِ الأَلْفَاظِ فِي الصحيحِ، بَعْضُهَا فِي صحيحَي البخاري ومسلمٍ، وَبَعْضُهَا فِي أَحَدِهِمَا، وَإِنَّمَا قَصَدْتُ الاخْتِصَارَ بِالإِشَارَةِ إِلَيْهَا، وَسَأَذْكُرُ مُعْظَمَهَا فِي أبوابها مِنْ هذا الكِتَابِ، إِنْ شَاءَ اللهُ تعالى.

Allah, the Exalted, has said:

360. Now the curse of Allah is upon wrong-doers (11 : 18)

361. And a crier in between them crieth: The curse of Allah is on evil-doers. (7 : 44)

Imam Nawawi says that it is evident from authentic traditions that the Holy Prophet (S.A.W.) has cursed the woman who uses wigs, and he (S.A.W.) has also cursed that woman whose profession is to provide wigs to other women. The Holy Prophet (S.A.W.) has disclosed that Allah, the Most High, has cursed the person who practices usuary. He (S.A.W.) has (also) cursed the artist who draws pictures. The Holy Prophet (S.A.W.) has also said that Allah the Most High has cursed a person who abolishes or reduces the limits of land. The Holy Prophet (S.A.W.) says that Allah the Exalted curses a person who steals even an egg; and also that Allah, the Most High may curse a person who curses his parents; and Allah may curse the person, who has slaughtered (an animal) in somebody's name other than Allah. The Holy Prophet (S.A.W.) said: May Allah the Most High, His angles and the entire humanity curse a person who introduces or invents some un-Islamic (contrary to Sharia) acts or provides shelter to such a person in the Holy City of Madina. The Holy Prophet (S.A.W.) also prayed: O Allah! Curse the tribes of Re'aln, Zakwan and 'Usaita, who have disobeyed Allah. the Most High and His Messenger (S.A.W.), the Holy Prophet (S.A.W.) also said: Allah the Most High, may curse the Jews, because they have converted the graves of their vencrable prophets into places of worship; and the Holy Prophet (S.A.W.) has cursed those males who make themselves look like females, and those females who make themselves look like males. All these traditions are authentic, quoted by *Imam Bukhari* and *Muslim* both and some by one of them. I have quoted a few only for brevity. Insha Allah, I shall quote in detail in the subsequent chapters of this book.

* * * * * * *

CHAPTER 266

PROHIBITION OF ABUSING MUSLIMS UNJUSTLY

قَالَ اللهُ تَعالى : وَالَّذِينَ يُؤْذُونَ الْمُؤْمِنِينَ وَالْمُؤْمِناتِ بِغَيْرِ ما اكْتَسَبُوا فَقَدِ احتَمَلُوا بُهتاناً وَإِثماً مُبِيناً [الأحزاب : ٥٨] .

Allah, the Exalted, has said:

362. And those who malign believing men and believing women undeservedly, they bear the guit of a slander and manifest sin. (33 : 58)

١٥٥٩ – وعن ابنِ مَسْعُودٍ رَضيَ اللهُ عَنْهُ قالَ : قالَ رَسُولُ اللهِ صَلَّى اللهُ عَلَيْهِ وسَلَّمَ : « سِبَابُ المُسْلِمِ فُسوقٌ ، وَقِتَالُهُ كُفْرٌ » متفقٌ عليه .

1559. Hazrat Ibn Mas'ud (R.A.A.) relates that the Holy Prophet (S.A.W.) said: Abusing a Muslims is a sin; and murder of a Muslim amounts to infidelity (Kufr). *(Bukhari and Muslim)*

١٥٦٠ – وعَنْ أبي ذَرّ رَضيَ اللهُ عَنْهُ أنّهُ سَمِعَ رَسُولَ اللهِ صَلّى اللهُ عَلَيْهِ وسَلَّمَ يقولُ : « لايَرمي رَجُلٌ رَجُلاً بِالفِسْقِ أوِ الكُفْرِ، إلّا ارتَدَّتْ عليهِ ، إنْ لَمْ يَكُن صَاحِبُهُ كذلكَ » رَواهُ البخاريُّ .

1560. Hazrat Abu Zarr (R.A.A.) reports that he heard the Holy Prophet (S.A.W.) saying: Nobody should call his brother an unbeliever or transgressor because if he is not like that his reproach would rebound upon the person who has said it. *(Bukhari)*

١٥٦١ – وعنْ أبي هُرَيْرَةَ رَضيَ اللهُ عَنْهُ أنَّ رَسُولَ اللهِ صَلَّى اللهُ عَلَيهِ وَسَلَّمَ قالَ : « المُتَسَابَّانِ مَاقَالا فَعَلى البَادِي مِنْهُما حتَّى يَعْتَدِيَ المَظْلُومُ » رواه مسلم .

1561. Hazrat Abu Hurairah (R.A.A.) relates that the Holy Prophet (S.A.W.) said: If two persons exchange abuses, the one who started it is to be blamed unless the other party might have transgressed. *(Muslim)*

١٥٦٢ – وعنهُ قالَ : أتِيَ النَّبيُّ صَلَّى اللهُ عليهِ وسَلَّمَ بِرجُلٍ قَدْ شَرِبَ قالَ : « اضرِبُوهُ » قالَ أبو هُرَيْرَةَ : فَمِنَّا الضَّارِبُ بِيدِهِ ، والضَّارِبُ بِنَعْلِه ، والضَّارِبُ بِثوبِهِ .فَلَمَّا انصَرَفَ ، قالَ بَعضُ القَوم : أخزاكَ اللهُ ، قالَ : « لاتَقُولُوا هذا ، لا تُعينُوا عليْه الشَّيطَانَ » رواهُ البخاريُّ .

1562. This Hadith has already been covered in S. No. 243 of Chapter 28.

١٥٦٣ – وعَنْهُ قالَ : سَمِعْتُ رسُولَ اللهِ صَلَّى اللهُ عَلَيْهِ وسَلَّمَ يقُولُ : « مَنْ قَذَفَ مَمْلُوكَهُ بِالزِّنى يُقامُ عليْهِ الحَدُّ يَومَ القِيَامَةِ . إلاَّ أنْ يَكُونَ كما قالَ » متفقٌ عليهِ .

1563. Hazrat Abu Hurairah (R.A.A.) reports that he heard the Holy Prophet (S.A.W.) say: A person who accuses his maid servant with adultery, will be subjected to the punishment of adultery on the Day of Judgement unless he happens to be true. *(Bukhari and Muslim)*

* * * * * * *

CHAPTER 267

PROHIBITION OF ABUSING THE DEAD WITHOUT JUSTIFICATION OR RELIGIOUS EXPEDIENCY

Imam Nawawi says that to foretell about the dire consequences of a dead persons sins and evil deeds is not permissible.

وَهوَ التَّحذِيرُ مِنَ الاقْتِداء به في بِدْعَتِه . وَفِسْقِهِ . وَنَحْوِ ذلكَ ؛ وَفيه الآيَةُ وَالأحاديثُ السَّابِقَةَ في الباب قبلَهُ .

١٥٦٤ – وعن عائشة رضي الله عنها قالت : قال رسول الله صلّى الله عليه وسلّم : « لاتسبّوا الأموات ؛ فإنّهم قد أفضوا ٣٠٧ إلى ما قدّموا » رواه البخاري .

1564. **Hazrat Ayesha** (R.A.A.) relates that the Holy Prophet (S.A.W.) said: Do not reproach or abuse dead persons for they are facing the consequences of what they had done in this world. *(Bukhari)*

* * * * * * *

CHAPTER 268

PROHIBITION OF TORTURING OR CAUSING ANNOYANCE

قال الله تعالى : وَالذين يُؤذُونَ المؤمنينَ والمؤمنات بغيرِ ما اكتسبُوا فقد احتملُوا بُهتاناً وإثماً مُبيناً [الأحزاب : ٥٨] .

Allah, the Exalted, has said.

363. And those who malign believing men and believing women undeservedly, they bear the guilt of slander and a manifest sin. (33 : 58)

١٥٦٥ – وعن عبد الله بن عمرو بن العاص رضي الله عنهما قال : قال رسول الله صلّى الله عليه وسلّم : « المُسلم مَن سَلِمَ المُسلمُونَ من لِسانه ويده ، والمهاجر مَن هجرَ ما نهى الله عنه » متفق عليه .

1565. **Hazrat Abdullah bin 'Amr bin Al 'Aas** (R.A.A.) reports that the Holy Prophet (S.A.W.) said: The perfect Muslim is one from whose tongue and hand all Muslims are immune, and (perfect) emigrant is one who leaves those things which Allah has prohibited.

(Bukhari and Muslim)

١٥٦٦ – وعنه قال : قال رسول الله صلّى الله عليه وسلّم : « مَن أحبَّ أنْ يُزحزحَ عَنِ النّار ، ويُدخلَ الجنّةَ ، فلتأتِه منيّتُهُ وهُوَ يُؤمنُ بالله واليومِ الآخرِ ، وليأتِ ٣٠٨ إلى النّاسِ الذي يُحبُّ أنْ يُؤتى إليهِ » رواه مسلم .

1566. This Hadis has been covered in S. No. 668 of Chapter 80.

* * * * * * *

CHAPTER 269

PROHIBITION OF HARBOURING ILL-FEELING AND NON-COOPERATION

قالَ اللهُ تعَالى : إنَّمَا المؤْمِنُونَ إخْوَةٌ [الحجرات : ١٠] . وقالَ تعالى : أذِلَّةٍ عَلى المُؤْمِنِينَ أعِزَّةٍ عَلى الكافِرِينَ [المائدة : ٥٤] . وقالَ تعالى : مُحَمَّدٌ رَسُولُ اللهِ ، وَالذِينَ مَعَهُ أشِدّاءُ عَلى الكُفَّارِ ، رُحَمَاءُ بَيْنَهُم [الفتح : ٢٩] .

Allah, the Exalted, has said:

364. The believers are naught else than brothers (49 : 10)

365. (A people) humble believers, stern toward disbelievers. (5 : 54)

366. Muhammad is the Messenger of Allah. And those with him are hard against the disbelievers and merciful among themselves. (48 . 29)

١٥٦٧ — وعنْ أنسٍ رَضيَ اللهُ عَنْهُ أنَّ النبيَّ صَلَّى اللهُ عليهِ وسَلَّمَ قالَ : « لاتبَاغَضُوا، ولَا تحَاسَدُوا ، ولَا تَدابَرُوا، ولَا تقَاطَعُوا ، وكُونُوا عِبَادَ اللهِ إخواناً ، ولَا يَحِلُّ لِمُسْلِمٍ أنْ يَهْجُرَ أخاه فوقَ ثلاثٍ » متفقٌ عليه .

1567. Hazrat Anas (R.A.A.) relates that the Holy Prophet (S.A.W.) said: Entertain no malice or envy nor indifference nor cut off relations; all the servants of Allah be brethern to each other. It is not permissible for a Muslim to keep away from his brother for more than three days. *(Bukhari and Muslim)*

١٥٦٨ — وعنْ أبي هُرَيْرَةَ رَضيَ اللهُ عَنْهُ أنَّ رَسُولَ اللهِ صَلَّى اللهُ عليهِ وسَلَّمَ قالَ : « تُفْتَحُ أبْوابُ الجَنَّةِ يَوْمَ الاثنَيْنِ وَيَوْمَ الخَمِيسِ ، فَيُغْفَرُ لِكُلِّ عَبدٍ لايُشْرِكُ بِاللهِ شَيْئاً، إلاَّ رَجُلاً كَانَتْ بَيْنَهُ وَبَيْنَ أخيهِ شَحْنَاءُ فيقالُ : أنظِرُوا هَذَيْنِ حَتَّى يَصطَلِحَا ! أنظِرُوا هَذَيْنِ حَتَّى يَصطَلِحَا ! » رواه مسلم .

وفي روايةٍ له : « تُعْرَضُ الأعْمالُ في كُلِّ يَومِ خَميسٍ وَاثنَيْنِ » وَذَكَرَ نَحْوَهُ .

1568. **Hazrat Abu Hurairah** (R.A.A.) reports that the Holy Prophet (S.A.W.) said: The gates of Paradise are opened on Mondays and Thursdays and every bondsman of Allah is forgiven who does not associate anybody with Allah, except a person who bears enmity towards a brother. With regard to them it is decreed that they be given respite till they make friends. *(Muslim)*

Another version of *Muslim* adds: Every Monday and Thursday the deeds of people are submitted to Allah.

* * * * * * *

CHAPTER 270

PROHIBTION OF JEALOUSY: IT MEANS TO WISH THE DEPRIVATION OF A FAVOUR WHETHER TEMPORAL OR SPIRITUAL FROM A PERSON

قَالَ اللهُ تعالى : أَمْ يَحْسُدُونَ النَّاسَ عَلى ماآتَاهُمُ اللهُ مِنْ فَضْلِهِ [النساء : ٥٤] .

Allah, the Exalted has said:

367. Or are they jealous of Mankind because of that which Allah of His bounty hath bestowed upon them? (4 : 54)

١٥٦٩ – وعَنْ أبي هُرَيْرَةَ رَضيَ اللهُ عَنْهُ أنَّ النبيَّ صَلّى اللهُ عليهِ وَسَلَّمَ قالَ : « إيَّاكُمْ وَالحَسَدَ ، فَإنَّ الحَسَدَ يَأْكُلُ الحَسَنَاتِ كَمَا تَأْكُلُ النَّارُ الحَطَبَ ، أوْ قَالَ : العُشْبَ » رواه أبو داود .

1569. **Hazrat Abu Hurairah** (R.A.A.) relates that the Holy Prophet (S.A.W.) said: Avoid jealousy for this destroys good deeds as fire destroys wood. *(Abu Daud)*

* * * * * * *

CHAPTER 271

PROHIBITION OF SPYING AND HEARING SOMEBODY'S TALK AGAINST HIS WISHES

قالَ اللهُ تَعَالى : وَلا تَجَسَّسُوا [الحجرات : ١٢] . وقالَ تعَالى : وَالّذِينَ يُؤْذُونَ المُؤْمِنِينَ وَالمُؤْمِنَاتِ بِغَيرِ مَااكْتَسَبُوا ، فَقَدِ احْتَمَلُوا بُهتَاناً وَإثْماً مُبِيناً [الأحزاب : ٥٨] .

Allah, the Exalted, has said:

368. And spy not (49 : 12)

369. And those who malign believing men and believing women undeservedly, they bear the guilt of slander and manifest sin. (33 : 58)

١٥٧٠ – وعَنْ أبي هُرَيْرَةَ رَضِيَ اللهُ عَنْهُ أنَّ رَسُولَ اللهِ صَلَّى اللهُ عليهِ وسلَّمَ قالَ : « إيَّاكُمْ وَالظَّنَّ ، فَإنَّ الظَّنَّ أكْذَبُ الحَديثِ ، وَلا تَحَسَّسُوا ، وَلا تَجَسَّسُوا وَلا تَنَافَسُوا ، وَلا تَحَاسَدُوا ، وَلا تَبَاغَضُوا ، وَلا تَدَابَرُوا ، وَكُونُوا عِبَادَ اللهِ إخْوَاناً كَمَا أمَرَكُمْ . المُسْلِمُ أخُو المُسْلِمِ ، لا يَظْلِمُهُ ، وَلا يَخْذُلُهُ وَلا يَحْقِرُهُ ، التَّقْوَى هٰهُنَا ، التَّقْوَى هٰهُنَا » وَيُشِيرُ إلى صَدْرِهِ « بِحَسْبِ امرىءٍ مِنَ الشَّرِّ أنْ يَحْقِرَ أخَاهُ المُسْلِمَ ، كُلُّ المُسْلِمِ عَلى المُسْلِمِ حَرَامٌ : دَمُهُ ، وَعِرْضُهُ ، وَمَالُهُ ، إنَّ اللهَ لا يَنْظُرُ إلى أجْسَادِكُمْ ، وَلا إلى صُوَرِكُمْ ، وَلَكِنْ يَنْظُرُ إلى قُلُوبِكُمْ » .

وفي رِوايةٍ : « لا تَحَاسَدُوا ، وَلا تَبَاغَضُوا ، وَلا تَجَسَّسُوا ، وَلا تَحَسَّسُوا وَلا تَنَاجَشُوا وَكُونُوا عِبَادَ اللهِ إخْوَاناً » .

وفي رِوايةٍ : « لا تَقَاطَعُوا ، وَلا تَدَابَرُوا ، وَلا تَبَاغَضُوا وَلا تَحَاسَدُوا ، وَكُونُوا عِبَادَ اللهِ إخْوَاناً » .

وفي رِوايةٍ : « لا تَهَاجَرُوا وَلا يَبِعْ بَعْضُكُمْ عَلى بَيْعِ بَعْضٍ »
رواه مسلم بكلِّ هذه الروايات ، وروى البخاريُّ أكثَرَها .

1570. Hazrat Abu Hurairah (R.A.A.) reports that the Holy Prophet (S.A.W.) said: Guard against suspicion, for suspicion is the greatest falsehood. Do not be inquisitive about other people's faults nor spy against others, nor hanker after a thing which others have (and you donot have), nor envy nor entertain ill-will nor indifference with each other, and O Allah's servants! be like brethren to each other as you have been commanded. A Muslim is the brother of another Muslim; he is not cruel towards him, nor he should humiliate him nor look down upon him. Here lies piety; here lies piety: said he (S.A.W.) pointing towards his chest. It is enough evil for a human being that he should look down upon a brother Muslim. Everyting of a Muslim is forbidden to another Muslim, his blood, his honour and his property. Allah the Most High does not look to your bodies or to your faces or to your (obvious) acts, but He looks to your hearts.

According to another version: 'Do not harbour envy or ill-will; and neither spy nor be inquisitive for other persons faults nor make bogus offers of prices to spoil bargain, and O Allah's servants! be brethren to each other.'

Another tradition says: 'Do not cut off relations with each other nor over-bid upon another's deal. *(Muslim)*

١٥٧١ – وعَنْ مُعَاوِيَةَ رضِيَ اللهُ عَنْهُ قالَ : سَمِعْتُ رَسُولَ اللهِ صَلَّى اللهُ عليهِ وسلَّم يَقُولُ : « إنَّكَ إنِ اتَّبَعْتَ عَوْرَاتِ المُسْلِمِينَ أفسَدْتَهُمْ ، أوْ كِدْتَ أنْ تُفسِدَهُم » حديثٌ صحيحٌ ،

رواهُ أبو داود بإسنادٍ صحيحٍ .

1571. **Hazrat Mu'awiah** (R.A.A.) relates that he heard the Holy Prophet (S.A.W.) say: If you go about probing about the faults of Muslims, you will create dissension and corrupt them. *(Abu Daud)*

١٥٧٢ – وعَنِ ابْنِ مسعودٍ رَضِيَ اللهُ عَنْهُ أنَّه أُتِيَ بِرَجُلٍ فَقِيلَ لَهُ : هذَا فُلانٌ تَقْطُرُ لِحْيَتُهُ خمراً ، فقالَ : إنَّا قَدْ نُهِينَا عَنِ التَّجَسُّسِ ، وَلَكِنْ إن يَظْهَرْ لَنَا شَيْءٌ ، نَأْخُذْ بِهِ . حَدِيثٌ حَسَنٌ صَحِيحٌ .

رواه أبو داود بإسْنادٍ عَلَى شَرْطِ البخاريّ ومسلمٍ .

1572. **Hazrat Abdullah bin Mas'ud** (R.A.A.) says that a man was brought before him and he was told; 'This man is so and so and his beard smells of liquor.' Hazrat Abdullah bin Mas'ud (R.A.A.) said. We have been forbidden to be inquisitive about (somebodys) faults; we can take cognisance of only such things which are evident.

(Abu Daud says that this tradition is sound and good.)

* * * * * * *

CHAPTER 272

PROHIBITION OF HARBOURING SUSPICION AGAINST MUSLIMS WITHOUT JUSTIFICATION

قَالَ اللهُ تَعَالى : يَا أَيُّهَا الَّذِينَ آمَنُوا اجْتَنِبُوا كَثِيراً مِنَ الظَّنِّ إنَّ بَعْضَ الظَّنِّ إثْمٌ [الحجرات : ١٢] .

Allah, the Exalted, has said:

370. O ye who believe! shun much suspicion; for lo! some suspicion is a crime. (49 : 12)

١٥٧٣ – وعنْ أبي هُرَيْرَةَ رضيَ اللهُ عَنْهُ أنَّ رَسُولَ اللهِ صَلَّى اللهُ عَلَيْهِ وسَلَّمَ قالَ : « إيَّاكُمْ وَالظَّنَّ ، فإنَّ الظَّنَّ أكذبُ الحَديثِ » متفقٌ عليه .

1573. Hazrat Abu Hurairah (R.A.A.) reports that the Holy Prophet (S.A.W.) has said. 'Shun suspicion, because suspicion is the biggest lie. This hadis has been partly covered in S. No. 1575 of Chapter 270. *(Bukhari and Muslim)*

* * * * * * *

CHAPTER 273

NOT TO LOOK DOWN UPON MUSLIM

قالَ اللهُ تَعَالَى : ﴿ يَا أَيُّهَا الَّذِينَ آمَنُوا لا يَسْخَرْ قَوْمٌ مِنْ قَوْمٍ ، عَسَى أَنْ يَكُونُوا خَيْراً مِنهُمْ وَلا نِسَاءٌ مِنْ نِسَاءٍ عَسَى أَنْ يَكُنَّ خَيْراً مِنْهُنَّ ، وَلا تَلمِزُوا أَنْفُسَكُمْ وَلا تَنَابَزُوا بالألقَابِ ، بِئسَ الاسْمُ الفُسُوقُ بَعْدَ الإيمَانِ ، وَمَنْ لم يَتُبْ فَأُولئِكَ هُمُ الظَّالِمونَ ﴾ [الحجرات : ١١] .

وقالَ تعَالى : ﴿ وَيْلٌ لِكُلِّ هُمَزَةٍ لُمَزَةٍ ﴾ [الهمزة : ١] .

Allah, the Exalted, has said:

371. O ye who believe! Let not a folk deride a folk who may be better than they (are), nor let women (deride) women who may be better than they are; neither defame one another, nor insult one another by nicknames. Bad is the name of lewdness after faith. And whoso turneth not in repentance, such are evil-doers. (49 : 11)

372. Woe unto every slandering traducer. (104 : 1)

١٥٧٤ – وعنْ أبي هُرَيْرَةَ رضيَ اللهُ عَنْهُ أنَّ رَسُولَ اللهِ صَلَّى اللهُ عليْهِ وسَلَّمَ قالَ : « بِحَسْبِ امرِئٍ مِنَ الشَّرِّ أنْ يَحقِرَ أخَاهُ المُسْلِمَ » رواه مسلم ، وقد سبق قريباً بطوله .

1574. This Hadis has already been covered in S. No. 1575 of Chapter 270.

١٥٧٥ـ وعَن ابنْ مسعُودِ رضيَ اللهُ عنه، عن النبيِّ صَلَّى اللهُ عليهِ وسَلَّمَ قالَ: «لايَدْخلُ الجنَّةَ مَنْ كانَ في قلبِه مِثْقَالُ ذرَّةٍ مِن كِبْرٍ!» فقَالَ رَجُلٌ: إنَّ الرَّجلَ يُحِبُّ أنْ يكُونَ ثوبُهُ حسَناً، ونَعْلُهُ حَسَنَة، فقال: «إنَّ اللهَ جَميلٌ يُحِبُّ الجمَالَ، الكِبْرُ بَطَرُ الحقِّ، وغَمْطُ النَّاسِ» رواه مسلم.

1575. This Hadis has been covered in S. No. 615 of Chapter 72.

١٥٧٦ ـ وعن جُنْدُبِ بنِ عبدِ اللهِ رضيَ اللهُ عنهُ قالَ: قالَ رسولُ اللهِ صلَّى اللهُ عليهِ وسلَّم: «قالَ رَجُلٌ: وَاللهِ لايَغْفِرُ اللهُ لِفُلان، فقالَ اللهُ عزَّ وَجَلَّ: مَنْ ذا الَّذي يتَألَّى عليَّ أنْ لاأغفِرَ لفُلانٍ! إنِّي قد غفَرْتُ لهُ، وأحبَطْتُ عمَلَكَ» رواه مسلم.

1576. Hazrat Jundub bin Abdullah (R.A.A.) relates that the Holy Prophet (S.A.W.) said: (Once) A man asserted: By Allah the Most High! Such and such person will not be forgiven by Allah. On this Allah, the Lord of Honour and Glory, said: 'Who is this man who swears in My name that I will not forgive So and So. I have forgiven him and have cancelled your good deeds. *(Muslim)*

* * * * * * *

CHAPTER 274

PROHIBITION OF REJOICING ON ANOTHER MUSLIM'S MISFORTUNE

قالَ اللهُ تعَالى: إنَّمَا المُؤْمِنُونَ إخْوَةٌ [الحجرات: ١٠]. وقال تعَالى: إنَّ الَّذينَ يُحبُّونَ أن تَشيعَ الفَاحِشَةُ في الَّذينَ آمَنُوا لهُمْ عذابٌ أليمٌ في الدُّنيَا وَالآخِرَةِ [النور: ١٩].

Allah, the Exalted, has said:

373. The believers are naught else than brothers. (49 . 10)

374. Lo! those who love that slander should be spread concerning those who believe, theirs will be a painful punishment in the world and the Hereafter (24 : 19)

١٥٧٧ – وعنْ وَاثِلةَ بْنِ الأَسْقَعِ رضيَ اللهُ عَنْهُ قالَ : قالَ رَسُولُ اللهِ صَلَّى اللهُ عليهِ وسَلَّمَ : « لاتُظْهِرِ الشَّمَاتَةَ لأَخيكَ ، فيَرْحَمَهُ اللهُ وَيَبْتَلِيَكَ » رواه الترمذي وقال : حديثٌ حسنٌ .

وفي البابِ حديثُ أبي هريرةَ السابقُ في باب التَّجَسُّسِ : « كُلُّ المُسْلِمِ عَلَى المُسْلِمِ حَرَامٌ » الحديثَ .

1577. Wasila bin Al-As-qa'a (R.A.A.) relates that the Holy Prophet (S.A.W.) said: Do not rejoice over the troubles of your brother lest Allah the Most High might have mercy on him and involve you in this trouble. (*Imam Tirmizi* has cited this tradition as good.)

* * * * * *

CHAPTER 275

ON PROHIBITION OF DERIDING A PERSON'S DESCENT WHICH HAS BEEN AUTHENTICATED BY SHARIA

قَالَ اللهُ تَعَالَى: وَالَّذِينَ يُؤْذُونَ الْمُؤْمِنِينَ وَالْمُؤْمِنَاتِ بِغَيْرِ مَا اكْتَسَبُوا فَقَدِ احْتَمَلُوا بُهْتَاناً ، وَإِثْماً مُّبِيناً [الأحزاب : ٥٨] .

Allah, the Exalted, has said:

375. And those who malign believing men and believing women undeservedly, they bear the guilt of slander and manifest sin. (33 : 58)

١٥٧٨ – وعَنْ أبي هُرَيْرَةَ رَضِيَ اللهُ عَنْهُ قَالَ : قالَ رَسُولُ اللهِ صَلَّى اللهُ عَلَيْهِ وَسَلَّمَ : « اثْنَتَانِ في النَّاسِ هُمَا بِهِمْ كُفْرٌ : الطَّعْنُ في النَّسَبِ ، وَالنِّيَاحَةُ عَلَى المَيِّتِ » رواه مسلم .

1578. Hazrat Abu Hurairah (R.A.A.) relates that the Holy Prophet (S.A.W.) said: The existence of two traits in people lead them to acts of ignorance. One is to taunt (somebody) on his family geneology, and the other is bewailing the dead. *(Muslim)*

* * * * * *

CHAPTER 276

PROHIBITION OF FLAW AND CHEATING

قَالَ اللهُ تَعَالَى : وَالَّذِينَ يُؤْذُونَ الْمُؤْمِنِينَ ، وَالْمُؤْمِنَاتِ ، بِغَيْرِ مَا اكْتَسَبُوا فَقَدِ احْتَمَلُوا بُهْتَاناً وَإِثْماً مُبِيناً [الأحزاب : ٥٨] .

Allah, the Exalted, has said:

376. And those who malign believing men and believing women undeservedly, they bear the guilt of slander and manifest sin. (33 : 58)

١٥٧٩ – وَعَنْ أَبِي هُرَيْرَةَ رَضِيَ اللهُ عَنْهُ أَنَّ رَسُولَ اللهِ صَلَّى اللهُ عَلَيْهِ وَسَلَّمَ قَالَ : « مَنْ حَمَلَ عَلَيْنَا السِّلاحَ ، فَلَيْسَ مِنَّا ، وَمَنْ غَشَّنَا ، فَلَيْسَ مِنَّا » رواه مسلم .

وفي رِوَايَةٍ لَهُ أَنَّ رَسُولَ اللهِ صَلَّى اللهُ عَلَيْهِ وَسَلَّمَ مَرَّ عَلَى صُبْرَةِ طَعَامٍ ، فَأَدْخَلَ يَدَهُ فِيهَا ، فَنَالَتْ أَصَابِعُهُ بَلَلاً ، فَقَالَ : مَا هَذَا يَاصَاحِبَ الطَّعَامِ ؟ » قَالَ أَصَابَتْهُ السَّمَاءُ يَارَسُولَ اللهِ : قَالَ : « أَفَلا جَعَلْتَهُ فَوْقَ الطَّعَامِ حَتَّى يَرَاهُ النَّاسُ ! مَنْ غَشَّنَا فَلَيْسَ مِنَّا » .

1579. Hazrat Abu Hurairah (R.A.A.) states that the Holy Prophet (S.A.W.) said: A person who takes up arms against us is not one of us and likewise the one who cheats us is not one of us. *(Muslim)*

According to another version of *Imam Muslim* (once) the Holy Prophet (S.A.W.) passed by a heap of corn and when he (S.A.W.) pushed his hand into it his (S.A.W.) fingers felt some moisture; On this He (S.A.W.) asked the grain dealer: 'O grain dealer! What is this? The dealer said. O Messenger of Allah! this grain has been drenched with rain.' The Holy Prophet (S.A.W.) said: Why it was not exposed on top so that people might see it? One who cheats is not one of us

١٥٨٠ – وَعَنْهُ أَنَّ رَسُولَ اللهِ ، صَلَّى اللهُ عَلَيْهِ وَسَلَّمَ ، قَالَ : « لا تَنَاجَشُوا » متفقٌ عليه .

1580. Hazrat Abu Hurairah (R.A.A.) relates that the Holy Prophet (S.A.W.) said: Do not raise prices in competition (to cheat). *(Bukhari and Muslim)*

١٥٨١ – وَعَنِ ابْنِ عُمَرَ رَضِيَ اللهُ عَنْهُمَا ، أَنَّ النَّبِيَّ صَلَّى اللهُ عَلَيْهِ وَسَلَّمَ نَهَى عَنِ النَّجَشِ . متفقٌ عليه .

1581. **Hazrat Ibn Umar** (R.A.A.) says that the Holy Prophet (S.A.W.) has prohibited raising prices in competition (with his brother in trade). *(Bukhari and Muslim)*

١٥٨٢ – وَعَنْهُ قَالَ : ذَكَرَ رَجُلٌ لِرَسُولِ اللهِ صَلَّى اللهُ عَلَيْهِ وَسَلَّمَ أَنَّهُ يُخْدَعُ فِي الْبُيُوعِ ؟ فَقَالَ رَسُولُ اللهِ صَلَّى اللهُ عَلَيْهِ وَسَلَّمَ : « مَنْ بَايَعْتَ ، فَقُلْ لاخِلابَةَ » متفقٌ عليه .

1582. **Hazrat Ibn Umar** (R.A.A.) relates: It was brought to the notice of the Holy Prophet (S.A.W.) that a man was often cheated in trade dealings. The Holy Prophet (S.A.W.) said to him 'When you enter into a bargain with somebody you tell him: There should be no cheating. *(Bukhari and Muslim)*

١٥٨٣ – وَعَنْ أَبِي هُرَيْرَةَ رَضِيَ اللهُ عَنْهُ قَالَ : قَالَ رَسُولُ اللهِ صَلَّى اللهُ عَلَيْهِ وَسَلَّمَ : « مَنْ خَبَّبَ زَوْجَةَ امْرِئٍ ، أَوْ مَمْلُوكَهُ ، فَلَيْسَ مِنَّا » رواه أبو داود .

1583. **Hazrat Abu Hurairah (R.A.A.)** reports that the Holy Prophet (S.A.W.) said: A person who plays false with somebody's wife or maid servants is not one of us. *(Abu Daud)*

* * * * * * *

CHAPTER 277

PROHIBITION OF BREACH OF PROMISE

قَالَ اللهُ تَعَالَى : يَا أَيُّهَا الَّذِينَ آمَنُوا أَوْفُوا بِالْعُقُودِ [المائدة : ١] .

وَقَالَ تَعَالَى : وَأَوْفُوا بِالْعَهْدِ إِنَّ الْعَهْدَ كَانَ مَسْئُولاً [الإسراء : ٣٤] .

Allah, the Exalted, has said:

377. O ye who believe! Fulfil your undertakings. (5 : 1)

378. And keep the covenant Lo! of the covenant it will be asked. (17 : 34)

١٥٨٤ – وعَنْ عَبْدِ اللهِ بْنِ عَمْرِو بْنِ الْعَاصِ رَضِيَ اللهُ عَنْهُمَا أَنَّ رَسُولَ اللهِ صَلَّى اللهُ عَلَيْهِ وَسَلَّمَ قَالَ : « أَرْبَعٌ مَنْ كُنَّ فيه ، كَانَ

مُنَافِقاً خالِصاً . وَمَنْ كانَتْ فيه خَصْلَةٌ مِنْهُنَّ ، كانَ فِيهِ خَصْلَةٌ مِنَ النِّفاقِ حَتَّى يَدَعَهَا : إذا اؤْتُمِنَ خَانَ ، وَإذا حَدَّثَ كَذَبَ ، وَإذا عَاهَدَ غَدَرَ ، وَإذا خاصمَ فَجَرَ » متفق عليه .

1584. This Hadis has already been covered in S. No. 695.

١٥٨٥ – وَعَنِ ابْنِ مَسْعُودٍ ، وَابْنِ عُمَرَ ، وَأَنَسٍ رَضِيَ اللهُ عَنْهُمْ قَالُوا : قَالَ النَّبِيُّ صَلَّى اللهُ عَلَيْهِ وَسَلَّمَ : « لِكُلِّ غادِرٍ لِوَاءٌ يَوْمَ القِيامَةِ ، يُقَالُ : هذهِ غَدْرَةُ فُلانٍ » متفقٌ عليهِ .

1585. Hazrat Ibn Mas'ud, Hazrat Ibn Umar and Hazrat Anas bin Malik (R.A.A.) report that the Holy Prophet (S.A.W.) said: For everyone who breaks his promise, there will be a flag (to mark him out) on the Day of Judgement, and it will be announced that this flag is the symbol of the breach of promise by so and so. *(Bukhari and Muslim)*

١٥٨٦ – وَعَنْ أبي سَعِيدٍ الخُدْرِيِّ رَضِيَ اللهُ عَنْهُ أَنَّ النَّبِيَّ صَلَّى اللهُ عَلَيْهِ وَسَلَّمَ قَالَ : « لِكُلِّ غادِرٍ لِوَاءٌ عِنْدَ اسْتِهِ يَوْمَ القِيامَةِ يُرْفَعُ لَهُ بِقَدْرِ غَدْرِهِ ، ألا وَلا غادِرَ أعْظَمُ غَدْراً مِنْ أمِيرِ عامَّةٍ » رواه مسلم

1586. Hazrat Abu Sa'eedKhudri (R.A.A.) relates that the Holy Prophet (S.A.W.) said: Every breaker of promise will have a standard fixed over his back on the Day of Judgement, the height of this standard will be according to the size of his breach of faith. Listen and beware! There is not bigger culprit of breach of promise than a ruler (who is not true to his people). *(Muslim)*

١٥٨٧ – وعنْ أبي هُرَيرَةَ رَضِيَ اللهُ عنهُ عنِ النبيِّ صَلَّى اللهُ عليهِ وسلَّم قالَ : قَالَ اللهُ تعالى : ثَلاثَةٌ أنا خَصْمُهُمْ يَوْمَ القِيامَةِ : رَجُلٌ أعْطَى بي ثُمَّ غَدَرَ ، وَرَجُلٌ بَاعَ حُرّاً فَأَكَلَ ثَمَنَهُ ، وَرَجُلٌ اسْتَأْجَرَ أجِيراً ، فَاسْتَوْفَى مِنْهُ ، وَلَمْ يُعْطِهِ أجْرَهُ » رواه البخاري

1587. Hazrat Abu Hurairah (R.A.A.) reports that the Holy Prophet (S.A.W.) said: Allah, the Most High, says: there will be three persons against whom I shall fight on the Day of Judgement: One, the person who makes a promise with an oath in My name and then breaks it; two, the person who sells a free man as a slave and appropriates his sale proceed and three, the person who engages a workman and having taken full work from him fails to pay him his dues.

(Bukhari)

* * * * * * *

CHAPTER 278

PROHIBITION OF REMINDING OF A FAVOUR

قَالَ اللهُ تَعَالَى : يَا أَيُّهَا الذِينَ آمَنُوا لاتُبْطِلُوا صَدَقَاتِكُمْ بالمَنِّ وَالأَذَى [البقرة : ٢٦٤]. وقالَ تَعَالَى: الَّذِينَ يُنْفِقُونَ أَمْوَالَهُمْ فِي سَبِيلِ اللهِ ثُمَّ لايُتْبِعُونَ ما أَنْفَقُوا مَنّاً وَلا أَذىً [البقرة : ٢٦٢] .

Allah, the Exalted, has said:

379. O ye who believe! Render not vain your almsgiving by repr-roach and injury. (2 . 264)

380. Those who spend their wealth for the cause of Allah and afterward make not reproach and injury to follow that which they have spent. (2 : 262)

١٥٨٨ – وعنْ أبي ذَرٍّ رَضِيَ اللهُ عنهُ عنِ النَّبيِّ صَلَّى اللهُ عليهِ وسلَّمَ قَالَ : « ثَلاثَةٌ لايُكَلِّمُهُمُ اللهُ يَوْمَ القِيَامَةِ ، وَلا يَنْظُرُ إِلَيْهِمْ ، وَلا يُزَكِّيهِمْ وَلَهُمْ عَذابٌ أَلِيمٌ » قالَ : فَقَرَأَهَا رسولُ اللهِ صَلَّى اللهُ عليهِ وسلَّمَ ثَلاثَ مَرَّاتٍ . قالَ أبو ذرٍّ : خابُوا وَخَسِرُوا مَنْ هُمْ يا رسولَ اللهِ ؟ قالَ المُسْبِلُ ، وَالمَنَّانُ ، وَالمُنْفِقُ سِلْعَتَهُ بالحَلِفِ الكَاذِبِ » رواه مسلم .

وفي روايةٍ له: « المسْبِلُ إزارَهُ » يَعْني : المسْبِلُ إزارَهُ وثَوْبَهُ أَسْفَلَ مِنَ الكَعْبَيْنِ للخُيَلاءِ » .

1588. This Hadis has already been covered by item No 794 of Chapter 119

* * * * * * *

CHAPTER 279

PROHIBITION OF PRIDE AND HAUGHTINESS

قَالَ اللهُ تَعَالَى : (فَلا تُزَكُّوا أَنْفُسَكُمْ هُوَ أَعْلَمُ بِمَنِ اتَّقَى)

[النجم : ٣٢] . وقال تعالى : ﴿إنما السبيل على الذين يظلمون الناس ويبغون في الأرض بغير الحق ، أولئك لهم عذاب أليم﴾ [الشورى: ٤٢].

Allah, the Exalted, has said:

381. Therefore ascribe not purity unto yourselves. He is best aware of him who wardeth off (evil). (53 : 32)

382. The way (of blame) is only against those who oppress mankind, and wrongfully rebel in the earth. For such there is a painful doom. (42 : 42)

١٥٨٩ – وعن عياض بن حمار رضي الله عنه قال : قال رسول الله صلى الله عليه وسلم : « إن الله تعالى أوحى إلي أن تواضعوا حتى لايبغي أحد على أحد ، ولايفخر أحد على أحد » رواه مسلم .

قال أهل اللغة : البغي : التعدي والاستطالة .

1589. Hazrat Ayaz bin Himar (R.A.A.) relates that the Holy Prophet (S.A.W.) said: Allah the Most High has revealed to me that you should adopt humility, so that nobody oppresses another, nor one should hold himself above another. *(Muslim)*

١٥٩٠ – وعن أبي هريرة رضي الله عنه أن رسول الله صلى الله عليه وسلم قال : « إذا قال الرجل : هلك الناس ، فهو أهلكهم » رواه مسلم .

1590. Hazrat Abu Hurairah (R.A.A.) reports that the Holy Prophet (S.A.W.) said: When a person says: People are dead (i.e. abuses or curses them); it is indeed he who suffers the most. *(Muslim)*

* * * * * * *

CHAPTER 280

NOT TO CUT OFF RELATIONS WITH THE MUSLIMS FOR MORE THAN THREE DAYS EXCEPT IN CAUSES OF UNPIETY AND IRRELIGIOUSNESS

قَالَ اللهُ تَعَالَى : إِنَّمَا الْمُؤْمِنُونَ إِخْوَةٌ فَأَصْلِحُوا بَيْنَ أَخَوَيْكُمْ [الحجرات : ١٠] . وقَالَ تَعَالَى : وَلَا تَعَاوَنُوا عَلَى الإِثْمِ وَالعُدْوَانِ [المائدة : ٢] .

Allah, the Exalted, has said:

383. The believers are naught else than brothers. Therefore make peace between your brothers. (49 : 10)

384. Help not one another unto sin and transgression. (5 : 2)

١٥٩١ - وَعَنْ أَنَسٍ رَضِيَ اللهُ عَنْهُ قَالَ : قَالَ رَسُولُ اللهِ صَلَّى اللهُ عَلَيْهِ وَسَلَّمَ : « لَا تَقَاطَعُوا . وَلَا تَدَابَرُوا . وَلَا تَبَاغَضُوا . وَلَا تَحَاسَدُوا ، وَكُونُوا عِبَادَ اللهِ إِخْوَاناً . وَلَا يَحِلُّ لِمُسْلِمٍ أَنْ يَهْجُرَ أَخَاهُ فَوْقَ ثَلَاثٍ » متفقٌ عليه .

1591. This Hadis has already been covered in S. No. 1570 of Chapter 271.

١٥٩٢ - وَعَنْ أَبِي أَيُّوبَ رَضِيَ اللهُ عَنْهُ أَنَّ رَسُولَ اللهِ صَلَّى اللهُ عَلَيْهِ وَسَلَّمَ قَالَ : « لَا يَحِلُّ لِمُسْلِمٍ أَنْ يَهْجُرَ أَخَاهُ فَوْقَ ثَلَاثِ لَيَالٍ : يَلْتَقِيَانِ ، فَيُعْرِضُ هذا وَيُعْرِضُ هذا ، وَخَيْرُهُمَا الَّذِي يَبْدَأُ بِالسَّلَامِ » متفقٌ عليه

1592. Hazrat Abu Ayub (R.A.A.) relates that the Holy Prophet (S.A.W.) said: It is not proper for a Muslim to keep away from his brother for more than three days so much so that when they meet they move away from each other. The better of them is one who is the first to salute the other. *(Bukhari and Muslim)*

١٥٩٣ - وَعَنْ أَبِي هُرَيْرَةَ رَضِيَ اللهُ عَنْهُ قَالَ : قَالَ رَسُولُ اللهِ صَلَّى اللهُ عَلَيْهِ وَسَلَّمَ : « تُعْرَضُ الأَعْمَالُ فِي كُلِّ اثْنَيْنِ وَخَمِيسٍ ، فَيَغْفِرُ اللهُ لِكُلِّ امْرِئٍ لَا يُشْرِكُ بِاللهِ شَيْئاً ، إِلَّا امْرَءاً كَانَتْ بَيْنَهُ وَبَيْنَ أَخِيهِ شَحْنَاءُ : فَيَقُولُ : اتْرُكُوا هذَيْنِ حَتَّى يَصْطَلِحَا » رواه مسلم .

1593. This Hadis has been covered in S. No. 1568 of Chapter 268

١٥٩٤ – وَعَنْ جَابِرٍ رَضِيَ اللهُ عَنْهُ قَالَ: سَمِعْتُ رَسُولَ اللهِ صَلَّى اللهُ عَلَيْهِ وَسَلَّمَ يَقُولُ: «إِنَّ الشَّيْطَانَ قَدْ أَيِسَ أَنْ يَعْبُدَهُ الْمُصَلُّونَ فِي جَزِيرَةِ الْعَرَبِ، وَلَكِنْ فِي التَّحْرِيشِ بَيْنَهُم» رواه مسلم .

1594. Hazrat Jabir (R.A.A.) relates that he heard the Holy Prophet (S.A.W.) say: The Satan has lost all hopes that the Muslims would worship (follow) him in the Arabian Peninsula; therefore he tries to bring about discord and non-cooperation between them. *(Muslim)*

١٥٩٥ – وَعَنْ أَبِي هُرَيْرَةَ رَضِيَ اللهُ عَنْهُ قَالَ: قَالَ رَسُولُ اللهِ صَلَّى اللهُ عَلَيْهِ وَسَلَّمَ: «لَا يَحِلُّ لِمُسْلِمٍ أَنْ يَهْجُرَ أَخَاهُ فَوْقَ ثَلَاثٍ، فَمَنْ هَجَرَ فَوْقَ ثَلَاثٍ، فَمَاتَ دَخَلَ النَّارَ».

رَوَاهُ أَبُو دَاوُد بإِسْنَادٍ عَلَى شَرْطِ الْبُخَارِيِّ وَمُسْلِم .

1595. Hazrat Abu Hurairah (R.A.A.) says that the Holy Prophet (S.A.W.) has said: It is not lawful for a Muslim to be angry with his brother for more than three days. If such a Muslim remained angry with his brother for more than three days, and he died during this interval he will go to hell. *(Abu Daud)*

١٥٩٦ – وَعَنْ أَبِي خِرَاشٍ حَدْرَدِ بْنِ أَبِي حَدْرَدٍ الْأَسْلَمِيِّ. وَيُقَالُ السُّلَمِيِّ الصَّحَابِيِّ رَضِيَ اللهُ عَنْهُ أَنَّهُ سَمِعَ النَّبِيَّ صَلَّى اللهُ عَلَيْهِ وَسَلَّمَ يَقُولُ: «مَنْ هَجَرَ أَخَاهُ سَنَةً فَهُوَ كَسَفْكِ دَمِهِ»

رواه أبو داود بإسناد صحيح .

1596. Hazrat Abu Khirash Hadrad bin Abu Hadrad Al-Aslami also known as Salmi Sahabi (R.A.A.) relates that he heard the Holy Prophet (S.A.W.) say: A person who boycotted his brother for a year is as if he had killed him. *(Abu Daud)*

١٥٩٧ – وَعَنْ أَبِي هُرَيْرَةَ رَضِيَ اللهُ عَنْهُ أَنَّ رَسُولَ اللهِ صَلَّى اللهُ عَلَيْهِ وَسَلَّمَ قَالَ: «لَا يَحِلُّ لِمُؤْمِنٍ أَنْ يَهْجُرَ مُؤْمِناً فَوْقَ ثَلَاثٍ، فَإِنْ مَرَّتْ بِهِ ثَلَاثٌ، فَلْيَلْقَهُ، فَلْيُسَلِّمْ عَلَيْهِ، فَإِنْ رَدَّ عَلَيْهِ السَّلَامَ، فَقَدْ اشْتَرَكَا فِي الْأَجْرِ، وَإِنْ لَمْ يَرُدَّ عَلَيْهِ، فَقَدْ بَاءَ بِالْإِثْمِ. وَخَرَجَ

المُسلِمُ مِن الهِجْرَة » رواه أبو داود بإسناد حسن . قال أبو داود : إذا كانتِ الهجْرَةُ لله تعَالى ، فلَيْسَ مِنْ هذا في شيء .

1597. **Hazrat Abu Hurairah** (R.A.A.) reports that the Holy Prophet (S.A.W.) said: It is not lawful for a Muslim to remain angry with another Muslim for more than three days. After three days he should go and meet him and salute him. If he reciprocates, both of them will share the recompense of reconciliation. If he (the second man) does not return the greeting he will be a sinner and the first man (who saluted him) will be absolved of the responsibility for the disruption of friendship between the two. *(Abu Daud)*

* * * * * * *

CHAPTER 281

PROHIBITION OF WHISPERING BY TWO PERSONS EXCLUDING A THIRD PERSON WITHOUT HIS CONSENT BUT IN AN EMERGENCY TO TALK WITH HIS PERMISSION

قَالَ اللهُ تعَالى : إنَّمَا النَّجْوَى مِنَ الشَّيْطان [المجادلة : ١٠] .

Allah, the Exalted, has said:

385. Lo! Conspiracy is only of the devil. (58 : 10)

١٥٩٨ — وَعَن ابْنِ عُمَرَ رَضِيَ اللهُ عَنْهُمَا أنَّ رَسُولَ اللهِ صَلَّى اللهُ عَلَيْهِ وَسَلَّمَ قَالَ : « إذا كَانُوا ثَلاثَةً ، فَلا يَتَنَاجَى اثْنَانِ دُونَ الثَّالِثِ » متفقٌ عليه

ورواه مالك في « المُوطأ » : عَنْ عَبْدِ اللهِ بْنِ دِينَارٍ قَالَ : كُنْتُ أنَا وَابْنُ عُمَرَ عِنْدَ دَارِ خَالِدِ بْنِ عُقْبَةَ الَّتي في السُّوقِ ، فَجَاءَ رَجُلٌ يُرِيدُ أنْ يُنَاجِيَهُ ، وَلَيْسَ مَعَ ابْنِ عُمَرَ أحَدٌ غَيْرِي ، فَدَعَا ابْنُ عُمَرَ رَجُلاً آخَرَ حَتَّى كُنَّا أرْبَعَةً ، فقالَ لي وَللرَّجُلِ الثَّالِثِ الَّذي دَعَا : اسْتَأخِرا شَيْئاً، فَإنِّي سَمِعْتُ رَسُولَ اللهِ صَلَّى اللهُ عَلَيْهِ وَسَلَّمَ يَقُولُ : «لايَتَنَاجَى اثْنَانِ دُونَ وَاحِدٍ » .

ورواه أبو داود وزَادَ : قَالَ أبُو صَالِح : قُلْتُ لابْنِ عُمَرَ : فَأرْبعَةً ؟ قَالَ : لايَضُرُّكَ » .

1598. Hazrat Ibn Umar (R.A.A.) relates that the Holy Prophet (S.A.W.) said: In a company of three persons two should not hold confidential talk excluding the third. *(Bukhari, Muslim and Abu Daud)*

Imam Abu Daud adds: Hazrat Abu Saleh relates: I asked (Hazrat) Ibn Umar: What if there be four persons? He said: In that case there is no harm. Imam Malik has reported in Muwatta that Abdullah Ibn Dinar relates. (Hazrat) Ibn Umar (R.A.A.) and I were together in the house of Khalid bin Uqbah, who was then in the market, when a man came to consult (Hazrat) Ibn Umar in confidence. As I was the only other person present, (Hazrat) Ibn Umar (R.A.A.) called another man in, which made us four, and asked the two of us to move away a bit, for he had heard the Holy Prophet (S.A.W.) say: 'Two persons should not hold confidential talk together, excluding a third man.'

١٥٩٩ – وَعَنِ ابْنِ مَسْعُودٍ رَضِيَ اللهُ عَنْهُ أَنَّ رَسُولَ اللهِ صَلَّى اللهُ عَلَيْهِ وَسَلَّمَ قَالَ : « إذا كُنْتُمْ ثَلاثَةً ، فَلا يَتَنَاجَى اثْنَانِ دُونَ الآخَرِ حَتَّى تَخْتَلِطُوا بالنَّاسِ ؛ مِنْ أَجْلِ أَنَّ ذلكَ يُحْزِنُهُ » متفقٌ عليه .

1599. Hazrat Ibn Mas'ud (R.A.A.) says that the Holy Prophet (S.A.W.) has said: Where there are three of you in a company, two should not hold confidential talks together till the number increases, lest the third man might feel annoyed. *(Bukhari and Muslim)*

* * * * * * *

CHAPTER 282

PROHIBITION OF CRUELTY TO WOMAN, SLAVE, BOY OR ANIMAL

قَالَ اللهُ تَعَالَى : وَبِالْوَالِدَيْنِ إِحْسَاناً ، وَبِذِي الْقُرْبَى ، وَالْيَتَامَى ، وَالْمَسَاكِينِ ، وَالْجَارِ ذِي الْقُرْبَى ، وَالْجَارِ الْجُنُبِ ، وَالصَّاحِبِ بِالْجَنْبِ ، وَابْنِ السَّبِيلِ ، وَمَا مَلَكَتْ أَيْمَانُكُمْ ؛ إِنَّ اللهَ لا يُحِبُّ مَنْ كَانَ مُخْتَالاً فَخُوراً [النساء : ٣٦] .

Allah, the Exalted, has said:

386. (Show) kindness unto parents, and unto near kindred, and orphans, and the needy, and unto the neighbour who is of kin (unto you) and the neighbour who is not of kin, and the fellow-traveller and the wayfarer and (the slaves) whom your right hands possess. Lo! Allah loveth not such as are proud and boastful. (4 : 36)

١٦٠٠ – وَعَنِ ابْنِ عُمَرَ رَضِيَ اللهُ عَنْهُمَا أَنَّ رَسُولَ اللهِ صَلَّى اللهُ عَلَيْهِ وَسَلَّمَ قَالَ : « عُذِّبَتِ امْرَأَةٌ فِي هِرَّةٍ سَجَنَتْهَا حَتَّى مَاتَتْ ، فَدَخَلَتْ فِيهَا النَّارَ ، لَاهِيَ أَطْعَمَتْهَا وَسَقَتْهَا ، إِذْ حَبَسَتْهَا ، وَلَا هِيَ تَرَكَتْهَا تَأْكُلُ مِنْ خَشَاشِ الأَرْضِ » متفقٌ عليه

1600. Hazrat Abdullah bin Umar (R.A.A.) relates that the Holy Prophet (S.A.W.) said: A woman was punished (tortured) because she shut up a cat till it died. On account of this she was doomed to hell. She had not given the cat anything to eat or drink when she confined it, nor did she free it to enable it pick up its food from among the insects and similar other creatures of the earth.

(Bukhari and Muslim)

١٦٠١ – وَعَنْهُ أَنَّهُ مَرَّ بِفِتْيَانٍ مِنْ قُرَيْشٍ قَدْ نَصَبُوا طَيْراً وَهُمْ يَرْمُونَهُ ، وَقَدْ جَعَلُوا لِصَاحِبِ الطَّيْرِ كُلَّ خَاطِئَةٍ مِنْ نَبْلِهِمْ ، فَلَمَّا رَأَوْا ابْنَ عُمَرَ تَفَرَّقُوا ، فَقَالَ ابْنُ عُمَرَ : مَنْ فَعَلَ هذا ؟ لَعَنَ اللهُ مَنْ فَعَلَ هذا ، إِنَّ رَسُولَ اللهِ صَلَّى اللهُ عَلَيْهِ وَسَلَّمَ لَعَنَ مَنِ اتَّخَذَ شَيْئاً فِيهِ الرُّوحُ غَرَضاً . متفقٌ عليه .

1601. Hazrat Ibn Umar (R.A.A.) says: that (once) he passed by some Quraish young men who had made a (living) animal a target and were shooting arrows at the bird which they had tied down. They had arranged with the owner of the bird that all the arrows that missed the target will become his property. When they saw Hazrat Ibn Umar (R.A.A.) they scattered. Hazrat Ibn Umar (R.A.A.) asked: Who has done this? May Allah's curse be upon the person who did this. The Holy Prophet (S.A.W.) has cursed the man who makes a living animal a target for shooting. *(Bukhari and Muslim)*

١٦٠٢ – وَعَنْ أَنَسٍ رَضِيَ اللهُ عَنْهُ قَالَ : نَهَى رَسُولُ اللهِ صَلَّى اللهُ عَلَيْهِ وَسَلَّمَ أَنْ تُصْبَرَ الْبَهَائِمُ . متفقٌ عليه .

1602. Hazrat Anas bin Malik (R.A.A.) relates that the Holy Prophet (S.A.W.) has forbidden making an animal a target for arrow shooting. *(Bukhari and Muslim)*

١٦٠٣ – وَعَنْ أَبِي عَلِيٍّ سُوَيْدِ بْنِ مُقَرِّنٍ رَضِيَ اللهُ عَنْهُ قَالَ : لَقَدْ رَأَيْتُنِي سَابِعَ سَبْعَةٍ مِنْ بَنِي مُقَرِّنٍ مَالَنَا خَادِمٌ إِلَّا وَاحِدَةٌ لَطَمَهَا أَصْغَرُنَا فَأَمَرَنَا رَسُولُ اللهِ صَلَّى اللهُ عَلَيْهِ وَسَلَّمَ أَنْ نُعْتِقَهَا .

رواه مسلم . وفي روايةٍ : « سابعَ إخوةٍ لي » .

1603. Hazrat Abu Ali Suwaed bin Muqrin (R.A.A.) states I was one of the seventh member of the Bani Muqrin tribe and between us we had only one servant. The youngest among us once slapped him. On this the Holy-Prophet (S.A.W.) commanded us to set him free. *(Muslim)*

١٦٠٤ – وعَنْ أبي مَسْعُودٍ البَدْرِيِّ رَضِيَ اللهُ عَنْهُ قَالَ : كُنْتُ أضرِبُ غُلاماً لي بالسَّوطِ ، فَسَمِعتُ صَوتاً من خَلفِي : « اعلَم أبَا مَسْعُودٍ » فلم أفهم الصَّوتَ مِنَ الغَضَبِ ، فلَمَّا دَنَا مِنِّي إذا هُوَ رَسُولُ اللهِ صَلَّى اللهُ عَلَيْهِ وَسَلَّمَ فإذا هُوَ يَقُولُ : « اعلَم أبَا مَسْعُودٍ أنَّ اللهَ أقدَرُ عَلَيكَ مِنكَ عَلَى هذا الغُلامِ » فَقُلْتُ : لا أضرِبُ مَملُوكاً بَعدَهُ أبداً .

وفي روايةٍ : فسَقَطَ السَّوْطُ مِنْ يَدِي مِنْ هَيْبَتِهِ .

وفي روايةٍ : فَقُلْتُ : يَا رَسُولَ اللهِ هُوَ حُرٌّ لِوَجْهِ اللهِ تعالى، فَقَالَ : « أمَا لَوْ لَمْ تَفْعَلْ ، لَلَفَحَتْكَ النَّارُ ، أوْ لَمَسَّتْكَ النَّارُ » رواه مسلم بهذهِ الرواياتِ.

1604. Hazrat Abu Mas'ud Badri (R.A.A.) relates: (Once) I was striking a slave with a whip when I heard a voice from behind me: 'Be careful! Abu Mas'ud'. I was so much enraged that I could not understand as to whose voice it was. Till the person came nearer, when I could know that it was the Holy Prophet (S.A.W.) and he (S.A.W.) was cautioning me: 'Abu Mas'ud! Be on your guard. (Stop, this is enough). Beware Abu Mas'ud, Allah the Most High, has greater power than you have on this slave, and I responded: I shall never beat a slave again (in future).

Another version says: 'Due to the reverence of the Holy Prophet (S.A.W.) the whip fell down from my hand,'

Yet another version says. 'O Messenger of Allah! I set him free for the sake of Allah.' The Holy Prophet (S.A.W.) remarked: If you had not freed him, you would have been burnt in the fire of Hell. *(Muslim)*

١٦٠٥ – وعَنِ ابْنِ عُمَرَ رَضِيَ اللهُ عَنْهُمَا أنَّ النَّبِيَّ صَلَّى اللهُ عَلَيْهِ وَسَلَّمَ قَالَ : « مَنْ ضَرَبَ غُلاماً له حَدّاً لم يأتِهِ . أو لَطَمَهُ . فإنَّ كَفَّارَتَهُ أنْ يُعتِقَهُ » رواه مسلم

1605. Hazrat Abu Umar (R.A.A.) reports that the Holy Prophet (S.A.W.) said. The atonement for beating or slapping a slave on the face, for no fault of his, is that he should be set free. *(Muslim)*

١٦٠٦ – وعَنْ هِشَامِ بْنِ حَكِيمِ بْنِ حِزَامٍ رَضِيَ اللهُ عَنْهُمَا أَنَّهُ مَرَّ بالشَّامِ عَلَى أُنَاسٍ مِنَ الأَنْبَاطِ . وَقَدْ أُقِيمُوا فِي الشَّمْسِ . وَصُبَّ عَلَى رُؤُوسِهِم الزَّيْتُ ! فَقَالَ : مَاهَذَا ؟ قِيلَ : يُعَذَّبُونَ فِي الخَرَاجِ . وَفِي رِوَايَةٍ : حُبِسُوا فِي الجِزْيَةِ . فَقَالَ هِشَامٌ : أَشْهَدُ لَسَمِعْتُ رَسُولَ اللهِ صَلَّى اللهُ عَلَيْهِ وَسَلَّمَ يَقُولُ : « إِنَّ اللهَ يُعَذِّبُ الَّذِينَ يُعَذِّبُونَ النَّاسَ فِي الدُّنْيَا » فَدَخَلَ عَلَى الأَمِيرِ. فَحَدَّثَهُ . فَأَمَرَ بِهِم فَخُلُّوا . رواه مسلم

1606. Hazrat Hisham bin Hakim ibn Hizam (R.A.A.) says that (Once he passed by a group of Nobtis (Non-Muslim peasants) in Damascus who had been made to stand in the sun, and over their heads olive oil had been poured. He inquired as to why they were subject to such treatment and was told. They are being tortured for the recovery of tax.

Another version says that it was for the recovery of jizya. On this Hazrat Hisham said: I bear witness that the Holy Prophet (S.A.W.) said. Allah will chastise those who torment people in this world. Then he went to (Amir bin Saad) the Governor, and apprised him of this tradition and consequently he ordered the men to be released. *(Muslim)*

١٦٠٧ – وعَنِ ابْنِ عَبَّاسٍ رَضِيَ اللهُ عَنْهُما قَالَ : رَأَى رَسُولُ اللهِ صَلَّى اللهُ عَلَيْهِ وَسَلَّمَ حِمَاراً مَوْسُومَ الوجْهِ . فأَنْكَرَ ذلكَ ؟ فَقَالَ : وَاللهِ لا أَسِمُهُ إلا أَقْصَى شَيْءٍ مِنَ الوجْهِ . وَأَمَرَ بِحِمَارِهِ . فَكُوِيَ فِي جَاعِرَتَيْهِ ، فهوَ أَوَّلُ مَنْ كَوَى الجَاعِرَتَيْنِ . رواه مسلم .

1607. Hazrat Ibn Abbas (R.A.A.) relates that the Holy Prophet (S.A.W.) was unhappy on seeing a donkey which had been tattooed on its face. Hazrat Ibn Abbas (R.A.A.) said: I shall tattoo my donkey on the part of its body farthest from the face, and he ordered it to be tattooed on its hips. Hazrat Ibn-i-Abbas was the first to mark the donkeys on their hips. *(Muslim)*

١٦٠٨ – وَعَنْهُ أَنَّ النَّبِيَّ صَلَّى اللهُ عَلَيْهِ وَسَلَّمَ : مَرَّ عَلَيْهِ حِمَارٌ قَد وُسِمَ فِي وَجْهِهِ . فَقَالَ : « لَعَنَ اللهُ الَّذِي وَسَمَهُ » رواه مسلم .

وفي رواية لمسلم أيضاً : نهى رَسُولُ اللهِ صَلَّى اللهُ عَلَيْهِ وَسَلَّمَ عن الضَّرْبِ في الوجهِ ، وعَنِ الوسْمِ في الوجهِ .

1608. Hazrat Jabir bin Abdullah (R.A.A.) says that once a donkey which had been tattooed on its face passed by the Holy Prophet (S.A.W.) who remarked: Allah's curse be on him who has tattooed it. *(Muslim)*

Imam Muslim also reports that the Holy Prophet (S.A.W.) forbade the beating or tattooing of an animal on its face.

* * * * * * *

CHAPTER 283

PROHIBITION OF TORTURING ANY LIVING CREATURE BY FIRE

١٦٠٩ – عَنْ أبي هُرَيْرَةَ رَضِيَ اللهُ عَنْهُ قَالَ : بَعَثَنَا رَسُولُ اللهِ صَلَّى اللهُ عَلَيْهِ وَسَلَّمَ في بَعْثٍ فَقَالَ : « إن وَجَدْتُمْ فُلاناً وَفُلاناً » لِرَجُلَيْنِ مِنْ قُرَيْشٍ سَمَّاهُمَا « فأحْرِقُوهُمَا بالنَّارِ » ثُمَّ قَالَ رَسُولُ اللهِ صَلَّى اللهُ عَلَيْهِ وَسَلَّمَ حِينَ أرَدْنَا الخُرُوجَ : « إنِّي كُنْتُ أمَرْتُكُمْ أنْ تُحْرِقُوا فُلاناً وَفُلاناً ، وَإنَّ النَّارَ لايُعَذِّبُ بِهَا إلا اللهُ ، فَإنْ وَجَدْتُمُوهُمَا فَاقْتُلُوهُمَا » رواه البخاري .

1609. Hazrat Abu Hurairah (R.A.A.) relates. 'The Holy Prophet (S.A.W.) sent us with a military force on an expedition, and asked us: If you find so and so, (naming two persons of the Quraish tribe) burn them in fire.' When we were about to march he (S.A.W.) said to us: I had asked you to burn so. and so. But it is only Allah the Master of Honour and Glory who punishes (a guilty person) with burning. So if you find them, behead them (and do not burn them). *(Bukhari)*

١٦١٠ – وعَنِ ابْنِ مَسْعُودٍ رَضِيَ اللهُ عَنْهُ قَالَ : كُنَّا مَعَ رَسُولِ اللهِ صَلَّى اللهُ عَلَيْهِ وَسَلَّمَ في سَفَرٍ ، فَانْطَلَقَ لِحَاجَتِهِ ، فَرَأيْنَا حُمَّرَةً مَعَهَا فَرْخَانِ ، فَأخَذْنَا فَرْخَيْهَا ، فَجَاءَتِ الحُمَّرَةُ فَجَعَلَتْ تَعْرِشُ فَجاءَ النَّبِيُّ صَلَّى اللهُ عَلَيْهِ وَسَلَّمَ فَقَالَ : « مَنْ فَجَعَ هذهِ بِوَلَدِها ؟ ! رُدُّوا وَلَدَهَا

إِلَيْهَا » وَرَأَى قَرْيَةَ نَمْلٍ قَدْ حَرَّقْنَاهَا . فَقَالَ : « مَنْ حَرَّقَ هذِهِ ؟ »
قُلْنَا : نَحْنُ . قَالَ : « إِنَّهُ لاَيَنْبَغِي أَنْ يُعَذِّبَ بِالنَّارِ إِلاَّ رَبُّ النَّارِ »
رواه أبو داود بإسناد صحيح .

1610. Hazrat Abdullah bin Mas'ud (R.A.A.) relates: We accompanied the Holy Prophet (S.A.W.) on a journey, at a halt when the Holy Prophet (S.A.W.) went away some-where for a while for some private work, we noticed a small red bird with two little birdies. We caught the little ones, and the mother-bird seeing this became perturbed and started beating the earth with its wings. By that time the Holy Prophet (S.A.W.) returned and asked: Who has caused trouble to this bird by catching hold of its youngs? Return them to her.' He (S.A.W.) also noticed a mound of ants which we had burnt down: He (S.A.W.) inquired. "Who has burnt down these ants? We answered: We have done this. He (S.A.W.) observed: It is not proper for anybody to torture (any creature) with fire except the Sustainer of the Hell (Allah the Almighty).

(Abu Daud)

* * * * * * *

CHAPTER 284

UNDESIRABILITY OF A PERSON OF MEANS TO EVADE PAYMENT TO CREDITOR ON DEMAND

قَالَ اللهُ تَعَالَى : (إِنَّ اللهَ يَأْمُرُكُمْ أَنْ تُؤَدُّوا الأَمَانَاتِ إِلَى أَهْلِهَا)
[النساء : ٥٨] . وقَالَ تَعَالَى : (فَإِنْ أَمِنَ بَعْضُكُمْ بَعْضاً فَلْيُؤَدِّ الَّذِي
اؤْتُمِنَ أَمَانَتَهُ) [البقرة : ٢٨٣] .

Allah, the Exalted, has said:

387. Lo! Allah commandeth you that ye restore deposits to their owners. (4 : 58)

388. Let him who is entrusted render back his trust when he is called upon to do so. (2 . 84)

١٦١١ — وَعَنْ أَبِي هُرَيْرَةَ رَضِيَ اللهُ عَنْهُ أَنَّ رَسُولَ اللهِ صَلَّى اللهُ
عَلَيْهِ وَسَلَّمَ قَالَ : « مَطْلُ الغَنِيِّ ظُلْمٌ . وَإِذَا أُتْبِعَ أَحَدُكُمْ عَلَى مَلِيءٍ
فَلْيَتْبَعْ » متفق عليه .
مَعْنَى « أُتْبِعَ » : أُحِيلَ .

1611. Hazrat Abu Hurairah (R.A.A.) relates that the Holy Prophet (S.A.W.) said: It is improper on the part of a person having means to avoid payment of his debt and if the repayment of debt due to any of you is undertaken by a person of means you should agree to the substitution. *(Bukhari and Muslim)*

* * * * * * *

CHAPTER 285

PROHIBITION OF ABJURING A GIFT BEFORE IT IS HANDED OVER TO THE DONEE AND TO GIVE CHARITY TO ONE'S OWN CHILDREN AND TO PURCHASE THE ARTICLE GIFTED FROM THE DONEE OR TO TREAT THE ARTICLE GIFTED AS ZAKAT OR KAFFARA AND TO PURCHASE SUCH THINGS FROM OTHER PERSON

١٦١٢ – عَنِ ابْنِ عَبَّاسٍ رَضِيَ اللهُ عَنْهُمَا أَنَّ رَسُولَ اللهِ صَلَّى اللهُ عَلَيْهِ وَسَلَّمَ قَالَ : « الَّذِي يَعُودُ فِي هِبَتِهِ كَالكَلْبِ يَرْجِعُ فِي قَيْئِهِ » متفقٌ عليه

وفي رِوَايَةٍ : « مَثَلُ الَّذِي يَرْجِعُ فِي صَدَقَتِهِ ، كَمَثَلِ الكَلْبِ يَقِيءُ ، ثُمَّ يَعُودُ فِي قَيْئِهِ فَيَأْكُلُهُ » .

وفي روايةٍ : « العَائِدُ فِي هِبَتِهِ كالعَائِدِ فِي قَيْئِهِ » .

1612. Hazrat Ibn Abbas (R.A.A.) reports that the Holy Prophet (S.A.W.) has said: The person who retracts a gift is like the dog which devours its vomitted stuff. *(Bukhari and Muslim)*

According to another tradition: A man who takes back his charity is like a dog which eats it own vomitted stuff.

١٦١٣ – وَعَنْ عُمَرَ بْنِ الخَطَّابِ رَضِيَ اللهُ عَنْهُ قَالَ : حَمَلْتُ عَلَى فَرَسٍ فِي سَبِيلِ اللهِ فَأَضَاعَهُ الَّذِي كَانَ عِنْدَهُ ، فَأَرَدْتُ أَنْ أَشْتَرِيَهُ ، وَظَنَنْتُ أَنَّهُ يَبِيعُهُ بِرُخْصٍ ، فَسَأَلْتُ النَّبِيَّ صَلَّى اللهُ عَلَيْهِ وَسَلَّمَ فَقَالَ : « لا تَشْتَرِهِ وَلا تَعُدْ فِي صَدَقَتِكَ وَإِنْ أَعْطَاكَهُ بِدِرْهَمٍ ، فَإِنَّ العَائِدَ فِي صَدَقَتِهِ كَالعَائِدِ فِي قَيْئِهِ » متفقٌ عليه

1613. **Hazrat Umar ibn Khattab** (R.A.A.) relates. 'I had dedicated a horse for the sake of Allah, but the person to whom I had given the horse was neglecting it, and as such I was thinking of buying it from him, believing that he would sell it cheap. Therefore (before doing so) I inquired about it from the Holy Prophet (S.A.W.) who said. Do not buy it and don't take back the thing which you have given in charity, even if he should be willing to sell it for a dirham, for this would amount to retracting your gift and the person who does that is like one who devours his own vomit. *(Bukhari and Muslim)*

* * * * * * *

CHAPTER 286

PROHIBITION OF MISAPPROPRIATION OF THE PROPERTY OF THE ORPHANS

قَالَ اللهُ تَعَالى: (إنَّ الَّذِينَ يَأْكُلونَ أَمْوَالَ اليَتَامى ظُلْماً إنَّمَا يَأْكُلُونَ فِي بُطُونِهم نَاراً وَسَيَصْلَوْنَ سَعِيراً) [النساء: ١٠]. وقَالَ تَعَالى: (وَلا تَقْرَبُوا مَالَ اليَتِيمِ إلا بِالَّتي هِيَ أَحْسَنُ) [الأنعام: ١٥٢]. وقَالَ تَعَالى: (وَيَسْأَلُونَكَ عَنِ اليَتَامَى قُلْ إصْلاحٌ لَهُمْ خَيْرٌ، وَإنْ تُخَالِطُوهُمْ فَإخْوَانُكُمْ، وَاللهُ يَعْلَمُ المُفْسِدَ مِنَ المُصْلِحِ) [البقرة: ٢٢٠].

Allah, the Exalted, has said:

389. Lo ! Those who devour the wealth of orphans wrongfully, they do but swallow fire into their bellies, and they will be exposed to burning flame. (4 : 10)

390. And approach not the wealth of an orphan save with that which is better. (6 : 152)

391. And they question thee concerning orphans. Say: To improve their lot is best. And if ye mingle your affairs with theirs, then (they are) your brothers. Allah knoweth him who spoileth from him who improveth. (2 : 220)

١٦١٤ ـ وعَنْ أبي هُرَيْرَةَ رَضِيَ اللهُ عَنْهُ عَنِ النَّبيِّ صَلَّى اللهُ عَلَيْهِ وَسَلَّمَ قَالَ: «اجْتَنِبُوا السَّبْعَ المُوبِقَاتِ! قَالُوا: يا رَسُولَ اللهِ وَمَا هُنَّ قال: «الشِّرْكُ باللهِ، وَالسِّحْرُ وَقَتْلُ النَّفْسِ الَّتي حَرَّمَ اللهُ إلاَّ بِالحَقِّ

وَأَكْلُ الرِّبَا ، وَأَكْلُ مَالِ الْيَتِيمِ . وَالتَّوَلِّي يَوْمَ الزَّحْفِ . وَقَذْفُ الْمُحْصَنَاتِ الْمُؤْمِنَاتِ الْغَافِلَاتِ » متفقٌ عليه .

1614. Hazrat Abu Hurairah (R.A.A.) relates that the Holy Prophet (S.A.W.) said: Avoid seven most dangerous things. The companions asked: O Messenger of Allah! What are these things. He (S.A.W.) answered: Making anybody or anything as partner with Allah; practising magic; killing without justification a living being whose life has been declared sacred by Allah; practising usury; misappropriating the property of an orphan; running away from the infidels in battle, and slandering chaste, innocent believing women. *(Bukhari and Muslim)*

* * * * * * *

CHAPTER 287

ABSOLUTE PROHIBITION OF PRACTISING USURY

قَالَ اللهُ تَعَالَى : (الَّذِينَ يَأْكُلُونَ الرِّبَا لا يَقُومُونَ إلاَّ كَمَا يَقُومُ الَّذِي يَتَخَبَّطُهُ الشَّيْطَانُ مِنَ المَسِّ . ذلِكَ بِأَنَّهُمْ قَالُوا : إِنَّمَا الْبَيْعُ مِثْلُ الرِّبَا ، وأَحَلَّ اللهُ الْبَيْعَ وَحَرَّمَ الرِّبَا ، فَمَنْ جَاءَهُ مَوْعِظَةٌ مِنْ رَبِّهِ فانْتَهَى فَلَهُ ماسَلَفَ وَأَمْرُهُ إلى اللهِ وَمَنْ عَادَ فأُولئِكَ أَصْحَابُ النَّارِ هُمْ فِيها خَالِدُونَ ، يَمْحَقُ اللهُ الرِّبَا وَيُرْبي الصَّدَقَاتِ) إلى قَوْلِهِ تَعَالَى : (يَا أَيُّهَا الَّذِينَ آمَنُوا اتَّقُوا اللهَ وَذَرُوا مَا بَقِيَ مِنَ الرِّبَا) [البقرة: ٢٧٥-٢٧٨].

وَأَمَّا الأَحَادِيثُ فَكَثِيرَةٌ في الصَّحِيحِ مَشْهُورَةٌ . مِنْهَا حَدِيثُ أَبي هُرَيرَةَ السَّابِقُ في الْبَابِ قَبْلَهُ

Allah, the Exalted, has said:

392. Those who swallow usury cannot rise up save as he ariseth whom the devil hath prostrated by (his) touch. That is because they say: Trade is just like usury; Whereas Allah permitteth trading and forbiddeth usury. He unto whom an admonition from his Lord cometh, and (he) refraineth (in obedience thereto), he shall keep (the profits of) that which is fast, and his affair (henceforth) is with Allah. As for him who returneth (to

usury) — Such are rightful owners of the fire. They will abide therein. Allah hath blighted usury and made almsgiving fruitful. Allah loveth not the impious and guilty. Lo! those who believe and do good works and establish worship and pay the poor-due, (Zakat) their reward is with their Lord and there shall no fear come upon them neither shall they grieve. O ye who believe! Observe your duty to Allah, give up what remaineth (due to you) from usury, if ye are (in truth) believers. (2 : 275–278)

١٦١٥ – وَعَنِ ابْنِ مَسْعُودٍ رَضِيَ اللهُ عَنْهُ قَالَ : « لَعَنَ رَسُولُ اللهِ صَلَّى اللهُ عَلَيْهِ وَسَلَّمَ آكِلَ الرِّبَا وَمُوكِلَهُ » رواه مسلم .

زاد الترمذي وغيره : « وَشَاهِدَيْهِ ، وَكَاتِبَهُ » .

1615. **Hazrat Abdullah bin Mas'ud** (R.A.A.) relates that the Holy Prophet (S.A.W.) cursed him who takes and him who pays interset. *(Muslim)*

Imam Tirmizi adds: And those who write and witness deeds involving the taking and paying of interest.

Note :— The Holy Prophet (S.A.W.) in one of his "Ruya-i-Sadiqa" (true dreams) has seen that in a stream of blood a man is swimming, and another man is standing on the bank with a stone in his hand. The first man when gets tired and wants to reach the bank, the second man aims a stone at him which strikes his mouth and goes into his stomach like a morsel, and as such this man after receiving the stone blow recedes (to the middle of the stream). The angel Gabriel explained that the man swimming in the stream of blood is a person who practices usury.

* * * * * * *

CHAPTER 288

PROHIBITION OF OSTENTATION

قَالَ اللهُ تَعَالَى : (وَمَا أُمِرُوا إِلَّا لِيَعْبُدُوا اللهَ مُخْلِصِينَ لَهُ الدِّينَ حُنَفَاءَ) [البينة : ٥] . وقالَ تَعَالَى : (لا تُبْطِلُوا صَدَقَاتِكُمْ بِالْمَنِّ وَالأَذَى . كَالَّذِي يُنْفِقُ مَالَهُ رِئَاءَ النَّاسِ) [البقرة : ٢٦٤] . وقالَ تعالى : (يُرَاؤُونَ النَّاسَ وَلا يَذْكُرُونَ اللهَ إِلَّا قَلِيلاً) [النساء : ١٤٢] .

Allah, the Exalted, has said:

393. And they are ordered naught else than to serve keeping religion pure for Him, as men upright. (98 . 5)

394. O ye who believe! Render not vain your almsgiving by reproaches and injury, like him who spendeth his wealth only to be seen of men and believeth not in Allah and the Last Day (2 : 264)

395. When they stand up to worship they perform it languidly and to be seen of men, and are mindful of Allah but little. (4 : 142)

١٦١٦ – وعن أبي هريرة رضي الله عنه قال : سمعت رسول الله صلى الله عليه وسلم يقول : « قال الله تعالى: أنا أغنى الشركاء عن الشرك ، من عمل عملا أشرك فيه معي غيري ، تركته وشركه » رواه مسلم .

1616. Hazrat Abu Hurairah (R.A.A.) relates that he heard the Holy Prophet (S.A.W.) say: Allah, the Most High, says: If anybody associates something with Me, I am not affected. If any one associates somebody with Me, in any way, I reject him and his act of associating anything with Me. *(Muslim)*

١٦١٧ – وعنه قال : سمعت رسول الله صلى الله عليه وسلم يقول : « إن أول الناس يقضى يوم القيامة عليه رجل استشهد ، فأتي به ، فعرفه نعمته ، فعرفها ، قال : فما عملت فيها ؟ قال : قاتلت فيك حتى استشهدت : قال كذبت ، ولكنك قاتلت لأن يقال : جريء ! فقد قيل ، ثم أمر به ، فسحب على وجهه حتى ألقي في النار . ورجل تعلم العلم وعلمه ، وقرأ القرآن ، فأتي به ، فعرفه نعمه فعرفها . قال : فما عملت فيها ؟ قال : تعلمت العلم وعلمته ، وقرأت فيك القرآن ، قال : كذبت ، ولكنك تعلمت ليقال : عالم ! وقرأت القرآن ليقال : هو قارئ ! فقد قيل ، ثم أمر به ، فسحب على وجهه حتى ألقي في النار . ورجل وسع الله عليه ،

وَأَعْطَاهُ مِنْ أَصْنَافِ المَالِ ، فَأُتِيَ بِهِ فَعَرَّفَهُ نِعَمَهُ ، فَعَرَفَهَا . قَالَ : فَمَا عَمِلْتَ فِيهَا ؟ قَالَ : مَاتَرَكْتُ مِنْ سَبِيلٍ تُحِبُّ أَنْ يُنْفَقَ فيها إِلَّا أَنْفَقْتُ فيهَا لَكَ . قَالَ : كَذَبْتَ ، ولكِنَّكَ فَعَلْتَ لِيُقَالَ : هو جَوَادٌ ! فَقَدْ قِيلَ ، ثُمَّ أُمِرَ بِهِ فَسُحِبَ عَلَى وَجْهِهِ ثُمَّ أُلْقِيَ فِي النَّارِ » . رواه مسلمٌ .

1617. Hazrat Abu Hurairah (R.A.A.) says that he heard the Holy Prophet (S.A.W.) say: The first person whose case will be adjudicated on the Day of Judgement, will be a martyr. He will be called and shown all the bounties which have been granted to him. He will recognise them (He will admit that he did have them) and then will be asked: what use did you make of the bounties? He will say: I carried on Jihad (fighting) in Thy cause till I was martyred, Allah will tell him: You are lying; you fought so that you might be known as brave man; and in fact you were known as such. It will be decided that he should be dragged on his face and thrown into the Hell. Next will be brought a man who had acquired knowledge and had studied the Quran. He will be shown the favours bestowed on him and will recognise them and will be asked: How did you use them? He will say. 'I acquired knowledge and taught it to others and read the Holy Quran for Thy pleasure. He will be told: 'You are a liar. Yor acquired knowledge only to be called a learned person and you read the Quran so that you might be called a Qari (reader), and so you were called. As per divine judgement he will also be dragged on his face and thrown into the Hell. Then another man will be brought forward on whom Allah the Most High will have granted him all kind of wealth and property in abundance. He will also be shown the favours bestowed upon him, which he will recognise. He will be asked: 'How did you use them'? He will say: I spent them in all the ways that Thou dost approve; And I spent them in all these ways so as to win Thy pleasure. He will be told: You are lying; you did all that so that you might be called a generous peerson and you were called as such. It will then he ordered that he may be dragged to the Hell. *(Muslim)*

١٦١٨ — وَعَنِ ابْنِ عُمَرَ رَضِيَ اللهُ عَنْهُمَا أَنَّ نَاساً قَالُوا لَهُ : إِنَّا نَدْخُلُ عَلَى سَلاطِينِنَا فَنَقُولُ لَهُمْ بِخِلافِ مَا نَتَكَلَّمُ إِذا خَرَجْنَا مِنْ عِنْدِهِمْ ؟ قالَ ابْنُ عُمَرَ رَضِيَ اللهُ عَنْهُمَا : كُنَّا نَعُدُّ هذا نِفَاقاً عَلَى عَهْدِ رَسُولِ اللهِ صَلَّى اللهُ عَلَيْهِ وَسَلَّمَ . رواه البخاري .

1618. This Hadis has been covered in S. No. 1546 f Chapter 258.

١٦١٩ – وعن جُنْدُبِ بنِ عبدِ اللهِ بنِ سُفْيَانَ رَضِيَ اللهُ عَنْهُ قالَ: قَالَ النَّبِيُّ صَلَّى اللهُ عَلَيْهِ وَسَلَّمَ: «مَنْ سَمَّعَ سَمَّعَ اللهُ بِهِ. وَمَنْ يُرَائِي يُرَائِي اللهُ بِهِ» متفق عليه.

وَرَوَاهُ مُسْلِمٌ أَيضاً مِنْ رِوَايَةِ ابْنِ عَبَّاسٍ رَضِيَ اللهُ عَنْهُمَا.

1619. Hazrat Jundub bin Abdullah bin Sufyan (R.A.A.) relates that the Holy Prophet (S.A.W.) said: A person who does some good work in order to boast, Allah the Most High will expose his faults and a person whose motive in doing some good deed is to show it, Allah the Most High will treat him as a hypocrite. *(Bukhari and Muslim)*

Imam Muslim has cited this on the authority of Hazrat Ibn-i-Abbas also.

١٦٢٠ – وَعَنْ أَبِي هُرَيْرَةَ رَضِيَ اللهُ عَنْهُ قَالَ: قَالَ رَسُولُ اللهِ صَلَّى اللهُ عَلَيْهِ وَسَلَّمَ: «مَنْ تَعَلَّمَ عِلْماً مِمَّا يُبْتَغَى بِهِ وَجْهُ اللهِ عَزَّ وَجَلَّ لا يَتَعَلَّمُهُ إِلاَّ لِيُصِيبَ بِهِ عَرَضاً مِنَ الدُّنْيَا، لَمْ يَجِدْ عَرْفَ الجَنَّةِ يَوْمَ القِيَامَةِ» يَعْنِي: رِيحَهَا. رواه أبو داود بإسنادٍ صحيحٍ. والأحاديثُ في الباب كثيرةٌ مشهورةٌ.

1620. This Hadis is the same as No. 1396 of Chapter 240.

Note:— Literally speaking hypocrisy means falsely making oneself appear to be virtuous or good; or in other words feigning to be better than one is, or to be what one is not, that is show and pomposity. The reality of human action lies in its intention and object. As such the goodness or badness of an act mostly depends upon intention. Hypocrisy shatters the very foundation of a man's actions or intentions. The real object of hypocrisy is that a person may display his goodness and piety and thus may create a goodwill among the people. On account of this Islam has called hypocrisy or "Rea" as imperceptible polytheism or "Shirk Khafi", because, according to the author, with the mixture of some worldly or secular objectives, in these acts, something more is associated along with Allah, the Master of Honour and Glory, as is evident from the traditions of the Holy Prophet (S.A.W.).

* * * * * * *

CHAPTER 289

THE THINGS WHICH ARE NOT SHOWING OFF

١٦٢١ ـ عَنْ أَبي ذَرٍّ رَضِيَ اللهُ عَنْهُ قَالَ: قِيلَ لِرَسُولِ اللهِ صَلَّى اللهُ عَلَيْهِ وَسَلَّمَ: أَرَأَيْتَ الرَّجُلَ يَعْمَلُ الْعَمَلَ مِنَ الخَيْرِ، وَيَحْمَدُهُ النَّاسُ عَلَيْهِ؟ قال: «تِلْكَ عَاجِلُ بُشْرَى المُؤْمِنِ» رواه مسلم .

1621. **Hazrat Abu Zarr** (R.A.A.) relates that the Holy Prophet (S.A.W.) was asked: 'O Messenger of Allah! What about a person who does some praiseworthy work and people praise him for the same? He (S.A.W.) answered: This is a prompt approbation of a Muslim's good work. *(Muslim)*

Note:-- This amounts to getting appreciation of one's good deeds in advance in this world.

* * * * * * *

CHAPTER 290

PROHIBITION OF LOOKING AT STRANGE WOMAN OR HANDSOME BOY WITHOUT JUSTIFICATION

قَالَ اللهُ تَعَالَى: (قُلْ لِلْمُؤْمِنِينَ يَغُضُّوا مِنْ أَبْصَارِهِمْ) [النور: ٣٠] وقَالَ تَعَالَى: (إِنَّ السَّمْعَ وَالْبَصَرَ وَالْفُؤَادَ كُلُّ أُولئِكَ كَانَ عَنْهُ مَسْئُولاً) [الإسراء: ٣٦]. وقَالَ تَعَالَى: (يَعْلَمُ خَائِنَةَ الأَعْيُنِ وَمَا تُخْفِي الصُّدُورُ) [غافر: ١٩]. وقَالَ تَعَالَى: (إِنَّ رَبَّكَ لَبِالْمِرْصَادِ) [الفجر: ١٤].

Allah, the Exalted, has said:

396. Tell the believing men to lower their gaze. (24 : 30)

397. The ear and the eye and the heart shall all be called to account. (17 : 36)

398. He knowth the traitor of the eyes, and that which the bosoms hide. (40 : 19)

399. Lo! thy Lord is ever watchful. (89 : 14)

١٦٢٢ – وَعَنْ أَبِي هُرَيْرَةَ رَضِيَ اللهُ عَنْهُ عَنِ النَّبِيِّ صَلَّى اللهُ عَلَيْهِ وَسَلَّمَ قَالَ: كُتِبَ عَلَى ابْنِ آدَمَ نَصِيبُهُ مِنَ الزِّنَا مُدْرِكٌ ذَلِكَ لَا مَحَالَةَ: الْعَيْنَانِ زِنَاهُمَا النَّظَرُ، وَالأُذُنَانِ زِنَاهُمَا الاسْتِمَاعُ، وَاللِّسَانُ زِنَاهُ الْكَلَامُ، وَالْيَدُ زِنَاهَا الْبَطْشُ، وَالرِّجْلُ زِنَاهَا الخُطَا، وَالْقَلْبُ يَهْوَى وَيَتَمَنَّى، وَيُصَدِّقُ ذَلِكَ الْفَرْجُ أَوْ يُكَذِّبُهُ»

متفقٌ عليه. وهذا لَفظُ مسلم، ورواية البُخاري مُختصرةٌ.

1622. Hazrat Abu Hurairah (R.A.A.) relates that the Holy Prophet (S.A.W.) said: A man commits adultery with his eyes when he looks at a strange woman; the adultery of the ears is listening to sexual dialogue; adultery of the tongue is talking about sex the adultery of the hand is to catch which is unlawful; and the adultery of the feet; is going towards a strange woman; the heart ardently desires adultery; and the sexual organs confirm or contradict the act. (This is *Imam Muslim's* account; the version of *Imam Bukhari* is shorter.)

١٦٢٣ – وَعَنْ أَبِي سَعِيدٍ الْخُدْرِيِّ رَضِيَ اللهُ عَنْهُ عَنِ النَّبِيِّ صَلَّى اللهُ عَلَيْهِ وَسَلَّمَ قَالَ: «إِيَّاكُمْ وَالْجُلُوسَ فِي الطُّرُقَاتِ!» قَالُوا: يَا رَسُولَ اللهِ مَالَنَا مِنْ مَجَالِسِنَا بُدٌّ: نَتَحَدَّثُ فِيهَا. فَقَالَ رَسُولُ اللهِ صَلَّى اللهُ عَلَيْهِ وَسَلَّمَ: «فَإِذَا أَبَيْتُمْ إِلَّا الْمَجْلِسَ، فَأَعْطُوا الطَّرِيقَ حَقَّهُ» قَالُوا: وَمَا حَقُّ الطَّرِيقِ يَا رَسُولَ اللهِ؟ قَالَ: «غَضُّ الْبَصَرِ، وَكَفُّ الأَذَى، وَرَدُّ السَّلَامِ، وَالأَمْرُ بِالْمَعْرُوفِ وَالنَّهْيُ عَنِ الْمُنْكَرِ» متفقٌ عليه.

1623. This Hadis is the same as No. 192 of Chapter 23.

١٦٢٤ – وَعَنْ أَبِي طَلْحَةَ زَيْدِ بْنِ سَهْلٍ رَضِيَ اللهُ عَنْهُ قَالَ: كُنَّا قُعُوداً بِالأَفْنِيَةِ نَتَحَدَّثُ فِيهَا فَجَاءَ رَسُولُ اللهِ صَلَّى اللهُ عَلَيْهِ وَسَلَّمَ فَقَامَ عَلَيْنَا فَقَالَ: مَالَكُمْ وَلِمَجَالِسِ الصُّعُدَاتِ؟ اجْتَنِبُوا مَجَالِسَ الصُّعُدَاتِ» فَقُلْنَا: إِنَّمَا قَعَدْنَا لِغَيْرِ مَا بَأْسٍ: قَعَدْنَا نَتَذَاكَرُ، وَنَتَحَدَّثُ. قَالَ: «إِمَّا لَا فَأَدُّوا حَقَّهَا: غَضُّ الْبَصَرِ، وَرَدُّ السَّلَامِ، وَحُسْنُ الْكَلَامِ» رواه مسلم.

«الصُّعُدَاتُ» بِضَمِّ الصَّادِ وَالْعَيْنِ، أَيْ: الطُّرُقَاتُ.

1624. Hazrat Abu Talha Zaid bin Sahl (R.A.A.) relates: (Once) we were sitting on a platform in front of our house when the Holy Prophet (S.A.W.) came and stood near us and asked "What has happend to you. Why are you sitting by the road side." We submitted: We only sit and converse and have no ulterior motive. He (S.A.W.) said. If you have to sit, then discharge your obligations of the road, namely, keep your eyes down, reply to salutation and talk decently. *(Muslim)*

١٦٢٥ – وعَنْ جَرِيرٍ رَضِيَ اللهُ عَنْهُ قَالَ : سَأَلْتُ رَسُولَ اللهِ صَلَّى اللهُ عَلَيْهِ وَسَلَّمَ عَنْ نَظَرِ الفَجْأَةِ فَقَالَ : « اصْرِفْ بَصَرَكَ » رواه مسلم .

1625. Hazrat Jarir (R.A.A.) says: I asked the Holy Prophet (S.A.W.) as to what should be done when our glance, accidentally falls (upon somebody forbidden) to look at. He (S.A.W.) said: Turn your eyes. *(Muslim)*

١٦٢٦ – وَعَنْ أُمِّ سَلَمَةَ رَضِيَ اللهُ عَنْهَا قَالَتْ : كُنْتُ عِنْدَ رَسُولِ اللهِ صَلَّى اللهُ عَلَيْهِ وَسَلَّمَ وَعِنْدَهُ مَيْمُونَةُ ، فَأَقْبَلَ ابْنُ أُمِّ مَكْتُومٍ ، وذلكَ بَعْدَ أَنْ أُمِرْنَا بِالحِجَابِ فَقَالَ النَّبِيُّ صَلَّى اللهُ عَلَيْهِ وَسَلَّمَ : « احْتَجِبَا مِنْهُ » فَقُلْنَا : يَا رَسُولَ اللهِ أَلَيْسَ هُوَ أَعْمَى : لا يُبْصِرُنَا ، وَلا يَعْرِفُنَا ؟ فَقَالَ النَّبِيُّ صَلَّى اللهُ عَلَيْهِ وَسَلَّمَ : « أَفَعَمْيَاوَانِ أَنْتُمَا أَلَسْتُمَا تُبْصِرَانِهِ !؟ » رواه أبو داود والترمذي وقَالَ : حَدِيثٌ حَسَنٌ صَحِيحٌ .

1626. Ummul Momineen Hazrat Umm Salamah (R A A.) relates that she was (once) sitting with the Holy Prophet (S.A.W.) along with Hazrat Maimuna (R.A.A.) when Hazrat Ibn Umm Maktum (R.A.A.) who was blind came there. This incident took place after we had been ordered to cover ourselves. The Holy Prophet (S.A.W.) asked us: Cover yourselves from him. We submitted 'O Messenger of Allah! Is he not blind and cannot see us nor recognise us. On this the Holy Prophet (S.A.W.) said: But you are not blind and can see him. *(Abu Daud and Tirmizi)*

١٦٢٧ – وَعَنْ أَبِي سَعِيدٍ رَضِيَ اللهُ عَنْهُ أَنَّ رَسُولَ اللهِ صَلَّى اللهُ عَلَيْهِ وَسَلَّمَ قَالَ : لاَ يَنْظُرُ الرَّجُلُ إِلى عَوْرَةِ الرَّجُلِ ، وَلاَ المَرْأَةُ إِلى

عَوْرَةِ المَرْأَةِ . وَلاَ يُفْضِي الرَّجُلُ إلى الرَّجُلِ في ثَوْبٍ وَاحِدٍ . وَلاَ تُفْضِي المَرْأَةُ إلى المَرْأَةِ في الثَّوْبِ الوَاحِدِ » رواه مسلم .

1627. Hazrat Abu Sa'id (R.A.A.) relates that the Holy Prophet (S.A.W.) said: A man must not look towards a woman's private parts, nor a woman should look at another woman's private parts; nor should two naked men or two naked women cover themselves under one cover. Because this thing can be the cause of some mischief.

(Muslim)

* * * * * * *

CHAPTER 291

PROHIBITION OF BEING ALONE WITH A STRANGE WOMAN

قال اللهُ تعالى : (وَإذَا سَأَلْتُمُوهُنَّ مَتَاعاً فَاسْأَلُوهُنَّ مِنْ وَرَاءِ حِجَابٍ) [الأحزاب :٥٣] .

Allah, the Exalted, has said:

400. And when ye ask of them (the wives of the Prophet) anything, ask it of them from behind a curtain. (33 : 53)

١٦٢٨ – وَعَنْ عُقْبَةَ بْنِ عَامِرٍ رَضِيَ اللهُ عَنْهُ أنَّ رَسُولَ اللهِ صَلَّى اللهُ عَلَيْهِ وَسَلَّمَ قَالَ : « إيَّاكُمْ وَالدُّخُولَ عَلَى النِّسَاءِ » ! فَقَالَ رَجُلٌ مِنَ الأنْصَارِ : أفَرَأيْتَ الحَمْوَ ؟ قالَ : « الحَمْوُ المَوْتُ ! » متفقٌ عليه .

1628. Hazrat 'Uqbah bin 'Aamir (R.A.A.) relates that the Holy Prophet (S.A.W.) said: Avoid visiting (stranger) women. A man from among the Ansar submitted: O Messenger of Allah! What about husband's brothers or in-laws? He (S.A.W.) said: These are death (for bed). *(Bukhari and Muslim)*

١٦٢٩ – وَعَنِ ابْنِ عَبَّاسٍ رَضِيَ اللهُ عَنْهُمَا أنَّ رَسُولَ اللهِ صَلَّى اللهُ عَلَيْهِ وَسَلَّمَ قَالَ : « لاَ يَخْلُوَنَّ أحَدُكُمْ بِامْرَأةٍ إلاَّ مَعَ ذِي مَحْرَمٍ » متفقٌ عليه .

1629. Hazrat Ibn 'Abbas (R.A.A.) reports that the Holy Prophet (S.A.W.) said. None of you should meet a (stranger) woman in privacy unless she is accompanied by a relative within the prohibited degrees.

(Bukhari and Muslim)

١٦٣٠ – وَعَنْ بُرَيْدَةَ رَضِيَ اللهُ عَنْهُ قَالَ : قَالَ رَسُولُ اللهِ صَلَّى اللهُ عَلَيْهِ وَسَلَّمَ : « حُرْمَةُ نِسَاءِ المُجَاهِدِينَ عَلَى القَاعِدِينَ كَحُرْمَةِ أُمَّهَاتِهِمْ ، مَا مِنْ رَجُلٍ مِنَ القَاعِدِينَ يَخْلُفُ رَجُلاً مِنَ المُجَاهِدِينَ فِي أَهْلِهِ ، فَيَخُونُهُ فِيهِمْ إلاَّ وَقَفَ لَهُ يَوْمَ القِيَامَةِ ، فَيَأْخُذُ مِنْ حَسَنَاتِه مَا شَاءَ حَتَّى يَرْضَى » ثُمَّ التَفَتَ إلَيْنَا رَسُولُ اللهِ صَلَّى اللهُ عَلَيْهِ وَسَلَّمَ فَقَالَ : « مَا ظَنُّكُمْ ؟ » رواهُ مسلم .

1630. Hazrat Buraidah (R.A.A.) relates that the Holy Prophet (S.A.W.) said. The sanctity of the women of those who go on Jihad in the cause of Allah, for those persons who stay behind at home, is like the honour of their mothers. A person who stayed at home and became the custodian of those on Jihad, but played foul with them, will on the Day of Judgement find the latter stand up and take away as much of his virtuous deeds as he likes till he is satisfied. Then the Holy Prophet (S.A.W.) turned to us and said: Now what do you think? (Imagine what good deeds he will not take). *(Muslim)*

* * * * * * *

CHAPTER 292

PROHIBITION OF MEN AND WOMEN MIMIC ONE ANOTHER IN DRESS AND BEHAVIOUR

١٦٣١ – عَنِ ابْنِ عَبَّاسٍ رَضِيَ اللهُ عَنْهُمَا قَالَ : لَعَنَ رَسُولُ اللهِ صَلَّى اللهُ عَلَيْهِ وَسَلَّمَ المُخَنَّثِينَ مِنَ الرِّجَالِ ، وَالمُتَرَجِّلاتِ مِنَ النِّسَاءِ .

وفي رواية : لَعَنَ رَسُولُ اللهِ صَلَّى اللهُ عَلَيْهِ وَسَلَّمَ المُتَشَبِّهِينَ مِنَ الرِّجَالِ بالنِّسَاءِ ، وَالمُتَشَبِّهَاتِ مِنَ النِّسَاءِ بِالرِّجَالِ . رواهُ البُخاري .

1631. Hazrat Ibn 'Abbas (R.A.A.) says that the Holy Prophet (S.A.W.) cursed males imitating females and females imitating males.

Another version says: The Holy Prophet (S.A.W.) has cursed men who make themselves like women and has cursed women who make themselves like men.

١٦٣٢ – وَعَنْ أَبِي هُرَيْرَةَ رَضِيَ اللهُ عَنْهُ قَالَ : لَعَنَ رَسُولُ اللهِ صَلَّى اللهُ عَلَيْهِ وَسَلَّمَ الرَّجُلَ يَلْبَسُ لِبْسَةَ المَرْأَةِ ، وَالمَرْأَةَ تَلْبَسُ لِبْسَةَ الرَّجُلِ . رواهُ أبو داود بإسناد صحيح .

1632. Hazrat Abu Hurairah (R.A.A.) relates that the Holy Prophet (S.A.W.) cursed men who dress like women and cursed women who dress like men. *(Imam Abu Daud* has cited his tradition on good authorities).

١٦٣٣ – وَعَنْهُ قَالَ : قَالَ رَسُولُ اللهِ صَلَّى اللهُ عَلَيْهِ وَسَلَّمَ : « صِنْفَانِ مِنْ أَهْلِ النَّارِ لَمْ أَرَهُمَا : قَوْمٌ مَعَهُمْ سِيَاطٌ كَأَذْنَابِ الْبَقَرِ يَضْرِبُونَ بِهَا النَّاسَ . وَنِسَاءٌ كَاسِيَاتٌ عَارِيَاتٌ مُمِيلاَتٌ مَائِلاَتٌ ، رُؤُوسُهُنَّ كَأَسْنِمَةِ الْبُخْتِ الْمَائِلَةِ لاَ يَدْخُلْنَ الْجَنَّةَ . وَلاَ يَجِدْنَ رِيحَهَا ، وَإِنَّ رِيحَهَا لَيُوجَدُ مِنْ مَسِيرَةِ كَذَا وَكَذَا » رواهُ مسلم

1633. Hazrat Abu Hurairah (R.A.A.) relates that the Holy Prophet (S.A.W.) said: There are two kinds of the inhabitants of the Hell whom I have not seen. One, persons holding whips like the tails of cows with which they will beat the people; and women who will have clothes on their persons, but will appear naked; and will twist their shoulders delicately and walk with waving motions. Their heads will appear like the humps of weddling she-camels. They will not enter Paradise nor perceive its fragrance though its fragrance is perceptible from such and such a distance. *(Muslim)*

* * * * * * *

CHAPTER 293

PROHIBITION OF IMITATING SATAN AND DISBELIEVERS

١٦٣٤ – عَنْ جَابِرٍ رَضِيَ اللهُ عَنْهُ قَالَ : قَالَ رَسُولُ اللهِ صَلَّى اللهُ عَلَيْهِ وَسَلَّمَ : « لاَ تَأْكُلُوا بِالشِّمَالِ ، فَإِنَّ الشَّيْطَانَ يَأْكُلُ وَيَشْرَبُ بِشِمَالِهِ » رواهُ مسلم .

1634. Hazrat Jabir (R.A.A.) relates that the Holy Prophet (S.A.W.) has said: Do not eat with your left hand, for Satan eats with his left hand. *(Muslim)*

١٦٣٥ – وَعَنِ ابْنِ عُمَرَ رَضِيَ اللهُ عَنْهُمَا أَنَّ رَسُولَ اللهِ صَلَّى اللهُ عَلَيْهِ وَسَلَّمَ قَالَ : « لاَ يَأْكُلَنَّ أَحَدُكُمْ بِشِمَالِهِ ، وَلاَ يَشْرَبَنَّ بِهَا . فَإِنَّ الشَّيْطَانَ يَأْكُلُ بِشِمَالِهِ وَيَشْرَبُ بِهَا » رواهُ مسلم .

1635. Hazrat Ibn 'Umar (R.A.A.) reports that the Holy Prophet (S.A.W.) has said: None of you should eat with left hand nor drink with it, for Satan eats with his left hand and drinks with it.

(Muslim)

١٦٣٦ – وَعَنْ أَبِي هُرَيْرَةَ رَضِيَ اللهُ عَنْهُ أَنَّ رَسُولَ اللهِ صَلَّى اللهُ
عَلَيْهِ وَسَلَّمَ قَالَ : « إِنَّ الْيَهُودَ وَالنَّصَارَى لَا يَصْبِغُونَ ، فَخَالِفُوهُمْ »
مُتَّفَقٌ عَلَيْهِ .

1636. Hazrat Abu Hurairah (R.A.A.) relates that the Holy Prophet (S.A.W.) said: The Jews and Christians do not dye their hair, therefore you should do its opposite.

Imam Nawawi says that one should dye his beard and white hair of the head red or yellow but not black. *(Bukhari and Muslim)*

* * * * * * *

CHAPTER 294

PROHIBITION OF DYEING HAIR BLACK BY MALES AND FEMALES

١٦٣٧ – عَنْ جَابِرٍ رَضِيَ اللهُ عَنْهُ قَالَ : أُتِيَ بِأَبِي قُحَافَةَ وَالِدِ
أَبِي بَكْرٍ الصِّدِّيقِ رَضِيَ اللهُ عَنْهُمَا يَوْمَ فَتْحِ مَكَّةَ وَرَأْسُهُ وَلِحْيَتُهُ
كَالثَّغَامَةِ بَيَاضاً ، فَقَالَ رَسُولُ اللهِ صَلَّى اللهُ عَلَيْهِ وَسَلَّمَ : « غَيِّرُوا
هَذَا وَاجْتَنِبُوا السَّوَادَ » رواه مسلم .

1637. Hazrat Jabir (R.A.A.) relates that Hazrat Abu Quhafah (R.A.A.) father of Hazrat Abu-Bakr (R.A.A.) was presented to the Holy Prophet (S.A.W.) on the day when Mecca fell. His head and beard were white like saghama grass. The Holy Prophet (S.A.W.) said: change this (its colour) but avoid black. *(Muslim)*

* * * * * * *

CHAPTER 295

PROHIBITION OF SHAVING PART OF HEAD AND PERMISSION FOR MALES TO SHAVE ENTIRE HEAD BUT NOT FEMALES

١٦٣٨ – عَنِ ابْنِ عُمَرَ رَضِيَ اللهُ عَنْهُمَا قَالَ : نَهَى رَسُولُ اللهِ
صَلَّى اللهُ عَلَيْهِ وَسَلَّمَ عَنِ الْقَزَعِ . متفق عليه

1638. Hazrat Ibn Umar (R.A.A.) says that the Holy Prophet (S.A.W.) has forbidden shaving only a part of the head and leaving unshaved another part. *(Bukhari and Muslim)*

١٦٣٩– وَعَنْهُ قَالَ : رَأَى رَسُولُ اللهِ صَلَّى اللهُ عَلَيْهِ وَسَلَّمَ صَبِيّاً قَدْ حُلِقَ بَعْضُ شَعْرِ رَأْسِهِ وَتُرِكَ بَعْضُهُ . فَنَهَاهُمْ عَنْ ذَلِكَ وَقَالَ : «احْلِقُوهُ كُلَّهُ ، أَوِ اتْرُكُوهُ كُلَّهُ» .

رواه أبُو داود بإسناد صحيح على شرط البُخاري ومُسلم .

1639. Hazrat Ibn Umar (R.A.A.) reports that the Holy Prophet (S.A.W.) saw a child with his head partly shaven and partly unshaven. He (S.A.W.) forbade this and told the child's elders to shave the whole of the head or leave the whole. *(Abu Daud)*

١٦٤٠– وَعَنْ عَبْدِ اللهِ بْنِ جَعْفَرٍ رَضِيَ اللهُ عَنْهُمَا أَنَّ النَّبِيَّ صَلَّى اللهُ عَلَيْهِ وَسَلَّمَ أَمْهَلَ آلَ جَعْفَرٍ رضي اللهُ عنه ثَلاثاً، ثُمَّ أَتَاهُمْ فَقَالَ : «لاَ تَبْكُوا عَلَى أَخِي بَعْدَ الْيَوْمِ» . ثُمَّ قَالَ : «ادْعُوا لِي بَنِي أَخِي» فَجِيءَ بِنَا كَأَنَّا أَفْرُخٌ فَقَالَ : «ادْعُوا لِيَ الْحَلاَّقَ» فَأَمَرَهُ ، فَحَلَقَ رُؤُوسَنَا. رواهُ أبوداود بإسنادٍ صحيحٍ على شَرْطِ البُخاريِّ ومُسْلِمٍ .

1640. Hazrat Abdullah bin Ja'far (R.A.A.) relates that the Holy prophet (S.A.W.) permitted the children of Hazrat Ja'far (R.A.A.) to mourn for him (after his martyrdom) for three days. (After three days) he (S.A.W.) came to them and said: Do not weep for my brother after today. Then he (S.A.W.) said: Bring my brother's sons to me. Due to the grief our condition was woeful like chicks. He then said: Send for a barber; and when he came, he (S.A.W.) directed him to shave our heads, which he did *(Abu Daud)*

١٦٤١– وَعَنْ عَلِيٍّ رَضِيَ اللهُ عَنْهُ قَالَ : نَهَى رَسُولُ اللهِ صَلَّى اللهُ عَلَيْهِ وَسَلَّمَ أَنْ تَحْلِقَ الْمَرْأَةُ رَأْسَهَا . رواهُ النَّسائي

1641. Hazrat Ali (R.A.A.) relates that the Holy Prophet (S.A.W.) forbade the shaving of the head of women. *(Nisai)*

* * * * * * *

CHAPTER 296

PROHIBITION OF USING WIGS, MARKING OF BODY AND FILING THE TEETH

قَالَ اللهُ تَعَالَى : إِنْ يَدْعُونَ مِنْ دُونِهِ إِلاَّ إِنَاثاً وَإِنْ يَدْعُونَ إِلاَّ شَيْطَاناً مَرِيداً لَعَنَهُ اللهُ وَقَالَ : لأَتَّخِذَنَّ مِنْ عِبَادِكَ نَصِيباً مَفْرُوضاً، وَلأُضِلَّنَّهُمْ ، وَلأُمَنِّيَنَّهُمْ . وَلآمُرَنَّهُمْ فَلَيُبَتِّكُنَّ آذَانَ الأَنْعَامِ ، وَلآمُرَنَّهُمْ فَلَيُغَيِّرُنَّ خَلْقَ اللهِ الآية [النساء : ١١٧-١١٩].

Allah, the exalted, has said:

401. They invoke in His stead only females; they pray to none else than Satan, a rebel, whom Allah cursed, and he said: Surely I will take of Thy bondmen an appointed portion. And surely I will lead them astray, and surely I will arouse desires in them, and surely I will command them and they will cut the cattle's ears, and surely I will command them and they will change Allah's creation. (4 : 117–119)

١٦٤٢ – وَعَنْ أَسْمَاءَ رَضِيَ اللهُ عَنْهَا أَنَّ امْرَأَةً سَأَلَتِ النَّبِيَّ صَلَّى اللهُ عَلَيْهِ وَسَلَّمَ فَقَالَتْ : يَا رَسُولَ اللهِ إِنَّ ابْنَتِي أَصَابَتْهَا الحَصْبَةُ . فَتَمَرَّقَ شَعرُهَا . وَإِنِّي زَوَّجْتُهَا . أَفَأَصِلُ فِيهِ؟ فَقَالَ : « لَعَنَ اللهُ الوَاصِلَةَ وَالمَوْصُولَةَ » متفقٌ عليه .

وفي روايةٍ : « الوَاصِلَةَ . وَالمُسْتَوْصِلَةَ » .

وَعَنْ عَائِشَةَ رَضِيَ اللهُ عَنْهَا نَحْوُهُ . متفقٌ عليه .

1642. Hazrat Asma' (R.A.A.) relates that a woman asked the Holy Prophet (S.A.W.): O Messenger of Allah! my daughter had smallpox, consequently she lost her hair. Now as I have married her, may I supply her wigs? The Holy Prophet (S.A.W.) said: Allah has cursed the manufacturer and the wearer of wigs.

(Bukhari and Muslim)

According to another version the Holy Prophet (S.A.W.) has cursed the maker of a wig and she who desired a wig.

The same tradition is reported by Hazrat Ayesha (R.A.A.).

(Bukhari and Muslim)

١٦٤٣ – وعَنْ حُميد بنِ عَبْدِ الرَّحْمٰنِ أنَّهُ سَمِعَ مُعَاوِيَةَ رَضِيَ اللهُ عَنْهُ عَامَ حجَّ عَلَى المنْبَرِ وتَنَاوَلَ قُصَّةً مِنْ شعْرٍ كَانَتْ فِي يَدِ حَرَسِيٍّ فَقَالَ: يَا أهْلَ المَدِينَةِ أيْنَ عُلَمَاؤُكُمْ؟! سَمِعْتُ النَّبِيَّ صَلَّى اللهُ عَلَيْهِ وَسَلَّمَ يَنْهَى عَنْ مِثْلِ هذهِ. وَيَقُولُ: إنَّمَا هَلَكَتْ بَنُو إسْرَائِيلَ حِينَ اتَّخَذَ هذهِ نِسَاؤُهُمْ» متفقٌ عليه.

1643. Hazrat Humaid bin Abdur Rahman (R.A.A.) relates that he heard from Hazrat Mu'awiah (R.A.A.) as saying from the pulpit in the year when he was on Pilgrimage, taking hold of a lock of hair from the hands of a servant: 'O people of Madina, where are your scholars? I have myself heard the Holy Prophet (S.A.W.) forbidding the use of this lock and say: 'The children of Israel were ruined when their women-folk took to this kind of thing. *(Bukhari and Muslim)*

١٦٤٤ – وعَنِ ابْنِ عُمَرَ رَضِيَ اللهُ عَنْهُ أنَّ رَسُولَ اللهِ صَلَّى اللهُ عَلَيْهِ وَسَلَّمَ لَعَنَ الْوَاصِلَةَ وَالْمُسْتَوْصِلَةَ. وَالْوَاشِمَةَ وَالْمُسْتَوْشِمَةَ. متفقٌ عليه.

1644. Hazrat Ibn 'Umar (R.A.A.) says that the Holy Prophet (S.A.W.) has cursed the maker and user of a wig and the tattoo maker and the one who gets tattooed. *(Bukhari and Muslim)*

١٦٤٥ – وعَنِ ابْنِ مَسْعُودٍ رَضِيَ اللهُ عَنْهُ قَالَ: لَعَنَ اللهُ الْوَاشِمَاتِ وَالْمُسْتَوْشِمَاتِ وَالْمُتَنَمِّصَاتِ. وَالْمُتَفَلِّجَاتِ لِلْحُسْنِ. المُغَيِّرَاتِ خَلْقَ اللهِ! فَقَالَتْ لَهُ امْرَأَةٌ فِي ذَلِكَ. فَقَالَ: وَمَا لِي لَا أَلْعَنُ مَنْ لَعَنَ رَسُولُ اللهِ صَلَّى اللهُ عَلَيْهِ وَسَلَّمَ وَهُوَ فِي كِتَابِ اللهِ؟! قَالَ اللهُ تَعَالَى: وَمَا آتَاكُمُ الرَّسُولُ فَخُذُوهُ وَمَا نَهَاكُمْ عَنْهُ فَانْتَهُوا [الحشر: ٧] متفقٌ عليه.

1645. Hazrat Ibn Ma'ud (R.A.A.) said. Allah has cursed female tattoo markers and those females who get tattooed, and those women who get their teeth filed (to make space between them) for beauty and those who have their superfluous hair plucked from their faces, and thus interfere in Allah's creation. A woman (Umm Yaqub) asked Hazrat Ibn Mas'ud (R.A.A.): 'What is all this? He answered: Why should I not curse those whom the Holy Prophet (S.A.W.) has cursed? Although this order exists in His book. (The Holy Quran) Allah, the

Most High says in His Book: And whatsoever the Messenger giveth you, take it. And whatsoever he forbiddeth, abstain from it.' (59 : 7)

(Bukhari and Muslim)

* * * * * * *

CHAPTER 297

PROHIBITION OF PLUCKING GRAY (WHITE) HAIR FROM BEARD OR HEAD, AND SHAVING OF BEARD BY A YOUNG MAN

١٦٤٦ – عَنْ عَمْرِو بْنِ شُعَيْبٍ ، عَنْ أَبِيهِ ، عَنْ جَدِّهِ رَضِيَ اللهُ عَنْهُ ، عَنِ النَّبِيِّ صَلَّى اللهُ عَلَيْهِ وَسَلَّمَ قَالَ : « لاَ تَنْتِفُوا الشَّيْبَ ؛ فَإِنَّهُ نُورُ الْمُسْلِمِ يَوْمَ الْقِيَامَةِ » حديث حسن . رَوَاهُ أَبُو دَاوُدَ ، وَالتِّرْمِذِيُّ ، وَالنَّسَائِيُّ بِأَسَانِيدَ حَسَنَةٍ . قَالَ التِّرْمِذِيُّ : هُوَ حَدِيثٌ حَسَنٌ .

1646. Hazrat 'Amr bin Shu'aib (R.A.A.) reports from his father and he from his father, that the Holy Prophet (S.A.W.) said Do not pluck away gray (white) hair, because they are the light of a Muslim on the Day of Judgement. *(Abu Daud and Tirmizi)*

١٦٤٧ – وَعَنْ عَائِشَةَ رَضِيَ اللهُ عَنْهَا قَالَتْ : قَالَ رَسُولُ اللهِ صَلَّى اللهُ عَلَيْهِ وَسَلَّمَ : « مَنْ عَمِلَ عَمَلاً لَيْسَ عَلَيْهِ أَمْرُنَا فَهُوَ رَدٌّ » رواه مسلم

1647. Hazrat Ayesha (R.A.A.) relates that the Holy Prophet (S.A.W.) said: A person who adopts an act which has not been approved by us, the said person or the act is rejected. *(Muslim)*

* * * * * * *

CHAPTER 298

PROHIBITION OF USING RIGHT HAND FOR CLEANING ORGAN OF URINATION AND CALL OF NATURE OR IMPURITIES AND TO TOUCH THEM WITH RIGHT HAND UNNECESSARILY

١٦٤٨ – عَنْ أَبِي قَتَادَةَ رَضِيَ اللهُ عَنْهُ عَنِ النَّبِيِّ صَلَّى اللهُ عَلَيْهِ وَسَلَّمَ قَالَ : « إِذَا بَالَ أَحَدُكُمْ ، فَلاَ يَأْخُذَنَّ ذَكَرَهُ بِيَمِينِهِ ، وَلاَ يَسْتَنْجِ بِيَمِينِهِ ، وَلاَ يَتَنَفَّسْ فِي الإِنَاءِ » .

متفقٌ عليه . وَفِي البَابِ أَحَادِيثُ كَثِيرَةٌ صَحِيحَةٌ .

1648. Hazrat Abu Qatadah (R.A.A.) relates that the Holy Prophet (S.A.W.) said: Do not touch your organ while urinating with your right hand, or employ it for washing or cleansing; and do not breathe into the vessel from which you drink (water or any other beverage). *(Bukhari and Muslim)*

* * * * * * *

CHAPPTER 299

PROHIBITION OF WEARING ONLY ONE SHOE OR ONE SOCK OR TO PUT ON SHOES OR SOCKS WHILE STANDING UNNECESSARILY

١٦٤٩ – عَنْ أَبِي هُرَيْرَةَ رَضِيَ اللهُ عَنْهُ أَنَّ رَسُولَ اللهِ صَلَّى اللهُ عَلَيْهِ وَسَلَّمَ قَالَ : « لاَ يَمْشِ أَحَدُكُمْ فِي نَعْلٍ وَاحِدَةٍ ، لِيَنْعَلْهُمَا جَمِيعاً ، أَوْ لِيَخْلَعْهُمَا جَمِيعاً » .

وفي رواية « أَوْ لِيُحْفِهِمَا جَمِيعاً » متفقٌ عَلَيْهِ

1649. Hazrat Abu Hurairah (R.A.A.) relates that the Holy Prophet (S.A.W.) said: Nobody should walk wearing only one shoe; he should wear both, or put off both.

Another version says: Or he should keep both the feet bare. *(Bukhari and Muslim)*

١٦٥٠ – وَعَنْهُ قَالَ : سَمِعْتُ رَسُولَ اللهِ صَلَّى اللهُ عَلَيْهِ وَسَلَّمَ يَقُولُ : « إِذَا انْقَطَعَ شِسْعُ نَعْلِ أَحَدِكُمْ فَلاَ يَمْشِ فِي الأُخْرَى حَتَّى يُصْلِحَهَا » رواهُ مسلم .

1650. Hazrat Abu Hurairah (R.A.A.) relates that he heard the Holy Prophet (S.A.W.) saying: When the strap of one of your shoes is broken, do not walk about with the other shoe in your foot till you have had the first one repaired. *(Muslim)*

١٦٥١ – وَعَنْ جَابِرٍ رَضِيَ اللهُ عَنْهُ أَنَّ رَسُولَ اللهِ صَلَّى اللهُ عَلَيْهِ وَسَلَّمَ نَهَى أَنْ يَنْتَعِلَ الرَّجُلُ قَائِماً .

رَوَاهُ أَبُو دَاوُدَ بِإِسْنَادٍ حَسَنٍ .

1651. Hazrat Jabir (R.A.A.) says that the Holy Prophet (S.A.W.) has forbidden a person from putting on his shoe while standing.

(Imam Abu Daud has cited this tradition on good proofs).

* * * * * * *

CHAPTER 300

PROHIBITION OF LEAVING FIRE OR LIGHT BURNING WHEN RETIRING

١٦٥٢ – عَنِ ابْنِ عُمَرَ رَضِيَ اللهُ عَنْهُمَا عَنِ النَّبِيِّ صَلَّى اللهُ عَلَيْهِ وَسَلَّمَ قَالَ: «لاَ تَتْرُكُوا النَّارَ فِي بُيُوتِكُمْ حِينَ تَنَامُونَ» متفق عليه

1652. Hazrat Ibn 'Umar (R.A.A.) relates that the Holy Prophet (S.A.W.) said: When you go to bed, do not leave a fire burning in your house (extinguish it). *(Bukhari and Muslim)*

١٦٥٣ – وَعَنْ أَبِي مُوسَى الأَشْعَرِيِّ رَضِيَ اللهُ عَنْهُ قَالَ: احْتَرَقَ بَيْتٌ بِالْمَدِينَةِ عَلَى أَهْلِهِ مِنَ اللَّيْلِ. فَلَمَّا حُدِّثَ رَسُولُ اللهِ صَلَّى اللهُ عَلَيْهِ وَسَلَّمَ بِشَأْنِهِمْ قَالَ: «إِنَّ هَذِهِ النَّارَ عَدُوٌّ لَكُمْ. فَإِذَا نِمْتُمْ. فَأَطْفِئُوهَا» مُتَّفَقٌ عَلَيْهِ

1653. This Hadis has already been covered in S. No. 161 of Chapter 16.

١٦٥٤ – وَعَنْ جَابِرٍ رَضِيَ اللهُ عَنْهُ عَنْ رَسُولِ اللهِ صَلَّى اللهُ عَلَيْهِ وَسَلَّمَ قَالَ: «غَطُّوا الإِنَاءَ. وَأَوْكِئُوا السِّقَاءَ. وَأَغْلِقُوا الْبَابَ. وَأَطْفِئُوا السِّرَاجَ. فَإِنَّ الشَّيْطَانَ لاَ يَحِلُّ سِقَاءً. وَلاَ يَفْتَحُ بَاباً. وَلاَ يَكْشِفُ إِنَاءً. فَإِنْ لَمْ يَجِدْ أَحَدُكُمْ إِلاَّ أَنْ يَعْرُضَ عَلَى إِنَائِهِ عُوداً. وَيَذْكُرَ اسْمَ اللهِ. فَلْيَفْعَلْ. فَإِنَّ الْفُوَيْسِقَةَ تُضْرِمُ عَلَى أَهْلِ الْبَيْتِ بَيْتَهُمْ» رواه مسلم.

1654. Hazrat Jabir (R.A.A.) relates that the Holy Prophet (S.A.W.) said. Cover up the containers, tie the opening of the leather water bag, shut the doors and put out the lamps, because the devil does not lift up the covering of a vessel, nor loosens the string of a leather water-skin, nor opens a closed door. If one does not find any thing to cover a vessel, he should place a piece of wood across it, or pronounce the name of Allah on it, it is enough. Sometimes a mouse (catches hold of an open oil lamp still burning) and burns down a house on top of its inmates. (Muslim)

* * * * * * *

CHAPTER 301

PROHIBITION OF OSTENTATION (IT IS AN ACT OR DEED USELESS BUT TIRESOME)

قَالَ اللهُ تَعَالَى : قُلْ مَا أَسْأَلُكُمْ عَلَيْهِ مِنْ أَجْرٍ وَمَا أَنَا مِنَ الْمُتَكَلِّفِينَ [ص : ٨٦] .

Allah, the Exalted, has said:

402. Say (O Muhammad, unto mankind): I ask of you no fee for this, and I am no imposter. (38 : 86)

١٦٥٥ – وَعَنْ عُمَرَ رَضِيَ اللهُ عَنْهُ قَالَ : نُهِينَا عَنِ التَّكَلُّفِ رَوَاهُ الْبُخَارِي .

1655. Hazrat Ibn 'Umar (R.A.A.) says: We have been asked not to strike an attitude. *(Bukhari)*

١٦٥٦ – وَعَنْ مَسْرُوقٍ قَالَ : دَخَلْنَا عَلَى عَبْدِ اللهِ بْنِ مَسْعُودٍ رَضِيَ اللهُ عَنْهُ فَقَالَ : يَا أَيُّهَا النَّاسُ مَنْ عَلِمَ شَيْئاً فَلْيَقُلْ بِهِ . وَمَنْ لَمْ يَعْلَمْ . فَلْيَقُلْ : اللهُ أَعْلَمُ . فَإِنَّ مِنَ الْعِلْمِ أَنْ تَقُولَ لِمَا لاَ تَعْلَمُ : اللهُ أَعْلَمُ . قَالَ اللهُ تَعَالَى لِنَبِيِّهِ صَلَّى اللهُ عَلَيْهِ وَسَلَّمَ : (قُلْ مَا أَسْأَلُكُمْ عَلَيْهِ مِنْ أَجْرٍ وَمَا أَنَا مِنَ الْمُتَكَلِّفِينَ) رواه البخاري

1656. Hazrat Masruq (R.A.A.) relates: Once we visited Hazrat Abdullah bin Mas'ud (R.A.A.) when he said to us: O people! A person who knows something, may talk about it and one who does not know (about the matter) should say: Allah, the Most High knows best, because when a person who has no knowledge of a matter says that Allah, the Most High knows best, is itself knowledge. Allah said to His Prophet. Say (O Muhammad) unto mankind: I ask of you no fee for this, and I am no imposter. (38 : 86) *(Bukhari)*

* * * * * * *

CHAPTER 302

PROHIBITION OF BEWAILING, BEATING OF FACE, TEARING OF CLOTHES, PLUCKING OF HAIR AND SHAVING OF HEAD ON DEAD BODY

١٦٥٧ – عَنْ عُمَرَ بْنِ الخَطَّابِ رَضِيَ اللهُ عَنْهُ قَالَ : قَالَ النَّبِيُّ صَلَّى اللهُ عَلَيْهِ وَسَلَّمَ : « المَيِّتُ يُعَذَّبُ فِي قَبْرِهِ بِمَا نِيحَ عَلَيْهِ » وَفِي رِوَايَةٍ : « مَا نِيحَ عَلَيْهِ » متفقٌ عَلَيْهِ .

1657. Hazrat 'Umar bin Al-Khattab (R.A.A.) relates that the Holy Prophet (S.A.W.) said: A dead person's corpse is tormented in the grave.

Another tradition says that a dead person is punished when somebody wails for it. *(Bukhari and Muslim)*

١٦٥٨ – وَعَنِ ابْنِ مَسْعُودٍ رَضِيَ اللهُ عَنْهُ قَالَ : قَالَ رَسُولُ اللهِ صَلَّى اللهُ عَلَيْهِ وَسَلَّمَ : « لَيْسَ مِنَّا مَنْ ضَرَبَ الخُدُودَ ، وَشَقَّ الجُيُوبَ ، وَدَعَا بِدَعْوَى الجَاهِلِيَّةِ » متفقٌ عليه .

1658. Hazrat Abdullah bin Mas'ud (R.A.A.) relates that the Holy Prophet (S.A.W.) said. A person who beats his face, tears his clothes and bewails his fate over a misfortune as was done in the days of ignorance, is not of us. *(Bukhari and Muslim)*

١٦٥٩ – وَعَنْ أَبِي بُرْدَةَ قَالَ : وَجِعَ أَبُو مُوسَى ، فَغُشِيَ عَلَيْهِ ، وَرَأْسُهُ فِي حِجْرِ امْرَأَةٍ مِنْ أَهْلِهِ ، فَأَقْبَلَتْ تَصِيحُ بِرَنَّةٍ فَلَمْ يَسْتَطِعْ أَنْ يَرُدَّ عَلَيْهَا شَيْئاً ؛ فَلَمَّا أَفَاقَ ، قَالَ : أَنَا بَرِيءٌ مِمَّنْ بَرِيءَ مِنْهُ رَسُولُ اللهِ صَلَّى اللهُ عَلَيْهِ وَسَلَّمَ : إِنَّ رَسُولَ اللهِ صَلَّى اللهُ عَلَيْهِ وَسَلَّمَ بَرِيءٌ مِنَ الصَّالِقَةِ ، وَالحَالِقَةِ ، وَالشَّاقَّةِ ! متَّفقٌ عليه .

1659. Hazrat Abu Burdah (R.A.A.) says that (once) Hazrat Abu Musa (R.A.A.) fell ill seriously and became unconscious. His head was in the lap of one of the woman of his family. (On seeing his serious condition) she started weeping in a loud voice. Hazrat Abu Musa (R.A.A.) could not stop her due to his weakness. But when he regained consciousness, he said: I detest what the Holy Prophet (S.A.W.) detested. He detested a woman who cried out loudly, or shaved her head, or tore her clothes. *(Bukhari and Muslim)*

١٦٦٠– وَعَنِ المُغِيرَةِ بْنِ شُعْبَةَ رَضِيَ اللهُ عَنْهُ قَالَ : سَمِعْتُ رَسُولَ اللهِ صَلَّى اللهُ عَلَيْهِ وَسَلَّمَ يَقُولُ : « مَنْ نِيحَ عَلَيْهِ ، فَإِنَّهُ يُعَذَّبُ بِمَا نِيحَ عَلَيْهِ يَوْمَ القِيَامَةِ » متفقٌ عليه .

1660. Hazrat Mughirah bin Shu'bah (R.A.A.) says that he heard the Holy Prophet (S.A.W.) say: A (dead) person, on whose death lamentation is uttered loudly, will be tortured for it till the Day of Judgement. *(Bukhari and Muslim)*

١٦٦١– وَعَنْ أُمِّ عَطِيَّةَ نُسَيْبَةَ – بِضَمِّ النُّونِ وَفَتْحِهَا – رَضِيَ اللهُ عَنْهَا قَالَتْ : أَخَذَ عَلَيْنَا رَسُولُ اللهِ صَلَّى اللهُ عَلَيْهِ وَسَلَّمَ عِنْدَ البَيْعَةِ أَنْ لاَ نَنُوحَ . متَّفَقٌ عليه .

1661. Hazrat Umm Atiyyah Nusaibah (R.A.A.) relates: The Holy Prophet (S.A.W.), while taking pledge, made us (the women) promise as part of the covenant, that we would not lament loudly on the dead. *(Bukhari and Muslim)*

١٦٦٢– وَعَنِ النُّعْمَانِ بْنِ بَشِيرٍ رَضِيَ اللهُ عَنْهُمَا قَالَ : أُغْمِيَ عَلَى عَبْدِ اللهِ بْنِ رَوَاحَةَ رَضِيَ اللهُ عَنْهُ . فَجَعَلَتْ أُخْتُهُ تَبْكِي . وَتَقُولُ : وَاجَبَلاَهُ . وَاكَذَا ، وَاكَذَا : تُعَدِّدُ عَلَيْهِ . فَقَالَ حِينَ أَفَاقَ : مَا قُلْتِ شَيْئاً إِلَّا قِيلَ لِي : أَنْتَ كَذَلِكَ ؟ ! رَوَاهُ البُخَارِي .

1662. Hazrat Nu'man bin Bashir (R.A.A.) says that when Hazrat Abdullah bin Rawaha (R.A.A.) went under a comma (in his illness), his sister (Umrah) started lamenting for him loudly thus: O thou mountain (The one holding towering personality among men) and such and such! (recounted his qualities). When he recovered his senses he said: Whatever you have said about me I was asked: Are you like this? *(Bukhari)*

١٦٦٣– وَعَنِ ابْنِ عُمَرَ رَضِيَ اللهُ عَنْهُمَا قَالَ : اشْتَكَى سَعْدُ بْنُ عُبَادَةَ رَضِيَ اللهُ عَنْهُ شَكْوَى ، فَأَتَاهُ رَسُولُ اللهِ صَلَّى اللهُ عَلَيْهِ وَسَلَّمَ يَعُودُهُ مَعَ عَبْدِ الرَّحْمَنِ بْنِ عَوْفٍ . وَسَعْدِ بْنِ أَبِي وَقَّاصٍ . وَعَبْدِ اللهِ بْنِ مَسْعُودٍ رَضِيَ اللهُ عَنْهُمْ ، فَلَمَّا دَخَلَ عَلَيْهِ ، وَجَدَهُ فِي غَشْيَةٍ فَقَالَ : « أَقَضَى ؟ قَالُوا : لاَ يَا رَسُولَ اللهِ . فَبَكَى رَسُولُ اللهِ صَلَّى اللهُ عَلَيْهِ وَسَلَّمَ . فَلَمَّا رَأَى القَوْمُ بُكَاءَ النَّبِيِّ صَلَّى اللهُ عَلَيْهِ

وَسَلَّمَ بَكَوْا، قَالَ : « أَلاَ تَسْمَعُونَ ؟ إِنَّ اللهَ لاَ يُعَذِّبُ بِدَمْعِ الْعَيْنِ ، وَلاَ بِحُزْنِ الْقَلْبِ، وَلَكِنْ يُعَذِّبُ بِهَذَا ، وَأَشَارَ إِلَى لِسَانِهِ « أَوْ يَرْحَمُ » متفقٌ عليه .

1663. This Hadis has been covered in S. No. 925 of Chapter 153.

١٦٦٤ — وَعَنْ أَبِي مَالِكٍ الأَشْعَرِيِّ رَضِيَ اللهُ عَنْهُ قَالَ : قَالَ رَسُولُ اللهِ صَلَّى اللهُ عَلَيْهِ وَسَلَّمَ : « النَّائِحَةُ إِذَا لَمْ تَتُبْ قَبْلَ مَوْتِهَا تُقَامُ يَوْمَ الْقِيَامَةِ وَعَلَيْهَا سِرْبَالٌ مِنْ قَطِرَانٍ ، وَدِرْعٌ مِنْ جَرَبٍ » رواهُ مسلم

1664. Hazrat Abu Malik Al Ash'ari (R.A.A.) relates that the Holy Prophet (S.A.W.) said: If a woman, who is given to lamenting loudly, does not repent and seek forgiveness before her death, she will be raised on the Day of Judgement wearing a coat of coaltar and a scarf of rust. *(Muslim)*

١٦٦٥ — وَعَنْ أُسَيْدِ بْنِ أَبِي أَسِيْدٍ التَّابِعِيِّ عَنِ امْرَأَةٍ مِنَ المُبَايِعَاتِ قَالَتْ : كَانَ فِيمَا أَخَذَ عَلَيْنَا رَسُولُ اللهِ صَلَّى اللهُ عَلَيْهِ وَسَلَّمَ ، فِي المَعْرُوفِ الَّذِي أَخَذَ عَلَيْنَا أَنْ لاَ نَعْصِيَهُ فِيهِ : أَنْ لاَ نَخْمِشَ وَجْهاً ، وَلاَ نَدْعُوَ وَيْلاً ، وَلاَ نَشُقَّ جَيْباً ، وَأَنْ لاَ نَنْشُرَ شَعْراً .

رَوَاهُ أَبُو دَاوُد بِإِسْنَادٍ حَسَنٍ .

1665. Hazrat Usaid bin Abu Usaid (R.A.) relates that a woman who took Oath of Allegiance at the hands of the Holy Prophet (S.A.W.) said: Among the matters about which the Holy Prophet (S.A.W.) took pledge from us, one was that we would not disobey him and will not scratch our faces, bewailing, tearing our garments and not loosening our hair. *(Abu Daud)*

١٦٦٦ — وَعَنْ أَبِي مُوسَى رَضِيَ اللهُ عَنْهُ أَنَّ رَسُولَ اللهِ صَلَّى اللهُ عَلَيْهِ وَسَلَّمَ قَالَ : « مَا مِنْ مَيِّتٍ يَمُوتُ ، فَيَقُومُ بَاكِيهِمْ ، فَيَقُولُ : وَاجَبَلاَهُ ، وَاسَيِّدَاهُ ، أَوْ نَحْوَ ذَلِكَ إِلاَّ وُكِّلَ بِهِ مَلَكَانِ يَلْهَزَانِهِ : أَهَكَذَا كُنْتَ ؟! » رَوَاهُ التِّرْمِذِي وَقَالَ : حَدِيثٌ حَسَنٌ .

1666. Hazrat Abu Musa Al-Ash'ari (R.A.A.) relates that the Holy Prophet (S.A.W.) said: When a person dies and one of his relatives laments for him saying: 'O the mount among men, O the chief and so on, Allah, the Most High, appoints two angels who pound him with their fists and ask him: 'Were you like this?' *(Tirmizi)*

١٦٦٧ـ وعن أبي هريرة رضي الله عنه قال: قال رسول الله صلى الله عليه وسلم: «اثنتان في الناس هما بهم كفر: الطعن في النسب. والنياحة على الميت» رواه مسلم.

1667. This Hadis has been covered in S. No. 1578 of Chapter 275.

* * * * * * * *

CHAPTER 303

PROHIBITION OF CONSULTING SOOTHSAYERS, FORTUNE TELLERS AND THOSE PERSONS WHO GIVE CLUE TO MISSING ARTICLES

١٦٦٨ـ عن عائشة رضي الله عنها قالت: سأل رسول الله صلى الله عليه وسلم أناس عن الكهان. فقال: «ليسوا بشيء» فقالوا: يا رسول الله إنهم يحدثونا أحياناً بشيء. فيكون حقاً؟ فقال رسول الله صلى الله عليه وسلم: «تلك الكلمة من الحق يخطفها الجني. فيقرها في أذن وليه. فيخلطون معها مائة كذبة» متفق عليه.

وفي رواية للبخاري عن عائشة رضي الله عنها أنها سمعت رسول الله صلى الله عليه وسلم يقول: «إن الملائكة تنزل في العنان ـ وهو السحاب ـ فتذكر الأمر قضي في السماء. فيسترق الشيطان السمع. فيسمعه. فيوحيه إلى الكهان. فيكذبون معها مائة كذبة من عند أنفسهم».

1668. **Hazrat Ayesha** (R.A.A.) relates: Some people solicited from the Holy Prophet (S.A.W.) information about soothsayers. He (S.A.W.) said: They are humbug and nonsense. The Companions asked: O Messenger of Allah! Sometimes they foretell something which comes true. The Holy Prophet (S.A.W.) explaining this said: That is something true which Satan hears by chance from the angels and which he conveys to his colleagues, and they mix a hundred falsehoods with it (and tell to the people). *(Bukhari and Muslim)*

Another report of *Imam Bukhari* says Hazrat Ayesha (R.A.A.) says that she heard the Holy Prophet (S.A.W.) say: The angels descend into the atmosphere with heavenly orders, talking of something that has been decreed in heaven, and the Satan over-hears this and thereafter communicates it to the soothsayers, who add a hundred falsehoods with it themselves (to convey to their clients).

١٦٦٩ – وَعَنْ صَفِيَّةَ بِنْتِ أَبِي عُبَيْدٍ ، عَنْ بَعْضِ أَزْوَاجِ النَّبِيِّ صَلَّى اللهُ عَلَيْهِ وَسَلَّمَ وَرَضِيَ اللهُ عَنْهَا عَنِ النَّبِيِّ صَلَّى اللهُ عَلَيْهِ وَسَلَّمَ قَالَ : « مَنْ أَتَى عَرَّافاً فَسَأَلَهُ عَنْ شَيْءٍ ، فَصَدَّقَهُ ، لَمْ تُقْبَلْ لَهُ صَلَاةٌ أَرْبَعِينَ يَوْماً » رَوَاهُ مُسْلِم .

1669. **Hazrat Safiyyah bint Abu Ubaid** (R.A.A.) relates on the authority of some of the wives of the Holy Prophet (S.A.W.) that he (S.A.W.) said: A person who goes to one who claims to tell him where he can find his lost property, and affirms the correctness of such a claiment, will lose the recompense of his prayers for forty days. *(Muslim)*

١٦٧٠ – وعَنْ قَبِيصَةَ بنِ المُخَارِقِ رَضِيَ اللهُ عَنْهُ قَالَ : سَمِعْتُ رَسُولَ اللهِ صَلَّى اللهُ عَلَيْهِ وَسَلَّمَ يَقُولُ : « العِيَافَةُ ، وَالطِّيَرَةُ ، والطَّرْقُ ، مِنَ الجِبْتِ » .

رَوَاهُ أبو داود بإسناد حسَن ، وقالَ : الطَّرْقُ ، هُوَ الزَّجْرُ ، أيْ : زَجْرُ الطَّيْرِ ، وهُوَ أنْ يَتَيَمَّنَ أوْ يَتَشَاءَمَ بِطَيَرَانِهِ ، فَإنْ طَارَ إلى جهةِ اليَمِينِ ، تَيَمَّنَ ، وَإنْ طَارَ إلى جهةِ اليَسَارِ تَشَاءَمَ : قالَ أبو داود : « وَالعِيَافَةُ » : الخطُّ .

1670. **Hazrat Qabaisah bin Al-Mukhariq** (R.A.A.) **says that he** heard the Holy Prophet (S.A.W.) say. **Fortune telling, drawing lots or** lives and flying birds to find good or bad omens **from the direction of** their flight, are all devillish practices. ***(Abu Daud)***

١٦٧١ – وَعَنْ ابْنِ عبَّاسٍ رَضِيَ اللهُ عَنْهُمَا قَالَ : قَالَ رَسُولُ اللهِ صَلَّى اللهُ عَلَيْهِ وَسَلَّمَ : « مَنِ اقْتَبَسَ عِلْماً مِنَ النُّجُومِ ، اقْتَبَسَ شُعْبَةً مِنَ السِّحْرِ زَادَ مَازَادَ » رَوَاهُ أَبو دَاود بإسناد صحيح .

1671. Hazrat Ibn Abbas (R.A.A.) relates that the Holy Prophet (S.A.W.) said: A person who learns a part of astrology is as if he learns magic, and the more he learns this, the more he learns of magic. *(Imam Abu Daud* has cited this on sound authority)

١٦٧٢ – وَعَنْ مُعَاوِيَةَ بْنِ الحَكَمِ رَضِيَ اللهُ عَنْهُ قَالَ : قُلْتُ يَارَسُولَ اللهِ إِنِّي حَدِيثُ عَهْدٍ بِجَاهِلِيَّةٍ ، وَقَدْ جَاءَ اللهُ تَعَالَى بِالإِسْلَامِ ، وَإِنَّ مِنَّا رِجَالاً يَأْتُونَ الْكُهَّانَ ؟ قَالَ : « فَلَا تَأْتِهِمْ » قُلْتُ : وَمِنَّا رِجَالٌ يَتَطَيَّرُونَ ؟ قَالَ : « ذَلِكَ شَيْءٌ يَجِدُونَهُ فِي صُدُورِهِمْ . فَلَا يَصُدُّهُمْ » قُلْتُ : وَمِنَّا رِجَالٌ يَخُطُّونَ ؟ قَالَ : « كَانَ نَبِيٌّ مِنَ الأَنْبِيَاءِ يَخُطُّ ، فَمَنْ وَافَقَ خَطَّهُ ، فَذَاكَ » رواه مسلم .

1672. This Hadis has been included in the Hadis vide S. No. 701 of Chapter 91

١٦٧٣ – وَعَنْ أَبِي مَسْعُودٍ الْبَدْرِيِّ رَضِيَ اللهُ عَنْهُ أَنَّ رَسُولَ اللهِ صَلَّى اللهُ عَلَيْهِ وَسَلَّمَ نَهَى عَنْ ثَمَنِ الْكَلْبِ ، وَمَهْرِ الْبَغْيِّ وَحُلْوَانِ الْكَاهِنِ » متفقٌ عليه

1673. Hazrat Abu Mas'ud Badri (R.A.A.) relates that the Holy Prophet (S.A.W.) has prohibited the use of the sale of a dog, the earning of a prostitute and the fee of soothsayer. *(Bukhari and Muslim)*

* * * * * * *

CHAPTER 304

PROHIBITION OF BELIEVING IN ILL OMENS

١٦٧٤ – عن انسٍ رَضِيَ اللهُ عَنْهُ قَالَ : قَالَ رَسُولُ اللهِ صَلَّى اللهُ عَلَيْهِ وَسَلَّمَ : « لاعَدْوَى ولا طِيَرَةَ وَيُعْجِبُنِي الفَأْلُ » قَالُوا : وَمَا الفَأْلُ ؟ قَالَ : « كَلِمَةٌ طَيِّبَةٌ » متفقٌ عليه

1674. Hazrat Anas (R.A.A.) says that the Holy Prophet (S.A.W.) said: There is neither infectious disease and nor bad omen, but I like good augury. The Companions asked him (S.A.W.) 'What is a good augury?' He (S.A.W.) answered: A good word. *(Bukhari and Muslim)*

١٦٧٥ – وَعَنِ ابْنِ عُمَرَ رَضِيَ اللهُ عَنْهُمَا قَالَ : قَالَ رَسُولُ اللهِ صَلَّى اللهُ عَلَيْهِ وَسَلَّمَ : لاعَدْوَى وَلا طِيَرَةَ ، وَإِنْ كَانَ الشُّؤْمُ فِي شَيْءٍ ، فَفِي الدَّارِ ، وَالمَرْأَةِ وَالفَرَسِ » متفقٌ عليه .

1675. Hazrat Ibn 'Umar (R.A.A.) relates that the Holy Prophet (S.A.W.) said: There is neither infection nor ill omen. Had there been any ill luck in any thing it would have been in a house, in a woman, or in a horse. *(Bukhari and Muslim)*

١٦٧٦ – وَعَنْ بُرَيْدَةَ رَضِيَ اللهُ عَنْهُ أَنَّ النَّبِيَّ صَلَّى اللهُ عَلَيْهِ وَسَلَّمَ كَانَ لايَتَطَيَّرُ . رَوَاهُ أَبُو داودَ بإسنادٍ صَحيحٍ .

1676. Hazrat Buraidah (R.A.A.) reports that the Holy Prophet (S.A.W.) never believed in omens. *(Imam Abu Daud* has cited this on sound authority.)

١٦٧٧ – وَعَنْ عُرْوَةَ بْنِ عَامِرٍ رَضِيَ اللهُ عَنْهُ قَالَ : ذُكِرَتِ الطِّيَرَةُ عِنْدَ رَسُولِ اللهِ صَلَّى اللهُ عَلَيْهِ وَسَلَّمَ فَقَالَ : أَحْسَنُهَا الفَأْلُ ، وَلا تَرُدُّ مُسْلِماً فَإِذا رَأَى أَحَدُكُمْ مَايَكْرَهُ ، فَلْيَقُلْ : اللَّهُمَّ لايَأْتِي بالحَسَنَاتِ إلاَّ أَنْتَ ، وَلا يَدْفَعُ السَّيِّئَاتِ إلاَّ أَنْتَ ، وَلا حَوْلَ وَلا قُوَّةَ إلَّا بِكَ » حَدِيثٌ صَحيحٌ رَوَاهُ أبو دَاوُد بإسنادٍ صَحيحٍ .

1677. Hazrat 'Urwah bin 'Aamir (R.A.A.) says: Once a mention was made of divination or the science of foretelling to the Holy Prophet (S.A.W.). He (S.A.W.) said: So far as it conveys a happy news, it is good, but even that should not deter a Muslim from his mission. If any of you may come across something unpallatable he should supplicate: 'O Allah! From Thee alone comes good and Thou alone canst repel evil. There is no strength to resist evil nor power to do good except through Thee. *(Abu Daud)*

* * * * * * *

CHAPTER 305

PROHIBITION OF DRAWING ANIMAL PICTURES ON BEDDINGS, STONES, CLOTH, PILLOWS, COINS, WALLS, CEILING, CURTAIN AND DRESS AND ORDER TO ERASE THEM

١٦٧٨ – عَنِ ابْنِ عُمَرَ رَضِيَ اللهُ عَنْهُمَا أَنَّ رَسُولَ اللهِ صَلَّى اللهُ عَلَيْهِ وَسَلَّمَ قَالَ: « إِنَّ الَّذِينَ يَصْنَعُونَ هٰذِهِ الصُّوَرَ يُعَذَّبُونَ يَوْمَ الْقِيَامَةِ، يُقَالُ لَهُمْ: أَحْيُوا مَا خَلَقْتُمْ » متفقٌ عليه .

1678. Hazrat Ibn 'Umar (R.A.A.) relates that the Holy Prophet (S.A.W.) said: Those people, who draw pictures will be punished on the Day of Judgement and (to render them helpless) they will be asked to put life into these things which they have made.

(Bukhari and Muslim)

١٦٧٩ – وَعَنْ عَائِشَةَ رَضِيَ اللهُ عَنْهَا قَالَتْ: قَدِمَ رَسُولُ اللهِ صَلَّى اللهُ عَلَيْهِ وَسَلَّمَ مِنْ سَفَرٍ وَقَدْ سَتَرْتُ سَهْوَةً لِي بِقِرَامٍ فِيهِ تَمَاثِيلُ فَلَمَّا رَآهُ رَسُولُ اللهِ صَلَّى اللهُ عَلَيْهِ وَسَلَّمَ ، تَلَوَّنَ وَجْهُهُ ! وَقَالَ: « يَا عَائِشَةُ ، أَشَدُّ النَّاسِ عَذَاباً عِنْدَ اللهِ يَوْمَ الْقِيَامَةِ الَّذِينَ يُضَاهُونَ بِخَلْقِ اللهِ ! » قَالَتْ: فَقَطَعْنَاهُ ، فَجَعَلْنَا مِنْهُ وِسَادَةً أَوْ وِسَادَتَيْنِ . متفقٌ عليه .

1679. Hazrat Ayesha (R.A.A.) says: Once when the Holy Prophet (S.A.W.) returned from a journey, he saw a curtain containing pictures hung on a platform in front of my house. On seeing this the Holy Prophet (S.A.W.) (became angry and) his face changed the colour and then said: O Ayesha,, on the Day of Judgement those persons who copy Allah's creation will be most severely punished. So I tore it up and made one or two pillow covers from it.

(Bukhari and Muslim)

١٦٨٠ – وَعَنِ ابْنِ عَبَّاسٍ رَضِيَ اللهُ عَنْهُمَا قَالَ: سَمِعْتُ رَسُولَ اللهِ صَلَّى اللهُ عَلَيْهِ وَسَلَّمَ يَقُولُ: « كُلُّ مُصَوِّرٍ فِي النَّارِ يُجْعَلُ لَهُ بِكُلِّ صُورَةٍ صَوَّرَهَا نَفْسٌ فَيُعَذِّبُهُ فِي جَهَنَّمَ » قَالَ ابْنُ عَبَّاسٍ: فَإِنْ كُنْتَ لَابُدَّ فَاعِلاً ، فَاصْنَعِ الشَّجَرَ وَمَالَا رُوحَ فِيهِ . متفقٌ عليه

1680. Hazrat Ibn Abbas (R.A.A.) relates that he heard the Holy Prophet (S.A.W.) say: Every Artist will be put in Hell. For every artist there will be a person appointed in respect of every one of his pictures which he made in the world, who will punish him for it in the Hell. *(Bukhari and Muslim)*

Ibn Abbas said: If it is unavoidable, draw pictures of trees and lifeless objects.

١٦٨١ ـ وَعَنْهُ قَالَ : سَمِعْتُ رَسُولَ اللهِ صَلَّى اللهُ عَلَيْهِ وَسَلَّمَ يَقُولُ : « مَنْ صَوَّرَ صُورَةً فِي الدُّنْيا، كُلِّفَ أَنْ يَنْفُخَ فِيهَا الرُّوحَ يَوْمَ الْقِيَامَةِ وَلَيْسَ بِنَافِخٍ » متفقٌ عليه .

1681. This Hadis has been included in S. No. 1544 of Chapter 260.

١٦٨٢ ـ وَعَنِ ابْنِ مَسْعُودٍ رَضِيَ اللهُ عَنْهُ قَالَ : سَمِعْتُ رَسُولَ اللهِ صَلَّى اللهُ عَلَيْهِ وَسَلَّمَ يَقُولُ : « إِنَّ أَشَدَّ النَّاسِ عَذَاباً يَوْمَ الْقِيَامَةِ الْمُصَوِّرُونَ » متفقٌ عليه .

1682. Hazrat Ibn Mas'ud (R.A.A.) says that he heard the Holy Prophet (S.A.W.) say: The severest punishment will be meted out on the Day of Judgement to the artists. *(Bukhari and Muslim)*

١٦٨٣ ـ وَعَنْ أَبِي هُرَيْرَةَ رَضِيَ اللهُ عَنْهُ قَالَ : سَمِعْتُ رَسُولَ اللهِ صَلَّى اللهُ عَلَيْهِ وَسَلَّمَ يَقُولُ : « قَالَ اللهُ تَعَالَى : وَمَنْ أَظْلَمُ مِمَّنْ ذَهَبَ يَخْلُقُ كَخَلْقِي ! فَلْيَخْلُقُوا ذَرَّةً أَوْ لِيَخْلُقُوا حَبَّةً ، أَوْ لِيَخْلُقُوا شَعِيرَةً » متفقٌ عليه .

1683. Hazrat Abu Hurairah (R.A.A.) says that he himself heard the Holy Prophet (S.A.W.) say: Allah, the Master of Honour says: Who can be worst tyrant than a person who although himself being a creation, attempts to imitate and become a creator like Me. Let him make an ant or a grain of barley. *(Bukhari and Muslim)*

١٦٨٤ ـ وَعَنْ أَبِي طَلْحَةَ رَضِيَ اللهُ عَنْهُ أَنَّ رَسُولَ اللهِ صَلَّى اللهُ عَلَيْهِ وَسَلَّمَ قَالَ : « لاتَدْخُلُ الْمَلائِكَةُ بَيْتاً فِيهِ كَلْبٌ وَلا صُورَةٌ » متفقٌ عليه .

1684. Hazrat Abu Talha (R.A.A.) relates that the Holy Prophet (S.A.W.) said: Angels do not visit a house in which there is a dog or a picture. *(Bukhari and Muslim)*

١٦٨٥ – وعن ابن عُمَرَ رضي اللهُ عنهُما قال: وعَدَ رَسُولَ اللهِ صلّى اللهُ علَيْهِ وسلّمَ جبريل أن يأتيه، فراثَ علَيْهِ حتّى اشتدَّ على رَسُولِ اللهِ صلّى اللهُ عليه وسلّمَ، فخرجَ فلقيهُ جبريلُ فشكا إليه، فقالَ: إنّا لاندخلُ بيتاً فيه كلبٌ ولا صورةٌ. رواه البخاري .

1685. Hazrat Ibn 'Umar (R.A.A.) relates that (Once) angel Gabriel promised to visit the Holy Prophet (S.A.W.) but he took considerable time in coming and this waiting proved to be very irksome to the Holy Prophet (S.A.W.) When he (S.A.W.) came out of his house he (S.A.W.) met angel Gabriel and complained to him on his being late. He said: We do not enter a house in which there is a dog or a picture. *(Bukhari)*

١٦٨٦ – وعَنْ عائِشَةَ رضيَ اللهُ عنها قالَتْ: واعدَ رَسُولَ اللهِ صلّى اللهُ علَيْهِ وسلّمَ جبريلُ علَيْهِ السّلامُ في ساعةٍ أنْ يأتيهُ، فجاءتْ تلكَ السّاعةُ ولم يأتِهِ! قالَتْ: وكانَ بيدِهِ عصاً، فطرحَها من يدِهِ وهوَ يقولُ: «ما يُخلِفُ اللهُ وعدَهُ ولا رُسُلُهُ» ثُمّ التفتَ، فإذا جروُ كلبٍ تحتَ سريرِه. فقالَ: «متى دخلَ هذا الكلبُ؟» فقُلتُ: واللهِ ما دريتُ بهِ، فأمرَ بهِ فأُخرجَ، فجاءهُ جبريلُ علَيْهِ السّلامُ: فقالَ رَسُولُ اللهِ صلّى اللهُ علَيْهِ وسلّمَ: «وعدتني، فجلستُ لكَ ولمْ تأتِني» فقالَ: منعني الكلبُ الذي كانَ في بيتِكَ، إنّا لاندخلُ بيتاً فيهِ كلبٌ ولا صورةٌ» رواه مسلم .

1686. Hazrat Ayesha (R.A,A.) says. Angel Gabriel once promised to visit the Holy Prophet (S.A.W.) sometime (during the night). When the time came, Angel Gabriel did not turn up. The Holy Prophet (S.A.W.) had stick in his hand which he (in utter disgust) threw away saying: Allah and His Messengers never commit a breach of promise. Then he noticed a dog lying underneath his (S.A.W.) wooden seat and asked: When did this dog come here? I said: By Allah! I did not see it come in He (S.A.W.) directed it to be put out and it was accordingly driven away. The angel Gabriel came and the Holy Prophet (S.A.W.) said to him: You had promised to visit me and I sat waiting for you but you did not come. He said: It was this dog which kept me away from coming to your house. We do not enter a house in which there is a dog or a picture. *(Muslim)*

١٦٨٧– وَعَنْ أَبِي الهَيَّاجِ حَيَّانَ بْنِ حُصَيْنٍ قَالَ : قَالَ لِي عَلِيُّ بْنُ أَبِي طَالِبٍ رَضِيَ اللهُ عَنْهُ : أَلا أَبْعَثُكَ عَلَى مَابَعَثَنِي عَلَيْهِ رَسُولُ اللهِ صَلَّى اللهُ عَلَيْهِ وَسَلَّمَ ؟ أَنْ لاتَدَعَ صُورَةً إِلاَّ طَمَسْتَهَا ، وَلا قَبْراً مُشْرِفاً إِلاَّ سَوَّيْتَهُ . رَوَاهُ مُسْلِمٌ .

1687. Abul Haiyyaj Haiyyan bin Husain relates: Hazrat Ali bin Abu Talib (R.A.A.) said to me: May I assign you a task which the Holy Prophet (S.A.W.) had assigned to me? Leave not a picture un-erased, and leave not a grave higher than a span unlevelled. *(Muslim)*

* * * * * * *

CHAPTER 306

PROHIBITION OF KEEPING A DOG, EXCEPT FOR GAME OR PROTECTION OF CATTLE AND CULTIVATION

١٦٨٨ – عَنِ ابْنِ عُمَرَ رَضِيَ اللهُ عَنْهُمَا : قَالَ سَمِعْتُ رَسُولَ اللهِ صَلَّى اللهُ عَلَيْهِ وَسَلَّمَ يَقُولُ : « مَنِ اقْتَنَى كَلْباً إِلاَّ كَلْبَ صَيْدٍ أَوْ مَاشِيَةٍ فَإِنَّهُ يَنْقُصُ مِنْ أَجْرِهِ كُلَّ يَوْمٍ قِيرَاطَانِ » متفقٌ عليه .

وفي رِوَايَةٍ : « قِيرَاطٌ » .

1688. Hazrat Ibn 'Umar (R.A.A.) relates that he heard the Holy Prophet (S.A.W.) say: A person who maintains a dog except for game or guarding cattle, shall be deprived of two qirats of his merit every day.

According to another tradition this quantity is one qirat. *(Bukhari and Muslim)*

١٦٨٩– وَعَنْ أَبِي هُرَيْرَةَ رَضِيَ اللهُ عَنْهُ قَالَ : قَالَ رَسُولُ اللهِ صَلَّى اللهُ عَلَيْهِ وَسَلَّمَ : « مَنْ أَمْسَكَ كَلْباً ، فَإِنَّهُ يَنْقُصُ كُلَّ يَوْمٍ مِنْ عَمَلِهِ قِيرَاطٌ إِلاَّ كَلْبَ حَرْثٍ أَوْ مَاشِيَةٍ » متفقٌ عليه .

وفي رواية لمسلم : « مَنِ اقْتَنَى كَلْباً لَيْسَ بِكَلْبِ صَيْدٍ . وَلا مَاشِيَةٍ وَلا أَرْضٍ ، فَإِنَّهُ يَنْقُصُ مِنْ أَجْرِهِ قِيرَاطَانِ كُلَّ يَوْمٍ » .

1689. Hazrat Abu Hurairah (R.A.A.) reports that the Holy Prophet (S.A.W.) said: A person, who maintains a dog, loses a qirat of his good deeds every day; unless he is maintained for the protection of his fields or cattle. *(Bukhari and Muslim)*

Imam Muslim's report says: A person who keeps a dog except for hunting or guarding crops or cattle, shall lose two qirats of his merit every day.

* * * * * * *

CHAPTER 307

PROHIBITION OF PUTTING A BELL ROUND THE NECK OF TRANSPORT ANIMALS OR TAKING A DOG ON A JOURNEY

١٦٩٠ – عَنْ أَبِي هُرَيْرَةَ رَضِيَ اللهُ عَنْهُ قَالَ : قَالَ رَسُولُ اللهِ صَلَّى اللهُ عَلَيْهِ وَسَلَّمَ: «لاتَصْحَبُ الْمَلائِكَةُ رُفْقَةً فيها كَلْبٌ أَوْجَرَسٌ»

رواه مسلم .

1690. Hazrat Abu Hurairah (R.A.A.) relates that the Holy Prophet (S.A.W.) said: Angels do not accompany a caravan which includes a dog or a bell. *(Muslim)*

١٦٩١ – وَعَنْهُ أَنَّ النَّبِيَّ صَلَّى اللهُ عَلَيْهِ وَسَلَّمَ قَالَ : «الجَرَسُ مَزَامِيرُ الشَّيْطَانِ» رَوَاهُ مُسْلِمٌ .

1691. Hazrat Abu Hurairah (R.A.A.) says that the Holy Prophet (S.A.W.) has said: The bell is one of the instruments of devils music. *(Muslim)*

* * * * * * *

CHAPTER 308

PROHIBITION OF RIDING A CAMEL WHICH EATS REFUSE OR FILTH

١٦٩٢ – عَنِ ابْنِ عُمَرَ رَضِيَ اللهُ عَنْهُمَا قَالَ : نَهَى رَسُولُ اللهِ صَلَّى اللهُ عَلَيْهِ وَسَلَّمَ عَنِ الجَلاَّلَةِ فِي الإبِلِ أَنْ يُرْكَبَ عَلَيْهَا .

رَوَاهُ أَبُو دَاوُدَ بإسْنَادٍ صَحِيحٍ .

1692. **Hazrat Ibn 'Umar (R.A.A.)** relates that the Holy Prophet (S.A.W.) has forbidden riding a **camel which eats refuse.**

(Imam Abu Daud **has cited this** with sound chain.)

* * * * * * *

CHAPTER 309

PROHIBITION OF SPITTING IN A MOSQUE, AND ORDER TO REMOVE IT IF FOUND AND TO KEEP A MOSQUE CLEAN

١٦٩٣ – عَنْ أَنَسٍ رَضِيَ اللهُ عَنْهُ أَنَّ رَسُولَ اللهِ صَلَّى اللهُ عَلَيْهِ وَسَلَّمَ قَالَ : « الْبُصَاقُ فِي الْمَسْجِدِ خَطِيئَةٌ ، وَكَفَّارَتُهَا دَفْنُهَا » متفقٌ عليه .

والمُرَادُ بِدَفْنِهَا إذا كَانَ المَسْجِدُ تُرَاباً أَوْ رَمْلاً وَنَحْوَهُ ، فَيُوَارِيهَا تَحْتَ تُرَابِهِ .قالَ أبو المحاسِنِ الرُّويَانِي مِنْ أَصْحَابِنَا في كِتَابِهِ «البحر» وقِيلَ : المُرَادُ بِدَفْنِهَا إخْرَاجُهَا مِنَ المَسْجِدِ ،أَمَّا إذا كَانَ المَسْجِدُ مُبَلَّطاً أَوْ مُجَصَّصاً، فَدَلَكَهَا عَلَيْهِ بِمَدَاسِهِ أَوْ بِغَيْرِهِ كَمَا يَفْعَلُهُ كَثِيرٌ مِنَ الجُهَّالِ ،فَلَيْسَ ذلكَ بِدَفْنٍ ، بَلْ زِيَادَةٌ فِي الخَطِيئَةِ وَتَكْثِيرٌ للقَذَرِ فِي المَسْجِدِ ، وَعَلَى مَنْ فَعَلَ ذلكَ أَنْ يَمْسَحَهُ بَعْدَ ذلكَ بِثَوْبِهِ أَوْ بِيَدِهِ أَوْ غَيْرِهِ أَوْ يَغْسِلَهُ .

1693. **Hazrat Anas** (R.A.A.) relates that the Holy Prophet (S.A.W.) said: Spitting in a Mosque is a sin and its expiation is to bury it

(Bukhari and Muslim)

Imam Nawawi says to bury a filth applies in case of mosque where there is sand or dust. Abul Mohasin Ruyani in his book "Bahr". says by burying means to throw away the filth outside the mosque. If the mosque has a pucca floor of lime plastered, the dirt should be washed away.

١٦٩٤– وَعَنْ عَائِشَةَ رَضِيَ اللهُ عَنْهَا أَنَّ رَسُولَ اللهِ صَلَّى اللهُ عَلَيْهِ وَسَلَّمَ رَأَى فِي جِدَارِ القِبْلَةِ مُخَاطاً ، أَوْ بُزَاقاً ، أَوْ نُخَامَةً ، فَحَكَّهُ . متفقٌ عليه .

1694. **Hazrat Ayesha Siddiqua** (R.A.A.) relates: If the Holy Prophet (S.A.W.) would see spittal or mucus from the nose or phlegm on the wall of mosque facing the Qibla (Mecca) he used to wipe it away. *(Bukhari and Muslim)*

١٦٩٥– وَعَنْ أَنَسٍ رَضِيَ اللهُ عَنْهُ أَنَّ رَسُولَ اللهِ صَلَّى اللهُ عَلَيْهِ وَسَلَّمَ قَالَ : « إِنَّ هٰذِهِ الْمَسَاجِدَ لَاتَصْلُحُ لِشَيْءٍ مِنْ هٰذَا الْبَوْلِ وَلَا الْقَذَرِ ، إِنَّمَا هِيَ لِذِكْرِ اللهِ تَعَالَى ، وَقِرَاءَةِ الْقُرْآنِ » أَوْ كَمَا قَالَ رَسُولُ اللهِ صَلَّى اللهُ عَلَيْهِ وَسَلَّمَ . رواه مسلم .

1695. **Hazrat Anas bin Malik** (R.A.A.) says that the Holy Prophet (S.A.W.) said: It is not proper to use the mosques for urinating and answering the call of nature. They are meant for the remembrance of Allah the Exalted, and the recitation of the Holy Quran as the Messenger of Allah (S.A.W.) has ordered. *(Muslim)*

* * * * * * *

CHAPTER 310

PROHIBITION OF FIGHTING AND CREATING NOISE AND DIS TURBANCE IN A MOSQUE; TO SEARCH MISSING ARTICLES OR TO SETTLE SALE, PURCHASE, WAGES AND OTHER MATTERS THEREIN

١٦٩٦– عَنْ أَبِي هُرَيْرَةَ رَضِيَ اللهُ عَنْهُ أَنَّهُ سَمِعَ رَسُولَ اللهِ صَلَّى اللهُ عَلَيْهِ وَسَلَّمَ يَقُولُ : « مَنْ سَمِعَ رَجُلاً يَنْشُدُ ضَالَّةً فِي الْمَسْجِدِ فَلْيَقُلْ : لَارَدَّهَا اللهُ عَلَيْكَ ، فَإِنَّ الْمَسَاجِدَ لَمْ تُبْنَ لِهٰذَا » رَوَاهُ مُسْلِم .

1696. **Hazrat Abu Hurairah** (R.A.A.) relates that he heard the Holy Prophet (S.A.W.) say: If anybody hears that somebody is searching his missing article in a mosque, then the former should say: May Allah not restore your missing article to you, for mosques are not meant for such purposes. *(Muslim)*

١٦٩٧– وَعَنْهُ أَنَّ رَسُولَ اللهِ صَلَّى اللهُ عَلَيْهِ وَسَلَّمَ قَالَ : « إِذَا رَأَيْتُمْ مَنْ يَبِيعُ أَوْ يَبْتَاعُ فِي الْمَسْجِدِ ، فَقُولُوا : لَاأَرْبَحَ اللهُ تِجَارَتَكَ ، وَإِذَا رَأَيْتُمْ مَنْ يَنْشُدُ ضَالَّةً فَقُولُوا : لَارَدَّهَا اللهُ عَلَيْكَ » .

رواه الترمذي وقال : حديثٌ حسنٌ .

1697. **Hazrat Abu Hurairah** (R.A.A.) reports that the Holy Prophet (S.A.W.) said: If you see a person settling a dealing in the mosque, then you should say to him: May Allah not make thy trade profitable, and if you see one searching his lost property in the mosque then say: May Allah not restore it to you. *(Imam Tirmizi* has cited this as good.)

١٦٩٨ – وَعَنْ بُرَيْدَةَ رَضِيَ اللهُ عَنْهُ أَنَّ رَجُلاً نَشَدَ فِي الْمَسْجِدِ فَقَالَ : مَنْ دَعَا إِلَى الجَمَلِ الأَحْمَرِ ؟ فَقَالَ رَسُولُ اللهِ صَلَّى اللهُ عَلَيْهِ وَسَلَّمَ : « لا وَجَدْتَ ؛ إِنَّمَا بُنِيَتِ الْمَسَاجِدُ لِمَا بُنِيَتْ لَهُ » رواه مسلم .

1698. Hazrat Buraidah (R.A.A.) relates that a man made enquiries about a missing camel in the mosque and said: Who was the person who enticed away the red camel? On this the Holy Prophet (S.A.W.) said: May you not find it. Mosques are built for the purpose for which they are built. *(Muslim)*

١٦٩٩ – وَعَنْ عَمْرِو بْنِ شُعَيْبٍ ، عَنْ أَبِيهِ ، عَنْ جَدِّهِ رَضِيَ اللهُ عَنْهُ أَنَّ رَسُولَ اللهِ صَلَّى اللهُ عَلَيْهِ وَسَلَّمَ نَهَى عَنِ الشِّرَاءِ وَالْبَيْعِ فِي الْمَسْجِدِ ، وَأَنْ تُنْشَدَ فِيهِ ضَالَّةٌ ، أَوْ يُنْشَدَ فِيهِ شِعْرٌ . رَوَاهُ أَبُو دَاوُدَ ، والتِّرمذي وقال : حَدِيثٌ حَسَنٌ .

1699. Hazrat 'Amr bin Shu'aib (R.A.A.) relates on the authority of his father and the latter on the authority of his grandfather that the Holy Prophet (S.A.W.) has forbidden sale and purchase and searching lost property or singing the poems in the mosque *(Abu Daud and Tirmizi. Imam Tirmizi* cited this as good.)

١٧٠٠ – وَعَنِ السَّائِبِ بْنِ يَزِيد الصَّحَابِي رَضِيَ اللهُ عَنْهُ قَالَ : كُنْتُ فِي الْمَسْجِدِ فَحَصَبَنِي رَجُلٌ ، فَنَظَرْتُ فَإِذَا عُمَرُ بْنُ الْخَطَّابِ رَضِيَ اللهُ عَنْهُ فَقَالَ : اذْهَبْ فَائْتِنِي بِهَذَيْنِ ، فَجِئْتُهُ بِهِمَا ، فَقَالَ : مِنْ أَيْنَ أَنْتُمَا ؟ فَقَالا : مِنْ أَهْلِ الطَّائِفِ ، فَقَالَ : لَوْ كُنْتُمَا مِنْ أَهْلِ الْبَلَدِ ، لأَوْجَعْتُكُمَا ، تَرْفَعَانِ أَصْوَاتَكُمَا فِي مَسْجِدِ رَسُولِ اللهِ صَلَّى اللهُ عَلَيْهِ وَسَلَّمَ ! رَوَاهُ الْبُخَارِي .

1700. Hazrat Sa'ib bin Yazid as Sahabi (R.A.A.) relates: I was in the mosque when someone threw a gravel at me. When I looked up, I found that it was Hazrat Umar bin Khattab (R.A.A.). He asked me: 'Go and fetch those two persons (who are talking so loudly in the mosque) to me. When I brought them up, he asked them: 'Where from you are coming'? They said: 'We are from Taif'. He (R.A.A.)

said: Had you been the residents of the town (Madina). I would have punished you, for talking so loudly in the mosque of the Holy Prophet (S.A.W.). *(Bukhari)*

* * * * * * *

CHAPTER 311

PROHIBITION OF ENTERING A MOSQUE AFTER EATING RAW ONIONS, GARLIC OR ANY OTHER BAD SMELLING ARTICLE AND WITHOUT REMOVING ITS BAD EFFECTS

١٧٠١ – عَنِ ابْنِ عُمَرَ رَضِيَ اللهُ عَنْهُمَا أَنَّ النَّبِيَّ صَلَّى اللهُ عَلَيْهِ وَسَلَّمَ قَالَ : « مَنْ أَكَلَ مِنْ هٰذِهِ الشَّجَرَةِ – يَعْنِي الثُّومَ – فَلَا يَقْرَبَنَّ مَسْجِدَنَا » متفقٌ عليه .

وفي روايةٍ لمسلم : « مَسَاجِدَنَا » .

1701. Hazrat Ibn Umar (R.A.A.) relates that the Holy Prophet (S.A.W.) said: A person who has eaten this vegetable i.e. garlic should not come near our mosque.

According to a report of *Imam Muslim*, "Our mosques".
(Bukhari and Muslim).

١٧٠٢ – وَعَنْ أَنَسٍ رَضِيَ اللهُ عَنْهُ قَالَ : قَالَ النَّبِيُّ صَلَّى اللهُ عَلَيْهِ وَسَلَّمَ : « مَنْ أَكَلَ مِنْ هٰذِهِ الشَّجَرَةِ ، فَلَا يَقْرَبَنَّا ، وَلَا يُصَلِّيَنَّ مَعَنَا » متفقٌ عليه .

1702. Hazrat Anas bin Malik (R.A.A.) states that the Holy Prophet (S.A.W.) has said: A person who has eaten this plant (garlic) should not come near us nor should he pray along with us.
(Bukhari and Muslim)

١٧٠٣ – وَعَنْ جَابِرٍ رَضِيَ اللهُ عَنْهُ قَالَ : قَالَ النَّبِيُّ صَلَّى اللهُ عَلَيْهِ وَسَلَّمَ : « مَنْ أَكَلَ ثُوماً أَوْ بَصَلاً ، فَلْيَعْتَزِلْنَا ، أَوْ فَلْيَعْتَزِلْ مَسْجِدَنَا » متفقٌ عليه .

وفي رواية لمُسْلِمٍ : « مَنْ أَكَلَ الْبَصَلَ ، وَالثوم ، وَالْكُرَّاث ، فَلَا يَقْرَبَنَّ مسجِدَنَا ، فَإِنَّ الْمَلَائِكَةَ تَتَأَذَّى مِمَّا يَتَأَذَّى مِنْهُ بَنُو آدَمَ »

1703. Hazrat Jabir (R.A.A.) reports that the Holy Prophet (S.A.W.) has said: A person who has eaten garlic or onion should keep himself away from us or he should not come near our mosques.
(Bukhari and Muslim)

Imam Muslim's version says: A person who has eaten garlic or onion or any other bad smelling thing should not approach our mosque for a thing which offends human beings also offends the angels.

١٧٠٤ – وَعَنْ عُمَرَ بْنِ الخَطَّابِ رَضِيَ اللهُ عَنْهُ أَنَّهُ خَطَبَ يَوْمَ الجُمُعَةِ فَقَالَ فِي خُطْبَتِهِ: ثُمَّ إِنَّكُمْ أَيُّهَا النَّاسُ تَأْكُلُونَ شَجَرَتَيْنِ مَا أَرَاهُمَا إِلاَّ خَبِيثَتَيْنِ: البَصَلَ، وَالثُّومَ. لَقَدْ رَأَيْتُ رَسُولَ اللهِ صَلَّى اللهُ عَلَيْهِ وَسَلَّمَ إِذَا وَجَدَ رِيحَهُمَا مِنَ الرَّجُلِ فِي المَسْجِدِ أَمَرَ بِهِ، فَأُخْرِجَ إِلَى البَقِيعِ، فَمَنْ أَكَلَهُمَا، فَلْيُمِتْهُمَا طَبْخاً. رواه مسلم.

1704. Hazrat Umar bin Al Khattab (R.A.A.) once delivered a sermon on a Friday (Prayer) and said: 'O people! When you eat garlic and onions, in my opinion these are very bad things. I have seen that when the Holy Prophet (S.A.W.) smelt the (foul) odour of either of these two things, he (S.A.W.) would expel that person from the mosque as far as (the graveyard of) Baqiah. Therefore anybody who wants to eat them, should rid them of their odour by cooking them. *(Muslim)*

* * * * * * *

CHAPTER 312

PROHIBITION OF SITTING WITH LEGS DRAWN UP AND THE KNEES TOUCHING THE ABDOMEN DURING FRIDAY SERMON FOR IT INVITES SLEEP, REMOVES THE CONCENTRATION TO HEAR SERMON AND CREATES APPREHENSION FOR BREAKING WUDU

١٧٠٥ – عَنْ مُعَاذِ بْنِ أَنَسٍ الجُهَنِيِّ، رَضِيَ اللهُ عَنْهُ. أَنَّ النَّبِيَّ صَلَّى اللهُ عَلَيْهِ وَسَلَّمَ. نَهَى عَنِ الحِبْوَةِ يَوْمَ الجُمُعَةِ وَالإِمَامُ يَخْطُبُ. رواه أبو داود، والترمذي وَقَالا: حَدِيثٌ حَسَنٌ.

1705. Hazrat Mu'az bin Anas Al Juhani (R.A.A.) says that the Holy Prophet (S.A.W.) has forbidden a person with his knees drawn up touching his abdomen while the Imam is delivering the Friday Sermon.
(Abu Daud and Tirmizi)

* * * * * * *

CHAPTER 313

PROHIBITION OF HAVING A HAIR OR NAIL CUT DURING THE FIRST TEN DAYS OF THE MONTH OF ZIL HAJ BY ONE INTENDING TO OFFER SACRIFICE

١٧٠٦ – عَنْ أُمِّ سَلَمَةَ رَضِيَ اللهُ عَنْهَا قَالَتْ : قَالَ رَسُولُ اللهِ صَلَّى اللهُ عَلَيْهِ وَسَلَّمَ : « مَنْ كَانَ لَهُ ذِبْحٌ يَذْبَحُهُ ، فَإِذَا أُهِلَّ هِلَالُ ذِي الحِجَّةِ، فَلَا يَأْخُذَنَّ مِنْ شَعْرِهِ وَلَا مِنْ أَظْفَارِهِ شَيْئاً حَتَّى يُضَحِّيَ » رَوَاهُ مُسْلِم

1706. Hazrat Ummul Momineen Umm Salamah (R.A.A.) relates that the Holy Prophet (S.A.W.) said: A person who has an animal and intends to offer a sacrifice (on the occasion of Eid-ul-Azha) should not have his hair cut or his nails trimmed during the first ten days of the month of Zil Haj, till he has offered his sacrifice. *(Muslim)*

* * * * * * *

CHAPTER 314

PROHIBITION OF TAKING AN OATH OF ANY CREATURE LIKE PROPHET, KA'BA OR ANTYHING BESIDE ALLAH, ANGELS, SKY, FOREFATHERS, LIFE, SOUL, HEAD, LIFE OF THE RULER, FAVOURS OF RULER, GRAVE OF SO AND SO AND TRUSTS ETC.

١٧٠٧ – عَنِ ابْنِ عُمَرَ ، رَضِيَ اللهُ عَنْهُمَا ، عَنِ النَّبِيِّ ، صَلَّى اللهُ عَلَيْهِ وَسَلَّمَ ، قَالَ : « إِنَّ اللهَ تَعَالَى يَنْهَاكُمْ أَنْ تَحْلِفُوا بِآبَائِكُمْ فَمَنْ كَانَ حَالِفاً ، فَلْيَحْلِفْ بِاللهِ ، أَوْ لِيَصْمُتْ » متفقٌ عليه .

وفي رواية في الصحيح : « فَمَنْ كَانَ حَالِفاً ، فَلَا يَحْلِفْ إِلَّا بِاللهِ ، أَوْ لِيَسْكُتْ » .

1707. Hazrat Ibn 'Umar (R.A.A.) relates that the Holy Prophet (S.A.W.) said: Allah, the Lord of Honour and Glory has forbidden you taking an oath of your fathers. A person who must take an oath, should swear by Allah or keep quiet. *(Bukhari and Muslim)*

١٧٠٨ – وَعَنْ عَبْدِ الرَّحْمٰنِ بْنِ سَمُرَةَ ، رَضِيَ اللهُ عَنْهُ قَالَ : قَالَ رَسُولُ اللهِ صَلَّى اللهُ عَلَيْهِ وَسَلَّمَ : « لَا تَحْلِفُوا بِالطَّوَاغِي ، وَلَا بِآبَائِكُمْ » . رواه مسلم .

1708. Hazrat Abdur Rahman bin Samurah (R.A.A.) reports that the Holy Prophet (S.A.W.) has said: You should not swear by your idols nor by your forefathers. *(Muslim)*

١٧٠٩ – وَعَنْ بُرَيْدَةَ رَضِيَ اللهُ عَنْهُ أَنَّ رَسُولَ اللهِ صَلَّى اللهُ عَلَيْهِ وَسَلَّمَ قَالَ : « مَنْ حَلَفَ بِالأَمَانَةِ ، فَلَيْسَ مِنَّا » .

حَدِيثٌ صَحِيحٌ ، رَوَاهُ أَبُو دَاود بإسناد صَحِيحٍ .

1709. Hazrat Buraidah (R.A.A.) relates that the Holy Prophet (S.A.W.) said: A person who swears by his integrity and not by Allah the Exalted is not of us. *(Abu Daud)*

١٧١٠ – وَعَنْهُ قَالَ : قَالَ رَسُولُ اللهِ ، صَلَّى اللهُ عَلَيْهِ وَسَلَّمَ : « مَنْ حَلَفَ ، فَقَالَ : إِنِّي بَرِيءٌ مِنَ الإِسْلاَمِ ، فَإِنْ كَانَ كَاذِباً ، فَهُوَ كَمَا قَالَ ، وَإِنْ كَانَ صَادِقاً ، فَلَنْ يَرْجِعَ إِلَى الإِسْلاَمِ سَالِماً » .

رواه أبو داود .

1710. Hazrat Buraidah (R.A.A.) relates that the Holy Prophet (S.A.W.) said: If a person takes an oath that if he does such and such act, or he is wrong, he may go out of Islam. then if he should turn out to be a liar he will be as he said (swore) and if he is proved to have spoken the truth then he will not come back to Islam without a stigma. *(Abu Daud)*

١٧١١ – وَعَنِ ابْنِ عُمَرَ رَضِيَ اللهُ عَنْهُمَا أَنَّهُ سَمِعَ رَجُلاً يَقُولُ : لاَ وَالْكَعْبَةِ ، قَالَ ابْنُ عُمَرَ : لاَ تَحْلِفْ بِغَيْرِ اللهِ ، فَإِنِّي سَمِعْتُ رَسُولَ اللهِ ، صَلَّى اللهُ عَلَيْهِ وَسَلَّمَ يَقُولُ : « مَنْ حَلَفَ بِغَيْرِ اللهِ ، فَقَدْ كَفَرَ أَوْ أَشْرَكَ » رواه الترمذي وقَالَ : حَدِيثٌ حَسَنٌ .

1711. Hazrat Ibn 'Umar (R.A.A.) says that he heard a man say: 'No, by Ka'ba,' as such Hazrat Ibn Umar warned him: 'Do not swear by anything other than Allah, for I have myself heard the Holy Prophet (S.A.W.) say: A person who swears by anything except Allah, is guilty of blasphemy or he (S.A.W.) said of associating something with Allah. (*Imam Tirmizi* has reported this tradition as good.)

* * * * * * *

CHAPTER 315

PROHIBITION OF KNOWINGLY TAKING A FALSE OATH

١٧١٢ – عَنِ ابْنِ مَسْعُودٍ رَضِيَ اللهُ عَنْهُ أَنَّ النَّبِيَّ صَلَّى اللهُ عَلَيْهِ وَسَلَّمَ قَالَ : « مَنْ حَلَفَ عَلَى مَالِ امْرِىءٍ مُسْلِمٍ بِغَيْرِ حَقِّهِ ، لَقِيَ اللهَ وَهُوَ عَلَيْهِ غَضْبَانُ » قَالَ : ثُمَّ قَرَأَ عَلَيْنَا رَسُولُ اللهِ صَلَّى اللهُ عَلَيْهِ وَسَلَّمَ مِصْدَاقَهُ مِنْ كِتَابِ اللهِ عَزَّ وَجَلَّ : (إِنَّ الَّذِينَ يَشْتَرُونَ بِعَهْدِ اللهِ وَأَيْمَانِهِمْ ثَمَناً قَلِيلاً) [آل عمران : ٧٧] إلى آخر الآية : مُتَّفَقٌ عَلَيْهِ

1712. Hazrat Abdullah bin Mas'ud (R.A.A.) relates that the Holy Prophet (S.A.W.) said: A person who swears falsely to take possession of Muslim's property unjustly, shall face the wrath of Allah on the Day of Judgement; and he (S.A.W.) cited the following verse from the Holy Quran in support of this statement.

> Lo! those who purchase a small gain at the cost of Allah's covenant, and their oaths, they have no portion in the Hereafter. Allah will neither speak to them nor look upon them on the Day of Resurrection, nor will He make them grow. Theirs will be a painful doom. (3 : 77) *(Bukhari and Muslim)*

١٧١٣ – وَعَنْ أَبِي أُمَامَةَ إِيَاسِ بْنِ ثَعْلَبَةَ الحَارِثِيِّ رَضِيَ اللهُ عَنْهُ أَنَّ رَسُولَ اللهِ صَلَّى اللهُ عَلَيْهِ وَسَلَّمَ قَالَ : « مَنِ اقْتَطَعَ حَقَّ امْرِىءٍ مُسْلِمٍ بِيَمِينِهِ ، فَقَدْ أَوْجَبَ اللهُ لَهُ النَّارَ . وَحَرَّمَ عَلَيْهِ الْجَنَّةَ » فَقَالَ لَهُ رَجُلٌ : وإِنْ كَانَ شَيْئاً يَسِيراً يَا رَسُولَ اللهِ ؟ قَالَ : « وَإِنْ كَانَ قَضِيباً مِنْ أَرَاكٍ » رَوَاهُ مُسْلِمٌ .

1713. Hazrat Abu Umamah Iyas bin Sa'labah Al Harisi (R.A.A.) relates that the Holy Prophet (S.A.W.) said: A person who usurps the right of a Muslim, by swearing (falsely) will be condemned by Allah the Exalted to the Hell and will be deprived of Paradise. A man asked: O Messenger of Allah! Even if it may be a small thing'? He (S.A.W.) answered: Even if it be the (smallest) twig of a bush tree. *(Muslim)*

١٧١٤ – وَعَنْ عَبْدِ اللهِ بْنِ عَمْرِو بنِ الْعَاصِ رَضِيَ اللهُ عَنْهُمَا عَنِ النَّبِيِّ صَلَّى اللهُ عَلَيْهِ وَسَلَّمَ قَالَ : « الْكَبَائِرُ : الإِشْرَاكُ بِاللهِ ، وَعُقُوقُ الْوَالِدَيْنِ ، وَقَتْلُ النَّفْسِ ، وَالْيَمِينُ الْغَمُوسُ » رواه البخاري

وفي رِوَايَةٍ : أنَّ أعْرَابِيّاً جَاءَ إلى النَّبِيِّ صَلَّى اللهُ عَلَيْهِ وَسَلَّمَ فَقَالَ : يَا رَسُولَ اللهِ مَا الكَبَائِرُ ؟ قالَ : «الإشْرَاكُ بِاللهِ» قالَ : ثُمَّ مَاذا ؟ قَالَ : «اليَمِينُ الغَمُوسُ» قُلْتُ : وَمَا اليَمِينُ الغَمُوسُ ؟ قَالَ : «الَّذِي يَقْتَطِعُ مَالَ امْرِئٍ مُسْلِمٍ !» يَعْنِي بِيَمِينٍ هُوَ فِيهَا كَاذِبٌ .

1714. Hazrat Abdullah bin 'Amr bin Al'Aas (R.A.A.) relates that the Holy Prophet (S.A.W.) said: These are major sins: (1) Associating somebody with Allah (2) disobeying parents (3) killing some body (4) and tendering a false oath. *(Bukhari)*

Another version of Imam Bukhari says: A man from the village came to the Holy Prophet (S.A.W.) and submitted: O Messenger of Allah! What are the major sins?' He (S.A.W.) answered: Associating anybody with Allah Most High. The man asked: and after that? The Holy Prophet (S.A.W.) replied: A false oath. I said: What is false oath. He (S.A.W.) said: which deprives a Muslim of his property i.e., taking oath while he is a liar.

* * * * * * *

CHAPTER 316

JUSTIFICATION FOR ACTION CONTRARY TO A SOUND OATH WHEN ITS CONTRAVENTION IS BETTER AND THEN PAYS EXPIATION FOR THE SAME

١٧١٥ – عَنْ عَبْدِ الرَّحْمَنِ بْنِ سَمُرَةَ رَضِيَ اللهُ عَنْهُ قَالَ : قَالَ لِي رَسُولُ اللهِ صَلَّى اللهُ عَلَيْهِ وَسَلَّمَ : «وَإِذَا حَلَفْتَ عَلَى يَمِينٍ ، فَرَأَيْتَ غَيْرَهَا خَيْراً مِنْهَا ، فَأْتِ الَّذِي هُوَ خَيْرٌ ، وَكَفِّرْ عَنْ يَمِينِكَ» متفقٌ عليه

1715. Hazrat Abdur Rahman bin Samurah (R.A.A.) reports that the Holy Prophet (S.A.W.) has told him that: If you take an oath for something and thereafter you learn about something then go after the better thing and expiate for the oath. The expiation for this violation of oath is either to free a slave or feed ten paupers for two times or provide clothes to ten (poor) persons. If he is not in a position to do any of these amends, then he should fast for three days.

(Bukhari and Muslim)

١٧١٦ – وَعَنْ أَبِي هُرَيْرَةَ رَضِيَ اللهُ عَنْهُ أَنَّ رَسُولَ اللهِ صَلَّى اللهُ عَلَيْهِ وَسَلَّمَ قَالَ : «مَنْ حَلَفَ عَلَى يَمِينٍ ، فَرَأَى غَيْرَهَا خَيْراً مِنْهَا ،

فَلْيُكَفِّرْ عَنْ يَمِينِهِ ، وَلْيَفْعَلِ الَّذِي هُوَ خَيْرٌ » رواهُ مسلم .

1716. **Hazrat Abu Hurairah** (R.A.A.) reports that the Holy Prophet (S.A.W.) has said: If a person has affirmed for a particular thing, and afterwards he finds somethiing better, then he should make amends (pay *Kaffara*) for contravening his oath, and do the better thing. *(Muslim)*

١٧١٧– وَعَنْ أَبِي مُوسَى رَضِيَ اللهُ عَنْهُ أَنَّ رَسُولَ اللهِ صَلَّى اللهُ عَلَيْهِ وَسَلَّمَ قَالَ : « إِنِّي وَاللهِ إِنْ شَاءَ اللهُ لَا أَحْلِفُ عَلَى يَمِينٍ ، ثُمَّ أَرَى خَيْراً مِنْهَا إِلَّا كَفَّرْتُ عَنْ يَمِينِي ، وَأَتَيْتُ الَّذِي هُوَ خَيْرٌ » متفقٌ عليه

1717. **Hazrat Abu Musa Ash'ari** (R.A.A.) relates that the Holy Prophet (S.A.W.) said: By Allah, if Allah so wills, I would not swear to do something, provided a better alternative becomes available which I would adopt and would make amends for oath. *(Bukhari and Muslim)*

١٧١٨– وَعَنْ أَبِي هُرَيْرَةَ رَضِيَ اللهُ عَنْهُ قَالَ : قَالَ رَسُولُ اللهِ صَلَّى اللهُ عَلَيْهِ وَسَلَّمَ : « لَأَنْ يَلَجَّ أَحَدُكُمْ فِي يَمِينِهِ فِي أَهْلِهِ آثَمُ لَهُ عِنْدَ اللهِ تَعَالَى مِنْ أَنْ يُعْطِي كَفَّارَتَهُ الَّتِي فَرَضَ اللهُ عَلَيْهِ » متفقٌ عليه

1718. **Hazrat Abu Hurairah** (R.A.A.) reports that the Holy Prophet (S.A.W.) said: If one of you should reamain adamant in his oath concerning his family (and thus be guilty of committing excess) then this is more sinful for him in the estimation of Allah than that he should make amends of this as prescribed by Allah the Exalted.

(Bukhari and Muslim)

* * * * * * *

CHAPTER 317

EXEMPTION FROM ATONEMENT FOR BREACH OF OATHS UTTERED BY WAY OF HABIT

قَالَ اللهُ تَعَالَى : (لَا يُؤَاخِذُكُمُ اللهُ بِاللَّغْوِ فِي أَيْمَانِكُمْ وَلَكِنْ يُؤَاخِذُكُمْ بِمَا عَقَّدْتُمُ الْأَيْمَانَ فَكَفَّارَتُهُ إِطْعَامُ عَشَرَةِ مَسَاكِينَ مِنْ أَوْسَطِ مَا تُطْعِمُونَ أَهْلِيكُمْ ، أَوْ كِسْوَتُهُمْ ، أَوْ تَحْرِيرُ رَقَبَةٍ فَمَنْ لَمْ

يجِدْ فَصِيَامُ ثَلاثَةِ أَيَّامٍ ، ذلكَ كَفَّارَةُ أَيْمانِكُمْ ، وَاحْفَظُوا أَيْمانَكُمْ) [المائدة : ٨٩] .

Allah, the Exalted, has said:

403. Allah will not take you to task for that which is unintentional in your oaths, but He will take you to task for the oaths which ye swear in earnest. The expiation thereof is the feeding of ten of the needy with the average of that wherewith ye feed your own folk or the clothing of them, or the liberation of a slave, and for him, who findeth not (the wherewithal to do so) then a three days' fast. This is the expiation of your oaths. (5 : 89)

١٧١٩ – وَعَنْ عَائِشَةَ رَضِيَ اللهُ عَنْهَا قَالَتْ : أُنزِلَتْ هَذِهِ الآيَةُ : (لايُؤَاخِذُكُمُ اللهُ بِاللَّغْوِ فِي أَيْمَانِكُمْ) فِي قَوْلِ الرَّجُلِ : لاوَاللهِ ، وَبَلَى واللهِ . رواه البخاري .

1719. Hazrat Ayesha Siddiqa (R.A.A.) relates that the above verse was revealed about persons who are in the habit of uttering phrases (oaths) like 'No by Allah;' and 'Yes! By Allah' (as a matter of habit) *(Bukhari)*

Note : It was customary among the Arabs that in order to give emphasis to their talking they would use phrases like 'No! By Allah' and 'Yes! By Allah', These are called unnecessary. As such Allah has exempted them from expiation.

* * * * * * *

CHAPTER 318

DISLIKING FOR SWEARING IN BUSINESS TRANSACTIONS THOUGH TRUE

١٧٢٠ – وَعَنْ أَبِي هُرَيْرَةَ رَضِيَ اللهُ عَنْهُ قَالَ : سَمِعْتُ رَسُولَ اللهِ صَلَّى اللهُ عَلَيْهِ وَسَلَّمَ يَقُولُ : « الحَلِفُ مَنْفَقَةٌ لِلسِّلْعَةِ ، مَمْحَقَةٌ لِلْكَسْبِ » متفقٌ عليه .

1720. Hazrat Abu Hurairah (R.A.A.) relates that he heard the Holy Prophet (S.A.W.) say: Too much swearing in business transactions may increase sales but (ultimately) it wipes out the profit and abundance. *(Bukhari and Muslim)*

١٧٢١ – عَنْ أَبِي قَتَادَةَ رَضِيَ اللهُ عَنْهُ أَنَّهُ سَمِعَ رَسُولَ اللهِ صَلَّى اللهُ عَلَيْهِ وَسَلَّمَ يَقُولُ : « إِيَّاكُمْ وَكَثْرَةَ الحَلِفِ فِي البَيْعِ ، فَإِنَّهُ يُنَفِّقُ ثُمَّ يَمْحَقُ » رواه مسلم .

1721. **Hazrat Abu Qatadah** (R.A.A.) relates that he heard the Holy Prophet (S.A.W.) say: Avoid too much swearing while selling (your goods) for, in the beginning it promotes business and then it brings all loss. *(Musllim)*

* * * * * * *

CHAPTER 319

DISLIKE FOR ASKING FOR A FAVOUR, EXCEPT HEAVEN IN THE NAME OF ALLAH, AND DISLIKE TO REFUSE WHO ASKS IN THE NAME OF ALLAH AND TO RECOMMEND IT

١٧٢٢ – عَنْ جَابِرٍ رَضِيَ اللهُ عَنْهُ قَالَ : قَالَ رَسُولُ اللهِ صَلَّى اللهُ عَلَيْهِ وَسَلَّمَ : « لايُسْأَلُ بِوَجْهِ اللهِ إلاَّ الجَنَّةُ » رواه أبو داود .

1722. Hazrat Jabir (R.A.A.) relates that the Holy Prophet (S.A.W.) said: Nothing should be asked in the name of Allah except Heaven. *(Abu Daud)*

١٧٢٣– وَعَنِ ابْنِ عُمَرَ رَضِيَ اللهُ عَنْهُمَا قَالَ : قَالَ رَسُولُ اللهِ صَلَّى اللهُ عَلَيْهِ وَسَلَّمَ : « مَنِ اسْتَعَاذَ بِاللهِ ، فَأَعِيذُوهُ ، وَمَنْ سَأَلَ بِاللهِ ، فَأَعْطُوهُ ، وَمَنْ دَعَاكُمْ ، فَأَجِيبُوهُ ، وَمَنْ صَنَعَ إِلَيْكُمْ مَعْرُوفاً فَكَافِئُوهُ ، فَإِنْ لَمْ تَجِدُوا مَا تُكَافِئُونَهُ ، فَادْعُوا لَهُ حَتَّى تَرَوْا أَنَّكُمْ قَدْ كَافَأْتُمُوهُ » حديثٌ صَحِيحٌ رواه أَبُو داود ، والنسائي بأسانيد الصحيحين .

1723. **Hazrat Ibn 'Umar** (R.A.A.) reports that the Holy Prophet (S.A.W.) said: A person who seeks shelter in the name of Allah may be given refuge, and a person who asks (for anything) in the name of Allah, his request may be granted and accept the invitation of a person who invites you, and reciprocate the good gesture of a person but if you cannot afford to do so then pray for him till you are satisfied that you have fully returned his favour. *(Imam Abu Daud and Nisai* have cited this with correct chains).

* * * * * * *

CHAPTER 320

PROHIBITION OF THE USE OF THE TITLE OF EMPEROR OR KING OF KINGS BY A KING AS IT SUITS ALLAH, THE EXALTED ONLY

١٧٢٤ – عَنْ أَبِي هُرَيْرَةَ رَضِيَ اللهُ عَنْهُ عَنِ النَّبِيِّ صَلَّى اللهُ عَلَيْهِ وَسَلَّمَ قَالَ : « إِنَّ أَخْنَعَ اسْمٍ عِنْدَ اللهِ عَزَّ وَجَلَّ رَجُلٌ تَسَمَّى مَلِكَ الأَمْلاكِ » متفقٌ عليه .

قال سُفْيَانُ بن عُيَيْنَةَ « مَلِكُ الأَمْلاكِ » مِثْلُ شَاهِنشَاه .

1724. Hazrat Abu Hurairah (R.A.A.) relates that the Holy Prophet (S.A.W.) said: The most disgraceful title in the estimation of Allah is for a person who calls himself King of kings (Shahinshah) or emperor. *(Bukhari and Muslim)*

* * * * * * *

CHAPTER 321

PROHIBITION OF EMPLOYING RESPECTABLE TITLE FOR HYPOCRITE AND INNOVATOR

١٧٢٥ – عن بُرَيْدَةَ رَضِيَ اللهُ عنهُ قَالَ : قَالَ رَسُولُ اللهِ صلَّى اللهُ عَلَيْهِ وَسَلَّمَ : « لاتَقُولُوا لِلْمُنَافِقِ سَيِّدٌ ، فَإِنَّهُ إِنْ يَكُ سَيِّداً ، فَقَدْ أَسْخَطْتُمْ رَبَّكُمْ عَزَّ وَجَلَّ » رواه أبو داود بإسنادٍ صحيحٍ .

1725. Hazrat Buraidah (R.A.A.) reports that the Holy Prophet (S.A.W.) said: Do not address a hypocrite by o'leader, because if he may be a leader, yet, you would arouse the wrath of your Lord Master of Honour and Glory. *(Abu Daud)*

* * * * * * *

CHAPTER 322

PROHIBITION OF ABUSING FEVER

١٧٢٦ – عَنْ جَابِرٍ رَضِيَ اللهُ عَنْهُ أَنَّ رَسُولَ اللهِ صلَّى اللهُ عَلَيهِ وسلَّم دَخَلَ على أُمِّ السَّائِبِ ، أَوْ أُمِّ المُسَيَّبِ فَقَالَ : « مَالَكِ يَا أُمَّ السَّائِبِ

ـ أَوْ يَا أُمَّ المُسَيَّبِ ـ تُزَفْزِفِينَ ؟ » قَالَتْ : الحُمَّى لابَارَكَ اللهُ فِيهَا !
فَقَالَ : « لاتَسُبِّي الحُمَّى ، فَإِنَّهَا تُذْهِبُ خَطَايَا بَنِي آدَمَ ، كَمَا يُذْهِبُ
الكِيرُ خَبَثَ الحَدِيدِ » رواه مسلم .

1726. Hazrat Jabir (R.A.A.) relates that the Holy Prophet (S.A.W.) visited Hazrat Umm Sa'ib or Ummul Musaiyab and asked her: What has happened to you, O Umm Sa'ib or Ummul Musaiyab? Why you are shivering? She answered: It is a fever; may Allah not bless it. He (S.A.W.) said to her: Do not abuse the fever, because it cleans the sins of the children of Adam as a furnace cleans the dirt of iron.

(Muslim)

* * * * * * *

CHAPTER 323

PROHIBITION OF ABUSING THE WIND AND WHAT TO SAY WHEN IT BLOWS STRONGLY

١٧٢٧ـ عَنْ أَبِي المُنْذِرِ أُبَيِّ بْنِ كَعْبٍ رَضِيَ اللهُ عَنْهُ قَالَ : قَالَ
رَسُولُ اللهِ صَلَّى اللهُ عَلَيْهِ وَسَلَّمَ : « لا تَسُبُّوا الرِّيحَ ، فَإِذَا رَأَيْتُمْ
مَاتَكْرَهُونَ ، فَقُولُوا : اللَّهُمَّ إِنَّا نَسْأَلُكَ مِنْ خَيْرِ هذِهِ الرِّيحِ وَخَيْرِ
مَافِيهَا وَخَيْرِ مَا أُمِرَتْ بِهِ ، وَنَعُوذُ بِكَ مِنْ شَرِّ هَذِهِ الرِّيحِ وَشَرِّ مَافِيهَا
وَشَرِّ مَا أُمِرَتْ بِهِ » رواه الترمذي وقَالَ : حَدِيثٌ حسنٌ صحيح .

1727. **Hazrat Abul Munzir Ubaiy bin Ka'ab** (R.A.A.) reports that the Holy Prophet (S.A.W.) said: Do not abuse the wind. If you find it unpleasant pray in these words:

'Allah, we beg from Thee something good from this wind, and the good that which is in it and the good of that for which it has been commanded, and we solicit Thy protection against the evil of this wind, and the evil that it contains and the mischief of that for which it has been commanded.

(Tirmizi)

١٧٢٨ـ وَعَنْ أَبِي هُرَيْرَةَ رَضِيَ اللهُ عَنْهُ قَالَ : سَمِعْتُ رَسُولَ اللهِ
صَلَّى اللهُ عَلَيْهِ وَسَلَّمَ يَقُولُ : الرِّيحُ مِنْ رَوْحِ اللهِ ، تَأْتِي بِالرَّحْمَةِ ،
وَتَأْتِي بِالعَذَابِ ، فَإِذَا رَأَيْتُمُوهَا فَلا تَسُبُّوهَا ، وَسَلُوا اللهَ خَيْرَهَا ،

واسْتَعِيذُوا باللهِ مِنْ شَرِّهَا » رواه أبو داود بإسنادٍ حسنٍ .

1728. **Hazrat Abu Hurairah** (R.A.A.) relates that he heard the Holy Prophet (S.A.W.) say: The wind is a blessing of Allah the Most High, it bears both His mercy and His wrath. Therefore, when you come across it do not abuse it, beg Allah for some good out of it, and His protection against its mischief.

(*Abu Daud* cited with sound chains)

١٧٢٩– وَعَنْ عَائِشَةَ رَضِيَ اللهُ عَنْهَا قَالَتْ : كَانَ النَّبِيُّ صَلَّى اللهُ عَلَيْهِ وَسَلَّمَ إذا عَصَفَتِ الرِّيحُ قَالَ : « اللَّهُمَّ إنِّي أسْألُكَ خَيْرَهَا ، وَخَيْرَ مَا فِيهَا ، وَخَيْرَ مَا أُرْسِلَتْ بِهِ ، وَأَعُوذُ بِكَ مِنْ شَرِّهَا ، وَشَرِّ مَا فِيها ، وَشَرِّ مَا أُرْسِلَتْ بِهِ » رواه مسلم .

1729. **Hazrat Ayesha Siddiqa (R.A.A.)** relates that when the wind used to blow furiously the Holy Prophet (S.A.W.) would supplicate:

O Allah, I beg Thee something good out of it, and the good of that which it contains and the good of the purpose for which it has been sent; and solicit Thy protection against its mischief and the mischief of that which it contains and the mischief of the purpose for which it has been sent.

(*Muslim*)

* * * * * * *

CHAPTER 324

DISLIKE FOR ABUSING COCK

١٧٣٠– عَنْ زَيْدِ بْنِ خَالِدٍ الجُهَنِيِّ رَضِيَ اللهُ عَنْهُ قَالَ : قَالَ رَسُولُ اللهِ صَلَّى اللهُ عَلَيْهِ وَسَلَّمَ : « لاتَسُبُّوا الدِّيكَ ، فإنَّهُ يُوقِظُ للصَّلاةِ » رواه أبو داود بإسناد صحيح .

1730. **Hazrat Zaid bin Khalid Juhani (R.A.A.)** relates that the Holy Prophet (S.A.W.) said: Do not abuse a cock for it wakes you up for your (morning) Prayer. (*Imam Abu Daud* has cited this with sound chains).

* * * * * * *

CHAPTER 325

PROHIBITION OF ATTRIBUTING RAIN TO A PARTICULAR STAR

١٧٣١ — عَنْ زَيْدِ بْنِ خَالِدٍ رَضِيَ اللهُ عَنْهُ قَالَ : صَلَّى بِنَا رَسُولُ اللهِ صَلَّى اللهُ عَلَيْهِ وَسَلَّمَ صَلاةَ الصُّبْحِ بِالحُدَيْبِيَةِ فِي إِثْرِ سَمَاءٍ كَانَتْ مِنَ اللَّيْلِ ، فَلَمَّا انصَرَفَ أَقْبَلَ عَلَى النَّاسِ ، فَقَالَ : « هَلْ تَدْرُونَ مَاذَا قَالَ رَبُّكُمْ ؟ » قَالُوا : اللهُ وَرَسُولُهُ أَعْلَمُ . قَالَ : قَالَ : أَصْبَحَ مِنْ عِبَادِي مُؤْمِنٌ بِي ، وَكَافِرٌ ، فَأَمَّا مَنْ قَالَ مُطِرْنَا بِفَضْلِ اللهِ وَرَحْمَتِهِ ، فَذَلِكَ مُؤْمِنٌ بِي كَافِرٌ بِالْكَوْكَبِ ، وَأَمَّا مَنْ قَالَ : مُطِرْنَا بِنَوْءِ كَذَا وَكَذَا ، فَذَلِكَ كَافِرٌ بِي مُؤْمِنٌ بِالْكَوْكَبِ » متفقٌ عليه .

1731. Hazrat Zaid bin Khalid (R.A.A.) says: It had rained during the previous night, next day the Holy Prophet (S.A.W.) led our morning Salat at Hudaibiyyah. At the end of the prayer addressing us the Holy Prophet (S.A.W.) said: Do you know as to what your Lord the Nourisher, has said?' The congregation said: Allah and His Messenger only know the best. He (S.A.W.) told us, Allah has said: 'This morning My servants have split up in two groups, one declaring its faith in Me and the other as dis-believing. The one who said: 'We have had this rain by the grace and mercy of Allah the Exalted, are believers in Me, and has rejected the stars; and the one who said: We got this rain with the help of such and such stars, denied Me and put his faith in the stars. *(Bukhari and Muslim)*

* * * * *

CHAPTER 326

PROHIBITION OF ADDRESSING A MUSLIM AS DISBELIEVER

١٧٣٢ — عَنِ ابْنِ عُمَرَ رَضِيَ اللهُ عَنْهُمَا قَالَ : قَالَ رَسُولُ اللهِ صَلَّى اللهُ عَلَيْهِ وَسَلَّمَ : « إِذَا قَالَ الرَّجُلُ لِأَخِيهِ : يَا كَافِرُ ، فَقَدْ بَاءَ بِهَا أَحَدُهُمَا ، فَإِنْ كَانَ كَمَا قَالَ وَإِلاَّ رَجَعَتْ عَلَيْهِ » مُتَّفق عليه .

1732. Hazrat Ibn Umar (R.A.A.) relates that the Holy Prophet (S.A.W.) said: When a man calls his brother as: 'O Kafir' (disbeliever) the epithet must devolve upon one of them. If the person thus addressed is such (then he is a disbeliever) otherwise it rebounds upon him who has said so. *(Bukhari and Muslim)*

١٧٣٣– وَعَنْ أَبِي ذَرٍّ رَضِيَ اللهُ عَنْهُ أَنَّهُ سَمِعَ رَسُولَ اللهِ صَلَّى اللهُ عَلَيْهِ وَسَلَّمَ يَقُولُ : «مَنْ دَعَا رَجُلاً بِالْكُفْرِ ، أَوْ قَالَ : عَدُوَّ اللهِ ، وَلَيْسَ كَذَلِكَ إِلاَّ حَارَ عَلَيْهِ» متفقٌ عليه .

1733. Hazrat Abu Zarr (R.A.A.) says that he heard the Holy Prophet (S.A.W.) say: If a person calls another person Kafir (disbeliever) or an enemy of Allah and the latter is not so, then, the epithet will rebound upon the former. *(Bukhari and Muslim)*

Translator's Note:

It is established from the traditions that the spoken words never die out and they remain preserved. Therefore to call somebody as a Kafir is not merely a joke; even a casual and unnecessary use of such words does have its effect.

Modern scientists are convinced that words spoken hundreds of years ago are alive somewhere in the atmosphere. They are trying to manufacture apparatus to catch such words. If they succeed, it will be another scientific proof of the truth of Islam and its principles and will revolutionise the mental level of mankind.

* * * * * * *

CHAPTER 327

PROHIBITION OF VULGAR AND LOOSE TALKING

١٧٣٤ – عَنِ ابْنِ مَسْعُودٍ رَضِيَ اللهُ عَنْهُ قَالَ : قَالَ رَسُولُ اللهِ صَلَّى اللهُ عَلَيْهِ وَسَلَّمَ : «لَيْسَ الْمُؤْمِنُ بِالطَّعَّانِ ، وَلا اللَّعَّانِ ، وَلا الْفَاحِشِ ، وَلا الْبَذِيِّ» رواه الترمذي وقال : حديثٌ حسنٌ .

1734. Hazrat Abdullah bin Mas'ud (R.A.A.) relates that the Holy Prophet (S.A.W.) said: A Muslim never taunts or curses or abuses nor resorts to vulgar talking. *(Tirmizi and Said it is sound)*

١٧٣٥– وَعَنْ أَنَسٍ رَضِيَ اللهُ عَنْهُ قَالَ : قَالَ رَسُولُ اللهِ صَلَّى اللهُ عَلَيْهِ وَسَلَّمَ : «مَا كَانَ الْفُحْشُ فِي شَيْءٍ إِلاَّ شَانَهُ ، وَمَا كَانَ الْحَيَاءُ فِي شَيْءٍ إِلاَّ زَانَهُ» رواه الترمذي وقال : حديثٌ حسن .

1735. **Hazrat Anas bin Malik (R.A.A.)** relates that the Holy Prophet (S.A.W.) said: Using foul language when mixed with any thing mutilates it, while decency, wherever it may be, beautifies it. *(Tirmizi)*

* * * * * * *

CHAPTER 328

DISLIKE FOR USING IRKSOME AND EXAGGERATED TERMS IN CONVERSATION

١٧٣٦ – عَنِ ابْنِ مَسْعُودٍ رَضِيَ اللهُ عَنْهُ أَنَّ النَّبِيَّ صَلَّى اللهُ عَلَيْهِ وَسَلَّمَ قَالَ : « هَلَكَ الْمُتَنَطِّعُونَ » قَالَهَا ثَلَاثاً . رَوَاهُ مُسْلِم .

1736. **Hazrat Abdullah bin Mas'ud** (R.A.A.) relates that the Holy Prophet (S.A.W.) said: The people who exaggerate are ruined. He repeated this thrice. *(Muslim)*

١٧٣٧ – وَعَنْ عَبْدِ اللهِ بْنِ عَمْرِو بْنِ الْعَاصِ رَضِيَ اللهُ عَنْهُمَا أَنَّ رَسُولَ اللهِ صَلَّى اللهُ عَلَيْهِ وَسَلَّمَ قَالَ : « إِنَّ اللهَ يُبْغِضُ الْبَلِيغَ مِنَ الرِّجَالِ الَّذِي يَتَخَلَّلُ بِلِسَانِهِ كَمَا تَتَخَلَّلُ الْبَقَرَةُ » .

رَوَاهُ أبو داودَ ، والترمذي ، وقال : حديثٌ حسن .

1737. **Hazrat Abdullah bin 'Amr bin Al 'Aas** (R.A.A.) reports that the Holy Prophet (S.A.W.) said: Allah the Exalted hates the person who twists his tongue in eloquence (while talking) as does a bull while eating extremely (fodder). *(Abu Daud and Tirmizi)*

١٧٣٨– وَعَنْ جَابِرِ بْنِ عَبْدِ اللهِ رَضِيَ اللهُ عَنْهُمَا أَنَّ رَسُولَ اللهِ صَلَّى اللهُ عَلَيْهِ وَسَلَّمَ قَالَ ; « إِنَّ مِنْ أَحَبِّكُمْ إِلَيَّ ، وَأَقْرَبِكُمْ مِنِّي مَجْلِساً يَوْمَ الْقِيَامَةِ ، أَحَاسِنَكُمْ أَخْلَاقاً ، وَإِنَّ أَبْغَضَكُمْ إِلَيَّ ، وَأَبْعَدَكُمْ مِنِّي يَوْمَ الْقِيَامَةِ ، الثَّرْثَارُونَ ، وَالْمُتَشَدِّقُونَ ، وَالْمُتَفَيْهِقُونَ »

رواه الترمذي وقال : حديثٌ حسن ، وقد سبق شرحُهُ في باب حُسْنِ الخُلُق

1738. **Hazrat Jabir bin Abdullah (R.A.A.)** relates that the Holy Prophet (S.A.W.) said: Dearest of you to me and the closest of you to me on the Day of Judgement will be Those of you who have best morals and the most hated to me and farthest from me on the Day of Judgement will be the most talkative, harsh in their tone and those persons who are haughty in talking. *(Tirmizi)*

* * * * * * *

CHAPTER 329

DISLIKE FOR SELF CONDEMNATION

١٧٣٩ – عَنْ عَائِشَةَ رَضِيَ اللهُ عَنْهَا عَنِ النَّبِيِّ صَلَّى اللهُ عَلَيْهِ وَسَلَّمَ قَالَ : « لَا يَقُولَنَّ أَحَدُكُمْ خَبُثَتْ نَفْسِي ، وَلَكِنْ لِيَقُلْ : لَقِسَتْ نَفْسِي » متفقٌ عليه .

1739. Hazrat Ayesha Siddiqa (R.A.A.) relates that the Holy Prophet (S.A.W.) said: None of you should say: My soul has vitiated (Khabusat), but he should say: My soul is not in order.
(Bukhari and Muslim)

* * * * * * *

CHAPTER 330

PROHIBITION OF CALLING GRAPES KARM

١٧٤٠ – عَنْ أَبِي هُرَيْرَةَ رَضِيَ اللهُ عَنْهُ قَالَ : قَالَ رَسُولُ اللهِ صَلَّى اللهُ عَلَيْهِ وَسَلَّمَ : « لَا تُسَمُّوا الْعِنَبَ الْكَرْمَ ، فَإِنَّ الْكَرْمَ الْمُسْلِمُ » متفقٌ عليه . وهذا لفظُ مسلم .

وفي رِوَايةٍ : « فَإِنَّمَا الْكَرْمُ قَلْبُ الْمُؤْمِنِ » وفي رواية للبخاري ومسلم : « يَقُولُونَ الْكَرْمُ ، إِنَّمَا الْكَرْمُ قَلْبُ الْمُؤْمِنِ » .

1740. Hazrat Abu Hurairah (R.A.A.) relates that the Holy Prophet (S.A.W.) said: None of you should call grapes Karm, for Karm is only a Muslim person. *(Bukhari and Muslim)* and these words are of Muslim.

Another version says: *Karm* is the heart of a Muslim.

Yet another version of Bukhari and Muslim says that the Holy Prophet (S.A.W.) said: 'People call grapes as *karm*, although it is only the heart of a true believer.'

١٧٤١ – وَعَنْ وَائِلِ بْنِ حَجَرٍ رَضِيَ اللهُ عَنْهُ عَنِ النَّبِيِّ صَلَّى اللهُ عَلَيْهِ وَسَلَّمَ قَالَ : « لَا تَقُولُوا : الْكَرْمُ ، وَلَكِنْ قُولُوا : الْعِنَبُ ، وَالْحَبَلَةُ » رواه مسلم .

1741. Hazrat Wayel bin Hajar (R.A.A.) reports that the Holy Prophet (S.A.W.) said: Do not call (grape) *Karm*, but call it Al Inab and Habala.

Note: Karm means grape. There are other words in Arabic langauge for grape, such as *'Inab* and *Habala*. But the word *Karm* has been ear-marked to denote the Muslim's heart, therefore it is not proper to use it for a fruit like grape.

* * * * * * *

CHAPTER 331

PROHIBITION OF ENUMERATING THE PHYSICAL CHARMS OF A WOMAN BEFORE A MAN EXCEPT IN CASE OF SOME RELIGIOUS REQUIREMENT LIKE MARRIAGE ETC.

١٧٤٢ – عَنِ ابْنِ مَسْعُودٍ رَضِيَ اللهُ عَنْهُ قَالَ : قَالَ رَسُولُ اللهِ صَلَّى اللهُ عَلَيْهِ وَسَلَّمَ : « لا تُبَاشِرِ المَرْأَةُ المَرْأَةَ ، فَتَصِفَهَا لِزَوْجِهَا كَأَنَّهُ يَنْظُرُ إِلَيْهَا » متفقٌ عليه

1742. Hazrat Abdullah bin Mas'ud (R.A.A.) relates that the Holy Prophet (S.A.W.) said: No woman should touch her private parts with those of another woman so that she may describe the latter's physical charms to her husband in such detail as if he was looking at her.

(Bukhari and Muslim)

* * * * * * *

CHAPTER 332

DISLIKE FOR A MAN SUPPLICATING LIKE 'O ALLAH YOU MAY FORGIVE IF YOU PLEASE BUT SHOULD SUPPLICATE WITH FULL CONFIDENCE

١٧٤٣ – عَنْ أَبِي هُرَيْرَةَ رَضِيَ اللهُ عَنْهُ أَنَّ رَسُولَ اللهِ صَلَّى اللهُ عَلَيْهِ وَسَلَّمَ قَالَ : « لايَقُولَنَّ أَحَدُكُمْ : اللَّهُمَّ اغْفِرْ لِي إِنْ شِئْتَ : اللَّهُمَّ ارْحَمْنِي إِنْ شِئْتَ ، لِيَعْزِمِ المَسْأَلَةَ ، فَإِنَّهُ لامُكْرِهَ لَهُ » . متفقٌ عليه .

وفي رواية لمسلم : « ولكن ليعزم ، وليعظم الرغبة ، فإن الله تعالى لا يتعاظمه شيء أعطاه » .

1743. Hazrat Abu Hurairah (R.A.A.) reports that the Holy Prophet (S.A.W.) said: One should not supplicate thus: 'O Allah, forgive me if Thou will; Allah have mercy on me if Thou will.' But one should be firm in his supplication, which should be made with full confidence and earnestness, for no one has the power to compel (Allah, the Almighty). *(Muslim)*

Another version of Muslim says: A supplicant should entreat earnestly with full confidence and should be earnest in his desire for acceptance of his prayer for nothing is too great for Allah to bestow.

١٧٤٤ – وعن أنس رضي الله عنه قال : قال رسول الله صلى الله عليه وسلم : « إذا دعا أحدكم ، فليعزم المسألة ، ولا يقولن : اللهم إن شئت ، فأعطني ، فإنه لا مستكره له » متفق عليه .

1744. Hazrat Anas bin Malik (R.A.A.) relates that the Holy Prophet (S.A.W.) said: When one of you is to supplicate he should do so with full confidence and should not say. 'O Allah, grant me if Thou will' for there is no power which can force Allah.

(Bukhari and Muslim)

* * * * * * *

CHAPTER 333

DISAPPROVAL OF SAYING 'WHATEVER ALLAH WILLS AND WHATEVER SO AND SO WILLS'

١٧٤٥ – عن حذيفة بن اليمان رضي الله عنه عن النبي صلى الله عليه وسلم قال : « لا تقولوا : ما شاء الله وشاء فلان ، ولكن قولوا : ما شاء الله ، ثم شاء فلان » رواه أبو داود بإسناد صحيح .

1745. Hazrat Huzaifah bin Al Yaman (R.A.A.) relates that the Holy Prophet (S.A.W.) said: 'Do not say what Allah wills and so and so wills but say: 'What Allah Wills. (and then after this)'what so and so wills'. *(Abu Daud with sound chains)*

* * * * * * *

CHAPTER 334

DISLIKE FOR CONVERSATION AFTER ISHA PRAYER

والمرادُ به الحديثُ الذي يكونُ مُباحاً في غيرِ هذا الوقت ، وفعلُه وتركُه سواءٌ ، فأمّا الحديثُ المُحرّمُ أو المكروهُ في غيرِ هذا الوقتِ ، فهُوَ في هذا الوقتِ أشدُّ تحريماً وكراهةً . وأمّا الحديثُ في الخيرِ كمُذاكرةِ العِلمِ وحِكاياتِ الصّالحينَ ، ومَكارِمِ الأخلاقِ ، والحديثُ مع الضّيفِ ، ومعَ طالبِ حاجةٍ ، ونحوُ ذلكَ ، فلا كراهةَ فيهِ ، بل هُوَ مُستحبٌّ ، وكذا الحديثُ لِعُذرٍ وعارضٍ لاكراهةَ فيهِ ، وقد تظاهرتِ الأحاديثُ الصّحيحةُ على كُلِّ ماذكرتُهُ .

Note:— *Imam Nawawi* says that the talking prohibited at this time is such which is lawful even after this time, and to talk or not to talk on such topics is of no importance. The talk which is unlawful at other times, is strictly forbidden at this time. In talks relating to good and beneficial matters like educational topics, accounts of pious persons, advocating virtues of good morals, conversation with the guest or needy persons, there is no objection or repugnance; rather such talks are desirable. Similarly in cases of some emergency or happening, there is no harm in talking. The subject matter described under this chapter is warranted by authentic traditions.

١٧٤٦ – عَنْ أبي برزةَ رَضِيَ اللهُ عنهُ أنَّ رَسُولَ اللهِ صَلّى اللهُ عَلَيهِ وَسَلَّمَ كانَ يكرهُ النّومَ قبلَ العِشاءِ والحديثَ بعدَها . متفقٌ عليه

1746. Hazrat Abu Barzah (R.A.A.) says that the Holy Prophet (S.A.W.) disliked to sleep before Isha prayer and talking after it.

(Bukhari and Muslim)

١٧٤٧ – وَعَن ابنِ عُمَرَ رَضِيَ اللهُ عَنهُما أنَّ رَسُولَ اللهِ صَلّى اللهُ عَلَيهِ وَسَلَّمَ صَلّى العِشاءَ في آخرِ حياتِهِ ، فلمّا سلّمَ ، قالَ : « أرأيتكُم ليلتَكُم هذهِ ؟ فإنَّ على رأسِ مائةِ سنةٍ لايبقى مِمّن هُوَ على ظَهرِ الأرضِ اليومَ أحدٌ » متفقٌ عليه

1747. Hazrat Ibn 'Umar (R.A.A.) relates that once towards the closing years of his life, the Holy Prophet (S.A.W.), when he had finished the Isha (night) prayer, said: Do you know something about this night of yours, for at the end of one hundred years from now no one, who is on the earth today, will survive. *(Bukhari and Muslim)*

١٧٤٨– وَعَنْ أَنَسٍ رَضِيَ اللهُ عَنْهُ أَنَّهمُ انْتَظَرُوا النَّبِيَّ صَلَّى اللهُ عَلَيْهِ وَسَلَّمَ ، فَجَاءَهُمْ قَرِيباً مِنْ شَطْرِ اللَّيْلِ فَصَلَّى بِهِم ، يعني العِشَاءَ ، قَالَ : ثُمَّ خَطَبَنَا فَقَالَ : « أَلا إِنَّ النَّاسَ قَدْ صَلُّوا ، ثُمَّ رَقَدُوا ، وَإِنَّكُمْ لَنْ تَزَالُوا في صَلاةٍ مَا انْتَظَرْتُمُ الصَّلاةَ » رواه البخاري

1748. This Hadis has already been covered in S. No. 1063 of Chapter 190.

* * * * * * *

CHAPTER 335

PROHIBITION OF A WOMAN REFUSING HERSELF TO HER HUSBAND WHEN HE CALLS HER WITHOUT RELIGIOUS EXCUSE

١٧٤٩ – عَنْ أَبِي هُرَيْرَةَ رَضِيَ اللهُ عَنْهُ قَالَ : قَالَ رَسُولُ اللهِ صَلَّى اللهُ عَلَيْهِ وَسَلَّمَ : « إِذا دَعَا الرَّجُلُ امْرَأَتَهُ إِلى فِرَاشِهِ[٣٣٦] فَأَبَتْ ، فَبَاتَ غَضْبَانَ عَلَيْهَا ، لَعَنَتْهَا المَلائِكَةُ حَتَّى تُصْبِحَ » متفقٌ عليه .

وفي رواية : حَتَّى « تَرْجِعَ » .

1749. This Hadis has already been covered in S. No. 281 of Chapter 35.

* * * * * * *

CHAPTER 336

ON PROHIBITION OF A WOMAN OBSERVING A VOLUNTARY FAST WITHOUT HER HUSBAND'S PERMISSION WHEN HE IS AT HOME

١٧٥٠– عَنْ أَبِي هُرَيْرَةَ رَضِيَ اللهُ عَنْهُ أَنَّ رَسُولَ اللهِ صَلَّى اللهُ عَلَيْهِ وَسَلَّمَ قَالَ : « لا يَحِلُّ للمَرْأَةِ أَنْ تَصُومَ وَزَوْجُهَا شَاهِدٌ إِلاَّ بِإِذْنِهِ ، وَلا تَأْذَنَ في بَيْتِهِ إِلاَّ بِإِذْنِهِ » متفقٌ عليه .

1750. This Hadis has already been covered in S. No. 282 of Chapter 35.

* * * * * * *

CHAPTER 337

ON PROHIBITION OF RAISING HEAD FROM BOWING AND PROSTRATION AHEAD OF THE IMAM

١٧٥١ — عَنْ أَبِي هُرَيْرَةَ رَضِيَ اللهُ عَنْهُ أَنَّ النَّبِيَّ صَلَّى اللهُ عَلَيْهِ وَسَلَّمَ قَالَ : « أَمَا يَخْشَى أَحَدُكُمْ إِذَا رَفَعَ رَأْسَهُ قَبْلَ الإِمَامِ أَنْ يَجْعَلَ اللهُ رَأْسَهُ رَأْسَ حِمَارٍ ! أَوْ يَجْعَلَ اللهُ صُورَتَهُ صُورَةَ حِمَارٍ » متفقٌ عليه .

1751. Hazrat Abu Hurairah (R.A.A.) relates that the Holy Prophet (S.A.W.) said: Do you not fear that if any of you raises his head (from his bowing or prostration) before the Imam does so, Allah will make his head like that of a donkey or will make his shape like that of a donkey. *(Bukhari and Muslim)*

* * * * * * *

CHAPTER 338

DISLIKING OF PLACING ONE'S HAND ON ONE'S WAIST DURING PRAYER

١٧٥٢ — عَنْ أَبِي هُرَيْرَةَ رَضِيَ اللهُ عَنْهُ قَالَ : نُهِيَ عَنِ الخَصْرِ فِي الصَّلاةِ . متفقٌ عليه .

1752. Hazrat Abu Hurairah (R.A.A.) says that the Holy Prophet (S.A.W.) has forbidden putting one's hand on his waist during prayer. *(Bukhari and Muslim)*

* * * * * * *

CHAPTER 339

UNDESIRABILITY OF JOINING PRAYER WHEN FOOD HAS BEEN SERVED AND ALSO WHEN ONE HAS TO ATTEND TO CALL OF NATURE

١٧٥٣ — عَنْ عَائِشَةَ رَضِيَ اللهُ عَنْهَا قَالَتْ : سَمِعْتُ رَسُولَ اللهِ صَلَّى اللهُ عَلَيْهِ وَسَلَّمَ يَقُولُ : « لاصَلاةَ بِحَضْرَةِ طَعَامٍ ، وَلا هُوَ يُدَافِعُهُ الأَخْبَثَانِ » رواه مسلم .

1753. Hazrat Ayesha (R.A.A.) relates that she heard the Holy Prophet (S.A.W.) say: Prayer is not (valid) when food has been served, similarly at the time when a person is in need of relieving himself one of the two filthy things (urination or stool). *(Muslim)*

* * * * * * *

CHAPTER 340

PROHIBITION OF LOOKING TOWARDS THE SKY WHILE PRAYING

١٧٥٤ – عَنْ أَنَسِ بْنِ مَالِكٍ رَضِيَ اللهُ عَنْهُ قَالَ: قَالَ رَسُولُ اللهِ صَلَّى اللهُ عَلَيْهِ وَسَلَّمَ: «مَابَالُ أَقْوَامٍ يَرْفَعُونَ أَبْصَارَهُمْ إِلَى السَّمَاءِ فِي صَلَاتِهِمْ!» فَاشْتَدَّ قَوْلُهُ فِي ذَلِكَ حَتَّى قَالَ: «لَيَنْتَهُنَّ عَنْ ذَلِكَ، أَوْ لَتُخْطَفَنَّ أَبْصَارُهُمْ!» رواه البخاري.

1754. **Hazrat Anas bin Malik** (R.A.A.) relates that the Holy Prophet (S.A.W.) said: what has happened to those people who raise their eyes and look towards the sky while praying. He cautioned the people for this, and asserted. Let them refrain from this or else they will lose their sight. *(Bukhari)*

* * * * * * *

CHAPTER 341

DISLIKE FOR LOOKING RIGHT AND LEFT DURING PRAYER WITHOUT EXCUSE

١٧٥٥ – عَنْ عَائِشَةَ رَضِيَ اللهُ عَنْهَا قَالَتْ: سَأَلْتُ رَسُولَ اللهِ صَلَّى اللهُ عَلَيْهِ وَسَلَّمَ عَنِ الالْتِفَاتِ فِي الصَّلَاةِ فَقَالَ: «هُوَ اخْتِلَاسٌ يَخْتَلِسُهُ الشَّيْطَانُ مِنْ صَلَاةِ الْعَبْدِ» رَوَاهُ الْبُخَارِي.

1755. Hazrat Ayesha (R.A.A.) relates: I (Once) asked the Holy Prophet (S.A.W.) about looking to the right or left during prayer. He (S.A.W.) said: It is a deception with which the Satan deceives a servant (worshipper) during his prayer. *(Bukhari)*

١٧٥٦ – وَعَنْ أَنَسٍ رَضِيَ اللهُ عَنْهُ قَالَ: قَالَ لِي رَسُولُ اللهِ صَلَّى اللهُ عَلَيْهِ وَسَلَّمَ: «إِيَّاكَ وَالالْتِفَاتَ فِي الصَّلَاةِ؛ فَإِنَّ الالْتِفَاتَ فِي الصَّلَاةِ هَلَكَةٌ، فَإِنْ كَانَ لَابُدَّ، فَفِي التَّطَوُّعِ لَا فِي الْفَرِيضَةِ» رواه التِّرمذي وقال: حديثٌ حسنٌ صَحيحٌ.

1756. **Hazrat Anas bin Malik** (R.A.A.) relates that the Holy Prophet (S.A.W.) said: Avoid looking in one direction or the other during prayer, for this is ruinous (a serious irregularity). If this could not be avoided, it might be ignored during voluntary prayer, but not during prescribed (Fard) prayers. *(Tirmizi).* He said it is sound and good.

* * * * * * *

CHAPTER 342

PROHIBITION OF FACING GRAVES DURING PRAYER

١٧٥٧– عَنْ أَبِي مَرْثَدٍ كَنَّازِ بْنِ الحُصَيْنِ رَضِيَ اللهُ عَنْهُ قَالَ : سَمِعْتُ رَسُولَ اللهِ صَلَّى اللهُ عَلَيْهِ وَسَلَّمَ يَقُولُ : « لاتُصَلُّوا إِلى القُبُورِ. وَلَا تَجْلِسُوا عَلَيْهَا » رواه مسلم .

1757. Hazrat Abu Marsad Kannaz bin Al-Husain (R.A.A.) says that he heard the Holy Prophet (S.A.W.) say: Do not face graves when praying nor sit on them. *(Muslim)*

* * * * * * *

CHAPTER 343

PROHIBITION OF PASSING IN FRONT OF A PRAYING PERSON

١٧٥٨– عَنْ أَبِي الجُهَيْمِ عَبْدِ اللهِ بْنِ الحَارِثِ بْنِ الصِّمَّةِ الأَنْصَارِيِّ رَضِيَ اللهُ عَنْهُ قَالَ : قَالَ رَسُولُ اللهِ صَلَّى اللهُ عَلَيْهِ وَسَلَّمَ : « لَوْ يَعْلَمُ المَارُّ بَيْنَ يَدَيِ المُصَلِّي مَاذا عَلَيْهِ لَكَانَ أَنْ يَقِفَ أَرْبَعِينَ خَيْراً لَهُ مِنْ أَنْ يَمُرَّ بَيْنَ يَدَيْهِ » قَالَ الرَّاوِي : لاأَدْرِي قَالَ أَرْبَعِينَ يَوْماً ، أَوْ أَرْبَعِينَ شَهْراً ، أَوْ أَرْبَعِينَ سَنَةً . متفقٌ عليه .

1758. Hazrat Abul Juhaim Abdullah bin Al Haris bin As-Sammah Al-Ansari (R.A.A.) relates that the Holy Prophet (S.A.W.) said: Had a person, who passes in front of a praying person, could realise the gravity of the sin, he would prefer to wait for forty rather than pass in front of the person engaged in prayer. The narrator says that he was not sure whether the Holy Prophet (S.A.W.) said forty days or forty months or forty years. *(Bukhari and Muslim)*

* * * * * * *

CHAPTER 344

REPUGNANCE OF OFFERING VOLUNTARY PRAYER AFTER IQAMAH HAS BEEN CALLED

١٧٥٩ – عَنْ أَبِي هُرَيْرَةَ رَضِيَ اللهُ عَنْهُ عَنِ النَّبِيِّ صَلَّى اللهُ عَلَيْهِ وَسَلَّمَ قَالَ : « إِذا أُقِيمَتِ الصَّلاةُ ، فَلا صَلاةَ إِلاَّ المَكْتُوبَةَ » رواه مسلم .

1759. Hazrat Abu Hurairah (R.A.A.) relates that the Holy Prophet (S.A.W.) said: When Iqamah (call for beginning the prayer) is called out, no prayer is permissible except the obligatory (Fard) one..
(Muslim)

* * * * * * *

CHAPTER 345

UNDESIRABILITY OF SPECIFYING ONLY FRIDAY FOR OBSERVING A FAST AND THE FRIDAY NIGHT FOR PRAYER

١٧٦٠ – عَنْ أَبِي هُرَيْرَةَ رَضِيَ اللهُ عَنْهُ عَنِ النَّبِيِّ صَلَّى اللهُ عَلَيْهِ وَسَلَّمَ قَالَ : « لا تَخُصُّوا لَيْلَةَ الجُمُعَةِ بِقِيَامٍ مِنْ بَيْنِ اللَّيَالِي ، وَلا تَخُصُّوا يَوْمَ الجُمُعَةِ بِصِيَامٍ مِنْ بَيْنِ الأَيَّامِ إِلاَّ أَنْ يَكُونَ فِي صَوْمٍ يَصُومُهُ أَحَدُكُمْ » رواه مسلم .

1760. Hazrat Abu Hurairah (R.A.A.) says that the Holy Prophet (S.A.W.) said. Do not specify the Friday night specially for optional prayers nor specify the day of Friday specially for observing a fast, unless it may happen to be one of the days on which a person usually observes a fast.
(Muslim)

١٧٦١ – وَعَنْهُ قَالَ : سَمِعْتُ رَسُولَ اللهِ صَلَّى اللهُ عَلَيْهِ وَسَلَّمَ يَقُولُ : « لايَصُومَنَّ أَحَدُكُمْ يَوْمَ الجُمُعَةِ إِلاَّ يَوْماً قَبْلَهُ أَوْ بَعْدَهُ » متفقٌ عليه .

1761. Hazrat Abu Hurairah (R.A.A.) reports that he heard the Holy Prophet (S.A.W.) say: None of you should fast only on Friday, but together with a day before or after it (Friday).
(Bukhari and Muslim)

١٧٦٢– وعَنْ مُحمَّد بن عبَّاد قال: سألتُ جابراً رَضِيَ اللهُ عَنْهُ: أنَهى النَّبِيُّ صلَّى اللهُ عَلَيْهِ وَسَلَّمَ عَنْ صَوْمِ الجُمُعَةِ ؟ قَالَ : نَعَمْ . متفقٌ عليه .

1762. Hazrat Muhammad bin 'Abbad (R.A.A.) relates: I asked Hazrat Jabir (R.A.A.): Did the Holy Prophet (S.A.W.) prohibit fasting only on Friday? He said: Yes. *(Bukhari and Muslim)*

١٧٦٣– وعَنْ أُمِّ المُؤْمِنِينَ جُوَيْرِيَةَ بِنْتِ الحَارِثِ رَضِيَ اللهُ عَنْهَا أنَّ النَّبِيَّ صَلَّى اللهُ عَلَيْهِ وَسَلَّمَ دَخَلَ عَلَيْهَا يَوْمَ الجُمُعَةِ وَهِيَ صَائِمَةٌ، فقَالَ : « أَصُمْتِ أَمْسِ ؟ » قَالَتْ : لا، قَالَ : « تُرِيدِينَ أنْ تَصُومِي غَداً ؟ » قَالَتْ : لا ، قَالَ : « فَأَفْطِرِي » رَوَاهُ البُخاري .

1763. Hazrat Ummul Momineen Juwairiah bint Haris (R.A.A.) relates that the Holy Prophet (S.A.W.) visited her on Friday when she was fasting. He (S.A.W.) asked her if she observed the fast yesterday? She said: 'No' He (S.A.W.) asked her whether she intended to observe the fast next day. She said: 'No'. He (S.A.W.) then said: Then break your fast (today). *(Bukhari)*

* * * * * * *

CHAPTER 346

PROHIBITION OF OBSERVING A SAUM-E-VISAL THAT IS A CONTINUOUS FAST LASTING FOR ONE OR MORE DAYS WITHOUT EATING OR DRINKING

١٧٦٤ – عَنْ أبي هُرَيْرَةَ وَعَائِشَةَ رَضِيَ اللهُ عَنْهُمَا أنَّ النَّبِيَّ صَلَّى اللهُ عَلَيْهِ وَسَلَّمَ نَهَى عَنِ الوِصَالِ . متفقٌ عليه .

1764. Hazrat Abu Hurairah (R.A.A.) and Hazrat Ayesha (R.A.A.) relate that the Holy Prophet (S.A.W.) has forbidden from *Saum-e-Visal*, i.e. the continuation of a fast for successive days (beyond one day. *(Bukhari and Muslim)*

١٧٦٥– وعَنِ ابْنِ عُمَرَ رَضِيَ اللهُ عَنْهُمَا قَالَ : نَهَى رَسُولُ اللهِ صَلَّى اللهُ عَلَيْهِ وَسَلَّمَ عَنِ الوِصَالِ . قَالُوا : إنَّكَ تُوَاصِلُ ؟ قَالَ : « إنِّي لَسْتُ مِثْلَكُمْ ، إنِّي أُطْعَمُ وَأُسْقَى » متفقٌ عليه ، وهذا لَفْظُ البُخاري.

1765. Hazrat Ibn 'Umar (R.A.A.) relates that the Holy Prophet (S.A.W.) forbade from *Saum-e-Visal.* The Companions said to him (S.A.W.). But you observe. He (S.A.W.) answered. 'I am not like you. I am given to eat and drink (by Allah). *(Bukhari and Muslim. This is the wording of Bukhari).*

* * * * * * *

CHAPTER 347

PROHIBITION OF SITTING ON A GRAVE

١٧٦٦ – عَنْ أَبِي هُرَيْرَةَ رَضِيَ اللهُ عَنْهُ قَالَ : قَالَ رَسُولُ اللهِ صَلَّى اللهُ عَلَيْهِ وَسَلَّمَ : «لأَنْ يَجْلِسَ أَحَدُكُمْ عَلَى جَمْرَةٍ ، فَتُحْرِقَ ثِيَابَهُ ، فَتَخْلُصَ إِلَى جِلْدِهِ خَيْرٌ لَهُ مِنْ أَنْ يَجْلِسَ عَلَى قَبْرٍ» رواه مسلم .

1766. Hazrat Abu Hurairah (R.A.A.) relates that the Holy Prophet (S.A.W.) said: It is better for a person to sit on burning coal by which his clothes may catch fire and the heat thereof may touch his skin, rather than that he sits on a grave. *(Muslim)*

* * * * * * *

CHAPTER 348

PROHIBITION OF CONSTRUCTING A STRONG GRAVE AND ERECTING A BUILDING OVER IT

١٧٦٧ – عَنْ جَابِرٍ رَضِيَ اللهُ عَنْهُ قَالَ : نَهَى رَسُولُ اللهِ صَلَّى اللهُ عَلَيْهِ وَسَلَّمَ أَنْ يُجَصَّصَ الْقَبْرُ ، وَأَنْ يُقْعَدَ عَلَيْهِ ، وَأَنْ يُبْنَى عَلَيْهِ . رواه مسلم .

1767. Hazrat Jabir (R.A.A.) relates that the Holy Prophet (S.A.W.) has forbidden that a grave should be made strong (of bricks and plaster) or durable or one should sit over it or the same should have a construction over it. *(Muslim)*

Note:— From authentic traditions, it is proved that to erect domes over graves or building mausoleum in graveyards, is strictly forbidden. The Holy Prophet (S.A.W.) has condemned those persons who build mosques over graves, and also those who light lamps on graves.

* * * * * * *

CHAPTER 349

STRICT PROHIBITION OF RUNNING AWAY OF A SLAVE FROM HIS MASTER

١٧٦٨ – عَنْ جَرِيرِ بْنِ عَبدِ اللهِ رَضِيَ اللهُ عَنْهُ قَالَ: قالَ رَسُولُ اللهِ صَلَّى اللهُ عَلَيْهِ وَسَلَّمَ: «أَيُّمَا عَبْدٍ أَبَقَ، فَقَدْ بَرِئَتْ مِنْهُ الذِّمَّةُ». رواه مسلم.

1768. Hazrat Jarir bin Abdullah (R.A.A.) relates that the Holy Prophet (S.A.W.) said: When a slave runs away from his master, he loses the protection (of Islam) in his favour. *(Muslim)*

١٧٦٩ – وَعَنْهُ عَنِ النَّبِيِّ صَلَّى اللهُ عَلَيْهِ وَسَلَّمَ: «إذا أَبَقَ الْعَبْدُ، لَمْ تُقْبَلْ لَهُ صَلاةٌ» رواه مسلم.

وفي رِوَايَةٍ: «فَقَدْ كَفَرَ».

1769. Hazrat Jarir (R.A.A.) reports that the Holy Prophet (S.A.W.) said: When a slave runs away from his master, his prayer is not accepted. *(Muslim)*

Another version says: He is guilty of infidelity.

* * * * * * *

CHAPTER 350

PROHIBITION OF INTERCESSION IN THE MATTER OF HUDOOD (PRESCRIBED PUNISHMENT UNDER SHARIAT LAW AGAINST GRAVE CRIMES)

قَالَ اللهُ تَعَالَى: الزَّانِيَةُ وَالزَّانِي فَاجْلِدُوا كُلَّ وَاحِدٍ مِنْهُمَا مِائَةَ جَلْدَةٍ وَلا تَأْخُذْكُمْ بِهِمَا رَأْفَةٌ فِي دِينِ اللهِ إِنْ كُنْتُمْ تُؤْمِنُونَ بِاللهِ وَالْيَوْمِ الآخِرِ [النور: ٢].

Allah, the Exalted has said:

404. The adulterer and the adulteress, scourge ye each one of them (with) a hundred stripes. And let not pity for the twain withhold you from obedience to Allah, if ye believe in Allah and the Last Day. (24 : 2)

١٧٧٠– وَعَنْ عَائِشَةَ رَضِيَ اللهُ عَنْهَا ، أَنَّ قُرَيْشاً أَهَمَّهُمْ شَأْنُ الْمَرْأَةِ الْمَخْزُومِيَّةِ الَّتِي سَرَقَتْ فَقَالُوا : مَنْ يُكَلِّمُ فِيهَا رَسُولَ اللهِ صَلَّى اللهُ عَلَيْهِ وَسَلَّمَ ؟ فَقَالُوا : وَمَنْ يَجْتَرِىءُ عَلَيْهِ إِلاَّ أُسَامَةُ بْنُ زَيْدٍ ، حِبُّ رَسُولِ اللهِ صَلَّى اللهُ عَلَيْهِ وَسَلَّمَ ، فَكَلَّمَهُ أُسَامَةُ فَقَالَ رَسُولُ اللهِ صَلَّى اللهُ عَلَيْهِ وَسَلَّمَ : « أَتَشْفَعُ فِي حَدٍّ مِنْ حُدُودِ اللهِ تَعَالَى ؟ » ثُمَّ قَامَ فَاخْتَطَبَ ، ثُمَّ قَالَ : « إِنَّمَا أَهْلَكَ الَّذِينَ قَبْلَكُمْ أَنَّهُمْ كَانُوا إِذَا سَرَقَ فِيهِمُ الشَّرِيفُ تَرَكُوهُ ، وَإِذَا سَرَقَ فِيهِمُ الضَّعِيفُ ، أَقَامُوا عَلَيْهِ الْحَدَّ ، وَايْمُ اللهِ لَوْ أَنَّ فَاطِمَةَ بِنْتَ مُحَمَّدٍ سَرَقَتْ لَقَطَعْتُ يَدَهَا » متفقٌ عليه .

وفي رِوَايَة « فَتَلَوَّنَ وَجْهُ رسولِ اللهِ صلَّى اللهُ عَلَيْهِ وسَلَّم » فَقَالَ : « أَتَشْفَعُ فِي حَدٍّ مِنْ حُدودِ اللهِ ! ؟ » قَالَ أُسَامَةُ : اِسْتَغْفِرْ لِي يَارَسُولَ اللهِ . قَالَ : ثُمَّ أَمَرَ بِتِلْكَ الْمَرْأَةِ ، فَقُطِعَتْ يَدُهَا .

1770. This Hadis has already been covered in S. No. 651 of Chapter 77.

* * * * * * *

CHAPTER 351

PROHIBITION OF EASING THE CALL OF NATURE AT PUBLIC THOROUGH FARES, PLACES OF SHADOW AND WATER POOLS ETC

قَالَ اللهُ تَعَالَى : وَالَّذِينَ يُؤْذُونَ الْمُؤْمِنِينَ وَالْمُؤْمِنَاتِ بِغَيْرِ مَا اكْتَسَبُوا فَقَدِ احْتَمَلُوا بُهْتَاناً وَإِثْماً مُبِيناً - [الأحزاب : ٥٨] .

Allah, the Exalted, has said:

405. And those who malign believing men and believing women undeservedly, they bear the guilt of slander and manifest sin. (33 : 58)

١٧٧١ – وَعَنْ أَبِي هُرَيْرَةَ رَضِيَ اللهُ عَنْهُ أَنَّ رَسُولَ اللهِ صَلَّى اللهُ عَلَيْهِ وَسَلَّمَ قَالَ : « اتَّقُوا اللَّاعِنَيْنِ » قَالُوا وَمَا اللَّاعِنَانِ ؟ قَالَ : « الَّذِي يَتَخَلَّى فِي طَرِيقِ النَّاسِ أَوْ فِي ظِلِّهِمْ » رواه مسلم

1771. Hazrat Abu Hurairah (R.A.A.) relates that the Holy Prophet (S.A.W.) said: Beware of two cursed practices. The Companions asked: What are the two cursed practices? He (S.A.W.) answered: A person answering the call of nature in a public thoroughfare or in a shady place (where people rest). *(Muslim)*

* * * * * * *

CHAPTER 352

PROHIBITON OF URINATION INTO STILL WATER (RESERVOIR OR POND)

١٧٧٢ – عَنْ جَابِرٍ رَضِيَ اللهُ عَنْهُ : أَنَّ رَسُولَ اللهِ صَلَّى اللهُ عَلَيْهِ وَسَلَّمَ نَهَى أَنْ يُبَالَ فِي المَاءِ الرَّاكِدِ . رواه مسلم .

1772. Hazrat Jabir (R.A.A.) relates that the Holy Prophet (S.A.W.) has forbidden urination into still water (reservoir or pond etc.). *(Muslim)*

* * * * * * *

CHAPTER 353

PROHIBITION OF PREFERRING ONE CHILD OVER ANOTHER IN THE MATTER OF GIFTS

١٧٧٣ – عَنِ النُّعْمَانِ بْنِ بَشِيرٍ رَضِيَ اللهُ عَنْهُمَا أَنَّ أَبَاهُ أَتَى بِهِ رَسُولَ اللهِ صَلَّى اللهُ عَلَيْهِ وَسَلَّمَ فَقَالَ : إِنِّي نَحَلْتُ ابْنِي هذا غُلاماً كَانَ لِي، فَقَالَ رَسُولُ اللهِ صَلَّى اللهُ عَلَيْهِ وَسَلَّمَ : « أَكُلَّ وَلَدِكَ نَحَلْتَهُ مِثْلَ هذا ؟ » فَقَالَ : لا ، فَقَالَ رَسُولُ اللهِ صَلَّى اللهُ عَلَيْهِ وَسَلَّمَ : « فَأَرْجِعْهُ » .

وفي رِوَايَةٍ : فَقَالَ رَسُولُ اللهِ صَلَّى اللهُ عَلَيْهِ وَسَلَّمَ : « أَفَعَلْتَ هَذَا

بِوَلَدِكَ كُلِّهِمْ ؟ » قَالَ : لا ، قَالَ : « اتَّقُوا اللهَ وَاعْدِلُوا فِي أَوْلادِكُمْ » فَرَجَعَ أَبِي ، فَرَدَّ تِلْكَ الصَّدَقَةَ .

وفي رِوَايَةٍ : فَقَالَ رَسُولُ اللهِ صَلَّى اللهُ عَلَيْهِ وَسَلَّمَ : « يَابَشِيرُ أَلَكَ وَلَدٌ سِوَى هذا ؟ » قَالَ : نَعَمْ ، قَالَ : « أَكُلَّهُمْ وَهَبْتَ لَهُ مِثْلَ هذا ؟ » قَالَ : لا ، قَالَ : « فَلاَ تُشْهِدْنِي إذاً فَإنِّي لا أَشْهَدُ عَلَى جَوْرٍ » .

وَفي رِوَايَةٍ « لا تُشْهِدْنِي عَلَى جَوْرٍ » .

وفي روايةٍ : « أَشْهِدْ عَلَى هذا غَيْرِي ! » ثُمَّ قَالَ : « أَيَسُرُّكَ أَنْ يَكُونُوا إلَيْكَ فِي البِرِّ سَوَاءً ؟ » قَالَ : بَلَى ، قَالَ : « فَلا إذاً » متفقٌ عليه .

1773. Hazrat Nu'man bin Bashir (R.A.A.) says that his father took him to the Holy Prophet (S.A.W.) and said. I had a slave whom I have gifted to this son of mine. The Holy Prophet (S.A.W.) inquired: Have you made a similar gift to each of your children? He said: No; whereupon the Holy Prophet (S.A.W.) said: 'Then take back (this gift).

Another version says: The Holy Prophet (S.A.W.) asked: Have you done this (favour) to each of your children? He answered: No. The Holy Prophet (S.A.W.) then said: Fear Allah and be fair to your offsprings. My father then came back and rescinded this gift.

Yet another version says that the Holy Prophet (S.A.W.) asked: O Bashir, have you other children beside this one? He answered: 'Yes Sir'. The Holy Prophet (S.A.W.) asked: Have you gifted (a slave) to each one of them? He said: 'No'. The Holy Prophet (S.A.W.) said: Then do not make me a witness for I do not want to be a witness for an injustice (cruelty).

One more version says: Do not make me witness for an injustice.

One more version says the Holy Prophet (S.A.W.) said. make some one else witness on this, and said: Do you like that all of your children may behave equally well towards you? My father said. 'Yes, Sir. Holy Prophet (S.A.W.) remarked: Then don't do (injustice) now?

(Bukhari and Muslim)

* * * * * * *

CHAPTER 354

PROHIBITION OF A WOMAN MOURNING ANYBODY FOR MORE THAN THREE DAYS EXCEPT HER HUSBAND FOR FOUR MONTHS AND TEN DAYS

١٧٧٤ – عَنْ زَيْنَبَ بِنْتِ أَبِي سَلَمَةَ رَضِيَ اللهُ عَنْهُمَا قَالَتْ : دَخَلْتُ عَلَى أُمِّ حَبِيبَةَ رَضِيَ اللهُ عَنْهَا زَوْجِ النَّبِيِّ صَلَّى اللهُ عَلَيْهِ وَسَلَّمَ حِينَ تُوُفِّيَ أَبُوهَا أَبُو سُفْيَانَ بْنُ حَرْبٍ رَضِيَ اللهُ عَنْهُ ، فَدَعَتْ بِطِيبٍ فِيهِ صُفْرَةُ خَلُوقٍ أَوْ غَيْرِهِ ، فَدَهَنَتْ مِنْهُ جَارِيَةً ، ثُمَّ مَسَّتْ بِعَارِضَيْهَا . ثُمَّ قَالَتْ : وَاللهِ مَالِي بِالطِّيبِ مِنْ حَاجَةٍ ، غَيْرَ أَنِّي سَمِعْتُ رَسُولَ اللهِ صَلَّى اللهُ عَلَيْهِ وَسَلَّمَ يَقُولُ عَلَى الْمِنْبَرِ : « لَا يَحِلُّ لِامْرَأَةٍ تُؤْمِنُ بِاللهِ وَالْيَوْمِ الآخِرِ أَنْ تُحِدَّ عَلَى مَيِّتٍ فَوْقَ ثَلَاثِ لَيَالٍ ، إِلَّا عَلَى زَوْجٍ أَرْبَعَةَ أَشْهُرٍ وَعَشْرًا » قَالَتْ زَيْنَبُ : ثُمَّ دَخَلْتُ عَلَى زَيْنَبَ بِنْتِ جَحْشٍ رَضِيَ اللهُ عَنْهَا حِينَ تُوُفِّيَ أَخُوهَا ، فَدَعَتْ بِطِيبٍ ، فَمَسَّتْ مِنْهُ ، ثُمَّ قَالَتْ : أَمَا وَاللهِ مَالِي بِالطِّيبِ مِنْ حَاجَةٍ ، غَيْرَ أَنِّي سَمِعْتُ رَسُولَ اللهِ صَلَّى اللهُ عَلَيْهِ وَسَلَّمَ يَقُولُ عَلَى الْمِنْبَرِ : « لَا يَحِلُّ لِامْرَأَةٍ تُؤْمِنُ بِاللهِ وَالْيَوْمِ الآخِرِ أَنْ تُحِدَّ عَلَى مَيِّتٍ فَوْقَ ثَلَاثٍ إِلَّا عَلَى زَوْجٍ أَرْبَعَةَ أَشْهُرٍ وَعَشْرًا » . متفق عليه .

1774. Hazrat Zainab bint Abu Salamah (R.A.A.) says: I visited Hazrat Umm Habibah (R.A.A.), wife of the Holy Prophet (S.A.W.) when her father Hazrat Abu Sufyan bin Harb (R.A.A.) had died. She sent for a yellow coloured perfume and applied it on one of her maid servants, and then rubbed it on her cheeks and said: By Allah! I did not need a perfume except that I had heard the Holy Prophet (S.A.W.) declare from the pulpit: It is not lawful for a woman who believes in Allah and the Last Day, that she should mourn a dead person for more than three days except in the case of her husband whom she can mourn for four months and ten days. Again Hazrat Zainab bint Abi Salamah (R.A.A.) visited (Ummul Momineen) Hazrat Zainab bint Jahash (R.A.A.) three days after the death of latter's brother; Hazrat Zainab Bint Jahash (R.A.A.) sent for some perfume and applied to her person, and remarked that: I did not need any perfume but I have heard from the Holy Prophet (S.A.W.) speaking from the pulpit that any woman who believes in Allah and the Day of Judgement, should not mourn a dead person for more than three days except her husband, on whose demise she can mourn for four months and ten days.'

(Bukhari and Muslim)

* * * * * * *

CHAPTER 355

MEETING A CARAVAN AHEAD TO MAKE PURCHASES FROM THE VILLAGE FOLK BY A CITY DWELLER AND OVER-BIDDING HIS BROTHER AND PROPOSING FOR HIS OWN MARRIAGE OVER THE PROPOSAL OF HIS BROTHER, EXCEPT WHEN HE HAS PERMITTED HIM TO DO SO OR HAS ABANDONED THE PROPOSAL. ALL THESE ACTIONS ARE UNLAWFUL

١٧٧٥ – عَنْ أَنَسٍ رَضِيَ اللهُ عَنْهُ قَالَ : نَهَى رَسُولُ اللهِ صلَّى اللهُ عَلَيْهِ وسَلَّمَ أَنْ يَبِيعَ حَاضِرٌ لِبَادٍ وَإِنْ كَانَ أَخَاهُ لأَبِيهِ وَأُمِّهِ .
متفقٌ عليه .

1775. Hazrat Anas (R.A.A.) relates that the Holy Prophet (S.A.W.) forbade that a citizen should sell for a villager (on commission) although he may be his real brother or father or mother.

(Bukhari and Muslim)

١٧٧٦ – وَعَنِ ابْنِ عُمَرَ قَالَ : قَالَ رَسُولُ اللهِ صَلَّى اللهُ عَلَيْهِ وَسَلَّمَ : « لا تَتَلَقَّوُا السِّلَعَ حَتَّى يُهْبَطَ بِهَا إِلَى الأَسْوَاقِ » متفقٌ عليه .

1776. Hazrat Ibn 'Umar (R.A.A.) relates that the Holy Prophet (S.A.W.) said: Do not purchase goods (from a caravan) by meeting it before it reaches the market. *(Bukhari and Muslim)*

١٧٧٧ – وَعَنِ ابْنِ عَبَّاسٍ رَضِيَ اللهُ عَنْهُمَا قَالَ : قَالَ رَسُولُ اللهِ صَلَّى اللهُ عَلَيْهِ وَسَلَّمَ : « لا تَتَلَقَّوُا الرُّكْبَانَ ، وَلا يَبِيعْ حَاضِرٌ لِبَادٍ ، فَقَالَ لَهُ طَاوُسٌ مَا : لايَبِيعْ حَاضِرٌ لِبَادٍ ؟ قال : لايَكُونُ لَهُ سِمْسَاراً .
متفقٌ عليه

1777. Hazrat Ibn Abbas (R.A.A.) reports that the Holy Prophet (S.A.W.) said: 'Do not go ahead to meet a trading caravan and purchase goods from them, nor a city dweller should act as agent for selling goods for a man from a village. Hazrat Ta'uṣ (R.A.A.) asked Hazrat Ibn Abbas: 'What is the meaning of a city dweller not selling the goods of man from a village? Hazrat Ibn-i-Abbas (R.A.A.) said: 'He should not act as his broker.' *(Bukhari and Muslim)*

Note:— During those days it was a common practice of some commission agents or brokers to meet a trading caravan outside the city and settle to purchase their goods at a lower price (without actually paying the price) and subsequently selling the same to the consumers in the city at a higher rate. These agents or middle men would pay to the caravan traders the lower price of the goods already agreed and would also claim commission or brokerage on these transactions. Thus these agents used to get double benefit on a transaction i.e. profit from the city purchasers and commission from the caravan traders.

١٧٧٨ – وَعَنْ أَبِي هُرَيْرَةَ رَضِيَ اللهُ عَنْهُ قَالَ : نَهَى رَسُولُ اللهِ صَلَّى اللهُ عَلَيْهِ وَسَلَّمَ أَنْ يَبِيعَ حَاضِرٌ لِبَادٍ ، وَلا تَنَاجَشُوا وَلا يَبِيعُ الرَّجُلُ عَلَى بَيْعِ أَخِيهِ ، وَلا يَخْطُبُ عَلَى خِطْبَةِ أَخِيهِ ، وَلا تَسْأَلُ الْمَرْأَةُ طَلاقَ أُخْتِهَا لِتَكْفَأَ مَا فِي إِنَائِهَا .

وفي رِوَايَةٍ قَالَ : نَهَى : رَسُولُ اللهِ صَلَّى اللهُ عَلَيْهِ وَسَلَّمَ عَنِ التَّلَقِّي وَأَنْ يَبْتَاعَ الْمُهَاجِرُ لِلأَعْرَابِي ، وَأَنْ تَشْتَرِطَ الْمَرْأَةُ طَلاقَ أُخْتِهَا : وَأَنْ يَسْتَامَ الرَّجُلُ عَلَى سَوْمِ أَخِيهِ ، وَنَهَى عَنِ النَّجْشِ وَالتَّصْرِيَةِ متفقٌ عليه .

1778. **Hazrat Abu Hurairah** (R.A.A.) says that the Holy Prophet (S.A.W.) has forbidden that a city dweller should act as commission agent for a man and forbade bogus purchases; and that a man should make an offer over the offer of his brother which is pending, or that he should make a proposal of marriage while the proposal of his brother (with the same party) is pending, or that a woman should try that her sister might be divorced so that she might step in her place.

Another version says: The Holy Prophet (S.A.W.) has forbidden meeting a trading caravan ahead (outside the city), or that a city dweller should act as a commission agent for the sale of the goods of a village folk or that a woman should make it a condition of marriage that a sister of hers (another woman) should be divorced, or that a person should offer a bogus high price without intention of purchasing, in order to corner the real purchaser to offer higher price and also has forbidden the accumulation of milk in the udder of an animal.

(Bukhari and Muslim)

١٧٧٩ – وَعَنِ ابْنِ عُمَرَ رَضِيَ اللهُ عَنْهُمَا ، أَنَّ رَسُولَ اللهِ صَلَّى اللهُ

عَلَيْهِ وَسَلَّمَ قَالَ : « لايَبِعْ بَعْضُكُمْ عَلى بَيْعِ بَعْضٍ ، وَلا يَخْطُبُ عَلى خِطْبَةِ أَخِيهِ إِلاَّ أَنْ يَأْذَنَ لَهُ » متفقٌ عليه وهَذا لَفْظُ مسلم .

1779. Hazrat Ibn 'Umar (R.A.A.) relates that the Holy Prophet (S.A.W.) said: None of you should make a bid to purchase when his brother (another person) has already made an offer; similarly he should not make a proposal for his marriage while a proposal of his brother (another person) is pending except when he is permitted to do so by him. *(Bukhari and Muslim.* This is the wording of *Muslim)*

١٧٨٠ – وَعَنْ عُقْبَةَ بْنِ عَامِرٍ رَضِيَ اللهُ عَنْهُ أَنَّ رَسُولَ اللهِ صَلَّى اللهُ عَلَيْهِ وَسَلَّمَ قَالَ : « المُؤْمِنُ أَخُو المُؤْمِنِ ، فَلاَ يَحِلُّ لِمُؤْمِنٍ أَنْ يَبْتَاعَ عَلَى بَيْعِ أَخِيهِ وَلاَ يَخْطُبَ عَلَى خِطْبَةِ أَخِيهِ حَتَّى يَذَرَ » رواهُ مسلم

1780. Hazrat 'Uqbah bin 'Aamir (R.A.A.) relates that the Holy Prophet (S.A.W.) said: A believer (Muslim) is a brother of another believer (Muslim), hence it is not lawful for a believer to make an offer to buy something while an offer of another brother (Muslim) for the same is pending. Similarly a Muslim should not propose to marry a woman while a proposal of his brother (another person) for the same woman is pending unless the former has withdrawn. *(Muslim)*

* * * * * * *

CHAPTER 356

PROHIBITION OF WASTING (SPENDING) MONEY ON ITEMS NOT APPROVED BY SHARIAH

١٧٨١ – عَنْ أَبِي هُرَيْرَةَ رَضِيَ اللهُ عَنْهُ قَالَ : قَالَ رَسُولَ اللهِ صَلَّى اللهُ عَلَيْهِ وَسَلَّمَ : « إِنَّ اللهَ تَعَالَى يَرْضَى لَكُمْ ثَلاَثاً ، وَيَكْرَه لَكُمْ ثَلاَثاً : فَيَرْضَى لَكُمْ أَنْ تَعْبُدُوه ، وَلاَ تُشْرِكُوا بِهِ شَيْئاً ، وَأَنْ تَعْتَصِموا بِحَبْلِ اللهِ جَمِيعاً وَلاَ تَفَرَّقُوا ، وَيَكْرَهُ لَكُمْ : قِيلَ وَقَالَ ، وَكَثْرَةَ السُّؤَالِ ، وَإِضَاعَةَ المَالِ » رواه مسلم

1781. Hazrat Abu Hurairah (R.A.A.) relates that the Holy Prophet said: Allah likes three things (practices) for you and similarly He dislikes three things (practices) for you. Pracitces liked for you are that you should worship Him, and should not associate anybody or anything with Him and that you should hold fast the rope of Allah (Islam) and should not get disunited; and He dislikes that you should be too much talkative or argumentative, accustomed to much asking and destroy property or wealth (extravagantly). *(Muslim)*

١٧٨٢– وَعَنْ وَرَّادٍ كَاتِبِ المُغِيرَةِ بْنِ شُعْبَةَ قَالَ : أَمْلَى عَلَيَّ المُغِيرَةُ فِي كِتَابٍ إِلَى مُعَاوِيَةَ رَضِيَ اللهُ عَنْهُ ، أَنَّ النَّبِيَّ صَلَّى اللهُ عَلَيْهِ وَسَلَّمَ كَانَ يَقُولُ فِي دُبُرِ كُلِّ صَلَاةٍ مَكْتُوبَةٍ : « لَا إِلَهَ إِلَّا اللهُ وَحْدَهُ لَا شَرِيكَ لَهُ ، لَهُ المُلْكُ وَلَهُ الحَمْدُ وَهُوَ عَلَى كُلِّ شَيْءٍ قَدِيرٌ ، اللَّهُمَّ لَا مَانِعَ لِمَا أَعْطَيْتَ ، وَلَا مُعْطِيَ لِمَا مَنَعْتَ ، وَلَا يَنْفَعُ ذَا الجَدِّ مِنْكَ الجَدُّ » وَكَتَبَ إِلَيْهِ أَنَّهُ « كَانَ يَنْهَى عَنْ قِيلَ وَقَالَ ، وَإِضَاعَةِ المَالِ ، وَكَثْرَةِ السُّؤَالِ ، وَكَانَ يَنْهَى عَنْ عُقُوقِ الأُمَّهَاتِ ، وَوَأْدِ البَنَاتِ ، وَمَنْعٍ وَهَاتِ » متفقٌ عَلَيْهِ .

1782. **Hazrat Warrad** (R.A.A.) the secretary of Hazrat Mughirah bin Sho'bah (R.A.A.) relates: Hazrat Mughirah dictated me a letter to Hazrat Amir Mu'awiah (R.A.A.) that the Holy Prophet (S.A.W.) used to supplicate at the end of each Fard (compulsory) prayer thus:

La ila-ha illal-laho wah-daho la sha-rika la-ho la-hul mul-ko wa la-hul ham-do wa huwa 'ala kul-li-shai-in Qadeer. Alla-hum-ma la mani'a lima a'tai-ta wa la mo'ti-ya lima mana'ta wa la yan-fa' zal-jad-da min-kal-jad.

'There is no god except Allah, who is Alone and has no associate. For Him is the sovereignty, and for Him is the praise and He has the power to do all that He wills.

O Allah! no one can stop that which Thou dost bestow, and no one can bestow that which Thou dost hold back, nor does the high status of anybody avail against Thee.

And also wrote to Hazrat Mu'awiah (R.A.A.) that the Holy Prophet (S.A.W.) forbade unnecessary talking and argumentation, destruction of property, and too much asking. He (S.A.W.) also used to forbid disobedience to mothers, burying girls alive, depriving somebody of his rights, and usurpation. *(Bukhari and Muslim)*

* * * * * * *

CHAPTER 357
PROHIBITION OF POINTING TOWARDS A MUSLIM WITH A WEAPON DELIBERATELY OR IN JOKE AND HANDING OVER AN UNSHEATHED SWORD

١٧٨٣ – عَنْ أَبِي هُرَيْرَةَ رَضِيَ اللهُ عَنْهُ عَنْ رَسُولِ اللهِ صَلَّى اللهُ عَلَيْهِ وَسَلَّمَ قَالَ : « لاَ يُشِرْ أَحَدُكُمْ إِلَى أَخِيهِ بِالسِّلاَحِ ، فَإِنَّهُ لاَ يَدْرِي لَعَلَّ الشَّيْطَانَ يَنْزِعُ فِي يَدِهِ ، فَيَقَعَ فِي حُفْرَةٍ مِنَ النَّارِ » مُتَّفَقٌ عليه .

وفي رِوَايَةٍ لِمُسْلِمٍ قَالَ : قَالَ أَبُو الْقَاسِمِ صَلَّى اللهُ عَلَيْهِ وَسَلَّمَ : مَنْ أَشَارَ إِلَى أَخِيهِ بِحَدِيدَةٍ ، فَإِنَّ المَلاَئِكَةَ تَلْعَنُهُ حَتَّى يَنْزِعَ ، وَإِنْ كَانَ أَخَاهُ لأَبِيهِ وَأُمِّهِ » .

1783. **Hazrat Abu Hurairah** (R.A.A.) reports that the Holy Prophet (S.A.W.) said: 'None of you should point at his brother (Muslim) with a weapon, for he is unaware lest Satan should make him let it loose (the weapon) from his hand, (and cause him injury or death) and may cause him (in consequence of injury or death) fall into the pit of Hell. *(Bukhari and Muslim)*

Imam Muslim's version says: Hazrat Abul Qasim Holy Prophet (S.A.W.)said: A person who pointed at a brother with a sharp edged weapon, is cursed by the angels till he keeps it away, although the person may be his real brother (and the former does not want to harm him).

١٧٨٤ – وَعَنْ جَابِرٍ رَضِيَ اللهُ عَنْهُ قَالَ : « نهَى رَسُولُ اللهِ صَلَّى اللهُ عَلَيْهِ وَسَلَّمَ أَنْ يُتَعَاطَى السَّيْفُ مَسْلُولاً » .

رَوَاهُ أَبُو دَاود ، والترمذي وقال : حديثٌ حَسَنٌ .

1784. **Hazrat Jabir** (R.A.A.) relates: 'The Holy Prophet (S.A.W.) has forbidden that anyone should hand over an unsheathed sword to another. *(Abu Daud and Tirmizi.* Later said this is good*)*

* * * * * * *

CHAPTER 358

UNDESIRABILITY OF LEAVING A MOSQUE AFTER AZAN AND BEFORE OFFERING FARD PRAYER EXCEPT WITH JUST EXCUSE

١٧٨٥ – عَنْ أبي الشَّعْثاءِ قال : كُنَّا قُعُوداً مَعَ أبي هُرَيْرَةَ رَضِيَ اللهُ عَنْهُ فِي المَسْجِدِ ، فَأذَّنَ المؤذِّنُ ، فَقَامَ رَجُلٌ مِنَ المَسْجِدِ يَمْشِي ، فَأتْبَعَهُ أبُو هُرَيْرَةَ بَصَرَهُ حَتَّى خَرَجَ مِنَ المَسْجِدِ ، فَقَالَ أبُو هُرَيْرَةَ : أمَّا هَذَا فَقَدْ عَصَى أبَا القَاسِمِ ، صَلَّى اللهُ عَلَيْهِ وَسَلَّمَ . رواهُ مسلم .

1785. **Hazrat Abu Sha'sa** (R.A.A.) says: We were once sitting with Hazrat Abu Hurairah (R.A.A.) in the mosque, when the Muezzin called the Azan; (Soon after this) a man stood up in the mosque and walked out. Hazrat Abu Hurairah (R.A.A.) followed him gazing at him till he left the mosque. Thereafter Hazrat Abu Hurairah (R.A.A.) remarked: This man has disobeyed the Holy Prophet Abul Qasim (Muhammad S.A.W.). *(Muslim)*

* * * * * * *

CHAPTER 359

UNDESIRABILITY OF REFUSING PERFUME WITHOUT DUE EXCUSE

١٧٨٦ – عَنْ أبِي هُرَيْرَةَ رَضِيَ اللهُ عَنْهُ قَالَ : قَالَ رَسُولُ اللهِ صَلَّى اللهُ عَلَيْهِ وَسَلَّمَ : « مَنْ عُرِضَ عَلَيْهِ رَيْحَانٌ ، فَلاَ يَرُدَّهُ ، فَإنَّهُ خَفِيفُ المَحْمِلِ ، طَيِّبُ الرِّيحِ » رواهُ مسلم .

1786. **Hazrat Abu Hurairah** (R.A.A.) reports that the Holy Prophet (S.A.W.) said: A person should not refuse to accept a gift of perfume for it is light in weight and has a good smell. *(Muslim)*

١٧٨٧ – وَعَنْ أنَسِ بْنِ مَالِكٍ رَضِيَ اللهُ عَنْهُ أنَّ النَّبِيَّ صَلَّى اللهُ عَلَيْهِ وَسَلَّمَ كَانَ لا يَرُدُّ الطِّيبَ . رواهُ البُخاري .

1787. **Hazrat Anas bin Malik** (R.A.A.) relates that the Holy Prophet (S.A.W.) never refused to accept a gift of perfume. *(Bukhari)*

* * * * * * *

CHAPTER 360

DISLKE FOR PRAISING A PERSON ON HIS FACE ABOUT WHOM IT IS FEARED THAT HE WILL FALL A PREY TO EVILS LIKE PRIDE ETC., AND IF THERE MAY BE NO RISK THEN IT IS PERMISSIBLE

١٧٨٨ – عَنْ أَبِي مُوسَى الأَشْعَرِيِّ رَضِيَ اللهُ عَنْهُ قَالَ : سَمِعَ النَّبِيُّ صَلَّى اللهُ عَلَيْهِ وَسَلَّمَ رَجُلاً يُثْنِي عَلَى رَجُلٍ وَيُطْرِيهِ فِي المِدْحَةِ، فَقَالَ : « أَهْلَكْتُمْ ، أَوْ قَطَعْتُمْ ظَهْرَ الرَّجُلِ » متفقٌ عليه .

1788. Hazrat Abu Musa Al-Ash'ari (R.A.A.) relates: The Holy Prophet (S.A.W.) heard a man who was exaggerating in praise of another person whereupon He (S.A.W.) said: 'You have killed him or you have broken his back. *(Bukhari and Muslim)*

١٧٨٩ – وَعَنْ أَبِي بَكْرَةَ رَضِيَ اللهُ عَنْهُ أَنَّ رَجُلاً ذُكِرَ عِنْدَ النَّبِيِّ صَلَّى اللهُ عَلَيْهِ وَسَلَّمَ ، فَأَثْنَى عَلَيْهِ رَجُلٌ خَيْراً ، فَقَالَ النَّبِيُّ صَلَّى اللهُ عَلَيْهِ وَسَلَّمَ : « وَيْحَكَ ! قَطَعْتَ عُنُقَ صَاحِبِكَ » يَقُولُهُ مِرَاراً « إِنْ كَانَ أَحَدُكُمْ مَادِحاً لاَ مَحَالَةَ ، فَلْيَقُلْ : أَحْسِبُ كَذَا وكَذَا إِنْ كَانَ يُرَى أَنَّهُ كَذَلِكَ وَحَسِيبُهُ اللهُ ، وَلاَ يُزَكَّى عَلَى اللهِ أَحَدٌ » متفقٌ عليه .

1789. Hazrat Abu Bakrah (R.A.A.) says once when a person was mentioned in the presence of the Holy Prophet (S.A.W.), another person praised him nicely. Holy Prophet (S.A.W.) said to the latter; Fie upon you, you have cut the throat of your companion. He (S.A.W.) repeated this several times and then said: 'If any of you has to praise somebody, he should (simply) say: I consider so and so as such and such, and if you consider him like this you will be accountable to Allah, and no one can be presented pure and pious before Allah.

(Bukhari and Muslim)

١٧٩٠ – وَعَنْ هَمَّامِ بْنِ الحَارِثِ ، عَنِ المِقْدَادِ رَضِيَ اللهُ عَنْهُ أَنَّ رَجُلاً جَعَلَ يَمْدَحُ عُثْمَانَ رَضِيَ اللهُ عَنْهُ ، فَعَمِدَ المِقْدَادُ ، فَجَثَا عَلَى رُكْبَتَيْهِ ، فَجَعَلَ يَحْثُو فِي وَجْهِهِ الحَصْبَاءَ ، فَقَالَ لَهُ عُثْمَانُ : مَا شَأْنُكَ ؟ فَقَالَ : إِنَّ رَسُولَ اللهِ صَلَّى اللهُ عَلَيْهِ وَسَلَّمَ قَالَ : « إِذَا رَأَيْتُمُ المَدَّاحِينَ ، فَاحْثُوا فِي وُجُوهِهِمُ التُّرَابَ » رَوَاهُ مسلم .

فَهَذِهِ الأَحَادِيثُ فِي النَّهْيِ ، وَجَاءَ فِي الإِبَاحَةِ أَحَادِيثُ كَثِيرَةٌ

صَحِيحَةٌ .

قَالَ العُلَمَاءُ : وَطَرِيقُ الجَمْعِ بَيْنَ الأَحَادِيثِ أَنْ يُقَالَ : إِنْ كَانَ المَمْدُوحُ عِنْدَهُ كَمَالُ إِيمَانٍ وَيَقِينٍ ، وَرِيَاضَةُ نَفْسٍ ، وَمَعْرِفَةٌ تَامَّةٌ بِحَيْثُ لا يَفْتَتِنُ ، وَلا يَغْتَرُّ بِذَلِكَ ، وَلاَ تَلْعَبُ بِهِ نَفْسُهُ ، فَلَيْسَ بِحَرَامٍ وَلاَ مَكْرُوهٍ ، وَإِنْ خِيفَ عَلَيْهِ شَيْءٌ مِنْ هَذِهِ الأُمُورِ ، كُرِهَ مَدْحُهُ فِي وَجْهِهِ كَرَاهَةً شَدِيدَةً ، وَعَلَى هَذَا التَّفْصِيلِ تُنَزَّلُ الأَحَادِيثُ المُخْتَلِفَةُ فِي ذَلِكَ . وَمِمَّا جَاءَ فِي الإِبَاحَةِ قَوْلُهُ صَلَّى اللهُ عَلَيْهِ وَسَلَّمَ لأَبِي بَكْرٍ رَضِيَ اللهُ عَنْهُ : « أَرْجُو أَنْ تَكُونَ مِنْهُمْ » أَيْ : مِنَ الَّذِينَ يُدْعَوْنَ مِنْ جَمِيعِ أَبْوَابِ الْجَنَّةِ لِدُخُولِهَا ، وفِي الحَدِيثِ الآخَرِ : « لَسْتَ مِنْهُمْ » ، أَيْ : لَسْتَ مِنَ الَّذِينَ يُسْبِلُونَ أُزُرَهُمْ خُيَلاءَ . وَقَالَ صَلَّى اللهُ عَلَيْهِ وَسَلَّمَ لِعُمَرَ رَضِيَ اللهُ عَنْهُ : « مَا رَآكَ الشَّيْطَانُ سَالِكاً فَجاً إِلاَّ سَلَكَ فَجاً غَيْرَ فَجِّكَ » وَالأَحَادِيثُ فِي الإِبَاحَةِ كَثِيرَةٌ ، وَقَدْ ذَكَرْتُ جُمْلَةً مِنْ أَطْرَافِهَا فِي كِتَابِ : « الأَذْكَارِ » .

1790. Hazrat Hammam bin Haris (R.A.A.) says on the authority of Hazrat Miqdad (R.A.A.) that a man started praising Hazrat Usman (R.A.A.) then Hazrat Miqdad sat down cross legged and began throwing pebbles into the mouth of the speaker. Hazrat Usman (R.A.A.) asked him: What is the matter with you? He said: The Holy Prophet (S.A.W.) said: when you notice a person praising somebody (on his face) then put the dust in his mouth.

Note:— Imam Nawawi says that all these traditions are about prohibition of praise, and that there are many traditions in justification of praise as well. The Ulema (learned persons) have said that in order to achieve a coherence between the two types of traditions, it should be seen whether the person praised is a man with firm conviction of faith and belief and a self denying man having thorough knowledge in ethics of religion, so much so that by being so praised, he may not get involved in some mischief, nor he may be deceived by it, nor he may feel happy on such praising, then in such a case this praise is neither unlawful nor abhorrent. If there be any apprehension of the presence of any of the drawbacks mentioned above, then to praise him is a very bad thing.

According to this clarification there are different kinds of traditions. As such, in justification of praise is a tradition wherein the Holy Prophet (S.A.W.) said about Hazrat Abu Bakr (R.A.A.) stating that: "I hope that you will be one of those persons who will be invited to enter the Paradise from all the doors."

And another tradition says: "You (Hazrat Abu Bakr R.A.A.) are not one of those persons who will not be invited to enter Paradise (because) you are one of those who let their trousers hang down in arrogance." (Hazrat Abu Bakr's cloth, trousers used to get dangling).

Another tradition about Hazrat Umar Farooq (R.A.A.) says. "Whenever the Satan notices you going on the road, he abandons that road, and takes up another path."

There are many traditions in support of justification of praising somebody, some of which have been mentioned by me in the book "Kitab-ul-Azkar."

* * * * * * *

CHAPTER 361

DISAPPROVAL OF EVACUATING A TOWN INFESTED WITH AN EPIDEMIC OR VISITING SUCH A TOWN

قَالَ تَعَالَى : أَيْنَمَا تَكُونُوا يُدْرِكْكُمُ الْمَوْتُ وَلَوْ كُنْتُمْ فِي بُرُوجٍ مُشَيَّدَةٍ [النساء : ٧٨] وقالَ تعالى : وَلاَ تُلْقُوا بِأَيْدِيكُمْ إِلَى التَّهْلُكَةِ [البقرة : ١٩٥] .

Allah, the Exalted, has said:

406. Wheresoever ye may be, death will overtake you, even though ye were in lofty towers. (4 : 78)

407. And be not cast by your own hands to ruin. (2 : 195)

١٧٩١ــ وَعَنِ ابْنِ عَبَّاسٍ رَضِيَ اللهُ عَنْهُمَا أَنَّ عُمَرَ بْنَ الْخَطَّابِ رَضِيَ اللهُ عَنْهُ خَرَجَ إِلَى الشَّامِ حَتَّى إِذَا كَانَ بِسَرْغَ لَقِيَهُ أُمَرَاءُ الأَجْنَادِ ــ أَبُو عُبَيْدَةَ بْنُ الْجَرَّاحِ وَأَصْحَابُهُ ــ فَأَخْبَرُوهُ أَنَّ الْوَبَاءَ قَدْ وَقَعَ بِالشَّامِ ، قَالَ ابْنُ عَبَّاسٍ : فَقَالَ لِي عُمَرُ : ادْعُ لِي الْمُهَاجِرِينَ

الأَوَّلِينَ ، فَدَعَوْتُهُمْ ، فَاسْتَشَارَهُمْ ، وَأَخْبَرَهُمْ أَنَّ الْوَبَاءَ قَدْ وَقَعَ بِالشَّامِ ، فَاخْتَلَفُوا ، فَقَالَ بَعْضُهُمْ : خَرَجْتَ لأَمْرٍ ، وَلاَ نَرَى أَنْ تَرْجِعَ عَنْهُ . وَقَالَ بَعْضُهُمْ : مَعَكَ بَقِيَّةُ النَّاسِ وَأَصْحَابُ رَسُولِ اللهِ صَلَّى اللهُ عَلَيْهِ وَسَلَّمَ ، وَلاَ نَرَى أَنْ تُقْدِمَهُمْ عَلَى هَذَا الْوَبَاءِ . فَقَالَ : ارْتَفِعُوا عَنِّي ، ثُمَّ قَالَ : ادْعُ لِي الأَنْصَارَ ، فَدَعَوْتُهُمْ ، فَاسْتَشَارَهُمْ ، فَسَلَكُوا سَبِيلَ الْمُهَاجِرِينَ ، وَاخْتَلَفُوا كَاخْتِلاَفِهِمْ . فَقَالَ : ارْتَفِعُوا عَنِّي . ثُمَّ قَالَ : ادْعُ لِي مَنْ كَانَ هَا هُنَا مِنْ مَشْيَخَةِ قُرَيْشٍ مِنْ مُهَاجِرَةِ الْفَتْحِ . فَدَعَوْتُهُمْ . فَلَمْ يَخْتَلِفْ عَلَيْهِ مِنْهُمْ رَجُلاَنِ ، فَقَالُوا : نَرَى أَنْ تَرْجِعَ بِالنَّاسِ ، وَلاَ تُقْدِمَهُمْ عَلَى هَذَا الْوَبَاءِ ، فَنَادَى عُمَرُ رَضِيَ اللهُ عَنْهُ فِي النَّاسِ : إِنِّي مُصْبِحٌ عَلَى ظَهْرٍ ، فَأَصْبِحُوا عَلَيْهِ . فَقَالَ أَبُو عُبَيْدَةَ بْنُ الْجَرَّاحِ رَضِيَ اللهُ عَنْهُ : أَفِرَاراً مِنْ قَدَرِ اللهِ ؟ فَقَالَ عُمَرُ رَضِيَ اللهُ عَنْهُ : لَوْ غَيْرُكَ قَالَهَا يَا أَبَا عُبَيْدَةَ ! — وَكَانَ عُمَرُ يَكْرَهُ خِلاَفَهُ — نَعَمْ نَفِرُّ مِنْ قَدَرِ اللهِ إِلَى قَدَرِ اللهِ ، أَرَأَيْتَ لَوْ كَانَ لَكَ إِبِلٌ ، فَهَبَطَتْ وَادِياً لَهُ عُدْوَتَانِ ، إِحْدَاهُمَا خَصِبَةٌ ، وَالأُخْرَى جَدْبَةٌ ، أَلَيْسَ إِنْ رَعَيْتَ الْخَصِبَةَ رَعَيْتَهَا بِقَدَرِ اللهِ ، وَإِنْ رَعَيْتَ الْجَدْبَةَ رَعَيْتَهَا بِقَدَرِ اللهِ ، قَالَ : فَجَاءَ عَبْدُ الرَّحْمَنِ بْنُ عَوْفٍ رَضِيَ اللهُ عَنْهُ ، وَكَانَ مُتَغَيِّباً فِي بَعْضِ حَاجَتِهِ ، فَقَالَ : إِنَّ عِنْدِي مِنْ هَذَا عِلْماً ، سَمِعْتُ رَسُولَ اللهِ صَلَّى اللهُ عَلَيْهِ وَسَلَّمَ يَقُولُ : « إِذَا سَمِعْتُمْ بِهِ بِأَرْضٍ ، فَلاَ تَقْدَمُوا عَلَيْهِ ، وَإِذَا وَقَعَ بِأَرْضٍ وَأَنْتُمْ بِهَا ، فَلاَ تَخْرُجُوا فِرَاراً مِنْهُ » فَحَمِدَ اللهَ تَعَالَى عُمَرُ رَضِيَ اللهُ عَنْهُ وَانْصَرَفَ . مُتَّفَقٌ عَلَيْهِ

1791. **Hazrat Ibn Abbas** (R.A.A.) relates that once Hazrat 'Umar ibn Khattab (R.A.A.) started for Syria. When he reached a place called Sargh, where Hazrat Abu Ubaidah bin Al Jarrah (R.A.A.), the Commander of the Muslim Army stationed and his companions met him and apprised him of the fact that Syria was infested with the epidemic of plague. Hazrat Ibn Abbas (R.A.A.) says that Hazrat Umar (R.A.A.) asked him to bring before him the earlier emigrants; and he accordingly called them. Hazrat 'Umar (R.A.A.) told them that an epidemic had broken out in Syria and sought their opinion; but they differed among themselves. Some of them said: 'You had started on a mission, and it is not proper to return home (without accomplishing it)'. Others said: 'You have among you the Companions of the Holy Prophet (S.A.W.) and many others, and as such it is improper to take them to the infested place.' Hazrat Umar (A.) then asked them to withdraw, and asked him to call the Ansar (local inhabitants of Madina). As such Hazrat Ibn Abbas (R.A.A.) called them, and Hazrat Umar (R.A.A.) consulted them and they followed the course of the Emigrants, and differed among themselves like them. So he asked them also to retire and asked Hazrat Ibn Abbas (R.A.A.) to call the leading Sheikhs of the Quraish out of those emigrants who were present at the conquest of Makkah. Accordingly Hazrat Ibn Abbas (R.A.A.) called them, and not any two of them differed in their views. They told him (with one voice): 'We think that you should return home taking back the people, and do not take the people into the epidemic (infested) land. Accordingly Hazrat 'Umar (R.A.A.) has it announced among the people that he would start for home the next morning. Next morning when all was ready, Hazrat Abu 'Ubaidah ibn Jarrah (R.A.A.) said to Hazrat Umar (R.A.A.): Are you running away from what has been decreed by Allah? Hazrat 'Umar (R.A.A.) replied: Abu 'Ubaidah (R.A.A.), I wish someone else had said this. Hazrat 'Umar (R.A.A.) did not like to be opposed by Hazrat Abu Ubaidah (R.A.A.). He continued: 'Yes, we are running away from (one) decree of Allah, to the other decree of Allah,' and said' 'Suppose you have some camels and you have to halt in a valley and the valley had two sides' One rich in greenery and the other dry and barren; then if you let your camels graze in the green part, would it not be by the will of Allah, or if you were to graze them in the dry part, would it not be by the will of Allah?' Hazrat Ibn Abbas (R.A.A.) continues: 'In the meantime Abdur Rahman bin Auf (R.A.A.) who had been away on some mission, arrived and said: 'I have some knowledge in this matter. I heard the Holy Prophet (S.A.W.) say: 'If you hear of (an epidemic of plague) in a land, then do not go there and if you happen to be in a land (where this epidemic has erupted), then do not run away from it. On hearing this Hazrat 'Umar (R.A.A.) praised Allah, the Exalted and returned from there. *(Bukhari and Muslim)*

١٧٩٢ – وَعَنْ أُسَامَةَ بْنِ زَيْدٍ رَضِيَ اللهُ عَنْهُ عَنِ النَّبِيِّ صَلَّى اللهُ عَلَيْهِ وَسَلَّمَ قَالَ : « إِذَا سَمِعْتُمُ الطَّاعُونَ بِأَرْضٍ ، فَلَا تَدْخُلُوهَا ، وَإِذَا وَقَعَ بِأَرْضٍ ، وَأَنْتُمْ فِيهَا ، فَلَا تَخْرُجُوا مِنْهَا » متفقٌ عليه .

1792. Hazrat Usama bin Zaid (R.A.A.) relates that the Holy Prophet (S.A.W.) said: 'If you hear of the prevalence of plague in a place, do not go there; and if it breaks out in the place where you happen to be, do not run away from there.' *(Bukhari and Muslim)*

* * * * * * *

CHAPTER 362

VEHEMENCE OF PROHIBITION OF MAGIC

قَالَ اللهُ تَعَالَى وَمَا كَفَرَ سُلَيْمَانُ وَلَكِنَّ الشَّيَاطِينَ كَفَرُوا يُعَلِّمُونَ النَّاسَ السِّحْرَ الآيَةَ [البقرة : ١٠٢] .

Allah, the Exalted, said:

408. Solomon disbelieved not: but the devils disbelieved, teaching mankind magic. (2 : 102)

١٧٩٣ - وَعَنْ أَبِي هُرَيْرَةَ رَضِيَ اللهُ عَنْهُ عَنِ النَّبِيِّ صَلَّى اللهُ عَلَيْهِ وَسَلَّمَ قَالَ : « اجْتَنِبُوا السَّبْعَ الْمُوبِقَاتِ » قَالُوا : يَا رَسُولَ اللهِ وَمَا هُنَّ ؟ قَالَ : « الشِّرْكُ بِاللهِ ، وَالسِّحْرُ ، وَقَتْلُ النَّفْسِ الَّتِي حَرَّمَ اللهُ إِلاَّ بِالْحَقِّ ، وَأَكْلُ الرِّبَا ، وَأَكْلُ مَالِ الْيَتِيمِ ، وَالتَّوَلِّي يَوْمَ الزَّحْفِ . وَقَذْفُ الْمُحْصَنَاتِ الْمُؤْمِنَاتِ الْغَافِلاَتِ » متفقٌ عليه .

1793. This Hadis has already been covered in S. No. 1614 of Chapter 286.

Note :— The Holy Quran has amply clarified the reality of magic or sorcery. It is an art which can be acquired through education and training. Magic is a visionery trick and legerdemain. As such magic does not survive long, as (the) Holy Quran has exposed its reality. As against this a miracle is ever lasting as established by the Holy Quran before the sane and wise persons who have accepted it. On the contrary magic is a practice of illiterate persons devoid of wisdom, among whom it is prevalent. (Translator)

* * * * * * *

CHAPTER 363

PROHIBITION OF CARRYING THE QURAN ON A JOURNEY THROUGH THE TERRITORY OF NON-BELIEVERS WHEN IT IS FEARED THAT IT WILL FALL INTO THE HANDS OF ENEMY

١٧٩٤ – عَنْ ابْنِ عُمَرَ رَضِيَ اللهُ عَنْهُمَا قَالَ: « نَهَى رَسُولُ اللهِ صَلَّى اللهُ عَلَيْهِ وَسَلَّمَ أَنْ يُسَافَرَ بِالْقُرْآنِ إِلَى أَرْضِ الْعَدُوِّ » متفقٌ عليه

1794. Hazrat Ibn 'Umar (R.A.A.) relates that the Holy Prophet (S.A.W.) has forbidden carrying of the Holy Quran on a journey through the enemy territory. *(Bukhari and Muslim).*

* * * * * * *

CHAPTER 364

PROHIBITION OF THE USE OF GOLD AND SILVER VESSELS FOR EATING, DRINKING AND PURIFICATION AND FOR OTHER PURPOSES

١٧٩٥ – عَنْ أُمِّ سَلَمَةَ رَضِيَ اللهُ عَنْهَا أَنَّ رَسُولَ اللهِ صَلَّى اللهُ عَلَيْهِ وَسَلَّمَ قَالَ: « الَّذِي يَشْرَبُ فِي آنِيَةِ الْفِضَّةِ إِنَّمَا يُجَرْجِرُ فِي بَطْنِهِ نَارَ جَهَنَّمَ » متفقٌ عَلَيْهِ.

وفي رِوَايةٍ لِمُسْلِمٍ: « إِنَّ الَّذِي يَأْكُلُ أَوْ يَشْرَبُ فِي آنِيةِ الْفِضَّةِ وَالذَّهَبِ ».

1795. This Hadis has already been given in No. 778 of Chapter 116.

١٧٩٦ – وعَنْ حُذَيْفَةَ رَضِيَ اللهُ عَنْهُ قَالَ: إِنَّ النَّبِيَّ صَلَّى اللهُ عَلَيْهِ وَسَلَّمَ نَهَانَا عَنِ الحَرِيرِ، وَالدِّيبَاجِ، وَالشُّرْبِ فِي آنِيَةِ الذَّهَبِ وَالْفِضَّةِ، وقال: « هُنَّ لَهُمْ فِي الدُّنْيَا وَهِيَ لَكُمْ فِي الآخِرَةِ » مُتَّفَقٌ عَلَيْهِ.

وفي روايةٍ في الصَّحِيحَيْنِ عَنْ حُذَيْفَةَ رَضِيَ اللهُ عَنْهُ: سَمِعْتُ رَسُولَ اللهِ صَلَّى اللهُ عَلَيْهِ وسَلَّمَ يقولُ: « لا تَلْبَسُوا الحَرِيرَ وَلا الدِّيبَاجَ، وَلا تَشْرَبُوا فِي آنِيَةِ الذَّهَبِ وَالْفِضَّةِ وَلا تَأْكُلُوا فِي صِحَافِهَا ».

1796. This Hadis has already been given in No. 777 of Chapter 116.

١٧٩٧- وَعَنْ أنس بن سِيرِينَ قالَ: كُنتُ مَعَ أنَس بن مالكٍ رَضِيَ الله عَنْهُ عِنْدَ نَفَرٍ مِنَ المَجُوسِ، فَجِيءَ بِفَالُوذَجٍ عَلى إنَاءٍ مِنْ فِضَّةٍ، فَلَمْ يَأكُلْهُ، فَقِيلَ لَهُ حَوِّلْهُ، فَحَوَّلَهُ عَلى إنَاءٍ مِنْ خَلَنْجٍ، وَجِيءَ بِهِ فَأكَلَهُ. رواه البيهقي بإسْنادٍ حَسَنٍ.

1797. Hazrat Anas bin Sirin (R.A.A.) relates: Once I was with Hazrat Anas bin Malik (R.A.A.) in the company of some magians when a sweet preparation was brought in a silver vessel, but Hazrat Anas (R.A.A.) refused to eat from this vessel. The man who had brought it was told, to change the vessel. Accordingly the vessel was changed and then the sweet preparation was eaten by Hazrat Anas (R.A.A.).

(Baihiqi)

Note :— All the Imams (scholers) are unanimous that to eat or drink from a silver or golden vessel is unlawful for men and women. Also ablution made from such a vessel or using perfume from it is unlawful.

* * * * * * *

CHAPTER 365

PROHIBITION OF PUTTING ON SAFFRON – COLOURED DRESS BY MEN

١٧٩٨- عَنْ أنس رَضِيَ اللهُ عَنْهُ قالَ: نَهَى النَّبيُّ صَلَّى اللهُ عَلَيْهِ وَسَلَّمَ أنْ يَتَزَعْفَرَ الرَّجُلُ. متفقٌ عليه.

1798. Hazrat Anas (R.A.A.) relates that the Holy Prophet (S.A.W.) has forbidden a male person from (wearing) saffron-coloured (dress).

(Bukhari and Muslim)

١٧٩٩- وعَنْ عبدِ اللهِ بنِ عَمْرِو بنِ العاصِ رَضِيَ اللهُ عَنْهُمَا قالَ: رَأى النَّبيُّ صَلَّى اللهُ عَلَيْهِ وَسَلَّمَ عَلَيَّ ثَوْبَيْنِ مُعَصْفَرَيْنِ، فقَالَ: «أمُّكَ أمَرَتْكَ بهذا؟» قلتُ: أغْسِلُهُمَا؟ قال: «بَلْ أحْرِقْهُمَا». وفي روايةٍ، فقالَ: «إنَّ هذا من ثِيَابِ الكُفَّارِ فلا تَلْبَسْهَا» رواه مسلم

1799. Hazrat Abdullah bin ‘Amr bin Al‘Aas (R.A.A.) relates: The Holy Prophet (S.A.W.) saw me wearing two pieces of saffron-coloured garments and asked. ‘Has your mother ordered you to wear these clothes?' I submitted: 'May I wash them out?' He (S.A.W.) added: But burn them.

Another version says: These are garments worn by the infidels, and therefore do not wear them. *(Muslim)*

Note :— The commentators have explained that the Holy Prophet (S.A.W.) meant by burning to get rid of the same by sale or handing over to some female as they were allowed to wear such clothes, and not to destroy them by burning.

* * * * * * *

CHAPTER 366

PROHIBITION OF VOWING SILENCE FOR A DAY TILL NIGHT

١٨٠٠ – عَنْ عَلِيٍّ رَضِيَ اللهُ عَنْهُ قَالَ : حَفِظْتُ عَنْ رَسُولِ اللهِ صَلَّى اللهُ عَلَيْهِ وَسَلَّمَ : « لا يُتْمَ بَعْدَ احْتِلامٍ ، وَلا صُمَاتَ يَوْمٍ إلى اللَّيْلِ » رواه أبو داود بإسنادٍ حسن .

1800. Hazrat Ali (R.A.A.) relates: 'I have preserved in my memory the saying of the Holy Prophet (S.A.W.) that: 'No one remains an orphan after he attains majority nor there is any sense in remaining silent from morning till night. *(Abu Daud* cited with good chains.)

١٨٠١ – وعَنْ قيسِ بنِ أبي حازِمٍ قالَ : دَخَلَ أبُو بكرٍ الصِّدِّيقُ رَضِيَ اللهُ عَنْهُ عَلى امْرأةٍ مِنْ أحْمَسَ يُقَالُ لَها : زَيْنَبُ ، فَرَآها لاتَتَكَلَّمُ . فقالَ : مالَها لاتَتَكَلَّمُ ؟ فقالُوا : حَجَّتْ مُصْمِتَةً ، فقالَ لها : تَكَلَّمِي فإنَّ هذا لايَحِلُّ ، هذا مِنْ عَمَلِ الجاهِلِيَّةِ ! فتَكَلَّمَتْ . رواه البخاري .

1801. Hazrat Qais bin Abu Hazim (R.A.A.) relates that once Hazrat Abu Bakr (R.A.A.) met a woman of Ahmas tribe who was known as Zainab; he found that she did not talk. He inquired as to why she did not speak? The people told him that she had sworn to be silent. He said: Speak to me as it is unlawful and an act of the days of Ignorance. Thereupon she started speaking. *(Bukhari)*

* * * * * * *

CHAPTER 367

IT IS UNLAWFUL TO ATTRIBUTE FATHERHOOD TO SOMEBODY ELSE BY A SON AND WRONG MASTERSHIP BY A SLAVE

١٨٠٢ – عَنْ سَعْدِ بنِ أبي وَقَّاصٍ رَضِيَ اللهُ عَنْهُ أنَّ النَّبِيَّ صَلَّى اللهُ عَلَيْهِ وَسَلَّمَ قَالَ : « مَنِ ادَّعَى إلى غَيْرِ أبِيهِ وَهُوَ يَعْلَمُ أنَّهُ غَيْرُ أبِيهِ ، فالجَنَّةُ عَلَيْهِ حَرَامٌ » متفقٌ عليهِ .

1802. Hazrat Sa'd bin Abi Waqqas (R.A.A.) relates that the Holy Prophet (S.A.W.) said: A person who attributes his fatherhood to someone other than his father, knowing that he is not his father, for such a person paradise will be forbiddn. *(Bukhari and Muslim)*

١٨٠٣ – وعَنْ أبي هُرَيْرَةَ رَضِيَ اللهُ عَنْهُ عَنِ النَّبِيِّ صَلَّى اللهُ عَلَيْهِ وَسَلَّمَ قَالَ : « لاتَرْغَبُوا عَنْ آبَائِكُمْ ، فَمَنْ رَغِبَ عَنْ أبِيهِ ،فَهُوَ كُفْرٌ » متفقٌ عليه .

1803. Hazrat Abu Hurairah (R.A.A.) relates that the Holy Prophet (S.A.W.) said: 'Do not feel ashamed of your relationship with your father because a person who turns away from his father commits infidelity (Kufr). *(Bukhari and Muslim)*

١٨٠٤ – وعَنْ يزيدَ بنِ شريكِ بنِ طارقٍ قالَ : رَأيْتُ عَلِيّاً رَضِيَ اللهُ عَنْهُ على المِنبَرِ يَخْطُبُ ، فَسَمِعْتُهُ يَقُولُ : لا وَاللهِ مَاعِنْدَنَا مِنْ كِتَابٍ نَقْرَؤُهُ إلاَّ كِتَابَ اللهِ ، وَمَا في هذهِ الصَّحِيفَةِ ، فَنَشَرَهَا فإذا فِيهَا أسْنَانُ الإبِلِ ، وَأشْيَاءُ مِنَ الجِرَاحَاتِ ، وَفِيهَا : قالَ رَسولُ اللهِ صَلَّى اللهُ عَلَيْهِ وَسَلَّمَ : « المَدِينَةُ حَرَمٌ مَابَيْنَ عَيْرٍ إلى ثَوْرٍ ، فَمَنْ أحْدَثَ فِيهَا حَدَثاً، أوْ آوَى مُحْدِثاً ،فَعَلَيْهِ لَعْنَةُ اللهِ وَالمَلائِكَةِ وَالنَّاسِ أجْمَعِينَ ، لايَقْبَلُ اللهُ مِنْهُ يَوْمَ القِيَامَةِ صَرْفاً وَلا عَدْلاً ، ذِمَّةُ المُسْلِمِينَ وَاحِدَةٌ ، يَسْعَى بِهَا أدْنَاهُمْ ، فَمَنْ أخْفَرَ مُسْلِماً،فَعَلَيْهِ لَعْنَةُ اللهِ وَالمَلائِكَةِ وَالنَّاسِ أجْمَعِينَ . لايَقْبَلُ اللهُ مِنْهُ يَوْمَ القِيَامَةِ صَرْفاً وَلا عَدْلاً ، وَمَنِ ادَّعَى إلى غَيْرِ أبِيهِ ، أوِ انْتَمَى إلى غَيْرِ مَوَالِيهِ ، فَعَلَيْهِ لَعْنَةُ اللهِ وَالمَلائِكَةِ

وَالنَّاسِ أَجْمَعِينَ ، لايَقْبَلُ اللهُ مِنْهُ يَوْمَ الْقِيَامَةِ صَرْفًا وَلا عَدْلاً » متفقٌ عليه .

1804. Hazrat Yazeed bin Shareek bin Tariq says that; I saw Hazrat Ali (R.A.A.) delivering a sermon from the pulpit wherein I heard him saying: 'By Allah! We have no other book but the Holy Quran which we read and ~~this book~~. When we open this book we find that it contains an account of the ages of the camels (Zakat limit), and some orders regarding indemnity for blood. This book also mentions that the Holy Prophet (S.A.W.) has said that the area from 'Aer mountain in Madina upto Saur mountain in Mecca is Haram area (a sancturay or sacred place). Therefore, anybody who introduces an innovation (in Islam) in this area, or gives shelter to an innovator, then Allah's, His angels' and the entire humanity's curse be upon him. Allah will not accept any expiation or compensation from him till the Day of Judgement. All the Muslims are equal in status and obligation. The lowest can offer protection. Any body who violates his protection and humiliates a Muslim, will be cursed by Allah, His angles and the entire humanity till the Day of Judgement, nor He will accept expiation or compensation from him. And a person who attributes wrong fatherhood to himself, or a slave who runs away from his master to somebody else, then Allah's, His angels' and the entire humanity's curse will be upon him. Allah will not accept any expiation or compensation from him. *(Bukhari and Muslim)*

١٨٠٥ — وَعَنْ أَبِي ذَرٍّ رَضِيَ اللهُ عَنْهُ أَنَّهُ سَمِعَ رَسولَ اللهِ صَلَّى اللهُ عليهِ وَسَلَّمَ يَقُولُ : « لَيْسَ مِنْ رَجُلٍ ادَّعَى لِغَيْرِ أَبِيهِ وَهُوَ يَعْلَمُهُ إلاَّ كَفَرَ ، وَمَنِ ادَّعَى مَالَيْسَ لَهُ ، فَلَيْسَ مِنَّا ، وَلْيَتَبَوَّأْ مَقْعَدَهُ مِنَ النَّارِ ، وَمَنْ دَعَا رَجُلاً بِالْكُفْرِ ، أَوْ قالَ : عَدُوَّ اللهِ ، وَلَيْسَ كَذَلِكَ إلاَّ حَارَ عَلَيْهِ » مُتَّفَقٌ عَلَيْهِ وَهَذا لَفظُ روايةِ مُسْلِمٍ .

1805. Hazrat Abu Zarr (R.A.A.) says that he heard the Holy Prophet (S.A.W.) say: A person who deliberately attributes somebody else as his father committed infidelity; and one who claimed a thing which does not belong to him, is not one of us. He should make his seat in the Hell. If a person calls another an unbeliever or an enemy of Allah, and he is not like that, the charge will revert on the accuser. *(Bukhari and Muslim)*

* * * * * * *

CHAPTER 368

SEVEREST ADMONITION FOR COMMITTING THOSE THINGS WHICH ARE PROHIBITED BY ALLAH AND HIS HOLY PROPHET (S.A.W.)

قالَ اللهُ تَعَالى : (فَلْيَحْذَرِ الَّذِينَ يُخَالِفُونَ عَنْ أَمْرِهِ أَنْ تُصِيبَهُمْ فِتْنَةٌ أَوْ يُصِيبَهُمْ عَذَابٌ أَلِيمٌ) [النور : ٦٣] . وقالَ تَعَالى : (وَيُحَذِّرُكُمُ اللهُ نَفْسَهُ) [آل عمران : ٣٠] . وقالَ تعَالى : (إِنَّ بَطْشَ رَبِّكَ لَشَدِيدٌ) [البروج : ١٢] . وقالَ تَعَالى : (وَكَذَلِكَ أَخْذُ رَبِّكَ إِذَا أَخَذَ الْقُرَى وَهِيَ ظَالِمَةٌ إِنَّ أَخْذَهُ أَلِيمٌ شَدِيدٌ) [هود : ١٠٢] .

Allah the Exalted has said:

409. And let those who conspire to evade orders beware lest grief or painful punishment befall them. (24 : 63)

410. Allah biddeth you beware of Him. (3 . 30)

411. Lo! the punishment of Thy Lord is stern. (85 : 12)

412. Even thus is the grasp of Thy Lord when He graspeth the townships while they are doing wrong. Lo! His grasp is painful, very strong. (11 : 102)

١٨٠٦ – وَعَنْ أَبِي هُرَيْرَةَ رَضِيَ اللهُ عَنْهُ أَنَّ النَّبِيَّ صَلَّى اللهُ عَلَيْهِ وَسَلَّمَ قَالَ : « إِنَّ اللهَ تَعَالى يَغَارُ ، وَغَيْرَةَ اللهِ أَنْ يَأْتِيَ الْمَرْءُ مَاحَرَّمَ اللهُ عَلَيْهِ » متفقٌ عليه .

1806. **Hazrat Abu Hurairah** (R.A.A.) reports that the Holy Prophet (S.A.W.) said: Allah, the Exalted, is Most self-respecting (very particular about His orders) and to challenge His self-respect is to do a thing which He has forbidden.

(Bukhari and Muslim)

CHAPTER 369

WHAT A PERSON SHOULD SAY OR DO WHO COMMITS PROHIBITED ACTS

قَالَ اللهُ تَعَالَى : (وَإِمَّا يَنْزَغَنَّكَ مِنَ الشَّيْطَانِ نَزْغٌ فَاسْتَعِذْ بِاللهِ) [فصلت : ٣٦] . وقَالَ تَعَالَى : (إِنَّ الَّذِينَ اتَّقَوْا إِذَا مَسَّهُمْ طَائِفٌ مِنَ الشَّيْطَانِ تَذَكَّرُوا فَإِذَا هُمْ مُبْصِرُونَ) [الأعراف : ٢٠١] . وقَالَ تَعَالَى : (وَالَّذِينَ إِذَا فَعَلُوا فَاحِشَةً ، أَوْ ظَلَمُوا أَنْفُسَهُمْ ، ذَكَرُوا اللهَ فَاسْتَغْفَرُوا لِذُنُوبِهِمْ ، وَمَنْ يَغْفِرُ الذُّنُوبَ إِلاَّ اللهُ ، وَلَمْ يُصِرُّوا عَلَى مَافَعَلُوا وَهُمْ يَعْلَمُونَ ، أُولَئِكَ جَزَاؤُهُمْ مَغْفِرَةٌ مِنْ رَبِّهِمْ ، وَجَنَّاتٌ تَجْرِي مِنْ تَحْتِهَا الأَنْهَارُ خَالِدِينَ فِيهَا ، وَنِعْمَ أَجْرُ الْعَامِلِينَ) [آل عمران : ١٣٥ ، ١٣٦] . وقال تَعَالَى : (وَتُوبُوا إِلَى اللهِ جَمِيعاً أَيُّهَا الْمُؤْمِنُونَ لَعَلَّكُمْ تُفْلِحُونَ) [النور : ٣١ .]

Allah, the Exalted has said:

413. And if a whisper from the devil reach thee (O Muhammad) then seek refuge in Allah. (41 : 36)

414. Lo! those who ward off (evil), when a glamour from the devil troubleth them, they do but remember (Allah's guidance) and behold them seers. (7 : 201)

415. And those who, when they do an evil thing or wrong themselves, remember Allah and implore forgiveness for their sins—Who forgiveth sins save Allah only?—and will not knowingly repeat (the wrong) they did. The reward of such will be forgiveness from their Lord, and Gardens underneath which rivers flow, wherein they will abide for ever—a bountiful reward for workers! (3 : 135—136)

416. And turn unto Allah together, O believers, in order that ye may succeed. (24 : 31)

١٨٠٧ — وَعَنْ أَبِي هُرَيْرَةَ رَضِيَ اللهُ عَنْهُ عَنِ النَّبِيِّ صَلَّى اللهُ عَلَيْهِ وَسَلَّمَ قَالَ : « مَنْ حَلَفَ فَقَالَ فِي حَلِفِهِ : بِاللاَّتِ وَالْعُزَّى ، فَلْيَقُلْ :

لاإلهَ إلاَّ اللهُ ، وَمَنْ قَالَ لِصَاحِبِهِ : تَعَالَ أُقَامِرْكَ ، فَلْيَتَصَدَّقْ » .

متفقٌ عليه

1807. Hazrat Abu Hurairah (R.A.A.) relates that the Holy Prophet (S.A.W.) said. A person who takes an oath and swears (by error): 'By Lat and Uzzah', should at once affirm. 'There is no god save Allah.' And one who invites his companions: 'Come let us gamble,' should (condone his sin) by giving charity.

(Bukhari and Muslim)

* * * * * * *

CHAPTER 370

MISCELLANEOUS TRADITIONS OF WISDOM AND KNOWLEDGE

١٨٠٨ – عَنِ النَّوَاسِ بنِ سَمْعَانَ رَضِيَ اللهُ عَنْهُ قَالَ : ذَكَرَ رَسُولُ اللهِ صَلَّى اللهُ عَلَيْهِ وَسَلَّمَ الدَّجَّالَ ذَاتَ غَدَاةٍ ، فَخَفَّضَ فِيهِ ، وَرَفَّعَ حَتَّى ظَنَنَّاه فِي طَائِفَةِ النَّخْلِ . فَلَمَّا رُحْنَا إِلَيْهِ ، عَرَفَ ذَلِكَ فِينَا ، فقالَ : « مَاشَأْنُكُمْ ؟ » قُلْنَا: يارَسُولَ اللهِ ذَكَرْتَ الدَّجَّالَ الْغَدَاةَ ، فَخَفَّضْتَ فِيهِ وَرَفَّعْتَ ، حَتَّى ظَنَنَّاه فِي طَائِفَةِ النَّخْلِ فقالَ : « غَيْرُ الدَّجَّالِ أَخْوَفُنِي عَلَيْكُمْ ؛ إنْ يَخْرجْ وأنَا فِيكُمْ ، فَأَنَا حَجِيجُهُ دونَكُمْ ؛ وَإِنْ يَخْرجْ وَلَسْتُ فِيكُمْ ، فَامْرُؤٌ حَجِيجُ نَفْسِهِ ، وَاللهُ خَلِيفَتِي عَلَى كُلِّ مُسْلِمٍ . إنَّه شَابٌّ قَطَطٌ عَيْنُهُ طَافِيَةٌ ، كأنِّي أُشَبِّهُهُ بِعَبْدِ الْعُزَّى بنِ قَطَنٍ ، فَمَنْ أَدْرَكَهُ مِنْكُمْ ، فَلْيَقْرَأْ عَلَيْهِ فَوَاتِحَ سُورَةِ الْكَهْفِ ؛ إنَّه خَارِجٌ خَلَّةً بَيْنَ الشَّامِ وَالْعِرَاقِ ، فَعَاثَ يَمِيناً وَعَاثَ شِمَالاً ، ياعِبَادَ اللهِ فَاثْبُتُوا » قُلْنَا : يارسولَ اللهِ وَمَا لُبْثُهُ فِي الأَرْضِ ؟ قالَ : « أَرْبَعُونَ يَوْماً : يَوْمٌ كَسَنَةٍ ، وَيَوْمٌ كَشَهْرٍ ، وَيَوْمٌ كجُمُعَةٍ ، وَسَائِرُ أَيَّامِهِ كَأَيَّامِكُمْ » قُلْنَا : يا رَسُولَ اللهِ ، فَذلكَ الْيَوْمُ الَّذِي كَسَنَةٍ أَتَكْفِينَا فِيهِ صَلاةُ يَوْمٍ ؟ قال : « لا ، أَقْدُرُوا لَهُ قَدْرَهُ » قُلْنَا : يَارَسُولَ اللهِ وَمَا إِسْرَاعُهُ فِي الأَرْضِ ؟ قالَ : « كَالْغَيْثِ اسْتَدْبَرَتْهُ الرِّيحُ ، فَيَأْتِي عَلَى

الْقَوْمِ ،فَيَدْعُوهُمْ ، فَيُؤْمِنُونَ بِهِ ، وَيَسْتَجِيبُونَ لَهُ فَيَأْمُرُ السَّمَاءَ فَتُمْطِرُ ، وَالْأَرْضَ فَتُنْبِتُ ، فَتَرُوحُ عَلَيْهِمْ سَارِحَتُهُمْ أَطْوَلَ مَا كَانَتْ ذُرىً ، وَأَسْبَغَهُ ضُرُوعاً ، وَأَمَدَّهُ خَوَاصِرَ ، ثُمَّ يَأْتِي الْقَوْمَ فَيَدْعُوهُمْ ، فَيَرُدُّونَ عَلَيْهِ قَوْلَهُ ، فَيَنْصَرِفُ عَنْهُمْ ، فَيُصْبِحُونَ مُمْحِلِينَ لَيْسَ بِأَيْدِيهِمْ شَيْءٌ مِنْ أَمْوَالِهِمْ ، وَيَمُرُّ بِالْخَرِبَةِ فَيَقُولُ لَهَا : أَخْرِجِي كُنُوزَكِ ، فَتَتْبَعُهُ كُنُوزُهَا كَيَعَاسِيبِ النَّحْلِ ، ثُمَّ يَدْعُو رَجُلاً مُمْتَلِئاً شَبَاباً فَيَضْرِبُهُ بِالسَّيْفِ ، فَيَقْطَعُهُ جِزْلَتَيْنِ رَمْيَةَ الْغَرَضِ ، ثُمَّ يَدْعُوهُ ،فَيُقْبِلُ ، وَيَتَهَلَّلُ وَجْهُهُ يَضْحَكُ ،فَبَيْنَمَا هُوَ كَذَلِكَ إِذْ بَعَثَ اللهُ تَعَالَى الْمَسِيحَ ابْنَ مَرْيَمَ ، صَلَّى اللهُ عَلَيْهِ وَسَلَّمَ ، فَيَنْزِلُ عِنْدَ الْمَنَارَةِ الْبَيْضَاءِ شَرْقِيَّ دِمَشْقَ بَيْنَ مَهْرُودَتَيْنِ ، وَاضِعاً كَفَّيْهِ عَلَى أَجْنِحَةِ مَلَكَيْنِ ، إِذَا طَأْطَأَ رَأْسَهُ ، قَطَرَ وَإِذَا رَفَعَهُ تَحَدَّرَ مِنْهُ جُمَانٌ كَاللُّؤْلُؤِ ، فَلَا يَحِلُّ لِكَافِرٍ يَجِدُ رِيحَ نَفَسِهِ إِلَّا مَاتَ ، وَنَفَسُهُ يَنْتَهِي إِلَى حَيْثُ يَنْتَهِي طَرْفُهُ ، فَيَطْلُبُهُ حَتَّى يُدْرِكَهُ بِبَابِ لُدٍّ فَيَقْتُلُهُ ، ثُمَّ يَأْتِي عِيسَى ، صَلَّى اللهُ عَلَيْهِ وَسَلَّمَ قَوْماً قَدْ عَصَمَهُمُ اللهُ مِنْهُ ،فَيَمْسَحُ عَنْ وُجُوهِهِمْ ،وَيُحَدِّثُهُمْ بِدَرَجَاتِهِمْ فِي الْجَنَّةِ ، فَبَيْنَمَا هُوَ كَذَلِكَ إِذْ أَوْحَى اللهُ تَعَالَى إِلَى عِيسَى صَلَّى اللهُ عَلَيْهِ وَسَلَّمَ أَنِّي قَدْ أَخْرَجْتُ عِبَاداً لِي لَا يَدَانِ لِأَحَدٍ بِقِتَالِهِمْ ، فَحَرِّزْ عِبَادِي إِلَى الطُّورِ . وَيَبْعَثُ اللهُ يَأْجُوجَ وَمَأْجُوجَ وَهُمْ مِنْ كُلِّ حَدَبٍ يَنْسِلُونَ ، فَيَمُرُّ أَوَائِلُهُمْ عَلَى بُحَيْرَةِ طَبَرِيَّةَ فَيَشْرَبُونَ مَا فِيهَا ، وَيَمُرُّ آخِرُهُمْ فَيَقُولُونَ : لَقَدْ كَانَ بِهَذِهِ مَرَّةً مَاءٌ ، وَيُحْصَرُ نَبِيُّ اللهِ عِيسَى ، صَلَّى اللهُ عَلَيْهِ وَسَلَّمَ ، وَأَصْحَابُهُ حَتَّى يَكُونَ رَأْسُ الثَّوْرِ لِأَحَدِهِمْ خَيْراً مِنْ مِائَةِ دِينَارٍ لِأَحَدِكُمُ الْيَوْمَ ، فَيَرْغَبُ نَبِيُّ اللهِ عِيسَى ، صَلَّى اللهُ عَلَيْهِ وَسَلَّمَ ، وَأَصْحَابُهُ ، رَضِيَ اللهُ عَنْهُمْ ، إِلَى اللهِ تَعَالَى ، فَيُرْسِلُ اللهُ تَعَالَى

عَلَيْهِمُ النَّغَفَ فِي رِقَابِهِمْ ، فَيُصْبِحُونَ فَرْسَى كَمَوْتِ نَفْسٍ وَاحِدَةٍ
ثُمَّ يَهْبِطُ نَبِيُّ اللهِ عِيسَى ، صَلَّى اللهُ عَلَيْهِ وَسَلَّمَ ، وَأَصْحَابُهُ رَضِيَ اللهُ
عَنْهُمْ ، إِلَى الأَرْضِ ، فَلاَ يَجِدُونَ فِي الأَرْضِ مَوْضِعَ شِبْرٍ إِلاَّ مَلأَهُ
زَهَمُهُمْ وَنَتْنُهُمْ ، فَيَرْغَبُ نَبِيُّ اللهِ عِيسَى ، صَلَّى اللهُ عَلَيْهِ وَسَلَّمَ ،
وَأَصْحَابُهُ رَضِيَ اللهُ عَنْهُمْ إِلَى اللهِ تَعَالَى ، فَيُرْسِلُ اللهُ تَعَالَى طَيْراً
كَأَعْنَاقِ الْبُخْتِ ، فَتَحْمِلُهُمْ ، فَتَطْرَحُهُمْ حَيْثُ شَاءَ اللهُ ، ثُمَّ يُرْسِلُ
اللهُ عَزَّ وَجَلَّ مَطَراً لاَ يَكُنُّ مِنْهُ بَيْتُ مَدَرٍ وَلاَ وَبَرٍ ، فَيَغْسِلُ
الأَرْضَ حَتَّى يَتْرُكَهَا كَالزَّلَقَةِ ، ثُمَّ يُقَالُ لِلأَرْضِ : أَنْبِتِي ثَمَرَتَكِ ،
وَرُدِّي بَرَكَتَكِ ، فَيَوْمَئِذٍ تَأْكُلُ الْعِصَابَةُ مِنَ الرُّمَّانَةِ ، وَيَسْتَظِلُّونَ
بِقِحْفِهَا ، وَيُبَارَكُ فِي الرِّسْلِ حَتَّى إِنَّ اللِّقْحَةَ مِنَ الإِبِلِ لَتَكْفِي الْفِئَامَ
مِنَ النَّاسِ ، وَاللِّقْحَةَ مِنَ الْبَقَرِ لَتَكْفِي الْقَبِيلَةَ مِنَ النَّاسِ ، وَاللِّقْحَةَ
مِنَ الْغَنَمِ لَتَكْفِي الْفَخِذَ مِنَ النَّاسِ ، فَبَيْنَمَا هُمْ كَذَلِكَ إِذْ بَعَثَ
اللهُ تَعَالَى رِيحاً طَيِّبَةً ، فَتَأْخُذُهُمْ تَحْتَ آبَاطِهِمْ ، فَتَقْبِضُ رُوحَ
٣٥٨
كُلِّ مُؤْمِنٍ وَكُلِّ مُسْلِمٍ ، وَيَبْقَى شِرَارُ النَّاسِ يَتَهَارَجُونَ فِيهَا
تَهَارُجَ الْحُمُرِ فَعَلَيْهِمْ تَقُومُ السَّاعَةُ ، رواه مسلم .

1808. **Hazrat Nawwas bin Sam'an (R.A.A.)** says that one morning the Holy Prophet (S.A.W.) said something about the Anti-Christ (Dajjal), and described him at times as mean and at times so huge that we thought that he might be just then present somewhere in the oasis (date-palm garden) close by. When we returned from the Holy Prophet (S.A.W.), he (S.A.W.) could notice our discomfiture, and asked us: What is the matter with you? We said: O Messenger of Allah (S.A.W.), when you talked about the Anti-Christ this morning at times you described him so low and at another time you talked of him as huge, so that we were led to believe that he might be present somewhere in the oasis (the date palm garden). He (S.A.W.) said: I am not so much worried about you as regards Anti-Chirst. If he appears while I am among you, I will defend you against him; but if he appears when I am no more between you, then everyone of you is to look after himself. And Allah will be the guardian of every Muslim in my absence. The Anti-Christ will be a young man with rough hair and one of his eyes will be protruded. I think that he might be resembling Abdul Uzza bin

Qatan. Any body who comes across him, should recite on him the opening verses of *Sura Al-Kahf* (Chapter 18). He will come from the road between Syria and Iraq, and will cause destruction and bloodshed on right and left. O the bondsmen of Allah, remain steadfast.

We submitted. O Messenger of Allah (S.A.W.)! How long will he remain on the earth?' He (S.A.W.) answered. '(For) forty days, but one day (of this spell) will be as long as a year, another day will be like a month, one day will be as long as a week and the rest of his days will be like your normal days. We submitted: O Messenger of Allah (S.A.W.)! On the day which will be as long as a year, will it be enough for us to offer the usual daily five prayers?' He (S.A.W.) answered: 'No, You should make an appropriate calculation of the duration of the day.' We further submitted. O Messenger of Allah (S.A.W.)! With what speed will he travel on the earth? He (S.A.W.) answered: (He will pass) like a cloud pushed by the wind. He. will (then) approach a people, and will invite them (to join him), and that nation will believe in him, and will accept his call. He will direct the sky which will shower rain on these people, the earth will produce plenty of greenery. When, in the evening the cattle of these people will come back to them, they will have fattened humps and their udders lengthened (with abundant milk), and their sides fully developed. Thereafter he will come to another people, and will ask them to obey him, but the said people will reject his call. The Anti-Christ will then leave them. Soon thereafter they will get famine stricken, and lose their property. The Anti-Christ will then pass through deserted place, and will call it to throw out its treasures, and its treasures will follow him like swarms of bees. After this he will call a youngman in blooming health. The Anti-Christ will strike him with his sword and cut him into two pieces These pieces will be placed separate from each other at a distance of an arrow target. He will then summon the dead person, who will return to life, and come back with a happy and smiling countenance While he will be in their midst (in this condition), Allah, the Exalted will send the Messiah (Christ) son of Mary, (Peace be upon him) who will descend (Upon the earth) near the Eastern white minaret in Damascus, clad in two saffron coloured garments, with his two hands resting on the arms of two angels. When he will bend his head, drops of water will fall from it, and when he will raise it, white drops like pearls will fall from it. A heretic (non-believer) who gets his smell will die; and his smell will go as far as his sight. He (Christ) will search the Anti-Christ and will catch hold of him at the gate of Lud (Lydda) (near Jerusalem), and will kill him. Hazrat Isa (Christ) will, thereafter, go to the people whom Allah has kept immune from the Anti-Christ. He will then wipe out their faces, and let them know their grades in paradise At this time Hazrat Isa (Christ) will receive a message from Allah, the Most High stating: 'I have brought out some servants of mine with whom nobody has power to fight. As such you take my servants in safety to Mount Tur (Sinai).

Allah, will then send Gog and Magog, who will descend from every height. (Ref: verse 96, Chapter 21, the Holy Quran). Their vanguard will pass over Lake Tabariah (Sea of Galilee) and drink up all its water; their rear-guard will also pass from there and will remark: At one time this place had water. The Prophet of Allah, Isa (Christ) (peace be upon him) and his companions will be besieged (and put to hardships) till a bull's head will appear to them better than hundred Dinars of yours today.

Then the Prophet of Allah, Hazrat Isa (Christ, Peace be upon him) and his companions (with whom Allah the Exalted will be pleased). will turn to Him, and will pray to Him, so that Allah, the Exalted will create a germ in the necks of these people (Gog and Magog) as a result of which they will all die suddenly by the next morning. Thereafter, the Prophet of Allah, Hazrat Isa (Christ, peace be upon him) and his companions, will descend from the mountain but will not find space equal to one span free from the dead bodies of the followers of Gog and Magog, and the offensive smell therefrom. Then the Prophet of Allah, Hazrat Isa (Christ, peace be upon him), and his companions will pray to Allah the Exalted, Who will send some birds as big as the necks of (huge) camels which will carry these (decomposed) dead bodies and drop them wherever Allah, wills. Thereafter, Allah will cause rain to fall whereby every dwelling place whether made of clay or of hair, will be thoroughly cleansed and look like a glass. Then the earth will be asked to produce its fruits and to return the bounties (deposited in its bosom). (As such there will be so much abundance and blessing) that a pomegranate will be sufficient to feed a party, which will be able to get shelter under the shade of pomegranate leaves. Milk will be so much in abundance that the produce of one she-camel will be enough to feed a big party and that of a cow will yield sufficient milk to cater for a tribe and that of a goat will be sufficient for a family. This time will pass when Allah, the Exalted will send a pleasant breeze which will touch the Muslims under their armpits, thereby every believer and Muslim will pass away (peacefully). After this only the debased type of people will be left who will practice sexual acts with women openly unabashedly like donkeys, and on such persons the Day of Judgement will dawn. *(Muslim)*

١٨٠٩ – وَعَنْ رِبْعِيِّ بْنِ حِرَاشٍ قَالَ : انطَلَقْتُ مَعَ أَبِي مَسْعُودٍ الأَنْصَارِيِّ إلى حُذَيْفَةَ بْنِ الْيَمَانِ رَضِيَ اللهُ عَنْهُمْ فَقَالَ لَهُ أَبُو مسعودٍ ، حَدِّثْنِي مَا سَمِعْتَ مِنْ رَسُولِ اللهِ صَلَّى اللهُ عَلَيْهِ وَسَلَّمَ ، في الدَّجَّالِ قَالَ : « إنَّ الدَّجَّالَ يَخْرُجُ ، وَإنَّ مَعَهُ ماءً وَنَاراً ؛ فَأَمَّا الَّذِي يَرَاهُ النَّاسُ ماءً فَنَارٌ تُحْرِقُ ، وَأَمَّا الَّذِي يَرَاهُ النَّاسُ نَاراً ، فَمَاءٌ بَارِدٌ عَذْبٌ ، فَمَنْ

أَدْرَكَهُ مِنْكُمْ ، فَلْيَقَعْ فِي الَّذِي يَرَاهُ نَاراً ، فَإِنَّهُ مَاءٌ عَذْبٌ طَيِّبٌ » فَقَالَ أَبُو مَسْعُودٍ : وَأَنَا قَدْ سَمِعْتُهُ . مُتَّفَقٌ عَلَيْهِ .

1809. Hazrat Rib'ie bin Hirash (R.A.A.) relates: Once I went with Hazrat Abu Mas'ud Ansari (R.A.A.) to Hazrat Huzaifah bin Al Yaman (R.A.A.) when Hazrat Abu Mas'ud (R.A.A.) said to him. Please, tell me what you heard from the Holy Prophet (S.A.W.) about the Anti-Christ. He said: When Anti-Christ will appear, he will have water and fire with him. The thing which the people may consider as water will actually be fire; and the thing which the people may consider as fire, will be the cool and sweet water. Therefore, anyone of you who happens to be at that time, should jump into that which he thinks as fire, for that will be sweet and palatable water. Hazrat Abu Mas'ud (R.A.A.) said. I have also heard this (from the Holy Prophet S.A.W.). *(Bukhari and Muslim)*

١٨١٠ – وَعَنْ عَبْدِ اللهِ بْنِ عَمْرِو بْنِ العَاصِ رَضِيَ اللهُ عَنْهُمَا قَالَ : قَالَ رَسُولُ اللهِ صَلَّى اللهُ عليه وَسَلَّمَ : « يَخْرُجُ الدَّجَّالُ فِي أُمَّتِي فَيَمْكُثُ أَرْبَعِينَ ، لا أَدْرِي أَرْبَعِينَ يَوْماً ، أَوْ أَرْبَعِينَ شَهْراً ، أَوْ أَرْبَعِينَ عَاماً . فَيَبْعَثُ اللهُ تَعَالَى عِيسَى ابْنَ مَرْيَمَ ، صَلَّى اللهُ عَلَيْهِ وَسَلَّمَ ، فَيَطْلُبُهُ فَيُهْلِكُهُ ، ثُمَّ يَمْكُثُ النَّاسُ سَبْعَ سِنِينَ لَيْسَ بَيْنَ اثْنَيْنِ عَدَاوَةٌ ، ثُمَّ يُرْسِلُ اللهُ ، عَزَّ وَجَلَّ ، رِيحاً بَارِدَةً مِنْ قِبَلِ الشَّامِ ، فَلا يَبْقَى عَلَى وَجْهِ الأَرْضِ أَحَدٌ فِي قَلْبِهِ مِثْقَالُ ذَرَّةٍ مِنْ خَيْرٍ أَوْ إِيمَانٍ إِلاَّ قَبَضَتْهُ ، حَتَّى لَوْ أَنَّ أَحَدَكُمْ دَخَلَ فِي كَبِدِ جَبَلٍ ، لَدَخَلَتْهُ عَلَيْهِ حَتَّى تَقْبِضَهُ ، فَيَبْقَى شِرَارُ النَّاسِ فِي خِفَّةِ الطَّيْرِ ، وَأَحْلامِ السِّبَاعِ لايَعْرِفُونَ مَعْرُوفاً ، وَلا يُنْكِرُونَ مُنْكَراً ، فَيَتَمَثَّلُ لَهُمُ الشَّيْطَانُ ، فَيَقُولُ : أَلا تَسْتَجِيبُونَ ؟ فَيَقُولُونَ : فَمَا تَأْمُرُنَا ؟ فَيَأْمُرُهُمْ بِعِبَادَةِ الأَوْثَانِ ، وَهُمْ فِي ذَلِكَ دَارٌّ رِزْقُهُمْ ، حَسَنٌ عَيْشُهُمْ ، ثُمَّ يُنْفَخُ فِي الصُّورِ ، فَلا يَسْمَعُهُ أَحَدٌ إِلاَّ أَصْغَى لِيتاً وَرَفَعَ لِيتاً ، وَأَوَّلُ مَنْ يَسْمَعُهُ رَجُلٌ يَلُوطُ حَوْضَ إِبِله فَيَصْعَقُ وَيَصْعَقُ النَّاسُ ، ثُمَّ يُرْسِلُ اللهُ – أَوْ قَالَ : يُنْزِلُ اللهُ – مَطَراً كَأَنَّهُ الطَّلُّ أَوِ الظِّلُّ ، فَتَنْبُتُ مِنْهُ أَجْسَادُ النَّاسِ ،

ثم ينفخ فيه أخرى فإذا هم قيام ينظرون ، ثم يقال : يا أيها الناس
هلم إلى ربكم ، وقفوهم إنهم مسؤولون ، ثم يقال : أخرجوا
بعث النار فيقال : من كم ؟ فيقال : من كل ألف تسعمائة
وتسعة وتسعين ؛ فذلك يوم يجعل الولدان شيبا ، وذلك يوم يكشف
عن ساق » رواه مسلم .

1810. Hazrat Abdullah Ibn 'Amr bin Al 'Aas (R.A.A.) relates that the Holy Prophet (S.A.W.) said: Anti-Christ will appear among my Umma (People), and will remain there for forty. It is not known as to whether he (S.A.W.) meant forty days or forty months or forty years. After this Allah the Exalted will send Hazrat Isa (Christ), the son of Mary (Peace be on him) who will search him and will kill him. Thereafter, all the human beings will remain alive for seven years. During these years there will be no ill-will even between two persons. Then Allah, the Lord of Honour and Glory, will send a cool breeze from the direction of Syria, which will not leave on this earth a single person in whose heart there will be an iota of faith or goodness but his soul will be taken possession of. Even if anyone of you goes (takes shelter) in some cave of a mountain, the said breeze will follow him there and the possession of his soul will be taken of. After this, there will remain only the worst type of people who will indulge in sexual activities like birds and will be like brutes in their behaviour. They will not recognize anything good nor will abstain from anything bad. Then Satan will come to them disguised as a human being and will ask them: 'Will you not obey me?' These people will ask him: What do you command us?' He (the Satan) will call upon them to worship idols. They will live their life (as idol-worshippers) and will have plenty of means of subsistence, and will lead a comfortable life. After this the trumpet (of Angel Israfeel) will be blown, and everyone who hears it, will turn his neck towards it, and will raise it. The first person to hear it will be a man who will be busy repairing the tank for drinking water for his camels. On hearing the sound he will become unconscious and others around him will become unconscious. Thereafter, Allah the Exalted will send or descend rain which will be like the drops of dew. This will enable people's bodies to grow. This will be followed by a second blow of the trumpet, which will make the people stand seeing. Then it will be said: O people, come forward before your Lord, make them stand, they will be questioned. Then it will be ordered: 'Separate from them those to be sent to the Hell. It will be submitted: 'How much (share of the Hell be separated). It will be said: 'Nine hundred and ninety nine out of each thousand (for Hell).' That will be the day which will make children old (verse 17 Chapter 74, Al Quran), and on the day when it falleth in earnest (Reference verse 42, Chapter 68, Al Quran). *(Muslim)*

١٨١١ – وَعَنْ أَنَسٍ رَضِيَ اللهُ عَنْهُ قَالَ : قَالَ رَسُولُ اللهِ صَلَّى اللهُ عَلَيْهِ وَسَلَّمَ : « لَيْسَ مِنْ بَلَدٍ إِلاَّ سَيَطَؤُهُ الدَّجَّالُ ، إِلاَّ مَكَّةَ وَالْمَدِينَةَ ؛ وَلَيْسَ نَقْبٌ مِنْ أَنْقَابِهَا إِلاَّ عَلَيْهِ الْمَلَائِكَةُ صَافِّينَ تَحْرُسُهُمَا، فَيَنْزِلُ بِالسَّبَخَةِ ، فَتَرْجُفُ الْمَدِينَةُ ثَلَاثَ رَجَفَاتٍ ، يُخْرِجُ اللهُ مِنْهَا كُلَّ كَافِرٍ وَمُنَافِقٍ » رواه مسلم .

1811. **Hazrat Anas bin Malik** (R.A.A.) relates that the Holy Prophet (S.A.W.) said: 'The Anti-Christ will overrun all cities except Makkah and Madina All the hill passes round the two cities (Makkah and Madina) will be guarded by the lines of angels to protect them. The Anti-Christ will land at Sabakhah, and the city of Madina will be rocked by earthquake thrice, as a result of which every disbeliever and hypocrite will be expelled from Madina.' *(Muslim)*

١٨١٢ – وَعَنْهُ رَضِيَ اللهُ عَنْهُ أَنَّ رَسُولَ اللهِ صَلَّى اللهُ عَلَيْهِ وَسَلَّمَ قَالَ : « يَتْبَعُ الدَّجَّالَ مِنْ يَهُودِ أَصْبَهَانَ سَبْعُونَ أَلْفاً عَلَيْهِمُ الطَّيَالِسَةُ » رَوَاهُ مسلم .

1812. **Hazrat Anas bin Malik** (R.A.A.) relates that the Holy Prophet (S.A.W.) said': Seventy thousand Jews of Ispahan wearing Satan Clothes will join Anti-Christ. *(Muslim)*

١٨١٣ – وَعَنْ أُمِّ شَرِيكٍ رَضِيَ اللهُ عَنْهَا أَنَّهَا سَمِعَتِ النَّبِيَّ صَلَّى اللهُ عَلَيْهِ وَسَلَّمَ يَقُولُ : « لَيَنْفِرَنَّ النَّاسُ مِنَ الدَّجَّالِ فِي الْجِبَالِ » رَوَاهُ مُسْلِمٌ .

1813. **Hazrat Umm Shareek** (R.A.A.) says that she heard from the Holy Prophet (S.A.W.) that people will run to the mountains (for shelter due to the fear of Anti-Christ.) *(Muslim)*

١٨١٤ – وَعَنْ عِمْرَانَ بْنِ حُصَيْنٍ رَضِيَ اللهُ عَنْهُمَا قَالَ : سَمِعْتُ رَسُولَ اللهِ صَلَّى اللهُ عَلَيْهِ وَآلِهِ وَسَلَّمَ يَقُولُ : « مَا بَيْنَ خَلْقِ آدَمَ إِلَى قِيَامِ السَّاعَةِ أَمْرٌ أَكْبَرُ مِنَ الدَّجَّالِ » رواه مسلم .

1814. Hazrat Imran bin Husain (R.A.A.) relates: 'I myself heard the Holy Prophet (S.A.W.) say: 'Since the creation of Adam till the Day of Judgement there is no greater calamity than the appearance of Anti-Christ.' *(Muslim)*

١٨١٥ – وعَنْ أبي سَعيدِ الخُدْرِيِّ رَضِيَ اللهُ عَنْهُ عَنِ النَّبيِّ صَلَّى عَلَيْهِ وَسَلَّمَ قالَ: «يَخْرُجُ الدَّجَّالُ فَيَتَوَجَّهُ قِبَلَهُ رَجُلٌ مِنَ المُؤْمِنِينَ فَيَتَلَقَّاهُ المَسَالِحُ: مَسَالِحُ الدَّجَّالِ، فَيَقُولُونَ لَه: إلى أَيْنَ تَعمِدُ؟ فَيَقُول: أعْمِدُ إلى هذا الَّذي خَرَجَ، فيقولُونَ له: أوَ مَا تُؤْمِن بِرَبِّنَا؟ فيقول: مابِرَبِّنا خَفَاءٌ! فيقولُونَ: اقْتُلُوه. فيقُول بَعْضُهُمْ لِبَعض أَلَيْسَ قَدْ نَهاكُمْ رَبُّكُمْ أَنْ تَقْتُلُوا أحَداً دونَه، فَيَنْطَلِقُونَ بِه إلى الدَّجَّالِ، فإذا رآه المُؤْمِنُ قالَ: يَا أَيُّهَا النَّاسُ إنَّ هذا الدَّجَّالُ الَّذي ذَكَرَ رَسُولُ اللهِ صَلَّى اللهُ عَلَيْهِ وَسَلَّمَ: فَيَأمُرُ الدَّجَّالُ بِهِ فَيُشَبَّحُ؛ فيَقولُ: خُذُوهُ وَشُجُّوهُ، فَيُوسَعُ ظَهْرُهُ وَبَطْنُهُ ضَرْباً، فيقولُ: أوَمَا تُؤمِنُ بي؟ فيَقُولُ: أنْتَ المَسيحُ الكَذَّابُ! فيُؤمَرُ بِهِ، فيُؤْشَرُ بالمِنْشَارِ مِنْ مَفْرِقِه حتَّى يُفَرِّقَ بَيْنَ رِجْلَيْهِ، ثُمَّ يَمْشي الدَّجَّالُ بَيْنَ القِطْعَتَيْنِ، ثُمَّ يقولُ لَهُ: قُمْ، فَيَسْتَوِي قَائِماً. ثُمَّ يقولُ لَهُ: أتُؤْمِنُ بي؟ فيقولُ: مَا ازْدَدْتُ فيكَ إلاَّ بَصيرةً. ثُمَّ يَقُولُ: يَا أَيُّهَا النَّاسُ إنَّهُ لايَفْعَلُ بَعْدِي بأحَدٍ مِنَ النَّاسِ، فيَأخُذُهُ الدَّجَّالُ لِيَذْبَحَهُ، فيَجْعَلُ اللهُ مَا بَيْنَ رَقَبَتِهِ إلى تَرْقُوَتِهِ نُحَاساً، فَلا يَسْتَطيعُ إلَيْهِ سَبيلاً، فيَأخُذُ بيَدَيْهِ وَرِجْلَيْهِ فيَقْذِفُ بِه، فيَحْسَبُ النَّاسُ أنَّما قَذَفَهُ إلى النَّارِ، وإنَّمَا أُلْقِيَ في الجَنَّةِ» فقالَ رَسُولُ اللهِ صَلَّى اللهُ عَلَيْهِ وَسَلَّمَ: «هذا أعْظَمُ النَّاسِ شَهادَةً عِنْدَ رَبِّ العَالَمينَ» رواه مسلم. وروى البخاريُّ بَعْضَهُ

1815. Hazrat Abu Sa'eed Khudri (R.A.A.) relates that the Holy Prophet (S.A.W.) said: 'When Anti-Christ will appear, a believer will go towards him, and will meet the guards of the Anti-Christ who will ask him: 'Where are you going?' He will say: 'I am going to this person who has appeared.' The guards will ask him: 'Do you not believe in our Lord? He will answer: Our Lord (Allah) has nothing to hide. (Then why should I recognize this liar as Lord). They will say: 'Kill him.' Some of them will say: 'Has not your lord forbidden to kill anybody without his permission?' So they will take this Muslim to the Anti-Christ. When the Muslim will see him, he will say: 'O People! This is the same Dajjal (Anti-Christ), as described by the Holy Prophet (S.A.W.). The Anti-Christ will order, his men. catch hold of this man, break his head and will get him thrashed on his bare back and stomach and will ask the man: 'Do you still not believe in me?' The Muslim will say: 'You are Anti-Christ, the Liar. Anti-Christ will then order that he should be sawn through from his skull to the joint of his legs. Anti-Christ will then walk between the two parts of his body and addressing these parts will say: 'Get up'. Thereupon (the two parts will join together) and the man will become whole and stand up. Then Anti-Christ will ask him: 'Do you believe (now) in me?' The Muslim will answer: 'I have now learnt something more about you.' And then this man will tell the people: 'O People! (Listen), now after me he (Anti-Christ) will not be able to harm anybody.' Thereafter, Anti-Christ will try to catch him to slaughter but Allah will make his neck from base to top made of brass, and Anti-Christ will not find any place to slaughter him. He will then catch hold of his hands and legs and throw him away. People will think that Anti-Christ has thrown him into the Hell, but in fact he had been thrown into the paradise. The Holy Prophet (S.A.W.) added: 'This man will have the highest grade of martyrdom in the estimation of the Lord of the worlds.)

(Muslim, Bukhari has reported some parts of it.)

١٨١٦ – وعَنِ المُغِيرَةِ بنِ شُعْبَةَ رضيَ اللهُ عنهُ قالَ : ماسألَ أحدَ رَسُولَ اللهِ صَلَّى اللهُ عَلَيْهِ وَسَلَّمَ عَنِ الدَّجَّالِ أكثرَ مِمَّا سألتُهُ ؛ وَإنَّهُ قالَ لي: «مَا يَضُرُّكَ ؟» قلتُ : إنَّهُمْ يقُولُونَ : إنَّ مَعَهُ جَبَلَ خُبْزٍ وَنَهرَ مَاءٍ ! قالَ : «هُوَ أهْوَنُ عَلَى اللهِ مِنْ ذلِكَ » متفقٌ عليه .

1816. Hazrat Mughirah bin Shu'bah (R.A.A.) says. No one enquired from the Holy Prophet (S.A.W.) about the Anti-Christ as much as I did, and he (S.A.W.) said: 'He will not harm you.' I submitted. 'O the Messenger of Allah (S.A.W.) it is said that there will be a mountain of bread and a stream of water with him (Anti-Christ). The Holy Prophet (S.A.W.) said: This is easier for Allah (to protect the Muslims from him). *(Bukhari and Muslim)*

١٨١٧ – وعَنْ أنَسٍ رضيَ اللهُ عَنْهُ قالَ : قالَ رَسُولُ اللهِ صَلَّى اللهُ عَلَيْهِ وَسَلَّمَ : «مَامِنْ نَبِيٍّ إلاَّ وَقَدْ أنْذَرَ أُمَّتَهُ الأعْوَرَ الكَذَّابَ ، ألا إنَّهُ أعْوَرُ . وَإنَّ رَبَّكُمْ عَزَّ وَجلَّ لَيْسَ بأعْوَرَ ، مَكْتُوبٌ بَيْنَ عَيْنَيْهِ ك ف ر» متفقٌ عليه

1817. Hazrat Anas bin Malik (R.A.A.) relates that the Holy Prophet (S.A.W.) said: 'Every prophet has warned his people against the one-eyed liar. Beware! (Indeed) he is one-eyed but your Lord is not one-eyed. Between the space of the eyes of the Anti-Christ will be written the letters 'KFR' (i.e. Kafir or unbeliever).

(Bukhari and Muslim)

١٨١٨ — وَعَنْ أَبِي هُرَيْرَةَ رَضِيَ اللهُ عَنْهُ قَالَ : قَالَ رَسُولُ اللهِ صَلَّى اللهُ عَلَيْهِ وَسَلَّمَ : « أَلَا أُحَدِّثُكُمْ حَدِيثاً عَنِ الدَّجَّالِ مَاحَدَّثَ بِهِ نَبِيٌّ قَوْمَهُ ! إِنَّهُ أَعْوَرُ ، وَإِنَّهُ يَجِيءُ مَعَهُ بِمِثَالِ الجَنَّةِ وَالنَّارِ ، فَالَّتِي يَقُولُ إِنَّهَا الجَنَّةُ هِيَ النَّارُ » متفقٌ عليه .

1818. Hazrat Abu Hurairah (R.A.A.) relates that the Holy Prophet (S.A.W.) said: Listen I will tell you something about Anti-Christ, which no other prophet has told his followers, and that he is one-eyed and that he will have with him something which will appear like Paradise and Hell. But the thing which he will call Paradise will in fact be the Hell, and the thing which he will call Hell, will be in fact Paradise. *(Bukhari and Muslim)*

١٨١٩ — وَعَنْ ابْنِ عُمَرَ رَضِيَ اللهُ عَنْهُما أَنَّ رَسُولَ اللهِ صَلَّى اللهُ عَلَيْهِ وَسَلَّمَ ذَكَرَ الدَّجَّالَ بَيْنَ ظَهْرَانَي النَّاسِ فَقَالَ : « إِنَّ اللهَ لَيْسَ بِأَعْوَرَ . أَلَا إِنَّ المَسِيحَ الدَّجَّالَ أَعْوَرُ العَيْنِ اليُمْنَى ، كَأَنَّ عَيْنَهُ عِنَبَةٌ طَافِيَةٌ » متفقٌ عليه

1819. Hazrat Ibn Umar (R.A.A.) relates that the Holy Prophet (S.A.W.) once described Anti-Christ before the people and said: 'Indeed Allah is not one-eyed, listen, the Anti-Christ will be blind of his right eye, which will look like a swollen grape.' *(Bukhari and Muslim)*

١٨٢٠ — وَعَنْ أَبِي هُرَيْرَةَ رَضِيَ اللهُ عَنْهُ أَنَّ رَسُولَ اللهِ صَلَّى اللهُ عَلَيْهِ وَسَلَّمَ قَالَ : « لَا تَقُومُ السَّاعَةُ حَتَّى يُقَاتِلَ المُسْلِمُونَ اليَهُودَ حَتَّى يَخْتَبِيءَ اليَهُودِيُّ مِنْ وَرَاءِ الحَجَرِ وَالشَّجَرِ ، فَيَقُولُ الحَجَرُ وَالشَّجَرُ : يَامُسْلِمُ هٰذا يَهُودِيٌّ خَلْفِي تَعَالَ فَاقْتُلْهُ ، إِلَّا الغَرْقَدَ فَإِنَّهُ مِنْ شَجَرِ اليَهُودِ » متفقٌ عليه .

1820. Hazrat Abu Hurairah (R.A.A.) relates that the Holy Prophet (S.A.W.) said: The Day of Judgement will not appear till the Muslims have had a fight with the Jews, till the Jews (in fear of Muslims) will seek shelter behind a rock or a tree and the said rock or tree, will call out: 'O Muslims, here is a Jew hidden behind me; come and kill him.' But the thorny tree called 'gharqad' will not do so, for it is a tree of the Jews. *(Bukhari and Muslim)*

١٨٢١ – وعَنْهُ رَضِيَ اللهُ عَنْهُ قالَ : قالَ رَسُولُ اللهِ صَلَّى اللهُ عَلَيْهِ وَسَلَّمَ : « والذي نَفْسِي بِيَدِهِ لاتَذْهَبُ الدُّنْيَا حَتَّى يَمُرَّ الرَّجُلُ بِالْقَبْرِ، فَيَتَمَرَّغَ عَلَيْهِ ، ويقولُ : يَا لَيْتَنِي مَكَانَ صَاحِبِ هذا الْقَبْرِ ، ولَيْس بِهِ الدِّيْنُ ؛ مَا بِهِ إلاَّ الْبَلاَءُ » . متفقٌ عليه .

1821. Hazrat Abu Hurairah (R.A.A.) relates that the Holy Prophet (S.A.W.) said: By Allah in Whose possession is my life, this world will not come to an end till a man passing by a grave will return and say: I wish I were in this grave in place of the person who lies in this grave. He will not say this for the sake of his faith, but will say so only out of desperation and misery. *(Bukhari and Muslim)*

١٨٢٢ – وَعَنْهُ رَضِيَ اللهُ عَنْهُ قالَ : قالَ رَسُولُ اللهِ صَلَّى اللهُ عَلَيْهِ وَسَلَّمَ : « لا تَقُومُ السَّاعَةُ حَتَّى يَحْسِرَ الْفُرَاتُ عَنْ جَبَلٍ مِنْ ذَهَبٍ يُقْتَتَلُ عَلَيْهِ ، فَيُقْتَلُ مِنْ كُلِّ مِائَةٍ تِسْعَةٌ وتِسْعُونَ ، فَيَقُولُ كُلُّ رَجُلٍ مِنْهُمْ : لَعَلِّي أَنْ أَكُونَ أَنَا أَنْجُو » .

وفي روايةٍ : « يُوشِكُ أَنْ يَحْسِرَ الْفُرَاتُ عَنْ كَنْزٍ مِنْ ذَهَبٍ ، فَمَنْ حَضَرَهُ فَلا يَأْخُذْ مِنْهُ شَيْئاً » متفقٌ عليه .

1822. Hazrat Abu Hurairah (R.A.A.) relates that the Holy Prophet (S.A.W.) said: The Last Day will not happen till a mountain of gold rises in the river Euphrates on which (large number of) people will be killed, as many as ninety nine out of a hundred (will be killed and only one will be spared); every one of them will say: 'May be I the one to be spared.'

Another version says: In the near future there will appear a treasure of gold from the river Euphrates. A person who happens to be present there should not take anything from this treasure.

(Bukhari and Muslim)

١٨٢٣ – وعَنْهُ قالَ : سَمِعْتُ رَسُولَ اللهِ صَلَّى اللهُ عَلَيْهِ وَسَلَّمَ يَقُولُ : « يَتْرُكُونَ الْمَدِينَةَ عَلَى خَيْرِ مَا كَانَتْ ، لايَغْشَاهَا إلاَّ الْعَوَافِي – يُرِيدُ : عَوَافِيَ السِّبَاعِ وَالطَّيْرِ – وَآخِرُ مَنْ يُحْشَرُ رَاعِيَانِ مِنْ مُزَيْنَةَ يُرِيدَانِ الْمَدِينَةَ يَنْعِقَانِ بِغَنَمِهِمَا فَيَجِدَانِهَا وُحُوشاً ، حَتَّى إذا بَلَغَا ثَنِيَّةَ الْوَدَاعِ خَرَّا عَلَى وُجُوهِهِمَا » متفقٌ عليه .

1823. Hazrat Abu Hurairah (R.A.A.) relates that he heard the Holy Prophet (S.A.W.) say: 'People will leave the holy city of Madina in excellent condition; nobody would inhabit it except beasts and birds. In the end, will come two shepherds of the Muzainah tribe, intending to enter Madina with their goats, but will find it full of wild beasts (and go away). When they will reach the hill known as Saniyya-tal-Wada'a, they will fall on their faces. *(Bukhari and Muslim)*

١٨٢٤ — وعَنْ أبي سَعيد الخُدْرِيِّ رَضِيَ اللهُ عَنْهُ أنَّ النَّبيَّ صَلَّى اللهُ عَلَيْه وَسَلَّمَ قالَ : « يَكُونُ خَليفَةٌ مِنْ خُلَفائِكُمْ في آخرِ الزَّمَانِ يَحْثُو المَالَ وَلا يَعُدُّهُ » رواه مسلم .

1824. Hazrat Abu Sa'eed Khudri (R.A.A.) relates that the Holy Prophet (S.A.W.) said: Near the Doomsday one of your Khalifas will distribute huge wealth without counting. *(Muslim)*

١٨٢٥ — وعَنْ أبي مُوسَى الأشْعَرِيِّ رَضِيَ اللهُ عَنْهُ أنَّ النَّبيَّ صَلَّى اللهُ عَلَيْهِ وَسَلَّمَ قال : « لَيَأْتِيَنَّ عَلَى النَّاسِ زَمَانٌ يَطُوفُ الرَّجُلُ فيه بالصَّدَقَةِ مِنَ الذَّهَبِ ، فَلا يَجِدُ أحَداً يَأْخُذُهَا مِنْهُ ، وَيُرَى الرَّجُلُ الوَاحِدُ يَتْبَعُهُ أرْبَعُونَ امْرَأَةً يَلُذْنَ بِهِ مِنْ قِلَّةِ الرِّجالِ وَكَثْرَةِ النِّسَاءِ » رواه مسلم .

1825. Hazrat Abu Musa Al-Ash'ari (R.A.A.) relates that the Holy Prophet (S.A.W.) said: A time will come when a man will go about with Zakat out of his stock of gold, to distribute (among the poor), but will not find anyone who would take it from him. Also there will be paucity of males and abundance of females so much so that it will be seen that a male will be followed by forty females seeking pleasure with him; *(Muslim)*

١٨٢٦ — وعَنْ أبي هُرَيْرَةَ رَضِيَ اللهُ عَنْهُ عَنْ النَّبيِّ صَلَّى اللهُ عَلَيْهِ وَسَلَّمَ قالَ : « اشْتَرَى رَجُلٌ مِنْ رَجُلٍ عَقَاراً ، فَوَجَدَ الَّذي اشْتَرَى العَقَارَ في عَقَارِهِ جَرَّةً فِيهَا ذَهَبٌ ، فقالَ لَهُ الَّذي اشْتَرَى العَقَارَ : خُذْ ذَهَبَكَ ، إنَّمَا اشْتَرَيْتُ مِنْكَ الأرْضَ ، وَلَمْ أشْتَرِ الذَّهَبَ ، وقالَ الَّذي لَهُ الأرْضُ : إنَّمَا بِعْتُكَ الأرْضَ وَمَا فِيهَا ، فَتَحَاكَمَا إلى رَجُلٍ ، فقالَ الَّذي تَحَاكَمَا إلَيْهِ : ألَكُمَا وَلَدٌ ؟ قالَ أحَدُهُمَا : لي غُلامٌ ، وقالَ الآخرُ : لي جَارِيَةٌ ، قالَ : أنْكِحَا الغُلامَ الجَارِيَةَ ، وَأنْفِقَا عَلى أنْفُسِهِمَا مِنْهُ وَتَصَدَّقَا » متفقٌ عليه .

1826. Hazrat Abu Hurairah (R.A.A.) relates that the Holy Prophet (S.A.W.) said: A person purchased a piece of land from another; the purchaser found in it a vessel filled with gold. So the purchaser said to the seller; 'Take your vessel of (gold) because I purchased only the land from you, and did not purchase this vessel of gold. The seller (the former owner of the land) said to him: 'I sold you land together with all that it contained.' Ultimately they took their dispute to a third person for decision. This man asked them: 'Have you any children?' One of them said: 'I have a boy; and the other said: I have a girl.' This man then said: Marry them (the boy and the girl) and spend the money on them and gift them.

(Bukhari and Muslim)

١٨٢٧ – وعَنْهُ رَضِيَ اللهُ عَنْهُ أَنَّهُ سَمِعَ رَسُولَ اللهِ صَلَّى اللهُ عَلَيْهِ وَسَلَّمَ يَقُولُ: «كانَتْ امْرَأَتَانِ مَعَهُمَا ابْنَاهُمَا، جَاءَ الذِّئْبُ فَذَهَبَ بِابْنِ إحْدَاهُمَا، فقالَتْ لِصَاحِبَتِهَا: إِنَّمَا ذَهَبَ بِابْنِكِ، وقالت الأُخْرَى: إِنَّمَا ذَهَبَ بِابْنِكِ، فَتَحَاكَمَا إلى دَاوُدَ، صَلَّى اللهُ عَلَيْهِ وَسَلَّمَ، فَقَضَى بِهِ لِلْكُبْرَى، فَخَرَجَتَا عَلَى سُلَيْمَانَ بنِ داودَ، صَلَّى اللهُ عليه وَسَلَّمَ، فَأَخْبَرَتَاهُ. فقالَ: ائْتُونِي بِالسِّكِّينِ أَشُقُّهُ بَيْنَهُمَا. فقالت الصُّغْرَى: لاتَفْعَلْ؛ رَحِمَكَ اللهُ، هُوَ ابْنُهَا. فَقَضَى بِهِ لِلصُّغْرَى» متفقٌ عليه .

1827. Hazrat Abu Hurairah (R.A.A.) relates that he heard the Holy Prophet (S.A.W.) say: There were two women, each had her child with her. A wolf came and took away the child of one of them. A woman said to her companion: The wolf has taken away your child. and the other replied: It was your child which the wolf has taken away. Ultimately they took their dispute to Prophet David (A.S.) and he decided in favour of the older woman. After this they passed by the Prophet Soloman (A.S.) and related to him what had happened. He said: (All right) bring me a knife, so that I may cut the child in two, and divide it between you. On this the younger woman cried out' Allah may have mercy on you! Please do not do this; the baby belongs to the other woman. (Hearing this) Prophet Soloman (A.S.) decided in favour of the younger one. *(Bukhari and Muslim)*

١٨٢٨ – وعَنْ مِرْدَاسٍ الأَسْلَمِيِّ رَضِيَ اللهُ عَنْهُ قالَ: قالَ النبيُّ صَلَّى اللهُ عَلَيْهِ وَسَلَّمَ: «يَذْهَبُ الصَّالِحُونَ الأَوَّلُ فَالأَوَّلُ، وَتَبْقَى حُثَالَةٌ كَحُثَالَةِ الشَّعِيرِ أَوْ التَّمْرِ، لايُبَالِيهِمُ اللهُ بَالَةً» رواه البخاري .

1828. Hazrat Mirdas al Aslami (R.A.A.) relates that the Holy Prophet (S.A.W.) said. The righteous and virtuous persons will die one by one earlier leaving behind the useless ones like the husk of barley or dates and Allah will not care for their lot. *(Bukhari)*

١٨٢٩ - وعَنْ رِفاعةَ بنِ رافعٍ الزُّرَقيِّ رَضِيَ اللهُ عَنْهُ قالَ: جاءَ جِبْريلُ إلى النبيِّ صَلّى اللهُ عَلَيْهِ وَسَلَّمَ قالَ: ماتَعُدُّونَ أَهْلَ بَدْرٍ فِيكُمْ؟ قالَ: «مِنْ أَفْضَلِ المُسْلِمِينَ» أوْ كَلِمَةً نَحْوَها. قالَ: «وكَذلِكَ مَنْ شَهِدَ بَدْراً مِنَ المَلائِكَةِ» رواه البخاري .

1829. Hazrat Rif'ah bin Rafi-'Az-Zuraqi (R.A.A;) relates that once the Angel Gabriel came to the Holy Prophet (S.A.W.) and enquired: How do you assess those among you who took part in the battle of Badr? He (S.A.W.) answered: They are reckoned as the best of Muslims (or some other words like that). Angel Gabriel said: The same is the status of those angels who participated in the battle of Badr. *(Bukhari)*

١٨٣٠ - وعَنِ ابنِ عُمَرَ رَضِيَ اللهُ عَنْهُما قالَ: قالَ رَسُولُ اللهِ صَلّى اللهُ عَلَيْهِ وَسَلَّمَ: «إذا أَنْزَلَ اللهُ تَعالى بِقَوْمٍ عَذاباً أَصابَ العَذابُ مَنْ كانَ فِيهِمْ، ثُمَّ بُعِثُوا عَلى أَعْمالِهِمْ» متفقٌ عليه .

1830. Hazrat Ibn 'Umar (R.A.A.) relates that the Holy Prophet (S.A.W.) said. 'When Allah inflicts punishment on a people it covers all the (members of that) people. But on the Day of Judgement they will be raised up according to their conduct in life.

(Bukhari and Muslim)

١٨٣١ - وعَنْ جابِرٍ رَضِيَ اللهُ عَنْهُ قالَ: كانَ جِذْعٌ يَقُومُ إلَيْهِ النَّبيُّ صَلّى اللهُ عَلَيْهِ وَسَلَّمَ، يَعْني في الخُطْبَةِ. فلَمّا وُضِعَ المِنْبَرُ، سَمِعْنا لِلْجِذْعِ مِثْلَ صَوْتِ العِشارِ حتّى نَزَلَ النَّبيُّ، صَلّى اللهُ عَلَيْهِ وَسَلَّمَ، فَوَضَعَ يَدَهُ عَلَيْهِ فَسَكَنَ .

وفي روايةٍ: فَلَمّا كانَ يَوْمُ الجُمُعَةِ قَعَدَ النَّبيُّ، صَلّى اللهُ عَلَيْهِ وَسَلَّمَ على المِنْبَرِ، فَصاحَتِ النَّخْلَةُ الّتي كانَ يَخْطُبُ عِنْدَها حَتّى كادَتْ أنْ تَنْشَقَّ .

وفي روايةٍ: فَصاحَتْ صِياحَ الصَّبيِّ، فَنَزَلَ النَّبيُّ، صَلّى اللهُ عَلَيْهِ وَسَلَّمَ، حَتّى أَخَذَها فَضَمَّها إلَيْهِ، فَجَعَلَتْ تَئِنُّ أَنِينَ الصَّبيِّ الّذي يُسَكَّتُ حَتّى اسْتَقَرَّتْ، قالَ: «بَكَتْ عَلى ماكانَتْ تَسْمَعُ مِنَ الذِّكْرِ» رَواه البخاريُّ .

1831. Hazrat Jabir (R.A.A.) relates: There was a trunk of a date tree on which the Holy Prophet (S.A.W.) would stand when delivering his sermon. After sometime a pulpit was set up in the mosque, and the Holy Prophet (S.A.W.) ascended this pulpit to deliver Friday sermon; then we heard the trunk cry out like the cry of a pregnant she-camel. The Holy Prophet (S.A.W.) came down from the pulpit and put his hand on the trunk, then it became peaceful.

Another version says: When on a Friday the Holy Prophet (S.A.W.) sat on the pulpit to deliver the sermon, the trunk of the date tree on which he used to rest while delivering sermon, started crying out, and it seemed that due to the pangs of separation it would rend asunder.

Yet another version says: It cried like the wailing of a child and the Holy Prophet (S.A.W.) came down and holding it grasped it and it began to sob like a child who is pacified by consolation. At last it was consoled. The Holy Prophet (S.A.W.) said: This trunk wept because it was deprived of hearing the sermon. *(Bukhari)*

١٨٣٢ – وعَنْ أبي ثَعْلَبَةَ الخُشَنِيِّ جُرْثُومِ بنِ نَاشِرٍ رَضِيَ اللهُ عَنْهُ عَنْ رَسُولِ اللهِ صَلَّى اللهُ عَلَيْهِ وَسَلَّمَ قالَ : « إن اللهَ تَعَالَى فَرَضَ فَرَائِضَ فَلا تُضَيِّعُوهَا ، وَحَدَّ حُدُوداً فَلا تَعْتَدُوهَا ، وَحَرَّمَ أشْيَاءَ فَلا تَنْتَهِكُوهَا ، وَسَكَتَ عَنْ أشْيَاءَ رَحْمَةً لَكُمْ غَيْرَ نِسْيَانٍ فَلا تَبْحَثُوا عَنها » حديثٌ حسن ، رواه الدَّارقُطْني وَغَيْرُهُ .

1832. Hazrat Abu Sa'laba Al Khushani Jursum bin Nashir (R.A.A.) relates that the Holy Prophet (S.A.W.) said. Allah the Exalted, has prescribed certain obligations which you should not destroy (ignore), and has likewise fixed certain limits which should not be transgressed, and has prohibited certain things which may not be committed; and has kept quiet about some matters simply as a matter of mercy for you, and not due to forgetfulness; so you should not be inquisitive about these things. (This is a good tradition, which *Dar Qutni* and others have quoted).

١٨٣٣ – وعَنْ عَبْدِ اللهِ بنِ أبي أوْفى رَضِيَ اللهُ عَنْهُمَا قالَ : غَزَوْنَا مَعَ رَسُولِ اللهِ صَلَّى اللهُ عَلَيْهِ وَسَلَّمَ سَبْعَ غَزَوَاتٍ نَأْكُلُ الجَرَادَ .

وفي روايةٍ : نَأْكُلُ مَعَهُ الجَرَادَ ، متفقٌ عليه .

1833. Hazrat Abdullah bin Abu Aufi (R.A.A.) says: We participated in seven battles along with the Holy Prophet (S.A.W.) and ate locusts.

Another version says: We ate locusts along with the Holy Prophet (S.A.W.). *(Bukhari and Muslim)*

١٨٣٤ – وعَنْ أبي هُرَيْرَةَ رَضِيَ اللهُ عَنْهُ أنَّ النَّبِيَّ صَلَّى اللهُ عَلَيْهِ وَسَلَّمَ قَالَ: « لا يُلْدَغُ المُؤْمِنُ مِنْ جُحْرٍ وَاحِدٍ مَرَّتَيْنِ » متفقٌ عليه

1834. Hazrat Abu Hurairah (R.A.A.) relates that the Holy Prophet (S.A.W.) said: A believer (Muslim) is not stung twice the same hole (that is he is not deceived twice). *(Bukhari and Muslim)*

١٨٣٥ – وعَنْهُ قَالَ: قَالَ رَسُولُ اللهِ صَلَّى اللهُ عَلَيْهِ وَسَلَّمَ: « ثَلاثَةٌ لا يُكَلِّمُهُمُ اللهُ يَوْمَ القِيَامَةِ وَلا يَنْظُرُ إلَيْهِمْ وَلا يُزَكِّيهِمْ وَلَهُمْ عَذَابٌ ألِيمٌ: رَجُلٌ عَلَى فَضْلِ مَاءٍ بِالفَلاةِ يَمْنَعُهُ مِنِ ابْنِ السَّبِيلِ، وَرَجُلٌ بَايَعَ رَجُلاً سِلْعَةً بَعْدَ العَصْرِ، فَحَلَفَ باللهِ لأخَذَهَا بِكَذَا وكَذَا، فَصَدَّقَهُ وَهُوَ عَلَى غَيْرِ ذَلِكَ، وَرَجُلٌ بَايَعَ إمَاماً لا يُبَايِعُهُ إلاَّ لِدُنْيَا، فَإنْ أعْطَاهُ مِنْهَا وَفَى، وَإنْ لَمْ يُعْطِهِ مِنْهَا لَمْ يَفِ » متفقٌ عليه .

1835. Hazrat Abu Hurairah (R.A.A.) reports that the Holy Prophet (S.A.W.) said: Allah, the Exalted, will not talk to three kinds of persons on the Day of Judgement, nor look at them, nor purify them, and for them is a dreadful punishment. One is a person who has with him excess water in a desert but he does not give it to a traveller: Two, a man who sells some articles to somebody after the *(Asr)* afternoon prayer and believing in him a man purchased the article at that price, though in reality its price was not so much; and three is one who takes the Oath of Allegiance to an Imam only for some worldly consideration, and he is faithful if the Imam gives him something, if he (Imam) does not give him anything he is unfaithful.

(Bukhari and Muslim)

١٨٣٦ – وعَنْهُ عَنِ النَّبِيِّ صَلَّى اللهُ عَلَيْهِ وَسَلَّمَ قَالَ: « بَيْنَ النَّفْخَتَيْنِ أرْبَعُونَ » قَالُوا: يَا أبَا هُرَيْرَةَ، أرْبَعُونَ يَوْماً؟ قَالَ: أبَيْتُ [٢]، قَالُوا: أرْبَعُونَ سَنَةً؟ قَالَ: أبَيْتُ. قَالُوا: أرْبَعُونَ شَهْراً؟ قَالَ: أبَيْتُ « وَيَبْلَى كُلُّ شَيءٍ مِنَ الإنْسَانِ إلاَّ عَجْبَ الذَّنَبِ، فِيهِ يُرَكَّبُ الخَلْقُ، ثُمَّ يُنَزِّلُ اللهُ مِنَ السَّمَاءِ مَاءً، فَيَنْبُتُونَ كَمَا يَنْبُتُ البَقْلُ » متفقٌ عَلَيْهِ .

1836. Hazrat Abu Hurairah (R.A.A.) says that the Holy Prophet (S.A.W.) said: The duration between the blowing of two trumpets (calls) is forty. The people asked: 'Well, Abu Hurairah is (this period)

forty days? He said: 'I am not definite.' The people said: Is it Forty years? He said: I am not sure. The people said: Is it forty months? He said: I am not sure, continuing he said: The Holy Prophet (S.A.W.) added: Everything of the human body will be destroyed except the last disc of the spine. On the Day of Judgement the creatures will be recreated on the basis of this bone. Then Allah will send down rain from the sky which will make the (dead) to grow like vegetables. *(Bukhari and Muslim)*

١٨٣٧ — وَعَنْهُ قَالَ : بَيْنَمَا النَّبِيُّ صَلَّى اللهُ عَلَيْهِ وَسَلَّمَ فِي مَجْلِسٍ يُحَدِّثُ الْقَوْمَ ، جَاءَهُ أَعْرَابِيٌّ فَقَالَ : مَتَى السَّاعَةُ ؟ فَمَضَى رَسُولُ اللهِ صَلَّى اللهُ عَلَيْهِ وَسَلَّمَ ، يُحَدِّثُ ، فَقَالَ بَعْضُ الْقَوْمِ : سَمِعَ مَا قَالَ ، فَكَرِهَ مَا قَالَ ، وَقَالَ بَعْضُهُمْ : بَلْ لَمْ يَسْمَعْ ، حَتَّى إِذَا قَضَى حَدِيثَهُ قَالَ : « أَيْنَ السَّائِلُ عَنِ السَّاعَةِ ؟ » قَالَ : هَا أَنَا يَا رَسُولَ اللهِ . قَالَ : « إِذَا ضُيِّعَتِ الْأَمَانَةُ ، فَانْتَظِرِ السَّاعَةَ » قَالَ : كَيْفَ إِضَاعَتُهَا ؟ قَالَ : إِذَا وُسِّدَ الْأَمْرُ إِلَى غَيْرِ أَهْلِهِ فَانْتَظِرِ السَّاعَةَ » رَوَاهُ الْبُخَارِي .

1837. Hazrat Abu Hurairah (R.A.A.) says: While the Holy Prophet (S.A.W.) was addressing the people in a meeting, a villager came there and asked: When the Doomsday will come? But the Holy Prophet (S.A.W.) continued his address (to the meeting). Some person from the audience said that the Holy Prophet (S.A.W.) had heard him but resented the villager's interruption, while some others said he (S.A.W.) did not hear him at all. However, when the Holy Prophet (S.A.W.) finished his speech, he (S.A.W.) asked: Where is the man who inquired about the Doomsday. The man submitted. It is I, O Messenger of Allah! The Holy Prophet (S.A.W.) said: 'When the trust is betrayed, be ready for the Doomsday. The questioner inquired: 'What is meant by the betrayal of trust?' The Holy Prophet (S.A.W.) answered; When the power to rule is entrusted to undeserving persons, then be ready for the Day of Judgement. *(Bukhari)*

١٨٣٨ — وَعَنْهُ أَنَّ رَسُولَ اللهِ صَلَّى اللهُ عَلَيْهِ وَسَلَّمَ قَالَ : « يُصَلُّونَ لَكُمْ ، فَإِنْ أَصَابُوا فَلَكُمْ ، وَإِنْ أَخْطَؤُوا فَلَكُمْ وَعَلَيْهِمْ » رَوَاهُ الْبُخَارِيُّ :

1838. Hazrat Abu Hurairah (R.A.A.) relates that the Holy Prophet (S.A.W.) said: Your leaders will lead you in prayer, then if they lead you correctly, this will earn merit for you. But if they go wrong, you will earn the merit, but they will suffer for the wrong. *(Bukhari)*

١٨٣٩ — وَعَنْهُ رَضِيَ اللهُ عَنْهُ : (كُنْتُمْ خَيْرَأُمَّةٍ أُخْرِجَتْ لِلنَّاسِ) قَالَ : خَيْرُ النَّاسِ لِلنَّاسِ يَأْتُونَ بِهِمْ فِي السَّلَاسِلِ فِي أَعْنَاقِهِمْ حَتَّى يَدْخُلُوا فِي الإِسْلَامِ.

1839. Hazrat Abu Hurairah (R.A.A.) referring to the Quranic verse: 'You are the best community that hath been raised up for mankind.' (3 : 110) says that the Holy Prophet (S.A.W.) said: 'The best persons for mankind are those who pull (recalcitrant) people with chains round their necks, till they join Islam. *(Bukhari)*

١٨٤٠ — وَعَنْهُ عَنِ النَّبِيِّ صَلَّى اللهُ عَلَيْهِ وَسَلَّمَ قَالَ : « عَجِبَ اللهُ عَزَّوَجَلَّ مِنْ قَوْمٍ يَدْخُلُونَ الْجَنَّةَ فِي السَّلَاسِلِ » رواهما البُخاري

1840. • **Hazrat Abu Hurairah** (R.A.A.) relates that the Holy Prophet (S.A.W.) said: Allah, the Master of Honour and Glory, is much pleased with the people who enter paradise with chains (that is they are imprisoned in chains and thereafter embrace Islam and in return get Paradise.) *(Bukhari)*

١٨٤١ — وَعَنْهُ عَنِ النَّبِيِّ صَلَّى اللهُ عَلَيْهِ وَسَلَّمَ قَالَ : « أَحَبُّ الْبِلَادِ إِلَى اللهِ مَسَاجِدُهَا . وَأَبْغَضُ الْبِلَادِ إِلَى اللهِ أَسْوَاقُهَا » رواه مُسلم

1841. Hazrat Abu Hurairah (R.A.A.) reports that the Holy Prophet (S.A.W.) said: To Allah the dearest places are the mosques, and the most unpleasant places are markets. *(Muslim)*

١٨٤٢ — وَعَنْ سَلْمَانَ الْفَارِسِيِّ رَضِيَ اللهُ عَنْهُ مِنْ قَوْلِهِ قَالَ : لَا تَكُونَنَّ إِنِ اسْتَطَعْتَ أَوَّلَ مَنْ يَدْخُلُ السُّوقَ ، وَلَا آخِرَ مَنْ يَخْرُجُ مِنْهَا ، فَإِنَّهَا مَعْرَكَةُ الشَّيْطَانِ ، وَبِهَا يَنْصِبُ رَايَتَهُ . رواهُ مسلم هكذا.

وَرَوَاهُ الْبَرْقَانِيُّ في صحيحه عَنْ سَلْمَانَ قَالَ : قَالَ رَسُولُ اللهِ صَلَّى اللهُ عَلَيْهِ وَسَلَّمَ : « لَا تَكُنْ أَوَّلَ مَنْ يَدْخُلُ السُّوقَ ، وَلَا آخِرَ مَنْ يَخْرُجُ مِنْهَا ، فِيهَا بَاضَ الشَّيْطَانُ وَفَرَّخَ » .

1842. Hazrat Salman Farsi (R.A.A.) says that if you have power or can help it, don't be the first to enter a market nor the last person to get out of it, because this place is the field of the activities of Satan, and the place where he hoists his flag. *(Muslim)*

Imam Barqani in his Sahih reports this Hadith thus: The Holy Prophet (S.A.W.) said: Do not be the first to enter the market nor the last to get out from there, because this is the place where Satan lays his eggs and hatches them.

١٨٤٣– وَعَنْ عَاصِمٍ الأَحْوَلِ عَنْ عَبْدِ اللهِ بْنِ سَرْجِسَ رَضِيَ اللهُ عَنْهُ قَالَ : قُلْتُ لِرَسُولِ اللهِ صَلَّى اللهُ عَلَيْهِ وَسَلَّمَ : يَا رَسُولَ اللهِ غَفَرَ اللهُ لَكَ ، قَالَ : « وَلَكَ » قَالَ عَاصِمٌ : فَقُلْتُ لَهُ : أَسْتَغْفَرَ لَكَ رَسُولُ اللهِ صَلَّى اللهُ عَلَيْهِ وَسَلَّمَ ؟ قَالَ : نَعَمْ وَلَكَ ، ثُمَّ تَلاَ هَذه الآية : واستغفرْ لِذَنبِكَ ، ولِلْمُؤْمِنِينَ وَالمُؤْمِنَاتِ [محمد : ١٩] ، رَوَاهُ مُسلم .

1843. Hazrat 'Asim Al-Ahwal (R.A.A.) reports on the authority of Hazrat Abdullah bin Sarjisa (R.A.A.) that the latter said to the Holy Prophet (S.A.W.) 'O Messenger of Allah! Allah has forgiven all your sins (if any). The Holy Prophet (S.A.W.) said: And your sins will also be remitted. Hazrat 'Asim continuing says. I said to Abdullah bin Sarjisa. Did the Holy Prophet (S.A.W.) ask for forgiveness for you? He said: Yes, and for you too; and recited the verse:

'And ask forgiveness for thy sins and for believing men and believing women. (47 : 19) *(Muslim)*

١٨٤٤– وَعَنْ أَبِي مَسْعُودٍ الأَنْصَارِيِّ رَضِيَ اللهُ عَنْهُ قَالَ : قَالَ النَّبِيُّ صَلَّى اللهُ عَلَيْهِ وَسَلَّمَ : « إِنَّ مِمَّا أَدْرَكَ النَّاسُ مِنْ كَلاَمِ النُّبُوَّةِ الأُولَى : إِذَا لَمْ تَسْتَحِ فَاصْنَعْ مَا شِئْتَ » رواهُ البُخَارِيُّ .

1844. Hazrat Abu Mas'ud Al Ansari (R.A.A.) relates that the Holy Prophet (S.A.W.) said that one of the sayings of former prophets, which has reached the people, is: If thou does not have modesty, then do what you like. *(Bukhari)*

١٨٤٥ – وَعَنْ ابْنِ مَسْعُودٍ رَضِيَ اللهُ عَنْهُ قَالَ : قَالَ النَّبِيُّ صَلَّى اللهُ عَلَيْهِ وَسَلَّمَ : « أَوَّلُ مَا يُقْضَى بَيْنَ النَّاسِ يَوْمَ القِيَامَةِ فِي الدِّمَاءِ » مُتَّفَقٌ عَلَيْهِ .

1845. Hazrat Abdullah bin Mas'ud (R.A.A.) relates that the Holy Prophet (S.A.W.) said that the first thing about human beings to be adjudicated on the Day of Judgement, will be the blood claim. *(Bukhari and Muslim)*

١٨٤٦ – وَعَنْ عَائِشَةَ رَضِيَ اللهُ عَنْهَا قَالَتْ : قَالَ رَسُولُ اللهِ صَلَّى اللهُ عَلَيْهِ وَسَلَّمَ : « خُلِقَتِ المَلاَئِكَةُ مِنْ نُورٍ ، وَخُلِقَ الجَانُّ مِنْ مَارِجٍ مِنْ نَارٍ ، وَخُلِقَ آدَمُ مِمَّا وُصِفَ لَكُمْ » رواهُ مسلم .

1846. **Hazrat Ayesha** (R.A.A.) relates that the Holy Prophet (S.A.W.) said: Angels were created from light (divine light), and Jinns from burning fire, and Hazrat Adam (A.S.) was created from that thing which you have already been told. *(Muslim)*

١٨٤٧– وَعَنْهَا رَضِيَ اللهُ عَنْهَا قَالَتْ: « كَانَ خُلُقُ نَبِيِّ اللهِ صَلَّى اللهُ عَلَيْهِ وَسَلَّمَ الْقُرْآنَ » رواهُ مُسْلِم فِي جُمْلَةِ حَدِيثٍ طَوِيلٍ.

1847. **Hazrat Ayesha** (R.A.A.) said that the conduct and character of the Holy Prophet (S.A.W.) was absolutely the Holy Quran. (*Muslim* has described this in an exhaustive tradition)

١٨٤٨– وَعَنْهَا قَالَتْ: قَالَ رَسُولُ اللهِ صَلَّى اللهُ عَلَيْهِ وَسَلَّمَ: « مَنْ أَحَبَّ لِقَاءَ اللهِ أَحَبَّ اللهُ لِقَاءَهُ، وَمَنْ كَرِهَ لِقَاءَ اللهِ كَرِهَ اللهُ لِقَاءَهُ » فَقُلْتُ: يَا رَسُولَ اللهِ. أَكَرَاهِيَةُ الْمَوْتِ؟ فَكُلُّنَا نَكْرَهُ الْمَوْتَ! قَالَ: « لَيْسَ كَذَلِكَ. وَلَكِنَّ الْمُؤْمِنَ إِذَا بُشِّرَ بِرَحْمَةِ اللهِ وَرِضْوَانِهِ وَجَنَّتِهِ أَحَبَّ لِقَاءَ اللهِ، فَأَحَبَّ اللهُ لِقَاءَهُ. وَإِنَّ الْكَافِرَ إِذَا بُشِّرَ بِعَذَابِ اللهِ وَسَخَطِهِ، كَرِهَ لِقَاءَ اللهِ، وَكَرِهَ اللهُ لِقَاءَهُ » رواهُ مسلم.

1848. **Hazrat Ayesha** (R.A.A.) relates that the Holy Prophet (S.A.W.) said: A person who loves to meet Allah, then Allah too loves to meet him; and a person who does not like meeting with Allah, then Allah too dislikes meeting him. Hazrat Ayesha (R.A.A.) continues. I asked: O Messenger of Allah! Does it mean (disliking to meet Allah) death? then what about which every one of us dislikes? He (S.A.W.) answered: It does not mean that. It means that when a Muslim is given the happy news of Allah's mercy, His pleasure and His Paradise, he feels pleased with the prospect of meeting Allah, and Allah is also pleased to meet him. But when a disbeliever (Kafir) is told of the chastisement and the displeasure of Allah, he does not like meeting Him, and then Allah too dislikes to meet him. *(Muslim)*

١٨٤٩– وَعَنْ أُمِّ الْمُؤْمِنِينَ صَفِيَّةَ بِنْتِ حُيَيٍّ رَضِيَ اللهُ عَنْهَا قَالَتْ: كَانَ النَّبِيُّ صَلَّى اللهُ عَلَيْهِ وَسَلَّمَ مُعْتَكِفاً. فَأَتَيْتُهُ أَزُورُهُ لَيْلاً، فَحَدَّثْتُهُ ثُمَّ قُمْتُ لأَنْقَلِبَ، فَقَامَ مَعِي لِيَقْلِبَنِي، فَمَرَّ رَجُلاَنِ مِنَ الأَنْصَارِ رَضِيَ اللهُ عَنْهُمَا. فَلَمَّا رَأَيَا النَّبِيَّ صَلَّى اللهُ عَلَيْهِ وَسَلَّمَ أَسْرَعَا. فَقَالَ صَلَّى اللهُ عَلَيْهِ وَسَلَّمَ: « عَلَى رِسْلِكُمَا إِنَّهَا صَفِيَّةُ بِنْتُ حُيَيٍّ » فَقَالاَ: سُبْحَانَ اللهِ يَا رَسُولَ اللهِ! فَقَالَ: « إِنَّ الشَّيْطَانَ

يَجْرِي مِنَ ابْنِ آدَمَ مَجْرَى الدَّمِ . وَإِنِّي خَشِيتُ أَنْ يَقْذِفَ فِي قُلُوبِكُمَا شَراً ـ أَوْ قَالَ : شَيْئاً ـ » متفقٌ عليه

1849. Hazrat Ummul Momineen Safiyyah bint Huyyi (R.A.A.) says. Once the Holy Prophet (S.A.W.) was in 'Itikaf' (withdrawing from wordly activities and devoting oneself wholly to the remembrance and worship of Allah in a corner of a mosque during the last ten days of Ramadhan) in mosque, and I went there to see him one night; and after having talked with him when I stood up to go back to my apartment. the Holv Prophet (S.A.W.) also stood up to accompany me and see me off. At this time two Ansaris passed nearby, and when they saw the Holy Prophet (S.A.W.) they accelerated their steps. The Holy Prophet (S.A.W.) asked them to halt and said: This is Safiyyah bint Huyyi (my wife). The Ansaris exclaimed: Holy is Allah! O Messenger of Allah. The Holy Prophet (S.A.W.) observed: Satan floats inside the body of a man along with the circulation of blood, and I apprehended lest this might create some evil (thoughts) in your minds, or he (S.A.W.) said: This may create something in your minds. *(Bukhari and Muslim)*

١٨٥٠ ـ وَعَنْ أَبِي الفَضْلِ العَبَّاسِ بْنِ عَبْدِ المُطَّلِبِ رَضِيَ اللهُ عَنْهُ قَالَ : شَهِدْتُ مَعَ رَسُولِ اللهِ صَلَّى اللهُ عَلَيْهِ وَسَلَّمَ يَوْمَ حُنَيْنٍ فَلَزِمْتُ أَنَا وَأَبُو سُفْيَانَ بْنُ الحَارِثِ بْنِ عَبْدِ المُطَّلِبِ رَسُولَ اللهِ صَلَّى اللهُ عَلَيْهِ وَسَلَّمَ . فَلَمْ نُفَارِقْهُ وَرَسُولُ اللهِ صَلَّى اللهُ عَلَيْهِ وَسَلَّمَ عَلَى بَغْلَةٍ لَهُ بَيْضَاءَ . فَلَمَّا التَقَى المُسْلِمُونَ وَالمُشْرِكُونَ وَلَّى المُسْلِمُونَ مُدْبِرِينَ . فَطَفِقَ رَسُولُ اللهِ . صَلَّى اللهُ عَلَيْهِ وَسَلَّمَ . يَرْكُضُ بَغْلَتَهُ قِبَلَ الكُفَّارِ ، وَأَنَا آخِذٌ بِلِجَامِ بَغْلَةِ رَسُولِ اللهِ . صَلَّى اللهُ عَلَيْهِ وَسَلَّمَ . أَكُفُّهَا إِرَادَةَ أَنْ لاَ تُسْرِعَ ، وَأَبُو سُفْيَانَ آخِذٌ بِرِكَابِ رَسُولِ اللهِ صَلَّى اللهُ عَلَيْهِ وَسَلَّمَ . فَقَالَ رَسُولُ اللهِ صَلَّى اللهُ عَلَيْهِ وَسَلَّمَ : « أَيْ عَبَّاسُ نَادِ أَصْحَابَ السَّمُرَةِ » قَالَ العَبَّاسُ . وَكَانَ رَجُلاً صَيِّتاً : فَقُلْتُ بِأَعْلَى صَوْتِي : أَيْنَ أَصْحَابُ السَّمُرَةِ ، فَوَاللهِ لَكَأَنَّ عَطْفَتَهُمْ حِينَ سَمِعُوا صَوْتِي عَطْفَةُ البَقَرِ عَلَى أَوْلاَدِهَا ، فَقَالُوا : يَا لَبَّيْكَ يَا لَبَّيْكَ . فَاقْتَتَلُوا هُمْ وَالكُفَّارُ ، وَالدَّعْوَةُ فِي الأَنْصَارِ يَقُولُونَ : يَا مَعْشَرَ الأَنْصَارِ ، يَا مَعْشَرَ الأَنْصَارِ ، ثُمَّ قَصُرَتِ الدَّعْوَةُ عَلَى بَنِي

الحارث بن الخزرج . فنظر رسول الله صلى الله عليه وسلم وهو
على بغلته كالمتطاول عليها إلى قتالهم فقال : « هذا حين حمي
الوطيس » ثم أخذ رسول الله صلى الله عليه وسلم حصيات ، فرمى
بهن وجوه الكفار ، ثم قال : « انهزموا ورب محمد » ، فذهبت
أنظر فإذا القتال على هيئته فيما أرى ، فوالله ما هو إلا أن رماهم
بحصياته ، فمازلت أرى حدهم كليلا ، وأمرهم مدبرا . رواه مسلم

1850. Hazrat Abul Fadhl Abbas bin Abdul Muttalib (R.A.A.) relates: I was with the Holy Prophet (S.A.W.) on the day of the battle of Hunain. I and Hazrat Abu Sufyan bin Al Haris bin Abdul Muttalib (R.A.A.) kept close to the Holy Prophet (S.A.W.) throughout on this day, and did not leave him (S.A.W.). The Holy Prophet (S.A.W.) was riding his white mule. When the Muslims clashed with the non-believers, they turned back and ran. (Majority among them was of newly converted Muslims). However, the Holy Prophet (S.A.W.) was applying spur to his mule to go ahead towards the non-believers. Hazrat Abbas (R.A.A.) says: I was holding the bridle of his (S.A.W.) mule trying to restrain it from becoming too fast, and Hazrat Abu Sufyan (R.A.A.) was holding the stirrup of the Holy Prophet (S.A.W.). The Holy Prophet (S.A.W.) asked me: O Abbas! Call the people of Samurah (who made the Convenant of Ridwan—*Baiat Ridwan).Hazrat* Abbas (R.A.A.) says: as I had a louder voice, I called out in my loudest voice: Where are the people of Samurah (those of the Convenant of Ridwan)? As such by Allah, on hearing my voice they ran towards the Holy Prophet (S.A.W.) like a cow running towards her calf. They started crying: Here we are, Here we are. And they started fighting the non-believers. At this very time leaders of Ansar were shouting: O people of Ansar, O people of Ansar, and thereafter calling Bani Haris bin Khazraj. The Holy Prophet (S.A.W.) raising his head, while sitting on his mule, surveyed the situation of the fighting, and said. Now the fighting is at its peak. After this the Holy Prophet (S.A.W.) threw some small pebbles on the faces of non-believers and said: 'By the Sustainer (Lord) of Muhammad (S.A.W.) they may be defeated.' After sometime I went to see the situation which was as before, but, By Allah! as soon as the Holy Prophet (S.A.W.) threw some pebbles, I noticed that the vehemence of the non-believers was abating, (and having been defeated), they ran away. *(Muslim)*

Note : In the battle of Hunain, although the Muslims outnumbered the non-believers, yet the newly converted Muslims were in majority in Muslim army. In the initial stage the onslaught of the non-believers they could not withstand, and ran away from the field. The older Muslims rallied under the leadership of the Holy Prophet (S.A.W.) and defeated the enemy. (Translator)

١٨٥١ – وَعَنْ أَبِي هُرَيْرَةَ رَضِيَ اللهُ عَنْهُ قَالَ : قَالَ رَسُولُ اللهِ صَلَّى اللهُ عَلَيْهِ وَسَلَّمَ : « أَيُّهَا النَّاسُ إِنَّ اللهَ طَيِّبٌ لاَ يَقْبَلُ إِلاَّ طَيِّباً ، وَإِنَّ اللهَ أَمَرَ الْمُؤْمِنِينَ بِمَا أَمَرَ بِهِ الْمُرْسَلِينَ ، فَقَالَ تَعَالَى : يَا أَيُّهَا الرُّسُلُ كُلُوا مِنَ الطَّيِّبَاتِ وَاعْمَلُوا صَالِحاً وَقَالَ تَعَالَى : يَا أَيُّهَا الَّذِينَ آمَنُوا كُلُوا مِنْ طَيِّبَاتِ مَا رَزَقْنَاكُمْ ثُمَّ ذَكَرَ الرَّجُلَ يُطِيلُ السَّفَرَ أَشْعَثَ أَغْبَرَ يَمُدُّ يَدَيْهِ إِلَى السَّمَاءِ : يَا رَبِّ يَا رَبِّ ، وَمَطْعَمُهُ حَرَامٌ ، وَمَشْرَبُهُ حَرَامٌ ، وَمَلْبَسُهُ حَرَامٌ ، وَغُذِيَ بِالْحَرَامِ ، فَأَنَّى يُسْتَجَابُ لِذَلِكَ ! ؟ » رواه مسلم .

1851. Hazrat Abu Hurairah (R.A.A.) relates that the Holy Prophet (S.A.W.) said. O people, Allah, is the Purest and the Neatest and He accepts nothing but the lawful and the purest. Allah has commanded the Muslims as He has commanded His Messengers. As such Allah the Most High has said:

O ye Messengers! Eat of the good things and do right. (23 : 51)

And has said: Eat of the good things wherewith We have provided you. (7 : 160).

Then he narrated the case of a man who set out on a very long journey: He is haggard, weary, covered with dust; he raises his hands towards the sky and prays: O My Lord, O My Lord! While he eats the unlawful food, and drinks the unlawful drinks, his dress is of unlawful (earning), his food procured unlawfully, then how, could his prayers be accepted? *(Muslim)*

١٨٥٢ – وَعَنْهُ رَضِيَ اللهُ عَنْهُ قَالَ : قَالَ رَسُولُ اللهِ صَلَّى اللهُ عَلَيْهِ وَسَلَّمَ : « ثَلاَثَةٌ لاَ يُكَلِّمُهُمُ اللهُ يَوْمَ الْقِيَامَةِ ، وَلاَ يُزَكِّيهِمْ ، وَلاَ يَنْظُرُ إِلَيْهِمْ ، وَلَهُمْ عَذَابٌ أَلِيمٌ : شَيْخٌ زَانٍ ، وَمَلِكٌ كَذَّابٌ ، وَعَائِلٌ مُسْتَكْبِرٌ » رواهُ مسلم

1852. This Hadis has already been covered in No. 617 of Chapter 72.

١٨٥٣ — وَعَنْهُ رَضِيَ اللهُ عَنْهُ قَالَ : قَالَ رَسُولُ اللهِ صَلَّى اللهُ عَلَيْهِ وَسَلَّمَ : « سَيْحَانُ وَجَيْحَانُ وَالفُرَاتُ وَالنِّيلُ كُلٌّ مِنْ أَنْهَارِ الجَنَّةِ » رواهُ مسلم .

1853. Hazrat Abu Hurairah (R.A.A.) relates that the Holy Prophet (S.A.W.) said: Sihan (Jexartes), Jihan (Oxus), Furat (Euphrates) and the river Nile, all are the canals (rivers) of Paradise. *(Muslim)*

١٨٥٤ — وَعَنْهُ قَالَ : أَخَذَ رَسُولُ اللهِ صَلَّى اللهُ عَلَيْهِ وَسَلَّمَ بِيَدِي فَقَالَ : « خَلَقَ اللهُ التُّرْبَةَ يَوْمَ السَّبْتِ ، وَخَلَقَ فِيهَا الجِبَالَ يَوْمَ الأَحَدِ ، وَخَلَقَ الشَّجَرَ يَوْمَ الاثْنَيْنِ ، وَخَلَقَ المَكْرُوهَ يَوْمَ الثُّلاثَاءِ ، وَخَلَقَ النُّورَ يَوْمَ الأَرْبِعَاءِ ، وَبَثَّ فِيهَا الدَّوَابَّ يَوْمَ الخَمِيسِ ، وَخَلَقَ آدَمَ صَلَّى اللهُ عَلَيْهِ وَسَلَّمَ بَعْدَ العَصْرِ مِنْ يَوْمِ الجُمُعَةِ فِي آخِرِ الخَلْقِ فِي آخِرِ سَاعَةٍ مِنَ النَّهَارِ فِيمَا بَيْنَ العَصْرِ إِلَى اللَّيْلِ » رواهُ مسلم .

1854. Hazrat Abu Hurairah (R.A.A.) relates: The Holy Prophet (S.A.W.) took hold of my hand and said: 'Allah, the Most High created the earth on Saturday, made mountains on the earth on Sunday, created trees on Monday, all unpleasant things on Tuesday, and light was created on Wednesday; Allah spread out animals on the earth on Thursday and created Hazrat Adam (A.S.) in the late afternoon (after 'Asr) on Friday in the wake of His Creation in the last hour of the day, between 'Asr (late afternoon) and the night. *(Muslim)*

Note : = The scholars say this Hadis is not sound.

١٨٥٥ — وَعَنْ أَبِي سُلَيْمَانَ خَالِدِ بْنِ الوَلِيدِ رَضِيَ اللهُ عَنْهُ قَالَ : « لَقَدِ انْقَطَعَتْ فِي يَدِي يَوْمَ مُؤْتَةَ تِسْعَةُ أَسْيَافٍ ، فَمَا بَقِيَ فِي يَدِي إِلا صَفِيحَةٌ يَمَانِيَةٌ » ؛ رواهُ البُخاري

1855. Hazrat Abu Sulaiman Khalid bin Waleed (R.A.A.) says: In the Battle of Mauta, seven swords were broken in my hand while in action, and in the end I had only a broad bladed (Small Yemeni) sword. *(Bukhari)*

١٨٥٦ — وَعَنْ عَمْرِو بْنِ العَاصِ رَضِيَ اللهُ عَنْهُ أَنَّهُ سَمِعَ رَسُولَ اللهِ صَلَّى اللهُ عَلَيْهِ وَسَلَّمَ يَقُولُ : « إِذَا حَكَمَ الحَاكِمُ ، فَاجْتَهَدَ ،

ثُمَّ أَصَابَ ، فَلَهُ أَجْرَانِ ، وإِنْ حَكَمَ وَاجْتَهَدَ ، فَأَخْطَأَ ، فَلَهُ أَجْرٌ » .

متفق عَلَيْه

1856. Hazrat 'Amr bin Al 'Aas (R.A.A.) relates that he heard the Holy Prophet say: When a ruler takes a decision after due consideration and enquiry, and this decision is proved to be just and right, such a ruler is entitled to double recompense, and when he comes to a decision with due care and enquiry but makes a mistake then he is entitled to a single reward. *(Bukhari and Muslim)*

١٨٥٧ – وَعَنْ عَائِشَةَ رَضِيَ اللهُ عَنْهَا أَنَّ النَّبِيَّ صَلَّى اللهُ عَلَيْهِ وَسَلَّمَ قَالَ : « الْحُمَّى مِنْ فَيْحِ جَهَنَّم فَأَبْرِدُوهَا بِالْمَاءِ » متفقٌ عليه

1857. Hazrat Ayesha (R.A.A.) relates that the Holy Prophet (S.A.W.) said. Fever is the diffusion of the heat of Hell. As such it should be cooled down with water. *(Bukhari and Muslim)*

١٨٥٨ – وَعَنْهَا رَضِيَ اللهُ عَنْهَا عَنِ النَّبِيِّ صَلَّى اللهُ عَلَيْهِ وَسَلَّمَ قَالَ : « مَنْ مَاتَ وَعَلَيْهِ صَوْمٌ ، صَامَ عَنْهُ وَلِيُّهُ » متفقٌ عَلَيْه .

1858. Hazrat Ayesha (R.A.A.) reports that the Holy Prophet (S.A.W.) said: If a person dies with obligation to make up some missing fasts, (then it is for) his heir (or close relations) to make up the missing fasts on his behalf. *(Bukhari and Muslim)*

Note : Imam Nawawi elucidating this tradition says that when a person dies with some defaults in fasting then it is lawful to fast on his behalf by his near relatives, whether heir or not.

But some other learned persons and theologians, like Imams Abu Hanifa, Malik and Shafi'ee, hold the view that it is not necessary to fast on behalf of a deceased person to make up the shortage of missing fasts but to pay ransom *(Fidya)* for each missing fast.

١٨٥٩ – وَعَنْ عَوْفِ بْنِ مَالِكِ بْنِ الطُّفَيْلِ أَنَّ عَائِشَةَ رَضِيَ اللهُ عَنْهَا حُدِّثَتْ أَنَّ عَبْدَ اللهِ بْنَ الزُّبَيْرِ رَضِيَ اللهُ عَنْهُمَا قَالَ فِي بَيْعٍ أَوْ عَطَاءٍ أَعْطَتْهُ عَائِشَةُ رَضِيَ اللهُ تَعَالَى عَنْهَا : وَاللهِ لَتَنْتَهِيَنَّ عَائِشَةُ ، أَوْ لأَحْجُرَنَّ عَلَيْهَا ، قَالَتْ : أَهُوَ قَالَ هَذَا ؟ قَالُوا : نَعَمْ ، قَالَتْ : هُوَ للهِ عَلَيَّ نَذْرٌ أَنْ لاَ أُكَلِّمَ ابْنَ الزُّبَيْرِ أَبَداً ، فَاسْتَشْفَعَ ابْنُ الزُّبَيْرِ إِلَيْهَا حِينَ طَالَتِ الْهِجْرَةُ . فَقَالَتْ : لاَ وَاللهِ لاَ أُشَفِّعُ فِيهِ أَبَداً ، وَلاَ

أَتَحَنَّثُ إِلَى نَذْرِي فَلَمَّا طَالَ ذَلِكَ عَلَى ابْنِ الزُّبَيْرِ كَلَّمَ الْمِسْوَرَ
ابْنَ مَخْرَمَةَ . وَعَبْدَ الرَّحْمَنِ بْنَ الأَسْوَدِ بْنِ عَبْدِ يَغُوثَ وَقَالَ لَهُمَا :
أَنْشُدُكُمَا اللهَ لَمَا أَدْخَلْتُمَانِي عَلَى عَائِشَةَ رَضِيَ اللهُ عَنْهَا . فَإِنَّهَا
لاَ يَحِلُّ لَهَا أَنْ تَنْذِرَ قَطِيعَتِي . فَأَقْبَلَ بِهِ الْمِسْوَرُ . وَعَبْدُ الرَّحْمَنِ
حَتَّى اسْتَأْذَنَا عَلَى عَائِشَةَ . فَقَالاَ : السَّلاَمُ عَلَيْكِ وَرَحْمَةُ اللهِ
وَبَرَكَاتُهُ ، أَنَدْخُلُ ؟ قَالَتْ عَائِشَةُ : ادْخُلُوا . قَالُوا : كُلُّنَا ؟ قَالَتْ :
نَعَمْ ادْخُلُوا كُلُّكُمْ . وَلاَ تَعْلَمُ أَنَّ مَعَهُمَا ابْنَ الزُّبَيْرِ . فَلَمَّا دَخَلُوا .
دَخَلَ ابْنُ الزُّبَيْرِ الْحِجَابَ . فَاعْتَنَقَ عَائِشَةَ رَضِيَ اللهُ عَنْهَا . وَطَفِقَ
يُنَاشِدُهَا وَيَبْكِي ، وَطَفِقَ الْمِسْوَرُ ، وَعَبْدُ الرَّحْمَنِ يُنَاشِدَانِهَا
إِلاَّ كَلَّمَتْهُ وَقَبِلَتْ مِنْهُ . وَيَقُولاَنِ : إِنَّ النَّبِيَّ صَلَّى اللهُ عَلَيْهِ وَسَلَّمَ
نَهَى عَمَّا قَدْ عَلِمْتِ مِنَ الْهِجْرَةِ ، وَلاَ يَحِلُّ لِمُسْلِمٍ أَنْ يَهْجُرَ أَخَاهُ
فَوْقَ ثَلاَثِ لَيَالٍ ، فَلَمَّا أَكْثَرُوا عَلَى عَائِشَةَ مِنَ التَّذْكِرَةِ وَالتَّحْرِيجِ .
طَفِقَتْ تُذَكِّرُهُمَا وَتَبْكِي . وَتَقُولُ : إِنِّي نَذَرْتُ وَالنَّذْرُ شَدِيدٌ .
فَلَمْ يَزَالاَ بِهَا حَتَّى كَلَّمَتِ ابْنَ الزُّبَيْرِ ، وَأَعْتَقَتْ فِي نَذْرِهَا ذَلِكَ
أَرْبَعِينَ رَقَبَةً . وَكَانَتْ تَذْكُرُ نَذْرَهَا بَعْدَ ذَلِكَ فَتَبْكِي حَتَّى تَبُلَّ
دُمُوعُهَا خِمَارَهَا . رواهُ البُخارِي .

1859. Hazrat Auf bin Malik bin Tufail (R.A.A.) says that Once Hazrat Ayesha (R.A.A.) was told that Hazrat Abdullah bin Zubair (R.A.A.) remarked in respect of a gift made by him to her, which she had distributed among the poor and needy, wherein he said: "If Hazrat Ayesha (R.A.A.) does not stop this practice, I shall stop sending (further gifts or stipends). She asked: 'Has he really said so?' And the people said: 'Yes!' Thereupon she declared: 'I swear in the name of Allah that I shall never talk to Abdullah bin Zubair.' When this period of their being not on speaking terms grew long, Hazrat Abdullah bin Zubair sent somebody to plead his case to her. But she (Ummul Momineen Hazrat Ayesha R.A.A.) refused to accept this recommendation and said: 'I shall not accept any recommendation on his behalf and will not annul my vow.' After the lapse of some more time Hazrat Abdullah bin Zubair grew impatient, and accordingly approached Hazrat Miswar bin Mukhramah and Hazrat Abdur Rahman bin Al Aswad bin Abd Yaghus and said to them: 'I call upon you in the name of Allah, the Most High, that you take me to Hazrat Ayesha (R.A.A.), for it is not lawful for her that she should take oath to cut off my relationship with her (as he was her nephew-sister's son). Accordingly Hazrat Miswar (R.A.A.) and Hazrat Abdur Rahman (R.A.A.) covering Hazrat Abdullah bin Zubair (R.A.A.) under their sheets took him to Hazrat Ayesha (R.A.A.) and called out: *As Salam-o-Alaikum Wa Rahmatullah Wa Barakatuhu* (Peace be on you and the mercy of Allah and His blessings). Have we your permission to come in?' She said: 'You may come in.' They further said: 'All of us?' She answered. Yes, all of you.' But Hazrat Ayesha (R.A.A.) did not know that Ibn Zubair was also with them. However when they went in, Ibn Zubair went straight behind the screen and holding on to his maternal aunt, Hazrat Ayesha (R.A.A.) started weeping and pleading his case in the name of Allah. His two companions Hazrat Miswar, and Hazrat Abdur Rahman also pleaded that she should talk to him and accept his apology. They further told her: 'Do you know that the Holy Prophet (S.A.W.) has forbidden cutting off relationship, and that it is not lawful for a Muslim to keep away from a brother Muslim for more than three days.' When they continued in their request, she also reminded them of the rights of kinship and broke down. She said: 'I have vowed and the atonement for the breach of this vow is very severe; but the two intermedisries continued their pleading till she yielded and talked to Hazrat Ibn Zubair. As an atonement for the breach of her vow, she had to free forty slaves. But afterwards whenever she remembered this episode, she would start weeping so much so that the sheet with which she covered her head, would become wet with tears. *(Bukhari)*

١٨٦٠ – وَعَنْ عُقْبَةَ بْنِ عَامِرٍ رَضِيَ اللهُ عَنْهُ أَنَّ رَسُولَ اللهِ صَلَّى اللهُ عَلَيْهِ وَسَلَّمَ خَرَجَ إِلَى قَتْلَى أُحُدٍ ، فَصَلَّى عَلَيْهِمْ بَعْدَ ثَمَانِ سِنِينَ كَالْمُوَدِّعِ لِلْأَحْيَاءِ وَالْأَمْوَاتِ ، ثُمَّ طَلَعَ إِلَى الْمِنْبَرِ ، فَقَالَ : إِنِّي بَيْنَ أَيْدِيكُمْ فَرَطٌ وَأَنَا شَهِيدٌ عَلَيْكُمْ ؛ وَإِنَّ مَوْعِدَكُمُ الْحَوْضُ . وَإِنِّي لَأَنْظُرُ إِلَيْهِ مِنْ مَقَامِي هَذَا . أَلَا وَإِنِّي لَسْتُ أَخْشَى عَلَيْكُمْ أَنْ تُشْرِكُوا ، وَلَكِنْ أَخْشَى عَلَيْكُمُ الدُّنْيَا أَنْ تَنَافَسُوهَا » قَالَ : فَكَانَتْ آخِرَ نَظْرَةٍ نَظَرْتُهَا إِلَى رَسُولِ اللهِ صَلَّى اللهُ عَلَيْهِ وَسَلَّمَ . متفقٌ عليه .

وفي رِوَايَةٍ : « وَلَكِنِّي أَخْشَى عَلَيْكُمُ الدُّنْيَا أَنْ تَنَافَسُوا فِيهَا ، وَتَقْتَتِلُوا فَتَهْلِكُوا كَمَا هَلَكَ مَنْ كَانَ قَبْلَكُمْ » قَالَ عُقْبَةُ : فَكَانَ آخِرَ مَا رَأَيْتُ رَسُولَ اللهِ صَلَّى اللهُ عَلَيْهِ وَسَلَّمَ عَلَى الْمِنْبَرِ .

وَفِي رِوَايَةٍ قَالَ : « إِنِّي فَرَطٌ لَكُمْ وَأَنَا شَهِيدٌ عَلَيْكُمْ وَإِنِّي وَاللهِ لَأَنْظُرُ إِلَى حَوْضِي الآنَ ، وَإِنِّي أُعْطِيتُ مَفَاتِيحَ خَزَائِنِ الأَرْضِ ، أَوْ مَفَاتِيحَ الأَرْضِ . وَإِنِّي وَاللهِ مَا أَخَافُ عَلَيْكُمْ أَنْ تُشْرِكُوا بَعْدِي وَلَكِنْ أَخَافُ عَلَيْكُمْ أَنْ تَنَافَسُوا فِيهَا » .

1860. **Hazrat 'Uqbah bin 'Aamir (R.A.A.)** relates that the Holy Prophet (S.A.W.) (once) visited the graves of the martyrs who fell in the Battle of Uhud and prayed for them eight years after the battle, as if he was saying goodbye to the present and departed souls. Then he ascended the pulpit and said: I am your fore-runner (going ahead of you) and I am a witness over you and our meeting shall be at the Reservoir (of Kausar), and I am looking towards it from this place. I am not worried about you that you will commit shirk (become guilty of associating somebody with Allah) but I am afraid that you might become enamoured of this world. Hazrat 'Uqbah bin 'Aamir (R.A.A.) says: This was my last opportunity of looking at the Holy Prophet (S.A.W.). *(Bukhari and Muslim)*

According to another version the Holy Prophet (S.A.W.) said: I fear that you might be lured by the attractions of this world, and start fighting among yourselves and be ruined as those nations before you were ruined. Hazrat 'Uqbah (R.A.A.) says: This was the last time that I saw the Holy Prophet (S.A.W.) on the pulpit!

Yet another version says: I am your precursor and am a witness on you. By Allah! I am looking at my reservoir (Kausar) just now; and I have been given the keys of the treasures in the earth or the keys of earth. By Allah, I am not worried that after me (when I pass over) you will associate somebody with Allah, but I am afraid that you might run after the world.

١٨٦١– وَعَنْ أَبِي زَيْدٍ عَمْرِو بْنِ أَخْطَبَ الأَنْصَارِيِّ رَضِيَ اللهُ عَنْهُ قَالَ صَلَّى بِنَا رَسُولُ اللهِ صَلَّى اللهُ عَلَيْهِ وَسَلَّمَ الْفَجْرَ ، وَصَعِدَ الْمِنْبَرَ ، فَخَطَبَنَا حَتَّى حَضَرَتِ الظُّهْرُ ، فَنَزَلَ فَصَلَّى ، ثُمَّ صَعِدَ الْمِنْبَرَ حَتَّى حَضَرَتِ الْعَصْرُ ، ثُمَّ نَزَلَ فَصَلَّى ، ثُمَّ صَعِدَ الْمِنْبَرَ حَتَّى غَرَبَتِ الشَّمْسُ ، فَأَخْبَرَنَا مَا كَانَ وَمَا هُوَ كَائِنٌ ، فَأَعْلَمُنَا أَحْفَظُنَا . رَوَاهُ مُسْلِمٌ .

1861. **Hazrat Abu Zaid 'Amr bin Akhtab Al-Ansari (R.A.A.)** says: (Once) the Holy Prophet (S.A.W.) led us the Fajr (Morning) Prayer then ascended the pulpit and delivered a sermon which lasted till the noon prayer time. He then came down from the pulpit, led us the noon (Zuhr) prayer, He again went on the pulpit and continued his sermon till the time of the late afternoon (Asr) prayer, when he came down and led the Asr Prayer. He again mounted the pulpit and continued his address untill the sunset. In the course of his address he talked about those things which had already happened and also about those things which are yet to happen. Therefore, the most learned persons among us are those persons who preserved these things in their memories. *(Muslim)*

١٨٦٢– وَعَنْ عَائِشَةَ رَضِيَ اللهُ عَنْهَا قَالَتْ : قَالَ النَّبِيُّ صَلَّى اللهُ عَلَيْهِ وَسَلَّمَ : «مَنْ نَذَرَ أَنْ يُطِيعَ اللهَ فَلْيُطِعْهُ ، وَمَنْ نَذَرَ أَنْ يَعْصِيَ اللهَ . فَلاَ يَعْصِهِ » رَوَاهُ الْبُخَارِي .

1862. Hazrat Ayesha (R.A.A.) relates that the Holy Prophet (S.A.W.) said: A person who has undertaken to obey Allah, should obey Him. But one who vows to disobey Allah, should not disobey Him. *(Bukhari)*

١٨٦٣– وَعَنْ أُمِّ شَرِيكٍ رَضِيَ اللهُ عَنْهَا أَنَّ رَسُولَ اللهِ صَلَّى اللهُ عَلَيْهِ وَسَلَّمَ أَمَرَهَا بِقَتْلِ الأَوْزَاغِ ، وَقَالَ : « كَانَ يَنْفُخُ عَلَى إِبْرَاهِيمَ » مُتَّفَقٌ عَلَيْهِ

1863. Hazrat Umm Shareek (R.A.A.) reports that the Holy Prophet (S.A.W.) ordered us to kill chameleon saying: 'It was he who was blowing (the fire kindled for burning) Prophet Abraham. *(Bukhari and Muslim)*

١٨٦٤ – وَعَنْ أَبِي هُرَيْرَةَ رَضِيَ اللهُ عَنْهُ قَالَ : قَالَ رَسُولُ اللهِ صَلَّى اللهُ عَلَيْهِ وَسَلَّمَ : « مَنْ قَتَلَ وَزَغَةً فِي أَوَّلِ ضَرْبَةٍ ، فَلَهُ كَذَا وَكَذَا حَسَنَةً ، وَمَنْ قَتَلَهَا فِي الضَّرْبَةِ الثَّانِيَةِ ، فَلَهُ كَذَا وَكَذَا حَسَنَةً دُونَ الأُولَى ، وَإِنْ قَتَلَهَا فِي الضَّرْبَةِ الثَّالِثَةِ ، فَلَهُ كَذَا وَكَذَا حَسَنَةً ».

وَفِي رِوَايَةٍ : « مَنْ قَتَلَ وَزَغاً فِي أَوَّلِ ضَرْبَةٍ ، كُتِبَ لَهُ مِائَةُ حَسَنَةٍ ، وَفِي الثَّانِيَةِ دُونَ ذَلِكَ ، وَفِي الثَّالِثَةِ دُونَ ذَلِكَ » . رَوَاهُ مُسْلِم .

1864. Hazrat Abu Hurairah (R.A.A.) relates that the Holy Prophet (S.A.W.) said: One who kills a chameleon in the first blow will have so much recompense to his credit; One who kills it in the second hit, will have so much recompense (less than the first), and the person who kills it in the third attempt will have so much recompense (i.e. less than the one who kills it in second stroke).

Another version says: He who kills a chameleon in the first attempt will be credited with recompense equivalent to a hundred good deeds, and if it is killed in the second attempt, the recompense will be less than that, and for killing it in the third stroke, the recompense will be less than the second.
(Muslim)

١٨٦٥ – وَعَنْ أَبِي هُرَيْرَةَ رَضِيَ اللهُ عَنْهُ أَنَّ رَسُولَ اللهِ صَلَّى اللهُ عَلَيْهِ وَسَلَّمَ قَالَ : « قَالَ رَجُلٌ لَأَتَصَدَّقَنَّ بِصَدَقَةٍ ، فَخَرَجَ بِصَدَقَتِهِ ، فَوَضَعَهَا فِي يَدِ سَارِقٍ ، فَأَصْبَحُوا يَتَحَدَّثُونَ : تُصُدِّقَ عَلَى سَارِقٍ ! فَقَالَ : اللَّهُمَّ لَكَ الْحَمْدُ لَأَتَصَدَّقَنَّ بِصَدَقَةٍ ، فَخَرَجَ بِصَدَقَتِهِ ، فَوَضَعَهَا فِي يَدِ زَانِيَةٍ ، فَأَصْبَحُوا يَتَحَدَّثُونَ : تُصُدِّقَ اللَّيْلَةَ عَلَى زَانِيَةٍ ! فَقَالَ : اللَّهُمَّ لَكَ الْحَمْدُ عَلَى زَانِيَةٍ ؟! لَأَتَصَدَّقَنَّ بِصَدَقَةٍ ، فَخَرَجَ بِصَدَقَتِهِ ، فَوَضَعَهَا فِي يَدِ غَنِيٍّ ، فَأَصْبَحُوا يَتَحَدَّثُونَ تُصُدِّقَ عَلَى غَنِيٍّ ! فَقَالَ : اللَّهُمَّ لَكَ الْحَمْدُ عَلَى سَارِقٍ ، وَعَلَى زَانِيَةٍ ، وَعَلَى غَنِيٍّ ! فَأُتِيَ فَقِيلَ لَهُ : أَمَّا صَدَقَتُكَ عَلَى سَارِقٍ ، فَلَعَلَّهُ أَنْ يَسْتَعِفَّ عَنْ سَرِقَتِهِ ، وَأَمَّا الزَّانِيَةُ فَلَعَلَّهَا تَسْتَعِفُّ عَنْ زِنَاهَا ، وَأَمَّا الْغَنِيُّ فَلَعَلَّهُ أَنْ يَعْتَبِرَ ، فَيُنْفِقَ مِمَّا آتَاهُ اللهُ »

رَوَاهُ الْبُخَارِيُّ بِلَفْظِهِ ، وَمُسْلِمٌ بِمَعْنَاهُ

1865. Hazrat Abu Hurairah (R.A.A.) relates that the Holy Prophet (S.A.W.) said: A man decided, I will give alms (tonight). Accordingly he set out with his alms and gave the same to a thief. In the morning, people started saying: Last night a thief was given alms. The man who gave alms prayed: Allah to Thee belongs all Praise. I shall now give alms again tonight. As such he went out with his alms and put the same in the hands of a whore. Next morning the people started talking, Last night alms were bestowed on a whore. The man, who gave alms supplicated: Allah, praise be to Thee who enabled me to give alms even to an whore, but nevertheless, I shall give alms once more. So he went out in the night (for the third time) with his alms, and this time he handed over the same to a rich man. Next day the people discussed: Alms were bestowed upon a rich man. He supplicated: Allah, I thank Thee for enabling me to give alms to a thief, an adulteress and to a rich man. He was told in his dream: Your alms to the thief might persuade him to stop his practice of stealing, and your alms to the adulteress might enable her to give up adultery and the rich man might get a lesson from your alms and start spending in charity out of the bounty which Allah has granted him.

(Bukhari narrated these words and *Muslim* narrated meaning it)

١٨٦٦ – وَعَنْهُ قَالَ : كُنَّا مَعَ رَسُولِ اللهِ صَلَّى اللهُ عَلَيْهِ وَسَلَّمَ فِي دَعْوَةٍ ، فَرُفِعَ إِلَيْهِ الذِّرَاعُ ، وَكَانَتْ تُعْجِبُهُ ، فَنَهَسَ مِنْهَا نَهْسَةً وَقَالَ : أَنَا سَيِّدُ النَّاسِ يَوْمَ الْقِيَامَةِ ، هَلْ تَدْرُونَ مِمَّ ذَاكَ ؟ يَجْمَعُ اللهُ الأَوَّلِينَ وَالآخِرِينَ فِي صَعِيدٍ وَاحِدٍ ، فَيَنْظُرُهُمُ النَّاظِرُ ، وَيُسْمِعُهُمُ الدَّاعِي ، وَتَدْنُو مِنْهُمُ الشَّمْسُ ، فَيَبْلُغُ النَّاسَ مِنَ الْغَمِّ وَالْكَرْبِ مَا لاَ يُطِيقُونَ وَلاَ يَحْتَمِلُونَ ، فَيَقُولُ النَّاسُ : أَلاَ تَرَوْنَ إِلَى مَا أَنْتُمْ فِيهِ إِلَى مَا بَلَغَكُمْ ، أَلاَ تَنْظُرُونَ مَنْ يَشْفَعُ لَكُمْ إِلَى رَبِّكُمْ ؟ فَيَقُولُ بَعْضُ النَّاسِ لِبَعْضٍ : أَبُوكُمْ آدَمُ ، وَيَأْتُونَهُ فَيَقُولُونَ : يَا آدَمُ أَنْتَ أَبُو الْبَشَرِ ، خَلَقَكَ اللهُ بِيَدِهِ ، وَنَفَخَ فِيكَ مِنْ رُوحِهِ ، وَأَمَرَ الْمَلاَئِكَةَ ، فَسَجَدُوا لَكَ وَأَسْكَنَكَ الْجَنَّةَ ، أَلاَ تَشْفَعُ لَنَا إِلَى رَبِّكَ ؟ أَلاَ تَرَى مَا نَحْنُ فِيهِ ، وَمَا بَلَغَنَا ؟ فَقَالَ : إِنَّ رَبِّي غَضِبَ غَضَباً لَمْ يَغْضَبْ قَبْلَهُ مِثْلَهُ ، وَلاَ يَغْضَبُ بَعْدَهُ مِثْلَهُ ، وَإِنَّهُ نَهَانِي عَنِ الشَّجَرَةِ ، فَعَصَيْتُ ، نَفْسِي نَفْسِي ، اذْهَبُوا إِلَى غَيْرِي ، اذْهَبُوا إِلَى نُوحٍ ، فَيَأْتُونَ نُوحاً فَيَقُولُونَ : يَا نُوحُ ، أَنْتَ أَوَّلُ الرُّسُلِ إِلَى أَهْلِ الأَرْضِ ، وَقَدْ سَمَّاكَ اللهُ عَبْداً شَكُوراً ، أَلاَ تَرَى إِلَى مَا نَحْنُ فِيهِ ، أَلاَ تَرَى إِلَى مَا بَلَغَنَا ، أَلاَ تَشْفَعُ لَنَا إِلَى رَبِّكَ ؟ فَيَقُولُ : إِنَّ رَبِّي غَضِبَ الْيَوْمَ غَضَباً لَمْ يَغْضَبْ قَبْلَهُ مِثْلَهُ ، وَلَنْ يَغْضَبَ بَعْدَهُ مِثْلَهُ ، وَإِنَّهُ قَدْ كَانَتْ لِي دَعْوَةٌ دَعَوْتُ بِهَا عَلَى قَوْمِي ، نَفْسِي نَفْسِي نَفْسِي ، اذْهَبُوا إِلَى غَيْرِي ، اذْهَبُوا إِلَى إِبْرَاهِيمَ . فَيَأْتُونَ إِبْرَاهِيمَ فَيَقُولُونَ : يَا إِبْرَاهِيمُ أَنْتَ نَبِيُّ اللهِ وَخَلِيلُهُ مِنْ أَهْلِ الأَرْضِ ، اشْفَعْ لَنَا إِلَى رَبِّكَ ، أَلاَ تَرَى إِلَى مَا نَحْنُ فِيهِ ؟ فَيَقُولُ لَهُمْ : إِنَّ رَبِّي قَدْ غَضِبَ الْيَوْمَ غَضَباً لَمْ يَغْضَبْ قَبْلَهُ مِثْلَهُ . وَلَنْ يَغْضَبَ بَعْدَهُ مِثْلَهُ ، وَإِنِّي كُنْتُ كَذَبْتُ ثَلاَثَ

كَذْبَاتٍ ، نَفْسِي نَفْسِي نَفْسِي ، اذْهَبُوا إِلَى غَيْرِي ، اذْهَبُوا إِلَى مُوسَى ، فَيَأْتُونَ مُوسَى ، فَيَقُولُونَ : يَا مُوسَى أَنْتَ رَسُولُ اللهِ ، فَضَّلَكَ اللهُ بِرِسَالاتِهِ وَبِكَلامِهِ عَلَى النَّاسِ ، اشْفَعْ لَنَا إِلَى رَبِّكَ ، أَلاَ تَرَى إِلَى مَا نَحْنُ فِيهِ ؟ فَيَقُولُ : إِنَّ رَبِّي قَدْ غَضِبَ الْيَوْمَ غَضَباً لَمْ يَغْضَبْ قَبْلَهُ مِثْلَهُ ، وَلَنْ يَغْضَبَ بَعْدَهُ مِثْلَهُ ، وَإِنِّي قَدْ قَتَلْتُ نَفْساً لَمْ أُومَرْ بِقَتْلِهَا ، نَفْسِي نَفْسِي نَفْسِي ، اذْهَبُوا إِلَى غَيْرِي ، اذْهَبُوا إِلَى عِيسَى . فَيَأْتُونَ عِيسَى ، فَيَقُولُونَ : يَا عِيسَى أَنْتَ رَسُولُ اللهِ وَكَلِمَتُهُ أَلْقَاهَا إِلَى مَرْيَمَ وَرُوحٌ مِنْهُ ، وَكَلَّمْتَ النَّاسَ فِي الْمَهْدِ ،اشْفَعْ لَنَا إِلَى رَبِّكَ ، أَلاَ تَرَى إِلَى مَا نَحْنُ فِيهِ ؟ فَيَقُولُ عِيسَى : إِنَّ رَبِّي قَدْ غَضِبَ الْيَوْمَ غَضَباً لَمْ يَغْضَبْ قَبْلَهُ مِثْلَهُ ، وَلَنْ يَغْضَبَ بَعْدَهُ مِثْلَهُ ، وَلَمْ يَذْكُرْ ذَنْباً ، نَفْسِي نَفْسِي نَفْسِي ، اذْهَبُوا إِلَى غَيْرِي ، اذْهَبُوا إِلَى مُحَمَّدٍ صَلَّى اللهُ عَلَيْهِ وَسَلَّمَ » .

وفي روايةٍ : « فَيَأْتُونِي فَيَقُولُونَ : يَا مُحَمَّدُ أَنْتَ رَسُولُ اللهِ ، وَخَاتَمُ الأَنْبِيَاءِ ، وَقَدْ غَفَرَ اللهُ لَكَ مَا تَقَدَّمَ مِنْ ذَنْبِكَ وَمَا تَأَخَّرَ ، اشْفَعْ لَنَا إِلَى رَبِّكَ ، أَلاَ تَرَى إِلَى مَا نَحْنُ فِيهِ ؟ فَأَنْطَلِقُ ، فَآتِي تَحْتَ الْعَرْشِ ، فَأَقَعُ سَاجِداً لِرَبِّي ، ثُمَّ يَفْتَحُ اللهُ عَلَيَّ مِنْ مَحَامِدِهِ ، وَحُسْنِ الثَّنَاءِ عَلَيْهِ شَيْئاً لَمْ يَفْتَحْهُ عَلَى أَحَدٍ قَبْلِي ثُمَّ يُقَالُ : يَا مُحَمَّدُ ارْفَعْ رَأْسَكَ ،سَلْ تُعْطَهْ ، وَاشْفَعْ تُشَفَّعْ ، فَأَرْفَعُ رَأْسِي ، فَأَقُولُ أُمَّتِي يَارَبِّ ، أُمَّتِي يَا رَبِّ ، فَيُقَالُ : يَا مُحَمَّدُ أَدْخِلْ مِنْ أُمَّتِكَ مَنْ لاَ حِسَابَ عَلَيْهِمْ مِنَ الْبَابِ الأَيْمَنِ مِنْ أَبْوَابِ الْجَنَّةِ وَهُمْ شُرَكَاءُ النَّاسِ فِيمَا سِوَى ذَلِكَ مِنَ الأَبْوَابِ» ثُمَّ قَالَ : «وَالَّذِي نَفْسِي بِيَدِهِ إِنَّ مَا بَيْنَ الْمِصْرَاعَيْنِ مِنْ مَصَارِيعِ الْجَنَّةِ كَمَا بَيْنَ مَكَّةَ وَهَجَرَ ، أَوْ كَمَا بَيْنَ مَكَّةَ وَبُصْرَى » مُتَّفَقٌ عليهِ

1866. Hazrat Abu Hurairah (R.A.A.) says: Once we participated in a feast along with the Holy Prophet (S.A.W.) where he had been offered a lamb's fore leg (duly cooked). He (S.A.W.) was pleased with it. He ate it as much as he liked. Afterwards he addressed us. 'I will be the leader of all the human beings on the Day of Judgement. Do you know what it is? On the Day of Judgement Allah will assemble all mankind, the first and last, on a wide and plain ground so that they may be visible to all those who may see, and everybody would be able to hear the caller as well. The sun will be nearest to them on the day and the people will undergo unbearable pain and grief which will be beyond their power. Then they will say to one another: Don't you know as to what has happened to you and how much have you suffered? Why Don't you try to find someone who could intercede for you with your Lord? Then they will say to each other: Adam is your father, (let us go to him), and they will go to him and say. O Adam (A.S.), you are the father of all mankind, Allah has created you with his own hands, and breathed into you His spirit and commanded the angels to bow down to you, and made the Paradise your dwelling place. Then will you not intercede for us with your Lord? You do not see our condition, and the magnitude of our suffering? Hazrat Adam (A.S.) will say: Today my Lord is enraged very much; He was never angry so much before, nor will He be so in future. He had prohibited me from (eating from a particular tree) but I disobeyed (His command). (I am worried about) myself, myself, myself. Go to someone else. (I suggest) you go to Nuh. The people will then go to Hazrat Nuh (Prophet Noah) and say: O Nuh, you are the first Messenger (Prophet from Allah) for the (whole) mankind on earth, and Allah has named you a grateful bondman. Do you not see our plight and our sufferings? Then why not you intercede with your Lord on our behalf. Prophet Noah will say: 'Today my Sustainer (Lord) is enraged very much; He was never angry so much in the past, nor will He be so in future. I had (only) one chance of supplication which I used for my people. (I am worried about) myself, myself, myself. Go to some one else, (I suggest) go to Abraham (Ibrahim A.S.). The people will then go to Hazrat Ibrahim (A.S.) and say: You are Allah's Prophet and Friend chosen from the inhabitants of the earth. Please do intercede for us with your Sustainer (Lord). Do you not see as to in what situation we are? He will tell them: Today my Sustainer Lord is enraged very much. He was never angry so much in the past, nor will He be so in future. Three falsehoods are attributed to me. (Reputed scholers refute the authenticity of reporting, of this portion). (I am worried about) myself, myself myself. Go to someone else; (I suggest) go to Moses. They will then go to Hazrat Musa (Moses), and say: O Moses, you are a Messenger of Allah. Allah honoured and distinguished you upon the people with His words and His message. Please do intercede for us with your Lord. Do you not see in what condition we are? Hazrat

Musa will say: Today my Sustainer Lord is enraged very much. He was never angry so much in the past, nor will He be so in future. I had killed a person whom I had not been ordered to kill. (I am worried about) myself, myself, myself. Go to someone else; (I suggest) you go to Hazrat Isa (Jesus Christ). They will accordingly go to Jesus, and will say to him: O Jesus, you are the Messenger of Allah, and His word, which He conveyed to Mary and His spirit, and you talked to people in your childhood from your cradle. Please intercede on our behalf with your Lord. Do you not see our condition in which we are? Hazrat Isa (Jesus Christ) will say: Today my Lord is enraged very much. He was never angry so much before, nor will He be so in future. Although Hazrat Isa would not mention any fault of him yet would say: (I am worried about) myself, myself, myself. Go to someone else, (I suggest you) go to Muhammad (S.A.W.).

Another version says: The Holy Prophet (S.A.W.) said. The people will come to me and will say: O Muhammad (S.A.W.) you are the Messenger of Allah, and the Last of all the prophets, and Allah has forgiven your all shortcomings (if any), the first and the last. Please intercede for us with your Lord. Do you not see our (pitiable) condition? Then I will proceed towards the *Arsh* (the throne), and shall fall down in prostration before my Lord. Then Allah will bestow upon me knowledge of His praise and glorification such as He had never told anyone before. Then it will be said: O Muhammad (S.A.W.), raise your head, and ask, you will be given, and intercede, your intercession will be accepted. Then I shall raise my head and will supplicate. O Lord, my people, O Lord, my people. Then it will be said: O Muhammad ! take into the Paradise through its gate on the right side such of your *Ummat* whose record is clear, and have nothing to account for: as regards the remainder, they will be admitted along with the other people through the various gates of Paradise. The Holy Prophet (S.A.W.) added: 'By Him in Whose possession is my life, the distance between the two shutters of the gates of Paradise is as much as the distance between Mecca (Makkah) and Hajar or Mecca (Makkah) and Busra.

(Bukhari and Muslim)

١٨٦٧ – وَعَنْ ابْنِ عَبَّاسٍ رَضِيَ اللهُ عَنْهُمَا قَالَ : جَاءَ إِبْرَاهِيمُ صَلَّى اللهُ عَلَيْهِ وَسَلَّمَ بِأُمِّ إِسْمَاعِيلَ وَبِابْنِهَا إِسْمَاعِيلَ وَهِيَ تُرْضِعُهُ حَتَّى وَضَعَهَا عِنْدَ الْبَيْتِ عِنْدَ دَوْحَةٍ فَوْقَ زَمْزَمَ فِي أَعْلَى الْمَسْجِدِ وَلَيْسَ بِمَكَّةَ يَوْمَئِذٍ أَحَدٌ وَلَيْسَ بِهَا مَاءٌ ، فَوَضَعَهُمَا هُنَاكَ ، وَوَضَعَ عِنْدَهُمَا جِرَاباً فِيهِ تَمْرٌ ، وَسِقَاءً فِيهِ مَاءٌ ، ثُمَّ قَفَّى إِبْرَاهِيمُ مُنْطَلِقاً ، فَتَبِعَتْهُ أُمُّ إِسْمَاعِيلَ فَقَالَتْ : يَا إِبْرَاهِيمُ أَيْنَ تَذْهَبُ وَتَتْرُكُنَا بِهَذَا

الوَادِي الَّذِي لَيْسَ فِيهِ أَنِيسٌ وَلاَ شَيْءٌ ؟ فَقَالَتْ لَهُ ذَلِكَ مِرَاراً ، وَجَعَلَ لاَ يَلْتَفِتُ إِلَيْهَا ، قَالَتْ لَهُ : آللهُ أَمَرَكَ بِهَذَا ؟ قَالَ : نَعَمْ . قَالَتْ : إِذاً لاَ يُضَيِّعُنَا ، ثُمَّ رَجَعَتْ ، فَانْطَلَقَ إِبْرَاهِيمُ صَلَّى اللهُ عَلَيْهِ وَسَلَّمَ ، حَتَّى إِذَا كَانَ عِنْدَ الثَّنِيَّةِ حَيْثُ لاَ يَرَوْنَهُ ، اسْتَقْبَلَ بِوَجْهِهِ الْبَيْتَ، ثُمَّ دَعَا بِهَؤُلاءِ الدَّعَوَاتِ، فَرَفَعَ يَدَيْهِ فَقَالَ : (رَبِّ إِنِّي أَسْكَنْتُ مِنْ ذُرِّيَّتِي بِوَادٍ غَيْرِ ذِي زَرْعٍ) حَتَّى بَلَغَ (يَشْكُرُونَ) وَجَعَلَتْ أُمُّ إِسْمَاعِيلَ تُرْضِعُ إِسْمَاعِيلَ ، وَتَشْرَبُ مِنْ ذَلِكَ المَاء ، حَتَّى إِذَا نَفِدَ مَا فِي السِّقَاءِ ، عَطِشَتْ ، وَعَطِشَ ابْنُهَا ، وَجَعَلَتْ تَنْظُرُ إِلَيْهِ يَتَلَوَّى ــ أَوْ قَالَ : يَتَلَبَّطُ فَانْطَلَقَتْ كَرَاهِيَةَ أَنْ تَنْظُرَ إِلَيْهِ ، فَوَجَدَتِ الصَّفَا أَقْرَبَ جَبَلٍ فِي الأَرْضِ يَلِيهَا ، فَقَامَتْ عَلَيْهِ ، ثُمَّ اسْتَقْبَلَتِ الْوَادِيَ تَنْظُرُ هَلْ تَرَى أَحَداً ؟ فَلَمْ تَرَ أَحَداً . فَهَبَطَتْ مِنَ الصَّفَا حَتَّى إِذَا بَلَغَتِ الْوَادِيَ ، رَفَعَتْ طَرَفَ دِرْعِهَا ، ثُمَّ سَعَتْ سَعْيَ الإِنْسَانِ المَجْهُودِ حَتَّى جَاوَزَتِ الْوَادِيَ ، ثُمَّ أَتَتِ المَرْوَةَ ، فَقَامَتْ عَلَيْهَا ، فَنَظَرَتْ هَلْ تَرَى أَحَداً ؟ فَلَمْ تَرَ أَحَداً ، فَفَعَلَتْ ذَلِكَ سَبْعَ مَرَّاتٍ . قَالَ ابْنُ عَبَّاسٍ رَضِيَ اللهُ عَنْهُمَا : قَالَ النَّبِيُّ صَلَّى اللهُ عَلَيْهِ وَسَلَّمَ : « فَذَلِكَ سَعْيُ النَّاسِ بَيْنَهُمَا » فَلَمَّا أَشْرَفَتْ عَلَى المَرْوَةِ سَمِعَتْ صَوْتاً ، فَقَالَتْ : صَهْ ــ تُرِيدُ نَفْسَهَا ــ ثُمَّ تَسَمَّعَتْ ، فَسَمِعَتْ أَيْضاً فَقَالَتْ : قَدْ أَسْمَعْتَ إِنْ كَانَ عِنْدَكَ غَوَاثٌ ، فَإِذَا هِيَ بِالمَلَكِ عِنْدَ مَوْضِعِ زَمْزَمَ ، فَبَحَثَ بِعَقِبِهِ ــ أَوْ قَالَ بِجَنَاحِهِ ــ حَتَّى ظَهَرَ المَاءُ ، فَجَعَلَتْ تُحَوِّضُهُ وَتَقُولُ بِيَدِهَا هَكَذَا ، وَجَعَلَتْ تَغْرِفُ المَاءَ فِي سِقَائِهَا وَهُوَ يَفُورُ بَعْدَ مَا تَغْرِفُ ، وفي روايةٍ : بِقَدْرِ مَا تَغْرِفُ . قَالَ ابْنُ عَبَّاسٍ رَضِيَ اللهُ عَنْهُمَا : قَالَ النَّبِيُّ صَلَّى اللهُ عَلَيْهِ وَسَلَّمَ : « رَحِمَ اللهُ أُمَّ إِسْمَاعِيلَ لَوْ تَرَكَتْ زَمْزَمَ ــ أَوْ قَالَ : لَوْ لَمْ تَغْرِفْ مِنَ المَاءِ ، لَكَانَتْ زَمْزَمُ عَيْناً مَعِيناً » قَالَ : فَشَرِبَتْ ،

وَأَرْضَعَتْ وَلَدَهَا ، فَقَالَ لَهَا المَلَكُ : لاَ تَخَافُوا الضَّيْعَةَ فَإِنَّ هَهُنَا بَيْتاً لِلَّهِ يَبْنِيهِ هَذَا الغُلاَمُ وَأَبُوهُ . وَإِنَّ اللهَ لاَ يُضَيِّعُ أَهْلَهُ . وَكَانَ البَيْتُ مُرْتَفِعاً مِنَ الأَرْضِ كَالرَّابِيَةِ تَأْتِيهِ السُّيُولُ ، فَتَأْخُذُ عَنْ يَمِينِهِ وَعَنْ شِمَالِهِ ، فَكَانَتْ كَذَلِكَ حَتَّى مَرَّتْ بِهِمْ رُفْقَةٌ مِنْ جُرْهُمٍ ، أَوْ أَهْلُ بَيْتٍ مِنْ جُرْهُمٍ مُقْبِلِينَ مِنْ طَرِيقِ كَدَاءٍ ، فَنَزَلُوا فِي أَسْفَلِ مَكَّةَ ، فَرَأَوْا طَائِراً عَائِفاً فَقَالُوا : إِنَّ هَذَا الطَّائِرَ لَيَدُورُ عَلَى مَاءٍ لَعَهْدُنَا بِهَذَا الوَادِي وَمَا فِيهِ مَاءٌ ، فَأَرْسَلُوا جَرِيّاً أَوْ جَرِيَّيْنِ ، فَإِذَا هُمْ بِالمَاءِ . فَرَجَعُوا ، فَأَخْبَرُوهُمْ ، فَأَقْبَلُوا وَأُمُّ إِسْمَاعِيلَ عِنْدَ المَاءِ ، فَقَالُوا: أَتَأْذَنِينَ لَنَا أَنْ نَنْزِلَ عِنْدَكِ ؟ قَالَتْ : نَعَمْ ، وَلَكِنْ لاحَقَّ لَكُمْ فِي المَاءِ ، قَالُوا : نَعَمْ . قَالَ ابْنُ عَبَّاسٍ : قَالَ النَّبِيُّ صَلَّى اللهُ عَلَيْهِ وَسَلَّمَ : « فَأَلْفَى ذَلِكَ أُمَّ إِسْمَاعِيلَ ، وَهِيَ تُحِبُّ الأُنْسَ ، فَنَزَلُوا ، فَأَرْسَلُوا إِلَى أَهْلِيهِمْ فَنَزَلُوا مَعَهُمْ ، حَتَّى إِذَا كَانُوا بِهَا أَهْلَ أَبْيَاتٍ ، وَشَبَّ الغُلاَمُ وَتَعَلَّمَ العَرَبِيَّةَ مِنْهُمْ وَأَنْفَسَهُمْ وَأَعْجَبَهُمْ حِينَ شَبَّ ، فَلَمَّا أَدْرَكَ ، زَوَّجُوهُ امْرَأَةً مِنْهُمْ ، وَمَاتَتْ أُمُّ إِسْمَاعِيلَ ، فَجَاءَ إِبْرَاهِيمُ بَعْدَ مَا تَزَوَّجَ إِسْمَاعِيلُ يُطَالِعُ تَرِكَتَهُ فَلَمْ يَجِدْ إِسْمَاعِيلَ ، فَسَأَلَ امْرَأَتَهُ عَنْهُ فَقَالَتْ : خَرَجَ يَبْتَغِي لَنَا – وَفِي رِوَايَةٍ : يَصِيدُ لَنَا – ثُمَّ سَأَلَهَا عَنْ عَيْشِهِمْ وَهَيْئَتِهِمْ فَقَالَتْ : نَحْنُ بِشَرٍّ ، نَحْنُ فِي ضِيقٍ وَشِدَّةٍ ، وَشَكَتْ إِلَيْهِ ، قَالَ : فَإِذَا جَاءَ زَوْجُكِ ، اقْرَئِي عَلَيْهِ السَّلاَمَ ، وَقُولِي لَهُ يُغَيِّرْ عَتَبَةَ بَابِهِ . فَلَمَّا جَاءَ إِسْمَاعِيلُ كَأَنَّهُ آنَسَ شَيْئاً فَقَالَ : هَلْ جَاءَكُمْ مِنْ أَحَدٍ ؟ قَالَتْ : نَعَمْ ، جَاءَنَا شَيْخٌ كَذَا وَكَذَا ، فَسَأَلَنَا عَنْكَ ، فَأَخْبَرْتُهُ ، فَسَأَلَنِي : كَيْفَ عَيْشُنَا ، فَأَخْبَرْتُهُ أَنَّا فِي جَهْدٍ وَشِدَّةٍ . قَالَ : فَهَلْ أَوْصَاكِ بِشَيْءٍ ؟ قَالَتْ : نَعَمْ أَمَرَنِي أَنْ أَقْرَأَ عَلَيْكَ السَّلاَمَ وَيَقُولُ : غَيِّرْ عَتَبَةَ بَابِكَ . قَالَ : ذَاكَ أَبِي وَقَدْ أَمَرَنِي أَنْ أُفَارِقَكِ ، الحَقِي بِأَهْلِكِ . فَطَلَّقَهَا ، وَتَزَوَّجَ مِنْهُمْ أُخْرَى ، فَلَبِثَ عَنْهُمْ إِبْرَاهِيمُ

ما شاءَ اللهُ ثُمَّ أتاهُمْ بعْدُ ، فلَمْ يجِدْهُ ، فدَخلَ على امرَأتِهِ . فسَألَ عنهُ . قَالَتْ : خرَجَ يبتَغي لَنا . قالَ : كَيفَ أنتُمْ ؛ وسَألَها عنْ عَيْشِهِمْ وهَيئَتِهِمْ . فقَالَتْ : نحنُ بخيرٍ وسَعةٍ وأثنَتْ على اللهِ تعَالى ، فقَالَ : ما طعَامُكُمْ ؟ قَالَتْ : اللَّحْمُ . قَالَ : فمَا شرَابُكُمْ ؟ قَالَتِ : المَاءُ . قالَ : اللّهُمَّ بَارِكْ لهُمْ في اللَّحْمِ والمَاءِ ، قَالَ النَّبيُّ صَلَّى اللهُ عَلَيْهِ وَسَلَّمَ : « ولَمْ يكُنْ لهُمْ يوْمَئِذٍ حَبٌّ ولَوْ كَانَ لهُمْ دَعَا لهُمْ فيهِ » قَالَ : فهُمَا لا يخلُو عليهِمَا أحدٌ بغيْرِ مكَّةَ إلاَّ لَمْ يُوافِقَاهُ .

وفي روايةٍ فجَاءَ فقَالَ : أينَ إسْمَاعِيلُ ؟ فقَالَتِ امرَأتُهُ : ذهَبَ يصِيدُ ، فقَالَتِ امرَأتُهُ : ألا تنزِلُ ، فتطْعَمَ وتشْرَبَ ؟ قَالَ : ومَا طعَامُكُمْ ومَا شرَابُكُمْ ؟ قَالَتْ : طعَامُنَا اللَّحْمُ ، وشرَابُنَا المَاءُ . قَالَ : اللّهُمَّ بَارِكْ لهُمْ في طعَامِهِمْ وشرَابِهِمْ — قَالَ : فقَالَ أبُو القَاسِمِ صَلَّى اللهُ عَلَيْهِ وَسَلَّمَ : «برَكَةُ دَعْوةِ إبْرَاهِيمَ صَلَّى اللهُ عَلَيْهِ وَسَلَّمَ» قَالَ : فإذا جاءَ زَوْجُكِ ، فاقرئي عَلَيْهِ السَّلامَ ومُريهِ يُثَبِّتْ عتَبَةَ بَابِهِ ، فلَمَّا جاءَ إسْمَاعِيلُ ، قَالَ : هلْ أتَاكُمْ منْ أحَدٍ ؟قَالَتْ: نعَمْ . أتانَا شيْخٌ حسَنُ الهيْئَةِ ، وأثنَتْ عليْهِ ، فسَألَني عنْكَ ، فأخبَرْتُهُ . فسَألَني كيْفَ عيْشُنَا ، فأخبَرْتُهُ أنَّا بخيرٍ . قَالَ : فأوْصَاكِ بشَيْءٍ ؟ قَالَتْ : نعَمْ . يقْرَأُ عليْكَ السَّلامَ ، ويَأمُرُكَ أنْ تُثَبِّتَ عتَبَةَ بَابِكَ . قَالَ : ذاكَ أبي ، وأنتِ العتَبَةُ أمرَني أنْ أمسِكَكِ ، ثُمَّ لبِثَ عنْهُمْ ماشاءَ اللهُ ، ثُمَّ جاءَ بعْدَ ذلكَ وإسْمَاعِيلُ يبْرِي نبْلاً لهُ تحتَ دَوْحَةٍ قريباً منْ زمْزَمَ ؛ فلَمَّا رآهُ ، قَامَ إليْهِ ، فصَنَعَ كمَا يصْنَعُ الوَالِدُ بالوَلَدِ ، والوَلَدُ بالوَالِدِ قَالَ يَا إسْمَاعِيلُ إنَّ اللهَ أمرَني بأمْرٍ ، قَالَ : فاصْنَعْ ما أمرَكَ ربُّكَ ؟ قَالَ : قَالَ : وتُعِينُني ، قَالَ : وأُعِينُكَ . قَالَ : فإنَّ اللهَ أمرَني أنْ أبْنيَ بيْتاً ههُنَا . وأشَارَ إلى أكَمَةٍ مُرْتَفِعَةٍ على ماحوْلَهَا . فعِنْدَ ذلكَ رفَعَ القَوَاعِدَ منَ البَيْتِ ، فجَعَلَ إسْمَاعِيلُ يأتي بالحِجَارَةِ ، وإبْرَاهِيمُ يبْني حتَّى إذا

ارْتَفَعَ الْبِنَاءُ . جَاءَ بِهَذَا الحَجَرِ فَوَضَعَهُ لَهُ فَقَامَ عَلَيْهِ . وَهُوَ يَبْنِي وَإِسْمَاعِيلُ يُنَاوِلُهُ الحِجَارَةَ وَهُمَا يَقُولانِ : رَبَّنَا تَقَبَّلْ مِنَّا إنَّكَ أَنْتَ السَّمِيعُ الْعَلِيمُ .

وَفِي رِوَايَة : إنَّ إبْرَاهِيمَ خَرَجَ بِإسْمَاعِيلَ وَأُمِّ إسْمَاعِيلَ ، مَعَهُمْ شَنَّةٌ فِيهَا مَاءٌ ، فَجَعَلَتْ أُمُّ إسْمَاعِيلَ تَشْرَبُ مِنَ الشَّنَّةِ ، فَيَدِرُّ لَبَنُهَا عَلَى صَبِيِّهَا حَتَّى قَدِمَ مَكَّةَ . فَوَضَعَهَا تَحْتَ دَوْحَةٍ ، ثُمَّ رَجَعَ إبْرَاهِيمُ إلَى أهْلِهِ ، فَاتَّبَعَتْهُ أُمُّ إسْمَاعِيلَ حَتَّى لَمَّا بَلَغُوا كَدَاءَ ، نَادَتْهُ مِنْ وَرَائِهِ : يَا إبْرَاهِيمُ إلَى مَنْ تَتْرُكُنَا ؟ قَالَ : إلَى اللهِ ، قَالَتْ : رَضِيتُ بِاللهِ ، فَرَجَعَتْ ، وَجَعَلَتْ تَشْرَبُ مِنَ الشَّنَّةِ ، وَيَدِرُّ لَبَنُهَا عَلَى صَبِيِّهَا حَتَّى لَمَّا فَنِيَ المَاءُ قَالَتْ : لَوْ ذَهَبْتُ ، فَنَظَرْتُ لَعَلِّي أُحِسُّ أحَداً ، قَالَ : فَذَهَبَتْ فَصَعِدَتْ الصَّفَا ، فَنَظَرَتْ وَنَظَرَتْ هَلْ تُحِسُّ أحَداً ، فَلَمْ تُحِسَّ أحَداً ، فَلَمَّا بَلَغَتِ الْوَادِي ، سَعَتْ ، وَأَتَتِ المَرْوَةَ ، وَفَعَلَتْ ذَلِكَ أشْوَاطاً ، ثُمَّ قَالَتْ : لَوْ ذَهَبْتُ فَنَظَرْتُ مَا فَعَلَ الصَّبِيُّ فَذَهَبَتْ وَنَظَرَتْ ، فَإذَا هُوَ عَلَى حَالِهِ كَأَنَّهُ يَنْشَغُ لِلمَوْتِ ، فَلَمْ تُقِرَّهَا نَفْسُهَا . فَقَالَتْ : لَوْ ذَهَبْتُ ، فَنَظَرْتُ لَعَلِّي أُحِسُّ أحَداً ، فَذَهَبَتْ فَصَعِدَتِ الصَّفَا ، فَنَظَرَتْ وَنَظَرَتْ ، فَلَمْ تُحِسَّ أحَداً حَتَّى أتَمَّتْ سَبْعاً ، ثُمَّ قَالَتْ : لَوْ ذَهَبْتُ ، فَنَظَرْتُ مَا فَعَلَ ، فَإذَا هِيَ بِصَوْتٍ ، فَقَالَتْ : أغِثْ إنْ كَانَ عِنْدَكَ خَيْرٌ ، فَإذَا جِبْرِيلُ صَلَّى اللهُ عَلَيْهِ وَسَلَّمَ فَقَالَ بِعَقِبِهِ هَكَذَا ، وَغَمَزَ بِعَقِبِهِ عَلَى الأَرْضِ ، فَانْبَثَقَ المَاءُ فَدَهِشَتْ أُمُّ إسْمَاعِيلَ ، فَجَعَلَتْ تَحْفِنُ — وَذَكَرَ الحَدِيثَ بِطُولِهِ .

رواه البخاري بهذه الرواياتِ كلها .

1867. Hazrat Ibn Abbas (R.A.A.) relates: Hazrat Ibrahim brought Hazrat Ismael and his mother while she was still nursing him, and put them under a big tree close to *Baitullah* (Ka'ba) or the House of Allah, just above the spring of Zam Zam in the upper part of the mosque. At that time nobody lived in Makkah as no water was found there. Prophet Hazrat Ibrahim brought both of them there, and left a bag of dates with them and water in a water-skin. Thereafter, turning away his face he marched off. His wife Hazrat Hajira, the Mother of (his son) Hazrat Ismail followed him and said: O Abraham, where are you going, leaving us in this wilderness (unfrequented valley) where there is no companion nor any provision (to subsist)? She repeated this several times, but Hazrat Ibrahim (A.S.) did not see back. Then Hazrat Hajira asked him: 'Has Allah commanded you to do this?' He answered, 'Yes.' She said. If so, then He will not let us ruin; and she returned back, and Prophet Ibrahim continued his march till he reached a place called Saniyah from where he was not visible to them. He (halted and) turned his face towards the direction of Ka'ba, raised his hands and supplicated:

> 'Our Lord! Lo I have settled some of my posterity in an uncultivable valley near unto Thy Holy House, Our Lord! that they may establish proper worship; so incline some hearts of men that they may yearn toward them, and provide Thou them with fruits in order that they may be thankful. (14 : 37)

Ismail's mother used to suckle Hazrat Ismail on her breast, and would herself subsist on the water (in the leather bag with her) till this became empty. She soon after felt thirsty and her baby (Hazrat Ismail) too. And due to intense thirst the child became much restless, and she had to see him turning over and over. Being unhappy to see him, she walked away (in one direction in search of water). Nearest to her was the Safa Hill, she ascended the hill, and looked all around the valley to see whether there was somebody (to help her) but she saw no one, and therefore, she descended from Safa and when she reached the valley, she raised the skirt of her apron and began running like a person in distress, and crossing the valley she ascended the top of the Hill of Marwah, and stood there looking for somebody, but she did not see anyone. Thus she did seven times. Hazrat Ibn Abbas (R.A.A.) relates that the Holy Prophet (S.A.W.) said: That is why people (Haj pilgrims) run between the two hills of Safa and Marwa (seven times). At last when she reached Marwa, for the seventh time, she heard a voice and she suddenly said to herself: Hark! and became more attentive, and said: (O Allah! At Last) I have heard your voice. I wish if my supplication could reach Thee! Soon she saw an angel near the Zam Zam. The angel struck the ground with his heel (or with his wings) which made the water sprout. Hazrat Hajira started digging out a hole like a cistern to contain the water, and began to fill her water-skin from it with her hands. While she was filling the leather bag with water, the same was sprouting with greater force. Hazrat Ibn Abbas (R.A.A.) relates that the Holy Prophet (S.A.W.) said: Allah may have mercy on the mother of (Hazrat) Ismail, had she left the spring of Zam Zam, as it was, (or she would not have filled her leather bag with water, then Zam Zam would have become a running rivulet for us). Hazrat Hajira drank this water

(while working) prayed: 'Our Lord! Accept from us (this duty) Lo! Thou, only Thou, art the Hearer, the Knower.' (2 : 127)

Yet another version says; Hazrat Ibrahim took Hazrat Ismail and his mother with him, and they had a water-skin with water. Hazrat Ismail's mother used to drink water from the waterskin, and fed the baby from her breast, till they reached Mecca (Makkah). Here Hazrat Ibrahim made his wife to sit under a big tree, and himself turned back to his house. Hazrat Ismail's mother followed him for some distance, till they reached the place known as 'Kadah'a; she called him from behind and said: O Ibrahim! On whose care you are leaving us? Hazrat Ibrahim said: 'In the care of Allah.' She said: Then I am fully contented with Allah, and she came back (to the place where she and her baby were living). She used to drink water from the water-skin, and giving suck to her child. When the water finished, she said to herself, I should better go and look around, if I can spot somebody. He (S.A.W.) said: She went and ascended the top of the Hill of Safa and looked around several times so that she may see somebody but did not see anyone. Then she came down the valley and ran to the hill of Marwa, and thus made several rounds. Then she thought! Let me go and see the child (as to) what has happened with him. When she went there, she found him on the throes of death. She could not stand this scene and found it difficult to control herself; she said to herself: Let me go and find out someone. She again went and ascended Safa and looked around again and again but did not see anyone. Thus she ran between Safa and Marwah totally seven times. She again said to herself: Let me go again and have a look and see what has happened (to the child), at this moment she heard a voice and she prayed: If you can do anything (good) then help me. Suddenly Hazrat Jibreel (Angel Gabriel) appeared and he struck the ground with his heel, and water began sprouting. Hazrat Ismail's mother (Hazrat Hajira) was awe stricken, and she started making boundary around the gushing water to preserve it. He then narrated the long remaining tradition. *(Bukhari* narrated all these versions).

١٨٦٨ – وَعَنْ سَعِيدِ بْنِ زَيْدٍ رَضِيَ اللهُ عَنْهُ قَالَ : سَمِعْتُ رَسُولَ اللهِ صَلَّى اللهُ عَلَيْهِ وَسَلَّمَ يَقُولُ : « الْكَمْأَةُ مِنَ الْمَنِّ ، وَمَاؤُهَا شِفَاءٌ لِلْعَيْنِ » متفقٌ عليه .

1868. Hazrat Sa'eed bin Zaid (R.A.A.) says that he heard the Holy Prophet (S.A.W.) say: Calyx are a species of Manna, and their water has got cure for the eye.' *(Bukhari and Muslim)*

* * * * * * *

CHAPTER 371

SOLICITING FORGIVENESS

قَالَ اللهُ تَعَالَى: وَاسْتَغْفِرْ لِذَنْبِكَ وَلِلْمُؤْمِنِينَ وَالْمُؤْمِنَاتِ [محمد: ١٩].
وقَالَ تَعَالَى: وَاسْتَغْفِرِ اللهَ إِنَّ اللهَ كَانَ غَفُوراً رَحِيماً [النساء: ١٠٦].
وقَالَ تَعَالَى: فَسَبِّحْ بِحَمْدِ رَبِّكَ وَاسْتَغْفِرْهُ إِنَّهُ كَانَ تَوَّاباً [النصر: ٣].
وقال تَعَالَى: لِلَّذِينَ اتَّقَوْا عِنْدَ رَبِّهِمْ جَنَّاتٌ تَجْرِي إلى قوله عزَّ وجلَّ:
وَالْمُسْتَغْفِرِينَ بِالأَسْحَارِ [آل عمران: ١٥-١٧]. وقال تَعَالَى: وَمَنْ يَعْمَلْ سُوءاً
أَوْ يَظْلِمْ نَفْسَهُ ثُمَّ يَسْتَغْفِرِ اللهَ يَجِدِ اللهَ غَفُوراً رَحِيماً [النساء: ١١٠].
وقالَ تَعَالَى: وَمَا كَانَ اللهُ لِيُعَذِّبَهُمْ وَأَنْتَ فِيهِمْ، وَمَا كَانَ اللهُ
مُعَذِّبَهُمْ وَهُمْ يَسْتَغْفِرُونَ [الأنفال: ٣٣]. وقالَ تَعَالَى: وَالَّذِينَ
إِذا فَعَلُوا فَاحِشَةً أَوْ ظَلَمُوا أَنْفُسَهُمْ ذَكَرُوا اللهَ فَاسْتَغْفَرُوا لِذُنُوبِهِمْ
وَمَنْ يَغْفِرُ الذُّنُوبَ إِلاَّ اللهُ وَلَمْ يُصِرُّوا عَلَى مَا فَعَلُوا وَهُمْ يَعْلَمُونَ
[آل عمران: ١٣٥] والآيات في الباب كثيرة مَعْلُومة.

Allah, the Exalted, said:

417. And ask forgiveness for thy sin. (47 : 19)

418. And seek forgiveness of Allah. Lo! Allah is ever Forgiving, and Merciful. (4 : 106)

419. Then hymn the praises of Thy Lord, and seek forgiveness of Him. Lo! He is ever ready to show mercy. (110 : 3)

420. For those who keep away from evil, with their Lord, are Gardens underneath which rivers flow, and pure companions and contentment from Allah. Allah is Seer of His bondmen. Those who say: Our Lord! Lo! we believe. So forgive us our sins and guard us from the punishment of Fire; The steadfast, and the truthful, and the obedient, those who spend (and hoard not), those who pray for pardon in the small hours of night. (3 : 15—17)

421. Yet whoso doeth evil or wrongeth his own soul, then seeketh pardon of Allah, will find Allah Forgiving, Merciful. (4 : 110)

422. But Allah would not punish them while thou wast with them, nor will He punish them while they seek forgiveness.
(8 : 33)

423. And those who, when they do an evil thing or wrong themselves, remember Allah and implore forgiveness for their sins — Who forgiveth sins save Allah only? — and will not knowingly repeat (the wrong) they did. (3 : 135).

١٨٦٩ – وَعَنِ الأَغَرِّ المُزَنِيِّ رَضِيَ اللهُ عَنْهُ أَنَّ رَسُولَ اللهِ صَلَّى اللهُ عَلَيْهِ وَسَلَّمَ قَالَ : « إِنَّهُ لَيُغَانُ عَلَى قَلْبِي . وَإِنِّي لأَسْتَغْفِرُ اللهَ فِي اليَوْمِ مِائَةَ مَرَّةٍ » رَوَاهُ مُسْلِم .

1869. Hazrat Agharr-Al Muzani (R.A.A.) says that the Holy Prophet (S.A.W.) said: Occasionally I feel a sort of heaviness over my heart, but I supplicate Allah for forgiveness a hundred times in a day. *(Muslim)*

١٨٧٠ – وَعَنْ أَبِي هُرَيْرَةَ رَضِيَ اللهُ عَنْهُ قَالَ : سَمِعْتُ رَسُولَ اللهِ صَلَّى اللهُ عَلَيْهِ وَسَلَّمَ يَقُولُ : « واللهِ إِنِّي لأَسْتَغْفِرُ اللهَ وَأَتُوبُ إِلَيْهِ فِي اليَوْمِ أَكْثَرَ مِنْ سَبْعِينَ مَرَّةً » رواه البخاري

1870. Hazrat Abu Hurairah (R.A.A.) says that he heard the Holy Prophet (S.A.W.) say: By Allah! I seek Allah's forgiveness and turn to Him in repentance more than seventy times a day. *(Bukhari)*

١٨٧١ – وَعَنْهُ رَضِيَ اللهُ عَنْهُ قَالَ : قَالَ رَسُولُ اللهِ صَلَّى اللهُ عَلَيْهِ وَسَلَّمَ : « وَالَّذِي نَفْسِي بِيَدِهِ لَوْ لَمْ تُذْنِبُوا ، لَذَهَبَ اللهُ تَعَالَى بِكُمْ ، وَلَجَاءَ بِقَوْمٍ يُذْنِبُونَ فَيَسْتَغْفِرُونَ اللهَ تَعَالَى فَيَغْفِرُ لَهُمْ » رواه مسلم .

1871. This Hadis has been dealt with as No. 422 of Chapter 51.

١٨٧٢ – وَعَنِ ابْنِ عُمَرَ رَضِيَ اللهُ عَنْهُمَا قَالَ : كُنَّا نَعُدُّ لِرَسُولِ اللهِ صَلَّى اللهُ عَلَيْهِ وَسَلَّمَ فِي المَجْلِسِ الوَاحِدِ مِائَةَ مَرَّةٍ : « رَبِّ اغْفِرْ لِي ، وَتُبْ عَلَيَّ إِنَّكَ أَنْتَ التَّوَّابُ الرَّحِيمُ » .

رواه أبو داود ، والترمذي وقال : حديث صحيح .

1872. Hazrat Ibn 'Umar (R.A.A.) relates: We could count the recitation of the supplication:

Rabbigh-firli wa tub alayya innaka antat Tawwa-bur Rahim.
O Lord, pardon me and turn to me wilh mercy for Thou art Oft-returning with compassion. Ever Merciful,
by the Holy Prophet (S.A.W.) for 100 times in one sitting.
(Abu Daud and Tirmizi)

١٨٧٣ — وَعَنِ ابْنِ عَبَّاسٍ رَضِيَ اللهُ عَنْهُمَا قَالَ : قَالَ رَسُولُ اللهِ صَلَّى اللهُ عَلَيْهِ وَسَلَّمَ : « مَنْ لَزِمَ الاسْتِغْفَارَ ، جَعَلَ اللهُ لَهُ مِنْ كُلِّ ضِيقٍ مَخْرَجاً ، وَمِنْ كُلِّ هَمٍّ فَرَجاً ، وَرَزَقَهُ مِنْ حَيْثُ لا يَحْتَسِبُ » رواه أبو داود .

1873. Hazrat Ibn Abbas (R.A.A.) relates that the Holy Prophet (S.A.W.) said: A person who has taken upon himself to regularly supplicate Allah for forgiveness, Allah provides deliverance from hardship, and grants relief from every sorrow and suffering and provides him sustenance from a source he cannot even imagine. *(Abu Daud)*

١٨٧٤ — وَعَنِ ابْنِ مَسْعُودٍ رَضِيَ اللهُ عَنْهُ قَالَ : قَالَ رَسُولُ اللهِ صَلَّى اللهُ عَلَيْهِ وَسَلَّمَ : « مَنْ قَالَ : أَسْتَغْفِرُ اللهَ الذي لاإلَهَ إلاَّ هُوَ الحَيَّ القَيُّومَ وَأَتُوبُ إلَيْهِ ، غُفِرَتْ ذُنُوبُهُ وَإِنْ كَانَ قَدْ فَرَّ مِنَ الزَّحْفِ» رواه أبو داود والترمذي والحَاكِمُ ، وَقَالَ : حَدِيثٌ صَحِيحٌ عَلَى شَرْطِ البُخَارِيِّ وَمُسْلِمٍ .

1874. Hazrat Ibn Mas'ud (R.A.A.) relates that the Holy Prophet (S.A.W.) said. He who supplicates:

Astaghfirulla-hal-lazi la ilaha illa huwal haiyal qaiyum wa atubo ilaihe.

'I solicit the pardon of Allah; there is no god except Allah, the Ever-living, the Ever-lasting, and I turn to Him in repentance;
'will have his sins remitted, even if he may have deserted the field of Jihad.
(Abu Daud, Tirmizi and Hakim. The latter said it is good according to standard of Bukhari)

١٨٧— وَعَنْ شَدَّادِ بْنِ أَوْسٍ رَضِيَ اللهُ عَنْهُ عَنِ النَّبِيِّ صَلَّى اللهُ عَلَيْهِ وَسَلَّمَ قَالَ : «سَيِّدُ الاسْتِغْفَارِ أَنْ يَقُولَ العَبْدُ : اللَّهُمَّ أَنْتَ رَبِّي ، لاإلَهَ إلاَّ أَنْتَ خَلَقْتَنِي وَأَنَاعَبْدُكَ ، وَأَنَا عَلَى عَهْدِكَ وَوَعْدِكَ مااسْتَطَعْتُ أَعُوذُ بِكَ مِنْ شَرِّ ما صَنَعْتُ ، أبوءُ لَكَ بِنِعْمَتِكَ عَلَيَّ ، وَأَبُوءُ بذَنْبِي ؛

فَاغْفِرْ لِي ، فَإِنَّهُ لا يَغْفِرُ الذُّنُوبَ إِلاَّ أَنْتَ . مَنْ قَالَهَا مِنَ النَّهَارِ مُوقِناً بِهَا ، فَمَاتَ مِنْ يَوْمِهِ قَبْلَ أَنْ يُمْسِي ، فَهُوَ مِنْ أَهْلِ الْجَنَّةِ ، وَمَنْ قَالَهَا مِنَ اللَّيْلِ وَهُوَ مُوقِنٌ بِهَا فَمَاتَ قَبْلَ أَنْ يُصْبِحَ ، فَهُوَ مِنْ أَهْلِ الْجَنَّةِ ، رواه البخاري .

1875. Hazrat Shaddad bin Aus (R.A.A.) relates that the Holy Prophet (S.A.W.) said: 'Istighfar' (Asking Allah's pardon or forgiveness) of the highest order is that a servant of Allah should say:

Alla-hum-ma anta Rab-bi, la i'la-ha il-la anta khalaq-tani wa ana abdu-ka wa ana 'ala 'ahdi-ka wa wa'adi-ka mas-ta-ta'to, a'oozo bika min shar-re ma sana'to, abu-o laka bi-ne'ma-tika 'alaiyya wa abu-o bi zam-bi, fagh-firli fa-in-nahu la yagh-fi-ruz-zunu-ba il-la anta.

'Allah, Thou art my only sustainer; there is no god save Thee; Thou hadst created me and I am Thy servant, and I try my best to fulfil my promise and my covenant with Thee, I seek Thy protection from the evil of that which I have done. I acknowledge the bounties that Thou hast bestowed upon me, and confess my sins; do Thou then pardon me, for verily none has the power to forgive save Thee alone.'

A person who supplicates with these words sincerely during the day, and if he dies before that very evening, will go to the paradise; and a person who supplicates with these words during the night faithfully believing in them, and if he dies before that very morning, will go to the paradise. *(Bukhari)*

١٨٧٦ – وَعَنْ ثَوْبَانَ رَضِيَ اللهُ عَنْهُ قَالَ : كَانَ رَسُولُ اللهِ صَلَّى اللهُ عَلَيْهِ وَسَلَّمَ إِذَا انْصَرَفَ مِنْ صَلاتِهِ ، اسْتَغْفَرَ اللهَ ثَلاثاً وَقَالَ : «اللَّهُمَّ أَنْتَ السَّلامُ ، وَمِنْكَ السَّلامُ ؛ تَبَارَكْتَ يَاذَا الْجَلالِ وَالإِكْرَامِ » قِيلَ لِلأَوْزَاعِيِّ – وَهُوَ أَحَدُ رُوَاتِهِ – : كَيْفَ الاسْتِغْفَارُ ؟ قَالَ يَقُولُ : أَسْتَغْفِرُ اللهَ ، أَسْتَغْفِرُ اللهَ . رواه مسلم .

1876. Hazrat Sauban (R.A.A.) says that the Holy Prophet (S.A.W.) after finishing his prayer, used to solicit forgiveness (from Allah) three times, and would further recite:

Astagh-fi-rul-lah, (Three times)

Al-lahum-ma antas salam, wa min-kas-salam, taba-rakta ya zal-ja-lali wal-Ik·am.

'Allah Thou art the Peace and from Thee is peace. Blessed art Thou, O Lord of Glory and Honour.'

Imam Auzai, one of the narrators of this tradition was asked: How did the Holy Prophet (S.A.W.) used to seek (Allah's) forgiveness?' He answered: He would say: *Astaghfirul-lah, astaghfirul-lah.* I beg Allah for forgiveness, I beg Allah for forgiveness. *(Muslim)*

١٨٧٧ — وَعَنْ عَائِشَةَ رَضِيَ اللهُ عَنْهَا قَالَتْ : كَانَ رَسُولُ اللهِ صَلَّى اللهُ عَلَيْهِ وَسَلَّمَ يُكْثِرُ أَنْ يَقُولَ قَبْلَ مَوْتِهِ : «سُبْحَانَ اللهِ وَبِحَمْدِهِ ، أَسْتَغْفِرُ اللهَ ، وَأَتُوبُ إِلَيْهِ » متفقٌ عليه

1877. Hazrat Ayesha (R.A.A.) relates that the Holy Prophet (S.A.W.) used to recite profusely before his death:

Subhan-Allah-e-wa-bi-hamdi-hi,As-tagh-firul-lah,wa atoobu ilaih.

Glory be to Allah and praise be to Him; I seek forgiveness of Allah and repent to Him. *(Bukhari and Muslim)*

١٨٧٨ — وَعَنْ أَنَسٍ رَضِيَ اللهُ عَنْهُ قَالَ : سَمِعْتُ رَسُولَ اللهِ صَلَّى اللهُ عَلَيْهِ وَسَلَّمَ يَقُولُ : « قَالَ اللهُ تَعَالى : يَا ابْنَ آدَمَ إِنَّكَ مادَعَوْتَنِي وَرَجَوْتَنِي غَفَرْتُ لَكَ عَلى ماكَانَ مِنْكَ وَلاأُبَالِي ، يَاابْنَ آدَمَ لَوْ بَلَغَتْ ذُنُوبُكَ عَنَانَ السَّمَاءِ ، ثُمَّ اسْتَغْفَرْتَنِي ، غَفَرْتُ لَكَ وَلا أُبَالِي ، يَاابْنَ آدَمَ إِنَّكَ لَوْ أَتَيْتَنِي بِقُرَابِ الأَرْضِ خَطَايَا ، ثُمَّ لَقِيتَنِي لاتُشْرِكُ بِي شَيْئاً ، لأَتَيْتُكَ بِقُرَابِها مَغْفِرَةً » رواه الترمذي وقَالَ : حَدِيثٌ حَسَنٌ .

1878. This Hadis has already been covered in S. No. 442 of Chapter 52.

١٨٧٩ — وَعَنِ ابْنِ عُمَرَ رَضِيَ اللهُ عَنْهُما أَنَّ النَّبِيَّ صَلَّى اللهُ عَلَيْهِ وَسَلَّمَ قَالَ : « يا مَعْشَرَ النِّسَاءِ تَصَدَّقْنَ ، وَأَكْثِرْنَ مِنَ الاسْتِغْفَارِ ؛ فَإِنِّي رَأَيْتُكُنَّ أَكْثَرَ أَهْلِ النَّارِ » قالَتِ امْرَأَةٌ مِنْهُنَّ : مَالَنَا أَكْثَرَ أَهْلِ النَّارِ ؟ قالَ : « تُكْثِرْنَ اللَّعْنَ ، وَتَكْفُرْنَ العَشِيرَ مَارَأَيْتُ مِنْ نَاقِصَاتِ عَقْلٍ وَدِينٍ أَغْلَبَ لِذِي لُبٍّ مِنْكُنَّ » قالَتْ : ما نُقْصَانُ العَقْلِ وَالدِّينِ ؟ قالَ : « شَهَادَةُ امْرَأَتَيْنِ بِشَهَادَةِ رَجُلٍ ، وَتَمْكُثُ الأَيَّامَ لا تُصَلِّي » رواه مسلم .

1879. Hazrat Ibn 'Umar (R.A.A.) relates that the Holy Prophet (S.A.W.) said: O ye the women folk give charity, and seek Allah's forgiveness more often, for I have seen the majority of you among the dwellers of the Hell. One of the women asked him: What was our fault for being in majority among the dwellers of the Hell? He (S.A.W.) answered: You are given to cursing too much and disobey your husband, and in spite of your deficiency in intelligence and in religion, I have not seen more destructive to capacity of knowledge and intellect of a man than you. The woman further requested: 'What is the deficiency in intelligence and matter of faith that we suffer from? He (S.A.W.) answered: The evidence of two women is equal to that of one man, and a woman cannot partake in prayer during her days of menses. *(Muslim)*

* * * * * * *

CHAPTER 372

WHAT ALLAH, THE EXALTED HAS PROVIDED FOR BELIEVERS IN PARADISE

قَالَ اللهُ تَعَالَى : إِنَّ الْمُتَّقِينَ فِي جَنَّاتٍ وَعُيُونٍ • ادْخُلُوهَا بِسَلَامٍ آمِنِينَ • وَنَزَعْنَا مَا فِي صُدُورِهِم مِّنْ غِلٍّ إِخْوَانًا عَلَى سُرُرٍ مُّتَقَابِلِينَ • لَا يَمَسُّهُمْ فِيهَا نَصَبٌ وَمَا هُم مِّنْهَا بِمُخْرَجِينَ [الحجر : ٤٥ – ٤٨]

وَقَالَ تَعَالَى: ﴿ يَا عِبَادِ لَا خَوْفٌ عَلَيْكُمُ الْيَوْمَ وَلَا أَنتُمْ تَحْزَنُونَ • الَّذِينَ آمَنُوا بِآيَاتِنَا وَكَانُوا مُسْلِمِينَ • ادْخُلُوا الْجَنَّةَ أَنتُمْ وَأَزْوَاجُكُمْ تُحْبَرُونَ • يُطَافُ عَلَيْهِم بِصِحَافٍ مِّن ذَهَبٍ وَأَكْوَابٍ وَفِيهَا مَا تَشْتَهِيهِ الْأَنفُسُ وَتَلَذُّ الْأَعْيُنُ وَأَنتُمْ فِيهَا خَالِدُونَ • وَتِلْكَ الْجَنَّةُ الَّتِي أُورِثْتُمُوهَا بِمَا كُنتُمْ تَعْمَلُونَ • لَكُمْ فِيهَا فَاكِهَةٌ كَثِيرَةٌ مِّنْهَا تَأْكُلُونَ [الزخرف : ٦٨ – ٧٣] .

وَقَالَ تَعَالَى : إِنَّ الْمُتَّقِينَ فِي مَقَامٍ أَمِينٍ • فِي جَنَّاتٍ وَعُيُونٍ • يَلْبَسُونَ مِن سُندُسٍ وَإِسْتَبْرَقٍ مُّتَقَابِلِينَ • كَذَلِكَ وَزَوَّجْنَاهُم بِحُورٍ عِينٍ • يَدْعُونَ فِيهَا بِكُلِّ فَاكِهَةٍ آمِنِينَ • لَا يَذُوقُونَ فِيهَا الْمَوْتَ إِلَّا الْمَوْتَةَ الْأُولَى وَوَقَاهُمْ عَذَابَ الْجَحِيمِ • فَضْلًا مِّن رَّبِّكَ ذَلِكَ هُوَ الْفَوْزُ الْعَظِيمُ [الدخان : ٥١ – ٥٧] .

وَقَالَ تَعَالَى: إِنَّ الأَبْرَارَ لَفِي نَعِيمٍ • عَلَى الأَرَائِكِ يَنْظُرُونَ • تَعرِفُ فِي وُجُوهِهِمْ نَضْرَةَ النَّعِيمِ • يُسْقَوْنَ مِنْ رَحِيقٍ مَخْتُومٍ • خِتَامُهُ مِسْكٌ وَفِي ذَلِكَ فَلْيَتَنَافَسِ المُتَنَافِسُونَ • وَمِزَاجُهُ مِنْ تَسْنِيمٍ • عَيْناً يَشْرَبُ بِهَا المُقَرَّبُونَ [المطففين : ٢٢ – ٢٨] . والآيَاتُ فِي البَابِ كَثِيرَةٌ مَعْلُومَةٌ .

Allah, the Exalted, has said:

424. Lo! those who ward off (evil) are among gardens, and water-springs. (And it is said unto them): Enter them in peace, secure. And we remove whatever rancour may be in their breasts. As brethren, face to face, (they rest) on couches raised. Toil cometh not unto them there, nor will they be expelled from thence. (15 : 45—48)

425. O my slaves! For you there is no fear this day, nor is it ye who grieve (ye) who believed Our revelations and were self-surrendered, Enter the Garden, ye and your wives, to be made glad. Therein are brought round for them trays of gold and goblets, and therein is all that souls desire and eyes find sweet. And ye are immortal therein. This is the Garden which ye are made to inherit because of what ye used to do. Therein for you is fruit in plenty whence to eat. (43 : 68—73)

426. Lo! those who kept their duty will be in a place secure amid gardens and watersprings, attired in silk and silk embroidery, facing one another. Even so (it will be). And we shall wed them unto fair ones with wide, lovely eyes. They call therein for every fruit in safety. They taste not death therein, save the first death. And He hath saved them from the doom of Hell, a bounty from thy Lord. That is the supreme triumph. (44 : 51—57)

427. Lo! the righteous verily are in delight, on couches, gazing, thou wilt know in their faces the radiance of delight. They are given to drink of a pure wine, sealed, whose seal is of musk—For this let (all) those strive who strive for bliss — and mixed with water of Tasnim, a spring whence those brought near to Allah drink. (83 : 22—28)

١٨٨٠ – وَعَنْ جَابِرٍ رَضِيَ اللهُ عَنْهُ قَالَ: قَالَ رَسُولُ اللهِ صَلَّى اللهُ عَلَيْهِ وَسَلَّمَ: «يَأْكُلُ أَهْلُ الجَنَّةِ فِيهَا، وَيَشْرَبُونَ، وَلا يَتَغَوَّطُونَ، وَلا يَمْتَخِطُونَ، وَلا يَبُولُونَ؛ وَلَكِنْ طَعَامُهُمْ ذَلِكَ جُشَاءٌ كَرَشْحِ

الْمِسْكِ ، يُلْهَمُونَ التَّسْبِيحَ وَالتَّكْبِيرَ ، كَمَا يُلْهَمُونَ النَّفَسَ » .

رواه مسلم

1880. Hazrat Jabir (R.A.A.) reports that the Holy Prophet (S.A.W.) said: The dwellers of Paradise will eat and drink but will not have to answer the call of Nature or to blow their noses or pass water. Their food will be digested resulting only in a belch or eructation smelling of musk. They will be taught glorification of Allah *(Subhan Allah)* and proclaiming His greatness (Allah-o-Akbar) as you are taught how to breath. ***(Muslim)***

١٨٨١ — وَعَنْ أَبِي هُرَيْرَةَ رَضِيَ اللهُ عَنْهُ قَالَ : قَالَ رَسُولُ اللهِ صَلَّى اللهُ عَلَيْهِ وَسَلَّمَ : « قَالَ اللهُ تَعَالَى : أَعْدَدْتُ لِعِبَادِيَ الصَّالِحِينَ مَا لاَ عَيْنٌ رَأَتْ ، وَلاَ أُذُنٌ سَمِعَتْ وَلاَ خَطَرَ عَلَى قَلْبِ بَشَرٍ . وَاقْرَؤُوا إِنْ شِئْتُمْ : فَلاَ تَعْلَمُ نَفْسٌ مَا أُخْفِيَ لَهُمْ مِنْ قُرَّةِ أَعْيُنٍ جَزَاءً بِمَا كَانُوا يَعْمَلُونَ [السجدة : ١٧] متفقٌ عليه

1881. Hazrat Abu Hurairah (R.A.A.) relates that the Holy Prophet (S.A.W.) said: Allah the Exalted says: I have prepared for my virtuous servants, (things) that which no eye has seen and, no ear has heard and no human mind has ever thought of. You may read the verse:

'No soul knoweth what is kept hid for them of joy, as a reward for what they used to do.' (32 : 17) ***(Bukhari and Muslim)***

١٨٨٢ — وَعَنْهُ قَالَ : قَالَ رَسُولُ اللهِ صَلَّى اللهُ عَلَيْهِ وَسَلَّمَ : « أَوَّلُ زُمْرَةٍ يَدْخُلُونَ الْجَنَّةَ عَلَى صُورَةِ الْقَمَرِ لَيْلَةَ الْبَدْرِ . ثُمَّ الَّذِينَ يَلُونَهُمْ عَلَى أَشَدِّ كَوْكَبٍ دُرِّيٍّ فِي السَّمَاءِ إِضَاءَةً : لاَ يَبُولُونَ . وَلاَ يَتَغَوَّطُونَ ، وَلاَ يَتْفُلُونَ . وَلاَ يَمْتَخِطُونَ . أَمْشَاطُهُمُ الذَّهَبُ ، وَرَشْحُهُمُ الْمِسْكُ ، وَمَجَامِرُهُمُ الأُلُوَّةُ — عُودُ الطِّيبِ — أَزْوَاجُهُمُ الْحُورُ الْعِينُ ، عَلَى خَلْقِ رَجُلٍ وَاحِدٍ ، عَلَى صُورَةِ أَبِيهِمْ آدَمَ سِتُّونَ ذِرَاعاً فِي السَّمَاءِ » متفقٌ عليه .

وفي رِوَايَةِ الْبُخَارِيِّ وَمُسْلِمٍ : آنِيَتُهُمْ فِيهَا الذَّهَبُ ، وَرَشْحُهُمُ الْمِسْكُ ، وَلِكُلِّ وَاحِدٍ مِنْهُمْ زَوْجَتَانِ يُرَى مُخُّ سُوقِهِمَا مِنْ وَرَاءِ

اللَّحْمِ مِنَ الحُسْنِ ، لاَ اخْتِلاَفَ بَيْنَهُمْ ، وَلا تَبَاغُضَ : قُلُوبُهُمْ قَلْبُ وَاحِدٍ ، يُسَبِّحُونَ اللهَ بُكْرَةً وَعَشِيّاً » .

قَوْلُهُ : « عَلَى خَلْقِ رَجُلٍ وَاحِدٍ » رواه بَعْضُهُمْ بِفَتْحِ الخَاءِ وَإِسْكَانِ اللاَّمِ ، وَبَعْضُهُمْ بِضَمِّهِما ، وَكِلاَهُمَا صَحِيحٌ .

1882. Hazrat Abu Hurairah (R.A.A.) relates that the Holy Prophet (S.A.W.) said: The first party of the dwellers of Paradise which will enter Paradise will be of those persons whose faces will be like the full moon, and those who follow them their faces will be like a shining star in the sky. They will not urinate, nor answer the call of nature, nor spitting, nor blow their noses. Their combs will be of gold and their perspiration will smell like musk. There fire pots will burn fragrant aloe-wood. Their wives will be the beautiful houries with large eyes. All the inmates will have identical habits and well-behaved. Their outstanding characteristics will be like their father Hazrat Adam (A.S.) and in height they will be as high as sixty arms length in the sky.
(Bukhari and Muslim)

According to another version of both the books. They will have golden vessels, their perspiration will smell like musk; every inmate of the Paradise will have two wives, whose beauty will be such that their nerve of the calf of their legs will be visible through their flesh. There will be no difference of opinion or malice between them; they will all be united in heart, glorifying Allah, every morning and evening.

١٨٨٣ – وَعَنِ المُغِيرَةِ بْنِ شُعْبَةَ رَضِيَ اللهُ عَنْهُ عَنْ رَسُولِ اللهِ صَلَّى اللهُ عَلَيْهِ وَسَلَّمَ قَالَ : « سَأَلَ مُوسَى ، صَلَّى اللهُ عَلَيْهِ وَسَلَّمَ رَبَّهُ ، مَا أَدْنَى أَهْلِ الجَنَّةِ مَنْزِلَةً ؟ قَالَ : هُوَ رَجُلٌ يَجِيءُ بَعْدَ مَا أُدْخِلَ أَهْلُ الجَنَّةِ الجَنَّةَ ، فَيُقَالُ لَهُ : ادْخُلِ الجَنَّةَ . فَيَقُولُ : أَيْ رَبِّ كَيْفَ وَقَدْ نَزَلَ النَّاسُ مَنَازِلَهُمْ ، وَأَخَذُوا أَخَذَاتِهِمْ ؟ فَيُقَالُ لَهُ : أَتَرْضَى أَنْ يَكُونَ لَكَ مِثْلُ مُلْكِ مَلِكٍ مِنْ مُلُوكِ الدُّنْيَا ؟ فَيَقُولُ : رَضِيتُ رَبِّ ، فَيَقُولُ : لَكَ ذَلِكَ وَمِثْلُهُ وَمِثْلُهُ وَمِثْلُهُ وَمِثْلُهُ ، فَيَقُولُ فِي الخَامِسَةِ : رَضِيتُ رَبِّ ، فَيَقُولُ : هَذَا لَكَ وَعَشَرَةُ أَمْثَالِهِ ، وَلَكَ مَا اشْتَهَتْ نَفْسُكَ ، وَلَذَّتْ عَيْنُكَ . فَيَقُولُ : رَضِيتُ رَبِّ ، قَالَ : رَبِّ فَأَعْلاَهُمْ مَنْزِلَةً ؟ قَالَ : أُولَئِكَ الَّذِينَ أَرَدْتُ ؛ غَرَسْتُ كَرَامَتَهُمْ

بِيَدِي ، وَخَتَمْتُ عَلَيْهَا ، فَلَمْ تَرَ عَيْنٌ ، وَلَمْ تَسْمَعْ أُذُنٌ ، وَلَمْ يَخْطُرْ عَلَى قَلْبِ بَشَرٍ » رواهُ مُسْلِم .

1883. Hazrat Mughirah bin Shu'ba (R.A.A.) relates that the Holy Prophet (S.A.W.) said: Hazrat Musa (Prophet Moses A.S.) asked his Lord: Allah! who will be of the lowest grade in the Paradise? Allah the Exalted said: It will be a person who will arrive when all the inmates of the Paradise will have entered the paradise. He will be asked to enter into the Paradise. But he will submit: My Lord (Sustainer), how can I enter when everyone has settled in his place and all places have been occupied. He will be asked: Would you like to have as much land as any king of the world had in his possession? He will say: O my Lord! I agree. He (Allah) will then tell him: You may have so much and (in addition) you may have so much, so much, so much more. On the mention of the fifth time, he will say: My Lord! I am safisfied. Allah, the Exalted will then tell him: You may have this and ten times more. (In addition to this) you will have whatever your heart desires, and your eyes feel sweet. He will say: O My Lord! I am satisfied. Prophet Moses then asked: My Lord, who will be of the highest order among the inmates of Paradise? Allah said: They will be the persons whom I shall honour with My own hands (Myself) and whose status will be sealed (attested) by Me. (I will bestow such things) which no eye has seen, no ear has heard and no human mind would have thought of. *(Muslim)*

١٨٨٤ – وَعَنِ ابْنِ مَسْعُودٍ رَضِيَ اللهُ عَنْهُ قَالَ : قَالَ رَسُولُ اللهِ صَلَّى اللهُ عَلَيْهِ وَسَلَّمَ : « إِنِّي لَأَعْلَمُ آخِرَ أَهْلِ النَّارِ خُرُوجاً مِنْهَا . وَآخِرَ أَهْلِ الْجَنَّةِ دُخُولاً الْجَنَّةَ . رَجُلٌ يَخْرُجُ مِنَ النَّارِ حَبْواً . فَيَقُولُ اللهُ عَزَّ وَجَلَّ لَهُ : اذْهَبْ فَادْخُلِ الْجَنَّةَ . فَيَأْتِيهَا . فَيُخَيَّلُ إِلَيْهِ أَنَّهَا مَلْأَى ، فَيَرْجِعُ ، فَيَقُولُ : يَا رَبِّ وَجَدْتُهَا مَلْأَى ، فَيَقُولُ اللهُ عَزَّ وَجَلَّ لَهُ : اذْهَبْ فَادْخُلِ الجَنَّةَ ، فَيَأْتِيهَا ، فَيُخَيَّلُ إِلَيْهِ أَنَّهَا مَلْأَى ، فَيَرْجِعُ . فَيَقُولُ : يَا رَبِّ وَجَدْتُهَا مَلْأَى ! فَيَقُولُ اللهُ عَزَّ وَجَلَّ لَهُ : اذْهَبْ فَادْخُلِ الْجَنَّةَ . فَإِنَّ لَكَ مِثْلَ الدُّنْيَا وَعَشَرَةَ أَمْثَالِهَا أَوْ إِنَّ لَكَ مِثْلَ عَشَرَةِ أَمْثَالِ الدُّنْيَا ، فَيَقُولُ : أَتَسْخَرُ بِي . أَوْ تَضْحَكُ بِي وَأَنْتَ الْمَلِكُ » قَالَ : فَلَقَدْ رَأَيْتُ رَسُولَ اللهِ صَلَّى اللهُ عَلَيْهِ وَسَلَّمَ ضَحِكَ حَتَّى بَدَتْ

نَوَاجِذُهُ فَكَانَ يَقُولُ : « ذَلِكَ أَدْنَى أَهْلِ الْجَنَّةِ مَنْزِلَةً » مُتَّفَقٌ عَلَيْهِ

1884. Hazrat Ibn Mas'ud (R.A.A.) relates that the Holy Prophet (S.A.W.) said. I know as to who will come out of the Hell last of all, or the last person to enter the Paradise. It will be a man who will come out of the Hell crawling on his buttocks. Allah, the Lord of Honour and Glory, will say to him: Go and enter the Paradise. He will go to the Paradise and think it is full. He will therefore return, and submit: My Lord! I find the Paradise full. Allah will say Go and enter the Paradise. In compliance with this order, he will again go and think that it is full. He will return and say: O my Lord! I find the paradise full. Allah the exalted, will say: Go and enter the Paradise. In compliance with this order he will again go and think that it is full. He will return and say: O My Lord! I found the Paradise full. Allah, the Exalted will say: Go and enter the Paradise. For you it is equivalent to the whole world and ten times more like it (or you have ten times the like of the world). He will submit: My Lord! Dost Thou joke with me and laugh at me although Thou are the Master? The narrator says: I noticed that the Holy Prophet (S.A.W.) while saying so, smiled so much so, that his last teeth became visible, and he was saying: Such will be the lowest in rank among the dwellers of Paradise.

(Bukhari and Muslim)

١٨٨٥ – وَعَنْ أَبِي مُوسَى رَضِيَ اللهُ عَنْهُ أَنَّ النَّبِيَّ صَلَّى اللهُ عَلَيْهِ وَسَلَّمَ قَالَ : « إِنَّ لِلْمُؤْمِنِ فِي الْجَنَّةِ لَخَيْمَةً مِنْ لُؤْلُؤَةٍ وَاحِدَةٍ مُجَوَّفَةٍ طُولُهَا فِي السَّمَاءِ سِتُّونَ مِيلاً . لِلْمُؤْمِنِ فِيهَا أَهْلُونَ ، يَطُوفُ عَلَيْهِمُ الْمُؤْمِنُ فَلاَ يَرَى بَعْضُهُمْ بَعْضاً » مُتَّفَقٌ عَلَيْهِ .

1885. Hazrat Abu Musa (R.A.A.) relates that the Holy Prophet (S.A.W.) said: A believer (Muslim) will have a tent inside the Paradise made from a hollowed pearl. The length of this tent will be sixty miles in the sky. All the members of the believer's family will live with him in this tent. The believer (Muslim) will walk inside this tent, and nobody will be able to see another. *(Bukhari and Muslim)*

١٨٨٦ – وَعَنْ أَبِي سَعِيدٍ الْخُدْرِيِّ رَضِيَ اللهُ عَنْهُ عَنِ النَّبِيِّ صَلَّى اللهُ عَلَيْهِ وَسَلَّمَ قَالَ : « إِنَّ فِي الْجَنَّةِ لَشَجَرَةً يَسِيرُ الرَّاكِبُ الْجَوَادَ الْمُضَمَّرَ السَّرِيعَ مِائَةَ سَنَةٍ مَا يَقْطَعُهَا » مُتَّفَقٌ عليه

وَرَوَيَاهُ فِي « الصَّحِيحَيْنِ » أَيْضاً مِنْ رِوَايَةِ أَبِي هُرَيْرَةَ رَضِيَ اللهُ عنه قَالَ : « يَسِيرُ الرَّاكِبُ فِي ظِلِّهَا مائَةَ سَنَةٍ مَا يَقْطَعُهَا » . مُتَّفق عَلَيْهِ

1886. Hazrat Abu Sa'eed Khudri (R.A.A.) relates that the Holy Prophet (S.A.W.) said: There is a tree in the Paradise under which a rider of a fast pony will not be able to cover the distance (from one end to the other) even in a hundred years. *(Bukhari and Muslim)*

This tradition has been reported by Hazrat Abu Hurairah (R.A.A.) also in these two Books.

١٨٨٧ – وعنه عن النبي صلى الله عليه وسلم قال: «إن أهل الجنة ليتراءون أهل الغرف من فوقهم كما تتراءون الكوكب الدري الغابر في الأفق من المشرق أو المغرب لتفاضل ما بينهم» قالوا: يا رسول الله، تلك منازل الأنبياء لا يبلغها غيرهم؟ قال: «بلى والذي نفسي بيده رجال آمنوا بالله وصدقوا المرسلين».

متفق عليه

1887. Hazrat Abu Sa'eed Khudri (R.A.A.) relates that the Holy Prophet (S.A.W.) said: The inmates of the Paradise will look towards the inmtaes of the upper mansions in the Paradise as you look at the bright stars from a distance in the eastern and western horizon. This will be so because there will be differences in the ranks of the inmates. The Companions asked: O Messenger of Allah! will these be the mansions of the Prophets where no other person will be able to reach? He (S.A.W.) said: Of course, but by Him in Whose possession is my life, there (in these mansions) will also be such persons who had faith in Allah and affirmed the righteousness of the Prophets.

(Bukhari and Muslim)

١٨٨٨ – وعن أبي هريرة رضي الله عنه أن رسول الله صلى الله عليه وسلم قال: «لقاب قوس في الجنة خير مما تطلع عليه الشمس أو تغرب» متفق عليه

1888. Hazrat Abu Hurairah (R.A.A.) relates that the Holy Prophet (S.A.W.) said: A small space in the Paradise equivalent to the distance between the two ends of a whip, would be better than the world and all that upon which the sun rises and sets.

(Bukhari and Muslim)

١٨٨٩ – وعن أنس رضي الله عنه أن رسول الله صلى الله عليه وسلم قال: «إن في الجنة سوقاً يأتونها كل جمعة. فتهب ريح الشمال. فتحثو في وجوههم وثيابهم، فيزدادون حسناً

وَجَمَالاً . فَيَرْجِعُونَ إِلَى أَهْلِيهِمْ ، وَقَدِ ازْدَادُوا حُسْناً وَجَمَالاً .
فَيَقُولُ لَهُمْ أَهْلُوهُمْ : وَاللهِ لَقَدِ ازْدَدْتُمْ حُسْناً وَجَمَالاً ! فَيَقُولُونَ :
وَأَنْتُمْ وَاللهِ لَقَدِ ازْدَدْتُمْ بَعْدَنَا حُسْناً وَجَمَالاً ! » رَوَاهُ مُسْلِمٌ .

1889. Hazrat Anas (R.A.A.) relates that the Holy Prophet (S.A.W.) said: In the Paradise there is a market to which the inmates of the Paradise will go every Friday. A breeze from the north will blow and spray perfume and other like things over their faces and clothes, enhancing their elegance and beauty; and when they will return to their family members, with improved looks and charm, the members of their families will say to them: You have become more handsome and more elegant. And they will in return say: By Allah, You too have become more handsome and beautiful in our absence *(Muslim)*

١٨٩٠ – وَعَنْ سَهْلِ بْنِ سَعْدٍ رَضِيَ اللهُ عَنْهُ أَنَّ رَسُولَ اللهِ صَلَّى
اللهُ عَلَيْهِ وَسَلَّمَ قَالَ : « إِنَّ أَهْلَ الْجَنَّةِ لَيَتَرَاءَوْنَ الْغُرَفَ فِي الْجَنَّةِ
كَمَا تَتَرَاءَوْنَ الْكَوْكَبَ فِي السَّمَاءِ » متفقٌ عَلَيْهِ .

1890. Hazrat Sahl bin Sa'd (R.A.A.) relates that the Holy Prophet (S.A.W.) said; The inmates of the Paradise will look at each others apartments as you see the stars in the sky. *(Bukhari and Muslim)*

١٨٩١ – وَعَنْهُ رَضِيَ اللهُ عَنْهُ قَالَ : شَهِدْتُ مِنَ النَّبِيِّ صَلَّى اللهُ
عَلَيْهِ وَسَلَّمَ مَجْلِساً وَصَفَ فِيهِ الْجَنَّةَ حَتَّى انْتَهَى ، ثُمَّ قَالَ فِي آخِرِ
حَدِيثِهِ : « فِيهَا مَا لاَ عَيْنٌ رَأَتْ ، وَلاَ أُذُنٌ سَمِعَتْ ، وَلاَ خَطَرَ عَلَى
قَلْبِ بَشَرٍ » ثُمَّ قَرَأَ تَتَجَافَى جُنُوبُهُمْ عَنِ الْمَضَاجِعِ إِلَى قَوْلِهِ
تَعَالَى : فَلاَ تَعْلَمُ نَفْسٌ مَا أُخْفِيَ لَهُمْ مِنْ قُرَّةِ أَعْيُنٍ .
رَوَاهُ البخاري .

1891. Hazrat Sahl bin Ss'd (R.A.A.) relates: I was present in a sitting along with the Holy Prophet (S.A.W.) full to the end. In this meeting he (S.A.W.) described the realities of the Paradise, and in the end said. In the Paradise there are things which no eye has ever seen, nor any ear has heard, nor has any human mind ever thought of. Then he recited:

> Who forsake their beds to cry unto their Lord in fear ana hope, and spend of what we have bestowed on them. No soul knoweth what is kept hid for them of joy, as a reward for what they used to do. (32 : 16—17) *(Bukhari and Muslim)*

١٨٩٢ـ وَعَنْ أَبِي سَعِيدٍ وَأَبِي هُرَيْرَةَ رَضِيَ اللهُ عَنْهُمَا أَنَّ رَسُولَ اللهِ صَلَّى اللهُ عَلَيْهِ وَسَلَّمَ قَالَ : « إِذَا دَخَلَ أَهْلُ الْجَنَّةِ الْجَنَّةَ يُنَادِي مُنَادٍ : إِنَّ لَكُمْ أَنْ تَحْيَوْا ، فَلاَ تَمُوتُوا أَبَداً ، وَإِنَّ لَكُمْ أَنْ تَصِحُّوا ، فَلاَ تَسْقَمُوا أَبَداً ، وَإِنَّ لَكُمْ أَنْ تَشِبُّوا فَلاَ تَهْرَمُوا أَبَداً ، وَإِنَّ لَكُمْ أَنْ تَنْعَمُوا ، فَلاَ تَبْأَسُوا أَبَداً » رواه مُسْلِم .

1892. Hazrat Abu Sa'eed (R.A.A.) and Hazrat Abu Hurairah (R.A.A.) report that the Holy Prophet (S.A.W.) said: When the inmates of the Paradise had entered it, a herald will announce. O the people of Paradise, you will live for ever, and will never die; you will always be in good health, and will not ever fall ill; you will remain always young, and will never grow old, and you will always be in comfort and will not ever come across any trouble. *(Muslim)*

١٨٩٣ـ وَعَنْ أَبِي هُرَيْرَةَ رَضِيَ اللهُ عَنْهُ أَنَّ رَسُولَ اللهِ صَلَّى اللهُ عَلَيْهِ وَسَلَّمَ قَالَ : « إِنَّ أَدْنَى مَقْعَدِ أَحَدِكُمْ مِنَ الْجَنَّةِ أَنْ يَقُولَ لَهُ : تَمَنَّ فَيَتَمَنَّى وَيَتَمَنَّى ، فَيَقُولُ لَهُ : هَلْ تَمَنَّيْتَ ؟ فَيَقُولُ : نَعَمْ ، فَيَقُولُ لَهُ : فَإِنَّ لَكَ مَا تَمَنَّيْتَ وَمِثْلَهُ مَعَهُ » رواه مُسْلِم .

1893. Hazrat Abu Hurairah (R.A.A.) relates that the Holy Prophet (S.A.W.) said: The least status which any one of you will get in the Paradise, will be that he will be asked: Express your desire; and then he will desire and desire. He will then be asked: Have you desired all? He will say: Yes. Then he will be told: You may have whatever you have wished, and so much more. *(Muslim)*

١٨٩٤ ـ وَعَنْ أَبِي سَعِيدٍ الْخُدْرِيِّ رَضِيَ اللهُ عَنْهُ أَنَّ رَسُولَ اللهِ صَلَّى اللهُ عَلَيْهِ وَسَلَّمَ قَالَ : « إِنَّ اللهَ عَزَّ وَجَلَّ يَقُولُ لأَهْلِ الْجَنَّةِ : يَا أَهْلَ الْجَنَّةِ ، فَيَقُولُونَ : لَبَّيْكَ رَبَّنَا وَسَعْدَيْكَ ، وَالْخَيْرُ فِي يَدَيْكَ ، فَيَقُولُ : هَلْ رَضِيتُمْ ؟ فَيَقُولُونَ : وَمَا لَنَا لاَ نَرْضَى يَا رَبَّنَا وَقَدْ أَعْطَيْتَنَا مَا لَمْ تُعْطِ أَحَداً مِنْ خَلْقِكَ ! فَيَقُولُ : أَلاَ أُعْطِيكُمْ أَفْضَلَ مِنْ ذَلِكَ ؟ فَيَقُولُونَ : وَأَيُّ شَيْءٍ أَفْضَلُ مِنْ ذَلِكَ ؟ فَيَقُولُ أُحِلُّ عَلَيْكُمْ رِضْوَانِي ، فَلاَ أَسْخَطُ عَلَيْكُمْ بَعْدَهُ أَبَداً » .

مُتَّفَقٌ عَلَيْهِ .

1894. Hazrat Abu Sa'eed Khudri (R.A.A.) relates that the Holy Prophet (S.A.W.) said: Allah, the Lord of Honour and Glory, will call the inmates of the Paradise, O Residents of Paradise! They will respond. Here we are, our Lord, and all good is in Thy Hands. He will ask them: Are you happy (satisfied)? They will answer: Why not, we may be happy our Lord! When you have bestowed upon us such bounties which you have not bestowed on any of your other creation. He will then say to them: Shall I not bestow upon you (something) even better than that? The inmates of the Paradise will inquire: What could be better than that? Allah will say. 'I bestow upon you My Pleasure and I shall never hereafter be angry with you.

(Bukhari and Muslim)

١٨٩٥ – وَعَنْ جَرِيرِ بْنِ عَبْدِ اللهِ رَضِيَ اللهُ عَنْهُ قَالَ : كُنَّا عِنْدَ رَسُولِ اللهِ صَلَّى اللهُ عَلَيْهِ وَسَلَّمَ فَنَظَرَ إِلَى الْقَمَرِ لَيْلَةَ الْبَدْرِ ، وَقَالَ : « إِنَّكُمْ سَتَرَوْنَ رَبَّكُمْ عِيَاناً كَمَا تَرَوْنَ هَذَا الْقَمَرَ ، لاَ تُضَامُونَ فِي رُؤْيَتِهِ » مُتَّفَقٌ عَلَيْهِ .

1895. This Hadis has already been covered in S. No. 1051 of Chapter 188.

١٨٩٦ – وَعَنْ صُهَيْبٍ رَضِيَ اللهُ عَنْهُ أَنَّ رَسُولَ اللهِ صَلَّى اللهُ عَلَيْهِ وَسَلَّمَ قَالَ : « إِذَا دَخَلَ أَهْلُ الْجَنَّةِ الْجَنَّةَ يَقُولُ اللهُ تَبَارَكَ وَتَعَالَى : تُرِيدُونَ شَيْئاً أَزِيدُكُمْ ؟ فَيَقُولُونَ : أَلَمْ تُبَيِّضْ وُجُوهَنَا ؟ أَلَمْ تُدْخِلْنَا الْجَنَّةَ وَتُنَجِّنَا مِنَ النَّارِ ؟ فَيَكْشِفُ الْحِجَابَ . فَمَا أُعْطُوا شَيْئاً أَحَبَّ إِلَيْهِمْ مِنَ النَّظَرِ إِلَى رَبِّهِمْ » رواه مُسْلِمٌ

قَالَ اللهُ تَعَالَى : إِنَّ الَّذِينَ آمَنُوا وَعَمِلُوا الصَّالِحَاتِ يَهْدِيهِمْ رَبُّهُمْ بِإِيمَانِهِمْ تَجْرِي مِنْ تَحْتِهِمُ الأَنْهَارُ فِي جَنَّاتِ النَّعِيمِ ، دَعْوَاهُمْ فِيهَا : سُبْحَانَكَ اللَّهُمَّ . وَتَحِيَّتُهُمْ فِيهَا سَلاَمٌ . وَآخِرُ دَعْوَاهُمْ أَنِ الْحَمْدُ لِلَّهِ رَبِّ الْعَالَمِينَ [يونس : ٩]

الْحَمْدُ لِلَّهِ الَّذِي هَدَانَا لِهَذَا وَمَا كُنَّا لِنَهْتَدِيَ لَوْلاَ أَنْ هَدَانَا اللهُ : اللَّهُمَّ صَلِّ عَلَى سَيِّدِنَا مُحَمَّدٍ وَعَلَى آلِ مُحَمَّدٍ ، كَمَا صَلَّيْتَ عَلَى إِبْرَاهِيمَ وَعَلَى آلِ إِبْرَاهِيمَ ، وَبَارِكْ عَلَى مُحَمَّدٍ ، وَعَلَى

آلِ مُحَمَّدٍ ، كَمَا بَارَكْتَ عَلَى إِبْرَاهِيمَ وَعَلَى آلِ إِبْرَاهِيمَ إِنَّكَ حَمِيدٌ مَجِيدٌ.

قَالَ مُؤَلِّفُهُ يَحِي النَّوَاوِيُّ غَفَرَ اللهُ لَهُ : «فَرَغْتُ مِنْهُ يَوْمَ الاثْنَيْنِ رَابِعَ عَشَرَ رَمَضَانَ سَنَةَ سَبْعِينَ وَسِتِّمِائَةٍ».

1896. Hazrat Suhaib (R.A.A.) relates that the Holy Prophet (S.A.W.) said: When the inmates of the Paradise will have entered the Paradise, Allah, the Master of Honour and Glory, will ask them: Do you want anything more that I should give you? They will submit. (O Allah)! Have you not made our faces shining? Have you not admitted us to the Paradise and saved us from the Hell? (What else is left to be desired?) Thereupon, the veil will be withdrawn, and the inmates of the Paradise will not have known anything dearer to them than looking at their Lord. *(Muslim)*

Allah the Exalted said.

Lo! those who believe and do good works, their Lord guideth them by their faith. Rivers will flow beneath them in the Gardens of Delight. Their Prayer therein will be: Glory be to Thee O Allah! and their greeting therein will be. Peace. And the conclusion of their prayer will be. Praise be to Allah, Lord of the Worlds! (10 : 10--11)

All praise is for Allah, who has guided us; and we would not have been properly guided, had Allah not guided us. 'O' Allah send salat (blessings) upon Our chief Muhammad and upon his family and followers as You sent salat (blessings) upon Ibrahim (Prophet Abraham) and his family and followers. O Allah! bless Muhammad, his family and followers as You blessed Ibrahim (Prophet Abraham), his family and followers and Indeed You are the Praised and the Respected.

Imam Nawawi, the compiler of this book says that he completed this compilation on Monday, the 14th Ramadan 670 A.H.

THE END

INDEX

B

N

P

Q

R

S

T

U

W

Y

Z